… Unto Heaven will I ascend

JACOB EPSTEIN'S INSPIRED YEARS 1930–1959

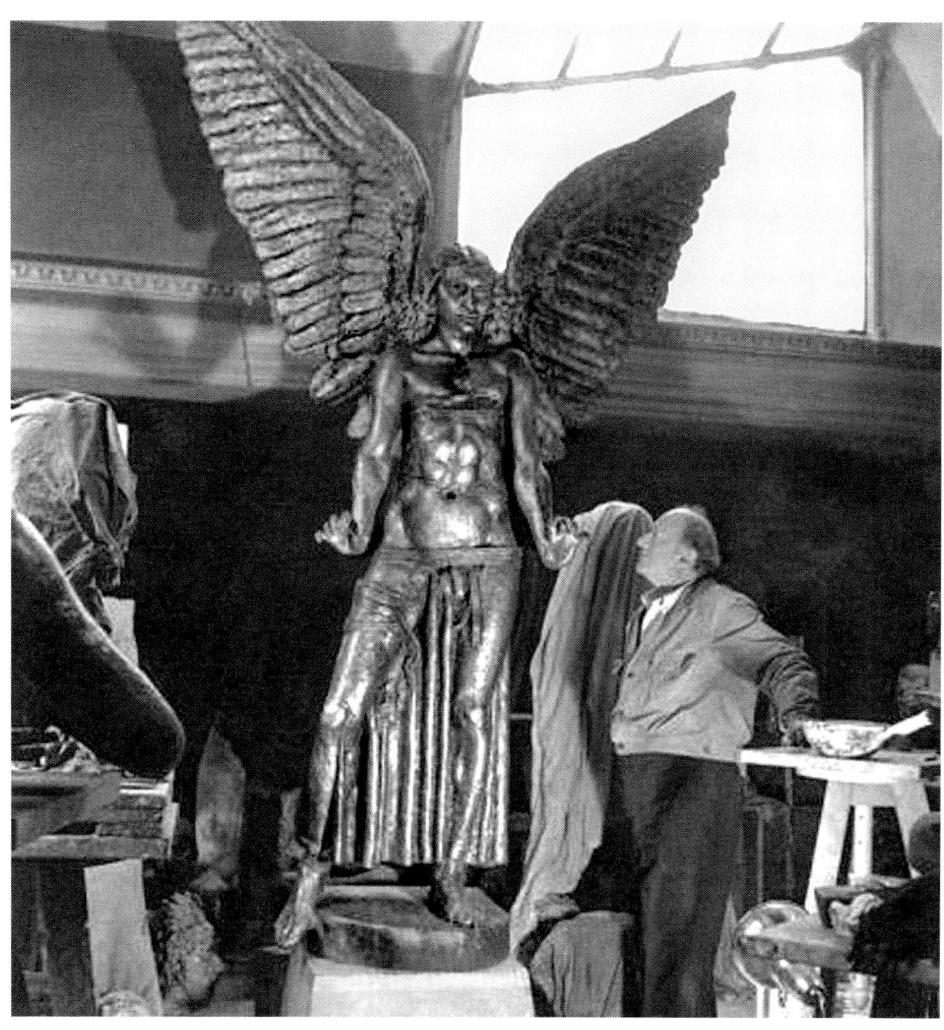

This volume is dedicated to the Epstein family and children, and in particular to Peggy Jean, Kitty and Jackie (God bless their souls), whom it was my privilege to meet

... Unto Heaven will I ascend

JACOB EPSTEIN'S INSPIRED YEARS 1930–1959

Raquel Gilboa

Paul Holberton publishing

ISBN 978 1 907372 49 0

British Library Cataloguing in Publication Data
A catalogue record for this book is available from the British Library

Produced by Paul Holberton publishing
89 Borough High Street, London SE1 1NL
www.paul-holberton.net

Images edited by Adi Kitov
Author's text edited before submission to the publisher
by Naomi Paz

Origination and printing by
E-graphic, Verona, Italy

FRONT COVER Epstein carving *Adam*, c. 1938–39 (see pp. 113ff.)

p. 2 Epstein in his studio with the bronze *Lucifer*, 1945 (see pp. 150ff.)

BACK COVER *The Crucifying Story*, 1933 (see p. 73)

CONTENTS

FROM THE FAMILY ALBUM

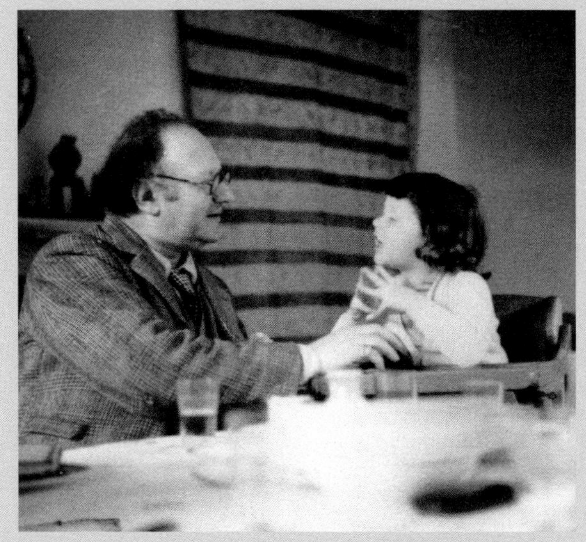

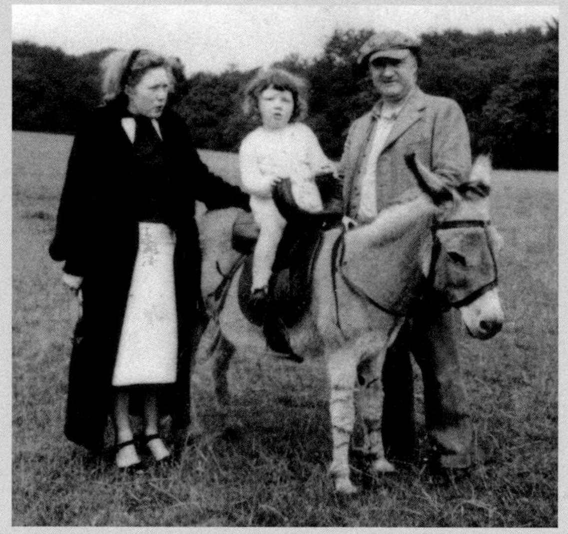

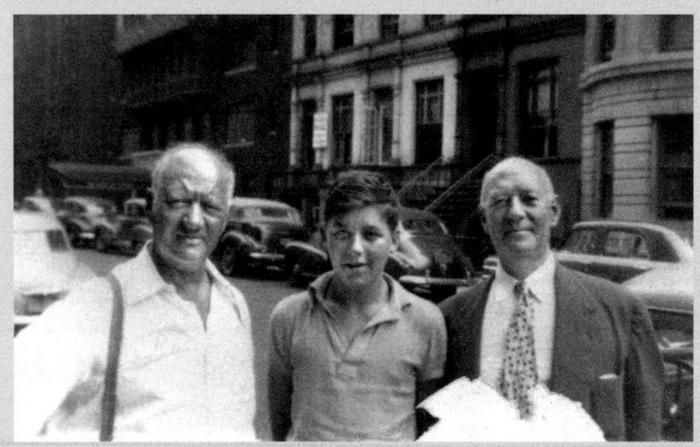

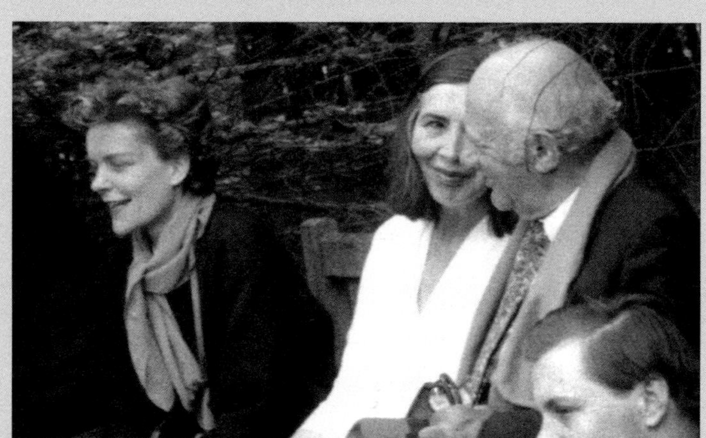

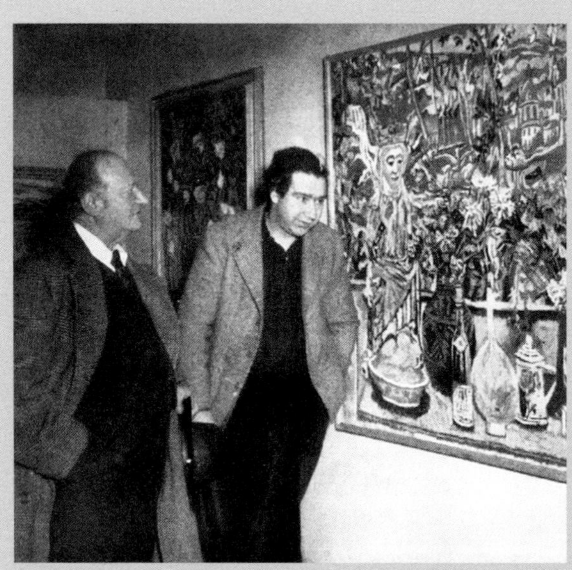

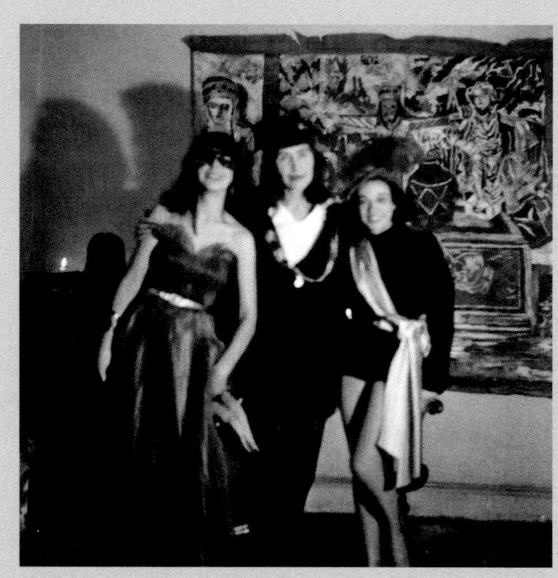

ACKNOWLEDGEMENTS

Although this volume was published after Epstein's children – Peggy Jean, Kitty and Jackie – had passed away, and therefore I cannot thank them directly, I wish nonetheless to acknowledge my gratitude to them. Many details are derived from the conversations and correspondence I had with them. I extend my gratitude to Epstein's living relatives, his granddaughter Leda Sloat and daughter-in-law Isabel Epstein, for their continuous encouragement extended over the period of research for this book.

The main source for information about Epstein, as well as for numerous images of works of art reproduced in this volume, is the archive in the New Art Gallery – Walsall, and there are not enough words to express my debt to its staff – directors Jo Digger and Stephen Snoddy, archivist Neil Lebeter, librarians Cheryl Jones and Litza Petraki, and assistant Elin Morgan. Additional help was extended to me by the Tate institutions – by the Library and the Archive in the Hyman Kreitman Reading Rooms, in which I was kindly aided by Krzysztof Cieszkowski, John Langdon, Chris Bastock and Jonathan Woodcock; and by Tate Enterprises and Tate Images, having the pleasure of unceasing cooperation of Clive Coward. I am indebted, too, to archivist Michael Phipps of the Henry Moore Foundation and archivist Claire Mayoh of the Henry Moore Institute for their help and good will.

Last but not least, I am grateful to Evelyn Silber, who proved throughout to be a supportive colleague, to Alexandra McFall-Dane for our conversation and permission to use her late husband's recollections, and John Finch for his further information on Epstein. Most of all, I extent my gratitude to David Glasser and the Ben Uri Gallery -The London Jewish Museum of Art for hosting the launching of my first volume, as well as their warm encouragement in regard to the publication of this volume.

I would like to thank, in alphabetical order, the cooperation of the following people (and their institutions), with the hope that no one has been forgotten:

In England: Perry Bonewell (Bolton Museum); Ingram Reid (Bonham's London); Griffin Co (Aberdeen Art Gallery); Sir Marc Cochrane; Niall Fairhead; Alexandra Gerstein (The Courtauld Institute); Robert Griffiths; David Herman; Jessica Hogg; Bettyann Holtzmann Kevles and Ellen Propp; Philip Hunt (National Galleries of Scotland); Kathryn Jones (Curator of Decorative Arts, The Royal Collection); Adina Kamien-Kashdan and Rachel Laufer (Israerl Museum in Jerusalem); Agi Katz (The Boundry Gallery); Roger Lovette; Roger Hull and Paul Webster (Liverpool Record Office); Jill Millard Shapiro; Beverley Cook, Charlotte Samuels and Sarah Williams (The Museum of London); Nick Nicholson (National Gallery of Australia in Canberra); Mike Pitts; Andrew Smart (A.C. Cooper Photographers); Bryn Sayles (Sotheby's, London) and Daniela Bachrach (Sotherby's, Tel-Aviv); Chris Smith (editorial director, Harper Collins).

Around the world: Francine Bouré (Musée des Beaux-Arts); Dianne Landry and Sym Corrigan (Dalhousie University); Jean England (The Church of the Ascension, Crownhill, Plymouth); Astrid Fendt (Staatliche Antikensammlungen und Glyptothek, Munich); Laura S. Griffith (Fairmount Park Art Association); Hillary S. Kativa (Historical Society of Pennsylvania); Isabelle Lawson (SNBA); Diane Ney (Washington National Cathedral); Dorothy Smith (The Jacob Rader Marcus Center of the American Jewish Archives); Steven Smith (The Historical Society of Pennsylvania); Dinah Voisin (Fiore de Henriquez estate).

Finally, I owe the completion of this project to the readers of the text and their illuminating comments: my dearest son Hed, who read the first draft, and Martin Ouvry, who read the last one; my editor in Israel Naomi Paz and Paul Holberton, who edited its final form; the devoted designer Laura Parker and my constant companion in Photoshop work Adi Kitov. In the light of the difficulties with public publishers regarding my previous book, and their unwillingness to risk what might be an unprofitable product, I decided not to approach them with this one and therefore this volume, too, is a private enterprise. Nor did I apply for grants from private or public bodies because – in spite of their acknowledgement of the quality of the first volume – I did not agree with their demand to reapply again for academic recommendations as, naturally, it is always from the same people. In the end, beside the hospitable consideration of Marc Rutter, it was my savings and those of my supportive husband Gideon that financed the publication of this book.

CLOCKWISE FROM TOP LEFT
(All from Peggy Jean's album unless otherwise stated)

Epstein and Jackie, late 1903s

Epstein, Peggy Jean and Leda 1939–40

Epstein and Kathleen with Sally Ryan, 1950s (NAGW)

Esther, Kathleen and Beth Lipkin, 1950s (NAGW)

Epstein and Theo, the opening of Theo's Exhibition (NAGW; clipping from *The Sphere*, 21 January 1950)

Epstein, Jackie and Irving Epstein in New York, 1949

FOREWORD: LETTER TO THE READER

There is only one true authority upon art, and that is the artist.
Besides him there is the art critic, the connoisseur and the enthusiast.
The art critic is a poor fellow; he might know so little and yet says so much.
The connoisseur knows much but often knows it too well; he may degenerate into a mere stamp collector.
The enthusiast is amiable but inherently a potential victim of deceit, or the servant of vogue and the slave of fashion.
(The sculptor Vernon Blake, *The Architectural Review*, March 1929, p. 101)

Humbly, I admit guilt. It is with modest ambition that I regard myself 'an authority upon art'. I am also a connoisseur of Epstein, in believing to know 'so much' about him and, through long study and research, in becoming knowledgeable about his art. However, I firmly believe that this second book, no more than my previous one (*Let There Be Sculpture: Jacob Epstein's Formative Years, 1880–1930*, London, 2009), does not descend into the enthusiast's pit of a mere stamp collection combined with blind adulation. I feel free to claim this because my writings on Epstein's art have not been directed or influenced by a priori dogma but, rather, by trying to understand what the artist actually executed, what were the artistic precedents that might have influenced him, and what he was attempting to convey.

The same attempt at understanding is applied here to his private life, which – as the credo of my books dictates – is an integral part of his art. I neither conform to conventions nor judge; I merely present facts and describe events, and offer my interpretations of the actions and deeds of the period. Much of the information comes from the archive material of family members, who, besides allowing me the free use of family photographs, kindly and patiently responded to my somewhat unorthodox method of research that, lacking an available expression, I term 'acquiring data with a tea-spoon'. This meant for them – after preliminary interviews that began in the mid 1980s with Peggy Jean, Kitty and Jackie – having to answer a constant flow of questions that arose concomitantly with the development of the text. Because their comments concerned the later years of Epstein's life, they became invaluable for this second volume. Jackie's main reservations were in regard to events that might appear controversial or the publication of which might hurt the family. I promised to present those private-life occurrences fairly, without any kind of censorship, but avoiding ungrounded speculation on what, ultimately, was irrelevant to his work. Jackie accepted this, and I believe my previous book successfully presented a text that respected Epstein's private life, with all the pros and cons that might be attributed to it. The present book is being written at a time when all three of Epstein's children are no longer with us; but the respectful attitude that I promised and kept to in the first book will, I hope, also be maintained here.

My book … *And There Was Sculpture*, which was completed in time to celebrate the fiftieth anniversary of Epstein's death, presented his life and work during the period that I considered to be his formative years (1880–1930). It introduced and discussed the development of his life and art up until he arrived at what can be defined as his own personal artistic language, in his last sculptures of that period, *Day* and *Night*, set above St James's Underground station in London. The argument of that book, valid also for this one, was that Epstein's art – both his pioneering stylized work and concomitantly the more naturalistic oeuvre – emanated from his persona in all its facets and dualities and therefore reflects it. The outcome of the first volume, therefore, was a new kind of 'non-traditional' biography, which did not conform to any established genre – being neither solely biographical (like Stephen Gardiner's *Epstein*) nor solely art-historical (like Evelyn Silber's books) – leaving some commentators with a sense of unease. My arbitrary division of Epstein's life into two periods and the particular years I had chosen, explained in the Epilogue of that book, were also questioned. Perhaps I had not been clear enough in justifying this hybridization and division respectively and therefore additional clarification on the raison d'être of both volumes follows.

I regard the carvings *Day* and *Night* (1928–29) not only as ending Epstein's formative years but also as marking a new beginning, as analysis reveals: their stylization – neither strictly geometric nor strictly archaizing – reflects the last stage of Epstein's development, manifesting the individual sculptural language with which he was to continue. Moreover, in the new era of the 1930s with which the present book begins, a younger generation of artists came to occupy a central position among London's artistic milieu. A seemingly new artistic philosophy was to impose in the 1930s a different perception of form; and Epstein, not being part of it, would be considered a 'traditionalist' and consigned to artistic isolation. For these reasons the period of the early 1930s marks a watershed, justifying the division that I have made of his oeuvre and initiating a new phase, discussed in this volume.

Although from both aspects – method and perspective – this volume continues the previous one, it stands in its own right as a separate entity owing to the enigmatic character of much of the later work and the chronological span of the sculptor's life that it discusses. The complexity of my task, as indeed of any biographer, has been aptly compared by an Israeli author to baking a doughnut:

> You observe personalities, whether alive or dead, and sense within them an ensconced enigma, something unfamiliar, a riddle – a hole. You start to surround this hole – to collect data, whatever had been written about him, the historical background – and you accumulate around it more and more dough, but all outwardly. At the end of the day you have told something but, paradoxically, if you haven't sinned against the person you have written about, and if this person had indeed been a great man, you are left with the fundamental riddle – the unsolved enigma of his life which, at best, you have managed to phrase better.[1]

In order to clarify both my 'baked doughnut' and where I stand in regard to Epstein and his work, I think it right briefly to rephrase, and add a little, to the perspective presented in my previous book.

In spite of the time gap between Epstein's actual life and my becoming acquainted with his work, we seem to share some similar cultural traits. 'Culture', as defined in *The Meaning of Modern Sculpture* by Epstein's contemporary R.H. Wilenski (London 1932), is "a state of mind that determines values". Our common cultural traits, Epstein's and mine, do not stem merely from being Jews, although this fact may add to a kind of common understanding and interpretation of phenomena, or to acknowledging some lines that are not to be crossed. It has more to do with a rebellion against Jewish orthodoxy and its religious bindings, and the adoption of universal secular ideas. This kind of diversion from Jewish orthodoxy, by and large, had its roots in the Bible, or in biblical values orientated towards creating a better society in a socialist sense, rather than in the Talmudic tradition that developed during later centuries. Such traits characterized many Jewish youngsters of Epstein's generation in Eastern Europe, as well as those who immigrated to America or Palestine. If Wilenski's definition is accepted, then 'cultural' Jews are secular Jews who possess a certain state of mind that determines a shared set of values; a person thus may culturally be a Jew and, at the same time, have no regard for religion. For the purposes of this research as a whole both Diaspora Epstein and Israeli I are cultural Jews.

However, whereas for the first volume, which ended in 1929, this had been a sufficient definition and, as one critic commented, "the Jewishness is not emphasised",[2] it is impossible for any research worthy of this name not to emphasize Jewishness in the context of the following years, when anti-Semitism was so openly expressed: it was the *bon ton* among the upper classes, slander in the mouths of hate-consumed clergy and an outlet of frustration for the man in the street. The element of religion, mainly as a consequence of a sense of group affiliation that derived from attacks on Jews, also infiltrated the consciousness of cultural Jews. Relevant for Epstein was the attitude prevalent among the literary and artistic classes, the so-called 'intelligentsia', to which he belonged; the common and quite popular coinage about 'one not being particularly anti-Semitic' was finding expression in its circles.[3] Anti-Semitism gradually became a philosophical ideology and a political policy intent on annihilating the Jewish 'race' around the world. Diaspora Jews in Europe paid dearly for this ideological-political atmosphere, though Epstein, in England, lived and witnessed it from a relatively sheltered place. There is no way in which one can ignore these facts and pretend that Epstein was merely an artist or an uninfluenced bystander, and therefore this aspect is given some weight in the present text.

In spite of my above-mentioned affiliation and identification with Epstein's culture, we do not share a similar cultural sense in regard to anti-Semitism, as it does not apply to Israelis brought up and living in a Jewish environment, albeit within a secular society. For us, anti-Semitism was and is something one learns about in history books. Anti-Semitism is only a Diaspora issue concerning 'The Jewish Problem', which, it was assumed, was solved by the establishment of the Israeli state, supposedly creating for the Jews a 'universal' Israeli entity – like that of the Turks or the French. Israelis in daily life do not relate to anti-Semitism, that is, until they go abroad and feel it when among the Gentiles; back in Israel, this feeling disappears. Jewish consciousness thus seems to be blurred in the Jewish state, surfacing, and often illogically increasing, when an Israeli lives abroad.

Consequently, it required an intellectual effort on my part to relate to Epstein's life within a society that had openly become increasingly anti-Semitic and, besides the difficulty of comprehending the period while seeking to penetrate into the enigma that is Epstein, I had to tread carefully with regard to an issue that Epstein himself had tried to suppress publicly, although indirectly admitting its existence:

> The average unfavourable criticism of my sculpture I had never put-down to anti-Semitism .... Artists are of all races and climes, and to band together in racial groups is ridiculous .... This pernicious radicalism in art should be forever banished (225).

The final issue regarding a biographer's perception of his protagonist, and one which I have not tackled before, is that of age. A young biographer writing about an elderly personality might be influenced by what his own age and age-mentality naturally dictate. It is hard to overcome preconceived ideas determined by the writer's own age and values (or personal culture, as defined above) or to make suggestions and assumptions without applying moral or social judgements regarding the protagonist and his actions. Luckily for both my protagonist and me, this book was written when I was approaching his age and, like Epstein, had acquired to some extent a degree of benevolence towards and tolerance of people's weaknesses, and also the ability to come to terms with things as they are.

This study, completed near the centenary of Epstein's most renowned work, *Rock Drill* (first version, 1913), attempts to follow the chronological order of things – works, private affairs and social occurrences – while grappling with the issue of 'how to incorporate chronologically a discussion on a sculpture in spite of its non-concomitant parameters', such as when it was commissioned, executed and presented. The outcome is not consistent for all the works; in some cases, where the general daily occurrences seem important, I have seen fit to deal separately with each sculptural parameter.

The main contribution of this research into Epstein's life and the sculptural work he executed after he had reached artistic maturity is observation of a kind seldom achieved before. It is based on what was termed above 'culture' – that out of which Epstein grew and which he never deserted, and the different one in which he lived: his art thus expresses his own interpretation of both 'cultures'. Whatever might have been Epstein's assumptions about his national and social position, or his "place in sculpture" (as he titled a chapter in his autobiography), the stature of his art and its validity for future generations remain open for discussion; I suggest, however, that no one will argue that Epstein's art is worthless. For my second book on this artistic rebel, whose work gave expression to human concerns and also to uncommon interpretations of so many subjects, I have chosen a title that reflects the aspirations of the angel Lucifer (Isaiah 14: 13–14), whose image Epstein so beautifully portrayed and which, to a great extent, reflects the aspirations of the artist himself – that of reaching a summit – *... Unto Heaven Will I Ascend: Jacob Epstein's Inspired Years (1930–1959)*.

1 Burshtein, 'Koreh Le'at', p. 14 (my abbreviation and rough translation).

2 Dennis Wardleworth, *The Art Book*, XVII/3, August 2010, p. 41.

3 See, for example, the discussion in T.S. Eliot's letter to Lionel Thrilling on his selection of Kipling's verse: "I am not aware that [Kipling] cherished any particularly anti-Semitic feelings. In any case, the interest of the poem lies in his criticism of the English than in any aversion to Jews." Thrilling replied: "As anti-Semitism goes these days, I suppose that Kipling is not – to use Mr Eliot's phrase – particularly anti-Semitic. I certainly should not think of isolating for discussion what kind of anti-Semitism he has, but only of mentioning, as one aspect of xenophobia, his queasy, resentful feelings about Jews": C. Ricks, *T.S. Eliot and Prejudice*, Berkeley 1989, pp. 26–27.

NOTES ON THE SOURCES

Two biographers, Richard Buckle and Stephan Gardiner, have written on Epstein. Buckle introduced information that, to a great extent, had been provided by Epstein's widow Kathleen; Gardiner added to it particularities deriving from papers left behind after her death, and more information that had been provided by Kathleen to various buyers and gallery owners.

Kathleen's comments to Richard Buckle were made during their conversations regarding the organization of Epstein's retrospective exhibition at the Festival of Arts in Edinburgh in 1962, and later on regarding his encompassing book on Epstein's oeuvre, as well as in response to questionnaires given to the Epstein's family members.[1] I realise that Kathleen would have wished to establish Epstein's reputation and, therefore, would had not disclosed anything that might shed an unfavourable light on him as a private person. However, regardless of any such personal concerns, it was frustrating to find her information on his work – the exact dates or circumstances of certain works – questionable.[2] Not that Kathleen had purposely intended to mislead; one has to take in account that at the time of researching Epstein's work (1961–62), Kathleen (b. 1901) was in her early sixties, and her memory might sometimes have failed her. She had entered the Epstein household, after the sudden death of Margaret Epstein, to find a total lack of order or records in regard to his works, and drawers and cupboards full of items of which she had only a vague knowledge or none at all. Moreover, Epstein cared little for the proper 'housekeeping' of his oeuvre, and even for the first catalogue of his work, by Haskell, there were no written records that could serve as a basis: it had to be composed with the help of Margaret's and Epstein's memories, and then only in 1930.[3] My task as a researcher, therefore, was to take into account the factors of style and subject-matter within the periods of the works' execution, as well as to consider any external matters relating to a specific work. This has sometimes resulted in a dating different from that previously assumed for some works (mainly drawings) and, associated with it, a different interpretation of the works.

Regarding the other sources used in this volume, I am immensely indebted to previous researchers and their publications on Epstein (books, journals and articles), even when I question their data or reject their conclusions. I mention here the basic sources in alphabetical order, commenting on their contribution in general. The notes in the main text expand this brief survey by presenting all the sources, including those cited from internet sites, which, owing to their quantity, it was impractical to include in the bibliography. This, conventionally, presents mainly published books.

MAIN PUBLICATIONS

Jacob Epstein, *Let There Be Sculpture*, London 1940
Citations in the main text of the present book are marked by page number thus: (128)

Jacob Epstein, *Epstein: An Autobiography*, London [1954], 1963
The *Autobiography* was a second edition of *Let There Be Sculpture*, with additional information in a 'Postscript', indicated here thus: (PS/342)

Richard Buckle, *Jacob Epstein: Sculptor*, London 1963
Unfortunately, the papers Buckle donated to the Henry Moore Institute (deposited after his death) now contains mainly information concerning the proceedings for Epstein's posthumous Edinburgh retrospective; the rest of Buckle's material, relating to his book on Epstein's life and work, has, as I am informed by Evelyn Silber, been destroyed.

Richard Buckle and Kathleen Epstein, *Epstein Drawings*, London 1962

Stephen Gardiner, *Epstein: Artist Against the Establishment*, London 1992
This provides a wealth of information on Epstein's private and commercial affairs.

Arnold Haskell, *The Sculptor Speaks*, London 1930
This is the most encompassing collection of Epstein's perceptions and opinions on art. Although the interviews with him ended in 1930, I found no divergence from Epstein's opinions expressed during the following years.

Evelyn Silber, *The Sculpture of Epstein*, London 1986
This is a concise account of Epstein's life and work, including an almost complete catalogue of his sculpture; items mentioned as being in private collections may have since changed hands. No serious research on Epstein can be done without referring to this book.

Evelyn Silber and Terry Friedman, *Jacob Epstein: Sculpture and Drawings*, exh. cat., Leeds City Art Galleries and Whitechapel Art Gallery, London 1987
This contains several articles on various aspects of Epstein's work. I am indebted to several of these, although not always in agreement with their statements and conclusions.

Henry Moore Early Carvings 1930–1940, exh. cat., essays by Henry Anne Garrould, Terry Friedman and David Mitchinson, Leeds City Art Galleries, 1982
This is a concise source for Moore's work of the period relevant to that of Epstein's.

R.H. Wilenski, *The Meaning of Modern Sculpture*, London 1932
This survey features concise explanations and a fluent everyday language without recourse to so-called 'professional jargon'. It is rare in discussing Epstein's work and its meaning as Wilenski comprehended it, beyond the discussion of mere forms.

R. Gilboa, *... And There Was Sculpture*, London 2009
Last but not least, reference to pages in my first volume on Epstein appears in square parentheses thus: [I/233]

LETTERS

All citations are verbatim.

Jane F. Babson, *The Epsteins: A Family Album*, Aylesbury 1984
This mostly consists of letters written by Margaret to her sister-in-law Sylvia (hereafter Babson, *The Epsteins*)

Jacob and Margaret Epstein's letters to Dr Adolph Oko, The Hebrew Union College Archive, Cincinnati (hereafter HUCAC)

Epstein's letters in the Epstein files, Tate (Gallery) Archive (hereafter TGA-)

Epstein's and Kathleen's letters in the Garman-Ryan-Epstein Collection, The New Art Gallery Walsall Archive (hereafter NAGW)

The Henry Moore Institute Archive (hereafter HMI)

Author's correspondence and conversations with Kitty Godley, Peggy Jean Lewis and her daughter Leda Sloat, John Finch, and Richard Buckle

MEMOIRS

David McFall, 'The Sculpture of EPSTEIN by Dr. Evelyn Silber published by Phaidon. With some personal recollections of the sculptor by David McFall R.A.', text deposited with the Royal Academy of Sculptors (also: http://davidmcfall.co.uk/Epstein.aspx); permission to quote kindly granted by the McFall Estate

Recordings of Peggy Jean, Jackie Epstein and Lynn Chadwick, all deposited in the archive of The New Art Gallery – Walsall.

Jacob Epstein: Rebel Angel
A film on Epstein produced by Central Television, in collaboration of the Arts Council of Great Britain, 1987 (hereafter *Rebel Angel*: Central TV). This offers an overview of Epstein's working life, including items filmed for newsreels. Not to be confused with Evelyn's Silber's catalogue by the same title.

Monitor 1: Jacob EpsteinA brief interview of about six minutes broadcast on the BBC radio on 2 February 1958. The recording was recently interwoven with photographs taken by G. Ireland into a new brief film production for England: (http://www.bbc.co.uk/archive/sculptors/12813.shtml) or in a more accessible universal form: http://www.youtube.com/watch?v = D_gYH5GnBNY.

KEY TO THE ILLUSTRATIONS

Illustrations of Epstein's works are indicated by [1]; his name is not indicated in the captions.
In those cases in which the suggested date of work differs from that traditionally given (the reasons for which are discussed in the text), the former has been placed between square brackets.

When there are several bronze replicas of works, the locations given here are – as far as possible and for the reader's advantage – those of public galleries, even if the reproduced photographs were received from other sources (all sources are mentioned in the Photographic Credits).

Comparative illustrations are given in figures (fig. 1).

1 Richard Buckle, A letter to the author, 30.9.1994; on questionnaires - Kitty Godley in a conversation with the author, 1985.

2 See my comment on a drawing in I/ 56, note 50. Additional disagreements are expressed in the course of this text.

3 Arnold Haskell, *The Sculptor Speaks*, London 1930, Appendix II.

CHAPTER 1

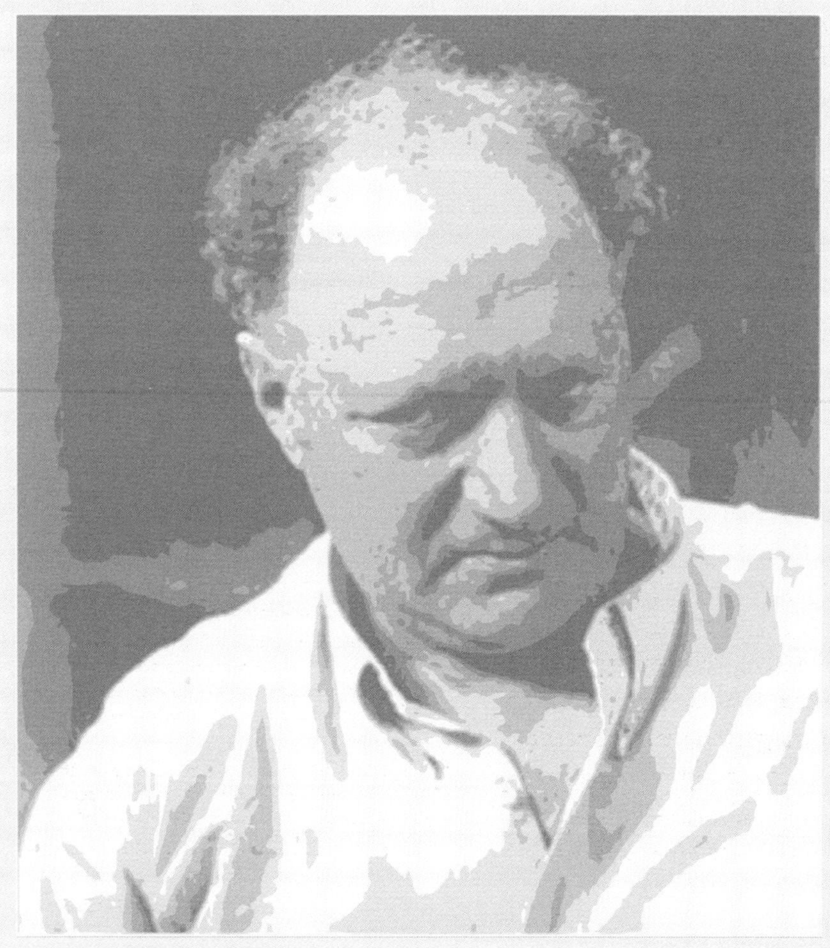

INTRODUCTION

JACOB EPSTEIN'S LIFE – FIRST PHASE, 1880–1929

As Epstein's life and work until 1930 are discussed in depth in ... *And There Was Sculpture*,[1] I offer here just a brief summary.

Born and educated in New York, Epstein completed his studies in Paris (1903–04) before settling in London (1905), where he married Margaret Dunlop (1906), becoming a British citizen in December 1910. In 1918 he fathered (by his model Meum Stewart Lindsell) his first child, Peggy Jean, whom he and Margaret adopted. In 1921 he met Kathleen Garman, who became his life-companion and the mother of his second family;[2] by 1927 they had two children, Theodore and Kitty.

Stories about Margaret's "constant harassment" of Kathleen – acting like a detective set on proving assumed infidelities, or spreading the rumour that one of the children was not Epstein's, and even setting fire to the house in Sydney Street, forcing Kathleen's move to 272 King's Road – were told by Kathleen's sister Helen.[3] This last rumour is surely untrue, for one cannot imagine Margaret, no matter how much she resented her rival, deliberately and methodically sending someone to carry out a crime that she herself could not perform because of her ill health. Earlier, certainly, she had committed a criminal act, shooting Kathleen in the shoulder (I/170), after which, in 1923, the two women reached a *modus vivendi*. For the rest of her life Margaret, who, according to her daughter Peggy Jean, would put up with anything so long as it contributed to Epstein's art, tolerated Kathleen's existence in Epstein's life, in a house not far away. Kathleen inspired Epstein to touch also upon Christian subjects, which he had not tackled before; her exquisite facial features inspired him to immortalize her in some of his best portraits. Epstein's and Kathleen's continued attachment was due also to her availability as a companion on visits to the theatre, to concerts and so on, and she was the mother of some of his children.

Towards the end of 1927 Epstein went to New York with his wife Margaret and daughter Peggy Jean but, despite rumours that he had left England for good, thus deserting Kathleen Garman, in late January 1928 he returned to England and to her.

The idea of a trip to New York in order to exhibit his work there might have occurred to Epstein some time around 1923, but the trip was finally decided upon when his contacts with his old friend, Dr Adolph Oko,[4] became more frequent. There was a long process of preparation. In January 1924 Oko began by establishing relations with the editor of *The Graphic*, who was apparently sympathetic to Epstein's work. The paper had already published an appreciation of Epstein and the editor suggested that Oko write an article that would stress that "the sculptor is not working for any sort of *reclama* [sic; mere publicity], but *is saying what is in him*, and that he must say at all costs". Moreover, on Epstein's approach to art he added: "I think this is a new point of view and needs saying",[5] a comment that reveals a different attitude from the usual American one, which tends toward *Reklame* or publicity for its own sake.

1 Raquel Gilboa, ... *And There Was Sculpture: Jacob Epstein's Formative Years (1880-1930)*, London 2009; hereafter [I/page].

2 'Life-companion' is used here to define Kathleen's relationship to Epstein. Considering how important she was to Epstein, I believe she does not deserve the somewhat derogatory title 'mistress'.

3 Gardiner, *Epstein*, p. 314. In the same breath Gardiner describes Helen's stories as "possibly subject to some exaggeration in telling".

4 On Dr Adolph Oko (1883–1944) and the New York exhibition, see I/178–79.

5 Letter from J.M. Bulloch, editor, to Dr Oko, 3 January 1924: HUCAC.

1
Madonna and Child, 1926–27
Bronze, life size
Riverside Church, New York

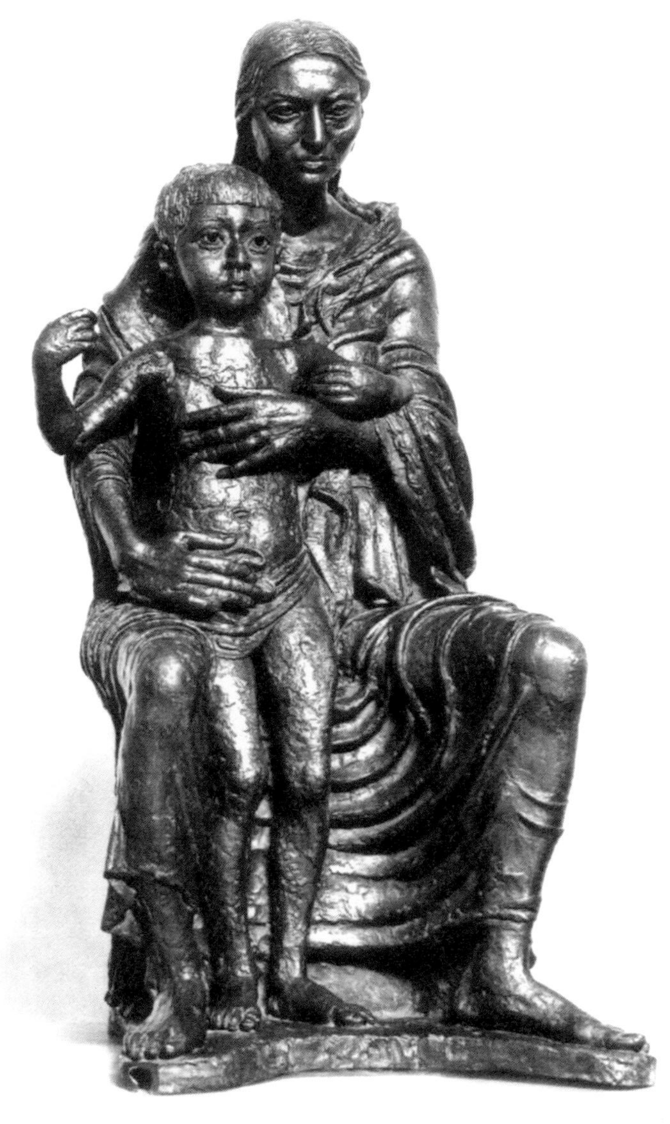

During the 1930s and up to his death in 1944, Oko was to some extent Epstein's confidant, playing a role similar to that of W.E. Ordway and John Quinn (in New York) and William Rothenstein (in London). In addition to commenting on the works, he lent a sympathetic ear (a 'wailing wall', as the Jewish idiom has it) to the woes that Epstein and Margaret recounted in their letters to him (cited here verbatim), among which figured gallery owners whose only idea was "to exploit artists financially"; Epstein's attempts to turn to other galleries were to no avail as they "are all the same".[6] Epstein's 1927 exhibition of sculptures in New York (I/179–85) had been a reasonable success; however, owing also to intrigues in the art world, he refused to remain in America even a short time longer for an intended exhibition in San Francisco, which eventually took place in May 1929 without him. In retrospect, one could say that the following comment at the time about his work justified Epstein's resentment of America's art world for its misapprehension and misinterpretation of his sculpture: "Next should come Jacob Epstein, who exhibits an enormous bronze *Mother and Child* [1]; it is larger than life size

6 Letter from Epstein to Dr Oko, 26 February 1930: HUCAC.

and no one will need a description after we mention the name Epstein. There are two starving figures, a terrible sight of tragedy."[7] Though with greater signs of appreciation, the work also elicited mixed feelings when presented in London, mainly in regard to its religious aspects:

> Madonna & Child drew the greatest storm of rage and approval. By this more than life-size bronze (a splayfooted gawky peasant girl wiping her enormous hands on the flanks of a wretched skinny child), babbitts were terrified. They said, one to another: "Well, I must say, I think it's blasphemous. Jesus looks positively Semitic! And when you remember the way Raphael painted the mother, it seems really shameful ... the man must be an atheist!" Aesthetes, on the other hand, became jubilant. "What strength," they murmured, "what superb nuance."[8]

It was on the selling of this huge work that Margaret Epstein's hopes for remaining in New York lay, as otherwise she would not be able to rent a studio (on a lease of not less than one year) to induce Epstein to stay in New York.[9] Although their financial situation improved slightly thanks to minor sales and an additional loan of $500,[10] as well as $200 paid for the sculptured head of Oko's wife,[11] it hardly covered the cost of the family trip.

As for Kathleen – it is doubtful whether anything could have completely healed the emotional strains inflicted on their relationship. Generally speaking, there is no going back to things as they used to be, and even healed wounds leave a scar: Kathleen experienced what she might have regarded as desertion – of herself and of their children. In late January 1928, in response to cables from Kathleen threatening to commit suicide with the children if he did not return immediately (I/186), Epstein made a hasty departure from New York, leaving behind Margaret and daughter Peggy Jean, who followed him after Margaret had arranged all the legal and financial matters of the exhibition. The status quo upon which Epstein's two families had relied until the end of the 1920s was temporarily shattered, and Margaret's resentful attitude toward Kathleen was now based on more substantial grounds than those of sheer jealousy.

Epstein arrived in London in time to see Henry Moore's first exhibition at the Warren Gallery, with 42 sculptures and 51 drawings,[12] and was delighted to discover a new artistic force that had little to do with Bloomsbury's production and was more in accord with his own concept of sculpture. Purchasing Moore's *Suckling Child*[13] and a Cumberland alabaster *Mother and Child* from the exhibition (and later on also *Composition* in Cumberland alabaster) was therefore Epstein's vote of confidence in the young artist. Moreover, he recommended Moore to the architect Charles Holden, to carve one of the 'Winds' plaques on the Underground Electric Company Building at 55 Broadway (above St James's Underground station), thereby bringing about Moore's first public commission, after which he would spread his artistic wings.

Soon after their return, in spring 1928, the Epsteins settled in the house that was to be Epstein's home for the rest of his life – 18 Hyde Park Gate (fig. 1). The house had previously been home to several artists, including the Jewish painter Solomon J. Solomon,[14] and possessed a studio at the rear with access from Queen's Gate Mews, which enabled Kathleen when she came to model for Epstein to avoid going through the house. As the Epsteins did not have the financial means to secure the lease, Philip Sayers loaned

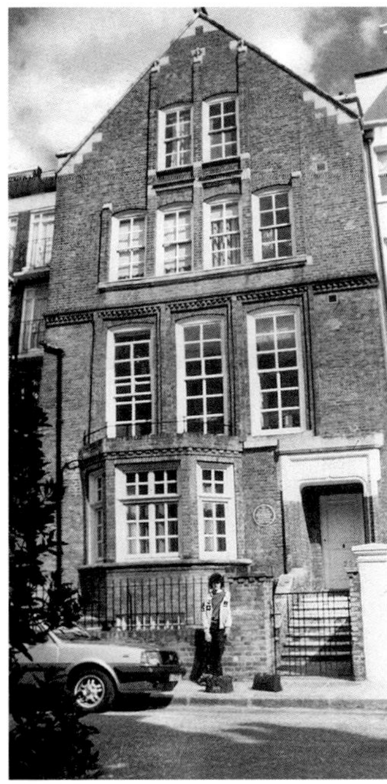

Fig. 1
Epstein's house, Hyde Park Gate, London

7 Joseph Pijoan, 'The Exposition of Contemporary Sculpture at San Francisco', *Parnasus*, vol. I, no. 5, May 1929, p. 10.

8 'Again, Epstein', *The Times*, Monday, 28 November 1927.

9 Letter from Margaret Epstein to Dr Oko, 14 November 1927: HUCAC.

10 Letter from Dr Oko to Epstein, 17 November 1927: HUCAC.

11 Letter from Epstein to Dr Oko, 7 January 1928: HUCAC. As arises from the letters, Oko was eager to sell Epstein's work whenever the opportunity arose. The reference to "Mrs Oko" was to his first wife, Pearl (Silber, *Sculpture of Epstein*, no. 124).

12 Berthoud, *Life of Henry Moore*, p. 69.

13 Oliver Brown's account (*Exhibition*, p. 110) states that it is the alabaster version. This cannot have been the case, however, because, according to Read (*Henry Moore: Sculpture and Drawings*, London 1944), the alabaster is dated 1930 – after Epstein's acquisition in 1928. The concrete version, however, was made in 1927 (Berthoud, *Life of Henry Moore*, p. 91). Epstein lent it for Moore's second exhibition in 1931, for which he wrote the catalogue introduction, and at which he bought the Cumberland alabaster *Composition* (another *Composition* from 1931 was acquired by Michael Ventris).

14 'Hyde Park Gate and Kensington Gate', *Survey of London: Volume 38: South Kensington Museums Area* (1975), pp. 26–38; http://www.british-history.ac.uk/report.aspx?compid=47515.

them money to cover it. Sayers is described as a "benevolent Irish collector, a dealer in Dublin";[15] in return, he bought Epstein's works at a reduced price.

In April 1929 Esther was born, the third child of Epstein and Kathleen, indicating that the distress caused by their separation had been eased by the profound attachment they felt for one another. Taking into account that they had started their relationship in 1921, the arrival of their children appears almost to be calculated – three years until the first-born, Theo (1924); almost the same span of time until the second child, Kitty (1927); and, after two more years, Esther (1929). By today's standards this is a well-planned family ("just a happy coincidence", contended his youngest son Jackie).[16] It is not known which of the two, Epstein or Kathleen, had initiated the idea of having children, whose legal status was determined by law and custom: their family name was Garman.

SECOND PHASE, 1929–30

The new house at 18 Hyde Park Gate had its own customs and timetable. Epstein's daily schedule in between his work and two families remained simple and constant over the years. A working day in his home, as David McFall recalls, started at 8 o'clock with breakfast:

> The table would be piled high with every available fruit like a harvest festival.
>
> Sculpture demands prolonged physical exertion and Epstein held that a full stomach was the prerequisite for stamina to start a working day on. The debris of porridge, kippers, sausage, bacon, eggs, toast and all were evidence of a hearty appetite.
>
> He would roar with derision at some item on the B.B.C. news – and then we [Epstein and McFall] would straight away get down to action.[17]

At noon Margaret brought in a tray with a light meal, as Epstein had his main meal with the family at 4–5 p.m. Afterwards, and almost every evening, a brief visit to Kathleen at her home, and twice a week – Wednesdays and Saturdays[18] – he stayed the night there, taking her out to dine. In later years, as Margaret's worsening health and immobility prevented her from frequent outings or attending cultural performances,[19] Epstein went with Kathleen to concerts, theatre and the ballet.

The handling of the financial affairs of the Epstein tribe was in Margaret's hands: she took care of Epstein's needs (including his taxi bills),[20] and also provided money for his second family; one can only guess how uncomfortable and even humiliating this must have been for Kathleen. Margaret herself must hardly have been satisfied with this small victory over her rival, as all the financial burden of sharing the needs of two families out of a meagre income and huge expenses fell upon her. In a letter to her sister-in-law Sylvia she mentions the burden of maintaining three households[21] – a weekend cottage in Epping Forest, Kathleen's household, and the Epsteins' big London house at 18 Hyde Park Gate. Epstein apparently made things worse by the impulse-buying of items for his ethnological collection and the generous gifts of flowers and exotic fruits he brought to Kathleen at every visit[22] – while paying less attention to her and the children's actual needs.

15 Gardiner, *Epstein*, p. 287, citing Peggy Jean.

16 A conversation with the author, 1998.

17 McFall, p. 3.

18 Wednesday and Saturday nights are mentioned by Gardiner (*Epstein*, pp. 227–28). Referring to a later period (1946–47), "Thursday evenings" are mentioned by John Finch, Margaret's last employee before she died in 1947: "Epstein always disappeared on Thursday evenings. I never dared ask where, but assumed it was to see Kathleen": letter to the author, 1 July 2006.

19 When Margaret met Epstein in 1903 she had thyroid deficiency disorder (then undiagnosed), and later also developed phlebitis and almost lost her legs: letter from Peggy Jean Epstein to the author, 18 April 2001.

20 Gardiner, *Epstein*, p. 307.

21 Babson, *The Epsteins*, p. 68.

22 Beth Lipkin in conversation with the author, 1986.

Not long after the Epsteins had settled in their new home, the Indian sisters Anita and Sunita, who had served as Epstein's models before his trip to New York, re-joined the household. Taking part in their daily lives, Sunita had an interest in the Epsteins' affairs and, being curious about Kathleen, on one occasion disguised herself as an Indian prince and arrived with a retinue at a restaurant where Epstein and Kathleen were dining; although they watched her spectacular entrance (so Kathleen reported to Richard Buckle),[23] neither of them recognised her. During 1928 (apparently before embarking on the project of *Day* and *Night)* Epstein made a series of drawings of Sunita, whose facial features had been immortalized in some of his most important previous works (*Rima*, 1925, and *Madonna and Child*, 1927). The drawings were presented in 1928 at the Godfrey Phillips Gallery in Duke Street, together with eight sculptures. Many of those drawings were included in Hubert Wellington's *Epstein, Seventy Five Drawings* (London 1929) – a book rejected for the American public, as the authorities in Washington pronounced it unsuitable for circulation.[24] Among the bronze portraits presented was that of Betty Joel, who would make a name for herself during the 1930s as a designer of modern furniture and is justly considered to have been the best avant-garde furniture designer of her epoch in England. As she belonged to the Leicester Gallery owner Godfrey Phillips's crowd,[25] she and the Epsteins developed a long and close relationship.

In their new home the Epsteins resumed their 'open house' gatherings of friends, artists and musicians on Sunday afternoons, forming what author and illustrator Kathleen Hale had much earlier defined as "a serious minded society", differing from Augustus John's more gregarious set (which she had joined after Epstein told her she must choose between them), adding that "they never mixed".[26] Although her memoirs refer to the late 1910s, when she met Peggy Jean's biological mother Meum Lindsell Stuart, the division of the avant-garde into 'societies' and their mutual exclusivity remained in effect for many years and, as will be elaborated upon further on, became even more rigid.[27]

On the threshold of the new decade, and throughout the 1930s, Arnold Haskell joined the gatherings in Epstein's house in order to write his book of dialogues with the artist, published as *The Sculptor Speaks* (London 1931), and from that time until Epstein's death they met almost weekly.

Haskell regarded his visits as "always valuable because of the extraordinary mixture of people gathered round the table – beautiful exotic models, writers, painters, musicians and politicians";[28] and in the 1940s the pianist Dorothy Moggridge would appear regularly.[29] Haskell briefly describes the gatherings held at the Epstein's big home in "the large airy room for all purposes", which was above the kitchen overlooking the street through the bay window:[30]

> In the large living room ... the table is fully laid for the friends who will come in. On the walls and around the room are the many treasures Epstein has accumulated. The only pictures on the walls are a vigorous series of paintings, flower pieces and nudes, by Matthew Smith .... There are a few Epsteins, a head of his wife, some heads of Peggy Jean and the mask of Meum. Through the glass doors can be seen two large Marquesan Idols.[31]

23 Buckle, *Epstein: Sculptor*, p. 182.

24 The decision was published as 'New Epstein Surprise: Drawings Banned in America', *Evening News*, 2 July 1929; cited in Gardiner, *Epstein*, p. 307.

25 Bernard Denvir, 'Obituary: Ewan Phillips', *The Independent*, 3 June 1994.

26 Hale, *A Slender Reputation*, p. 54.

27 Haskell, *Balletomane at Large*, p. 54.

28 Haskell, *In His True Centre*, p. 87.

29 Moggridge, a known pianist, worked during the 1930s for the BBC Television Orchestra in their 'Soiree Musicale'.

30 Gardiner, an architect by profession, describes the house and its functions in detail: Gardiner, *Epstein*, pp. 285–88.

31 Haskell, *The Sculptor Speaks*, p. 1.

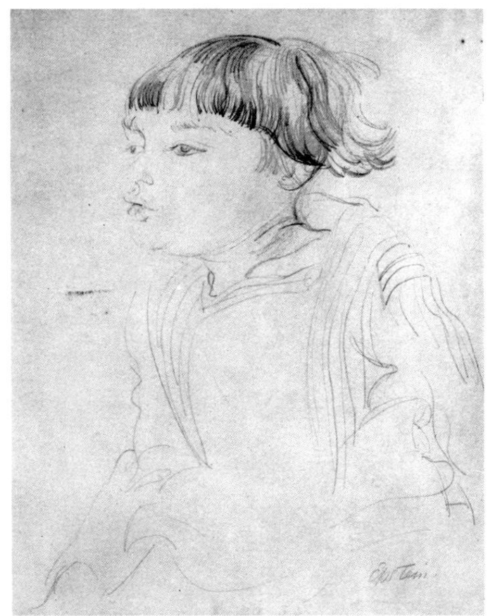

2
Theo (Theodore Garman), 1930
Pencil, 380 x 302 mm
GREC-NAGW

Margaret Epstein "conducted" these gatherings in which, as in the previous years described by Hale, the atmosphere "was one of great respect and deference, almost idolatry" towards Epstein and towards the hostess, "Hugely fat and with dyed red hair, who was a warm 'earth mother' figure whom I loved".[32]

Haskell described positively the lively atmosphere of the house in the 1930s, its guests and the many art works on the walls and furniture, as well as Epstein's welcoming of any interruptions of the conversations by his daughter Peggy Jean. However, the scrutinizing eyes of Ethel Mannin, undoubtedly coming from a more affluent background, saw the dust of ages all around, a shabby room with a garish light and the "cheapest kind of tea things".[33] Alongside expressions of her respect for the sculptor, the picture she conveyed was that of an artist's poverty. The Epsteins, whose daily needs did not require expensive "tea things" or any other bourgeois commodities acquired for their own sake, resented this upper-class depiction of their life. An old acquaintance, J.K. Feibleman, claimed that "Epstein's house, whether by design or accident, was always the typical madhouse of the famous Bohemian artist".[34]

Daughter Peggy Jean was always part of these social gatherings, as well as of the Epsteins' Easter visits during the 1930s to Paris.[35] Epstein loved the constant presence of this child of his and, being generally fond of having children around, was pleased that "the house was always streaming with children".[36] He was not a Victorian father whose children "were to be seen and not heard, painted and glared into silence", as Augustus John is said to have preferred them.[37] Epstein adored children whoever they were, and an anecdote told by his sister Sylvia attests to this: during 1926 he was working on Rabindranath Tagore's portrait and, considering him a holy person, Epstein was envisaging depicting a kind of halo over his head. At one of his sittings, however, Sunita's son Enver came into the studio and went up to Tagore, and "Tagore shuddered, pulling his hand away from the child; Jacob saw it".[38] There is no halo in Tagore's portrait.

A brief preliminary note on Epstein's attitude to his own children is in order here.

Epstein's love and affection for his children with Margaret is attested by its many expressions in his letters over the years. However, it is not easy to assess his feelings towards his second family's children, in spite of his strong emotional attachment to their mother. Until the mid 1940s, when they were living close by and he was making portraits of them, the Garman children had little involvement with Epstein's life, and, moreover, Epstein seems to have been very reserved concerning his second family with people outside his immediate circle or even with those closest to him. Thus, to his friend and ophthalmologist Dr Blake he wrote of an intended visit to his clinic of "the small girl Kitty Garman with her mother Kathleen Garman who has sat for me a great many times".[39] For reasons that will be elaborated upon further on, for many years Kathleen's children left no mark on his daily life or his sculpture. Therefore, at this stage, I provide only a few general remarks on them.

According to Buckle, Theo (b. 1924) adored his father.[40] The two extant drawings of Theo are from 1930, when he was about six years old [2], and there are no known other drawings, nor were any sculptural portraits made of him.[41] For Epstein, who modelled his other children to excess, and in particular Peggy Jean, this seems quite "out of character".[42]

Margaret's second child and the youngest of the Epsteins, Jackie (b. 1934), hardly knew Theo – regrettably, as he said – because Kathleen "kept him in the back".[43] Sylvia,

32 Hale, *A Slender Reputation*, p. 54.
33 Mannin, *Confessions and Impressions*, pp. 149–51.
34 Feibleman, *Philosophers Lead Sheltered Lives*, p. 102.
35 Judy Collins in conversation with Peggy Jean: Tate Archive (Hyman Kreitman Research Centre), TAV 4794.
36 McFall, p. 10.
37 Holroyd, *Augustus John*, p. 535.
38 Babson, *The Epsteins*, p. 60.
39 HMI: 24/1990/14. Undated, but Kitty was fifteen around 1940.
40 Buckle, *Epstein: Sculptor*, p. 332. Buckle's information had been acquired from Kathleen and, apparently, that is the impression she desired to produce.
41 One of the drawings (not that illustrated here) had been included in Epstein, *Epstein Drawings*, no. 49.
42 "Out of character" was his youngest son Jackie's expression when we discussed this phenomenon in 1998.
43 Interview with the author in 2007.

Epstein's youngest sister, living in New York, who paid her brother a visit after World War II, noted that "Jacob and Theo did not get along together".[44] Although Epstein "thought the world" of his children, as Peggy Jean remarked,[45] his somewhat peculiar relationship with Theo seems to be reflected, perhaps unconsciously, in the phrasing regarding this son in one of his letters to his daughter Peggy Jean, mentioning that Kathleen "has *her boy* who isn't at all well".[46] In later years Kathleen commented to the poet Samuel Menashe that "the father had had no joy in the son".[47]

Kitty [3], the middle child and said to have been a fragile baby, was born almost immediately before Epstein's three-month trip to New York (1927). When he left, Kathleen sent Kitty to live with her grandmother in the Garmans' house, Black Hall, Herefordshire,[48] with the child coming only rarely to London for visits. Kitty's childhood memories of her father are those of an impressive figure in a black leather cap who seldom came to visit her at her grandmother's house in the north, and "I was frightened of him".[49] When in later years she came to live in London with her mother, she modelled for several drawings and portrait sculptures. A closer relationship between Kitty and her father developed in the late 1940s when, after her divorce, she and her two baby girls came to live with him for a while. This, to a limited extent, compensated for the years of detachment and enabled her to get to know him better. Epstein's sister Sylvia remarked that, although many of their relatives resembled Epstein's mother Mary, "only Kitty in Jacob's family looks like his mother",[50] which makes one wonder whether Epstein also saw this resemblance.

Esther, Kathleen's youngest (b. 1929), of whom apparently no drawing exists, "was loved dearly", according to Sylvia, and her half-sister Peggy Jean and half-brother Jackie are in accord. One of her portraits, presented further on, is among Epstein's masterpieces. Immediately after she was born she was sent to Kathleen's nanny, Ada Newbould, in Sheffield, remaining there until she was seven years old (about 1936). Grandmother Garman then moved to Harting in the south with Kitty, and Esther joined her; when the old lady died Kitty joined Esther at Ada's house in spite of her dislike for Ada.[51] All Kathleen's three children spent their school holidays with Ada, while their mother remained in London.

One may assume that Kathleen was not happy about her own and her children's social status; but after her father's death in 1923 she was financially, and perhaps also emotionally, entirely dependent on Epstein. Besides being a figure of international fame in the artistic and cultural milieu to which she (as well as her sisters Mary and Lorna and Communist brother Douglas) chose to belong, her life-companion and the domineering person who had fathered her children was after all basically a charming and caring person. And most of all he adored her, and was devoted to her – albeit, as explained below, on his own fundamentally biblical terms. At this stage of the exposition, it is enough to suggest that Epstein may have attempted to clarify his attitude to Kathleen in a drawing of a biblical scene given to her as a personal gift.[52] Kathleen titled it '*The Blessing*', in which, she explained, "the Patriarch [is] transmitting his blessings to the awed child, the mourning woman and the stillness of the desert night".

The drawing [4] depicts a tent in which an elderly man, "the Patriarch", is blessing the grown-up daughter while "the mourning woman" stands with her hands covering her face; a silhouette of three little children of different ages, drawn in a few vague lines, features in the background. An interpretation of the biblical scene that suits the

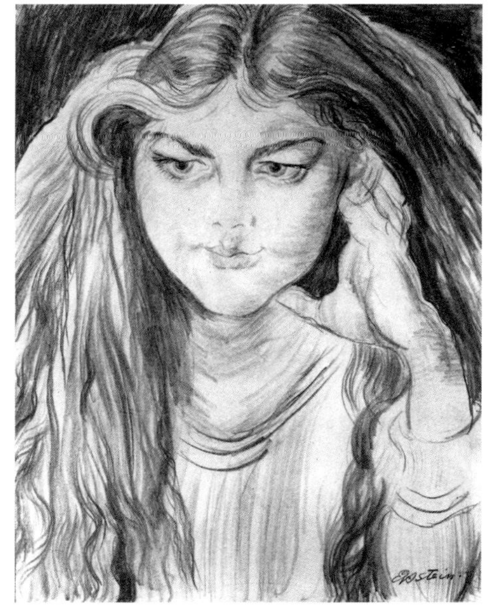

3
Kitty, 1937
Pencil, 750 x 600 mm
GREC-NAGW

44 Babson, *The Epsteins*, p. 63.

45 Peggy Jean interviewed in *Rebel Angel* – Central TV.

46 Letter from Epstein to Peggy Jean (by then living in America), 20 January 1950, after Margaret's death, when his second family became part of his daily life. Theo was by then living in Kathleen's previous home: TGA 8716-20 (my emphasis).

47 Connolly, *The Rare and the Beautiful*, p. 229.

48 Letter from Epstein to Kathleen, 1927: NAGW, NY-16 rtf: "I ask you how our little girl is".

49 Conversation with the author, 1985. Rose's remark (*Daemons and Angels*, p. 183) that she met her father for the first time when she was seven years old was not mentioned, and my impression was that, though infrequently, she saw her father throughout her childhood.

50 Babson, *The Epsteins*, p. 60. When I met Kitty during the mid 1980s, with her slim figure and big bright eyes, I did not see this resemblance. Margaret, on the other hand, did resemble her (Babson, *The Epsteins*, p. 20).

51 Connolly, *The Rare and the Beautiful*, pp. 92–93.

52 Epstein, *Epstein Drawings*, no. 44. Kathleen dates the drawing, which was never exhibited, to 1927. Further on I contest this date on grounds of style and in the context of Epstein's work of the period (it is one of several cases in which I do not agree with her dating; e.g., I/56, ftn. 51). In this case, Epstein's artistic interest in Bible stories and his work on biblical subjects began in 1929–30; in 1927–28 he drew mainly nudes (published in Wellington, *Epstein, Seventy Five Drawings*), most of them of his model Sunita. There are no biblical subjects in his work during 1927, and in style [4] differs from the earlier drawings of Sunita, but is well attuned with those of his Old Testament drawings of 1930–31.

4
The Blessing, 1930 [1927]
Pencil and wash, 58 x 44.5 cm
GREC-NAGW

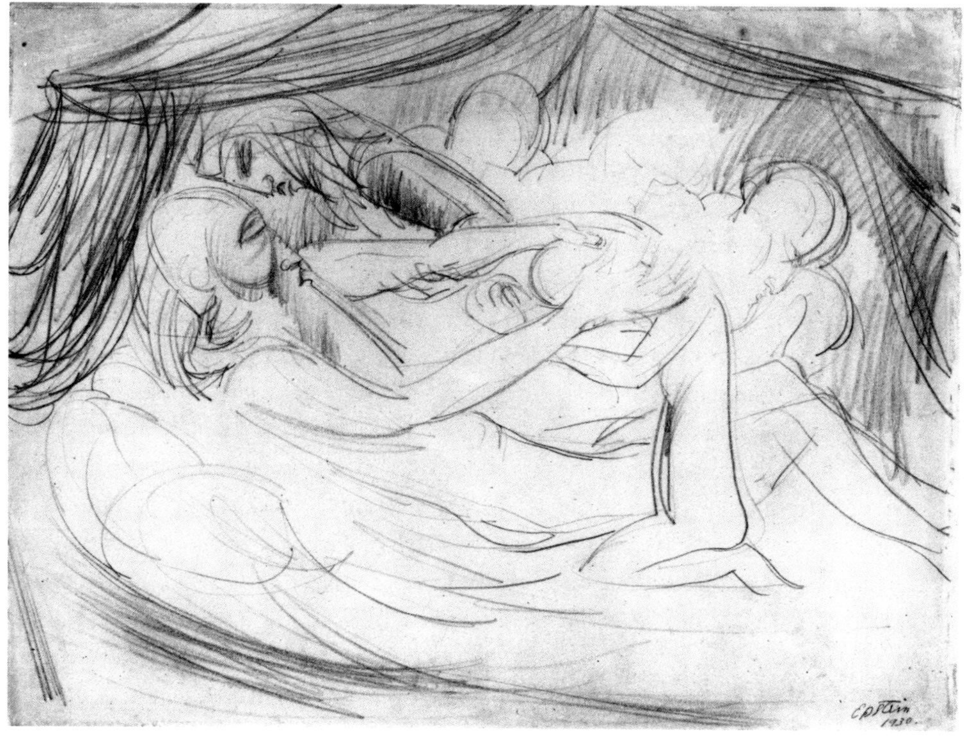

context, unpleasant as it may have been for the mourning mother of the three children in the background of the drawing, as for the living one in Epstein's second family, is that a kind of preference (the blessing) is given to the first-born child.[53]

Biblical reference in Epstein's life both private and professional stemmed not only from his engagement with biblical subjects during this period but also, as I have suggested in the Foreword (p. 9), from his particular state of mind (which I have termed 'Jewish culture'). This biblical level of being seems to have been noted at the time also by his sitters, one of whom, Lady Anne Tree, stated: "He was an Old Testament figure, or the reincarnation of one".[54] And indeed the biblical Jacob had two wives and two other women who served as surrogate mothers, like Epstein. The somewhat naive illustration [4] may hint, I suggest, at Kathleen's anxieties about her family's precarious social position.

EPSTEIN'S OEUVRE AND ITS NATURE

Epstein has been described as "a man of wide culture, fond of poetry and music, an exceptional collector of primitive art, especially African".[55] Such a neutral, though favourable description, which can be parallelled elsewhere, does not reveal the contradictions within which he lived and worked – an American living in England, a conscious Jew who utilized Christian symbols, a skilful modeller who introduced direct carving into England, and a modernist who eventually came to dislike abstraction for its own sake. The outcome of it all was that he did not fit neatly into the artistic categories of his time. In order to emphasize the individuality of the artist and his work I have chosen to present a brief outline of the theme of procreation in his work – a subject

53 A point discussed in my conversation with Kitty, 1985.

54 Gardiner's interview (*Epstein*, p. 426).

55 In the list of artists in Compton, *British Art*, p. 264.

with which Epstein had been obsessed during his formative years (as elaborated upon in the discussion of them in the first volume) and one, as we will see, which to some extent is expressed also in his first carved work of 1930. By the end of 1929, besides producing many traditional portraits albeit in his own expressive manner, Epstein had experimented with various styles, and mastered them all – the simplified but still traditional forms of the eighteen sculptures for the British Medical Association building in the Strand [5], made partly by direct carving and thus introducing this technique into England in 1908; the introduction of non-European influences when he plunged into symbolical subjects in his direct carvings during the early 1910s [6 – *Maternity*], and a similar amalgam in his most renowned work, the 1912 *Monument in Memory of the Late Oscar Wilde*;[56] the influences of primitive art and their stylization in the carvings of the Pett Level works of 1913–16 [7 – *Flenite Female*]; and a return to more naturalistic, almost Rodinesque, modelled forms in the post-WW1 large bronzes [8 – *Visitation*; 1925]. The end of these formative years, 1928–29, is marked by a return to direct carving [9 – *Night*] for London's St James Underground station, projecting his eclectic choice of form and iconography from the enormous repertoire he had accumulated.

I have deliberately not included his best-known work, *The Rock Drill* (1913–16), the first ever assemblage combining a ready-made component and sculpture, which was an outstanding work not only for its period, but also for the future direction of art. The reason for this exclusion (despite my suggestion of it as again conveying the idea of procreation – albeit in a different perception, medium and technique – I/128), is that it was Epstein's first and last experimental work, after which he returned to the traditional methods of carving and modelling.

Whatever had been the artistic trend during the period under discussion, almost every large sculpture that Epstein produced between the 1930s and the 1950s aroused a public outcry, causing one critic to state that "a new carving by Mr. Epstein – good, bad or indifferent – can still steal the headlines when criminal assault, private or political, is out of season".[57] These decades of artistic notoriety combined with personal hardships are elaborated upon here mainly in order to clarify his work, because a cornerstone of the approach I have taken is the idea that Epstein's oeuvre cannot be completely divorced from his personal life or the period in which he lived and worked. Unfortunately, information regarding the personal or artistic considerations of his work made after the 1930s is not to be found in the books written during his lifetime,[58] nor in his autobiography of 1940, to which, in 1954, he added a postscript. Faithful to his own statement that "my work is there, that is enough",[59] the task of searching for and finding the artist's ideas within the work has to be achieved mainly through analysing his sculptures in the context of their era, and indicating the possible sources of influence available to him at the time.

The interpretations of the works presented stem from some specific premises (explained in my previous book, I/11–14) that should be briefly recapitulated:

• Epstein was very well informed in humanistic studies and art history. His admirers have noted this: "He has an active interest in aesthetic theory, and I have heard him display considerable knowledge of the history of art in conversations with the late Bernard Van Dieren at the Café Royale".[60] As well as being aware of the cultural trends of his time, Epstein's reading and knowledge of other subjects too was broad:

56 'Agreement between Jacob Epstein of 72 Cheyne Walk Chelsea in the county of London, sculptor (hereinafter called "The Sculptor") on one part and Roberts Ross of the Reform Club Pall-Mall (hereinafter called "The Client",' with Stephen Grange, dramatic author, signing as witness: HMI, 45/1990/3.

57 Watson, *Art Lies Bleeding*, London 1939, p. 16.

58 Arnold Haskell's book seems to be the only relevant one, but it belongs to the early 1930s; little of the person is disclosed in Laurie Lee's 'Introduction' in a later book, written in the last years of Epstein's life, G. Ireland, *Epstein: A Camera Study of the Sculptor at Work*, London 1957.

59 Haskell, *The Sculptor Speaks*, p. 8.

60 Feibleman, *Philosophers Lead Sheltered Lives*, p. 101.

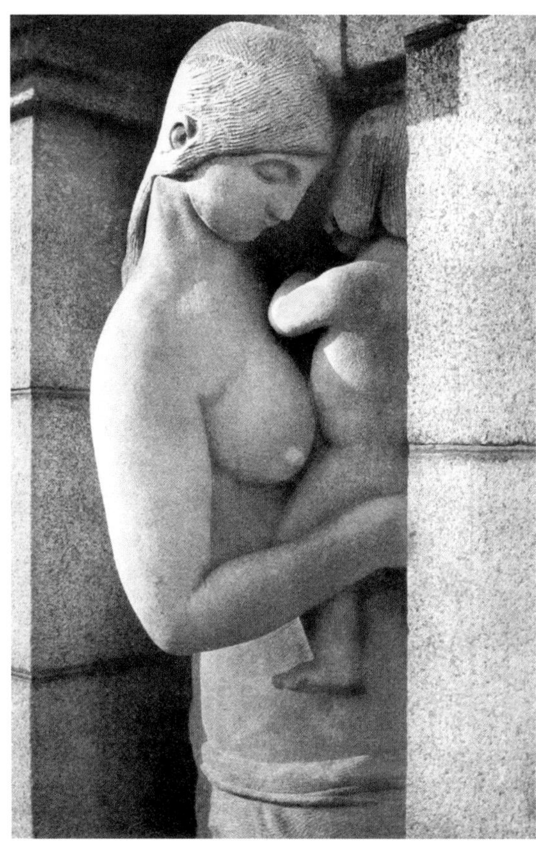

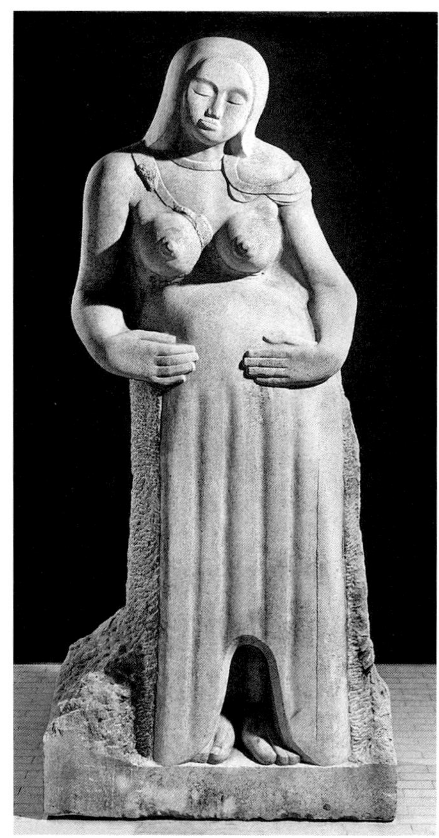

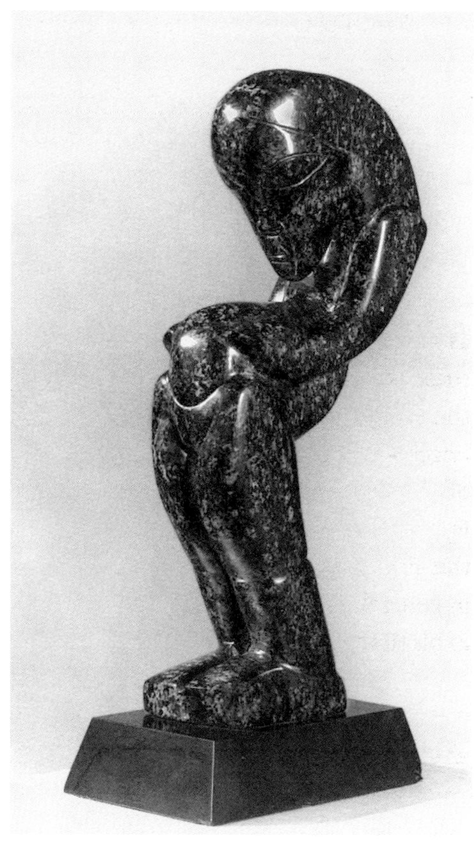

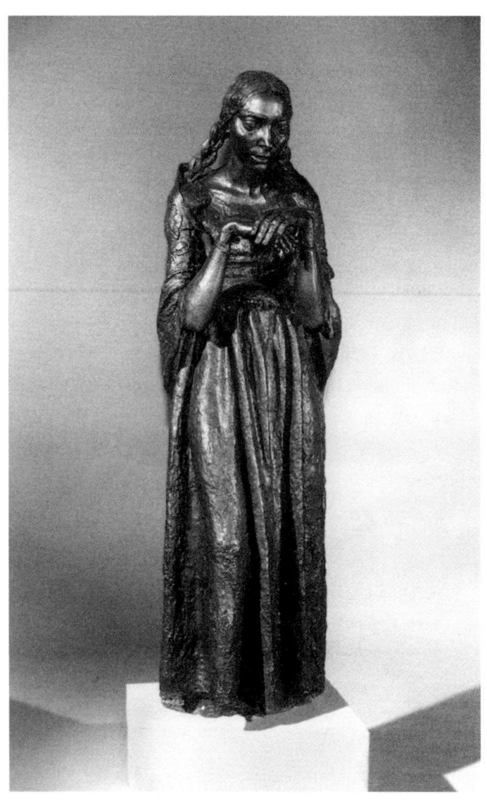

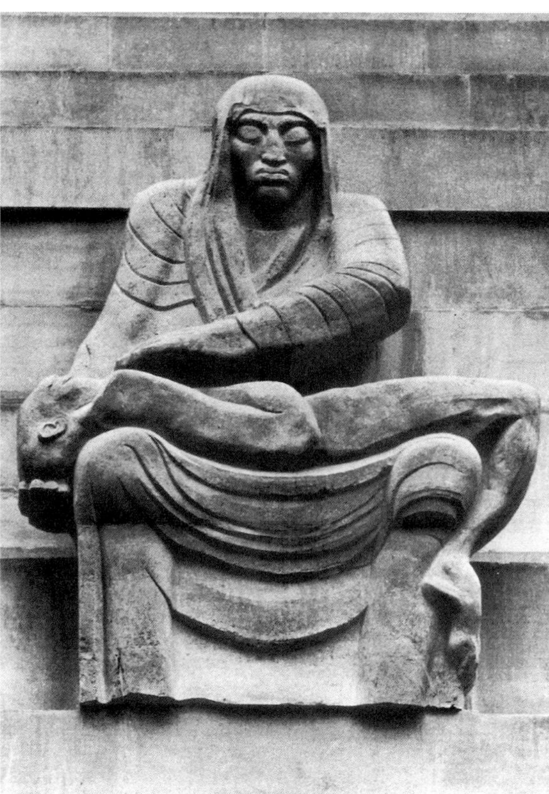

5
Maternity, 1907–08
Portland stone, H. 210–12 cm
Zimbabwe House (former British Medical Association Building), London; destroyed

6
Maternity, 1912
Hoptonwood stone, H. 206 cm
Leeds City Art Gallery

7
Female Figure in Flenite, 1913
Serpentine, H. 60.9 cm
Tate, London

8
The Visitation, 1926
Bronze, H. 165 cm
Tate Gallery, London

9
Night, 1929
Portland stone blocks,
275 x 275 x 100 cm
London Underground Electric Railways Headquarters, Westminster

Mrs. Epstein would return home from her visit to their friend's second-hand bookshop [Moshe Oved, discussed further on] with an armful of books. These were placed by Epstein's bed, and he would pick them one after the other. The books might be almost anything: novels by D.H. Lawrence, textbooks on entomology, histories of the Chinese people .... Epstein read and retained knowledge ... he generally understood what he was talking about regardless of the preconditions of the subject.[61]

His knowledge embraced all that concerned the subjects of his work – images as an expression of religious or abstract ideas – as is evident from the titles given to these works. As Epstein rarely discussed his sources, proof of them has to be found in the sculptures themselves – following the idea that art derives from art and its influences – whether they were those of tradition, or exceptional examples that, because of their rarity, captured the artist's mind. The aim here is to try and determine, through Epstein's work, what might have influenced him regardless of the rarity or popularity of the influential element. The assumption on which this study rests is that Epstein knew, in general terms and relating to his own work, all the essentials of art that were known in his time.

• Epstein's approach to the question of the appropriate form in which to express an abstract idea was based on his understanding of both content and technical means, resulting in a mandate of his own making:

I make no formula, and only when I see something to be done in abstract form that better conveys *my meaning* than natural forms, then I use it;[62] [adding elsewhere] it is not only the visual that stimulates an artist's conceptions.[63]

He expressed his ideas through a principal motif that embodied *essence*, offering an *implicit* symbolism,[64] often characterized by free forms resulting from the breakdown (abstraction) or disintegration (stylization) of natural forms in order to express the symbolic meaning inherent in them. Examination of his oeuvre shows that when Epstein wanted to express an abstract idea he tended to stylize the forms (*Genesis*); but when he wished to stress a human individuality within the idea, he executed the work naturalistically (*Visitation*).[65]

• An ambiguity in Epstein's work, generally overlooked, is that of content. On the one hand he was a revolutionary artist who in his work expressed universal ideas; on the other, he was the only sculptor of his time whose work projected his interpretation of ideas that emanated from what has previously been termed 'Jewish culture' (p. 9). The irony of this ambiguity – universality and Jewish culture – is that the 'Jewishness' they perceived in his sculptures of Christian subjects was generally received with antagonism by Gentiles, while the Jewish world of the time ignored his work because of its universality, which might also expressed through Christian motifs. As a result of this ambiguity there was confusion as to whether Epstein should be regarded as a 'Jewish artist' or not. Epstein insistently refused to be tagged 'a Jewish sculptor': "I have never joined in all-Jewish exhibitions of art .... I am most often annoyed rather than flattered to be told that I am the best or foremost Jewish artist. Surely to be an artist is enough" (225).[66]

61 Finch, email letter to the author, 1 July 2009.

62 Letter from Epstein to John Quinn, the American art collector, cited in Reid, *The Man From New York*, p. 299 (my emphasis).

63 Ibid., p. 237.

64 The idea of 'implicit symbolism' is taken from Hinks, *Myth and Allegory in Ancient Art*, p. xliii. With it Hinks contrasts 'explicit symbolism', in which an issue is presented through a specific event of a story, with an allegorical as well as descriptive character. The explicit symbolic expression became part of an iconographic tradition understood by the viewer.

65 Epstein specifically makes this distinction when he talks about *Visitation* (1925) and *Genesis* (1930): Haskell, *The Sculptor Speaks*, p. 63.

66 This was said in the 1940s. In 1913, however, he went with the painter David Bomberg to Paris in order to choose works by Jewish artists of the School of Paris to be presented in 'The Jewish Section' of an exhibition in the Whitechapel Gallery: Cork, *Vorticism*, I, p. 121.

In light of Epstein's resentment at being artistically classified by race (and from the 1930s on, this was to become an acute issue), a brief elaboration is needed in regard to artistic classification by culture – in other words, how one relates to the state of mind that distinctively reflects Jewishness in art.

The question whether there is a cultural phenomenon that justifies the tag 'Jewish art' was and still is disputed. Studies have previously claimed that the Jewishness of Jewish art is "characterized by the fact that it is made by Jewish artists and by its content",[67] overly stressing an accident of birth combined with subject-matter. The most recent reasonable definition, which corresponds to the notion of a 'culture' which I find to apply to Epstein, states that "until a better definition is found, Jewish art may probably be best defined as an art bearing a strong stamp of Jewish culture expressed deliberately or in an involuntary manner".[68]

Considering Epstein's work from the viewpoint of 'Jewish art' may have little validity, because if by 'art' we mean the style and means of expression (line, colour, form) that distinguish one art from another, then there is no Jewish style in art (and this point will be expanded upon later, when discussing philosophical notions of the 1930s). The Jews' artistic means of expression were borrowed from the peoples amongst whom they lived. However, 'Jewish art' may have meaning as a *cultural* term, as can 'Christian art', regardless of the artistic means employed.

The important issue seems to be whether and how, because of his state of mind, he introduced Jewish notions into the expression of his subject-matter, and what were the values he projected ('culture' in the sense used above) even in works with Christian subjects.

Creating so many works on Christian subjects does not imply that he was probably a Messianic Jew (a naïve perception suggested to me in the past). On the contrary, it emerges from this study that, while Epstein consistently sought some kind of spiritual meaning in his Christian subjects, in his art he gave them a Jewish interpretation and, therefore, Epstein is *culturally* a Jewish artist.

THE NEW AGE: A GENERAL PROLOGUE TO THE 1930s

I. THE SOCIAL SCENE

In order to understand the milieu within which Epstein was functioning, I will summarize here several issues regarding London's intellectual environment in his time. This somewhat lengthy exposition is necessary because Epstein's work is interwoven with these issues and, I suggest, they influenced it in a way that, in turn, conveys his reactions to them.

The years between the wars, when referring in particular to the cocoon of London's so-called intelligentsia, might be justly titled 'the Morbid Age', as indeed a recent study is titled.[69] This morbidity, which we now perceive in a past we can only read about, is manifested in different outlooks found within London's intellectual, literary and cultural hegemony, which may or may not have been echoed in the rest of the country. One may also regard as morbid naivety (though stemming from the most generous impulses of humanity) the political dream of a movement for democratic action supported by all

67 Posèq, 'The Hanging Carcass Motif and Jewish Artists', *Jewish Art*, xvi, 1990–91, p. 139.

68 Posèq, *Soutine; His Jewish Modality*, p. xxviii.

69 Overy, *The Morbid Age: Britain Between the Wars*, London 2009.

people of goodwill (the League of Nations) as well as the aesthetic dream in which art would be appreciated by the masses, yet produced at a high level of sensitivity.[70] To what extent did England share these European dreams? "The truth is that it is impossible to discover what the English people are really feeling and thinking, about the war or about anything else", commented Orwell when summing up Malcolm Muggeridge's book *The Nineteen Thirties*, which mainly reflects on the political issues of the period.[71] This comment illuminates the difficulty in choosing how to assess those years and what to emphasize about them, in view of the many and differing opinions.

Where literature is concerned, the period reflects a certain temperamental similarity among noted authors and intellectuals, as well as among the generally well-to-do intelligentsia, which amounts to a pessimistic outlook on life, seeing its prospects as wavering between Communism and Fascism; this was a mood seemingly contradicting the relatively affluent years and euphoric atmosphere being enjoyed by many until the crash of the stock market in 1929. Thus, for example, T.S. Eliot's poem 'We are the Hollow Men' describes a very upper-class social gathering, and up to a point it can be regarded as a lament over the decadence of Western civilization. The English translation of Oswald Spengler's great treatise on the rise and fall of civilizations, *The Decline of the West*, published in 1926–28, convinced many readers of that period that they were living through the dying days of a civilization that had lost all creativity and power. And yet, "when one looks back at the 1920s, nothing is queerer than the way in which every important event in Europe escaped the notice of the English intelligentsia", commented George Orwell.[72] Thus, the Russian revolution eluded the English, because throughout those years Russia for them meant Tolstoy, Dostoyevsky and exiled counts driving taxi-cabs, but not gulags; Italy meant picture galleries, ruins, churches and museums, but not blackshirts; Germany meant films, nudism and psychoanalysis, but not Hitler, of whom hardly anyone had heard until 1931. British consciousness between the death of Lenin (January 1924) and the Ukraine famine (1932–33) remained unaffected, in spite of Malcolm Muggeridge's unauthorized visit to the area in early 1933 that exposed the planned and deliberate famine brought about by the forced collectivization of agriculture. 'Dictatorship of the proletariat' had become the dictatorship of Joseph Stalin, he claimed,[73] explaining how the dictatorship of Stalin had developed into a "dictatorship of the General Idea". His conclusion that "If the General Idea is fulfilled it can only be by bringing into existence a slave state" angered the 'Left' – including also the Epsteins? No source available – which saw Russia and its revolution as a paradigm of hope for post-war Europe.

On 24 October 1929, the Wall Street Crash shattered the glow of capitalism, plunging the USA into an economic depression, affecting the rest of the world by precipitating the calling-in of American loans to other countries and the imposing of customs barriers to stop the import of foreign goods, thereby contributing to unemployment and governmental instability in Europe. It is little wonder that the following decade saw the rise in Germany of a third-party platform in the form of Nazism. This would lead Germany out of the Depression sooner than other countries, throwing the rest of Europe into a state of panic, because the Depression elsewhere did not end until World War II began.

Where England is concerned, there are two opposing historical images of the Depression in the 1930s. On one hand there were 2.5 million unemployed men (25%

70 Julian Symons, 'The Heart of a Dream', in *The Thirties: A Dream Revolved*, p. 55. Symons's book reflects mainly on the political and intellectual (chiefly literary) panorama of the period.

71 George Orwell, 'The Limit to Pessimism', in *Collected Essays, Journalism and Letters*, vol. 1, pp. 533–35; Malcolm Muggeridge, *The Nineteen Thirties*, London 1940.

72 Ibid., p. 508.

73 Muggeridge, 'Famine in the North Caucasus', etc.

of the workforce in 1933), and on the other hand prosperity in the south,[74] particularly in London, which escaped the Depression that decimated industries elsewhere in Britain, and its middle class prospered.[75] The city epitomized the new post-war England, "belonging far more to the age itself than to this particular island; America, I supposed, was its real birthplace".[76] In 1931 London's cultural life was enriched by the inauguration of the Royal Ballet at its home in Sadler's Wells. The entertainment sphere had been enriched by the talking movies, produced in all countries, but this to some extent formed a language barrier that hindered cultures from communicating through film, previously achieved in silent movies by means of gestures and facial expressions.

Public entertainment extended beyond the local music halls and cinema, and for the first time outdoor activities in open spaces were made possible for a wider population, who could now travel in motor vehicles to rural locations far beyond the walking reach of a railway station. This all contributed to a freer attitude to the naked body: "The 1930s saw the growth of nudism under labels such as 'naturalism' or 'gymnosophy', a pursuit of harmony with nature and untrammelled and non-erotic meeting of humans as nature intended then to be", suggests Timothy Wilcox,[77] adding that "the aesthetic of the human body promoted in naturalism often drew on ancient Greek models". It is thus not surprising that the then modern assimilation of these models of 'harmony with nature', as will be elaborated upon further on, attracted people to the simplified classicism of Aristide Maillol.

The class system of London 'society' remained as it had been – mostly impenetrable and to a growing extent openly anti-Semitic. On this last issue among his own milieu, as far as I could gather, Epstein remained silent; the temperament that had caused him to explode against anti-Semitic remarks on his work in his early years in London was now tamed.[78] As for the rest of the country, the stress of unemployment, low wages and a reduced standard of living elicited social unrest that found an outlet in two opposing political notions. On the one hand, Communism began attracting a large number of followers, mainly from the lower classes but also among the intelligentsia; both social sectors were looking for a more benevolent social order – models for which they believed the new Russian regime possessed – to ease the burden that fell mainly on the less fortunate sectors of the population. On the other hand, many among the upper classes and the more fortunate ordinary folk were deterred by this social unrest and favoured the sense of order offered by state supremacy or Fascism (in its original form and in line with its early manifestation in Mussolini's Italy). Its appeal, to which anti-Semitism was later added, led to the formation of Fascist political movements. The rift between these two ideologies in Britain later resulted in bitter clashes between the English supporters of authoritative Fascism and their democratic Socialist opponents.

In this atmosphere as described above, English Jews, who during the mid 1930s numbered about 300,000 (less than 1% of the population), were living in a peculiar situation. There were important differences between English and European Jews, who constituted a larger minority (Germany), up to almost 10% of the population (Poland). "The Polish Jew knows why he suffers; he is a Jew. But the German Jews do not even know for what they are suffering; many of them are no longer conscious of being Jews," explained Dr Chaim Weizmann in England.[79] The Jews in England of the period may be regarded as belonging to one or other categories: the affluent and intellectual circles

74 For more on this, see http://www.20thcenturylondon.org.uk/server.php?show=nav.41.

75 The government, as became apparent, was confused in coping with the Depression between 1931 and 1933, but things changed a little for the better with the Special Areas Act of 1934, which tried to attract light industries to 'distressed' areas with the construction of 500,000 council houses and the encouragement of new industries such as chemicals and electrical goods. In fact, people with secure jobs benefited from the Depression because prices fell and they could buy more.

76 J.B. Priestley, *English Journey*, [1934]. pp. 371–75.

77 Timothy Wilcox, *Day in the Sun*, pp. 9–11.

78 "Lord Alfred Douglas summoned Jacob Epstein before a Magistrate in Marlborough Street Police Court to-day for using threats toward him on Dec. 9, 1913, claiming that he received a letter signed 'Epstein' which said: 'If you attack my monument to Oscar Wilde in any way derogatory to me in England, I shall have you in court. Should you disregard this warning, I shall spoil the remains of your beauty double quick'": cable sent to *The New York Times*, 2 January 1914, published on 3 January. Epstein was not legally represented, but consented to be bound over for the sum of £100 to keep the peace for six months. Douglas went on in 1920 to found a magazine, *Plain English*, in which he printed numerous anti-Jewish pieces.

79 Sacks, *The Intelligent Man's Guide To Jew-Baiting*, pp. 12, 40.

were in most cases 'Germans', while the ordinary middle class were 'Polish'. According to this metaphorical division Epstein was both – 'German' in his intellectual and artistic notions, and 'Polish' in his Jewish roots and perceptions. In regard to his art, however, he was not slow to notice that it was the English upper middle class that most resented his work, and he commented on it:

> One might wonder what is that strikes at them in my sculpture, what profoundly rooted beliefs and shibboleths are disturbed … and can only be understood by relating it to something fundamental going far deeper than the sculpture or painting involved (127).
>
> I do not see myself as a martyr, but what has always astonished me was the bitterness of the attacks on my statues. Their cause I am unable to fathom (175).

Epstein, I suggest, had failed to grasp the obvious. If, as he said, he did not put the criticism of his sculpture down to anti-Semitism (225), he did not care to explain his audiences' insecurity when confronting an unfamiliar phenomenon in which (as remarked already in 1924, and tagged by Epstein as a "piece of Aryanism"), when "surrounded by Epstein's sculptures, the Aryan is in the face of an alien Genius".[80]

For both sorts of Jews it was the rise to power of Fascism in its political manifestations that started the final (one hopes) saga of Jewish tribulations in the modern era. Mussolini became Prime Minister of Italy in 1922, but it was not until 1935 that the Fascist government published his book *Fascism, Doctrine and Institutions* (written in 1932),[81] and by that time its philosophical basis was only just being explored in treatises from university professors, explaining also the socialistic ideology of Fascism. The German imitation (rising to power in 1933) displayed the same features of distorted socialism and national fervour.

By mid 1930 England had three separate Fascist groups, two of which, in reply to a questionnaire, had declared their uncompromising hostility towards the Jews. Only Sir Oswald Mosley's group professed to have no anti-Semitic bias; moreover, when Mosley started his new party after leaving Labour in 1931, he was reported to have Jewish bodyguards.[82] Generally speaking, however, once the potential of using anti-Semitism as a pawn in the political game had appeared, it would be asking too much of politicians not to exploit it. By the mid 1930s, following Hitler's anti-Semitic precedent in Germany, Mosley's group of blackshirts (the British Union of Fascists, or BUF) was reflecting this change in the accentuation of the anti-Semitic attitude.

A noted writer of the period, D.H. Lawrence, went further in condemning the political thinking in England, stating that the whole of the Liberal Democratic tradition was, in fact, "essentially Jewish in nature", which was an accusation, not a compliment.[83] In the same vein of castigating the Liberal tradition, T.S. Eliot wrote (1934), "What is still more important [in society] is unity of religious background, and reasons of race and religion combine to make any large number of free-thinking Jews undesirable".[84] Eliot, as judged by Leonard Woolf (Virginia Woolf's Jewish husband, a friend of Eliot), "was slightly anti-Semitic in the sort of vague way which is not uncommon" – otherwise described (see above, p. 9), as "not being particularly anti-Semitic". Eliot, as suggested by another commentator, would probably have denied this quite genuinely;[85] and indeed

80 Signed by 'Rusticus', *The New Age*, February 1924; cited I/223.

81 Ardita Publishers, Rome. http://www.worldfuturefund.org/wffmaster/Reading/Germany/mussolini.htm.

82 Sacks, *The Intelligent Man's Guide To Jew-Baiting*, pp. 11–12.

83 For comment on Jewish refugees coming to England, see Holmes, *Anti-Semitism in British Society*, p. 214. Holmes also points to Lawrence's *Kangaroo* (1923) and *The Virgin and the Gipsy* (1930) as conveying the same idea.

84 In a series of lectures delivered at the University of Virginia in 1933, published in London in 1934 under the title *After Strange Gods: A Primer of Modern Heresy*.

85 Suggested by Peter Ackroyd (*T.S. Eliot*, p. 304).

in the early 1940s Eliot was actively helping Jewish refugees from Germany and Austria to re-settle in Britain and America.[86] During the 1950s a warm relationship developed between Epstein and the poet (discussed further on).

The most prominent anti-Semite in the London art world was Wyndham Lewis, Epstein's acquaintance from the good old days of Vorticism in the mid 1910s, who respected Epstein and appreciated his art;[87] his is an interesting case in the development of anti-Semitism. In his writings after 1926 (*The Art of Being Ruled*, in a chapter entitled 'Fascism as an Alternative'), Lewis had been advocating a viable system to counter liberalism and "bourgeois" democracy. Far preferable to Lewis was the idea of authoritative leaders who would "assume responsibility for the ignorant millions", and replace the exploitation of "the weaknesses of the Many" with "the exploitation of the intelligence of the Few". Throughout the 1930s Lewis continued to support Nazism – in his most notorious pro-Nazi document *Hitler* (1931) – and later on attacked Communism in *The Old Gang and The New Gang* (1933), *Left Wings over Europe; or How to Make a War about Nothing* (1936), and *Count Your Dead: They Are Alive* (1937). However, a visit in 1937 to Berlin, where he became aware of German militarism, and a visit to the Warsaw ghetto and the experience of Kristallnacht (9–10 November 1938), triggered a change in Lewis's politics. On the eve of World War II he retracted his position – in *The Hitler Cult and The Jews: Are They Human?* (1939), which received a favourable review in London's *Jewish Chronicle* entitled 'Justice for the Jew'.

II. PHILOSOPHICAL ASPECTS IN ART

Whereas in their early stages the Italian and British Fascist movements had propagated a social order based on the supremacy of the State over the individual, in Germany another ingredient had been added to the development of Nazi ideology – the marking of a certain group among the white European race as 'Aryans', and claiming its superiority over all other Europeans and non-Europeans.

In my previous book, dealing with Epstein's formative years, I coined the expression 'the Aryan Sun' for the nineteenth century's cultural-philosophical notion of an Indo-European original religion (I/96–97). Devoid of any racially discriminatory ideology this notion had been accepted by English intellectuals too, and expressed not only in Epstein's carvings of 1909–12 and but also in the same period in the work of Eric Gill.[88] I shall employ the term 'Aryan Sun' again (with an explanation of its English aspect) for the 1930s and 1940s because, to my mind, Epstein's sculpture of those years constituted a kind of response to the racist ideology that the 'New Age' of the 1930s had introduced into the concept, although the word 'sun' itself appears in the title of only one of his sculptures of this period – the final (1935) form of *Sun God*, conceived in 1910.

The 'New Age' of this movement culminated in the perception of "pure blood", elaborated upon in a book by Alfred Rosenberg (one of the principal ideologues of the Nazi party) entitled *Der Mythus des zwanzigsten Jahrhunderts* (The myth of the twentieth century; 1930). The titular "myth" in the book refers to the myth of blood which, under the sign of the swastika, strives to put an end to racial chaos and advocates the recognition of the Aryan German folk as a superior race, destined to rule inferior societies. Under this ideology, the book rejected modern artistic notions, retreating instead into a kind of

86 This is the other side of the coin, revealed in a previously unknown cache of letters from Eliot to Horace Kallen. Moreover, in letters written after the war (*Modernism/Modernist*, January 2003), Eliot also voiced support for the State of Israel.

87 In his letter to Beatrice Hasting (1914) he urges her to disconnect herself from the intellectual circle to which he himself wanted to belong (T.E. Hulme's), claiming that "They are pretty boring folk; Epstein is the only individual in that little set who does anything or has any personality": Rose, *The Letters of Wyndham Lewis*, p. 65.

88 Epstein's carvings included *Sun God* and *Sun Goddess Crouching*. See I/87–110.

Neo-Classicist Realism. Thus, whereas in the political sphere the polarity was presented as 'Fascism vs. Communism', in the sphere of art it became 'Aryan vs. Semitic'. To a lesser extent politically, but with a distinct social, artistic and racial tint, these oppositions existed in England, too. Owing to the passing of time and the arrival of new audiences who, as it is said, "knew not Joseph" (Exodus 1: 8), some explanation is required in this regard, and that of the influential opinions of Herbert Read, expressed during the early 1930s.

Unlike Roger Fry with his "significant form", the term proposed in *Vision and Design* (London, 1921; based on Clive Bell's theory in *Art*, 1915), which served in fact to dismiss any kind of art that did not conform to his own ideas, Read distinguished between different kinds of valid art, though not hiding which kind he himself preferred, and in the case of sculpture (inspired by Henry Moore) he required 'truth to material'. However, both men's theories meant that any 'form' might be acceptable, as long as it did not project content or idea. In the early 1930s, consistently with the prevailing atmosphere in Europe, and particularly in England, Read regarded form and its evolution as an Aryan domain:[89]

> It may be old-fashioned to believe in the racial factor in art, or in anything else but politics, but though art in a very real sense is universal … nevertheless certain types of art have characterized certain types of people …. The Semites, in fact, are not expressive at all in plastic modes – that is to say, they are not original or 'creative' in them. *Relatively speaking, there is no Jewish art.*

Stating that Semites are neither original nor inventive in regard to form is not necessarily anti-Semitic nor, when uttered by a Jew, is it "a pathetic example of Jewish self-denigration",[90] but simply the truth. Unlike other peoples, the Jews were basically a people of the given 'word' (on Mt Sinai), and later on of 'the book', and felt no need to translate their knowledge or ruling ideology into images, a practice more suited to illiterate societies. The Jewish nation's means of popular communication, oral or written, was not a visual one but textual.

Read continues:

> The Jew still retains the essential mobility of temperament, the inquietude … [when] he takes to plastic art … the art he creates is a distinctive art. *It has not the same respect for forms as Aryan art*; it avoids the definite and static. It is essentially romantic, and is not ashamed of its romanticism. It sees in painting, not a means of interpreting the outer world, but as means of expressing the inner self. That is why it uses the essential types of individualist art – lyricism and symbolism.

Read identified Jewish art, which "relatively speaking" does not exist, as distinctively expressionistic; as conveying moods and inner feelings expressed through colours and stylized forms rather than through mere formal organizations. I assume that his notions were derived from observing "the School of Paris" (a term then used derogatorily),[91] as he stresses the differences between Picasso (although not French, yet still "Germanic")[92] and Chagall (embodying the universal Jew, the most renowned Jewish member of the School of Paris).

Are Read's definitions or appreciations of Jewish artists' art of the 1930s derogatory? Yes, if one is insulted by racial epithets or when "the racist implications of this genteel

89 Read, *The Meaning of Art*, p. 79; the italics in these citations are mine.

90 As claimed by Charles Spencer in his introduction to the catalogue of the exhibition *Jewish Art* (Glasgow, 1979), in relation to Berenson's view mentioned below.

91 See Posèq, *Soutine: His Jewish Modality*, p. xix.

92 Read, *The Meaning of Art*, p. 213.

practice of art criticism ... are revealed as loaded terms";[93] no, if one is within Read's period and his definitions of art that also embrace other peoples – because for him (and his attitude is purely aesthetic) the characteristic style of the northern latitudes (northern Europe) is expressionistic, too, just as "it is also a characteristic style of the Jews".[94] The argument of an implicit racial anti-Semitism in Read's case, therefore, seems out of place, assuming that no offence or derogatory attitude was intended towards "expressionism" or the "northern latitudes". Moreover, if 'form' is the gospel, then indeed there is no defined 'Jewish form' or a 'Jewish style', but rather an expressionistic mode that due to an emphasis on internal content is distinctively Jewish. However, according to Charles Spencer,[95] "Englishness in art is positively recognisable, whether Blake, Hogarth, Turner or Hockney; so is Frenchness, Italianness, Scottishness, and most certainly so is Jewishness". Nevertheless, he adds, since there have been some two thousand years of neglect by the Jews of the visual arts, it is only in the last hundred years that individuals "have made statements which can only adequately be described as Jewish". In regard to Read's "Germanic" Picasso, however, Epstein might have had some reservations, as he commented that Picasso's Jewish "strain" was the drive behind his artistic innovations.[96] And it is this very factor, of innovations within the two kinds of artistic styles, that seems to be lacking in Read's eloquent review.

Read's ideas, reflecting a common attitude for which he seems to have laid the philosophical grounds, recur also in the writings of another renowned art critic, Bernhard Berenson, who remarked that the Jews had never revealed any originality, nor expressed anything recognizably Jewish.[97] Although these critics reach the same conclusion, their ideas stem from opposing viewpoints: Read advocated a positive perception of modern art, whereas Berenson, a conservative who disapproved of modern art, saw in it a decline of form; and it was precisely in this modern kind of art that Jewish artists acquired their fame. The same perception of 'expressionism', almost half a century later, seems to be at work in Dennis Farr's survey of English art, in which Epstein's work as a whole is presented as manifesting a "vehement expressionist character rooted in Epstein's *virile temperament*, which he inherited from his Central European Jewish ancestry".[98]

III. THE ARTISTIC SCENE

One of the unfortunate occurrences of the period for Epstein and his Bohemian milieu of 'oldies' was the closure of the Café Royal in Regent Street (renovated in 1928). With its disappearance, London's intelligentsia lost its legendary meeting-place. By the time it was reinstated in 1930, 'Bohemia' had already become dispersed among various clubs, and it was in these that its members continued their intellectual cultural discussions. Moreover, the avant-garde circle during the 1930s had expanded as growing numbers of young artists and artisans tired to acquire status in the art world. "The ten thousand artists in England form not so much a profession as a species .... Their trade is one of the few that is allowed to preserve the oriental practice of bargaining ... the purchaser [then] claims the righteous satisfaction of a patron. From his greengrocer he has simply ordered what he required, but he has 'helped' the man who has supplied him with a picture or carving."[99] This, apparently, still is the art-buyer's situation, on which I do not intend to dwell, although it will occasionally

93 Barker, 'The Primitive Within: The Question of Race in Epstein's Career 1917–1929', p. 44. Her article deals mainly with the period of the 1920s, but the citation is from Read's book of 1933.

94 Read, *Contemporary British Art*, p. 27.

95 Unnamed art critic (a correspondent of the *Jewish Chronicle* and a lecturer in the Spiro Ark), 'The roots of modern Jews', http://www.somethingjewish.co.uk/articles/844_about_the_spiro_ark.htm.

96 Epstein in an interview with the *Jewish Chronicle*, London, 25 February 1916.

97 Bernhard Berenson, *Aesthetics and History in The Visual Arts*, New York [1948] 1956, pp. 178–79.

98 Dennis Farr, *English Art, 1870–1940*, p. 220. My italics indicate my astonishment that expressionism is viewed necessarily as "virile"; as I share Epstein's roots and tendencies, I wonder whether this book is also "virile".

99 Watson, *Art Lies Bleeding*, p. 60.

be mentioned in regard to the sale of Epstein's work. Artist-public or artist-critic relations, on the other hand, are a more important subject for our discussion because it is in these spheres that the artist's reputation and his place in history are determined.

It is customary, and rightfully so, to present the full or partial scope of developments in modern art of the first half of the twentieth century as a succession of artistic movements, and Epstein is usually placed among the pioneers of modern sculpture in the mid 1910s, thanks to his extraordinary carvings and then the famous assemblage of a ready-made and a stylized plaster figure in *The Rock Drill* (1913–15). This sculpture is regarded as his most significant contribution to the successive modernist movements of the early twentieth century. After World War I, European artists continued their quest for form: the first metal sculptures of the Constructivists in the early 1920s introduced a new perception of line, volume and space, configured by thin metal strings, bound metal bars or flat metal sheets. In the presentation of figures, Constructivism enabled sculptural elements to become discontinuous through the circumscribing of vacuums and holes; the sense of mass thus became diffused, almost irrelevant. These experiments in form, however, were not restricted to a certain kind of medium, but were carried out also in carving and modelling, whilst *retaining the essence of an idea* (for example, Naum Gabo's metal heads and Jacques Lipchitz's sculptured and modelled couples of the mid 1920s).

Unlike his European contemporaries, Epstein did not continue to experiment and indeed abandoned his engagement with mechanical and geometrical forms, probably because of their analogy to machinery that reminded everyone of the war. He dismantled his *Rock Drill* because it projected "the terrible Frankenstein monster we have turned ourselves into" (163). His first post-World War I work was a bronze human figure on naturalistic lines, his *Risen Christ* (presented in 1920), marking his return to modelling, which was considered by contemporary artists and art critics in England as a traditional and less noble technique than direct carving; Epstein's 'fault' lay in this notion of 'carving vs. modeling'.[100] This dichotomy between the main sculptural media, as formulated during the mid 1910s in the writings of Gaudier-Brzeska for *Blast* and by Eric Gill in the 1920s,[101] had been followed by the young Henry Moore in 1926 ("Modelling is modulation of surfaces .... Sculpture is relation of masses"),[102] long after the European art world (except Brancusi, who continued to work with masses) had developed the different media and formal conceptions mentioned above, and a different (Cubist) approach to the less 'noble' modelling.

However, in the 1930s Frank Dobson stated that this kind of dichotomy "isn't one for the sculptor", adding that "this growing tendency to dogmatize on stone carving ... seems to be as devastating as any academic theory has ever been".[103] Epstein, for his part, argued against Moore's approach, saying that "in carving the suggestion for the form of the work often comes from the shape of the block ... while in modelling the artist is entirely unfettered by anything save the technical difficulties of his own chosen subject".[104] Even harsher than Epstein was Stanley Casson, who claimed that "these artists (Moore, Hepworth & co. in Cornwall) reflect a tendency in modern sculpture which is much applauded [truth to material] .... It is a retrograde tendency ... a translation of art into craft [wherein] the sculptor ... will be driven to choose stones or boulders or tree trunks for their fancied resemblance to the forms he desires".[105]

100 Wittkower, *Sculpture: Processes and Principles*, p. 251.

101 See Zilczer, 'The Theory of Direct Carving in Modern Sculpture', p. 46.

102 Notebook no. 6, Henry Moore Foundation; cited by Friedman, *Henry Moore Early Carvings 1920–1940*, p. 23.

103 An interview with Casson in the 1930s, cited from *Carving Mountains*, exh. cat., Kettle's Yard, p. 14.

104 Haskell, *The Sculptor Speaks*, p. 61.

105 Casson, *XXth Century Sculptors*, p. 20.

Another commentator,[106] relating to Epstein's work with the two media, pointed to an interesting phenomenon: "By a strange coincidence it happens that the critics of the leading serious newspapers have discovered that there are two Jacob Epsteins: one is a powerful and expressive modeller for reproduction in bronze, and the other is, or perhaps believes [he is]ffinacnial, the sculptor hero of a bad novel", and he categorically stressed: "There are no two Jacob Epsteins. What these writers fail to see is, that in [Epstein's] exhibition which puzzles them by its twofold aspect, the sculptor is dealing on the one hand with portraits of living persons and, on the other, with the imaginative rendering of a creative idea". In the same vein of twofold aspects was a critique by Thomas Craven of the mid 1930s: for him one was expressive, epitomized by Rodin (here he echoes Herbert Read), one decorative, typified by Brancusi. Craven viewed the former as "a communicative instrument", conveying an idea inseparable from the flow of life experience, whereas the latter was epitomized by "a prayerful brass-polisher" whose art was produced by "spending years on a simple void form, smoothing and caressing it with maternal pride, in order to pretend that he has reduced the structure of the universe to its eternal symbol – the egg".[107] Epstein, no doubt, would have rejected this evaluation of Brancusi's art because for him Brancusi, of all modern sculptors, was "the man who brought the greatest individual touch into sculpture" (252). Yet Epstein did not deny that in the last analysis Brancusi's smooth surfaces remained, to a great extent, attuned to the sculptural achievements of Maillol, and that his work had become "a formula" that inspired "imitators and followers by the hundred", and these indeed may have turned his kind of art into the decorative production stigmatized by Craven.

In this dichotomy, which only strengthened in the 1930s, Epstein lost the battle against his colleagues. He did not write treatises in order to explain his approach; during the 1920s he mainly modelled, and in carving he adopted an artistic path that contradicted the contemporary tendency to what Orwell called "meaningless" works,[108] because his carvings introduced his personal notions into his executed subjects.

There is another presence, however, in this debate: it has been pointed out that since the days of Ruskin English art criticism had always contained "an innate moralism", in which a work of art that the critic disliked "is frequently characterized as something actually wicked, rather than as something trivial, vulgar or foolish".[109] Thus emotional expression was considered "vulgar", because the avoidance of emotional expression suited the English nature; as the painter Augustus John once remarked, "the only English thing about me is my horror of showing emotion".[110] Beautiful forms, on the other hand, were considered the paragon of art: "Read often speaks of beauty as though it were a kind of Platonic Absolute existing somewhere or other in its own right and in no way dependent on human appreciation," noted George Orwell.[111]

Taking into account the morality implicitly involved, one may suggest that whatever the nature and medium of Epstein's personal artistic expression might have been, critics would have condemned them anyway, given their own personal "innate moralism" eschewing the display of emotion. Attitudes towards Epstein's work during the 1920s and onwards centred around his being 'literary' (in other words, conveying an idea), but also around his uncommon 'immoral' presentation of his "most personal feelings in sympathy with the grief and agony of oppression". Thus, his "maidens"

106 Leman Hare, 'Much Ado About "Genesis"', pp. 176–77.

107 Craven, *Modern Art*, p. 297. The American publication (Simon & Shuster) came out in January 1934.

108 Orwell, 'Inside the Whale', *Collected Works*, vol. I, p. 507: "In 'cultured' circles art-for-art-saking extended practically to a worship of the meaningless".

109 Lucie-Smith, *Art of the 1930s*, p. 170.

110 Holroyd, *Augustus John*, p. 563, citing a letter from John to Mary Keene.

111 George Orwell, Review of Herbert Read's collection of essays, *A Coat of Many Colours*, *Poetry Quarterly*, Winter 1945; *Collected Essays, Journalism and Letters*, vol. 2, pp. 48–52.

were viewed as "tragic and deeply wrought by emotion", and his men were seen to "cringe and grieve".[112] Those who disliked Epstein's approach were as much outraged by the sculpture's content as they were by his artistic style. Perhaps this aspect may explain why Epstein occupies such a central place in Wilenski's book, *The Meaning of Modern Sculpture*, whereas other commentators concentrating on mere form tend to minimize his contribution,[113] and some English critics even totally ignore him.[114] In view of what has been said above in regard to the dichotomy between form and idea, I was amused to read in the mid 1980s in *The Times* a comment by the English writer Peter Ackroyd to the effect that American artists concentrated on form and technical means rather than on content and meaning. Apparently, times and *The Times* have changed, but during the 1920s and 1930s in England the debate on the nature of art continued, more or less, along the lines of 'form vs. expression'.

The sculptural outcome of English preference for form devoid of content during the 1920s and 1930s was a flood of female nudes and torsos supposedly influenced by Maillol, which for the sake of convenience I will call 'the harmony school', because this indeed is the sense they projected – harmonious proportions of smooth bodies. "In fact, it is indisputably Maillol's influence [over that of Rodin's essentially individual art] that has proved to be the most formative in the field of representational art in the present century, not only in France but in other parts of Europe", suggested the art critic E.H. Ramsden in 1953.[115] Epstein, on the other hand, commented that this influence had been exerted "in a manner that does [no] justice to Maillol himself, who is an artist first and last, and not a theorist".[116] On the threshold of the 1930s, artists, in particular those close to the Bloomsbury set (Gill, Dobson, Underwood), were producing smooth bodies carved or modelled on Maillolesque lines even when to some degree stylized, often with expressionless faces and most of them bearing symbolical names that could be easily renamed with no relevance to the figure presented – for example Gill's torso of a naked woman entitled *Mankind*, or Frank Dobson's more stylized naked women *Cornucopia* (1925–27), and *Truth* (1930). None of these once popular works engaged with the European artistic ferment of the 1920s noted above.

The quantity of dismissive criticism of Epstein written during the 1930s casts a disturbing shadow on what had been an impressive career. It has led one commentator to declare: "The long years of adverse criticism naturally put him on the defensive with art historians, curators, journalists and the like – whom he regarded as parasites, unless they praised him unequivocally".[117] In an atmosphere of polarized attitudes to art and polite anti-Semitism at the end of the 1920s growing rather less polite thereafter, the outsider Jew Epstein deliberately allowed himself to become estranged from London's art world. He made a great amount of portraiture, only some of which is to be mentioned or presented here; and he responded to society's attitude towards him in a series of carvings on symbolic themes that also reflected personal conflicts. Their execution was rarely impulsive because, as Epstein himself declared, a work on a grand scale "is often the result of years of planning, musing upon and developing. It is not only the visual that stimulates an artist's conceptions. Sometimes a poem or a piece of music will evoke a complete image in the most striking fashion" (PS/237). These works included the monumental *Genesis* (1930) and *Primeval Gods* (1931–33); the smaller carvings *Chimera* and *Elemental* (1932); *Behold the Man* (1934–35); *Consummatum Est*

112 Casson, *Some Modern Sculptors*, p. 113. On Epstein's art see the chapter entitled 'Epstein and Dramatic Sculpture', pp. 113–77. Such condemnation of empathy with grief (shared by other critics) might have been influenced by the fact that, as Casson mentions, the sculptor himself was "in origin one of an oppressed race".

113 For example, Giedion-Welcker, *Contemporary Sculpture: An Evolution in Volume*; Selz, *Modern Sculpture: Origins and Evolution*; Burnham, *Beyond Modern Sculpture*; Trier, *Form and Space*.

114 For example, Underwood, *A Short History of English Sculpture*; Read, *The Art of Sculpture*, and *The Origins of Form in Art*.

115 Ramsden, *Thames and Variations*, p. 15.

116 Haskell, *The Sculptor Speaks*, p. 130.

117 McFall, p. 2.

(1938–39); *Adam* (1938) and *Jacob and the Angel* (1940); the bronze *Lucifer* (1944–45) and again a carving, *Lazarus* (1947). One cannot ignore the symbolic names of these sculptures, despite Epstein confusing the issue by saying that the names were usually given mainly for the purpose of the catalogue.[118] The following discussion, involving both general affairs and strictly artistic observation, will reveal that in each case the name has a definite relation to the sculpture's theme and essence, as well as to the personal concerns of the sculptor. It was only during the 1950s, following the trauma and emotional shock of World War II, that new requirements for the expression of ideas and emotions rather than for mere forms with which to play renewed the demand for 'an Epstein' and his kind of 'content' sculpture, mainly in public commissions. Epstein, by then in his seventies, was flooded with work, and his sculpture – which employed Christian imagery to convey universal ideas of consolation and hope to a war-weary England – became newly relevant, gaining him the status of grand old master of English sculpture.

118 McFall, p. 73.

CHAPTER 2

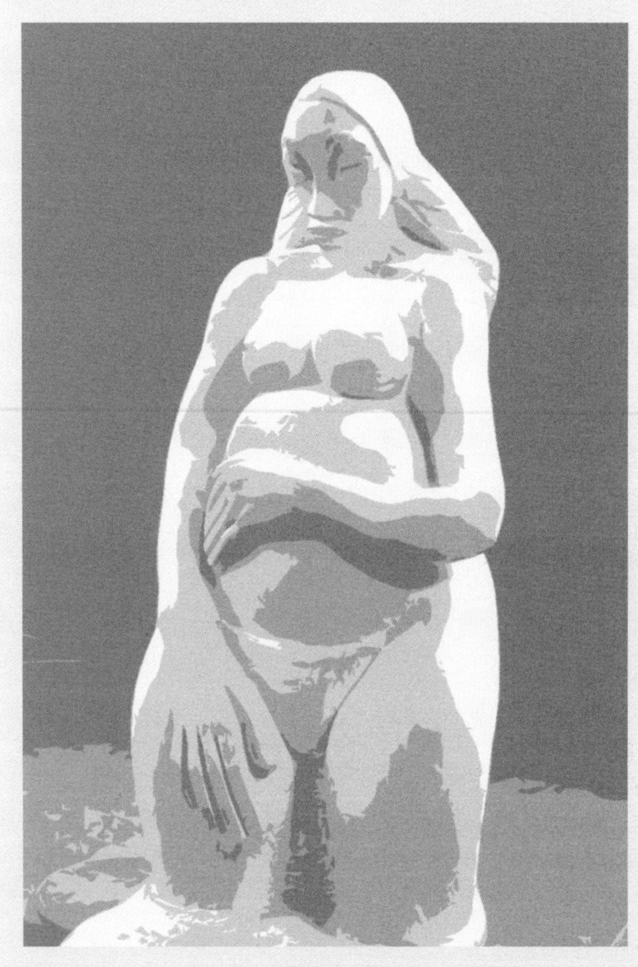

FAREWELL TO THE ARYAN SUN (1930–32)

TOWARDS A NEW PATH

1929 had been a stormy year for Epstein following the public uproar greeting his sculptures *Day* and *Night* (on which he worked under "miserable conditions for over six months [and] got badly paid and bringing a stream of condemnations when exposed to the public"),[1] and ended with an unpleasant personal setback: Epstein was informed by Lady Jones of her purchase of a bust of Mrs Epstein from the King's Gallery, King's Road, Chelsea. His inspection determined that it was a cement cast – not made by him. In July 1929 he began an action against the proprietors, International Depositories Ltd., but on 17 October 1930 the action was decided against him. "From the ways things went at this trial it looked as if I were the criminal, one who by his villainous accusations made other people suffer," was Epstein's conclusion in his sarcastic account of what had gone on in court (141). Throughout his life Epstein had held a high opinion of his own importance as an artist, and he did not hesitate to compare his recent struggle to that of his friend Oko's 'Spinoza Society' to obtain recognition of the great philosopher: "The living Epstein struggles with all the forces united against him; their struggles are over dead Jews," Epstein wrote, concluding, "He who is equally great is alive and at the corner of his life when it is a question of whether he will be free to do his future and greatest work or not."[2] The unpleasant affair did not deter him from continuing to work. At the very end of the year he was included in the 'Modern and African Sculpture' show held in November-December at the Sydney Burney Gallery (13 St James's Place), which also exhibited works by Zadkine, Sidney Gordin, Maillol, Hepworth, John Skeaping and Dobson, as well as African sculpture.

At the threshold of the 1930s, two characteristics of Epstein's *Day* and *Night* produced for the Underground Building may be noted. The first, as discussed above, is that he ignored the dominant trend of the 1920s, of form divorced from idea, for his figures demonstrated, almost shouted, the notion of 'idea' as an essential element in sculpture. *Night* evoked the subject of the Pièta, while *Day* presented on a public building the uncommon sculptural theme of a father-son relationship. Influenced by Epstein's precedent, the father-son theme was soon to be taken up by other artists of his generation during the 1930s,[3] notably by Eric Gill in his *Prospero and Ariel* executed shortly afterwards for Broadcasting House (1931).[4] Epstein's response to Gill's mainstream works, as will be elaborated upon further on, would be delivered in two stages – an immediate one at the beginning of the decade and another one at its end.

The second characteristic of *Day* and *Night* relates to the issue of 'form': these two sculptures present what may be regarded as the last phase of Epstein's eclectic choice of forms from different periods and civilizations, transforming them into a personal

1 Letter from Epstein to Dr Oko, 26 February 1930: HUCAC.

2 Letter from Epstein to Dr Oko, 13 February 1924: HUCAC.

3 See I/194–95 and Ramsden, *Themes and Variations*.

4 For a more detailed discussion of the influence of Epstein's work on that of Gill, see I/88–89.

expression in the final product. Useful in this respect is an evaluation provided on the threshold of the 1930s by one of the few critics who favoured his work: "Learned men tell us there is nothing Assyrian or African about his art and no resemblance to archaic rock carving. But if Epstein has taken his studies of these works so deeply into his art that they cannot be identified, it only increases the suspicion that there is something new as well and alien to our habits of thought in his sculpture."[5]

The carvings that followed after 1930 are less obvious in regard to form, harder to decipher in regard to meaning, but easier to trace the sources for: several of them reflect precedents found in Epstein's earlier work. Criticism of them has been polarized, altering with the time and with the critic.[6] One opinion expressed towards the end of the twentieth century stated that "the evaluation of an artist and his co-initiates tended rather to be made in terms of degrees of technical innovations assessed apart from representation as such", and therefore Epstein's "occasional carvings – strange and ambitious though they mostly are" seemed to be exceptions amongst his main work, the portraits, by which he was judged as a representational sculptor.[7] Wilenski, on the other hand, writing at a time (before 1931) when his oeuvre of carvings constituted the paragon of modern sculpture in England, stated that "his [Epstein's] contribution to modern sculpture consists entirely in his carvings".[8]

Genesis, the first carving of the new era of Epstein's second phase in life and work, seems to justify both opinions: it is "strange and ambitious" and it may be regarded as a unique contribution to England's modern art of the period. Among all of his carvings, however, it seems to be the one that has generated the greatest number of journalistic comments and artistic evaluations as well as vitriolic comments.

It had been conceived in 1929, and, as the chronology of his personal life indicates, it coincided with and responded to Kathleen's third pregnancy. During her first he was engaged in carving *Rima* (I/173), while her second pregnancy had been reflected in the bronze *Visitation* (I/177). Apparently, Epstein had desired to commemorate this most recent occurrence in a carving that presented the full naked pregnant body, and for this he needed a pregnant model in the studio.[9] Pregnancy in art is usually represented covered by clothing, and as such it had been drawn and carved by Epstein as *Maternity* for the decoration of the BMA building (1907–08), in which a young Caucasian woman with a swollen belly exposes her breasts [10]. Epstein's detailed study of the phenomenon, of the naked natural contours, of the body completely exposed, seen from different angles,[10] seems to reflect the happy coincidence of his encounter with two sisters, the half-black/half-Jewish Esther and Rebecca,[11] of whom he later made bronze portraits.[12] The studies, drawn in naturalistic lines, related to *Genesis* are supposed to be of Rebecca [11], as noted on the verso of another drawing [12].[13]

Following these studies merely of a model in a state of pregnancy, Epstein's preliminary thoughts for the sculpture seem to have been drawn on a wide page of 76.3 cm, wider than his regular pages (*c.* 55 cm).[14] From the outset Epstein divided the page into two sections [13],[15] intending to reflect on each a different stage in the process of his thought. The suggestion that the still naturalistic left side was directed towards a sculptural concept appears justified by the style of the straightened head (inclined in previous drawings) and by its minimized facial details and by the design of the left

5 James Bone, 'Mr Epstein's Alien Sculpture', *The Guardian*, 23 July 1929; reprinted in 'Past Notes' in the same newspaper, 23 July 1993.

6 "They all were circling in their varying states of distress," suggests A.M. Wagner (*Mother Stone*, pp. 193–205), discussing criticism from various quarters, in particular regarding Epstein's *Genesis*. She cites Epstein's contemporaries the artists Paul Nash and Frank Dobson and the artist-critic Roger Fry, and a retrospective view of the 1960s by Michael Freed.

7 Harrison, *English Art and Modernism*, p. 205.

8 Wilenski, *The Meaning of Modern Sculpture*, p. 5.

9 I doubt whether a pregnant Kathleen would have been interested in posing, or whether an angered Margaret would have tolerated it.

10 In addition to the more 'conventional' drawing presented here, Evelyn Silber kindly drew my attention to "the drawing of a seemingly pregnant seated woman, seen full frontal with her legs slightly splayed, seen from head to mid-calf", sold, Christie's, 12 May 1989, lot 58.

11 Buckle, *Epstein: Sculptor*, p. 174.

12 Silber, *Sculpture of Epstein*, nos. 196, 197 (1930).

13 My assumption presupposes also that the execution of the carving started in late 1929. The drawings would have to have been made earlier, while the bronze portraits date to 1930.

14 This was presented in Silber and Friedman, *Jacob Epstein*, p. 230 (though erroneously giving different dimensions, 57 x 44.6 cm), and therefore it is definitely not "a prime piece of evidence [which] has so far been omitted": Wagner, *Mother Stone*, p. 212.

15 "I can confirm [the page] arrived possibly actually folded or flat but with evidence of having been folded for a long period," replied Silber in answer to my question about the page's condition, adding: "A curator would never fold a previously unfolded drawing": letter to the author, 28 August 2010.

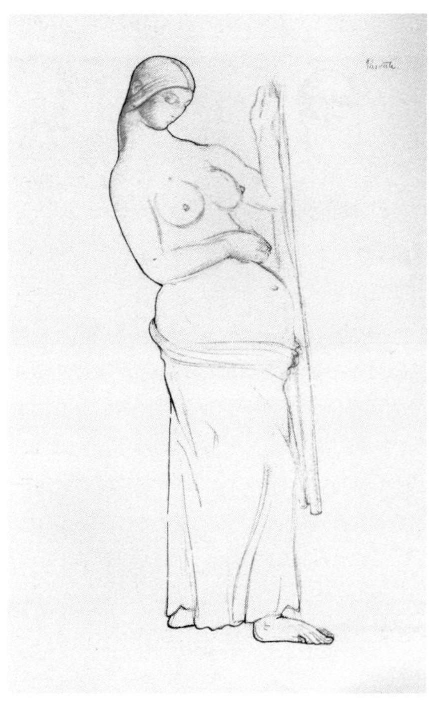

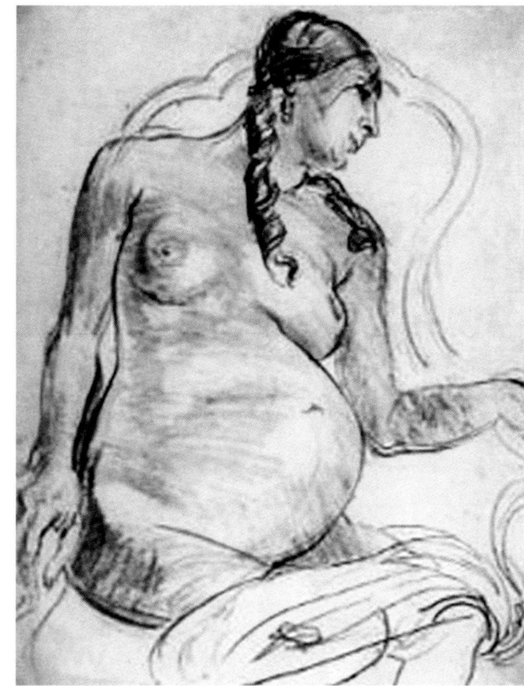

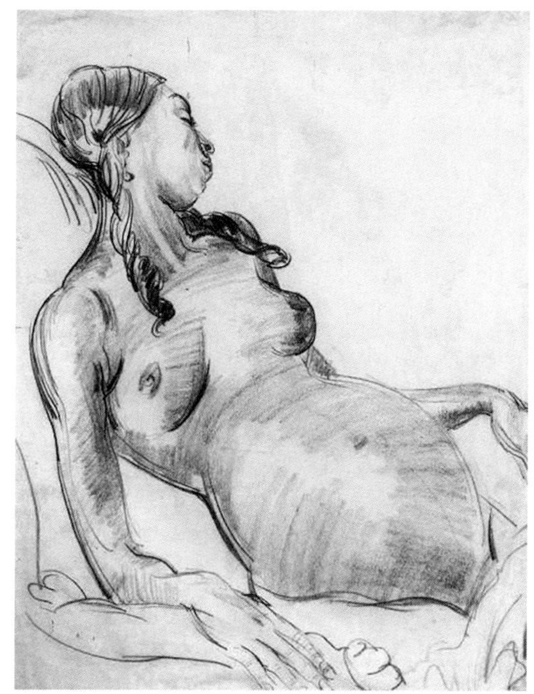

10
Maternity, 1907
Pen and ink and pencil,
50 x 30.5 cm
GREC-NAGW

11
Maternity, 1929
Pencil, 57 x 47 cm
GREC-NAGW

12
Rebecca (as inscribed in pencil on the reverse), 1929
Pencil, 53 x 410 cm
GREC-NAGW

13
Two studies for 'Genesis', 1929
Pencil, 76.3 x 50.6 cm
Birmingham Museums and Art Gallery

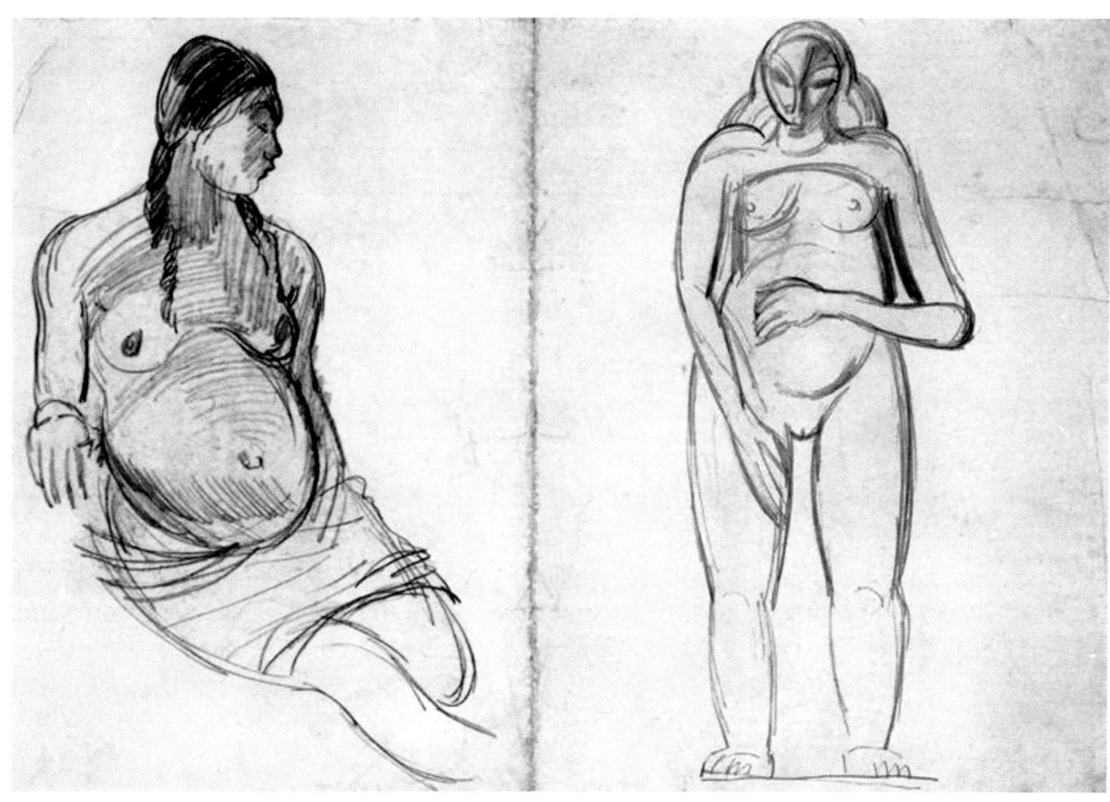

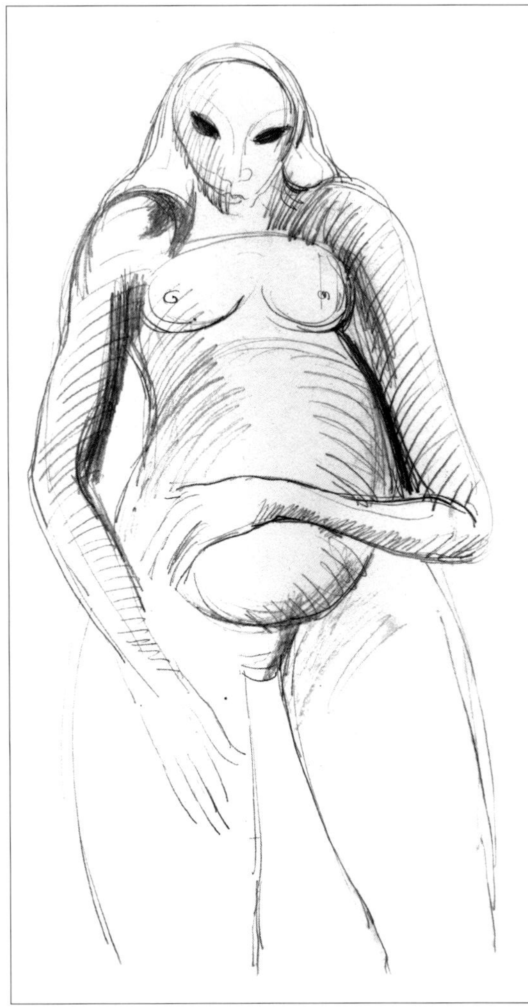

14
Study for 'Genesis', 1929 [1930]
Pencil, 50.8 x 38 cm
Private collection

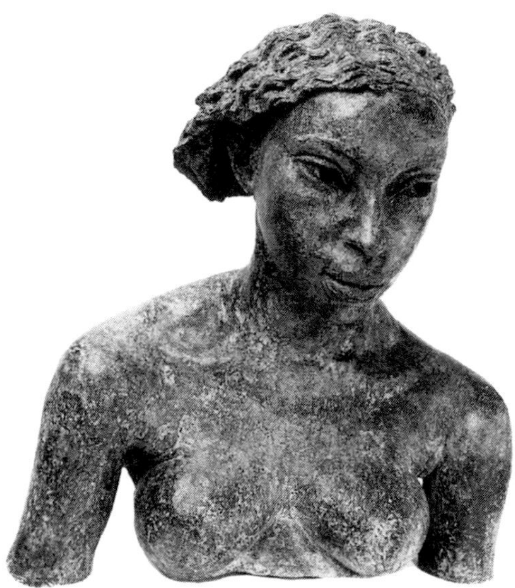

14a
Lydia, 1st portrait, 1929–30
Bronze, H. 52 cm
Private collection

hand, which is now reduced to three lines on the thigh, close to the swollen belly. On the other half of the page Epstein developed a different concept by stylizing the form into a standing frontal figure holding her swollen belly, thus laying the groundwork for elements in the pose of the sculpture to be – the ovoid head, pointed jaw, accentuatedly slanting eyes, nose narrowed to a straight rectangle, and the division of the hair into two parts. The vulva in this drawing has a slight mark on its outer labia, probably indicating an intention to carve it in a similar way to *Sun God Crouching* (1910).[16] Another drawing [14], which might be considered as the last survivor in this sequence of drawings, bears no traces of the human model, and apparently is a development of the previous drawing [13] with greater stylization: the lower parts of the exaggerated thighs are clear (though there is no attention to the lower legs), while the upper part is darkened by hatching, thus conveying the sense of a body inclined backwards – as it was indeed in the finished sculpture.[17]

This last drawing, given to Kathleen as a present,[18] seems to justify my argument that, like many of his other works, Epstein's *Genesis* reflects a personal state of affairs, which, in this instance, is one connected to Kathleen's third pregnancy. All these drawings (and there were probably more on the subject) clearly contradict Epstein's statement that he "worked on this figure [*Genesis*] with no hesitation, and with no preliminary studies" (163), which would be true only if by preliminary study detailed preparation were meant. Silber mentions (with no reference to her race) that "I have met at least one woman, Dorothy Warren, who as a young art student (not pregnant) modelled for Epstein's life drawings related to *Genesis*",[19] and one may observe that another African model, *Lydia* [14a], whose bronze portrait had been executed in the relevant period of 1929–30, might have inspired the slanted eyes, long face and expressive mouth both in Epstein's drawings [13, 14] and in the sculpture itself.

The sculpture, however, is not a direct 'transcription' of any of its suppositious models; indeed it appears that Epstein purposely combined different details from different models in order not to relate it to any particular one, thus eliminating the personal and achieving the universality the sculpture conveys. If in my introduction

16 I/99, pl. 47, presents the front view; here [57] is a side view.

17 Wagner, *Mother Stone*, pp. 212–13, suggests a different order of execution of the drawings – with Epstein jumping from the first page to another, and then returning to the other half of the first page – with no regard for the figures' pose and without proposing a convincing argument for stylistic continuity.

18 Epstein, *Epstein Drawings*, pl. 54 (dated incorrectly as 1931).

19 Epstein, *Epstein Drawings*, note 15.

I presented in Epstein's work three "dualities", or "ambiguities", as I called them (pp. 22–23), here in *Genesis* he seems to express yet another one, that of combining what one may regard as contradictory conceptions – Eve, the biblical mother of the human race, according a 'white' legend adopted in Europe, depicted with African facial features. One is left to wonder whether these contrasting elements in the mixed race of his Jewish-African models of the period, Esther and Rebecca, inspired him to express this mixture in his *Genesis*.

Responding to the art around him, and the tendency to smooth, vague and expressionless female nudes, Epstein felt "the necessity for giving expression [in *Genesis*] to the profoundly elemental in motherhood, the deep down instinctive female without the trappings and charm of what is known as feminine" (163). The last phrase, I suggest, alludes to Epstein's first reaction in this decade against Gill's as well as others' conception of the Ur-mother who begets life, expressed in artistic representations that earlier (p. 33) I termed the 'harmony school'. Leon Underwood's harmonious *Eve* (1923) waves the apple attribute to distinguish her from just a seated naked woman; Eric Gill entitled two delicate small figures (*c*. 80 cm high) expressing the same idea *Mankind* and *Eve*. *Mankind* is a beheaded torso of a naked woman represented down to the knees in a classical pose; more relevant to us is *Eve* (1928), an extrovert nude figure, with European facial features displaying an Archaic Greek smile. She is depicted as if arising from folds of drapery with her arms held behind her back, accentuating her frontal nakedness, adorned with a pearl-like necklace that sets off her alluring vague smile (fig. 2), thus personifying what Epstein referred to as "the trappings of femininity". Epstein's *Genesis* differs from Gill's work not only in size but also, fundamentally, in form, and not least in her expression, which conveys a kind of confused introspection, thus fulfilling Epstein's artistic contention: "*My* feminine would be the eternal primeval feminine, the mother of the race" (162).

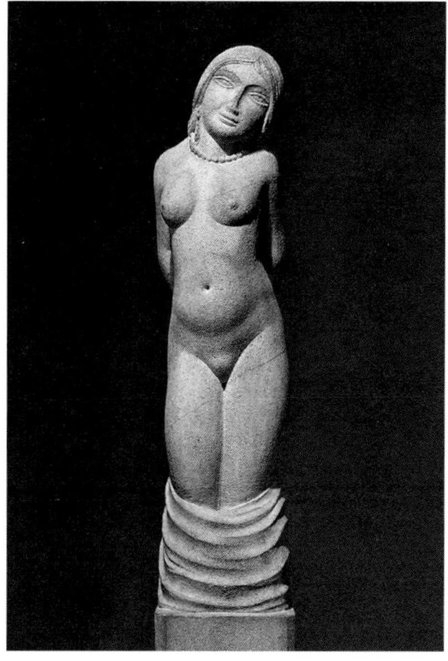

Fig. 2
Eric Gill
Eve, 1928
Bath stone, 73.7 x 15.2 x 15.2 cm
Tate

Maternity was a subject that had featured in Epstein's work from the beginning, expressed in various styles,[20] and therefore it is not strange that Kathleen's pregnancy should have renewed his interest in it. During this period of the 1930s, however, the accent in his carving was different: for the first time it was not a representation simply of a universal theme, but of one connected with and emanating from his own culture; this trend would become evident in most of the works he was to create during this decade. The carving was started toward the end of 1929 in his cottage at Epping Forest, where "It is raining all the time. I have nothing to read except an old Bible. I keep reading *Genesis* and made some drawings," as he wrote to Kathleen.[21] Throughout 1930, on "a block of Seravezza marble" which he had bought in Paris he attacked the "sympathetic material … with my aim very clearly defined in my mind" (162–63). When the block was moved to his London studio Epstein wrote: "[I] am at work now on a marble figure for which I must have time. Time and means to carry on."[22] Epstein carved what Margaret described as "a new thing of his own for six months which always brings a time of famine [no income] – the sacrifice a genius makes in his lifetime for doing what at the moment pleases himself best – which will ultimately be regarded like the *Madonna* as the summit of his achievement. It is *a femme ancient* [sic] in marble, very large."[23]

20 *Maternity* (1907), *Maternity* (1912) and the two *Flenit* figures (1913–14) are all belly-swollen females. *Madonna and Child* (1927) and *Night* (1929) are mothers.

21 Buckle, *Epstein: Sculptor*, p. 189. I did not find this letter in the NWAG archive.

22 Letter from Epstein to Dr Oko, 26 February 1930: HUCAC.

23 Letter from Margaret to Dr Oko, 22 March 1930: HUCAC.

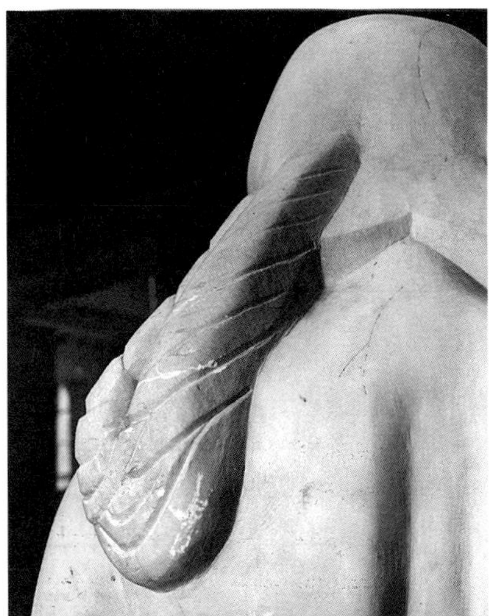

15a
Genesis, 1929–30 (detail)

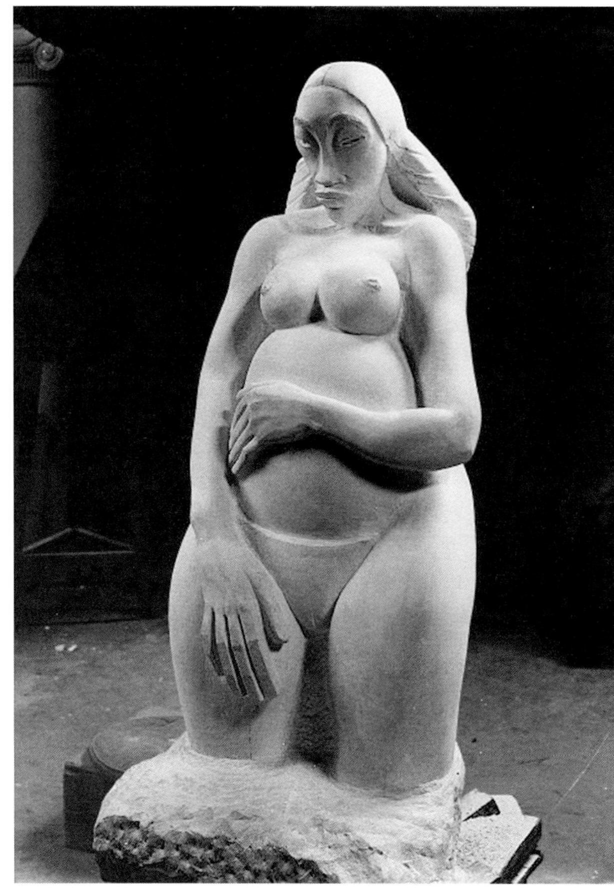

15b
Genesis, 1929–30
Seravezza marble, H. 162.5 cm
Whitworth Art Gallery, Manchester

In March 1930, while still busy with his carving, he started another project that stemmed from the same cultural nexus – illustrations of the Old Testament. As the illustrations must have been made over a long period, I will first discuss the carving, mainly because, as I stressed above, I regard it as marking a new direction in Epstein's sculpture.

EPSTEIN'S REBIRTH

I. GENESIS, 1930

Genesis's figure [15b] has an elongated 'S' shape, with a downward-inclined head and an accentuated, heavy, rounded belly supported by hugely disproportionate thighs sprouting out of a flat mass representing the earth. The head has coarse, semi-primitive, stylized facial features with protruding lips, and the hair is depicted as two masses (evident in the drawn model and also in the stylized figure [13]) on which the plaits are marked in low relief, serving as the only decorative element [15a]. The hand positions diverge slightly from the *Venus Pudica* pose: the palm of the left hand is folded across the belly rather than the breasts and, while recalling the classical pose, the right hand is near the vulva, touching the thigh with its unnaturally long palm. The enlarged proportions of the hands echo Epstein's similar sculptural treatment of the hands in the *Risen*

Christ; in both cases Epstein sought to draw the viewer's attention to them, as Rodin did to the hands of his *Burghers of Calais*.

An interesting small illustration of the period, inscribed *Genesis* II [15c], seems to have been drawn after the execution of the large carving, as it projects a sense of conclusion rather than a process of thinking. Unusually among the *Genesis* drawings, it is inscribed and signed, and probably purposely made as a present after the completion of the sculpture.

Epstein's figure rises upwards just above the knees, and a precedent for this idea can be found in what apparently had been the outcome of Sunita's last modelling sessions for him, a bronze figure entitled *Reclining Goddess* [16], which has legs posed similarly to those in *Genesis*, with the earth element at the feet.[24]

This reclining presentation seems to have been influenced by Henry Moore's favourite subject, corresponding with it while at the same time retaining a sense of individuality quite distinct from Moore's universality. Was it deliberately intended to refer to Moore? Or was it just Epstein's experiment with a pose?[25]

Although a sympathetic Wilenski comprehended *Genesis*'s "undeniably primeval and profound" form as significant of the idea expressed and appropriate to its name,[26] in his analysis of its formal qualities he criticized the diverse, unhomogeneous plastic languages employed: homogeneity was the period's prerequisite for a harmonious artistic treatment ('non-glyptic' was a term used by by another commentator).[27] Nowadays such a quality would not excite remark, but according to contemporary perceptions Wilenski had a point: the smooth rounded belly and breasts are not in accord with the quadrangular treatment of the palms and fingers, nor with the stylized features of the head and its details. However, Wilenski seems to have misjudged the pose, and perhaps the low positioning of the sculpture in the gallery may have influenced his observation

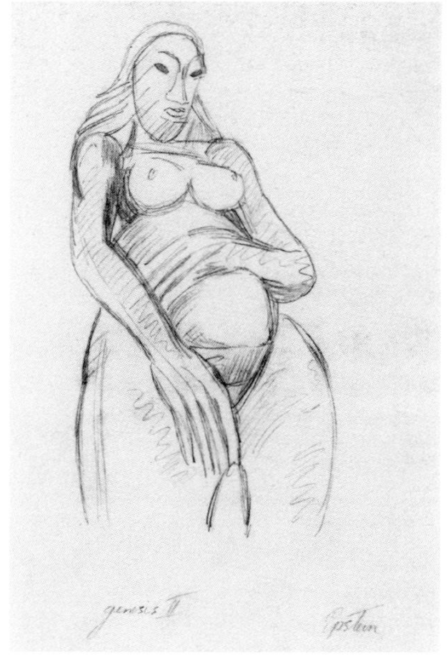

15c
Genesis II, 1929
Pencil, 265 x 155 mm
Private collection

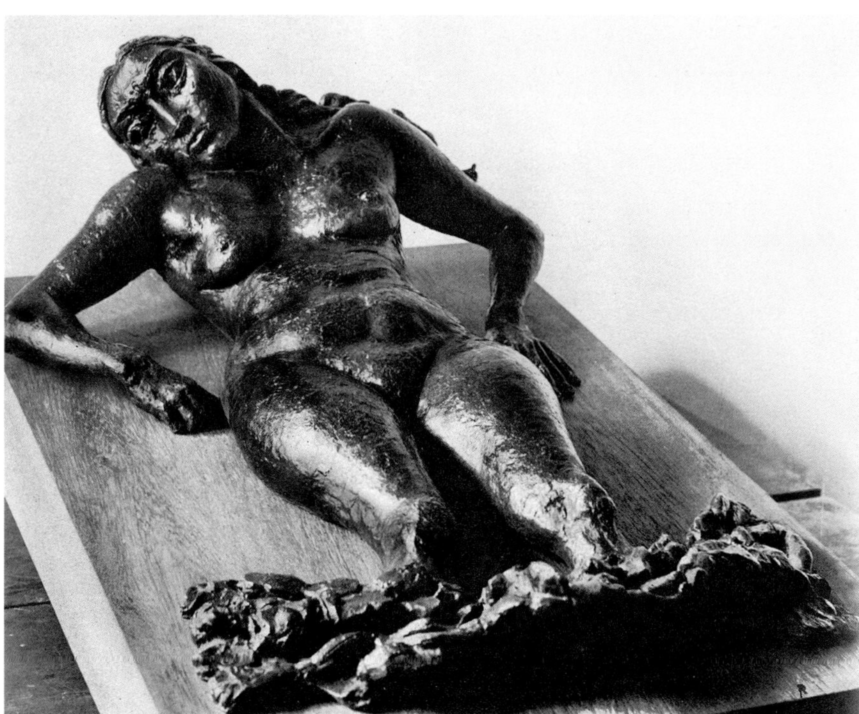

16
Reclining Goddess, 1929–30 [1931]
Bronze, H. 76 cm
Formerly Shinman collection

24 Silber, *Sculpture of Epstein*, no. 206. Both sculptures are dated in Haskell's catalogue to 1931, but *Genesis* had been finished in 1930 and presented in early 1931, whereas *Reclining Goddess* was presented only in 1933 (at Leicester Galleries). I suggest that this late presentation of *Reclining Goddess* was in order to avoid its comparison with the carving and does not reflect its execution date. I believe it was made before the carving, in early 1930, because dating it to 1931 means that the earth element had been made after the carving, against Epstein's customary order of carving following bronze.

25 Oddly enough, details from the Leicester Galleries' catalogue of Moore's work (exh. no. 704, June 1939) present three reclining figures – no. 38, *Reclining Nude* (probably the one mentioned by Silber and presented in 1933) and two that were not catalogued by Silber (and therefore no images of which are available), nos. 39 and 40, *Reclining Negress*. I think all of them might have been made well before 1931. The outcome of this survey seems to confirm my suggestion that, where subject matter was concerned, Epstein had been influenced by Moore more than previously assumed.

26 R.H. Wilenski, *The Observer*, 8 February 1931, cited in Epstein, *Let There Be Sculpture*, p. 312.

27 Parkes, *Art of Carved Sculpture*, pp. 134–35.

that "the flow of the lines downward suggests a falling body rather than an organization rising upward from the ground". Whether one likes it or not, the natural flow of lines in advanced pregnancy, due to gravity, is that of a drooping belly, and no artist can rectify this even when attempting to show a rising body. *Genesis* therefore expresses to the letter Epstein's declared intentions: "From that broad thighs and buttocks ascend, base solid and permanent for her who is to be the bearer of man. She feels within herself the child moving, her hand instinctively and soothingly placed where it can feel this enclosed new life so closely bound with herself" (162).

Epstein's "eternal primeval feminine, the mother of the race" was not so named explicitly after the biblical Eve; it was intended to accentuate the figure's universal message rather than attaching her to a particular myth. 'Genesis' (in Hebrew) conveys what the O.E.D. tells us – "mode of formation or generation" – and that is how the first book of the Old Testament is titled in all its non-Hebrew versions, but the Hebrew title repeats the first word, *Be'reshit* – 'in a beginning'.[28] Epstein's choice of name, therefore, might reflect his reaction against Gill's depiction of an Eve while also tacitly implying that, from a philosophical vantage-point, for him the generation process began with the very tangible female-creator rather than with the abstract God-creator. I have discussed elsewhere this uncommon outlook with reference to other sculptures of pregnant women carved during the 1910s, under the title *Mythic Motifs*.[29] Pregnancy, in that study, was regarded as giving explicit expression to the creative force of the woman. I suggested that these pregnant figures implicitly conveyed the male's envy of this force, what Freud called "womb-envy". The 1910s sculptures, created during the period when Epstein had as yet no offspring, were stylized to anonymous universality, whereas Epstein's work relating to the subject of pregnancy in 1925 and 1930, although essentially conveying the same motifs, was allowed to have a human face, probably because by the end of this period he had fathered four children. Consequently, it is easier to relate to *Genesis*, because the figure of the primordial mother of the race is touching and, to my mind, also sentimental.[30] Moreover, her face expresses a kind of very human confusion, rather than conveying a sense of being "a concealing mask ... a device of transformation and alienation".[31]

Genesis was a large-scale carving for which Epstein was not commissioned. Thus, in his second phase in life he set out on a new path as an independent creator of works for which he could never be sure of finding buyers, because the famous carver of publicly commissioned works of 1908–29 was to be ignored for the next two decades. It was the public's neglect, however, that gave birth to his new artistic persona – a creator who now began to fulfil his self-definition declared already in 1916 – "a Jew with a burning desire to do something worth perpetuating for my race".[32] This independence also meant that 1930 was financially not a very successful year: out of ten portraits registered,[33] only about six were commissioned by clients; four were of models he had to pay. An important one among those was Sunita's portrait, entitled *Israfel*,[34] discussed further on. The year ended more auspiciously: Epstein was one of three official representatives of British sculpture at the seventeenth Venice Biennale (4 May – 4 November 1930), presenting nine exhibits, beside Henry Moore and John Skeaping with seven exhibits each – a venue that gave all of them their break into the international artistic scene. However, it was to be Epstein's last invitation to international exhibitions outside Britain, as his stature in England had

28 'A' is the literal translation; the commonly used 'the' is an interpretation. See Gilboa, *Intercourses in the Book of Genesis*, p. 39.

29 Gilboa, *Mythic Motifs in Jacob Epstein's Sculptural Work*.

30 *Contra* Silber, *Epstein*, p. 50: "*Genesis* is totally unsentimental and un-erotic, but its descriptive banality conflicts with the mystery it is supposed to embody".

31 Wagner, *Mother Stone*, p. 220. Wagner devotes a long discussion (pp. 212–20) to Picasso's masks, to their African origin and to Lévi-Strauss's anthropological definition of masks as "a device of transformation and alienation" (p. 220), but I wonder whether this has anything to do with Epstein's declared intention to express the opposite.

32 Interview with *The Jewish Chronicle*, 25 February 1916, p. 14.

33 Counted from Silber, *Sculpture of Epstein*.

34 Silber, *Sculpture of Epstein*, no. 199.

begun to be severely impacted by a younger generation of sculptors.

In early February 1931 *Genesis* was presented at the Leicester Galleries, coinciding with gunshots fired at *Day* on the Underground Building, hitting the "father's right forearm and the chest of the child".[35] As for the way *Genesis* was viewed by the wider public, the few headlines that Epstein chose to cite in his autobiography (308–11) read: "Epstein's Bad Joke in Stone"; "Mongolian Moron that is Obscene"; "Mr. Epstein's Latest – And his Worst"; "Coarse and Repellent".

The carving left audiences bewildered. One letter among the many conveys the general public's reaction: "... an open insult to motherhood and degrading to that which throughout the ages has been protected and held sacred".[36] Even when there were more sympathetic attitudes, however, they failed to grasp what Epstein had presented: "No one seriously disputes that Epstein is a master of his medium of expression. It is the idea made manifest in his work that is so violently disturbing the criticasters [sic]. What can he mean, and what is his motive?"[37] The question of motive gains weight when it is considered together with the layout of Epstein's exhibition in the Leicester Galleries – *Genesis* in the midst of the space, surrounded by bronze portraits the titles of which were chosen so "as to suggest that their sitters are Jews ... [and] as much as the calculated conjunction of objects, this too is a self-conscious move".[38]

An interesting exchange of opinion that demonstrates the artist's inner vision or perception of beauty can be found in Epstein's interview with the critic of *The Daily Mail*, who concluded his article by declaring that "Epstein is a law to himself":

> Critic: What need was there to give the lady such an ugly face?
> Epstein: Ugly! ... You say ugly, but I don't agree with you. It is not ugly for me. I pursue only my own ideas, not anybody else's.

Unfortunately, as one critic commented, "there is a tendency, at least in this country, to condemn any work of art, if the subject-matter [is considered to] be not beautiful ... the question raised by *Genesis* is not whether its originality shocks some people, but simply whether it does convey the idea of a Primitive Dawn; if it does so, surely that it is a great achievement".[39]

The positive reaction of several women writers to the sculpture was quite surprising;[40] apparently, they favoured the idea of the dawn of humanity being conveyed by a female. And so it did to me when I first encountered this white carved marble, arousing within me tender feelings, inducing me to caress the swollen belly softly and murmur in Epstein's mother-tongue, "*mameleh*".

It was during these days of scandal that two writers published pieces in favour of Epstein and his work. The art critic R.H. Wilenski, in early March 1930, published an article entitled 'People You Would Like to Know – Jacob Epstein', in which he described the person Epstein as he knew him:

> The world thinks of him [as] truculent and flamboyant, but he is extremely simple and extremely shy ... like most of his work, he creates the impression of being considerably over life-size ... he has a soft, nervous voice ... tenderness is a quality unsuspected by the general public.[41]

35 *Star*, 2 February 1931; cited in Gardiner, *Epstein*, p. 319.

36 Kathleen L. Bounstead, President of The Mothers Union, 16 February 1931; cited in Brown, *Exhibition*, p. 116.

37 M. Lazoff, *Manchester Guardian*, 22 April 1931.

38 Wagner, *Mother Stone*, p. 207.

39 Lehman Hare, 'Much Ado About "Genesis"', p. 178.

40 Cited in Wagner, *Mother Stone*, pp. 226–28.

41 Wilenski, 'People You Would Like to Know'.

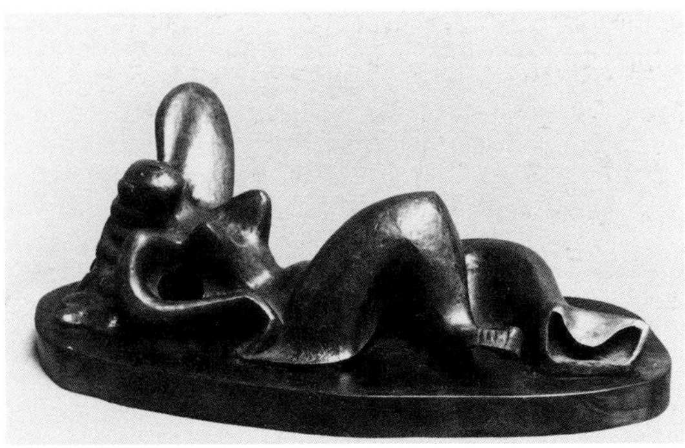

Fig. 3
Leon Underwood
Mother Earth, 1930
Bronze, 23 x 55 x 27 cm
Private collection

Even more important was the initiative of Arnold Haskell, who, in 1927, had been nominated as a reader for William Heinemann Ltd. Haskell's first suggestion in this capacity was for a book on Epstein, "whose every work caused a violent sensation".[42] Haskell's conversations with Epstein were collected and published under the title *The Sculptor Speaks*, attempting to explain Epstein and his work to the uninitiated, hostile public, who were overwhelmed by the huge white marble with non-Caucasian features bearing a biblical title.

Not long after the public presentation of *Genesis*, on Monday 13 April 1931, *The Times* announced that *Genesis* had received a favourable review (in *The Manchester Guardian*) and found a purchaser.[43] With what may be regarded as a touch of cynicism, the favourable piece ended with "There is surely room for it in the world of art" and named Mr and Mrs Alfred Charles Bossom of London as the buyers, for £5,000. No less interesting is *The Times'* report on the purchaser who, like Epstein, was a Jew who had emigrated from the US, and whose artistic taste and oeuvre were obviously very (perhaps too) modern for English taste:

> An architect, an alderman, a man of wealth is clever little Purchaser Bossom. Like Sculptor Epstein he is of Semitic descent. His wealth derived from his conception and industrious execution of the idea of building skyscrapers like a graduated pile of boxes with the smallest on top — the 'set back' style to provide air and light.[44]

In Britain, so *The Times* continued with a similar tint of cynicism, modern architect Bossom is a member of the London County Council and chairman of the Committee of the Royal Society of Arts for the Preservation of Ancient Cottages, in one of which he apparently dwells; and that is why the Bossoms "may plant *Genesis*, obviously unsuitable for an Ancient Cottage, in their own garden" – probably because his offer to place it on loan to the Tate Gallery had been refused. Mrs Bossom subsequently sent it on tour around the country to collect money for charity, and it successfully drew huge crowds and donations.[45] Noble as her intention had been (Epstein was understandably angry at the sculpture being presented in a trade show),[46] when Epstein became aware that she meant to take it to America, he sarcastically wondered whether she intended to show it on Coney Island. I agree with Gardiner's comment that this initiative, which attracted much publicity, introduced a similar idea "into some others' minds, for which Epstein suffered later".

The reactions of fellow artists to *Genesis* were subtly acidulous in praising Epstein's portraits in the exhibition while condemning the carving. It is worth recalling the arguments of what I have termed 'the harmony school', because the Fry-Bell concept of 'meaningful form' of the mid 1910s, anchored in the ultra-simple classicism of Maillol's work, was continued to a large extent during the 1930s by the very influential Herbert Read, who stated:[47]

> Art is most simply and most usually defined as an attempt to create pleasing forms. Such forms satisfy our sense of beauty, and the sense of beauty is satisfied when we are able to appreciate a unity or harmony of formal relations among our sense-perceptions.

42 Haskell, *In His True Centre*, p. 87.

43 http://www.time.com/time/magazine/article/0,9171,752830,00.html#ixzz0ZeS3gmSU

44 He designed the Seaboard National Bank in New York (Seaboard's President, Samuel Bayne, was his father-in-law) and the Magnolia Petroleum Building in Dallas, Texas.

45 Details of the tour are described in Gardiner, *Epstein*, p. 326.

46 'Angry Epstein', *The Manchester Guardian*, 13 December 1931.

47 Read, *The Meaning of Art*, p. 18.

Frank Dobson (dubbed by Fry "a true sculptor")[48] stated that "restless sculpture is an abomination".[49] However, is not a "restless" sculpture one also capable of conveying a sense of excitement? A propos restlessness, a comparison between Epstein's *Genesis* and Leon Underwood's *Mother Earth* created during the same period (1930–31) (fig. 3) reveals Underwood's gradual departure from 'harmony school' production (typified by his above-mentioned *Eve* of 1923) towards more complex configuration, while his 'restless', edgy forms in a reclining figure (undoubtedly following Moore's favourite pose) contrast with the smooth and tranquil lines of *Genesis*. Yet I cannot not find any instance of anyone calling it a 'restless abomination' and, therefore, it seems that the 'restlessness' was determined more by the idea reflected than by the forms used.

Furthermore, Underwood's small wood-carving *Regenesis* (fig. 4) – a figure consisting of successive masses of different planes at different angles, in a very 'restless' combination of forms reflecting Cubist lines – is regarded as an interesting case of animosity toward a fellow sculptor's work, expressing in sculpture rather than in an article an angry response to Epstein's bulky sculptured figure.[50] Haskell summed up the issue with the putdown, "there has been a recent case of a nonentity trying to steal a little notoriety with a piece of carpentry labelled with a name very like the *Genesis*".[51] The irony, I suggest, is that in comparison with Underwood's other, generally less than daring nudes of the period, *Regenesis*, seen today, strikes me as his most intricate and perplexing work.

Another case of a colleague "trying to steal a little notoriety" might be that of Paul Nash, a painter turned art critic (as Roger Fry had been in the 1920s), only in a more assiduous and harmful way – not only through articles but also by forming groups that, in the long run, attempted and to a great extent succeeded in sidelining Epstein and his work, especially from what were regarded as 'developments' in art. In December 1930 Nash became the art critic for the *Weekend Review* and later on, in April 1931, also for *The Listener*.[52] Borne forward on the popular wave of 'Epstein-bashing' (by then almost a national sport of the gutter press, in response to every presented carving),[53] Nash published in the *Weekend Review* (18 April 1931) a long article that Epstein, in his autobiography, would regard as a postmortem on *Genesis* and on himself. Discussing "pure form" and the fact that Epstein's work did not correspond to it, Nash stated that "Epstein is the only artist among us who *wants* to shock. His work is definitely *épatant*."[54] Epstein's reply, published in the same paper (25 April), was not just a response to a hostile colleague whose art he did not appreciate because he belonged to "that school of aesthetics and critics commonly supposed to reside in the neighbourhood of Gordon Square", but a valid assessment of the deficiencies in the art of the painter turned critic. In regard to the particular point of "wants to shock", Epstein's reply was: "I might assert, with as much authority, that Mr. Nash paints anaemic pictures in order not to shock or hurt people's feelings" (229).

Even years later and after Epstein's death, when his carvings' merits both as forms and as expressions of ideas become more obvious to viewers, Nash's allegation of Epstein's intention to shock the public was surprisingly repeated by John Rothenstein, particularly in regard to *Genesis* – "a proneness to aggressive distortion, to an anti-humanism, in fact, that was calculated to alienate almost any public of the pre-war period ... (perhaps designed especially to shock)".[55]

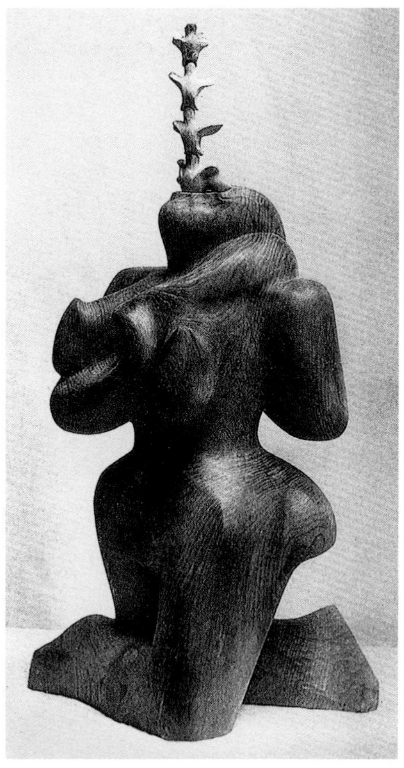

Fig. 4
Leon Underwood
Regenesis, c. 1930
Elmwood, 83.8 cm
Private collection

48 *Dial*, 24 June 1920; cited in Epstein, *Let There Be Sculpture*, p. 229.

49 Jason and Thompson-Pharoah, *The Sculpture of Frank Dobson*, p. 48.

50 Silber, *Sculpture of Epstein*, p. 50. It was also a "corrective", according to Underwood (cited by Wagner, *Mother Stone*, p. 233). Wagner elaborates on Underwood's motives, but these are beyond the scope of this discussion.

51 Haskell, *The Sculptor Speaks*, pp. 140–41. Wagner attributes the statement to Epstein with the unvalidated claim that it "certainly had Epstein's approval and may have stemmed from the artist himself": Wagner, *Mother Stone*, p. 233, note 115.

52 Nash turned to art criticism to supplement his declining income from his art; for a brief survey of Nash's publications, see Harrison, *English Art and Modernism*, pp. 234–38.

53 "A new carving by Mr. Epstein – good, bad or indifferent – can still steal the headlines when criminal assault, private or political, is out of season": Watson, *Art Lies Bleeding*, p. 16.

54 Epstein could not include extracts from this article in his autobiography, as Nash in 1940 did not permit it (229).

55 John Rothenstein's introduction to the 1952 Arts Council exhibition catalogue, *Epstein*. He makes a point of mentioning that some of Moore's carved figures were outstanding creations, surely among the finest carvings made in England since the Reformation.

II. THE NEW ARTISTIC GENERATION

To what extent might Epstein have been aware of Nash's attempts (through his second occupation as a journalist) to form a new modern art movement, referred to as the 'Hampstead Highbrows' and intended to supersede the old avant-garde of the 'Chelsea Bohemians'? It seems he was aware of it, although in his above-mentioned response to Nash he reacted only against Nash's art and not against the art politics that he promoted. There was nothing novel in Nash's waving a different artistic flag, or in his desire to form a group; that indeed had been the regular state of the arts since the English Impressionists and the Camden Town Group broke away from the Royal Academians just when Epstein came to England; and Epstein himself had been a founding member of the London Group.

Epstein's artistic isolation at the beginning of the 1930s was a consequence, to a significant extent, of the rise of a new artistic milieu, a milieu which included Henry Moore (recently married). This milieu grew, acquired its fame and established its unity around one essential conception – that of abstract art. Its members' homes and studios, centred in London's Hampstead, formed an unprecedented artistic environment, fostering an atmosphere "resembling workshops in Quattrocento Italy";[56] it provided these modernists with a sort of neighbourhood club where they could exchange ideas and technical innovations. They were fortunate to have in their midst the talented art critic and propagandist Herbert Read, whose influence in the early 1930s overshadowed that of Roger Fry. He promoted their art in his many articles and writings, insisting on "truth to materials". Epstein's response to this old slogan in a new guise was: "There is so much talk now of material that I can foresee as logical conclusion an exhibition of stones".[57]

The ferment of the energetic younger generation in Hampstead was to a great extent bad news for the mature and ageing Epstein. Perhaps he nurtured an unconscious envy of the comradeship in art of a kind he himself had hardly known (only during the 1910s, and even this had been limited) and in which, at this stage of his life, he could not participate, both because of his age and and because of his differing approach. He gradually estranged himself even from Moore. A decade later he wrily commented on the state of the arts in the England of the 1930s that manifestos "are got out in the best futurist, surrealist manner, imitating political party cries and slogans, and even Groups [sic] give themselves military titles like 'Unit 1' or 'Cell 33'" (250). Epstein omitted the name of the most relevant group, and the first one to have put his art in the shade, the Seven and Five, established by Nash and headed by Ben Nicholson,[58] and devoted above all to abstract art. Although regarding abstract art as extremely useful for experimentation, Epstein denied its value as an end in itself, arguing that its possibilities of pure form were limited "like the patterns in a children's kaleidoscope".[59] Moreover, he commented, it had become the last word in *chic* in the service of applied art, "and no middle-class home will be complete without this [modern-designed] radiator or telephone sculpture", pointing to his vacuum-cleaner as "modernist art".[60] However, once the focus of art had shifted from the figurative to the non-figurative, the progress from stylization (to which Epstein's work belonged) to the abstraction of form and later on to the creation of form in an absolute sense – form for form's sake – was so rapid as to

56 Read, 'British Art 1930–1940', p. 5.

57 Haskell, *The Sculptor Speaks*, p. 135. Indeed we may note Carl Andre's sculpture of a pile made from bricks (1966), acquired by and presented at the Tate Gallery in 1976.

58 In retrospect, their exhibition in February 1933 at the Leicester Galleries was defined as "no more than a genteel exhibiting group masquerading as avant-garde": Lewison, 'Going Modern and Being British', p. 67.

59 Haskell, *The Sculptor Speaks*, p. 44.

60 Ibid., p. iii.

seem inevitable.[61] Epstein, with the advent of these new terms and tendencies, was left out or, as he probably would have put it, left himself out.

Following the disintegration of the Seven and Five, Nash formed the group 'Unit 1', which included several members of the Seven and Five who, unlike Nicholson, had not committed themselves solely to abstract art. The new group embraced several artistic trends, adapting Continental influences to the objects and idioms of English art. They found in Herbert Read a vehement supporter, who during the 1930s wrote in praise of their work,[62] and later on became to some extent also involved in selling it.[63] The first and only exhibition of Unit 1, for which Herbert Read produced a book of statements and photographs,[64] was held at the Mayor Galleries in April 1934. In a letter to the editor of *The Times* in 2 June 1934 Nash, co-founder of both groups, claimed that the distinctive aim of the latter one was that it was composed of eleven individuals seeking the "expression of a truly contemporary spirit, for that thing which is recognised as peculiarly of today". The exhibition attracted more public attention than Fry's second Post-Impressionist exhibition (1912),[65] thus threatening to overturn Bloomsbury's claim to lead the avant-garde. However, unlike the informal Bloomsbury group, who maintained their personal ties throughout, Unit 1 disbanded, as tension between its members prevented them from achieving artistic coherence; their personal contacts, on the other hand, remained close in spite of their different artistic preferences.

Only one member of the new generation, Henry Moore, captured the attention of Epstein. Initially Epstein had admired Moore's art but he gradually developed a certain animosity towards it and towards Moore himself. Despite their work sharing some common aspects, their contacts later on left a sour taste with Epstein, as I will briefly note here, with more to follow.

Not long after the presentation of *Genesis*, Henry Moore's second solo exhibition was presented in April 1931 at the Leicester Galleries, Epstein's habitual showplace. Since his resignation from the post of teacher of sculpture at the Royal College of Art in January 1930, in order to make up for the loss of his salary Moore "had set himself a target of thirty sculptures a year",[66] mostly reclining and "mother & child" figures, and these, by April 1931, amounted to a substantial body of work. Epstein lent to Moore's exhibition the sculptures that he had bought – notably the alabaster *Suckling Child* (1930; stated as made after the concrete version of 1928) – and, as the gallery's proprietor Oliver Brown recalled, the exhibition "was greatly helped by the offer of Jacob Epstein to write a note on his work for the catalogue".[67] Epstein's correspondence before the exhibition indicates a close relationship between the two artists and, besides helping Moore to promote his work by presenting it to would-be buyers, Epstein had handwritten an introduction, which had then been typed, and read and approved by Moore:[68]

> Dear Moore,
> Thanks for the typed copy. I'm glad you like it & think it will do. I will make a few small additions. I meant to include something about "architectural work". I believe your show will be a great success as it ought to be.
> Am looking forward to seeing you & Mrs Moore on Sunday [at Epstein's open-house gatherings; see pp. 17–18].
> Could I have "All that matters" & the other small carvings & keep [them] until

61 See also Ramsden, *Themes and Variations*, p. 15.

62 In the books *Art Now* (1933), *Art and Industry* (1934), *Surrealism* (1936), *Art and Society* (1937), in addition to a great number of magazine articles published in England and abroad.

63 As can be seen in some of his letters to Ben Nicholson (TGA 8717.1.2.3620, for example).

64 Read, *UNIT 1*, London 1934.

65 Compton, *British Art in the 20th Century*, pp. 214–15.

66 Berthoud, *The Life of Henry Moore*, p. 108.

67 Brown, *Exhibition*, p. 110.

68 Cited from 'All you need is friends', *The Art Newspaper*, no. 85, October 1998. The exact date (March 1931) was kindly provided by Michael Phipps, archivist of the Henry Moore Foundation.

> the exhibition when I'd be only too pleased to show them. I'd like to show them to some friends on Sunday who might be useful [in buying] during the exhibition.
>
> With greetings from Mrs. Epstein.
> Sincerely yours,
> J. Epstein.

And he adds at the bottom a remark about the unpopularity of his own recently presented work:

> You know "Genesis" failed to pass the test at the Tate. My friends (old friends)[69] the board of trustees said they could not find a place for it & so declined to have it on loan. The crowding I suppose was only in their minds.

Moore's second exhibition, amidst the admiration of artistic circles, was a success despite the tag "cult of ugliness" having been applied to it.[70] His *Reclining Figure* (1929) became and has since remained a key example of his most renowned theme, developed during the following years in various forms, sizes and media. The subject itself was of no novelty in art; Moore, however, stylized the forms of his figures while retaining the basic pose of their Mexican precedent, the rain-god Chacmool. His work influenced Leon Underwood, who executed his figures mainly in cast bronze, giving round smooth surfaces to edgy and stylized masses, retaining the 'harmony school' tendency to give his reclining figures vague symbolical names, such as *Dawn* or *Mother Earth* (fig. 3).

In the foreword to Moore's catalogue Epstein praised his work, stating: "Before these works I ponder in silence", and declaring that "for the future of Sculpture in England Henry Moore is vitally important".[71] However, and in spite of his praise, he had reservation about the new artistic concept that had replaced Fry's 'significant form', hinting at this through the word 'if': "If sculpture is truly 'the relation of masses', here is the example for all to see". Another reservation seems to have been directed towards the notion of divorcing form from content which, at this stage of Moore's work, was not yet obvious: "The Forces within the works project upon our minds what the sculptor wishes to convey", which for Epstein fundamentally meant – an idea.

In his discussions with Haskell he expanded his praise:

> Henry Moore is the one important figure in contemporary English sculpture .... What is clearly expressed is a vision rich in sculptural invention, *avoiding the banalities of abstraction* and concentrating upon those enduring elements that constitute great sculpture .... Even the smallest works of Moore have an impressive and remote grandeur.[72]

Moore's short-lived period of what one could perhaps term "the banalities of abstraction" was yet to come (mere objects, strings – his compositions of 1933–34), after which he to some extent returned to 'idea', resuming his search for form within his main subjects, the mother-and-child and reclining figures. In that intervening period, however, these two great artists became estranged, due both to their differing artistic directions and to their different social milieux. After 1933 Moore's work developed, in differing degrees of stylization, simplified organic, fluid, biomorphic forms, reminiscent

69 Epstein, in all probability, was referring to J.B. Manson, director of the Tate Gallery, with whom he had had close contact during their studies in Paris (1903–04), sharing a work studio. Later on they were members of the then avant-garde Camden Town Group. In 1917 Manson declared Epstein to be "the only sculptor in England": Silber, *Epstein*, p. 33. In later years, Manson became a notoriously anti-modernist director of the Tate, and he is not mentioned in Epstein's biography.

70 *The Morning Post*, 11 April 1931.

71 Cited in Berthoud, *The Life of Henry Moore*, pp. 110–11.

72 Haskell, *The Sculptor Speaks*, pp. 135–36 (my italics).

of Hans Arp's style while retaining his own constant subjects – the female body and the reclining figure. Thus Moore departed from Epstein's kind of art and its sources, coming under the influence of other trends in a search for new forms for their own sake.

Although Epstein was one of the first to acclaim Henry Moore, and Moore never forgot this, or Epstein's generosity,[73] it was only later, as Arnold Haskell suggested, when, during the 1930s, critics began to use Moore to denigrate Epstein, that their friendship suffered; he claimed that Moore played no part in this, as "it would be impossible to meet a man of greater humanity and integrity".[74]

By contrast to Epstein in his almost complete artistic isolation, Henry Moore cooperated with his colleagues, in particular Ben Nicholson, corresponding throughout the years about his work and planning his participation in exhibitions.[75] Meanwhile another factor that contributed to Epstein's sense of being pushed aside was the way critics harped on about his art as being essentially non-English. Thus, while slightly mocking Read's praise of the new generation headed by Moore, the art historian E.G. Underwood praised the veteran Eric Gill because "his work is in the purest English tradition" but found in Epstein's art that "there is practically nothing English …. [His art] is vigorous, dynamic even; one hesitates to call it romantic because that is an epithet appropriate only to European art, but it is wholly exotic, and for this reason cannot appropriately be dealt at length in a history of English sculpture."[76]

How was Epstein to cope with his inceasing alienation from the London art scene and from his audience? One consolation might have been Arnold Haskell's book of conversations with Epstein, *The Sculptor Speaks*, published in 1931, which proved to be a success (fig. 5). In mid May the English public had the opportunity to see Epstein's large bronze *Madonna and Child*, which returned to England after being shown in New York and elsewhere.[77] It had been bought by the American sculptor Sally Ryan and was displayed on loan at the Tate Gallery. Ryan's optimistic view of it in early 1938 was that "it will probably be on view at the Tate Gallery indefinitely, as I have no intention of leaving London permanently for some years at least".[78]

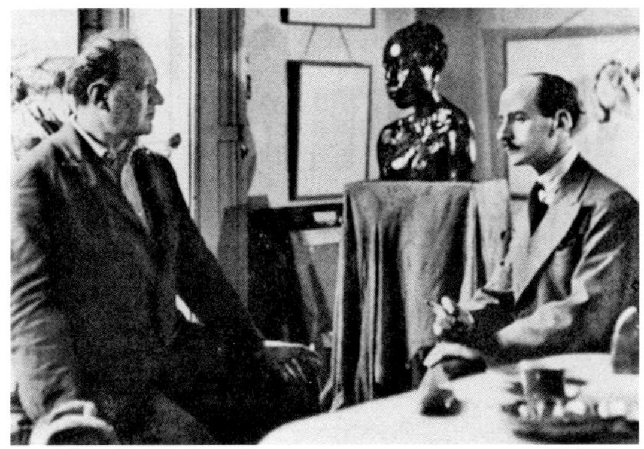

Fig. 5
Epstein and Haskell in Epstein's studio
Photograph from Arnold Haskell, *In His True Centre*, London 1951, p. 59

There is a saying that changes in art predict political changes, a saying that appears to suit the tumultuous years of the 1930s, where developments in art resulted in polarities that anticipated political polarization. As for the artists themselves, most of them (also within the younger generation described above) could to different extents have been termed Left-wing. Epstein's old colleague Wyndham Lewis, almost alone among the older generation of his milieu, had been notably right-wing (see Introduction, p. 28). After World War I Lewis turned to literature, and this became his main occupation during the 1930s, following his second book, *The Apes of God* (1930), a satire on amateurism in general and Left-wing Bloomsbury amateurism in particular. After the success of the National Socialists in winning seats in the German Reichstag, Lewis travelled to Berlin in November 1930 to find a German publisher for *The Apes of God*, and had the satisfaction of watching Goebbels and Goering rallying a crowd of twenty thousand from a balcony at the Berlin Sport Palace. Returning to London, Lewis dismissed Nazi anti-Semitism as a mere sideshow, a "racial red herring". When the Second Spanish Republic was declared on 14 April 1931, a horrendous future was destined for Spain, casting a heavy shadow over Europe, including England. On these two subjects – Nazism (as a manifestation of

73 Obituary, *The Sunday Times*, 23 August 1959.
74 Haskell, *Balletomane at Large*, p. 54.
75 For example, a letter to Nicholson, dated 28 March 1937: TGA- 8717.1.2.3023.
76 Underwood, *A Short History of English Sculpture*, p. 154.
77 *The Times*, 21 May 1931.
78 Press cutting in the Tate Archive, unidentified source.

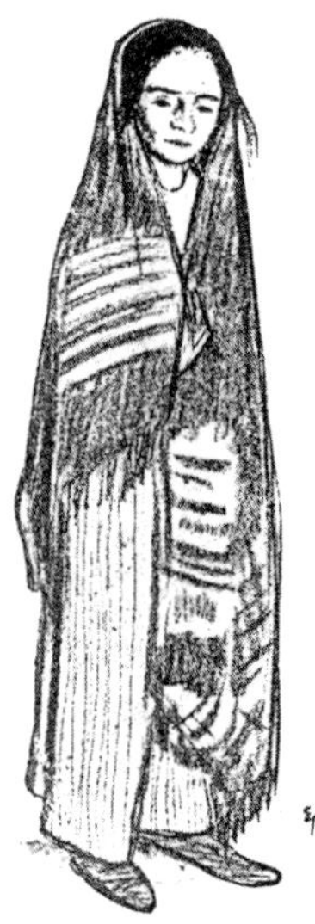

17
The Little Sister
H. Hapgood, *The Spirit of the Ghetto*, p. 260

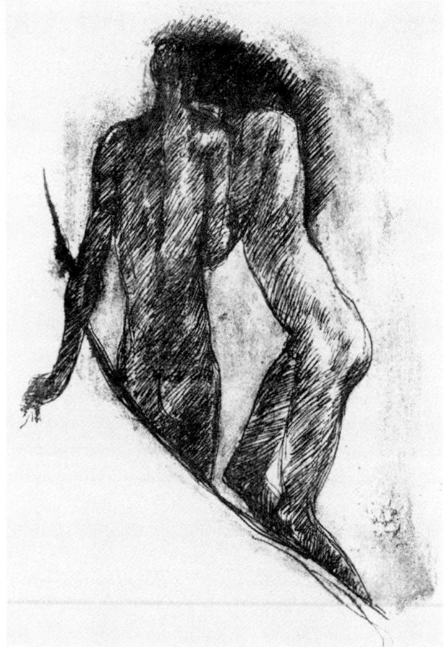

18
Drawing from Walt Whitman, *Calamus* 1904 [1901]
Pen and ink and wash, 310 x 203 mm
KE 6

authoritarian doctrine in Germany and Italy) and republicanism (representing democracy) – the two former colleagues in the Vorticist period now stood on different sides of the fence, retaining a dislike of the Bloomsbury set as their only artistic and social common denominator.

In February 1931, concomitant with the shock created by the presentation of a Hebrew concept in *Genesis*, another kind of shock occurred, triggering a chain of events (mentioned above, p. 27) that was to have a direct impact on British society and eventually an indirect impact on Epstein's work. On 28 February Sir Oswald E. Mosley resigned from the Labour Party, launching the following day the New Party, which advocated a new national policy to meet the economic crisis brought about by the Great Depression. "At the beginning Mosley had a regular bodyguard of Jewish prize-fighters [e.g., Kid Lewis] as Fascism was not then thought of as anti-Semitic," recalled George Orwell,[79] adding that Mosley did not embrace anti-Semitism until about 1933 or 1934. Mosley was denied the opportunity to establish his party when a surprise election was suddenly called in 1931. All the New Party candidates, including Mosley himself, lost their seats in Parliament, a fact that one may assume the socialist Epsteins did not deplore. Meanwhile Epstein had his own artistic reaction to the political stress caused by these events.

EPSTEIN'S RE-FOUND GODS

I. ILLUSTRATIONS OF THE OLD TESTAMENT

Epstein's plunge in 1930 into his Jewish culture during the carving of *Genesis*, and afterwards during 1931, is manifested and explicitly expressed in his drawings for the Old Testament: "In 1931 I made a series of drawings for the Old Testament. I became so absorbed in the text and in the countless images evoked by my readings, a new world passed in vision before me. I lost no time in putting it on paper" (166).

Fifty-four drawings were exhibited in May 1932 at the Redfern Gallery, for which a catalogue was produced, and about 35 more were added later,[80] all now dispersed to the point of being almost untraceable. Therefore, when attempting to explain Epstein's personal attitudes and intentions, I will refer mainly to the titles given by Epstein himself in the authorized catalogue, and to the biblical verses that he saw fit to cite or indicate.

The exhibition included only Old Testament subjects because, suggests Gardiner, "the search for the Messiah is more in tune with [Epstein's] art than the Messiah found".[81] As for the drawings that were made later, the few I could find relate mostly to the historical events described in the Old Testament. Some of these are claimed to refer to the New Testament; I shall later express my reservations in regard to this claim.

Stylistically, these 54 drawings clearly present a development in Epstein's rendering of the figure on a paper support – from the naturalistic, illustrative presentation of his New York drawings for Hutchinson Hapgood's *The Spirit of the Ghetto* (1902) [17] and from the Parisian drawings, with minimal figures in freer dark-ink contours, for Walt Whitman's

79 Letter from Orwell to Julia Symonds, 25 October 1947: *Collected Essays, Journalism and Letters*, vol. IV, no. 95, pp. 383–84.

80 See Redfern Gallery 1932 and Felsenstein, 'Epstein as a Book Illustrator', p. 285, note 40. I found several on the internet, most owners unidentified.

81 Gardiner, *Epstein*, p. 317, explaining why no New Testament drawings were included.

Calamus poems (1904) [18]. In these Bible drawings he reached a kind of abstraction, as I would call it, in spite of Epstein's deprecation of abstract art (p. 46). He conveyed his perceptions, I suggest, by creating an unrealistic atmosphere expressed by only a few pencilled or inked contour lines and a few patches of light, almost transparent, colour. Nevertheless, and in spite of the almost elusive treatment, the illustrations convey the essence of the subject rather than staging events or individualizing persons.

As the catalogue makes clear, the collection's dominant subject, under various titles, is that of the "patriarch", with eight drawings bearing this title; five relate in one way or another to the Almighty, and three to Adam and Eve. Several subjects Epstein depicted more than once (for example, Absalom), others only once, and among these some rarely if ever depicted by other illustrators (for example, *Moses with his Ethiopian wife* [19]). Even with subjects also treated by other artists, Epstein arrived at a different interpretation and succeeded in exposing new facets that reflected his own ideas. The selection of drawings I discuss below includes some that touch upon a complex philosophical issue; others, unsurprisingly in this study, reflect Epstein's personal concerns.

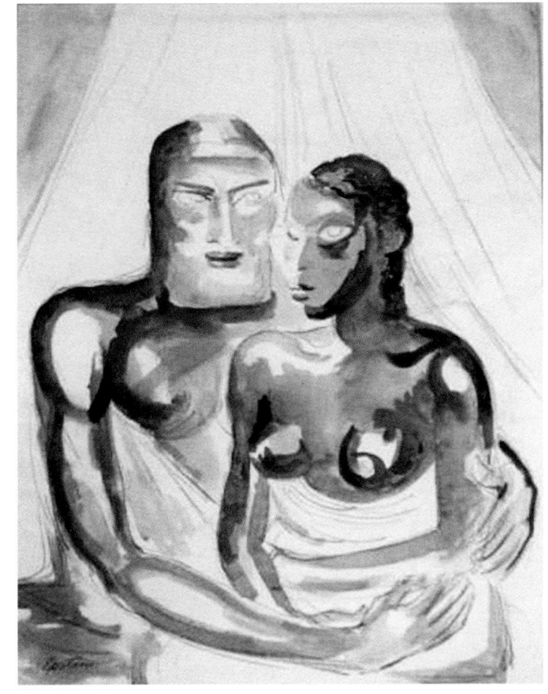

19
Moses with his Ethiopian wife, 1931
Pencil and watercolour, 570 x 430 mm
Private collection, on loan to NAGW

And the Spirit of God Moved upon the Face of the Waters [20] raises the problematic question how a Jewish artist may depict God, and in the case of this verse, Genesis 1:2, how to interpret the 'something' hovering above the waters.[82] Epstein's choice was to present the common European image of an angel as God's "spirit", and this choice is 'explained' in another drawing entitled *Messenger of Creation*;[83] this is not God himself. Its role as "messenger" was the explanation Epstein gave for utilizing a winged figure in his carving for the tomb of Oscar Wilde,[84] and it applies in these drawings equally. The common conceptual basis of the drawing [20] and the carved messenger on the tomb is evident in their floating pose and in the similar Egyptian aura of their facial features – the thick lips, slit-closed eyes, hairstyle and the unified forehead and long nose.

Another illustration, this time anthropomorphizing the deity, *The Hand of God* [21] features the pointing finger of an outstretched hand, echoing Michelangelo's famous fresco and paying homage to the great artist, whom Epstein admired. In *And God Blessed the Seventh Day* [22], God is presented as an old bearded man, enclosed by a circle which in its lower part has an added wave that may allude to the yin-yang symbol, signifying harmony. His hands are raised in the almost universal manner of blessing. This particular drawing seems to have been influenced by a watercolour, *God blessing the Seventh Day*, by another artist whom Epstein admired – William Blake (fig. 6); both works have at the centre a bearded man looking downwards and raising his hands. The hand gestures in Epstein's drawing, however, also hint at the traditional Jewish manner of blessing the candles on the Sabbath eve; the eyes are almost closed, with palms facing the viewer in the gesture used by Jewish women when blessing the candles.

The subject that seems to dominate the entire set of Epstein's drawings (whether or not included in the exhibition) is that of the patriarch and his relationships, whether between the father and his sons or between God and his subjects. Repeatedly addressing the theme of father and son during this drawing enterprise continued a theme that had been introduced by Epstein in 1929 in his carving *Day*; indeed one of the drawings not included in the exhibition, entitled *Biblical Subject*, was in Haskell's possession and was chosen for his book on Epstein (p. 91), undoubtedly because it echoed the composition of father and son carved in *Day*.

82 The Hebrew word for that 'something' can refer either to a spirit or to a wind; English translations have it as an elusive 'God's spirit' or a physical 'God's wind', meaning an awesome wind, the added 'God' suggesting a superlative. This interpretation of that 'something' as a natural phenomenon had been suggested by the Jewish scholar Abraham Ibn Ezra (late 11th–mid 12th century), as noted in J. Skinner's popular *Critical Commentary on Genesis* (Edinburgh 1910) and in recent times in E.A. Speiser's *Genesis* (Anchor Bible, 1964).

83 Redfern Gallery 1932, no. 40.

84 Haskell, *The Sculptor Speaks*, p. 20.

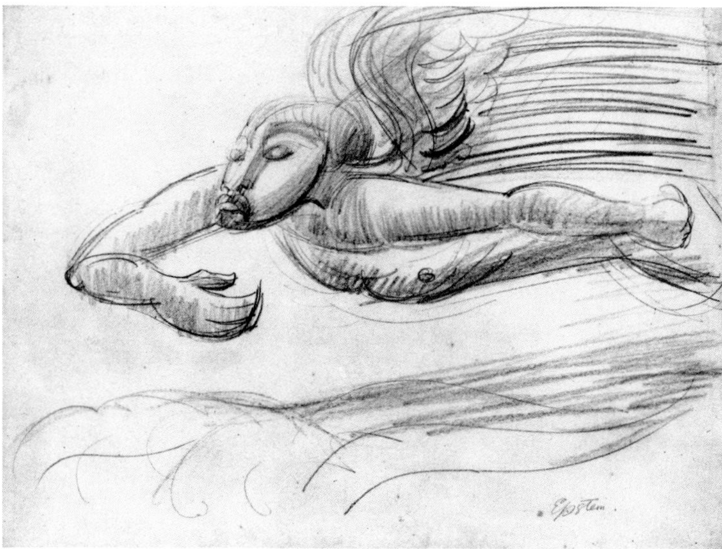

20
And The Spirit of God Moved Upon The Face Of The Waters, 1931 [1930]
Pencil, 44.5 x 57.8 cm
Formerly Shinman collection

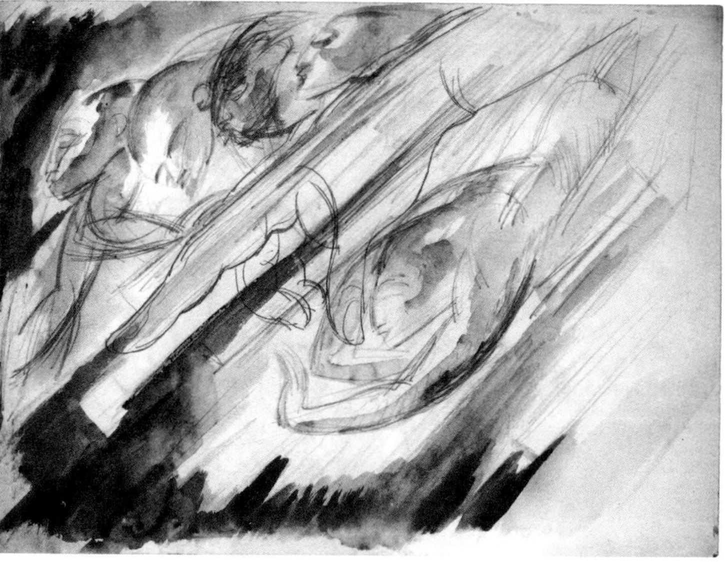

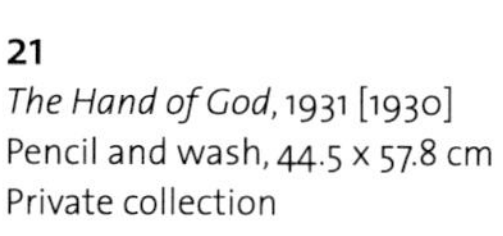

21
The Hand of God, 1931 [1930]
Pencil and wash, 44.5 x 57.8 cm
Private collection

22
And God Blessed the Seventh Day, 1931
Pen, ink and wash, 43 x 57 cm
Private collection

Fig. 6
William Blake
God Blessing the Seventh Day, 1805
Watercolour, 42 x 35.5 cm
Private collection

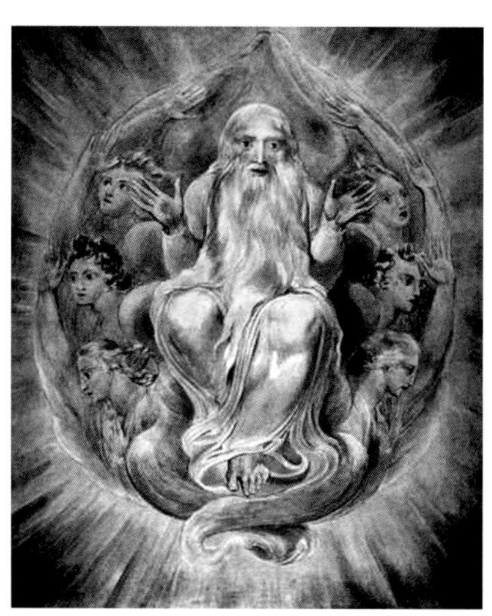

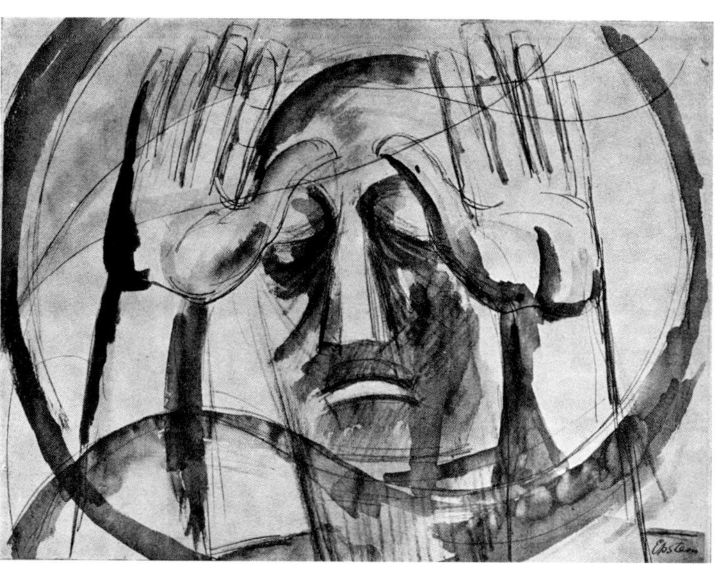

Of the eight drawings in the catalogue entitled *Patriarchal Group*,[85] two – *Noah and two of his sons* and *Jacob and the sons of Leah* – convey a special facet of fatherhood. These two titles are rare if not unique in the general range of Bible illustrations. These and two more subjects of equal rarity reflect, I suggest, a particular state of affairs in Epstein's life at the time.

Noah is a common subject in art, but Noah and two of his sons is a peculiar subject because Noah was well known to have had three sons. The illustration [23] presents a father figure embracing the shoulders of his two sons. To his right is a bearded figure looking down, wearing a kind of multicoloured garment (echoing Joseph's coat of many colours in Genesis), marking him as Shem, considered to be the forefather of the Semitic peoples; to Noah's left is a smooth-faced figure with a fair complexion who, in the manner depicted on many Greek vase paintings, exposes his chest and legs, marking him as Japheth, considered to be the forefather of the Europeans. The last son, Ham, considered to be the father of the African peoples, is the one omitted; he is redundant to a scene in which the father embraces the two sons who, in Epstein's world at the time, were involved in a conflict that might influence the future of the part of the human race to which their descendants belonged. Epstein's choice of subject was, I suggest, a response to the growing anti-Semitism in England, as well as to the ideology that emphasized conflict between Aryans and Semites rather than acknowledging both as members of the same family. Epstein's Jewish consciousness – usually dormant because he regarded himself first and foremost as an artist – had been awakened by forces beyond his control: he later recalled Albert Einstein's comment: "I thought I was a physicist, I did not bother about being a Jew until Hitler made me conscious of it" (95).

Jacob and the Sons of Leah evokes, I suggest, Epstein's personal sphere. The sons of the biblical Jacob presented are those of the first wife, Leah, who, in the biblical story, is not the beloved wife (Rachel) but rather the one who, for many years, established Jacob's family. Regarding Epstein's feelings for his children, I have suggested above an interpretation of a drawing made in 1930 and given to Kathleen [4]. It expressed, through a biblical scene, his attitude towards his second family. Epstein seems to have made a distinction between his original family, which always came first, and his second family – of which, to a great extent, he was deprived, mainly by distance. This was despite his love and adoration of the mother – allegorized in another drawing in the exhibition, which illustrates an elderly man embracing a younger woman surrounded by flowers: the drawing was given to Kathleen as a token of love and thus suitably titled *Song of Solomon*.[86] Closing the catalogue of the exhibition, as if saying 'last but not least', is the drawing *Leah*, another unprecedented artistic presentation – the biblical Jacob's first wife, who had to share him with a beloved younger wife.[87]

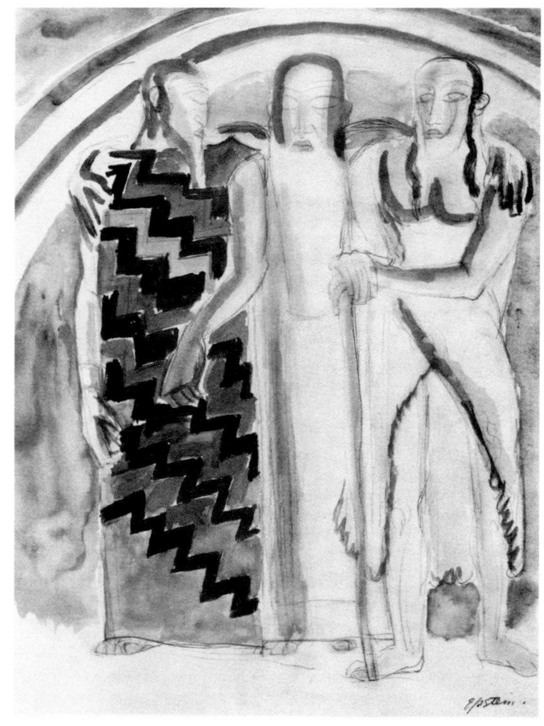

23
Noah and two of his sons, 1931
Pencil and watercolour, 438 x 572 mm
Victoria and Albert Museum, London

To Haskell's question "What is a fine drawing?",[88] Epstein replied that it depended whether the artist had "an interesting mind with something original to express", and whether that idea could be better expressed "by the use of [drawing rather than] any other technique". In sum, what to expect in a fine drawing, suggested Epstein, was "harmony between the actual expression and the means used". It was Epstein's "actual expression" that, by and large, led to the unfavourable reaction when he presented the set of 54 drawings at the Redfern Gallery (23 February – 19 March 1932). "It seemed that

85 In Redfern Gallery 1932, eight drawings entitled *Patriarchal Group* (nos. 6, 15, 30, 34, 35, 52, 53), and an affiliated subject, *Jacob and the Sons of Leah* (no. 30).

86 Buckle, *Epstein: Sculptor*, no. 41 (erroneously dated 1923). In Redfern 1932 it is no. 23, and another one under that title is no. 7.

87 Redfern Gallery 1932, no. 54; unfortunately I could not trace this drawing.

88 Haskell, *Black on White*, pp. 22–23.

I had again committed some kind of blasphemy," commented Epstein. The disapproval had been directed towards both his non-traditional style and his interpretation of his subject-matter, inasmuch as he had in both respects disregarded commonly accepted conceptions of biblical figures evolved in a long artistic iconography. The author and critic Cyril Connolly identified this issue, praising Epstein for "scraping off the accretions of Anglo-Hellenic good taste that generations of Etonian bishops have allowed to accumulate on the subjects of their exegesis".[89] In an apt comparison, he summed up the virtue of Epstein's biblical figures by saying: "At last we see them as Blake would have drawn them had Blake been a Jew".

'The Jewish Blake' Epstein did not present pleasant pictures; they are stern in their content, "with patriarchal harshness";[90] and even after many years of changes in the perception of art they are still regarded as laden with "passion and sexuality and with a frightening intensity rarely seen in religious subject-matter".[91] Epstein's stance towards biblical figures and events, as is very clear from the drawings, was not a religious one; one may even term them secular. His approach, however, accorded with a traditional method of Jewish exegesis, that is, engaging with Bible stories as paradigms or metaphors for pressing contemporary events.[92] This method also constitutes the basis of his sculptural work – one of adding his own interpretation to the old perceptions, in a manner reflecting his intellectual preoccupations as well as his personal atitudes.

Into the nexus of family relationships expressed in the Bible drawings a new spice had been introduced during 1931 – the person who inspired Epstein's sculptures produced during 1932, and who is indirectly referred to in another Old Testament drawing, discussed further on. As Epstein's work and life were interwoven to such a degree that it is sometimes difficult to determine the correlation of an event and the work reflecting it, this would seem to be the right place to introduce her.

Isabel Nicholas,[93] born in East London in 1912 and brought up in Liverpool, arrived back in London at the age of eighteen intending to study painting, but dropped out of the Royal Academy of Arts course in London in 1930, leaving herself penniless and in a need of a job. Some time in 1931, at the recommendation of a Jewish girlfriend who later immigrated to Palestine, she approached Epstein, by then in his fifties, who immediately accepted her as a model. Like Epstein's model Sunita before her, and owing to her similar impoverished condition, in due course she became a member of the Epstein household, living there and sharing a room with Peggy Jean, who, most of the time, was a boarder at Dartington Hall School. Isabel took part in the family's life, went with them at Easter to Paris, and joined them at weekends in their cottage in Epping Forest, where Epstein, at the time, was engaged in his watercolours of biblical themes. Her stay with the Epsteins enabled her to develop her own drawing abilities, reflecting her obsession with animals, to the delight and interest of Epstein, who went with her and Peggy Jean to London Zoo to observe them.[94] Isabel was an exotic beauty, and said to be irresistible – "tall, lithe, superbly proportioned … full mouth, high cheek-bones, and heavy-lidded, slanting eyes, from which shone forth a gaze of exceptional, though remote, intensity".[95] For Peggy Jean she was like a sister, for Mrs Epstein like another daughter.[96] For Epstein, during the next two years, she would become much more than that, despite his great love for Kathleen – as expressed in a beautiful drawing depicting an elderly

89 Connolly, 'The Sculptor Paints', p. 101.

90 See also Gaunt, 'Epstein's Bible Drawings', pp. 290–91.

91 Lovatt, 'Epstein's Bible', p. 43.

92 In Judaic tradition this is usually done by the Rabbi, who interprets the *Parasha* (the chosen Bible chapter for the prayer) every Saturday in synagogue, adding his own opinion on, and alluding to, contemporary occurrences.

93 All details about her were taken (as is) from her memoirs, deposited in the Kaiman Kreitman Research Centre, Tate's Kit-Accession, TGA 9612. Unfortunately, her remarks on Epstein, his work and their relationship leave many lacunae. Isabel later married composer Ian Rawsthorne and took his name.

94 *Rebel Angel* – Central TV.

95 For citations of several commentators on Isabel see Martin Gayford, *The Daily Telegraph*, 25 July 1998.

96 With hindsight, Peggy Jean (in a recorded interview with the author) thought that Margaret's acceptance of such a beautiful person into the household was a means to divert Epstein's attention from Kathleen. She said that Margaret's main objection to Kathleen, whom she called "the witch", was the permanence of her relationship with Epstein, which she regarded as a threat to her home.

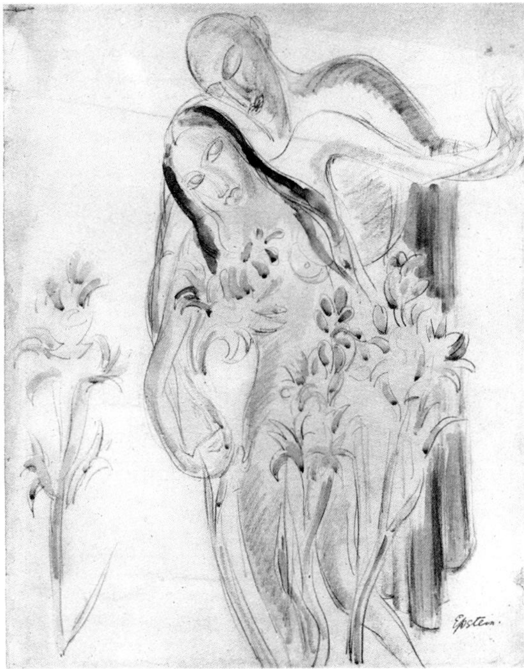

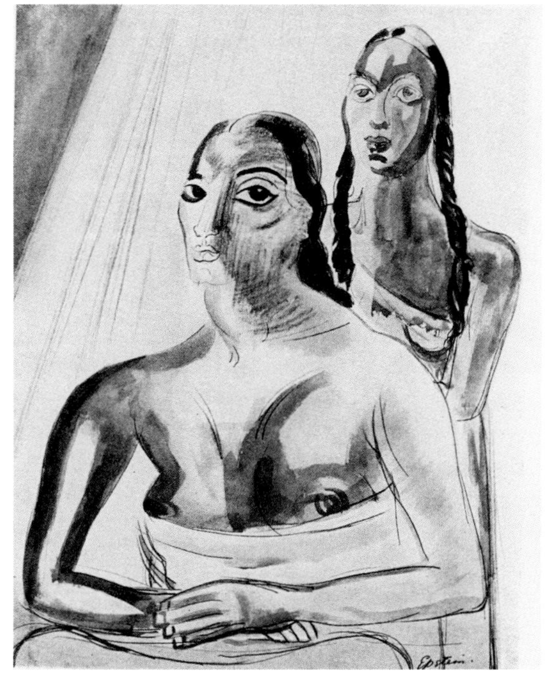

man embracing a flourishing woman under the disguise of a biblical theme [24]. Unlike the drawings on biblical subjects discussed above, the following one may illuminate this interesting facet of Epstein's life during this period.

It depicts a subject described in Genesis, 30: 3, that has rarely – if ever – been selected for illustration, *Rachel and Bilhah* [24a]. The drawing has two figures: seated is Jacob's beloved wife Rachel, depicted as a sensuous mature woman with breasts exposed, while the modestly dressed Bilhah with her maiden's braids resting on her chest (echo-ing Epstein's bronze *Visitation* of 1925) stands behind her. There was a celebrated representation of Rachel on her own by Gustave Doré, but the combination of one of Jacob's wives with the maid who would bear the children for her that she could not conceive is unique. This subject, I suggest, may have reflected a personal state of affairs in which, while devoting one drawing to the dutiful and loyal wife no. 1 through the metaphor of Leah, Epstein drew his sensuous beloved wife no. 2 in front of a looming shadow – the younger Isabel Nicholas who had entered his life. An argument in support of this interpretation can be drawn from a comparison between *Isabel, 1st portrait* [25] and *Kathleen, 3rd portrait* [26], made during the same year,[97] in which, for the first time since he had begun to model her, Kathleen is presented in a bust that exposes her breasts, thus giving both sculptures a similar pose; but while Kathleen is draped in a transparent dress, Isabel is naked.

The busts thus seem to be a parallel exercise in modelling, but while Kathleen's face projects a pondering and serious mood, Isabel's face projects confidence, accentuated by a tint of cynicism in the expression of her mouth. It does not take a very shrewd eye to notice the difference in the expressions, and no doubt Kathleen too observed it. This perhaps is why in that same year, as if to reach a kind of equilibrium in his mind between these two beautiful women, Epstein executed *Kathleen, 4th portrait* [27], a head and shoulders of a smiling and somewhat childlike Kathleen with two maiden's braids

24
Songs of Solomon, 1931
Pen, ink and wash, 570 x 430 mm
Formerly Shinman collection

24a
Rachel and Bilhah
Pen, ink and wash, 570 x 430 mm
Private collection

97 Silber, *The Sculpture of Epstein*, no. 221, suggests Kathleen's portrait is 1931 and Isabel's 1932, which, I suggest, is too late considering she started to model for him in 1931.

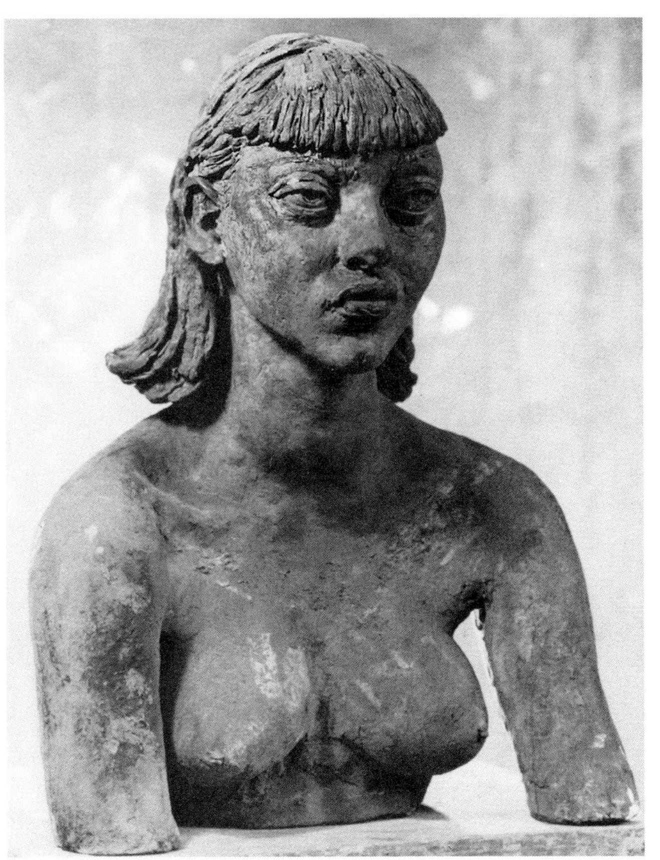

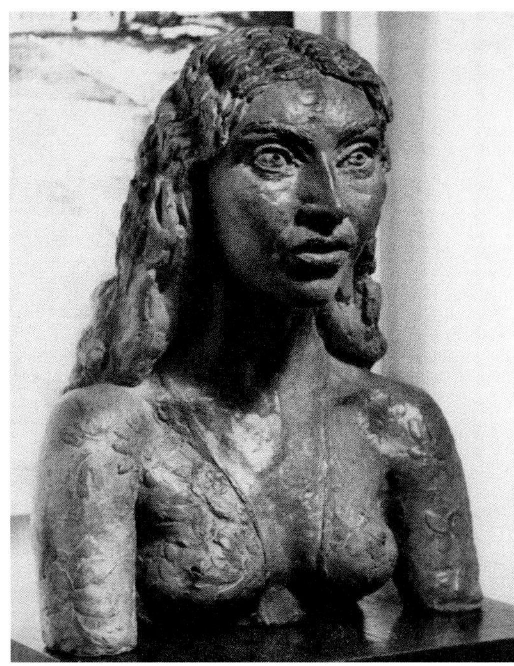

25
Isabel, 1st portrait, 1931 [1932]
Bronze, H. 53.3 cm
Private collection

26
Kathleen, 3rd portrait, 1932
Bronze, H. 38.5 cm
Private collection

27
Kathleen, 4th portrait, 1932
Bronze, H.38.5 cm
Private collection

28
Isabel, 2nd portrait, 1932
Bronze, H.70.6 cm
Private collection

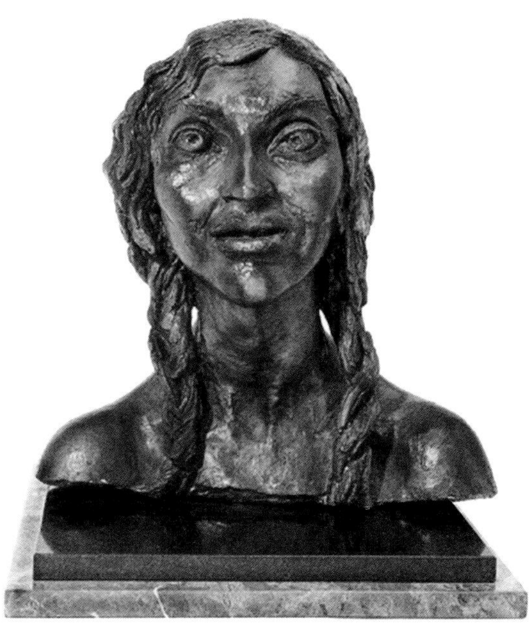

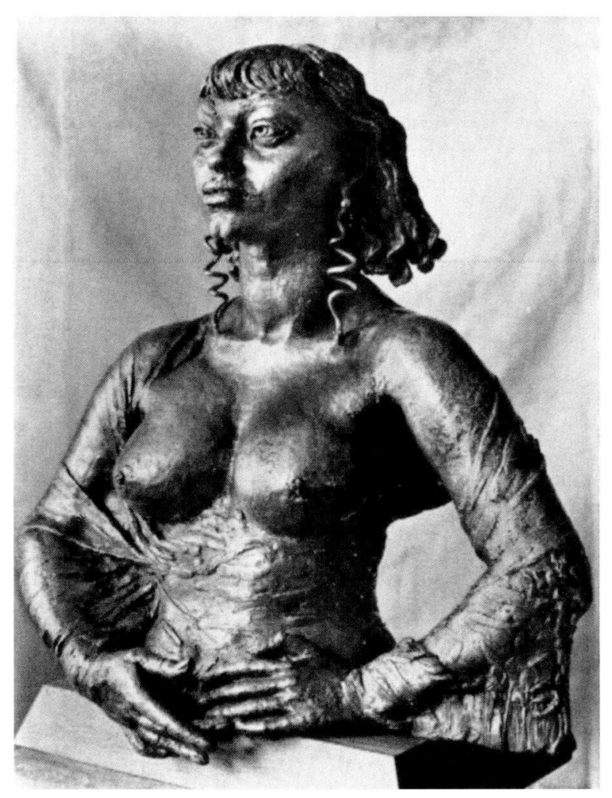

resembling those in the drawing of Bilhah [24]. In contrast, *Isabel, 2nd portrait*, also made toward the end of 1932, is a very sensuous work [28], given her exposed breasts and long ringlet-like earrings.

The two portraits of Isabel, the first one plain and then the more sensuous one, echo the two stages of Epstein's work on Kathleen's first two portraits – a plain and a sensuous one – made when they had met in the early 1920s (I/167). One is left wondering whether Kathleen, like Margaret before her, had sensed what was developing between the artist and his model. All four portraits were presented in May 1933 in Epstein's exhibition at the Leicester Galleries.

II. A NEW 'SUN' ENTITY

Epstein's sculptural activity in 1931 seems to reflect a change in his state of mind that occasioned a return to the consideration of his own culture. The first sign of his altering his previous approach to the subject of the 'Sun' seems to be a drawing made during the same period and in the same style as the illustrations to the Old Testament, but totally unrelated to them. It depicts a vivid figure like his carving *Sun God* [29]. The philosophical change it indicates manifested itself in a sculptural work that, like a Janus head, had two different profiles.

The first of these consisted of the outcome of alterations made to the older carving *Sun God*, begun in 1910 during his friendship and involvement with Eric Gill in an artistic endeavour that I termed 'the Aryan Sun' (I/90–91); it had remained unsold in his studio. During 1929–30, when Haskell held his conversations with Epstein, he noticed that Epstein had renewed work on it. Epstein claimed that it "has been put away for over twenty years",[98] probably hinting that its full development was as yet incomplete. However, the new work on it did not at any stage alter its basic characteristics. Carved on one side of a thin, almost square block, a naked male figure stands with legs astride, arms outstretched to the sides, elbows bent to raise the forearms, the palms open with the thumbs pointing up to the temples. From a recessed line surrounding the oval face, the sun-like hair-halo forms a square wave that touches the edge of the block. The almost naturalistic details of the slender figure are executed in relatively low relief on the thin mass of the body, which accentuates the impact of its phallus.

In its last stage of the work in 1931 [30a], Epstein left the figure and its details alone but deepened the surroundings and thus increased the relief, adding an interesting stylization – pubic hair which echoed Michelangelo's treatment of the same part of the body in his *David*. But the addition of pubic curls to the figure, I suggest, was not a mere toying with allusion to a revered artist, but was intended to emphasize the god's function of procreation: the viewer's eye is attracted to the very organ responsible for it, and thus the young pagan sun-god resumes his ancient role as the Giver of Life.[99]

This last stage of *Sun God* may be regarded as Epstein's final contribution to his involvement during the 1910s with the pagan notion of 'the Aryan Sun', and with its implicit idea of the absolute supremacy of the unpartnered procreating male god. Now, although not totally divorcing himself from the concept of male domination (being

98 Haskell, *The Sculptor Speaks*, p. 138.

99 For comprehensive discussion of this issue, see I/90.

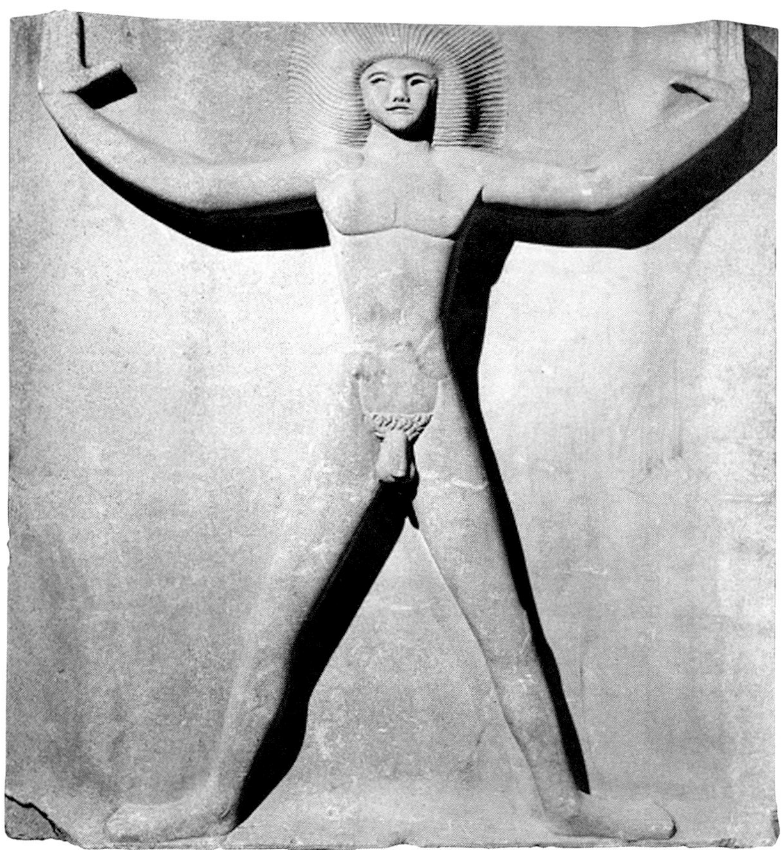

30a
Sun God, 1931
Hoptonwood stone, 213.4 x 198 x (at the top) 35.5 cm
Metropolitan Museum, New York

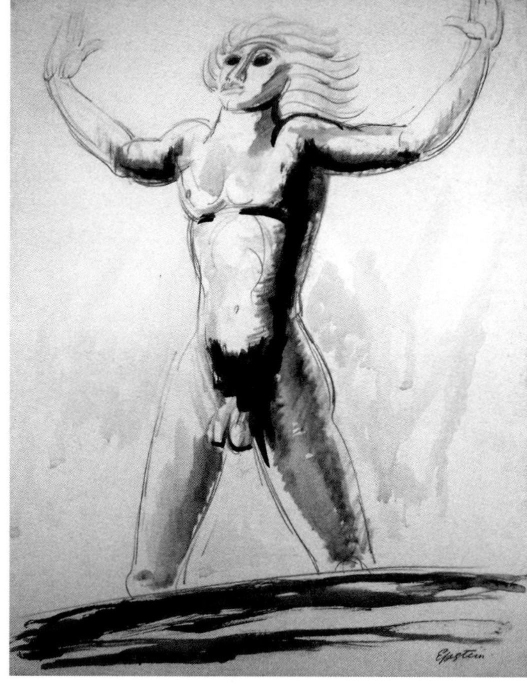

29
Sun God, 1931
Pencil and watercolour on paper, 570 x 430 mm
Private collection, on loan to NAGW

himself male), he set his mind on expressing a different outlook, presenting what may be termed 'a biblical perception of procreation', in which there was collaboration of the sexes in order to procreate: on the same dimensions of another square block – later to be glued to the back of *Sun God*[100] – he depicted a huge father-figure bearing on his chest the small figure of a woman giving birth and her offspring. He thereby produced a family group which he entitled *Primeval Gods* [30/b] and which, he declared, he had completed in three months.[101]

The deep relief on the added block features a colossal image of a man, whose shoulders and vertically downstretched arms with bent palms form a frame that encloses two small figures – a woman resting on his belly, above the genitalia, and a child emerging from her vagina, attached to his chest. The 'staging' of small figures on the chest of a large male figure is a motif common in Polynesian art (fig. 7),[102] and an echo of the influence of 'primitive' art on Epstein at an earlier time.

If one recalls Wilenski's comment on the "unhomogeneous" forms of *Genesis* (see p. 41), then in *Primeval Gods* Epstein went even further in this diversity, with each of the figures displaying its own style. Thus the colossal man (which I regard as 'the father') seems to echo Epstein's *Day*, at least as far as the archaic treatment of the head is concerned. However, in this presentation, the limbs lack the geometrical bulk of *Day*, resembling (particularly in the shoulders) Moore's rounded edges (a not unnatural exchange of

100 This fact is not mentioned in other texts. However, the straight line dividing the blocks and the glue can be seen all around the two blocks. The top planes of the two blocks – forming the backgrounds – are almost equal in width, while differing in the depth of the reliefs; *Primeval Gods* is the heavier one. A more complex point is its unclear date of execution – Silber mentions 1931–33, based on *Sun God* being mentioned by Haskell, and in May 1933 the entire complex was exhibited at the Leicester Galleries.

101 *Rebel Angel* – Central TV.

102 The God-Creator Tangaroa, Cook Islands (wood, H. 69 cm) or from Doroto Islands (wood, H. 117 cm); both items reached The British Museum at the end of the nineteenth century. See Fagg, *Tribal Image*, nos.75, 76.

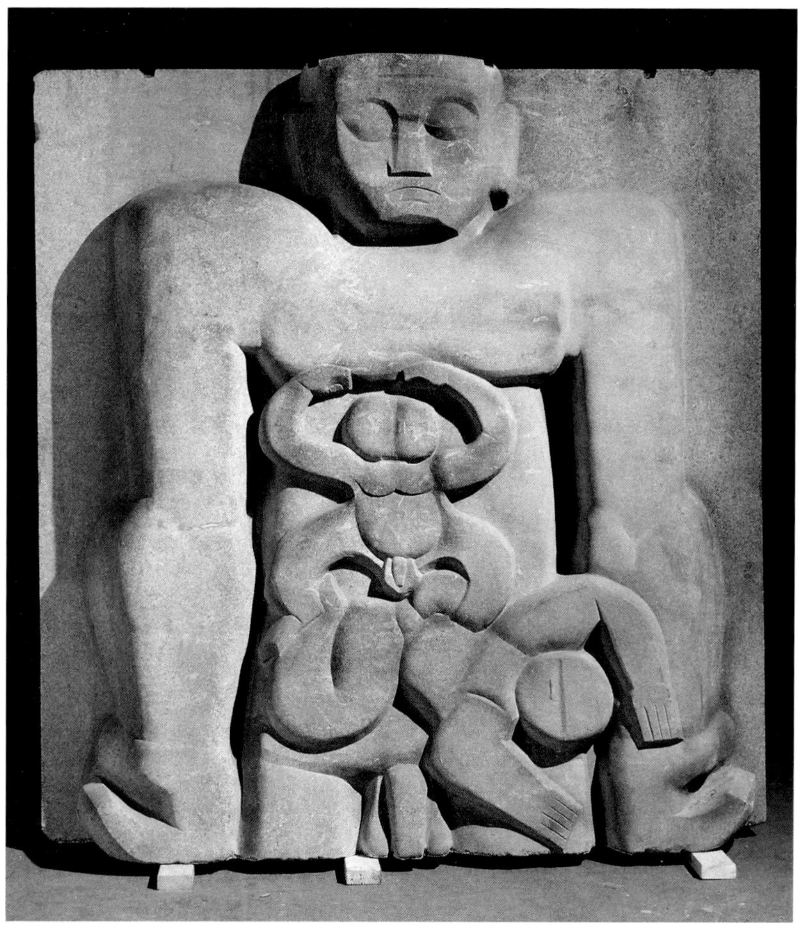

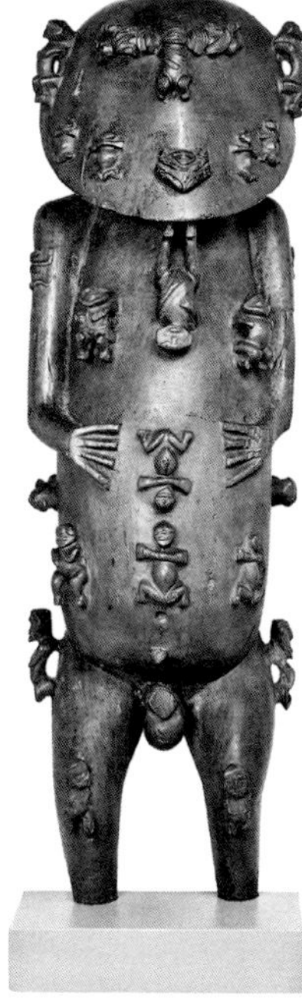

30b
Primeval Gods, 1931–33
Hoptonwood stone,
213.4 x 198 x (at the top) 35.5 cm
Metropolitan Museum, New York

Fig. 7
The God-Creator Tangaroa
Wood, H. 69 cm
Cook Islands
The British Museum

31
Birth, 1913
Stone, 30.5 x 26.5 x 10.2 cm
Leeds City Art Galleries

influences between two great artists) and conveying the sense of a stone naturally eroded by water. A different stylization is evident in the small figures, with elements reduced into almost flat planes with few details, obviously recalling 'primitive' art and Epstein's work during the 1910s – notably his carving of a similar subject, *Birth* [31].

The carving on this big block continued during 1932, and, hoping to show it in his exhibition of 1933 mentioned above, he wrote to his friend Dr Oko:[103]

> At the moment I am carving [two indecipherable words] of gods; my exhibition will be of Gods stone carvings & portraits & studies of women & I expect it to be the largest show I've had at the Leicester; it may take place Easter end of March or April.

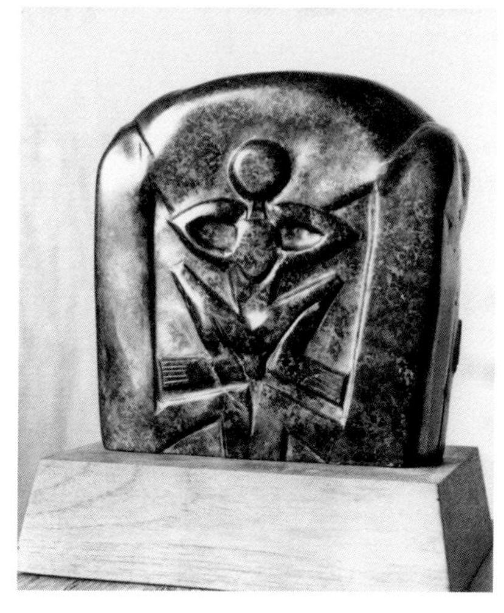

The composition of *Primeval Gods*, I suggest, is by far the most intricate and condensed work that Epstein had carved up until that point, embracing three figures that each projects, by its sheer size, a very distinct social order. The size of the birthling, equalling that of the woman who has begotten him, bestows on the composition a symbolistic aura, accentuated by the way the colossal male figure towers above the smaller maternal unit towards which his look is directed. Undoubtedly, in accordance with the social order since primordial times, he is the most important figure – the god-creator. The inverted woman delivering her offspring towards him, however, inserts her hand in

103 Letter from Epstein to Dr Oko, 22 February 1933: HUCAC.

his palm in a gesture symbolic of cooperation, and the frontal offspring supported by the father's chest enables an interpretation of the composition as meaning 'we are all in this'. This perception is reinforced by the sculpture's title: it is not 'a' primordial god, as the impact of the male's size overshadowing the others might suggest, but 'gods'. They, including the female, are the gods of the primordial family unit, thus following the notion expressed by the great progenitrix Eve, when she boasted that, like God, she had "created" a child (Genesis 4: 1). Given this biblical aura, *Primeval Gods* was probably carved concurrently with, or immediately after, the series of Old Testament drawings – particularly, as I have already pointed out, because the subject of the patriarch was a prominent one among the drawings.

CHAPTER 3

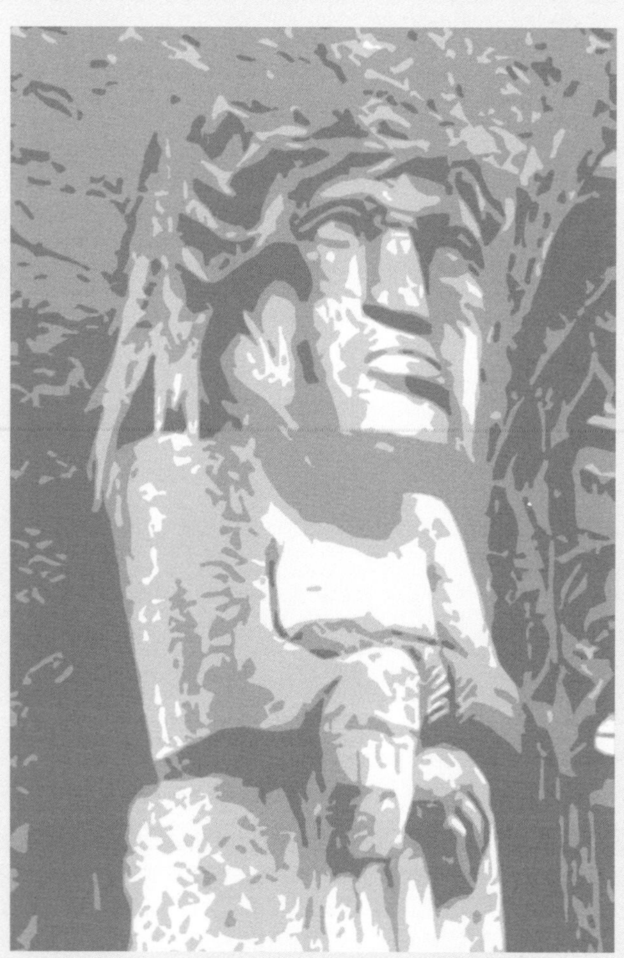

FLOWERS AND EVIL (1933–38)

CERBERUS AWAKENS

I. MADRIGALS

The years leading up to World War II were loaded with political and cultural events, and for Epstein with personal conflicts, to the extent that a separation between public and individual affairs is almost impossible. In this chapter, therefore, I have attempted to interweave these events while also seeking to retain a chronological order.

Generally speaking, most of the events that were to influence the public and its state of mind in the following years are grounded in 1932. The social situation during that economically harsh year, with as yet no government solutions in sight, enabled Oswald Mosley to rise to power once again. After his failure in the 1931 elections he had returned from a study tour of Europe's 'new movements', of Italy's Benito Mussolini and others, convinced that Fascism rather than Socialism was the way forward for him and for Britain; and, as a result of German influence, he had now added anti-Semitism to his political platform. He united the existing British Fascist movements to form the British Union of Fascists (BUF),[1] claiming a membership as high as 50,000 and receiving the support of the *Daily Mail* and *Daily Mirror* – two newspapers with a wide circulation.[2] The often disrupted BUF meetings, and its members' frequent involvement in violent confrontations, particularly with Communist and Jewish groups and especially in London, led Mosley to establish a corps of black-uniformed paramilitary stewards, dubbed Blackshirts. Epstein used to take Peggy Jean for walks in Hyde Park and listen to the orators, getting into a heated argument when someone made an anti-Semitic remark, and being stopped by a scared Peggy Jean, who would drag him away. A wry point came up in Peggy Jean's conversation:[3] among the schools she attended was an Anglican one which had two Jewish pupils – herself and Mosley's daughter from his first (Jewish) wife; the proclaimed Jew, Peggy Jean, was blond, while the so-called Aryan girl had dark hair.

For the nation, however, there were two achievements that brought a more optimistic hue to the closure of the year: British scientists John Cockcroft and Ernest Walton succeeded in splitting an atom of lithium in a Cambridge laboratory, thus inaugurating a new phase in human existence; and on 19 December the BBC Empire Service (in 1988 renamed 'The World Service') began transmission, thus firing the opening salvo of mass media in the global village.

On the literary plane, Aldous Huxley's *Brave New World*, published in 1932, foretold a utopia in which, using biotechnology and improving humanity by means of eugenics, the world eliminated all mental problems and stress. Seeking to exploit the anxieties of his bourgeois audience in regard to both Soviet Communism and Henry Ford-like

1 The British Fascists (1923; originally operating under the name British Fascisti); the National Fascisti (1924); Imperial Fascist League (1929). These small movements, whose members often moved from one to another, were paid little attention by the wider political establishment, being viewed as little more than an adult version of the Scouts. Until the BUF in 1932 they had few policies beyond admiration for Mussolini and virulent anti-Communism.

2 Horrie, 'Revealed: The Fascist Past of the Daily Mirror'. Among Mosley's followers were the novelist Henry Williamson, military theorist J.F.C. Fuller and the future 'Lord Haw Haw', William Joyce. The BUF existed until 1940, when it was banned by the authorities.

3 Recorded interview with the author, 1989.

American capitalism, the book suggested that the price of universal happiness would be the sacrifice of the most hallowed stumbling-stones of our culture – motherhood, home, family, freedom, even love. This vision, commented Orwell later, "seemed possible and even imminent before Hitler appeared".[4]

A glimpse at the horrendous conditions in Europe, which those who were looking for jobs or needed to keep them had to endure, had been eloquently illustrated in George Orwell's *Down and Out in Paris and London* published that year; but the harshest conditions, as noted, had hit Germany. It is little wonder that Epstein's, as well as Europe's, fears materialized in January 1933, when Hitler gained substantial seats in Germany's parliament with his promise that his was the right way out of the economic catastrophe. Hitler joined the government and, after being appointed Chancellor, outlawed the rival Communist party by enforcing the Enabling Act, which gave him absolute dictatorship for the next four years. Gradually and increasingly atrocities were committed against Jews, Communists and modern artists, motivating them to flee Germany. Many amongst them arrived as a first wave of refugees in England (a second wave, as discussed later, would come just before the outbreak of war). The regimes in Germany and Russia did not favour modern art, regarding it as negative and preferring traditional representational modes. Despite the differences between these two regimes, the rationale behind their rejection of modern art was the same: their understanding that "the aesthetic foundation upon which all 'modern art' had been built – *the notion that an artist's individual conscience or sensitivity can lead to personal or universal redemption* – was in direct opposition to the corporate view of culture".[5] It is of no surprise, therefore, that the implicit meaning of modern art, perceived as the stand of the individual against the multitude (labelled as 'proletariat' or 'folk'), was violently repudiated by both Stalin and Hitler.[6] Outside Germany, this campaign served to de-legitimize modern art and to tar modernist artists around the world not only as anti-Fascist but, I suggest, also as anti-materialist.[7] This latter notion was an issue that touched the sensibilities of affluent Americans who, for their part, sought to delay America's direct response against Hitler's atrocities as much as possible, continuing to do business with Germany.

Artistic circles in England extended a helping hand to art refugees in order to enable them to remain in England, in spite of the publicly acknowledged concern that an influx of (mainly Jewish) arrivals might become "an irritant", as Stanley Baldwin contended at a rally in support of German refugees at the Albert Hall.[8] Two influential artistic figures among those refugees who came to England were the discipline-crossing art historian Aby Warburg, arriving with his enormous library of books and papers on the history of art (now housed at the Warburg Institute, London) and the architectural historian Nikolaus Pevsner, renowned for the valuable books he edited on art – *The Pelican History of Art* and the 46-volume *Buildings of England*.

Among many others[9] were the architect Walter Gropius, of the Bauhaus, who had left Germany in 1934 after the school was attacked by the Nazis as a "Cathedral of Marxism"; the artist brothers Anton Pevsner and Naum Gabo; and the painter-sculptor Kurt Schwitters, closely associated with the Dada movement (and later on with Constructivism). The art refugees who found asylum in London brought with them

4 Orwell, 'Notes on the Way', on religion, or lack of it, first published in *Time and Tide*, 30 March and 6 April 1940; *Collected Essays, Journalism and Letters*: http://orwell.ru/library/articles/notes/english/e_notew.

5 Elliot, 'The Battle for Art', p. 31 (my italics).

6 London's Hayward Gallery presented a major Council of Europe exhibition in November 1995, *Art and Power: Europe under the Dictators, 1930–1945*.

7 Platt, *Art and Politics in the 1930s*, p. vii.

8 Conservative Party leader (1923–1937) and former Prime Minister.

9 For a more comprehensive list, in particular of Jewish artists, see Dickson and MacDougall, *Forced Journeys: Artists in Exile in Britain c. 1933–1945*, which includes 25 artists.

their own works of art as well as French modern works, which enriched the stock of the London dealers, noted Oliver Brown of the Leicester Galleries, who presented at the end of 1934 "an important German artist", Max Liebermann, whose work had not previously been known in England.[10]

At this point, where the issue is of extending help, I note a less discussed and less publicized aspect of Einstein – that of coming to the aid of other artists in their time of need. Although the first instances to which I refer belong to earlier periods, Epstein's accompanying comments on art in his letters, in cases where documentation exists, help us to understand the person and his outlook.

The first noted artist he had tried to help (in 1915) was Benjamin Coria,[11] appealing in a letter to a well-established Jewish artist in London, Alfred Wolmark:[12]

> I have a friend in London, a Jewish painter, Benjamin Coria by name. He comes from Mexico, knows no English & is at this moment absolutely destitute. He has few friends & is a very decent chap & artist of talent. He has no push of any sort .... I had helped him as much as I could but you know my difficulties. [13]

Another artist he tried to help was Horace Brodsky.[14] In sharing with him common interests (such as a friendship with Gaudier-Brzeska, and opinions on the position of the artist in the world), Epstein somewhat bitterly agreed to give him a recommendation (1925):

> Certainly use my name as reference if you think it will have any influence; most likely it won't. The more one knows about 'art'[,] at any rate the practice of it, the less your advice is wanted.
>
> The great thing is to be an art critic, or someone who bothers himself about art[,] not actually does it.[15]

Two interesting cases during the 1930s involved female artists – the sculptor Antonietta Raphaël,[16] whose work Epstein unsuccessfully tried to get exhibited at the Redfern Gallery in the mid 1930s, and the painter Clara Klinghoffer,[17] for whom he signed (30 May 1939) a letter of recommendation to a school in the United States in which he stated: "I consider Miss Clara Klinghof[f]er an artist of great talent – a painter & draughtswoman of the first order & with her understanding of painting and drawing, well qualified to teach either".

His encouragement of Moore has already been mentioned. Less well-known is his help to the Scottish painter Alexander Galt, who in his lifetime "eschewed the bright lights of society .... The sculptor Jacob Epstein befriended Galt in the 1930s, which helped the latter's reputation."[18] Another instance, during the 1950s (elaborated below), was Epstein's assistance to the sculptor Fiore De Henriquez.

A particularly interesting case is that of the Russian-born sculptor Abraham Melnikov (1892–1960), who emigrated from British Mandatory Palestine to London, seeking a new phase in his sculptural career.[19] He followed notions introduced by Epstein, namely seeking inspiration in non-European and archaic art, in his case that of Mesopotamia and Egypt (see fig. 8).[20] In 1936 he approached the Ben Uri Gallery in London looking for professional help, and made contact with Epstein, who had been one of its patrons. It

10 Brown, *Exhibition*, p. 121.

11 On Benjamin Coria's life there is almost no information. Prior to his coming to London from Mexico, he taught at the Academia de San Carlos, Mexico City.

12 Alfred Wollmark (1877–1961) was born into a Jewish family in Warsaw, emigrated to London, becoming a British citizen in 1894. A painter and designer of pottery and stained glass, his early work was of scenes of Jewish life in East London, later becoming one of the pioneers of post-Impressionism in England.

13 Letter from Epstein to Alfred Wollmark, 30 April 1915, TGA-721/38a, addressed to "dear Wollmark", asking whether "a Jewish fund that could be formed on Coria's behalf? Do you know of any? Or Jewish people that could buy one of his watercolours, because he is Jewish if for no other reason." On 7 May 1915 Epstein thanks Wollmark for what he is doing for Coria: TGA-721/39.

14 Painter Horace Brodsky (or Brodzky; 1885–1969) was born in Australia and lived in London until 1915. After seven years in the USA, he returned to England in 1923, where he remained until his death.

15 Letter from Epstein to Horace Brodsky, 10 March 1925; TGA 949.2.4.

16 The sculptures of Antonietta Raphaël (1895–1975) are characterized by full, rounded shapes, and said to echo the French sculptor Aristide Maillol, to whose work she turned, but with sensitivity far from the academicism that characterizes Gill's work and towards which Epstein remained indifferent. Her expressionistic paintings, imbued with memories of Jewish rites, were rich in Fauvist colouring, and this might have drawn Epstein to her work.

17 Clara Klinghoffer (1900–1970) became a famous painter overnight at the age of nineteen, and is universally recognized as one of the greatest English female painters, hailed as "the girl who could draw like Raphael" (*Women of Today*, 1932). In 1933 she exhibited at the Leicester Galleries, *Paintings & Drawings by Clara Klinghoffer* (exh. no. 537), and her work is included in the Tate collection.

18 C. Gregory, 'Human Camera Comes Out of the Shadows', *The Scotsman*, 6 July 2004.

19 Owing to political intrigues among Palestine's Jews, Melnikov was unable to find an outlet for his talents, as no Jewish institution would have engaged him for the very few artworks commissioned at the time, so he went to England in 1936.

20 As a commission from Alfred Mond, 1st Baron Melchett, Melnikov had carved the renowned *Roaring Lion* in the Galilee, commemorating the settlers' fight. Another public work, *Awakening Judah* (1925), is now in the National Park, Ramat-Gan, Israel.

is not known to what extent Epstein could or did help him, himself living on the verge of bankruptcy; however, Epstein is mentioned in Melnikov's letters to his daughter,[21] stating that Epstein often visited him in his London studio.

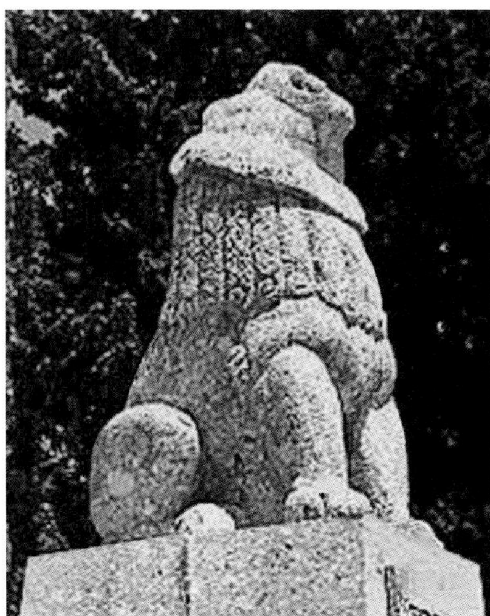

Fig. 8
Abraham Melnikov
The Roaring Lion, 1934
Galilean granite, H. 150 cm
Tel-Hai, Israel

The events of 1933 accompanied a change among the intelligentsia, which included Epstein's artistic counterparts of long ago, the Bloomsbury set. Cambridge graduate Anthony Blunt, in retrospect, summed up the previous and recent artistic and social affairs thus:

> Anything to do with content was irrelevant. We had occasionally defended it ... as in the case of Epstein's *Rima*, 'because it was modern art'. But I remember that on the whole we did not regard Epstein as a very good a sculptor as Bourdelle [sic] .... [That belief in 'pure form' was strong to the extent of] demeaning even Gauguin as Romantic, which was a bad thing ....
>
> Then, quite suddenly, in the autumn term of 1933, Marxism hit Cambridge ... almost all my younger friends had joined the communist party and Cambridge was literally transfromed overnight.[22]

The intellectual polarity, Fascism vs. Marxism, became an ideological rift in which the artistic milieu, by and large and to various degrees, tended to the Left; Epstein, a long-time socialist, was part of this and yet, following his own imperative taken long before (I/23–24), he remained outside the main circles interested in politics. In Kathleen's family the Left had a strong hold: her brother Douglas and her brother-in-law Ernest Wishart were Communists, establishing a publishing company with proclaimed Communist interests.

The Fascist era that started in 1933 saw the publication of a new novel by H.G. Wells, *The Shape of Things to Come*,[23] catching people's imagination with its speculative prediction of future events from 1933 until 2106, including the prophecy of a second world war set to break out in January 1940. A feeble Nazi Germany – so Wells had perceived the new regime – being incapable of systematic murder of the Jews on a great scale, would therefore set about "unorganized" persecutions and pogroms "everywhere in Europe" during the chaotic 1950s; world chaos would eventually end with a creation of a peaceful European utopia with a global *lingua franca*. The Jews, against their historical tendency to avoid assimilation, would be absorbed into the general society, losing their separate identity. In retrospect, this last prediction, as well as Wells's rejection of the Zionist idea during a period in which it had started to gain momentum, is quite tantalizing.

During the 1930s, since his exhibition of 1931 at the Leicester Galleries that had included *Genesis*, Epstein held an exhibition of his works every second year. In 1931 he had received only three commissioned portraits, but by the end of 1932 he had altogether about nine (not a very good state of affairs to be in amidst the Depression), in addition to the portraits of personal interest to him – those of Kathleen and Isabel mentioned above.[24] For his intended exhibition in 1933 he prepared three small intricate carvings created during 1932, although only two were eventually presented. His daughter Peggy Jean told him to make them larger, as someone would probably steal such small things.[25] Epstein does not comment on these works in his autobiography, either because they were small or

21 Seen by Nathan Zach, who knew Melnikov from his studies in England (see Nathan Zach, *From Year to Year it's* ... [in Hebrew], Tel Aviv 2010, p. 156). Zach claims that he had seen several of Epstein's letters left in Melnikov's estate (conversation with the author, May 2011), but I could not find them when Melnikov's papers were auctioned on 1 June 2011.

22 Blunt, 'From Bloomsbury to Marxism', pp. 165–66. Professor of the History of Art at the University of London and later Director of the Courtauld Institute of Art and Surveyor of the King's Pictures, Blunt had been affected too. In the mid 1980s he was exposed as a member of the Cambridge Five (a group of spies working for the Soviet Union from some time in the 1930s to at least the early 1950s; see Miranda Carter, *Anthony Blunt: His Lives*, New York 2001).

23 H.G. Wells, *The Shape of Things to Come*, London 1933.

24 It is hard to estimate how long it took him to produce a portrait, as it depended on several factors: number of sittings required, interval period between sittings and sitter's ability to sit for a long time.

25 Leda, Epstein's granddaughter, citing her mother Peggy Jean (email, 20 January 2008): "She can't remember him saying anything [about those carvings specifically, but] he was always joking around".

perhaps because they reflected personal concerns. The genesis of their development from idea to form, as was Epstein's approach, as well as their order of execution, is therefore unknown, and the following offers a necessarily arbitrary account of the sculptures and drawings made during 1932 for the exhibition of 1933.

The three carved sculptures were conceived while the Epstein household, with Isabel as part of it, continued its routine of living in the city amidst its political fermentation, and spending weekends and holidays in their cottage 'Deerhurst' amidst the flora of Epping Forest that Epstein loved to paint. It was the forest, suggests Buckle, as the rationale behind these carvings, that put into Epstein's head the idea of carving several primitive woodland spirits or demons, because in it "he heard ancient voices".[26] Whatever may have been Epstein's personal demons during this period, he did not need to turn to legends of a terrifying Cerberus or elusive creatures in order to become stressed while Fascism and racism were rearing their ugly heads. One had only to hear about the establishment of the UBF and listen to the inner Jewish warning voices, voices of the kind that had driven his parents out of Europe after the pogroms – "My father and mother had come to America on one of those great waves of immigration that followed persecution and pogroms in Czarist Russia and Poland," wrote Epstein in his autobiography (11).

I. SMALL CARVINGS IN STONE

By 1932 Kathleen was in her early forties, having been part of Epstein's life for over a decade already and, as noted above, still modelling for him. Their close attachment continued and so, apparently, did the difficulties and misunderstandings in their relationship, on the reasons for which one can only speculate. Like everything else in Epstein's life, their problems seem to be echoed in his work, both in sculpture and drawings, and here I relate them according to the relevant issue, starting with sculpture.

One common and notable feature of the 1932–33 carvings, besides their small scale, was their being free of a pedestal. Epstein had adopted this approach in one of his earliest surviving sculptures (*Baby Asleep*, 1904), but not until 1932 did he place his figures directly on the floor, in such a way that the base of the sculpture and the standing viewers shared the same platform, resulting in a new perspective for them – they had to look down. Another common denominator was the projection of anguish and mental stress. While the stress conveyed by the first sculpture to be discussed can be interpreted as reflecting personal preoccupations, the other two may, I suggest, have conveyed fears that arose from the social atmosphere within which he lived.

The largest of the three and, as I suggested above, the most personal one, is *Woman Possessed* – only 107 cm long [32]. Carved in Hoptonwood stone it presents a woman's supine nude figure, her torso arched upwards. The body is stylized, with minimalist details; the facial elements do not convey emotion, although the closed eyes and the slightly separated lips may indicate anguish and suffering. The posture of the raised pelvis that flattens the belly is maintained by the pressing down of the heels, shoulders and head. The folded arms with raised elbows and clenched fists, a universal sign of anger, are pulled towards the ground as if attempting to gain additional support. The

26 Buckle, *Epstein: Sculptor*, p. 192.

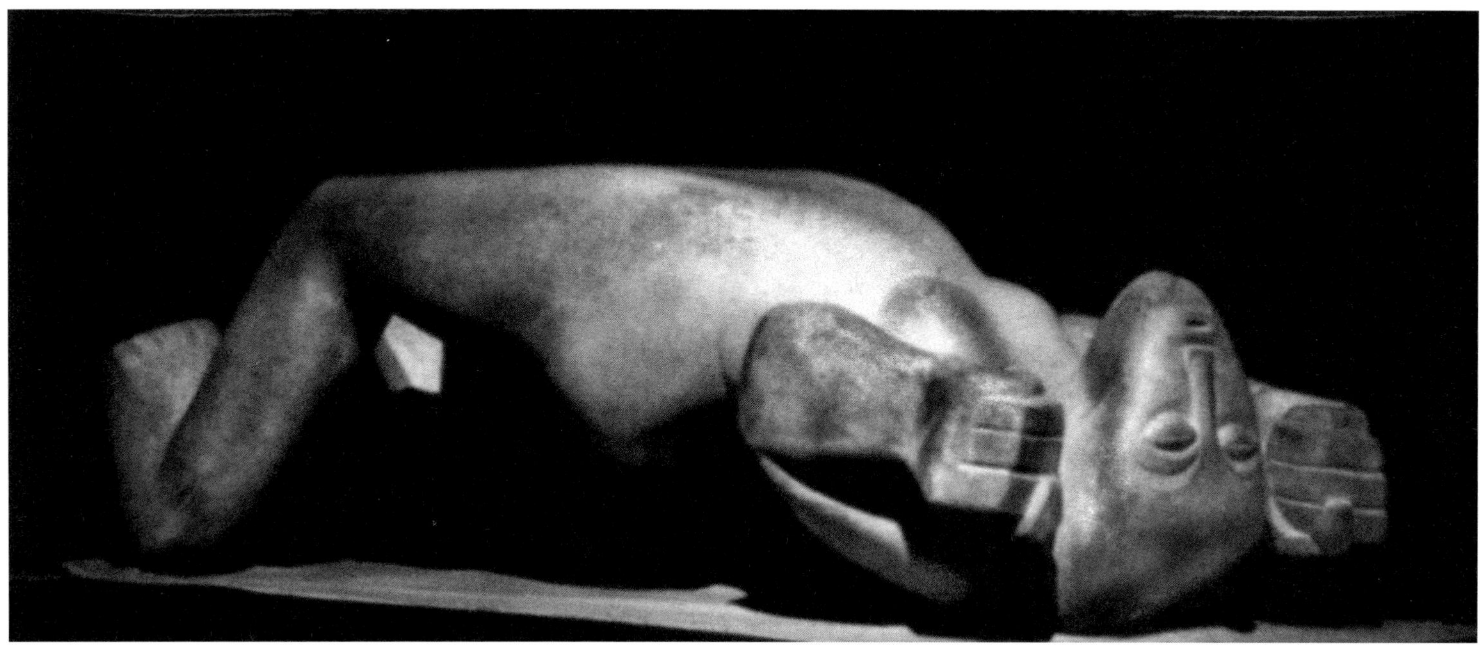

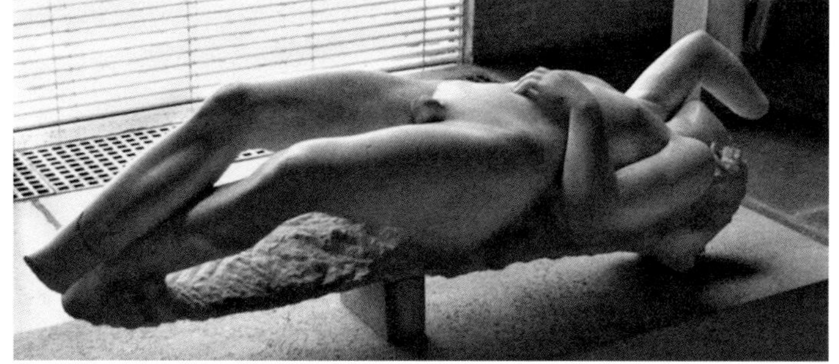

32
Woman Possessed, 1932
Hoptonwood stone, 33.3 x 102.2 x 45.1 cm
Courtesy of the National Gallery of Australia, Canberra

Fig. 9
Niobid, *c.* 320 BC
Marble, 156 cm
Courtesy of the Glyptothek, Munich

depiction, therefore, is that of a figure in a posture that cannot be maintained. Through this dynamic posture, so unlike that of his other massive carvings, Epstein achieved a unique sculptural reflection of the momentary; in this sense, I suggest, no comparison can be made with other artists' works of the period presenting a horizontal female.[27]

The outcome of Epstein's search for his own sculptural interpretation of the horizontal position resulted, as I have already mentioned (p. 41), in the maquette reflecting Sunita's natural pose in *Reclining Goddess* [16]. The stylized carving of *Woman Possessed*, on the other hand, is an unnatural pose, probably influenced by classical representations of Niobids – Niobe's sons in death agony, as they were slain by Apollo's arrows in retaliation for their mother's insult to his mother (fig. 9). Although these precedents are of males whereas Epstein's figure is that of a woman, both concepts convey the same sense of stress, suspense and also of defeat.

Regarding the message in *Woman Possessed* – or the idea that Epstein was trying to convey – Buckle was reminded of Lydia Sokolova's movement at the climax of Massiene's production of Stravinsky's *Rite of Spring*, where the pose of the very last moment of the chosen woman before her collapse expresses "her union with her god".[28] Epstein had

27 A comparison with Giacometti's *Femme égorgée*, made in the same year, 1932, is suggested by David J. Getsy ('Fallen Woman', pp. 115–29), merely because both sculptures express a stressful state and directly touch the floor. Getsy does not claim that Giacometti knew Epstein's sculpture.

28 Buckle, *Epstein: Sculptor*, p. 192.

seen the performance in Covent Garden in 1929,[29] but I doubt whether a secular Epstein would have had such a metaphysical intention. Following the approach suggested here, of his work reflecting also his personal life, there is room to regard the figure in *Woman Possessed* as a metaphorical Kathleen, whose stress conveys the unspecified problems that they were experiencing, for which, according to Gardiner, Epstein blamed himself.[30] What might have 'possessed' Kathleen is unknown and, as there are no direct sources, one can only speculate. It might have been a vague suspicion about Isabel, but was more likely to have been the death of their fourth child, the victim of an infant cot-death that happened while Kathleen was playing the piano in the same room.[31] As the gaps between their children were of about three years (see p. 14), it makes sense that after Esther (born 1929) they might have had another baby by 1931–32, and its death could have been a source of stress, corresponding to the suggested artistic precedent in the Niobids (mental anguish caused by bereavement) – a source of stress in particular because the medical community of the time did not recognise such deaths as a medical syndrome but related them to neglect or – worse – to a criminal offence.[32]

A source of stress for Kathleen could also have been the state of illegitimacy that their by-now maturing children were beginning painfully to grasp. When I met Kitty (1985), she mentioned the burden of being illegitimate and I had the impression that she was holding a grudge against her father for not doing something to rectify it. I was on the brink of asking her, "What has your mother done about it?" when I was 'saved' by the entrance of her husband, the Honourable Wayne Godley, which ended the intimate conversation, preventing me from digging deeper into an over fifty-year-old wound. To some extent, and through his work, Epstein may have attempted to explain himself in regard to legitimacy through the biblical illustration mentioned earlier [4].

No less stressful for Kathleen was the issue of provisioning and maintaining a home because, for all personal purposes and daily issues, she was left largely alone to confront her problems, and the small sums allocated to her by Margaret Epstein were never sufficient, taking into account that 1932 had been the worst of the Depression years, in which unemployment had reached its highest levels. The stress created by lack of money no doubt affected her relationship with Epstein. Therefore, in addition to carving *Woman Possessed* – a figure that acknowledges Kathleen's mental and physical fatigue and (as Buckle suggested) perhaps also the sacrifices she was making – Epstein drew, in between his work on the small sculptures that convey stressful situations, a series of drawings that seem to reflect their state of affairs through images from her culture – his first drawings of Christian entities.

Kathleen made a point of including them in *Epstein Drawings*, a book published after his death. In the introduction to the book Richard Buckle stated that a unifying factor for the drawings lay in their provenance from the collection of the sculptor's wife (as she had since become). Surprisingly, many of them were made before the end of World War I, before Epstein had even met Kathleen, but there are almost no drawings from the later period when Kathleen was living with Epstein and was a constant witness to his work. The particular drawings under discussion are explained as the "very few drawings from the Gospel", made in 1930–31. Exceptional in their content for this period (as Epstein usually did not oscillate between subjects, unless they were commissioned – and these

29 Two drawings dated to 1929 attest to Epstein's attendance at this performance, but neither has this particular pose (Silber and Friedman, *Jacob Epstein*, p. 234, fig. 87). Massiene actually presented Nijinsky's choreography, which Epstein had seen in Paris in 1913 (attested to by his daughter Kitty); therefore the mere pose – if indeed it remained part of the ballet – might have been long imprinted in Epstein's mind. The subject will be mentioned later in regard to other sculptures.

30 Gardiner, *Epstein*, p. 332. Gardiner does not cite Epstein's exact words, however.

31 This child had never been mentioned in any of my contact with Epstein's children. The event was recounted by Dr Valerie Cowie, the psychiatrist who befriended Kathleen and Theo, to Cressida Connolly in *The Rare and the Beautiful*, p. 199.

32 'Cot death' began to be recognized in the 1950s. However, it was not until 1969 that a definition of Sudden Infant Death Syndrome (SID) became widely accepted.

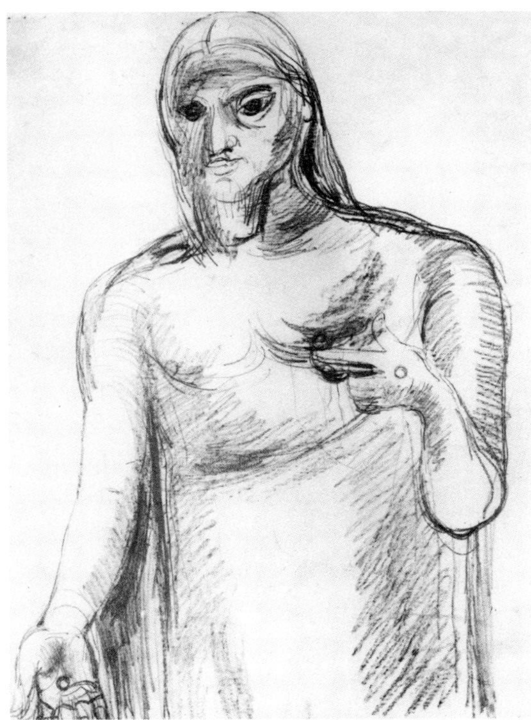

33
Noli Me Tangere, 1932 [1930]
Pencil, 582 x 445 mm
GREC-NAGW

drawings were not), they correspond to Kathleen being a Christian. Buckle's claim that all the drawings in the book were given to her as a gift because of their rarity, quality, uniqueness etc., makes sense, but gives no indication that some might have been given to her because they expressed a personal interest or had a bearing on the state of affairs existing between them. This omission, I suggest, was contrived by Kathleen in order to cast only a positive light on their lives together, and was covered up, in the case of the 'Christian' drawings, by placing them irrespective of the order of their execution among drawings that seem to belong to different periods. This, I believe, is the case with the four drawings that I suggest to be from 1932 – nos. 50, 53, 55, 56. A reading of these four drawings is suggested below, in which their assumed order and date differ from those in Kathleen's notes.

'Couples' is a subject upon which Epstein hardly ever touched – only in rare depictions of biblical scenes and in a few stylized male-female figures from his Vorticist period. His only drawing of a couple relating to one another in a human manner that I know is *One Hundred Pillars of the Sacred Temple*, depicting in naturalistic lines an embracing couple (1910; I/97). The drawings on Christian subjects made during the 1930s and given to Kathleen, three of which feature couples, are discussed here in the order and context in which I believe they were executed. My main argument is the continuity of subject and artistic development that they convey.

No. 50, entitled *Noli Me Tangere*, is still a solitary figure – a standing Jesus detached from any surroundings, with the traditional long hair and robe, and the stigmata on both hands [33]. The drawing, in both the contours and the condensed hatching, is executed in a rough pencil. The slanted dark eyes are large within the round face and the lips are closed. The head is darkened on either side to the extent that its expression in the lighter strip of nose and mouth seems to convey stress and anger rather than the friendly warning indicated in the Gospel: when Jesus, after the Resurrection, meets his sceptical mother or Mary Magdalene or both together (it varies in the traditional illustrations) and they wish to verify that it is truly him, he kindly, not angrily, warns them, 'Do not touch me!' Another departure from the traditional iconography is the position of the wound: although the text (John 19: 34) does not specify on which side Jesus was pierced, in many images it is represented on his proper right side – such as in Grünewald's Isenheim Altar and Raphael's Mond *Crucifixion* in the National Gallery, London, to name just two. In Epstein's drawing, the stigmatized left hand points to a wound on the left side of the chest, a little above the heart – the organ in which love is assumed to dwell. How is one to interpret this variation? Kathleen does not attribute any significance to it, but I would regard it as expressing Epstein's view of his personal situation, because, besides having been generally stigmatized as an artist, he has now also been hurt as a man – as the lover of his woman – and he suffers a wound inflicted by her upon his heart. This interpretation tacitly claims that within their relationship Epstein metaphorically regarded himself as a Christ figure, a martyr, a person tortured for clinging to his own beliefs, whether artistic or personal, the personal aspect being mainly his decision to remain with his legal wife rather than to be with Kathleen. Is my interpretation valid? I believe it is, because the other three drawings, also claimed by Kathleen to represent Christian subjects, seem to support it.

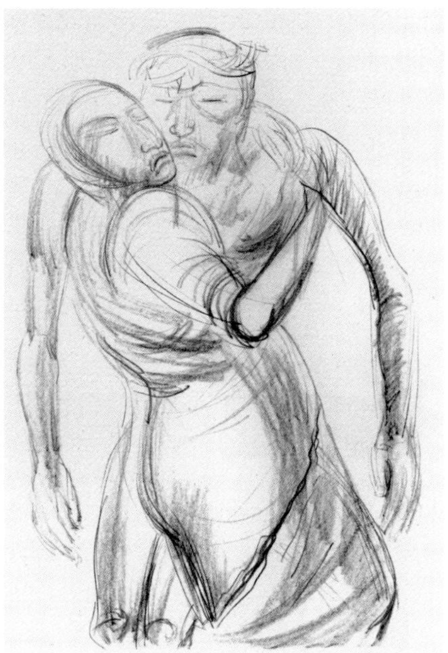

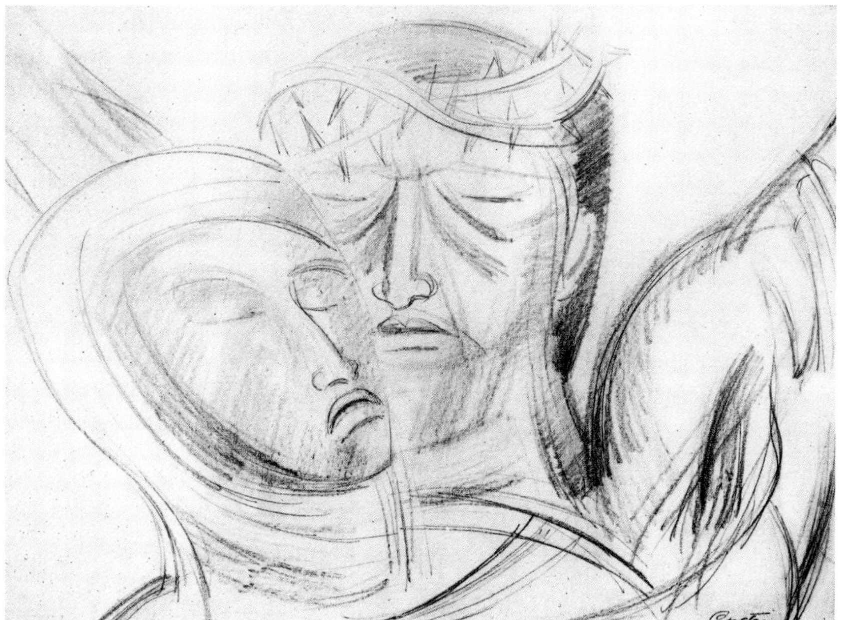

34
Pietá – Two Figures, 1932
Pencil, 582 x 445 mm
Private collection

35
Pietá – Two Heads, 1932
Pencil, 445 x 580 mm
GREC-NAGW

No. 56, entitled *Pietà – Two Figures* [34], a rough, unsigned sketch with the characteristics of many of Epstein's preliminary studies for a subject, has two figures – a naked man standing upright, his hands hanging helplessly by his sides, while a dressed female clings to him, her left hand around his neck and her right one on his upper arm; their eyes are closed and their lips drop, expressing discomfort, sorrow or desperation. Important elements (repeated in the following drawings) are the man's head crowned with an unclear decoration and the woman's head with an undetailed top that may indicate a headdress. The subject is clarified in a more elaborated drawing, entitled *Pietà – Two Heads* [35], with the same poses and same crown on the head as in [34]; both pairs of eyes are closed, the man's partly drawn arms are raised and the woman clings to him. The male figure is unmistakably Jesus since he wears the crown of thorns; the woman's head is bandaged in a manner recalling the 'barbe' under the chin forming part of the late medieval or Renaissance wimple in which the Virgin Mary was depicted.[33]

'Pietà' is a term more commonly used to describe the Virgin holding her dead son on her lap, but these drawings feature a helpless woman clinging to a man crowned with thorns. The titles given by Kathleen to these compositions would seem to be misleading, for they do not convey grief at a death but rather perhaps a sense of shame, or of being pointed at. In their difficult circumstances, each suffering from their own problems, Epstein and Kathleen both required caring, a mutual *pietà*.

The last drawing [36], no. 53, closing this series of Christian motifs from the 1930s, is similar in style to the Old Testament drawings discussed above – a few pencil lines and the elements accentuated with wash.[34] Its title, *Jesus and John*, as in the previous cases seems to be misleading. The figure of Jesus is clear and recognisable by the conventional presentation of his hair, and is related to the previous drawings in its facial elements – the large slanted eyes and closed lips. The figure supposed to be John is merely sketched, but the impression is rather that of a delicate female head, similar to those in the previous drawings – with the closed eyes and lips depicted in delicate pencil

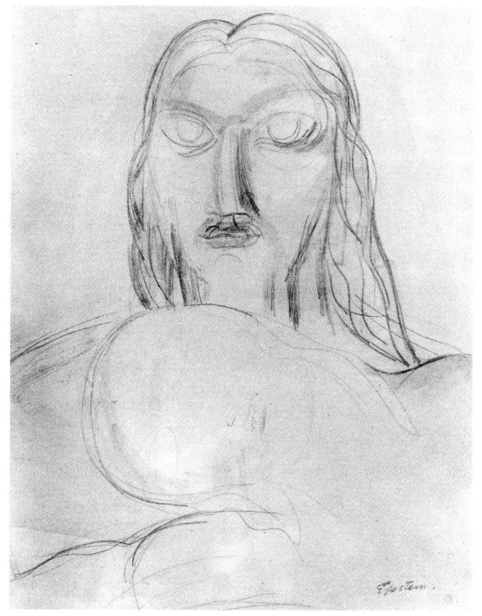

36
Jesus and John, 1932 [1930]
Pencil and wash, 483 x 382 mm
Birmingham Art Gallery

33 There are examples among Dürer's drawings, for example *St Anne*, 1519, brush on grey primed paper, 39.5 x 29.2 cm, Graphische Sammlung Albertina, Vienna.

34 Unfortunately, the drawing is reproduced only in black and white, and not having seen it in the original I cannot assess the play of pencil and coloured wash.

outline and wash. What is actually presented here, in spite of its given title, is a kind of Jesus with a woman's head resting on his chest, and the atmosphere conveyed is that of conciliation and tranquillity. Did Epstein and Kathleen eventually reach this state? The answer, in light of the events that followed, is not simple; however, the dating of these drawings, in view of the above argument, is suggested as 1932.

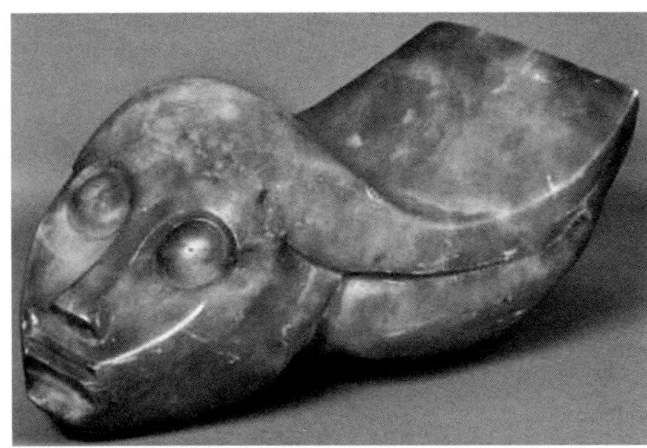

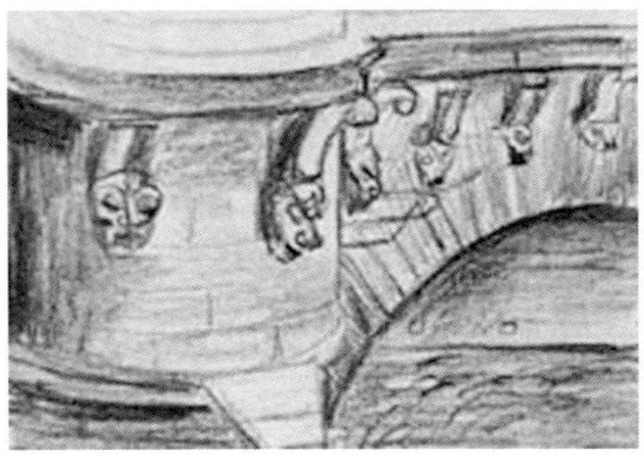

37
Chimera, 1932
Alabaster, H. 10 cm, L. 26 cm
Formerly Shinman collection

38
Pont Neuf, 1930s
Pencil, 14 x 19 cm
Private collection (courtesy of the Boundary Gallery)

To return to the sculptural work of this stressful period, the second carving, *Chimera* [37], is a small piece only 26 cm in length, although its title refers to a monster – a creature of substantial size composed of different animal parts. Buckle does not discuss Epstein's intentions, but defines it merely as a creature "eddying doubtfully and mindlessly round corners, like a fish among rocks".[35] The small sculpture has a long curved neck ending in a human head, with facial features geometrically stylized (like those in *Woman Possessed*), large rounded eyes that seem to be looking at the world in awe, and a long narrow rectangular and flattened nose over narrow closed lips. The overall impression is that of a gargoyle, and the artistic idea may have stemmed from a small sketch of the Pont Neuf that Epstein had done during one of the family's visits to Paris [38]. Epstein's interpretation of a gargoyle's purpose – namely, to watch protectively over a building – inverts its traditional task, because the sculptural outcome projects an inner fear within the creature rather than a threat to the outer world. Was Epstein hinting at an inversion in society in which the guardians are frightened rather than frightening?

Elemental [39a], the last of this group of carvings, is suggested by Buckle to be reminiscent of an anecdotal boss in a Gothic cloister several times enlarged, and he adds: "There emerged from the stone a huddled, fearful male creature clutching his knees to his chin and keeping his eyes tight closed against the winds of Hell".[36] The viewer, however, sees the stressful face looking up as if awaiting catastrophe – or salvation.

The figure's raised folded legs and hands clutching ankles echo Epstein's stone carving *Sun Goddess Crouching* [40], created, like the first version of *Sun God*, at the height of his 'Aryan Sun' period in 1910 (I/98). While it retains the outline of the square block, Epstein gave this figure of his sun-goddess non-European facial features and a restraint on its movement – created by the hands clutching the ankles and the backward-pulled elbows – so it has the appearance of an extrovert figure inclining forward while exposing her genitalia. The same pose, but set within an oval frame of stone, is presented in *Elemental* [39c], but the intensity of the ball it makes turns it into an introvert figure, closing into itself and barely exposing its phallus. The raised horizontal head gazes upwards, as if searching for release from the tension of terror, and the pupils of the eyes are expressed by holes. The figure displays a kind of despair, one more profound than is expressed by the introvert pose of Epstein's great spiritual mentor Rodin in a work entitled *Despair* (fig. 11).

This fairly small carving in alabaster, 80 cm high, was never exhibited during Epstein's lifetime.[37] Being unpolished, it leaves room for the claim that it had remained unfinished,[38] and part of the figure – the section between the legs – seems incomplete to the extent that in photographs the male genitalia are hardly visible [39b]. Perhaps this is why Epstein decided not to include it in his 1933 exhibition at the Leicester Galleries.

In April 1933, at the Mayor Gallery, London saw the first exhibition by the Surrealists, offering a new approach to the application of the imagination and incorporating

35 Buckle, *Epstein: Sculptor*, p. 191. The reason for his silence on Epstein's intentions is unclear, but he could have acquired information on this period's carvings from Kathleen.

36 Buckle, *Epstein: Sculptor*, p. 189.

37 Silber, *Sculpture of Epstein*, no. 225, p. 52: "It does not seem included in his Leicester Galleries exhibition in May 1933, and it was virtually unknown until its inclusion in the Edinburgh Memorial exhibition in 1961. It is described as: 'pent-up primitive man'" (*Jacob Epstein, A Catalogue of the Collection of Edward P. Shinman*).

38 Buckle, *Epstein: Sculptor*, p. 191.

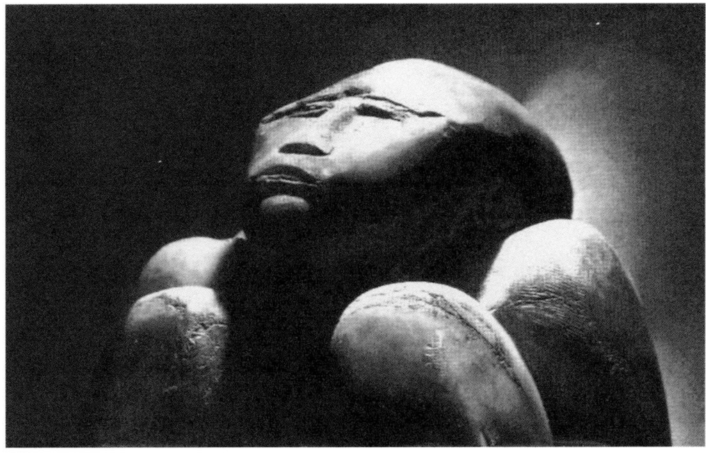

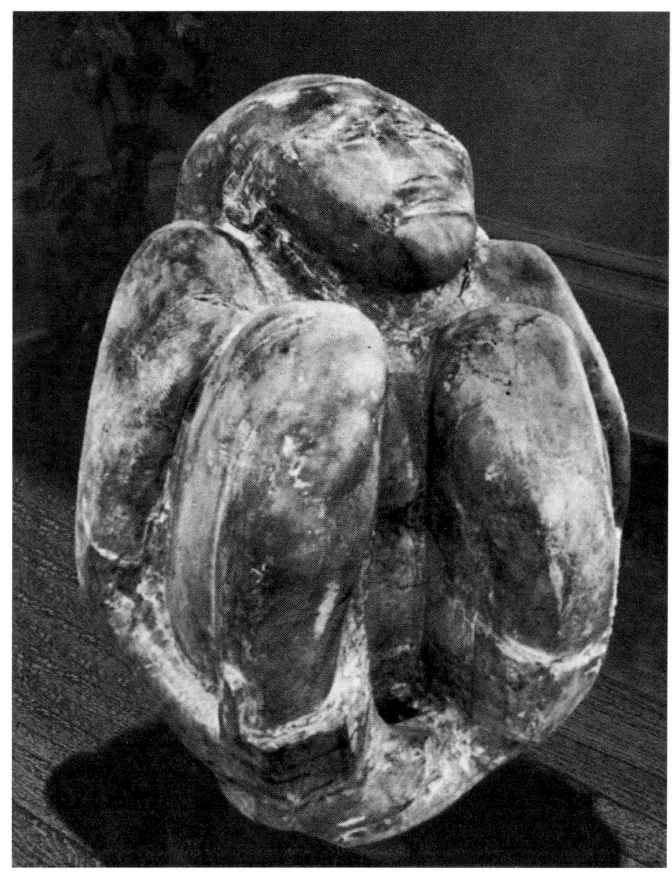

39a
Elemental (detail of head), 1932
Alabaster, H. 81 cm
Private collection

39b
Elemental (front), 1932

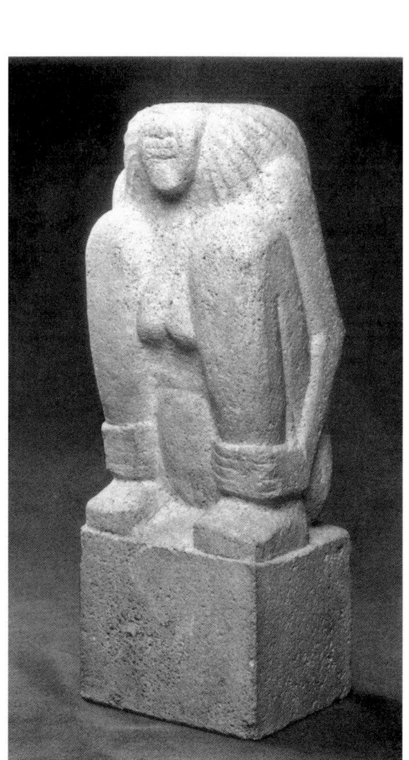

40
Sun Goddess crouching (front), 1910? [1912]
Limestone, H. 37 cm
Courtesy of Nottingham City Museums and Galleries

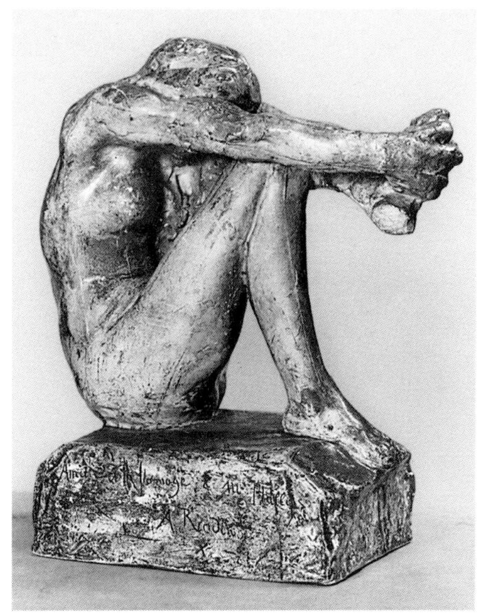

Fig. 11
August Rodin
Despair, 1890
Plaster, H. 27.9 cm
Bethnal Green Museum, London

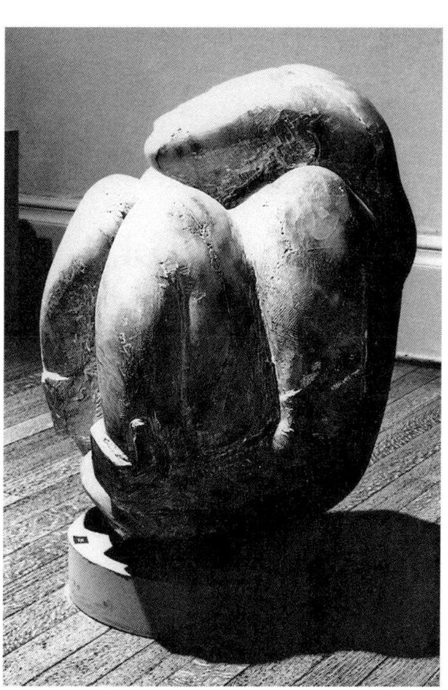

39c
Elemental (side view), 1932

subconscious as well as conscious impressions within the artist's treatment of his subjects. "London has been talking & the press writing up the first large exhibition of Surrealist sculpture & paintings. As a phenomenon of the period & as I am in no way prejudiced or incoherent [intolerant?] of new forms of art I go to have a look at it", wrote Epstein in one of the unpublished drafts of his biography.[39] As this is his only written reaction to his colleagues and the new artistic groups, I cite from it at length.

> ... a group of what I recognise from the much published photographs as the literary leaders & exhibitors of this group, as new groups use now the propaganda methods of political agitators. I hear their polemists & adherents. This group of revolutionaries evidently have nothing better to do this morning than getting together amongst these works; they stand with a self-satisfied air & when I enter the gallery there is a stir amongst them almost of challenge. Why?
>
> I go about amongst the pictures & statues & as I am with a friend perhaps I am not approached[,] although carefully trailed at a little distance by one of the group detailed to watch me.
>
> I look naturally with eagerness to find something good & I do but it is here & there displayed on the walls amongst the silly products of our modern stupidities; [it is] decorative work from New Guinea. Why these ancient primitive works should be allied with crudeness & pretence is beyond me.
>
> A table placed in one of the galleries has about [sic] a notice asking visitors to place their Surrealist bands upon it. I deposit my catalogue. I would like to deposit the whole little band of Spanish French & English 'surrealists' themselves there[,] for [???]ting they are 'surrealist'.

Had Epstein been blind to the possibilities in the new "phenomenon of the period"? It makes sense that he could not have foreseen that Surrealist art had prophesized and established the grounds for what in more recent times has become 'visual culture'.[40] The only explanation that I can suggest for his closed attitude is to refer to another trait of our common roots, that of Polish Jews (and I suspect that Epstein would not have liked it), which dictates that one should 'not wash one's dirty linen in public'. Moreover, there existed a general attitude that regarded the need for any psychological treatment as an admittance of failure; and Surrealism (in its first stage), by giving expression to the unconsciousness and by exploring one's fears and tribulations, does just that – and in a very explicit way. Epstein, as we have already seen (for example in the Old Testament and New Testament illustrations), seems to have found an outlet for his mental stress by means of *implicit* symbolism rather than through direct, extrovert (or exhibitionist) representations.

On Moore's work, on the other hand, Surrealism seems to have had quite an influence early on, although he adjusted the Surrealist theories to his own ideas about form. Thus, Moore's favourite reclining figure subject was given a Surrealist aura in several of his 1934 works by re-arranging the body into parts and giving their forms a less obvious reference to their natural counterpart.[41] The Surrealist influence on him was prolonged,[42] and in 1936, during the 'International Surrealist Exhibition' held from 11 June to 4 July at the New Burlington Galleries in London, he signed the Surrealist Manifesto, becoming in 1937 a member of the English Surrealist group.

39 NAGW archive.

40 The expression 'visual culture' encompasses recent art products that combine all kinds of artistic means, media and images, quite often focusing on aspects of culture that rely on and are influenced (in most cases) by already existing visual images. 'Visual arts', on the other hand (the common coinage, also in Epstein's day), refers to traditional means of execution and criticism in which work in each medium is treated separately.

41 *Henry Moore: Early Carvings 1920–1940*, fig. 40, p. 33, and no. 30, p. 72.

42 *Henry Moore: Early Carvings 1920–1940*, p. 36. Stating this, however, does not diminish the impact of surrealism on Moore in regard to psychological aspects of human concerns, in spite of his trying to disguise the factor of 'idea' in his later sculptures and drawings. See Kamien-Kazhdan, 'Unveiling Moore's Enigma', pp. 13–16.

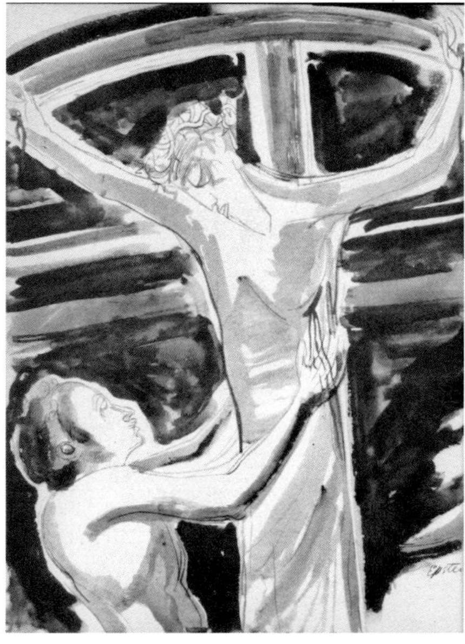

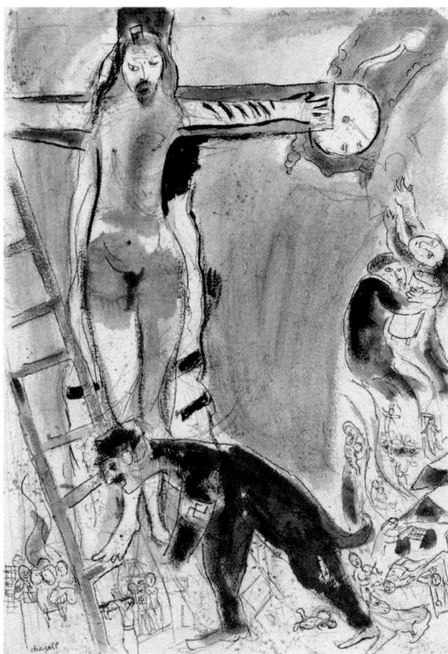

41
The Crucifying Story, 1933
Pen and wash, from Mosheh Oyved, *The Book of Affinity,* p. 23

Fig. 12
Marc Chagall
Apocalypse in Lilac, c. 1945–47
Gouache on paper, 51.1 x 36 cm
Courtesy of Ben Uri Gallery
The Jewish Museum of Art, London

Although Surrealism had no influence on Epstein's sculpture, in his illustrations for *The Book of Affinity,*[43] written during the tumultuous year of 1933 by his old friend and acquaintance Mosheh Oved (1885–1958), he had to cope with the demands of the book's Surrealist and hallucinatory atmosphere, for all its concrete ambience of events reflecting Jewish affairs. The text is a parable in vindication of the Jews, depicting them as creators of world harmony amidst pogrom-like attacks. As the subtitle indicates, the book was written and "ministered by Ahaviel", a female angel whose name in Hebrew means 'God loves me',[44] and it recounts the protagonist's struggle against 'He-She', a lion who is identified as the "Standard-Bearer of Affinity". An illustration for the chapter entitled 'The Crucifying Story' [41] is interesting as the only direct representation of a Crucifixion by Epstein that I have been able to find; and needless to say it does not follow convention. The Surrealist background is expressed both by detaching the event from any socio-geographical iconography and by the cross being off-centre and framed by a bow, giving the impression that it is actually detached from the crucified figure. It makes sense that Epstein would treat this loaded subject of the Crucifixion from within a purely Jewish context, not only because Jesus was a Jew but also because it corresponded to the words printed on the back: "I used to lift up my eyes to him, *and there was understanding between us*" (my italics).

If my dating of 1932 for the previous drawings [33–36] with Christian motifs is correct, then this illustration is only slightly later. Whilst the previous figures of Jesus, I suggested, might be read a metaphor for Epstein himself, here Jesus as a bearded man is not only a Jew talking to another Jew ("My disciples and followers have let me down, and I have come back to my People, whom I never left"), but his martyrdom stands for the Jews "who are representing this to the last drop of blood and last splinter of bone".

In 1938, Chagall would depict a crucified Jesus with all the Jewish religious accessories,[45] and later still – summing up this apocalyptic period – his last crucified Jesus, to some extent and by contrast to his heavy oil paintings (it is in gouache; fig. 12), resembles Epstein's light touch of drawings on paper of Jewish subjects.

43 Frontispiece and six illustrations in Oyved, *The Book of Affinity,* p. 23. Here I use the Hebrew form of the author's name, as written in Epstein, *Let There be Sculpture,* p. 110.

44 The name Ahaviel is moulded on the pattern of the common Hebrew name Azriel (e.g. Jeremiah 36: 26), meaning 'God helps me'.

45 *The White Crucifixion,* 1938, oil on canvas, 154.3 x 139.7 cm, The Art Institute of Chicago.

Epstein did no sculptural work during this period of 1933 in which he executed all these illustrations. Moore, on the other hand, was carving extensively throughout the decade, between seven and twenty works a year![46] Epstein's presence on the artistic stage, therefore, was maintained by earlier works, presented in May 1933 at the Leicester Galleries. The exhibition was entitled 'Carvings and Bronzes by Jacob Epstein'. In addition to *Chimera* and *Woman Possessed* of 1932, there were also carvings from bygone days – *Female Figure in Flenite* and *Figure in Flenite* (mid 1910s; lent by Mrs G.E. Rogers, and not for sale), and the more recent two-sided block of *Sun God* and *Primeval Gods*, both achieved during 1931–33. In a period that regarded carving as *the* noble form of sculpture, the visitors to the exhibition could follow the evolution of Epstein's carved forms in different styles over the years, all of them being expressions of ideas rather than beautiful objects or interesting forms for their own sake. The carvings, however, were surrounded by outstanding bronze portraits, as if to accentuate the difference between portraying a face and expressing an idea.[47] It was the *tour de force* of an artist underestimated by his colleagues – the only positive, albeit brief, note of the period I have found is that which, noting the Epstein-Moore connection in these sculptures, headlined the exhibition as "Epstein at his best".[48] As this exhibition followed the introduction of the new voice of Surrealism in April, it was sidelined by the new phenomenon and its exhibits remained unsold. An anonymous critique that I have found reads:

> If Mr. Epstein chooses to carve large lumps of Hopton Wood stone with an arrangement of simplified human figures, and announces that they are 'Primeval Gods', that is his affair. From the angle of design, there is nothing remarkable about these clumsy works; it is just the brute force of their execution that redeems them from sheer dullness. Neither they, nor the 'Elemental' figure, mildly suggestive of an attack of tetanus, nor yet the 'Chimera' vaguely recalling a bucolic gargoyle on some rustic parish church, were the things for which Mr. Epstein's later Exhibition in Leicester Galleries, London, ought to be remembered.

The critic then sings the praises of the portraits.[49]

The author of the critique was clearly indifferent to Epstein's non-portraiture work, partly because it did not follow the recent developments in form mentioned above and also, I suggest, because the critic had failed to find any kind of development in Epstein's approach to the expression of ideas. During this same period Herbert Read published another book, *Art Now*, in which, in addition to his previous advocation of 'truth to material', he attempted "to trace that gradual change in the *philosophy of beauty*" (my italics); Epstein was not among the artists he mentioned to prove his point.[50] As to the legitimate aim of promoting "beauty", in particular the beauty that Read found in the works of his favourite artists, I cite without further comment Orwell's response:[51] "Read often speaks of beauty as though it were a kind of Platonic Absolute existing somewhere or other in its own right and in no way dependant on human appreciation"; referring to the recurring forms of Read's favourite artists, he adds: "Any shape, any sound, any colour, any smell becomes odious through too much repetition, because repetition fatigues the senses to which beauty must make its appeal".

46 *Henry Moore: Early Carvings 1920–1940*, p. 30.

47 The works included one of his friend's wife, Mrs Edward Good (*A Portrait of a Lady*), one of the above-mentioned author and founder of the Ben Uri Gallery Moshe Oved, and the above-mentioned busts of Isabel and Kathleen.

48 Anon., *The Jewish Chronicle*, 5 May 1933, p. 19.

49 Anon., 'Little Tin Gods', *Connoisseur*, XCI, June 1933, p. 407.

50 The few English artists mentioned were mainly those Read promoted – Paul Nash, Henry Moore, Ben Nicholson, Barbara Hepworth and, from Epstein's old milieu, Wyndham Lewis and Edward Wandsworth.

51 Orwell, 'A Review of Herbert Read's Essays: A Coat of Many Colours', published in *Poetry Quarterly*, Winter 1945; *Collected Essays, Journalism and Letters*, vol. 2, no. 14, pp. 48–52; mentioned in my Introduction, p. 32.

III. POLITICAL, ARTISTIC AND PERSONAL MATTERS

Some time in early July 1933, in all probability on account of the school holidays, which the Garman children spent at the home of Kathleen's nanny, Ada Newbould, Kathleen went to Martigues for two months to help her sister Helen who, in late 1931, had given birth.[52] Although among the Garman sisters it would regularly be Kathleen who was called to give a helping hand, this time (with the baby no longer a new-born), the trip might have been an excuse to take a break. Indeed, help could just as well have been extended by another of the Garman siblings who was already in Martigues: sister Mary and her husband Roy Campbell with their children were still living there, and brother Douglas's wife Jeanne and her sister Lisa had also arrived for a visit.[53] Epstein, so it seems, accepted the excuse of the baby, and no objection to Kathleen's trip is recorded in his letters. As there are no letters by Kathleen for that period, it is hard to say how or whether she had been impressed by the liberated approach of her sister Mary who, as a married woman, had once had a lesbian relationship with Vita Sackville-West and now resumed the pattern by having an affair with her brother's wife.[54] In Epstein's one remaining letter of the period,[55] he addresses her as "My sweet girl, my loving girl", telling her that he has been busy during the days but the nights were dragging; he writes of a possible acquisition of "the Nefertiti" (a mask he wanted and later acquired, claiming that it resembled Kathleen; fig. 13), and of his plans for work for which Kathleen would model, ending his letter with "How I long for you again my darling one, my sweet one in whom all my hope for happiness lies", asking her to write to him. There is no doubt that, in spite of tensions, complaints, and Isabel's temporary seductive presence, Kathleen had always been the love of his life.

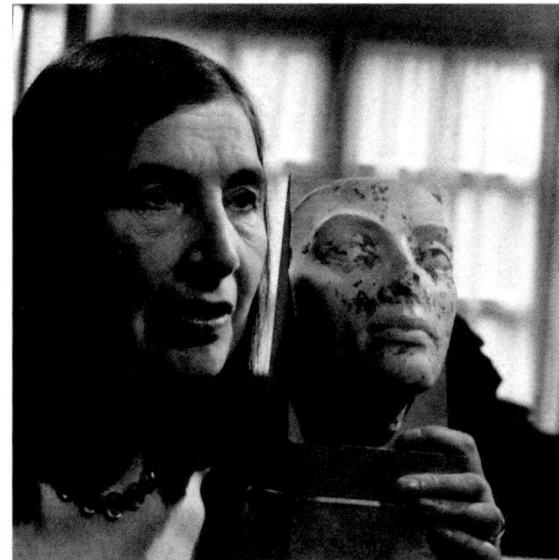

Fig. 13
Kathleen and the Nefertiti mask that Epstein regarded as projecting her

Isabel was a talented painter: "intelligent and attractive enough to divert [Epstein's] attention from Kathleen", suggests Gardiner, who seems to regard every model who came to the house as potential seductress.[56] In spite of the growing closeness between them, in particular where art was concerned, Isabel "found him rather silent on the subject of art; [but] one thing came over clearly: his views on it were decided and unattached to those of others".[57] Unfortunately for research, she did not elaborate further.

Epstein thus remained during the summer months at his home in Hyde Park Gate with wife Margaret and model Isabel who was staying in Peggy Jean's room, or during the weekends at his cottage in Epping Forest. Gardiner, who interviewed Isabel at length,[58] quotes her comment that, by painting scenes of the forest herself, she may have started him (and Peggy Jean) off into doing floral watercolours. Epstein, however, reported that this new direction was accidental, inspired by the attractive colours of the trees, and that the August heat that made sculpture an unpleasant task.[59] The only change in his routine during this year had been the Epsteins' move in 1933 from their Epping Forest cottage at no. 49 Baldwin's Hill, which they had rented in 1928, to 'Deerhurst', no. 50 Baldwin's Hill, a bigger place almost opposite no. 49.[60]

Kathleen returned in September 1933 and, whether or not Epstein's drawing [36] indeed reflects a conciliation, their problems apparently still existed. This seems to have been the period during which Kathleen found in London a kind of comfort in female companionship – with the Jewish-Canadian pianist Beth Lipkin, whom "she befriended";[61] this description was resented by Beth, as it suggested to her "patronization by Kathleen

52 Gardiner, *Epstein*, p. 331. In 1930 Kathleen's sister, Helen, married Marius Jean-Baptiste Polge, and in 1931 bore him a daughter, Katherine Francesca (later to become the poet Laurie Lee's wife).

53 Connolly, *The Rare and The Beautiful*, pp. 119–21. In 1928 the Campbells went to live in the French province of Martigues, leaving the place in 1933. They, as well as others, followed Augustus John, who had settled there as early as 1910 (Holroyd, *Augustus John*, p. 317). Connolly (pp. 113–30) mentions a long list of the artists and intellectuals who favoured the place.

54 Connolly, *The Rare and the Beautiful*, p. 120: "and Mary's letters attest to a brief romance". An unfortunate mistake (by an anonymous writer) relates this affair to Kathleen: see http://en.wikipedia.org/wiki/Kathleen_Garman

55 Undated; NAGW archive.

56 Gardiner, *Epstein*, p. 325.

57 Isabel's memoirs, Tate Archive, Kit-Accession, TGA 9612.

58 Gardiner, *Epstein*, pp. 325–26.

59 Epstein's explanation was published in *The Lincolnshire Herald*, 12 January 1933.

60 This house, and the group of four cottages, nos. 29–35, are listed buildings. In 1950 Epstein finally left Loughton: http://www.hillsamenitysociety.co.uk/detail/disctrail.htm.

61 Gardiner, *Epstein*, p. 374.

… which is totally offensive both to Kathleen and to me … we were close friends and played duets together, and I taught Esther [piano]".[62] Their common musical interests drew them close, and undoubtedly Kathleen was pleased with the love, respect and even adoration that Beth bestowed upon her.

For Epstein, lacking public commissions throughout the decade, the harsh economic climate meant a greater dependence on portraiture, which, in these cash-strapped times, did not enrich him; altogether in the previous decade he had had about 56 commissions, approximately five or six per year. An episode involving Augustus John seems to belong to this period: on an unspecified date in the 1930s, probably at the height of the Depression, Epstein and Kathleen met him in the street. "In answer to the question, Epstein said that he was doing good work but could not sell it and was very poor." John at once took out a cheque-book and wrote him a cheque, "which we will never refer to again'.[63] Despite becoming distant from Epstein after World War I, John had retained his regard for Epstein's work and, having come into inheritances in 1930 and 1939,[64] he could afford such generosity. In contrast, Epstein's financial situation was shaky.[65] Besides the usual expenses for two households and Peggy Jean's tuition fees – "I hated her living away as she now goes to boarding school & seems happy & interested" – he admitted to piling up "endless debts" to his bronze founders. Throughout this period, in spite of the government spending in 1933 and 1934 that was intended to stimulate the economy, the economic climate was harsh. It seems that even commissions for portraits of famous people became rare. Silber's catalogue of Epstein's work indicates about ten portraits made during 1933, of which about seven seem to be those of models and only three paid for. The Leicester Gallery's next catalogue of exhibitions for June – a month after the closing of Epstein's exhibition – held an advertisement inviting people to get their portraits done by him.

In late 1933 Epstein also became somewhat involved with politics, both indirectly and directly. The indirect occasion was related to the artist Arthur Lett-Haines's desire to organize an exhibition of contemporary British art at the Anglo-German Club and to include Epstein in it.[66] Epstein declined his written invitation out of suspicion regarding the motives of the club;[67] and to his rejection Epstein added: "I do not wish to have any works of mine borrowed to exhibit there".[68] Epstein ended his rejection by hoping that "your exhibition will have every success".

Epstein's more direct participation in political affairs was due to the escalating situation in Spain, to which the Fascist phenomenon that had already started in Italy and Germany had spread. On 19 November 1933, the right-wing parties, with the newly created La Falanga, won the elections in Spain. In reaction, the Artists' International Association (AIA) was founded in London – an organization that embraced all styles of art, both modernist and traditional, aiming to promote "the international unity of artists against Imperialist War on the Soviet Union, Fascism, and colonial oppression".[69] It was the only art organization that both Epstein and Henry Moore joined. It established a "refugee committee" in an attempt to help persecuted artists come to England, and from 1935 it held a series of large group exhibitions on political and social themes, opening with an exhibition entitled 'Artists against Fascism and War'.[70] It is not clear to what extent Epstein was personally involved in these activities; all that I have found is

62 Letter from Beth Lipkin to Gardiner: NAGW–BL/1/4/4/32, after the publication of his book.

63 Holroyd, *Augustus John*, p. 671, note 86.

64 Ibid., p. 553.

65 Letter from Epstein to Dr Oko, 22 February 1933: HUCAC.

66 Arthur Lett-Haines (1894–1978) was a British painter who was part of a London artistic circle that included D.H. Lawrence, the Sitwells and Wyndham Lewis – namely, the right wing of the artistic world.

67 Letter from Epstein to Norman Horstein, 5 December 1933: TGA, 871.22.

68 Letter from Epstein to Arthur Lett-Haines, 7 December 1933, TGA, 8317.1.1.1050.

69 See Radford, *Art for a Purpose*, p. 2.

70 The AIA supported the left-wing Republican side in the Spanish Civil War through exhibitions and other fund-raising activities. Many of those linked with the Association, such as the painter Duncan Grant, were also pacifists.

that, in 1937, together with Moore and other artists who had joined the organization, he signed letters in support of its British section.[71]

In 1933 Epstein had occasion to meet several interesting people and make their portraits. First and foremost was his old friend Dr Adolph S. Oko, who had been unable to help with Epstein's exhibition in New York in 1927 (I/182). Apparently, that incident had been explained and forgiven, and their relationship warmed during Oko's stay in England (1933–38). In 1935 Epstein did a portrait of Oko's second wife, Dorothy,[72] whom Oko had 'stolen' from the president of the Hebrew Union College; it was after this that Oko resigned from the College and came to England.[73] During his time in England, in which he devoted himself to his research on Spinoza (see also I/179),[74] the Okos were welcomed by the Epsteins, who, apparently, cared very little about the so-called indecency of the affair. After his return to the States, following the outbreak of war, Oko became a driving force in the publication of Epstein's autobiography in America and in the selling of his portraits, until his death in 1944.

In September 1933 Albert Einstein arrived in England from mainland Europe, having been put on a list of assassination targets with a "$5,000 bounty" on his head, while a German magazine included him in a list of the enemies of Germany under the heading "not yet hanged".[75] He stayed at the home of Commander Oliver Locker-Lampson, Conservative MP and ally of Winston Churchill, who offered him a safe place to stay in the Norfolk countryside, in a small hut on Roughton Heath in Cromer, that contained a piano on which Einstein played.[76] Epstein was invited to come for several days and do Einstein's portrait. A photograph taken on 19 September (fig. 14a) shows Einstein with his host (on the horse), and an "unknown" person standing behind them, who, judging from the facial features and his typical cap, I believe to be Epstein (see fig. 14b).[77]

In the first sitting in the hut (sittings lasted two hours every morning), Einstein smoked his pipe, creating a cloud that prevented Epstein from seeing anything of the sitter. Consequently, for the second sitting Einstein was asked to smoke only during the break. "Einstein appeared dressed very comfortably in a pullover with his wild hair floating in the wind. His glance contained a mixture of the humane, the humorous, and the profound. This was a combination which delighted me. He resembled the ageing Rembrandt", wrote Epstein (94). Although Epstein had to hasten his work and considered it not to have been carried "to completion", it became his most popular piece, being reproduced over the years in about thirty-five copies. "More can be learned of the personality of Epstein from his bust of Einstein than from any other of his works. The confrontation of these two shy beings both making order out of chaos, two Jews dabbling in the raw matter of Genesis, marks an epoch in the history of the modern spirit," suggested Golding when writing on the great figures of the era.[78]

Epstein's contacts with another aspect of his roots, the national movement of the Jews, were sparse. During early 1927, as he stated, "Zionism was not the acute question it became later and I had not thought about it" (146). By the 1930s, however, Zionism had become an acute question not only in H.G. Wells's futuristic book *The Shape of Things to Come* but also for the British Mandate in Palestine. In December 1933, following Einstein's portrait, Epstein started a portrait of one of Zionism's prominent figures, Dr Chaim Weizmann.[79] Generally, Epstein was cordial with his sitters and often conversed with

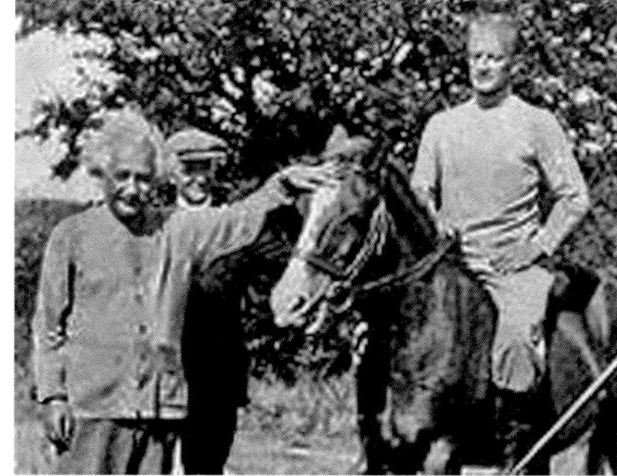

Fig. 14a
Einstein in Roughton Heath

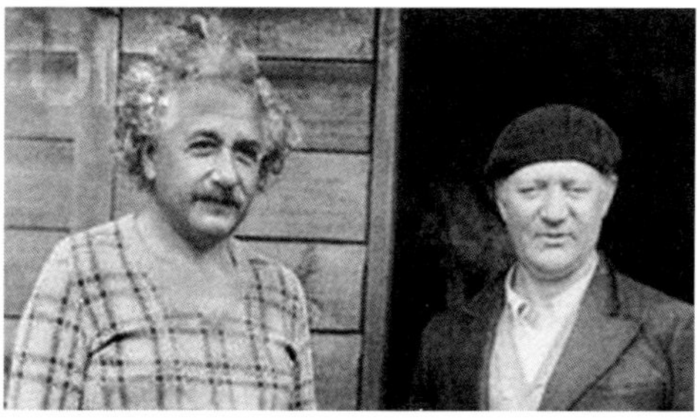

Fig. 14b
Einstein and Epstein in front of the cabin in Roughton Heath, October 1933

71 Berthoud, *Life of Henry Moore*, p. 145.

72 Silber, *Sculpture of Epstein*, no. 266

73 http://www.americanjewisharchives.org/aja/FindingAids/oko.htm.

74 Adolph S. Oko (1883–1944). In England Oko completed his Spinoza bibliography, and back in America he founded Societas Spinozana and later became a trustee of Domus Spinozana in The Hague. In 1923 Epstein did his portrait (Silber, *Sculpture of Epstein*, no. 137) and in 1926 that of his first wife, Pearl (no. 174).

75 Isaacson, *Einstein: His Life and Universe*, pp. 407–10.

76 http://www.bbc.co.uk/norfolk/kids/science/az_alberteinstein.shtml.

77 This suggestion derives from a comparison especially of the chins; fig. 13b shows Epstein and Einstein standing in front of the cabin on 6 October 1933.

78 Golding, 'Epstein', pp. 219–20.

79 Dr Chaim Azriel Weizmann, a lecturer in chemistry at Manchester University, developed the ABE-process, which produces acetone through bacterial fermentation. During World War I, from 1916 until 1919, he was Director of the British Admiralty laboratories, researching synthetic rubber and high-octane gasoline, and inventing the chemical formula that enabled Britain to produce more effective explosives. See Adams, *Arms and the Wizard*.

them. But Weizmann (who in 1948 became the first President of the State of Israel), is not mentioned by Epstein in his autobiography among the personalities who had impressed him during sittings; and for his part Weizmann, somewhat amused, summed up the nature of their contact in a letter:[80]

> I'm getting some rest by sitting about 3 hours a week for the sculptor Epstein. Jimmy [J.E.A. de Rothschild] ordered my ''ead' as a birthday present to me. I have never indulged in these personal vanities, but this time it would have offended Jim and I'm to sit. It's rather fascinating to watch a first-class artist and to see how the clay assumes life under his hands. At present the head begins to look like a cross between Shmarya Levin [another prominent Zionist leader] and the devil. I suppose it will become myself later on.

With no new sculptures in 1933 Epstein regarded himself as practically "giving up sculpture for the time being" (namely carving). However, an outlet that had started as "a mere diversion" in his forest cottage grew into an immersion in a passion, "and I could not think of nothing else but painting". He dedicated to this passion the chapter 'Watercolours of Epping Forest' in his autobiography (165), in which he describes going into the forest with his daughter Peggy Jean (and actually also with – unmentioned – Isabel), "and we did not have to walk far before seeing something worth painting". Altogether he painted sixty works only of flowers for his first exhibition on the theme, and "went on painting, and painted three hundred more". Their style is interesting, because in seemingly free strokes they echo the flower drawings of his friend Matthew Smith, who, no doubt, exerted some artistic influence. This book cannot offer coloured images, but it may suffice to say that the impact of both artists' flower drawings lies in the use of strong, brilliant and contrasting colours, with paint laid on generously and confidently – a complete diversion from what had been the conventional approach to flower painting when Smith had started his own style. The difference between them, however, lies in Smith's often controlled presentation of flora in a vase and within a setting, whereas Epstein generally presents simply flowers, by themselves, as if 'framing' a detail taken from a field.

Epstein's drawings were presented in the Christmas exhibition (December 1933) at the Tooth Gallery, and the exhibition was a sell-out: it was a pleasant ending to a not very successful year in which his sculptural work had been ignored. In view of the events to come, Epstein's experience in the woods, followed by his great success with the paintings, may have finally ignited a sexual consummation between Epstein and Isabel, as Isabel had till then felt that "he was rather a puritan about that kind of thing".[81] However, Epstein's puritanism seems to have been overcome, as in February 1934 he and Isabel conceived a child (born at the end of October 1934). During early 1934 Isabel had presented her own watercolours at Arnold Haskell's Valenza Gallery in Conduit Street, successfully. All her drawings were sold, and she acquired a reputation that was to help her later on when she moved to Paris and joined the cultural scene there.

The coming year was thus to bring the Epsteins a happy domestic addition, albeit in less happy circumstances. "One has to draw a distinction between what was said before

80 Letter from Dr Chaim Weizmann to Lola Hann, Hamburg, 8 January 1934, *The Letters and Papers of Chaim Heizmann*, vol. XVI, ed. G. Sheffer, Jerusalem 1978. Kindly provided by the Weizmann Institute Archive.

81 Gardiner, *Epstein*, p. 326.

and what after 1934," George Orwell stated later,[82] and I suspect his assessment was partly derived from the mood of the nation (described further on). Political affairs and Epstein's personal ones toward the end of 1934 became interwoven.

The reaction in England to the expansion of the German army and navy and the creation of its air force in October can be defined, in retrospect, as mild. In the autumn of 1934 a branch of the League of Nations Union in Ilford, Essex, organized a ballot of the British electorate, announcing the results in the early summer of 1935.[83] More than 11 million people, or approximately 38% of the adult population of the country, took part. Five questions covering several national issues were asked, and the fifth was:

> Do you consider that, if a nation insists on attacking another, the other nations should combine to compel it to stop, by
> (a) economic and non-military measures? (Over 90% said yes)
> (b) if necessary, military measures? (About 70% said yes).

A not very sweeping majority therefore (6.8 million), was in favour of military action, but only as a last resort to stop an aggressor; while more than two million were against fighting even then; and the remainder abstained on the issue. The answers reflect public opinion during the year in which Germany, the defeated combatant of World War I, was steadily developing into an increasingly threatening force, whose extent, apparently, was not well estimated either by the public or by its government, as barely a year after the ballot (November 1935) Churchill needed to warn Prime Minister Stanley Baldwin not to underestimate German air-power.

Within the Epstein family, Isabel's pregnancy that had begun in February ended in a very happy result for Margaret, who found a way round any official adoption of the child, with all the potential unpleasantness (and, given their advanced age, also probable rejection) that it might entail. On the due period, when the 'situation' required visibility, Margaret strapped a pillow to her stomach pretending to be pregnant. Although, when reading about it, this seemed to me ridiculously unbecoming for Margaret in her sixties, but Peggy Jean confirmed the story, explaining it by the state of her mental health: "Mommy was, by then, very ill!"; but, in view of what was coming, I consider that this pretence of being pregnant had been carefully planned by Margaret. In September Isabel "spent some time in the country, changed her name to Epstein by deed poll".[84] A Jamaican doctor working in Surbiton, who came regularly to the house to treat Margaret, undertook to 'deliver' the baby.[85] Isabel gave birth to Jackie under her new surname, 'Epstein', and Jackie's birth certificate (October 1934) could therefore state that "margaret [sic] Epstein of Independent means, of 24 Hamlet Gardens, Ravenscourt Park, W.6." gave birth to a boy, and that "maggie Johnson Robertson [had been] Present at the birth, [at] 20 Paragon Grove, Surbiton".[86] Margaret, so it appears, had beaten the system and was registered in England as Jackie's natural mother, while Peggy Jean's mother Meum Lindsell Stewart had had to go to France to deliver her, and later the baby had to be adopted legally.

As in the case of Epstein's first daughter, Peggy Jean, immediately after his birth Jackie was left by Isabel with the Epsteins. After recovering from the birth she went to Paris, but the rest of her highly interesting life and the company she kept are beyond

82 Letter from George Orwell to a friend, 29 October 1948: *Collected Essays, Journalism and Letters*, vol. IV, p. 450.

83 McCarthy, 'Democratising British Foreiogn Policy', and see also http://www.chu.cam.ac.uk/archives/education/churchill_era/exercises/appeasement/part_B2.php.

84 Gardiner, *Epstein*, p. 337.

85 Peggy Jean's elaboration on my text on family members, sent to her on 18 November 2001.

86 Cited from a photocopy kindly provided by Jackie Epstein.

the scope of this book. It suffices to say that she met the foreign correspondent Sefton Delmer, later to become her first husband, and later still married (separately) two composers, Constant Lambert and Alan Rawsthorne. As Isabel Rawsthorne she became a painter of repute, and designed the sets for two ballets, *Tiresias* (1952) and *Madame Chrysanthème* (1955).[87]

Isabel's detachment from her son was carried to the point of erasing him from her consciousness, and although in later years she was living not far away Jackie never saw her. Moreover, when Susan Crosland interviewed her, asking if she ever saw Jackie, she replied: "Who's Jackie?"[88] All she chose to remember from the old days with Epstein was Peggy Jean as "blonde and pretty and jolly", and very little about the household, saying that "Hyde Park Gate seemed more like a *pension* than a home".

Thus Margaret had another child who was legally hers; but unlike baby Peggy Jean, who, in less affluent days, had slept during her first years in her parents' room, listening to Margaret reading to Epstein [I/18], baby Jackie had his own room with a governess.[89] The financial situation at the Epsteins' house became tighter with the addition of a new baby and a governess, as there were not enough commissioned portraits during this year; the catalogue indicates ten, of which two were of models and thus about eight paid for; one commission was from an old acquaintance, George Bernard Shaw.[90]

Surprisingly, Kathleen was not aware that Jackie was biologically Epstein's child, believing him to be adopted. Did this new baby, brought into Epstein's life and legally recognized as his son not long after the death of their own baby (see p. 67), increase the tension that already existed between Epstein and Kathleen? Was this tension due to the mere presence of the baby or to the fact that, as Epstein told her, the child bore his name whereas their children did not? In view of the claim of constant attempts by Margaret to cause a rift between Epstein and Kathleen,[91] it is curious as to why she made no direct or indirect attempt to divulge to Kathleen the truth about Epstein's own child (and thus expose his infidelity to her) – unless it was out of fear for the legitimate status of 'her' baby.

BEHOLD THE MAN

By 1935 Hitler had begun threatening France and England to the extent that the tiny British Communist party, hardly even a recognized entity, whose main activity lay in libelling the Labour Party, needed to become patriotic and capitalist, with slogans such as 'Defence of Democracy' and 'Stop Hitler'. Whether it was related to these events or not, members of the Independent Fascist League defiled Epstein's Hudson Memorial [I/174] in Hyde Park.

Hitler's order for Germany's rearmament on 16 March, as a way to lift Germany out of the Depression, stimulated its economy between 1933 and 1935, with unemployment dropping from 6 million to 1 million. The notorious German concentration camps started to be built, and in April 'non-Aryan' writers were prohibited from being published. A renowned anecdote in this respect was the attempt to translate J.R.R. Tolkien into German. The German publishing house inquired whether Tolkien was of *Arisch* (Aryan) origin. An infuriated Tolkien responded with a reply that has since become legendary:

87 Buckle, *Epstein: Sculptor*, p. 209, mentioning her portrait. In all probability, it was owing to Kathleen's influence on his text that he did not mention her involvement with Epstein.

88 Letter from Susan Crosland to Peggy Jean, 22 July 1978: NAGW. Crosland (1927–2011) was a renowned freelance author for several newspapers, specializing in writing features and profile articles, and was made a Trustee of the National Portrait Gallery by Prime Minister Wilson. She wished to write Epstein's biography, in which she saw "the central theme as The Artist in Revolt". Her plans were not realised, as in 1977, during her research, her husband Tony Crosland, then foreign secretary, died aged fifty-eight following a stroke, and she became engaged in writing his biography instead.

89 Interview with the author, 1998.

90 On Shaw as a sitter and his arguments with the Epsteins, see Gardiner, *Epstein*, p. 336.

91 Gardiner, *Epstein*, p. 314.

> Thank you for your letter .... I regret that I am not clear as to what you intend by *arisch*.
>
> I am not of *Aryan* extraction: that is Indo-Iranian; as far as I am aware none of my ancestors spoke Hindustani, Persian, Gypsy, or any related dialects. But if I am to understand that you are enquiring whether I am of *Jewish* origin, I can only reply that I regret that I appear to have *no* ancestors of that gifted people.[92]

The year 1935, however, was not one of acute political issues only, as in it the literary world gained its most important innovation, when Penguin Publishing introduced the first paperbacks, making reading affordable and portable for the masses. However, those grim ideas that had been once the domain of the few who could afford to purchase the books that contained them were now thanks to this new state of literary affairs able to reach the many. One would have liked to believe that positive published ideas could perhaps have influenced the course of history; but as we know this did not happen, in spite of all the published warnings.

In view of the above-described political atmosphere, and in particular regarding its 'Jewish aspect', it is not surprising that in his next work Epstein carved a particular Jew in a peculiar situation. The growing anti-Semitism in Germany, mirrored also in England, involving a discourse on Jews as the cause of the world's social problems and in particular as the harbingers of disparaged modern art, may have induced in the Jew and artist Epstein a sense of being pointed at. In order to express his situation and what he felt about it, both as a Jew and as an artist, he needed to find a suitable vehicle within European iconography. He resorted to the most obvious images of Jesus, at the moment of being crowned with thorns and being pointed at. Epstein's self-identification with Jesus has already been suggested in regard to the drawings given to Kathleen (p. 69), and thus there would be no novelty in this repeated use of the Jesus paragon for personal purposes. However, during the carving of the sculpture in the mid 1930s, the national aspect also came into play: "As in all [Epstein's] work racial feelings are somehow there and one is aware of a further conception of the race of Christ suffering through the centuries and terribly in our day", observed art critic James Bone.[93]

So far, Epstein's carved sculptures of figures had not exceeded natural proportions; his *Venus* I and II (1914–16), including their bases of doves, as well as the square block of *Sun God* and *Primeval Gods* (1931–33), were about two metres in height. In 1934, however, Epstein entered a phase in which he created what can be termed colossal figures, one after the other. He explained this fascination with huge dimensions:

> When I see these great monoliths lying ready for the butcher's hand, as it were, I instantly have a sentimental feeling of pity that the fate of a noble block of stone should be so ignominious [to be sliced up and used for interior decoration]. Knowing that this stone could contain a wonderful statue moves me to purchase it and rescue it, even though at the moment I have no definite idea for it.
>
> Never mind – that will come (168).

And eventually, with the aid of unpleasant reality, it came.

92 Carpenter, *Letters of J.R.R. Tolkien*, no. 30, p. 37 (italics in original). No. 29 is the cover letter that Tolkien wrote to his publisher concerning this correspondence, in which he refused to give any declaration whatsoever of his racial origins. I am grateful to Chris Smith, Editorial Director, Harper-Collins, for leading me to this letter. It has become renowned to the extent of being included in Wikipedia.

93 'Epstein's New Sculptures – Behold the Man', *Manchester Guardian*, 7 March 1935; cited in Epstein's autobiography (172).

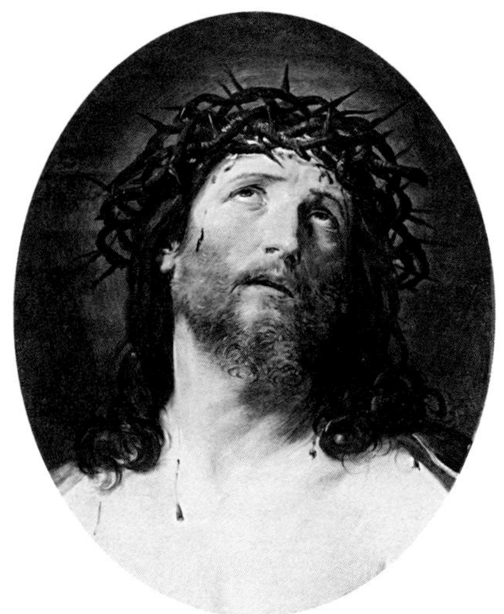

Fig. 15
After Guido Reni
Ecce Homo, c. 1640–49
Oil on wood, 56 x 42.8 cm
National Gallery, London

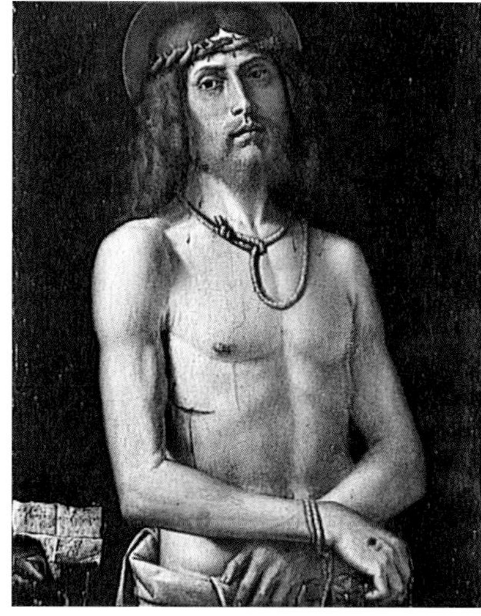

Fig. 16
Bartolomeo Montagna
Ecce Homo, 1500–07
Oil on poplar wood, 55 x 43 cm
Musée du Louvre, Paris

Epstein explained that he "wished to make an 'Ecce Homo', a symbol of man, bound, crowned with thorns and facing with [a] relentless and over-mastering gaze of pity and prescience our unhappy world" (168). He had before him a wide repertoire of imagery on the subject, but it seems that his idea required a presentation unlike the common one of Christ with an upraised face and agonized expression (such as Guido Reni's [fig. 15]). Epstein's Christ, as he described it, would address the viewer and therefore required a thoughtful expression rather than a suffering one; one precedent that might have influenced him was Bartolomeo Montagna's representation, which he had seen in the Louvre (fig. 16).

While leaving it to the viewer to describe this work, as he had no intention of doing so himself (169), Epstein "gave himself up wholly to a realisation of lines and planes, what critics are fond of calling "the formal relations [as] the plastic aim was always of paramount importance and the 'preaching' side secondary" (168). By the word "preaching" Epstein was hinting with a tint of cynicism at the vocabulary used by the professional 'guild' formed by his critics.

The sculpture, bearing the English title *Behold the Man* (rather than the traditional Latin *Ecce Homo*) [42a], towers three metres high, of which the head with its crown of thorns occupies almost one third. As these are not naturalistic proportions, the sculpture conveys the aura of a symbol stronger than any effect of realism. The treatment of the body is unique as well: the chest is narrowed in order to allow the folded and bound hands to rest on the legs, while the edge of the rope that binds them touches the floor. The elements within the elongated trapezoid head are carved in sharp geometric angles – the almond-shaped eyes sunk under the flat forehead, the flat rectangle of the nose, and the curved upper lip closing on the lower protruding bottom one above a trapezoid chin. The expression of the face transmits a sense of disdain rather than the "gaze of pity" that Epstein claimed to have intended, and one wonders whether the resentment felt by viewers of the work did not stem from that disdain. The execution of the sculpture was an arduous task and, while carving, he found the stone to be the toughest, most difficult piece he had ever tackled. The result, also due to its configuration, which retained the frame of the block, was, as his friend Matthew Smith commented, that "You have made a heavy stone seem heavier" (168).

There is a difference between what people saw in the mid 1930s and the sculpture that the viewer e ncounters today in its permanent place in the old cathedral ruins at Coventry: seen from below, with the figure set on a high pedestal, the head acquires a reasonable proportion [42c]. At the time, however, either in the showroom or, as it was never sold, in Epstein's studio standing on wooden beams that created a space underneath into which baby Jackie was fond of crawling,[94] an onlooker of average height was faced with a huge, towering figure with a disproportionate head and an austere face with blank eyes and clenched lips [42b]. Consequently, standing close to it gave the viewer an uneasy feeling; hence, despite a favourable description of the sculpture by one commentator, his remark that the sculpture was unsuitably exhibited was a logical one.[95] The sculpture had been presented while still unfinished at the Leicester Galleries in March 1935, and it remained in the studio, being worked on in different periods, "whenever I could" (169); he was still working on it in the late 1940s.[96]

94 Jackie Epstein's conversation with the author.

95 *The Daily Telegraph*, signed T.W.E [Earp], cited in Epstein, *Let There Be Sculpture*, p. 170.

96 Silber, *Sculpture of Epstein*, p. 177.

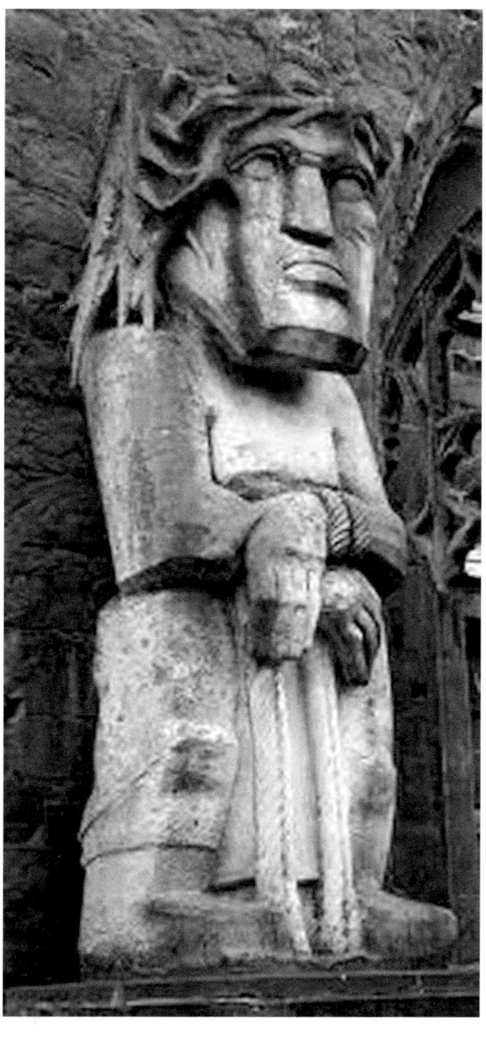

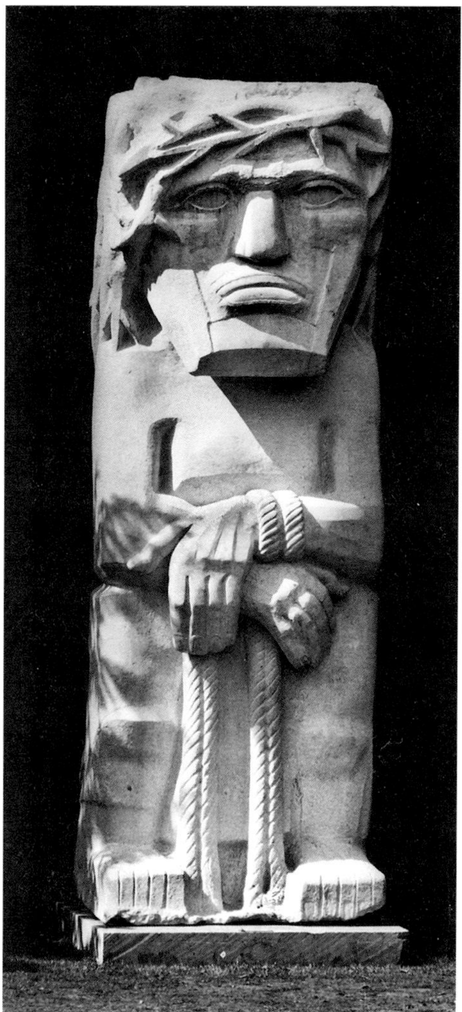

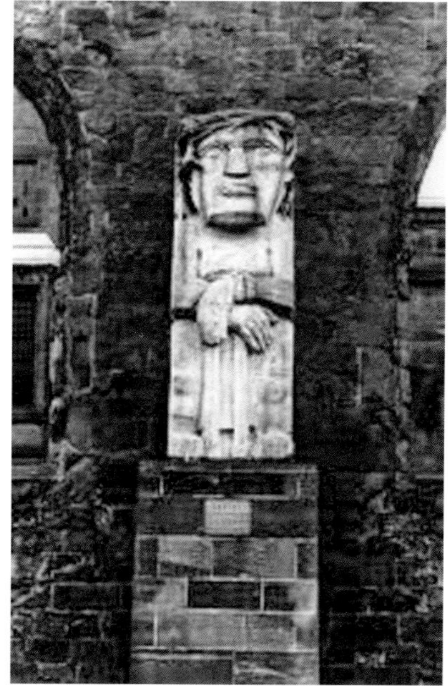

42a
Behold the Man (profile), 1934–35
Subiaco stone, H. 300 cm
Coventry Cathedral ruins

42b
Behold the Man (in the gallery)

42c
Behold the Man (seen on the pedestal)

Some of the newspapers had a field day with their vitriolic comments on Epstein's largest work (one of the sculptures most vehemently attacked, as Epstein noted), directed partly at the form of the figure but mainly at Epstein's presentation of Jesus and its implications for Christians. Thus, *The Sunday Pictorial* described it as "A statue that should be hidden"; *The Daily Mirror* refused to publish a photograph and was praised by its readers when it published their unfavourable comments on the work, mainly as an "insult to religion".[97] Anthony Blunt reacted against this supposed "insult", placing Epstein's *Behold the Man* among other manifestations in art of religious feeling amidst a general public indifference. Pointing to William Blake as an example of the expression of personal religious views in art, Blunt regarded *Behold the Man* as Epstein's particular as well as personal contribution to revitalizing European religious art with "an infusion of dark blood", and stated the need to clear away "much sentimentality and clap-trap from the idea of religious art".[98] A comparison to Epstein's *Risen Christ* of 1917 is in order here. Both sculptures project a kind of reproach by the man Jesus to the atrocities inflicted by men upon men: in the first this relates to the horrendous casualties of World War I; in the second, I suggest, it condemns the crimes and insults directed against Jesus's people which, eventually, in the period of *The Risen Christ*, would lay the ground for another

97 Ibid., p. 169.

98 Blunt, 'Epstein and Religious Art', cited in Epstein, *Let There Be Sculpture*, p. 174. Gardiner regards it as an indirect anti-Semitic comment; I disagree and give another explanation to Blunt's words.

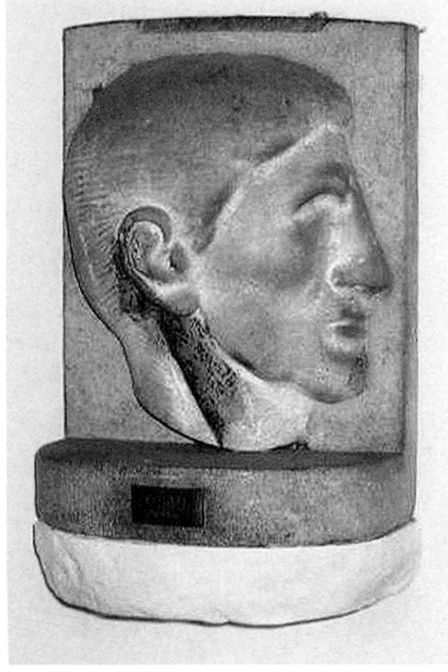

43
Canon Mortlock
Marble relief
Church of St Vedast, Foster Lane, London

war. In both cases the people's resentment of the work had been aroused by the unconventional approach to Jesus's image, in the first instance against its modernism and in the second against a monumentality influenced by non-European art – what Blunt had called the "dark" infusion. Aware of this argument, Epstein justified the Jesus he had depicted by contending that it was attuned to and acceptable by "an orthodox Christian ... who really thinks about religion and sees it as a living force".[99]

The period of the 1930s, with its strained atmosphere – though this, in its early stages, seemed to be of concern mainly to Jews – saw the formation of an unusual alliance, in which Epstein's *Behold the Man* had a part to play, though only once the outcome of racial hatred and anti-Semitism had become obvious to all. Indeed the subsequent history of *Behold the Man* has its hilarious side. Canon Charles Bernard Mortlock was contemptuous of Judaism,[100] which he described in 1936 as a "monstrous creation of human ingenuity", and in the context of the Crucifixion he apostrophized the Jews as "God killers". Nonetheless, with a good Christian heart he felt deeply for the Jews suffering persecution under Hitler, and in January 1943, during a service in Westminster Abbey, had offered up special prayers for the Jewish people. During these troubled times he came to Epstein to have his portrait done; Epstein was after all considered to be the best portraitist in England, and a friendship developed between them. Whether because he genuinely wanted to 'save' Epstein's soul, or because he wished to have *Behold the Man* for the Church, he tried to persuade Epstein to convert to his kind of Christianity (Anglo-Catholic), telling him that this would enable him to acquire the carving for the Church.[101] Epstein politely declined, and therefore the work remained Epstein's (although, following its display at an exhibition in Battersea Park in 1948, it remained in a keeper's garden until a more suitable place could be found).[102]

However, upon hearing of Epstein's death, the next Sunday Canon Mortlock descended from his pulpit and stepped into the nave, asking the congregation to join him in a prayer for "brother Jacob Epstein who died unbaptized". On 10 November 1959, he delivered the address at the memorial service organized by Kathleen at St Paul's Cathedral. Mortlock's relief portrait by Epstein is currently situated in an alcove in the garden of his church, St Vedast's, Foster Lane, near St Paul's Cathedral, accompanied by a plaque inscribed A *bas-relief of Canon* C.B. *Mortlock by his friend Jacob Epstein* [43].

After Epstein's death, *Behold the Man* was entrusted by Lady Epstein to the hands of Canon Mortlock who, during his own lifetime, could not find a suitable place for it.[103] On his death it was bequeathed to the organ-builder Noel Mander, who "never regarded it as a personal gift but as in trust".[104] Mander tried to get Westminster City Council to place it in the south-east corner of St Margaret's churchyard, but was told it would constitute a potential hazard as people might step off the pavement into traffic to get a better view. Another suggested site, in Cannon Street near St Paul's Churchyard, was rejected by the Royal Fine Arts Commission on the grounds that "it would be out of keeping and out of scale" with its surroundings.[105] A more acid comment came from the critics' 'guild': John Piper[106] wrote to the secretary that he agreed "with Henry Moore that it should be seen low down in a jungle of leaves or undergrowth – if that is what he said".[107] The work's eventual location resulted from Mander's perception that for a sculpture representing the Man of Sorrows he should find a ruin, and therefore he suggested to the authorities that it be placed in the ruined cathedral at Coventry. After

99 Haskell, 'Epstein's "Behold the Man"'.

100 For more on Canon Mortlock, see http://www.mortlock.info/encyclopedia/Corbel.rtf. I am indebted to Robert Griffiths (transmitter of the article on Mortlock) for further details on the Mortlock-Epstein connections and for the photograph of the relief.

101 Peggy Jean's comment to the author, 3 March 2005: "Mortlock was willing to buy the statue, if Jacob would become a Christian".

102 Gardiner, *Epstein*, p. 478.

103 Mortlock tried to place the sculpture in several churches; the last one to reject it, toward Epstein's final year, was that of Selby: unidentified newspaper clipping, 20 April 1959, Tate Archive.

104 This and the following information is taken from Mander's letter to his son Edmund (signed "Pa", 1992); photocopy courtesy of Robert Griffith.

105 Gardiner, *Epstein*, p. 477.

106 John Egerton Christmas Piper (1903–1992); his path crossed Epstein's when he was asked to design the stained-glass windows for the new Coventry Cathedral, for which Epstein made *St Michael and the Devil*.

107 Gardiner, *Epstein*, p. 519. On the basis of this hearsay report Gardiner blamed Moore (at the time a commissioner on the RFAC) for sabotaging the installation of *Behold the Man* in London.

considerable delay, caused by Moore's exhibition being held in Coventry,[108] it was accepted, in spite of Moore's objection that the proposal "is inappropriate", and moved there to its permanent site in 1969; as can be seen, the transfer was not an easy one (figs. 17a–b).

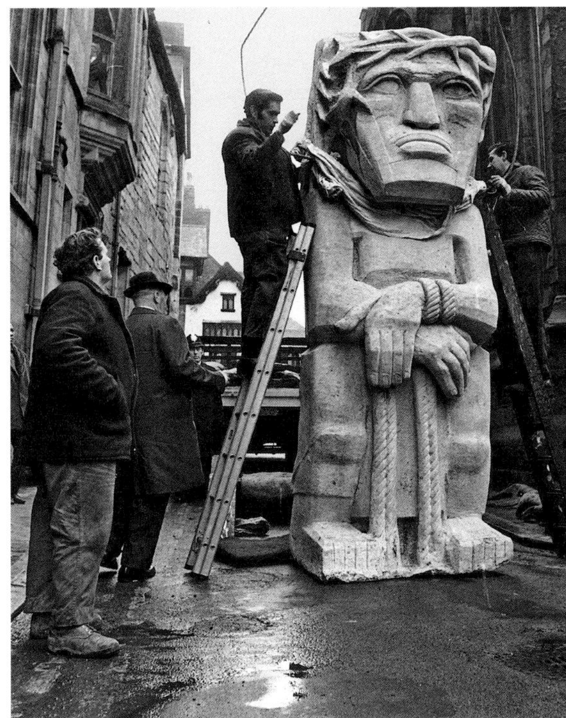

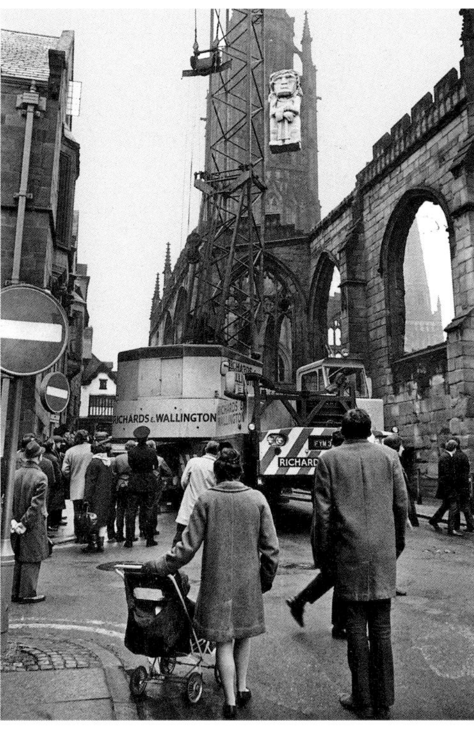

Figs. 17a–b
Moving *Behold the Man in*to the ruins of Coventry Cathedral, 1969
NAGW Archive

1935 had been quite an unpleasant year for Epstein, given the atmosphere in the art world. In January the quarterly review *Axis* began to appear, advocating abstract art and continuing to present it within the international context until its closure in 1937.[109] This publication followed *Unit 1*, published in 1934, and preceded *Circle*, in 1937. Needless to say, Epstein remained an outsider uninvolved in this artistic ferment.

In his personal life the situation also worsened, and the tension between Kathleen and Epstein reached a peak in March 1935, when Kathleen found out that Jackie was not simply adopted but was Epstein's natural son by another woman. Gardiner tells of a white-faced Kathleen, standing at the top of the stairs, whispered to the arriving Beth Lipkin: "He's had another child ..." – attributing this detail to Beth Lipkin. She, on the other hand, categorically denied it: "All you say about what occurred inside the house is a total fabrication .... I have never given you such account in any interview".[110]

The exposure of the secret left a bitter feeling. It had been the eleven-year-old Theo who, seeing in a newspaper an article on Epstein's exhibition of March 1935 (which beside the centrepiece *Behold the Man* included portraits of Jackie), first read Epstein's revelation that Jackie was his son. While Kathleen and Epstein could work out between them how to settle their future together, the sensitive Theo from this point onwards resented his father, who continued to come to his mother's house as if nothing had happened. There was never to be much fondness between father and son; their relationship remained at best civil, although in later years they bore a mutual respect for one another's art.

Epstein and Kathleen's attachment continued nonetheless, although it seems to have acquired a different hue, which, I believe, is not uncommon among couples who remain together for a long period – namely, it begins with an infatuation that develops into love, and in time turns into a friendship that tolerates indiscretions and, at the end of the road, settles into shared notions and memories. Epstein and Kathleen, as I understand it, seemed to have reached a point at which their mutual love acquired a kind of understanding that enabled them to tolerate Epstein's indiscretions, and later on also tolerate those of Kathleen. Gardiner speculates on Kathleen's reasons for continuing their relationship in spite of the betrayal, and to my mind the most convincing

108 Gardiner, *Epstein*, p. 520, note 478; this and the following had been told to Gardiner by Noel Mander, 7 June 1991.

109 Read, 'British Art 1930–1940'.

110 Gardiner, *Epstein*, p. 374, note 510; letter from Beth Lipkin to Gardiner, 12 January 1993: NAGW–BL/1/4/4/32.

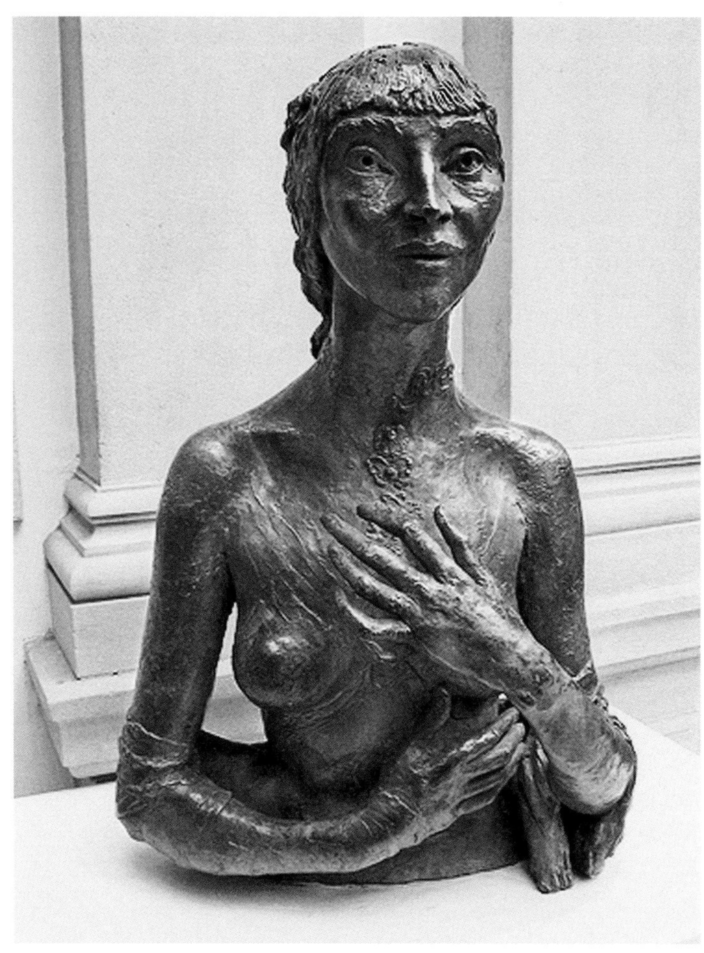

45
Kathleen, 5th portrait, 1935
Bronze, H. 76.2 cm
Bristol Museum and Art Gallery

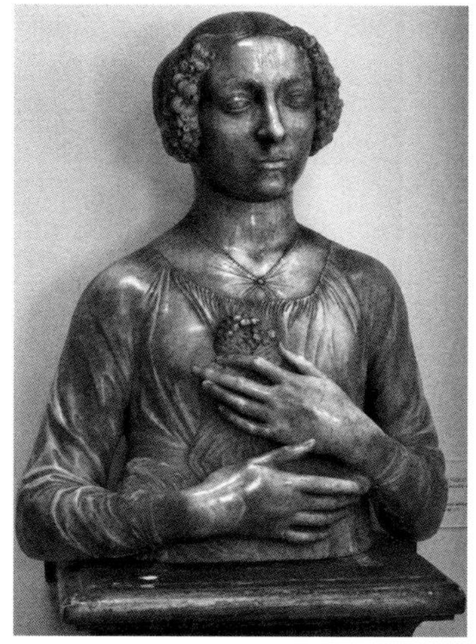

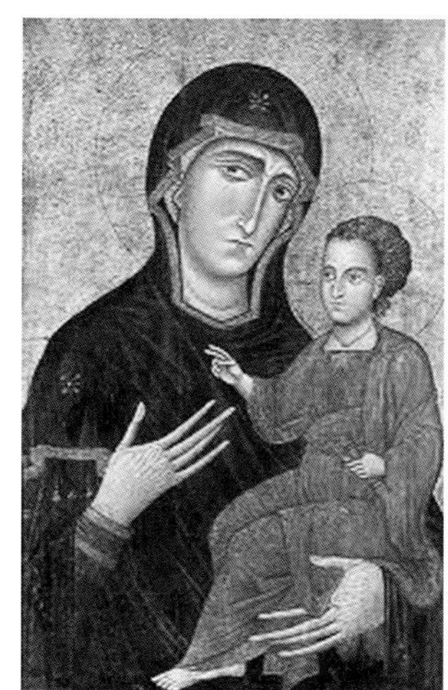

Fig. 18
Andrea del Verrocchio
Lady with primroses, 1475–80
Marble, H. 61 cm
Bargello Museum, Florence

Fig. 19
Berlinghiero
Madonna and Child, 1228–36
Tempera on wood, gold ground,
80.3 x 53.7 cm
Metropolitan Museum, New York

of these was the similarity that all parties could have perceived between Kathleen's new situation and that of Margaret: both women had had to come to terms with Epstein's personal needs in order to serve his art; had Kathleen left him, it would have suggested that she was less devoted to him than Margaret. It is also doubtful whether an angry and insulted Kathleen could have actually afforded to leave the man whom, after all, she both cherished and knew to love her dearly. Whether it was Kathleen's love and Isabel's disappearance that helped (as Gardiner suggests), or her having three children to raise with no other source of income (her father had left her out of his will), Kathleen remained with Epstein. Peggy Jean "doesn't remember Epstein having affairs after Isabel, although he had models, but only for his work, as he was too busy with Kathleen, Margaret and his work".[111]

Perhaps as a sort of atonement he made a Madonna-like fifth portrait of Kathleen, which I consider to be the most beautiful of the series [45], and in which I speculate that Epstein's allusion to the Madonna is not accidental. While the pose and hand gestures recall those of Verrocchio's marble bust *Lady with Primroses* (fig. 18), Kathleen's expressive and very long pianist's fingers are accentuated like those of a Byzantine Madonna (fig. 19). This hand gesture was repeated in her next two portraits, and is featured in only two other portraits by Epstein of women.[112]

111 Letter from Leda Sloat to the author with Peggy Jean's comments, 15 July 2006. However, she adds: "BUT we don't know".

112 *Betty Peters* and *Deirdre*, in Silber, *The Sculpture of Epstein*, nos. 307 and 314, respectively.

The relationship endured, and Kathleen lived to reap the fruits of her devotion and tolerance, because in the years to come (after Margaret's death) Jackie would be, in all things that mattered and until her death, more her son than Margaret's.

Epstein, however, had little time to dwell on his personal woes, as in April 1935 he found himself engaged in the start of a major art war (42–55). In early 1935 the Southern Rhodesia government took over the British Medical Association building, and the High Commissioner proclaimed Epstein's figures to be undesirable. The announcement in the press on 28 April was "of so insulting a nature" (42) that Epstein replied in a letter to the editor of *The Observer* (5 May), saying that the sculptures were never intended to be "topical" but to have "a universal appeal, even perhaps to be understood in Southern Rhodesia". The Rhodesian response was that "Anatomy for British Medical Association, yes. But do these figures indicate the product of Southern Rhodesia? No. It is a question of what is appropriate."

Several personalities from the artistic world joined the "acrimonious discussion" between Epstein and the Southern Rhodesian authorities, writing letters to the papers, and Sir Eric Maclagan, the director of the Victoria and Albert Museum, circulated a petition for the preservation of the statues. Among the protestors were the Samuels, purchasers of Epstein's work, to whom I found a note of thanks about "your signature to a letter in *The Times*, 10 May 1935, when you signed with other 8 Readers of Art protesting against the removal or mutilation of my Strand Statues".[113] A notable missing signatory was that of the Royal Academy, which, as one of its members, Walter Sickert, wrote, "ought to have summoned an emergency meeting, and sent a request asking to be allowed to make a representation to the King on the subject". The President of the Royal Academy refrained from adding his signature, even after Sickert's resignation. Epstein, apparently, was not surprised:

> I myself, in commenting on the President's refusal to sign the memorial in support of the statues, recalled that a former President of the Royal Academy signed a memorial for the removal of my Hudson Panel in Hyde Park. One president signs a memorial against one of my statues, and another refuses to sign for. This is the spirit of the Royal Academy!

A later echo of the affair of Epstein's sculptures can be heard from Henry Moore, who had also been maltreated by the Royal Academy, when Richard Cork came to interview him in the 1980s just before an exhibition:[114]

> And suddenly, when I cited Epstein's notorious Strand statues, Moore's mood changed to fury .... Almost half a century later, Moore was still vehement about the Royal Academy's disgraceful refusal to back Epstein in his attempt to stop the tragic mutilation of the Strand statues. "I'll never forgive them for that," he exploded.

113 Letter from Epstein to the Samuels, no date, TGA.9012/ 1–17. Mr and Mrs Samuels were art collectors from Liverpool, who purchased his work from the gallery during the 1930s, and in the 1940s they became friendly enough to purchase directly from Epstein. They also encouraged the Israeli sculptor Melnikov (see pp. 63–64), providing another common denominator between him and Epstein.

114 R. Cork, 'Hitler, Mothers, Navelgazing: Richard Cork recalls the revealing day he spent with sculptor Henry Moore', *The Independent, Sunday*, 14 February 2010.

Under the combined pressure of intelligent opinion (including that of his good old friend Muirhead Bone, who had already 'saved' him from the outrage of public opinion in the cases of the Hudson Memorial [1925] and *Day and Night* [1929]), the statues remained in place for another two years.

By the end of 1935 Epstein had produced an unsold carving and about six commissioned portraits (the remainder were portraits of models and family members), not enough to support two families. Kathleen, who needed money to go to Martigues to her sister Helen (probably a much needed break after the exposure of the Isabel affair), had not received it from Epstein by the time she left, and an apologetic Epstein wrote to her later that he was sending her a money order,[115] also for her holiday trip to Paris. In this letter he seeks to reassure her of his love and longing for "my darling one, my great one in whom all my happiness lies", while he himself was "in a spiritually low state", adding: "Why didn't I go with you to Paris? ... Of course you are going to the Louvre without me is a betrayal by myself of what I wanted to do for years[,] but there it is; I am to blame." And as he knew well that Kathleen always attracted people around her, he adds: "Write to me and tell me minutely of the new and fascinating persons you've met".

In September 1935 the political situation and current events were becoming increasingly threatening, with the swastika now the official symbol of Nazi Germany and the Nuremberg Laws depriving German Jews of citizenship. On 3 October, the Italian armed forces began their invasion of Ethiopia, and the League of Nations started the slow process of imposing sanctions, which were ineffective because neither Britain nor France took any serious action against Italy (for example by blocking Italian access to the Suez Canal). Even actions such as the Italians' use of a chemical weapon did little to change the League's passive approach to the situation. All sanctions announced by the League were lifted after the Italians captured the Ethiopian capital of Addis Ababa on 5 May 1936, and Haile Selassie, "Emperor of Abyssinia [Ethiopia]", left the country on 1 May 1936 for England, where Epstein (at the request of Commander Locker-Lampson, who had hosted Einstein two years previously) sculpted his bust in 1936 (101–02). The status of his sitter required that Epstein come to him in the Abyssinian Legation. He tried to realise the Commander's hope that the popularity of the bust would raise funds for the Emperor's struggle to achieve his country's liberation, but, "As it turned out, my bust had no popularity, and was only a matter of great expense to myself", and when Epstein wrote his autobiography in 1940 he noted that the work was still in his possession.

A more satisfying artistic commission arriving at the end of the year, executed in early 1936, was Epstein's first and only work for the theatre – a ballet. In late 1935 Mrs Laura Henderson, owner of the Windmill Theatre,[116] agreed to stage a ballet, *David*, that had been written much earlier by Poppoea Wanda. Wanda explained its rationale:[117]

> The Ballet "David" was written for two reasons. 1) I have always had an intense interest in and a great admiration for the Jews, and 2) the title role seemed to me eminently suitable to that great classical dancer Anton Dolin.
>
> I wanted the Ballet to be as Jewish as possible; its décor, costumes and music must all be work of Jews, and the 23rd Psalm in episode three must be sung in Hebrew.

115 Letter from Epstein to Kathleen, 11 September 1935: NAGW – BL/1/3/2/7.

116 In 1930 Laura Henderson bought the Palais de Luxe and formed a new company, the Windmill Theatre Co Ltd., almost completely rebuilding it as a theatre. The Windmill is also famous for being the only theatre in London that never closed during the war, except for the twelve compulsory days between 4 and 16 September 1939, during the blitz: see Matthew Lloyd's site, www.arthurlloyd.co.uk.

117 The programme for *David* produced by the company, TGA-8225.6.150.

… I am proud of my collaborators, Jacob Epstein [curtain], Bernard Meninsky [setting], Maurice Jacobsen [music] and Horinsky, our Cantor, a goodly army of names, and distinctively Jewish, but I am obliged to admit that the choreographer, Kate Lester, and I lack that distinction [and apparently so did Dolin].

David is a ballet consisting of six episodes in the life of its protagonist, through which it conveys scenes from Jewish history – the gradual growth from shepherd youth to being anointed and receiving the 'call'; the grown man who becomes a king and dances before the Ark of the Covenant. There is no mention in it of Goliath, and therefore Epstein's remark that his first scheme had "included the famous Goliath encounter"[118] is unclear. This famous encounter appears only on the cover of the programme, drawn by Bernard Meninsky – a young David holding the head of Goliath.[119]

"Ushered by Anton Dolin,"[120] Epstein designed a drop-curtain in which he presented his own interpretation of the scenes from David's life. "Tireless I made a curtain depicting David upon his throne singing his psalms in front of Jehovah," he wrote, devoting "considerable more time to the wish than the theatre usually demands & my compensation lay in the enthusiasm & excitement of the ballet audience which followed the showing of the curtain".

A brief anecdote is in order here. The colourful Mrs Henderson arrived with her deputy Vivian van Damm to see "how a man could earn so much in a short space of time, merely with the stroke of a brush or the whack of a sculptor's chisel".[121] Entering into the semi-darkness of his studio they saw only a ladder:

> "Is Mr. Epstein anywhere around here?"
> "You can never tell," came a gruff voice from the top of the ladder.
> "Well, we want to see him," I persisted.
> "WHO does?" boomed back the voice from up there.
> At this stage Mrs Henderson's patience could not be contained.
> "Go on, Mr. Van Damm," she burst out, "be Rude to him".
>
> During the entire meeting, Epstein shouting down to us, he never did consent to come down off the ladder, but went on painting the first theatre front cloth he ever had painted – a work of art.

The curtain was described as having nine panels [46].[122] Epstein claimed that he had himself executed all the "75 figures that appear and all the actual painting" with a brilliance of colouring like a "Russian ikon".[123] He managed to present within the panels an entire panorama of subjects and figures, with items occasionally intruding from one panel into a neighbouring one. The question of how one is to read the curtain as a whole is problematic, because not all the scenes appear to be connected with King David. However, in the treatment of the whole rectangle, the layout of the panels can be perceived as conveying a naively stylized structural tabernacle – a central space surrounded on all sides. This central scene has rectangular side-posts on either side, alluding to columns, each 'column' having three scenes. An oval shape tops the tabernacle, and a narrow panel with two scenes frames the central scene at the bottom. Thus the work seems to correspond to the first part of the comforting prophecy of Amos (9: 11), "In that day I raise up the tabernacle of David which is fallen, and I will close up the

118 *The Daily Telegraph*, 18 November 1935.

119 Bernard Meninsky (1891–1950) was a fellow Jewish artist. During World War I he joined the Royal Fusiliers, the unit to which Epstein was posted in 1917 (I/149), intended to fight with General Edmund Allenby in Palestine. They remained friends, and the Meninskys attended the Sunday musical gatherings at the Epstein's home: Nora Meninsky's memoirs, TGA 20077/7/2-8. Meninsky was Epstein's daughter Kitty's teacher at the Central School of Arts and Crafts (now St Martin's) in the late 1940s.

120 This is what Epstein states in an unpublished draft for his autobiography, entitled *Curtain for Ballet*: NAGW.

121 The following description derives from Van Damm, *Tonight and Every Night*, p. 77, and Van Damm, *We Never Closed*, p. 75. I am greatly indebted to Jill Millard Shapiro for the information.

122 Described in *The Times*, 14 January 1936. The curtain was reproduced in *The Sketch*, 15 January 1936, p. 105 (reprinted in Friedman and Silber, *Jacob Epstein*, fig. 77, p. 207), and a photograph of Epstein standing in front of it [46] was reproduced in *The Sphere*, 18 January 1936.

123 Letter from Epstein to *The Daily Telegraph*, 18 November 1936.

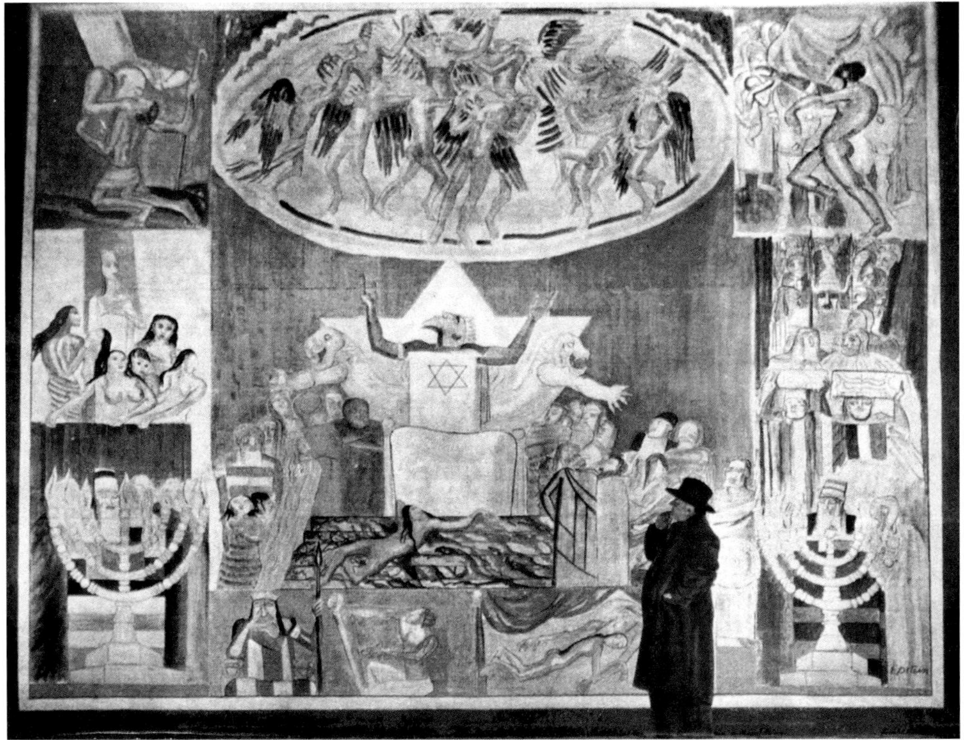

46
Drop-curtain for the ballet *David*, 1936
10 x 8.35m (30 x 25 ft)
Destroyed (illustration taken from ballet catalogue)

breaches thereof" (King James Bible translation). As the prophecy states, there are no breaches around this tabernacle, as the centre is enclosed.

As this book does not dwell on Epstein's drawings that are not related directly to his life and his non-portraiture sculptural work, I shall just mention briefly what I regard as important in the heart of the tabernacle – the central panel.[124] King David is seated on a throne, the upper part of its back of which is designed as the Star of David; two roaring lions (the lion being the symbol of the Judean kingdom) behind the king's back protrude forwards and sideways above two groups of people, and a crowd stands behind the throne. The configuration of what has been termed in later periods a 'star of David' had no symbolic meaning in biblical times, and only comparatively recently has it became a national symbol. I suggest, therefore, that by utilizing this recently adopted symbol and repeating it again on the king's chest, Epstein wished to emphasize an identification of the biblical king (who is also considered to be an ancestor of Jesus) and the Jewish people.

The curtain was considered a great success, and Epstein paid homage to other artists who had worked for the stage: "I was of course following in the tradition of Diaghilef ballets in which Picasso & Matisse & Rouault [were] designing curtains & scenic sets". He deplored England's lacking "a school of stage designs deriving from artists pictures & sculptures & not leave this field with its opportunities for work".

The curtain's end was tragic. Margaret reported: "I believe the curtain Jacob did for the ballet of *David and Goliath* [sic] is going to America this next week .... Dolin I believe is trying to sell it [and in the margin]: Everyone is selling here what is not rivetted to their person[.] Rockefeller Centre is about the kind of place that would have space hanging it").[125] The curtain was dispatched to America by Vivian van Damm, but the ship was

124 As far as I can decipher from the photograph, the other panels depict. young David being anointed by the Prophet Samuel (top left) and, as a mature king, dancing in front of the Ark (top right); playing in his youth the harp to King Saul (bottom left), and as an old man being warmed by the young Abishag (bottom right). The side-columns, as I call them, have two more scenes in each, the lower part similarly presenting people lighting the Temple *Menorah* (the candelabrum designed and made by Bezalel during the wanderings in the desert). The second level of the left column-panel shows a group of women, one exposing her breasts (Friedman, 'Epstein and the Theatre', note 123, suggests it is Bathsheba) and on the right side – above two people carrying what seem to be stones, another group of figures of which the central one – with square beard and pointed head with horns at the front – seems to be a non-Hebraic figure.

125 Margaret confirms "The owner is Mrs. Laura Henderson here in London": letter from Margaret to her sister-in-law Sylvia, December 1941; cited in Babson, *The Epsteins*, p. 54.

torpedoed on route and the Epstein curtain was no more.[126] Whether or not Epstein had been paid a large sum for the work, as Mrs Henderson claimed, his financial troubles did not diminish.

In February 1936 Epstein received from Oko an advance of £25 for his wife Dorothy's portrait, which Epstein hoped "does her justice".[127] Epstein's situation worsened towards the end of April to the extent that he was willing to cut his regular prices for an immediate payment. Thus, after reporting to Oko on a common friend who was ailing, the composer Bernard van Dieren,[128] who "seems in a terrible way & it's painful to talk to Frida [his wife]"), Epstein asked: "Would it be asking the impossible Oko if you would send me [another] £100 on the portrait of Mrs Oko. I am in troubles over my overdrafts at the bank & things are very very slow with me monetary".[129]

From 11 June to 4 July the International Surrealist Exhibition was held at the New Burlington Galleries in London. The exhibition was an Anglo-French project organized by (among others) Henry Moore, Paul Nash and Herbert Read, the last explaining its rationale in the catalogue thus: "A nation which has produced two such superrealists as William Blake and Lewis Carroll is to the manner born. Because our art and literature is the most romantic in the world, it is likely to become the most superrealistic."[130] With more than a touch of romanticism in his own work, Epstein conceived Romanticism differently, although his unfavourable comment on the British Surrealist exhibition in 1933 was mild in comparison to others' christening of the International as "the Marx Brothers of art".[131] However, when Read wrote in the catalogue that this movement was "a desperate act of men too profoundly convinced of the rottenness of our civilisation to want to save a shred of its respectability", he touched upon a nihilism in which Epstein had no interest and which, I suggest, in the end even Moore avoided, in spite of his having been without doubt influenced by Surrealism (see p. 72).

At the same time as the exhibition, the oxymoron 'surreal reality' reached the political sphere with horrendous impact: the Spanish civil war became an international affair, and a particular interest was taken by London's intelligentsia in what has been regarded as a war between good and evil.[132] The British Labour Party expressed its support for the Spanish Republic, and Stalin agreed to help the Republican forces; several days later Hitler agreed to extend help to the Nationalists, and the struggle between factions in Spain thus became a full-out civil war exacerbated by international involvement.

On the whole, British artists in the 1930s openly took sides on such issues, revealing themselves consistently as humane liberals – in their opposition to the events such as the shocking Moscow Trials (1936) and the Munich appeasement treaties (1937–38),[133] protesting both during and at the climax of the Spanish civil war, until 1 April 1939, when General Franco announced its end. In *Homage to Catalonia* (1937) George Orwell reveals how this war became a quasi-mythological cause to which artists from all across Europe and America rallied, almost always in support of the Left (apart from Roy Campbell, Epstein's brother-in-law, described as "a freakishly Quixotic feudalist").

As for Epstein, he had joined other artists in support of the International Artists Association that had announced a peace campaign against Fascist aggression (p. 76). Might the obvious Fascist tendencies of the upper classes in London and of its media

126 Van Damm, *We Never Closed*, p. 75. Van Damm, however, claims that it was sent for its protection rather than for its intended sale.

127 Letter from Epstein to Dr Oko, 9 February 1936: HUCAC.

128 Van Dieren wrote on Epstein's art: Van Dieran, *Epstein*, London 1920.

129 Letter from Epstein to Dr Oko, 1 April 1936, HUCAC.

130 See Read, 'Introduction', p. 13; http://www.romanianculture.org/downloads/Surrealism%20Catalogue.pdf

131 Symons, 'Surrealism and the AIA', in *The Thirties*, p. 86.

132 After the Spanish dictator Miguel Primo de Rivera was forced to resign on 28 January 1930, the political situation in Spain became characterized by unrest. Its exposition is beyond the scope of this text, and only the main events are mentioned. The chronology follows data from ttp://www.spartacus.schoolnet.co.uk/SPAchronology.htm.

133 Mellers and Hildgard, 'The Cultural Setting', p. 42.

have influenced his involvement, albeit on a small scale, with certain Jewish institutions? It is certainly possible, although I have not been able to discover when precisely he began his relationship with the Ben Uri Gallery which, at that time, was the most important Jewish art outlet. The earliest documented date of his involvement is provided by the catalogue to the 'Annual Exhibition of Works by Jewish Artists', 21 June – 5 July 1936, in which he is mentioned as a patron.[134]

During May 1936 another project appeared on the horizon, arising from the publisher George Macy's admiration of Epstein's flower drawings, which he wanted to produce as prints for his Limited Edition Club (Madison Avenue, New York). A deal was concluded to produce six of the watercolours "to feel out the market", with the originals to be returned to Epstein for his intended exhibition.[135] Another contract with Macy to produce "a series of drawings", an unspecified number of illustrations for an English translation of Baudelaire's *Fleurs du Mal* for his Club (to be delivered by 1 July 1937), was signed on 1 June 1936.[136] However, at the time, and for a long period afterwards, Macy's letters about the project were only intermittently answered by Epstein – both regarding this project and another, of illustrating *The Merchant of Venice*; Margaret, who took over the correspondence, said that Epstein preferred *King Lear*. It took Macy over two years and at least one more visit to Paris to finalize the Baudelaire project, which was eventually exhibited in December 1938.

On the family front things were not made easy by the Epsteins having to care simultaneously for a toddler and a vivacious teenager. Darlington Hall, the last English boarding school to which Peggy Jean was sent (in order to give Margaret space to handle Epstein's affairs), did not do her any good: "They taught her to smoke & drink at 13, among other things".[137] Margaret consequently tried to help her by getting "Miss Betty Joel a good friend of mine to take Peggy Jean into her beauty correspondence business". Joel had been a furniture designer influenced by the modern movement;[138] her professional fame reached its peak in the 1930s, but Peggy Jean, working in the office, did not at the time appreciate the privilege of being within this kind of environment.[139] Joel was for Margaret more than a mere friend – she was a confidante who, as noted above, tried to help in times of need. In addition to these household troubles, there was the awful affair of their German refugee governess, Gertrude, engaged for little Jackie: she was exposed as a Nazi supporter, saluting while she listened to his speeches on the radio, having first ensured that no one apart from Peggy Jean was around. In the few months that Peggy Jean worked with Joel she had also gone to clubs to dance, and she celebrated her last governess's disappearance by dancing all night long. A slight tone of regret can be detected when Margaret adds:[140]

> Jacob feels when he comes home at 7 a.m. [from Kathleen's house] & he sees PJ getting out of her taxi, that perhaps his life has influenced her. He feels this very much. That's why he has an idea of consenting to this scheme of her going to you for a while ... [adding later on] She had an unusually stormy upbringing.

Making up her mind to send Peggy Jean to Sylvia in New York towards the end of May 1936, hoping that she would study art at Epstein's old school, the Art Students League,

134 The next mention I have found is in the 1940 catalogue; both catalogues are in the National Art Library (pressmark 200 B.B.). Unfortunately neither the Library nor the Ben Uri Gallery have all the catalogues.

135 Gardiner (*Epstein*, pp. 347–51) elaborates on this issue (data taken from documents from the publisher deposited in the Henry Ransom Center, Austin, Texas), which is beyond the scope and subject of this book.

136 NAGW – BL/1/1/2/2.

137 Letter from Margaret to Sylvia (seven pages long), August 1936; cited in Babson, *The Epsteins*, pp. 44–45. The following details are taken from this letter.

138 Epstein did the first portrait of Betty Joel (1896–1985) in 1928 (Silber, *Sculpture of Epstein*, no. 184), and the second one, entitled *La Belle Juive*, in 1930 (no. 198).

139 Conversation with the author, 1993.

140 Letter, see note 137.

may have ignited in the ageing Margaret's mind the idea of making her will. She left all her possessions to her husband, and "if my said husband shall not be living at my death" she appointed her friend and confidante Miss Betty Joel as her executor, leaving all her property "in trust for my son Jacob and my daughter Madge (generally known as Peggy Jean)".[141]

Gardiner details the heavy mental and financial burden on Margaret during this period, in a year in which only two portraits were commissioned, about which she wrote to Sylvia:

> At the moment we are in the hands of money lenders [for a debt of £2600] .... Our income is so irregular & so fantastically spent you would get the astonishment of your life if you had a glance at it .... One gets so infernally busy in an artist's household when he has 3 establishments & the intake does not suffice for 1.[142]

At the end of May the portrait for Oko was ready: "You know[,] when you asked me to do the portrait I said it would be £300. I want it now to be £200 and if [you] could make the 2nd payment now of £100 that would settle the commission. You have of course paid me £100 leaving £100 due."[143] As if to rub salt into his monetary wounds, after thanking Oko for the cheque sent he reports that he had heard that his "flower paintings in New York (of which show I don't benefit as I sold the paintings outright) were sold at £60 each; some profit for the dealers"; he himself had received an average of £20.[144]

Peggy Jean was sent to New York to live with her Aunt Sylvia. Between August and October, therefore, Epstein had to live without his little girl, who had matured into quite a wild teenager and, with her blond curls and graceful manner, resembled her biological mother Meum. His attitude to the whole affair and his love for his daughter is reflected in Margaret's next letter:[145]

> He is not angry with me about it – her going to New York I mean any more. His rages go off like a child's, but he opens every letter with a New York stamp on it all the same just as if they were his own. It's about my Peggy Jean, he thinks & he just opens them the darling! That shows he is anxious about her.

The most interesting part of these two long letters, however, somewhat overshadowed by Margaret's long description of Peggy Jean's misbehaviour, is a more intricate matter. At the end of the first one Margaret mentions contacts in the US that might lead to commissions for Epstein, allowing them to join Sylvia and Peggy Jean in New York. She adds about that prospect that "He [Epstein] can't get out of his mix [with Kathleen] in a hurry – but some day we might pick up the little Jacob and the three of us make a run for it, as we did in 1927. Then it failed, *but he had not quarrelled with her so much then*, but next time it would succeed I think."[146] Was Margaret deluding herself that Epstein was ready to leave Kathleen? Not entirely, I suggest, because into this period of quarrels between them fits Epstein's remark in a letter to Oko in which he states, but without specifying the reasons, that he prefers to stay in Deerhurst "to get away from London for as long as I can'.[147]

141 A photocopy of her will, kindly provided by Peggy Jean's daughter Leda.

142 See note 138.

143 Letter from Epstein to Dr Oko, 30 May 1936: HUCAC.

144 Letter from Epstein to Dr Oko, 12 June 1936: HUCAC.

145 Letter from Margaret to Sylvia, October 1936; cited in Babson, *The Epsteins*, p. 48.

146 Babson, *The Epsteins*, p. 45 (my italics); from the same letter.

147 Letter from Epstein to Dr Oko, Monday (estimated as 1936, given its place in the bundle of letters): HUCAC.

The story of Peggy Jean's period in New York is quite amusing, although it had been far less amusing at the time for the adults involved. Her behaviour there, apparently, was not an improvement on what it had been at home. Sylvia's details – such as, "she used to walk in the apartment in the nude, just like she did at home [as if] she did not know the difference", or of her having accumulated debts of $10,000 – were, however, rejected by Peggy Jean in our conversation. Peggy Jean commented instead on Sylvia's Hollywood-style imagination and added that she had never walked around naked at home, and that her debts actually amounted to "only" $1000.

Sylvia sent a letter on 19 September urging the Epsteins to take back their daughter, but she was not at all eager to return home. Margaret's first reply was a cable in which she "had to write what was in his mind when he opened and read" Sylvia's letter; then she sent a calmer reply,[148] trying to explain to Sylvia their situation, in which Epstein "is most awfully hard up at the moment and he had a fear that he would not be able to pay for Peggy Jean's stay in New York so I had to caution Peggy Jean through you about dress". And after citing the enormous sum of $10,000 that Sylvia had reported, she added: "He goes about in rags pretty much as I do as you have seen. We live such a busy life we never think of a stitch of clothes, but Peggy Jean is a gay young thing and I try to get her what I can."

The Epsteins, Jacob in particular but no less so Margaret, were warm and affectionate parents, and their first-born Peggy Jean was very dear to them. When Epstein was away from London in 1924, doing a portrait of the author Joseph Conrad and feeling moody, he "wired for my five-year-old Peggy Jean to come", and on her arrival "things looked better". Both parents indulged their daughter with almost everything she wanted, involving her in their social life at home even as a child, as Nora Meninsky observed: "I remember that on one occasion Paul Robeson was there, and he was playing with Peggy Jean – Epstein's little daughter".[149] In one of Haskell's interviews with Epstein their conversation "was interrupted by the entrance of Peggy Jean, and Epstein became entirely a father".[150] In later years, as David McFall recalls, "the house was always full of children, they would scamper around the tea-table and chase each other under the grand-piano. No one scolded them, they were cherished. Epstein beamed with delight at their antics."[151]

A brief break is in order here, to explain further Epstein's complicated position between his two families and their offspring. The Epsteins' fond attitude, later extended to their son Jackie, was an uncommon phenomenon in artistic and intellectual circles. The intellectual code regarded fondness towards children as suburban or bourgeois, perceiving parenthood as a distraction from the serious pursuit of culture. As Cyril Connolly famously wrote, "There is no more sombre enemy of good art than the pram in the hall". Literary intellectuals in the first half of the twentieth century tended to opt for childlessness or even child neglect (Wyndham Lewis's son and daughter were given away); in the Bloomsbury set Vanessa Bell was quite an exception merely in having children.[152]

While the Epsteins came from the lower middle classes (Margaret's father was a farmer and Epstein's a small-scale businessman), and both were raised by their own mothers, Kathleen, by contrast, was the daughter of a respected doctor who had been

148 Letter from Margaret to Sylvia, 2 October 1936 (only four pages); cited in Babson, *The Epsteins*, pp. 47–48.

149 Nora Meninsky's memoir, TGA-20077/7/1.

150 Haskell, *The Sculptor Speaks*, p. 9.

151 McFall, p. 10.

152 Connolly, *Enemies of Promise*, p. 116. See Carey, *The Intellectuals and the Masses*, on Wyndham Lewis p. 170.

a pillar of his community; she had been brought up in a manor house and raised by a governess and a nanny. She regarded herself as belonging to the 'intellectuals', having acquaintances among them since her arrival in London in the early 1920s: "She sang, played the piano … and was attuned to all the arts and knew how to draw them all into the supreme art of life".[153] Kathleen's approach to her own children was to send the two girls with their prams away and continue with her intellectual life. "It was wonderful to have her as a friend, but because of the sparring I wouldn't have liked to be a child of hers", said the young American poet Samuel Menashe, who was befriended by Kathleen when in England during and after the war.[154]

As clichéd as the following claim may sound, I believe that the family and the father's attitude are ultimately determined by the mother. There could be no better support for this claim and for the attitudes mentioned above than Margaret's and Kathleen's different attitudes to their children and Epstein's response to them. Among Kathleen's children, Theo was the only one who was able to see his father regularly – although during his often 'pop in' visits Epstein spent almost all his time with Kathleen, rather than parenting Theo – because Theo was the only one of Kathleen's children whom she kept with her in London. The reason why she did so is a matter for speculation. Perhaps it was because Theo was born while her father, who objected to Epstein, was either still alive or had only just died (the dates are unclear), and she could not send the baby to her home in the north; or perhaps she wanted to establish a countermeasure to Epstein's strong attachment to Peggy Jean, counting on the common male vanity of wanting male progeny. If this was her motivation, it did not work – Epstein remained, to the end of his life, strongly attached to his oldest daughter.

Both Theo and Esther adored Kathleen in spite of what one may term her 'neglect', probably because "she was cheerful in her sadness";[155] and the growing children understood that a factor in her sadness was her side-street existence, outside their father's life, and, as a result, their own social status. Kitty, however, who was frightened of her mother's temper and her sarcasm, seems to have been the only one to have spoken of the less pleasant aspects of Kathleen's motherhood: "I think she wanted us – her daughters – to excel, but she did not want us to succeed, because she had to be the queen".[156] Epstein's attitude to these children during most of their childhood and adolescent years was attuned to Kathleen's. The one and only instance I have found of Epstein expressing in writing his care for one of their common children occurs in an early letter from New York (1927), after receiving the news that Kathleen had sent baby Kitty to live with her grandmother in the north: "… and when I ask you how *our* little girl is, you will just say 'damn his impertinence', and that you no doubt think serves me right".[157] Indeed legally they were hers and bore her surname, and it was up to her to decide how and where they were going to be. Epstein had to come to terms with Kathleen's attitude. However, his poor or non-existent relationship with Kathleen's daughters improved when, after Margaret's death, they lived closer to him.

After failure to find "a situation" for her in New York so that she could stay there, Peggy Jean returned to England at the end of October. The sorry end to her American trip must have affected her. Realising she was a burden on her parents, she set out to lend a helping hand by learning to decipher Epstein's handwriting and saving the expense

153 Letter from Paolo Vivante to Cressida Connolly, 3 November 2002: NAGW – CC/1/5/2/2.

154 Connolly, *The Rare and the Beautiful*, p. 229. Samuel Menashe (1925–2011) was a young American poet who studied in London in the 1940s after the war. His first book, *The Many Named Beloved* (published by Victor Gollancz in London, 1961) gained wide acclaim in Britain. He was later included in the Penguin Modern Poets series (vol. 7 of the 2nd series, 1966: *Poems by Donald Davie, Samuel Menashe, and Allen Curnow*).

155 Letter from Paolo Vivante to Cressida Connolly: see note 153.

156 Connolly, *The Rare and the Beautiful*, p. 184.

157 NAGW – NY.16.rtf (postmark 7 January 1928); my italics). Apparently he had accepted her decision to keep him out of her decisions regarding the children, perhaps after realising that even after having children with her he was not going to leave Margaret; I found no other letter mentioning her children as also his.

of having her father's memoirs typed by doing it herself. Epstein, through the literary agent Spencer Curtis Brown, had signed a contract with the publisher Michael Joseph to write an autobiography,[158] but with no precise deadline. He wrote hastily on small pads of bluish paper, sometimes two or three versions of a chapter, and so also his foreword, which was eventually not included,[159] and some other chapters that perhaps should have been. With sculptural works that required completion and other issues that required his attention, time passed. Meanwhile, during the last months of 1936 and into the following year, Peggy Jean devotedly continued her typing job, the results of which will be discussed in another chapter.

October 1936 was an eventful month as far as the political situation in England was concerned. On 4 October, Oswald Mosley's Blackshirts marched in London, deliberately into the Jewish populated East End, disseminating anti-Semitic and anti-Communist slogans. They were confronted by Communists, Anarchists, trade unionists and East End residents, who endeavoured to prevent the march by putting up makeshift barricades in the surrounding streets. A final confrontation took place in Cable Street, and Mosley was forced to retreat to the City of London. This 'BATTLE OF CABLE STREET' was regarded as a popular triumph against English fascism and commemorated in a celebratory mural. Two days later, on 6 October, Mosley was in Berlin, where he secretly married Diana Guinness (née Mitford) in the home of the senior Nazi propaganda officer, Joseph Goebbels; Adolf Hitler was one of the guests. Mosley explained his relations with the two heads of Fascist states thus: "Mussolini and Hitler were interested in our movement, not because our policies were similar – the aims of these intensely national movements in each country were widely divergent – but because we were strongly opposed to Communism, and unlikely to quarrel with any European country which had no intention of challenging British interests".[160] Mosley and other right-wingers tagged as 'Communists' all those who protested against his marches and gatherings. As a measure of protection against Mosley's 'soldiers', the Public Order Bill, announced in December, prohibited the wearing of uniforms by political bodies in Britain, effective from 1 January 1937.

Mosley's policy of not quarrelling with other countries as long as their actions did not affect England – no matter the atrocities they committed – was not unique to him (see p. 88). Indeed Mosley found precedent and support for it in the position that the Jewish Prime Minister Disraeli had taken in an analogous case, when the Turks were slaughtering Bulgarians. Disraeli had claimed in August 1876 that "Our duty at this critical moment is to maintain the Empire of England";[161] Mosley told his opponents they "should not confuse this question with anti-Semitism, or they will find themselves in deep water".[162] When in the elections next year Mosley's BUF, standing in three Left-wing strongholds in East London, received almost a quarter of the votes, he seemed to have proved that military non-involvement and fear of another war were stronger than social or humanitarian concerns.

On 2 November 1936, the BBC inaugurated the world's first regular television service, broadcasting news of a loss that saddened many – the fire that destroyed the Crystal Palace built to house the Great Exhibition of 1851. Epstein suffered a personal loss during this November, the death of his older brother, Lois. This was the brother whom Epstein's mother had called upon to help him while he was a student in Paris,[163] and to whom the

158 Probably in 1936, suggests Gardiner (*Epstein*, p. 335).

159 NAGW archive.

160 Mosley, *My Life*, p. 299 (my italics).

161 Rathbone, 'Gladstone, Disraeli and the Bulgarian Horrors'.

162 Mosley, *My Life*, p. 283.

163 Babson, *The Epsteins*, p. 8.

collector John Quinn supposedly delivered Epstein's huge granite sculpture *Mother and Child* (1915) [I/174–75]. When Epstein's autobiography was published, Margaret wrote to Sylvia, sending a copy that Lois's son Ebner eventually inherited: "I will send you a copy as 'to the most charming of all the Epsteins to me in New York, Lois'. I must not ever forget how he supplied us with luxuries in every way [in New York in 1927] and helped where he could. What a pity he was finished off so soon", adding that Scots do not forget those who have helped them.[164]

One positive event somewhat compensated for an otherwise rather unpleasant period. A German attempt to further ties between British and German artists had led to an invitation to the London Group to hold their exhibition of that year also in Berlin – but under the condition that Jewish artists would not be included. The London Group, a brainchild of Epstein (among others), who gave it its name in 1913, officially rejected the offer, and Epstein wrote a letter in support of the decision to the media, declaring that the whole scheme was "nothing more than an attempt to enlist the support of British artists in the cause of Nazi propaganda". After banning Jewish artists and pushing German artists into exile, the Nazi regime was now attempting "to disguise propaganda as a love of culture"; and he ended his letter with the call to all British artists to do "their utmost to check the attempt".[165]

However, while those artists with modernist tendencies boycotted the scheme, members of the Royal Society of Portraits, after 'checking the attempt', were enthusiastic to participate, as their traditional art did not clash with Nazi artistic notions.

The end of 1936 saw Epstein's December exhibition of flower drawings, with a catalogue listing 39 titles. The exhibition included one drawing lent by Oko, who wished Epstein "luck". Epstein replied that he would need it, as his income was quite meagre;[166] that entire year, as Silber's catalogue of works indicates, he had done only seven commissioned portraits.

CONSUMMATUM EST

On 2 January 1937, after thanking Oko for his loan, Epstein wrote that he was beginning new work on two portraits that he had promised, which "delays my carving work I'd rather be at".[167] In his autobiography Epstein describes how this carving, started towards the end of 1936, had been conceived (176):

> The unworked alabaster block lies prone on its length, and I consider whether I should raise it, but decide to leave it where it is. I can conceive any number of works in it. I can conceive a single figure or a group of figures. I have been listening to Bach's B minor Mass. In the section Crucifixus, I have feeling of a tremendous quiet, of awe … in this mood I conceive my 'Consummatum Est' …. I see immediately the upturned hands, with the wounds in the feet, stark, crude, with the stigmata. I even imagine the setting for the finished figure, a dim crypt, with a subdued light on the semitransparent alabaster.

Epstein's ideas on the nature of alabaster here expressed apply not only to his first but equally to the following works he would make in this material. The natural shades

164 Letter from Margaret to Sylvia, December 1940; cited in Babson, *The Epsteins*, p. 56.

165 *The Evening Standard*, 2 December 1936; cited in Rose, *Demons and Angels*, p. 199.

166 Letter from Epstein to Dr Oko, undated (estimated as November/December): HUCAC.

167 Letter from Epstein to Dr Oko, 2 January 1937: HUCAC.

47
Consummatum Est, 1936
Alabaster, 61 x 223.5 x 81.3 cm
Scottish National Gallery of Modern Art, Edinburgh

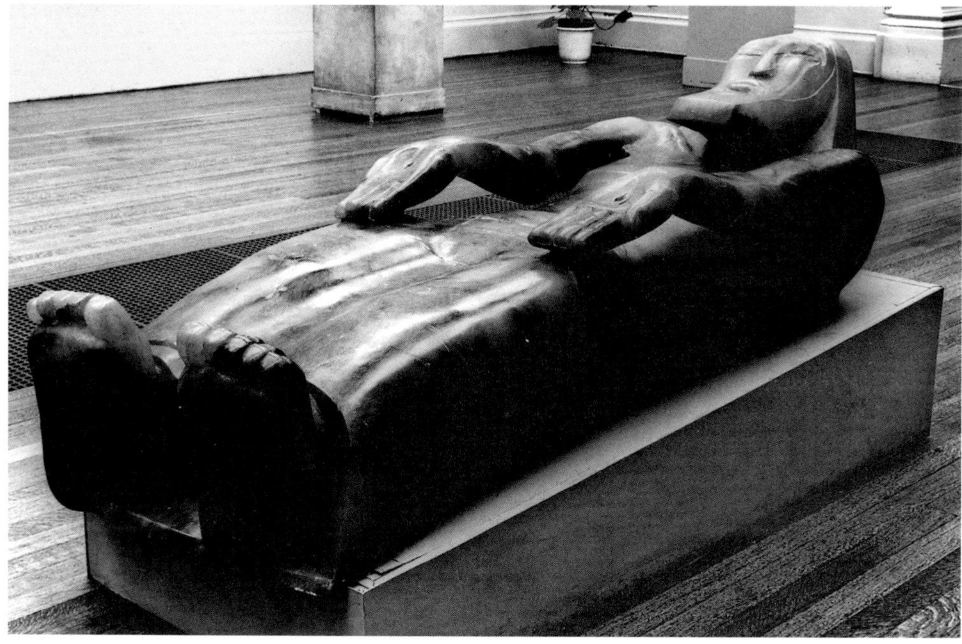

of alabaster, graduating from dark brown to light transparent yellow, gave the artist the opportunity to use the light shades for the head, bestowing on it a spiritual essence, while retaining the darker earthy ones for the legs and body. Epstein had long been interested in transparent effects: in his student days in Paris he had wished to make a sculpture in marble, "transparent so the light would glow through".[168]

Sculpting in alabaster is an old English practice: it had begun in the Middle Ages, centred in Nottingham, where a style of decoration was established that spread to France.[169] The material was widely used in English churches, darker pieces being applied to the walls and lighter pieces serving for figure sculpture, the body usually being painted, while the face and hands would be left in the natural colour of the mineral.[170] Epstein's innovation in the use of alabaster, however, was to involve all the natural colours of the stone in one sculpture.

The figure in *Consummatum Est* [47] is that of a man with a beard, uncommon in representations of Jesus. His static pose is that of a supine body with elements that indicate distress – the raised head, the extended hands exposing to the viewer the palms with the stigmata, and the flexed toes.

To this work Epstein dedicated the longest discussion in his autobiography, explaining at length the work process (176–78), from which I cite a crucial remark (177):

> The sculptor with his vision, planning, working, laying loving hands upon the willing and love-returning stone, the creation of a work, the form embodying an idea, strange copulation of spirit and matter, the intellect dominating hammer and chisel – the conception that at last becomes a piece of sculpture.

One is left to wonder whether the uncommonly long explanation given, in particular Epstein's insistence on form embodying an idea, was deliberately delivered in order to mask the influence of or similarity to a precedent by a fellow artist, whom he had begun to resent because this artist divorced forms from ideas, adopting abstraction.

168 Letter from Epstein to Ordway, 8 February 1904 NYPL; cited in I/51.

169 W. Stevenson, 'Art in Alabaster Preserved in France, Considered in its Relationship to the Nottingham School of Alabasters', *Transactions of the Thoroton Society*, vol. 11, 1907, pp. 89–98.

170 *Alabaster*, London, 14 August 1930, p. 5. The unnamed editor counts in the introduction 34 churches that used panels of this material. Twelve alabaster sculptures of the Apostles (H. 44–49.5 cm) originally destined for the church of Zamora in Spain are now at the Victoria and Albert Museum, London; see Bedford, R.P., 'An English Set of Twelve Apostles in Alabaster', *Burlington Magazine*, LXII, 1923, p. 131.

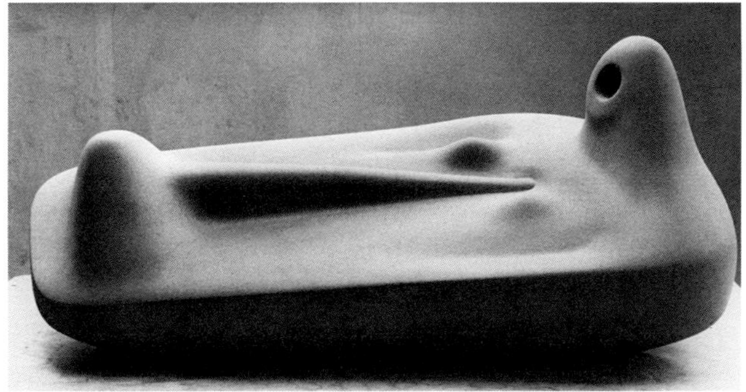

Fig. 20
Henry Moore
Reclining figure, 1934–35
Corsehill stone, 62.5 cm long
Henry Moore Foundation

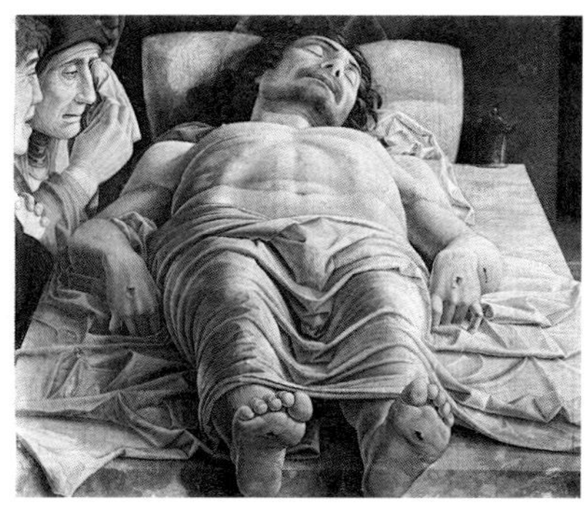

Fig. 21
Andre Mantegna
Lamentation over the Dead Christ, 1490
Tempera on canvas, 68 x 81 cm
Pinacoteca di Brera, Milan

In 1934–35 Moore created an exceptional version of his favourite subject, *Reclining figure* [fig. 20], in which, as a recent viewer has stated, the pose is a sort of universal situation any man might recognise, because "the sculpture appears to represent a man lying in a bath, his arms at his sides, staring down at his own erection".[171] Moore's figure is distinctly out of character, not only in its obvious sexual reference or in the display of a sense of humour (even in the hole in the head reflects an air of surprise) but also in the static disposition of the masses, such that the lower part of the stylized figure is entirely parallel to the floor, like a flat tablet with slightly protruding elements. His other reclining figures of this period (and later on) present what one may term Moore's mannerisms, in which there is a kind of inner movement within the masses even when they are not hollowed or separated out.[172] For a long period this carving was kept out of public notice,[173] but Epstein could have seen it in Moore's studio. There were contacts, though limited, between the two during 1935, which enabled Epstein to have some knowledge of Moore's work and his personal affairs: "It was a pleasure meeting you the other night & I hope Mrs Moore is getting better of her accident".[174] One occasion on which Epstein might have had a brief glimpse of it was when it was shown at the Leicester Galleries in November 1936.[175]

In this version of his reclining figure motif, just this once during his early years, Moore seems to have retreated from the notion of divorcing form from idea, as the work obviously does convey an idea.[176] Did Epstein grasp the opportunity to play on, or hint at, this diversion? If my theory of a connection between Moore's *Reclining Figure* and *Consummatum Est* is valid, then this is Epstein's second work in which Moore's influence may be noted (the first being the stylized curves in *Primeval Gods*; see p. 58), despite the two artists' estrangement.

An anecdote told by William Roberts may shed some light on this estrangement: when Roberts came to see one of Epstein's exhibitions of a later period, he saw Epstein "sticking the red spots that signify a sale, upon his own work. Henry Moore, who had been inspecting the exhibition, remarked as he left to Brown [proprietor of the gallery], 'Remember me to Epstein'. For me the thought of Moore being remembered to Epstein had a slight tinge of irony."[177]

Epstein's *Consummatum Est*, with its raised head and outstretched arms exposing the stigmata on the palms and lying almost on the floor, has nothing in common with St John's description of the occasion when Jesus uttered these words, on the cross, after drinking the vinegar (19: 30). Seeking a precedent in Christian art for a supine pose in

171 Searle, 'Henry Moore: Smooth Operator'.

172 The first appearance of the apple-like head with a hole was in 1933, and in 1934 Moore introduced the reclining figure as a composition of parts. See Read, *Henry Moore: Sculpture and Drawings*.

173 It originally belonged to Irina Moore and has remained in the Moore family, kept in their own secure storage. It was not presented even in the exhibition to celebrate the opening of The Henry Moore Centre for the Study of Sculpture and The Henry Moore Sculpture Gallery at the re-opening of Leeds City Art Gallery in November 1982, as the catalogue testifies.

174 Letter from Epstein to Henry Moore, 15 March 1935. The letter, as well as information in the previous and the following notes, was kindly provided by Michael Phipps, Archivist, The Henry Moore Foundation.

175 The HMF records show that "one copy of the catalogue with pencil annotations shows that item 9 is this sculpture", annotated as "Reclining Figure, Corsehill stone", without mentioning any date. However, in Herbert Read's first biography of Moore (1944), which includes a photograph of this very work, there are no other reclining figures in Corsehill stone made during these particular years of 1935–36. Three other exhibitions in this period in London that might have presented it are mentioned in Moore's list of exhibitions (Lewison, *Circle*, p. 49), but their catalogues do not indicate the presence of this particular work either. Between 1972 and 2002 it was presented in six Moore exhibitions, but only abroad. Its exposure anew in England was in London in 2008 (*Henry Moore Family Collection: Ideas for Sculpture*, Hauser & Wirth Gallery).

176 Little has been written on the work of Moore's later years, during which it obviously embodied the notion of 'idea'. One intriguing study is Kamien-Kazhdan, 'Unveiling Moore's Enigma', pp. 13–19.

177 W. Roberts: 'Dealers and Galleries: The Leicester Galleries'.

this context is therefore futile, and, though it represents a quite different moment, the closest precedent – known to both Epstein and Moore – seems to be Mantegna's painting *Lamentation over the Dead Christ* (fig. 21). Mantegna's supine Christ is viewed from the legs, and to a great extent this angle accentuates the covered penis, which attracts attention even before the viewer is aware of the motionless head and the palms facing helplessly downward. In Epstein's sculpture the living head is raised up, and the upward-facing palms are resolutely stretched out to reveal the stigmata. Both *Consummatum Est* and Moore's *Reclining Figure* seem to require viewing from the same vantage point as Mantegna's painting; however, in regard to 'idea', *Consummatum Est* has links to Mantegna's representation of Jesus's tribulations, whereas Moore's *Reclining Figure* lacks any Christian connotation.

Epstein's Christ is not merely a helpless figure; to a certain degree, I suggest, and like its maker, it questions, reproaches and probably relates to another meaning of the Latin word *consummatum* – summing up or adding up; and what is summed up, I believe, is his attitude towards Epstein and his people (178):

> The feet are weary from having trod the earth in vain, the hands with their wounds turned to the sky, the face calm with all the suffering drained away. Like the enigmatic stones of a far island that face the sea, my stone will face the sky and give no answer.

Consummatum Est and many bronze portraits were presented at the Leicester Galleries in October. Its accusatory content was clearly understood: "The sensationalism implicit in this bulk, no less than its symbolical 'content', is intimidating".[178] Epstein's summary of the opening of the exhibition was rather mild: "From the first day opinion was violently divided. As I never go to the private views and hate seeing my works in galleries surrounded by the curious, I had only reports of how it was received & for the most part I understood there was a feeling, at least, of respect";[179] but this is not what one could read the next day in most of the papers. As had been the case with *Ecce Homo*, the uneasiness and main resentment of the broad public was towards Epstein's untraditional expression of Christian iconography. "A disgusting travesty; An outrage of Christian ideas" were some of the titles cited by Epstein in his autobiography. In an unprecedented act of art criticism, *The Sunday Dispatch* sent their sports editor to review it.[180] As the alabaster was presented together with bronze portraits, the so-called respectable critics (tagged by Epstein as "sterile minds") wavered between their condemnation of Epstein's carving ("Mantegna's 'dead Christ' which might seem to bear upon the question, bears heavily the wrong way for Mr. Epstein's because it makes no attempt to embody the emotional content of the words")[181] and praise for the portraits, which caused Epstein to react: "Certainly, were I as good as these critics say, I could not possibly be as bad as they make out" (184). On the other hand, given the highly stylized features of the body, fully in accord with the notions of those whom Epstein termed "sterile minds", *Consummatum Est* is probably Epstein's most abstract carving of his later years.

Once Epstein realised that this work would never be placed in a cathedral or basilica, and since he refused to place it with an art gallery to be sold, he predicted that "Most likely for a decade or two the work will remain in my studio, to be forgotten by all save myself" (178). He was wrong; only five years later the carving was acquired by William

178 H. Gordon Porteous, *The New English Weekly*, 28 October 1937.

179 A draft of the autobiography, which, I suggest, was included in the printed book because ultimately it did not truthfully convey the lukewarm reception of the work: NAGW.

180 John Macadam, 31 October 1937; cited in Epstein, *Let There be Sculpture*, p. 180.

181 'Entertainments – Consummatum Est', *The Times*, 22 October 1937.

Cartmell, acting on behalf of the owners of the Louis Tussaud gallery in Blackpool.

Epstein's sense of exhaustion expressed in his sculpture through the image of Christ was justified by unfolding events: the world news provided little consolation. At the end of January Stalin started the second round of purge-trials in which leaders of the Communist Party were sentenced to death; on 8 June he continued with the execution of army leaders. In March Pope Pius XI published the anti-Nazi encyclical *Mit brennender Sorge* and the anti-Communist encyclical *Divini redemptoris*, condemning both totalitarian States and their ideologies. Spanish Fascism acquired in April its most renowned stigma when the German Luftwaffe destroyed the Basque town of Guernica. England's political groups were torn between the two evils, and for a while January's bleak news from Russia put the Left on a kind of hold. The coronation on 12 May 1937 of George VI (following the abdication of Edward VIII) could be seen as inducing a slight Right-wing tendency in public opinion; both royal brothers embraced Germany, reinforcing the British public's appeasement tendencies of the previous year. The Communists were not the only ones who opposed Fascism, and 1937 saw the involvement of writers and artists in anti-Fascist actions, particularly in regard to Spain. 'Save Spain' rallies were organized, the first of them as a benefit concert at the Albert Hall for the National Joint Committee for Spanish Refugees in Aid of the Basque Refugee Children's Fund, sponsored by W.H. Auden, Virginia Woolf and H.G. Wells, among others, with the programme cover designed by Pablo Picasso.

Epstein had his own personal battle to fight – a renewed attack on the MBA statues that had started immediately after George VI's coronation. Removal of some of the decorations attached to the statues had caused small pieces of the works to fall. A head was reported to have fallen, and it was alleged that a woman had been hit by it, or it had narrowly missed her. The Southern Rhodesian authorities used this as an excuse to begin demolition of the statues, and once the issue had become a matter of public safety it silenced even the Royal Fine Arts Commission, which "two years earlier gave Epstein an assurance that his works would not be removed".[182] Muirhead Bone's option, to "restore any decayed stones" (as carried out on the colleges of Oxford almost every year without obliterating the sculptures on their buildings), was rejected.[183] An interesting plea to preserve them by relocating them, a solution that had not been seriously considered by any authority, was heard from Epstein's erstwhile colleague, Eric Gill:

> I should have thought it obvious from any point of view that these statues were very beautiful works, and not from any merely studio or aesthetic point of view ... it seems to me clear they should be removed completely, however difficult and expensive such a job might be .... There are not a great number of beautiful or even interesting sculptures in London buildings, and I think the removal of these particular works in the nature of a national misfortune.[184]

I discussed this episode in my previous book (I/196–97) and the question of whether other options existed to save the statues is beyond the scope of the present one. It suffices to mention that the architect of the building, Charles Holden, stated that the Rhodesian authorities had decided that there was no other option but to remove the ailing parts of the stone, and that everything possible had been done to preserve the rest.[185] At the end of the day, Epstein's conviction was that the statues would have been better preserved

182 Letter from T.E. Earp, in *The Daily Telegraph*, 23 June 1937.

183 *The Times*, 28 June 1937.

184 Letter from Eric Gill, in *The Daily Telegraph*, 27 August 1937.

185 RIBA, AHP/26/25/1 (ii-iii).

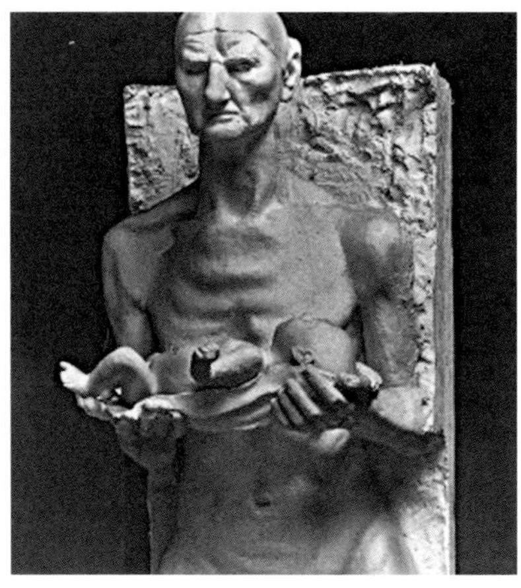

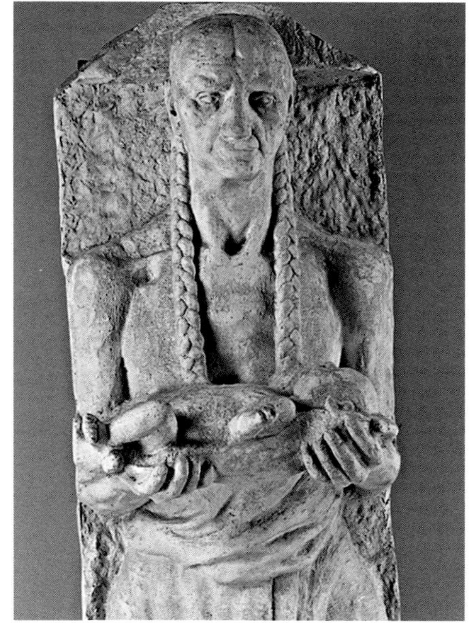

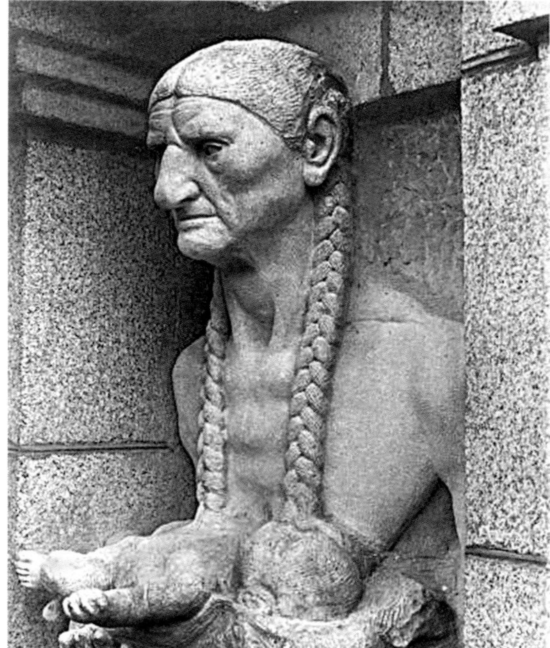

48a
Infancy, 1907–08, BMA building: preparatory plaster, 1907–08

48b
Plaster made before destruction, 1937
The Israel Museum, Jerusalem

48c
Infancy, 1907–08, BMA building: stone carving (detail), 1907–08

had he been given permission to bring his own moulders to work on precise copies instead of Bone's workers, who had made "complete travesties of the originals" (55).

He was probably right as far as making exact plaster copies of the originals was concerned, as a comparison between the three versions of *Infancy* seems to demonstrate: [48a] is the plaster made in 1907, out of which the carving (with added pigtails and skirt) had been made [48c];[186] the plaster made by Bone's moulders [48b] seems to have eliminated the fine facial details and their expression as well as other small elements.[187]

Deploring "the mutilated fragments of my [carved] decorations", while an understandable lament by their maker, is not quite the reaction of the neutral viewer: nowadays, if one stands in front of the building in the afternoon, when the sunset rays shine on it, the remains of the sculptures can be seen and perceived as beautiful antiques. The outcome of the negotiations in 1937, nonetheless, left Epstein embittered, and he seems to have cut contacts with Holden, apparently without accepting his arguments for the necessity of the treatment carried out on the decorations (I/196–97).

In Easter 1937 (falling that year in March) Epstein and Margaret with Peggy Jean visited Paris, as it had been their custom to do every year during the 1930s;[188] this was to be their last visit together before the war. While sitting in a café they were approached by Norman Hornstein, a medical student at Edinburgh University, who invited Peggy Jean to a concert. As they were leaving the next day she declined his invitation, but he followed them to London, "courting and proposing to PJ".[189] They got married in late October 1937, when Peggy Jean became eighteen. Margaret was ecstatic with happiness and relief: "She took all my time up from Jackie & Hubby. Now I have a new son to look after her half & half. We are partners in it."[190] Some of Margaret's wishes for her daughter while she was still in her wild phase had now come true at last; and while expressing these wishes she expressed the credo by which she herself lived:

186 See also I/80.

187 This plaster and also that of *Maternity* were donated by Kathleen to the Israel Museum, Jerusalem. See http://www.imj.org.il/imagine/collections/results.asp?searchType=simple&words=epstein&ArtistE=on.

188 Peggy Jean in a recorded interview with Judy Collins, 6 July 1987: TGA – TAV 479A.

189 Peggy Jean's daughter Leda Sloat summing up their meeting: correspondence with the author, 27 March 2011.

[opposite page]

190 Letter from Margaret to Sylvia, 13 October 1937; cited in Babson, *The Epsteins*, p. 49.

191 Letter from Margaret to Sylvia, August 1936; cited in Babson, *The Epsteins*, p. 44.

192 Letter from Margaret to Sylvia, 13 October 1937; cited in Babson, *The Epsteins*, p. 49.

193 Letter from Leda, Norman's daughter, to the author.

Some day PJ should get married of course. Perhaps some nice Doctor, Jewish-Scot or Jewish or Scot, who would understand her & then she would be heroically good. She would be happy with children I think. Once she gets over the all for enjoyment-period & see that the unselfish life is the life of great happiness come what may.[191]

Part of the attraction that Norman held for the Epsteins, and in particular for Margaret, was his socialist tendencies; writing to Aunt Sylvia, Margaret admits that "at first I was afraid he was too beautiful, but Communism has been his religion and that has kept him good I think … he is the only one of PJ's admirers that Epstein really liked."[192] Epstein made a portrait of his son-in-law, entitled *Young Communist*, a title that later caused Norman a lot of trouble in McCarthy's America.[193] At the outbreak of war Norman joined the Army. Peggy Jean already had two children by then. One day, after taking the children for a visit to the hospital in which their father was serving, upon returning she found that their home had been bombed by the Germans. She therefore moved with the children to live with the Epsteins, and her sculptor father was able to do their portraits.

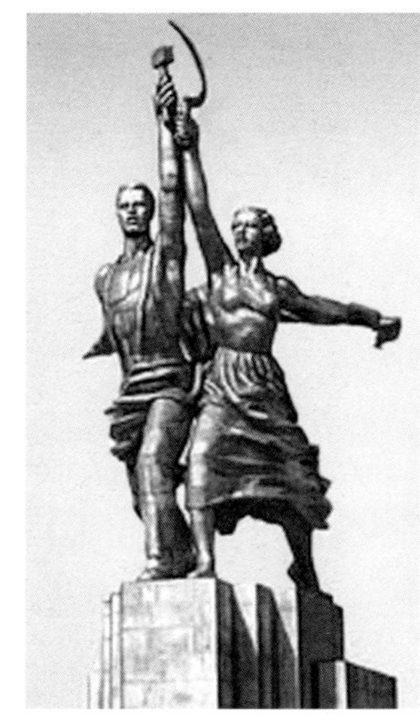

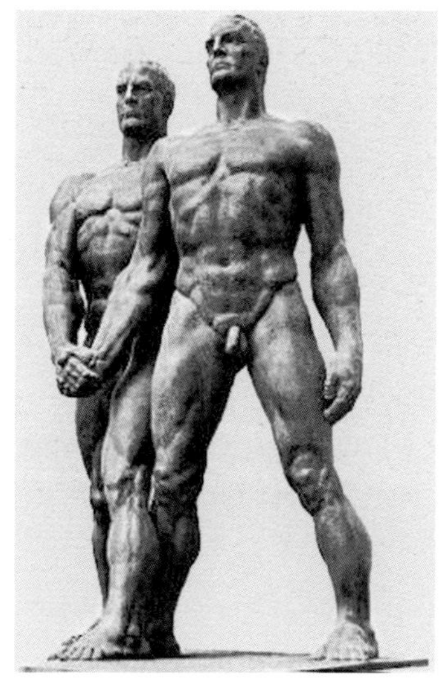

Fig. 22
Vera Mukhina
Energy in Movement, 1937
For the Russian Pavilion, Paris
Stainless steel, H. 2.40 m

Fig. 23
Josef Thorak
Comradeship, 1937
For the German Pavilion, Paris

How much of the public's attention had the BMA controversy that had so deeply wounded Epstein occupied? Probably not as much as the news about the marriage of the Duke of Windsor (formerly Edward VIII) to Mrs Wallis Warfield Simpson in France on 3 June. The couple may have arrived in the country beforehand, mingling with the visitors at the opening of the Paris Exhibition (25 May–25 November 1937), which boasted 38 rival displays – many of them making political statements by advertising the virtues of their art and 'way of life' to the 31.2 million visitors.

As the exhibition was taking place during the Spanish Civil War, the Spanish Pavilion attracted much attention. The pavilion, set up by the Republican government, displayed Pablo Picasso's famous painting *Guernica* – a depiction of the horrors of war, in commemoration of the bombing of the Spanish town of Guernica on 26 April that year. The main architectural attractions, however, were the German and Soviet Pavilions set up on either side of the Eiffel Tower, both huge and deliberately symbolic, and both presenting symbolic sculpture.

The Soviet pavilion was crowned with a sculpture by Vera Mukhina (fig. 22). It represented "energy in movement" – man and woman charging ahead, united in their drive towards a target – and later became a national symbol. It was executed along naturalistic lines, stylized mainly in the lower part of the garments.

There were two groups of sculptures at the entrance to the main hall of the German Pavilion, each 7 m tall; the one most relevant, entitled *Comradeship*, represented two nude men in neo-classical style executed by the sculptor Josef Thorak (fig. 23). The proportions were grossly exaggerated at the thighs and chest in order to convey power and strength rather than classical beauty; such exaggeration of the classical had become a characteristic of most Nazi art and architecture.

Unlike Mukhina's sculpture, which conveyed motion, Thorak's figures were static – no movement in the firm and intimidating German stand. It would be a matter of

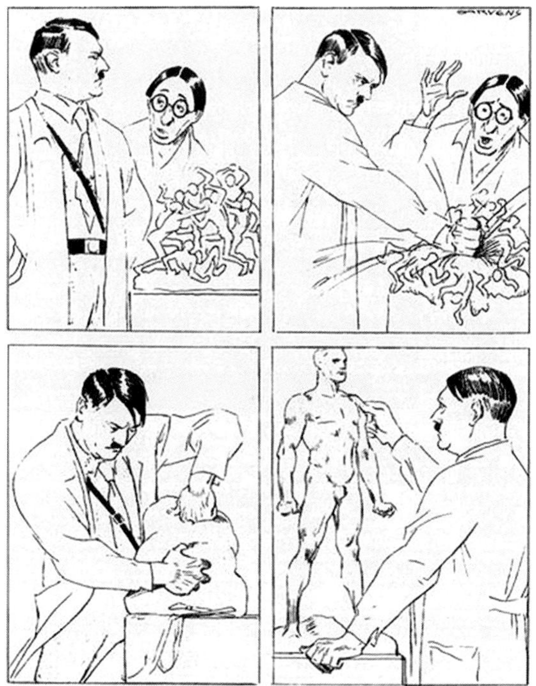

Fig. 24
O. Gravens
Der bildhauer Deutschland; Kladderadatsch, 49, 1933, p. 7

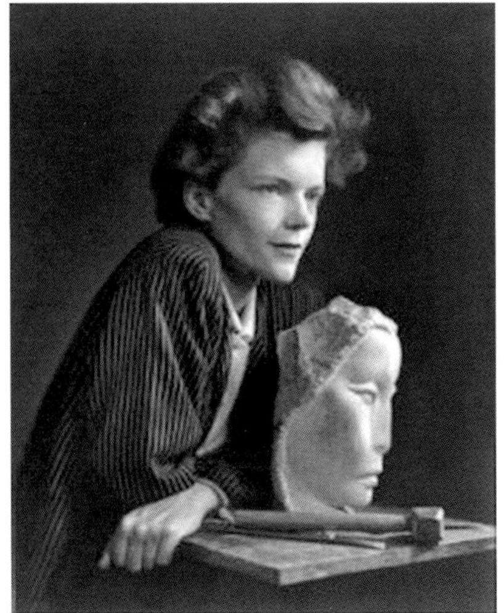

Fig. 25
Sally F. Ryan
NAGW archive

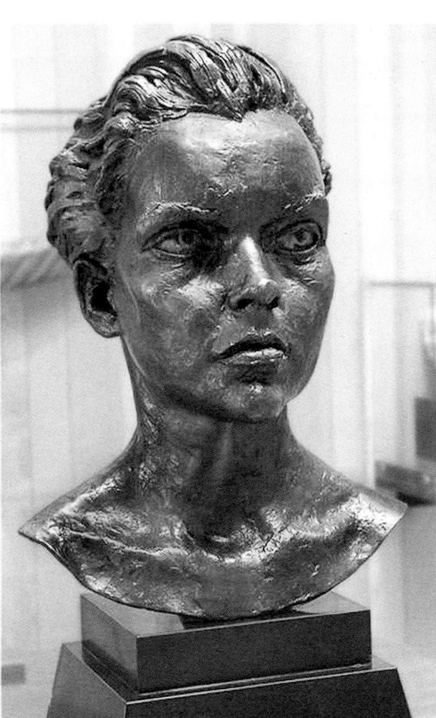

49a
Sally Ryan, 1937
Bronze, H. 39 cm
GREC-NAGW

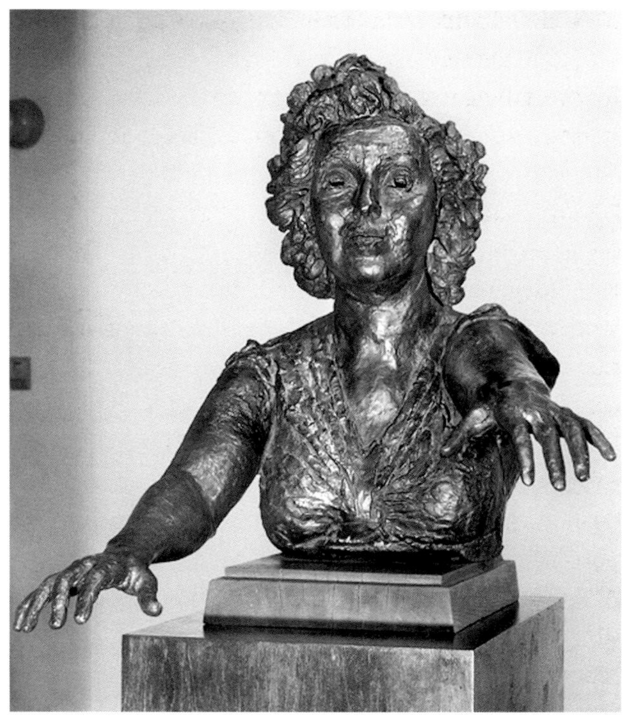

49b
Ellen Ballon, pianist, 1938
Bronze, 66 x 58.4 x 72.8 cm
Dalhousie University Art Gallery, Halifax, Canada

debate, which of these two conceptions more effectively expressed comradeship, and what in particular was expressed in the German one. Thorak's figures seem to mirror the Nazi ideal of manhood, as expressed in a propaganda drawing – the leader moulding a great heroic figure (similar to those in the sculpture) out of his weak multitude of small people (fig. 24).

Both projects, German and Soviet, are relevant because they seem to have left an impression on Epstein, who might have been with Margaret in Paris during the exhibition. If unable to see them *in situ*, he no doubt saw photographs of them. The impression they left on him, I suggest, would become evident in his work later on.

Some time in 1937 the twenty-one-year-old American sculptor Sally F. Ryan (fig. 25) arrived in England with her companion, the Canadian pianist Ellen Ballon (1898–1969), and commissioned a portrait of herself from Epstein. She was the granddaughter of Thomas Fortune Ryan, a highly successful entrepreneur and patron of the arts, a member of the circle of the young Epstein's benefactor Ordway, and also that of his supporter during the 1910s John Quinn. Her route to Epstein might alternatively have been through Kathleen's Canadian companion Beth Lipkin, a piano player too (see p. 76). Epstein hardly ever flattered his sitters by trying to make them look more pleasing than they were or regarded themselves to be. However, I find in Sally's portrait [49a], which successfully projects her inner strength, a subtle treatment of her jaw that minimizes the impression of her very elongated chin and thus gives her a more pleasant appearance. She liked her portrait and ordered one also of Ellen, whom Epstein depicted in a bust with arms outstretched, as if she were playing the piano [49b].[194] Although not a pupil of his,[195] Ryan became more than a client – a family friend, a buyer of his work who hosted him at her home when he visited New York, and in later years collaborated with

194 Silber, *Sculpture of Epstein*, no. 294. Ballon eventually settled in Canada.

195 As suggested by Rose, *Demons and Angels*, p. 212. Another one suggested to be "his only pupil" is Astrid Zidower (Buckle, *Epstein: Sculptor*, p. 6), whom Buckle recommended for the making of the statue of Orpheus that now sits on the terrace at Harewood. Epstein, as Beth Lipkin testified to the author, had no pupils.

his widow Kathleen in establishing the Garman-Ryan Collection. The collection is now settled in the New Art Gallery–Walsall, which has become an important research centre for everything to do with Epstein. The three foreign women left England when the war started, each to their own homes in Canada and the States.

Hardly a month after their display of grandeur at the world exhibition, the Nazi regime organized a tour of exhibitions of modern art around Germany, under the title *Entartete Kunst* (degenerate art), consisting of works by modernist artists, many of them Jewish, who had flourished during the Weimar Republic (1919–33) and had been expelled or had fled between 1933 and 1935 (see p. 62). In all, twenty-two such local exhibitions were organized between 1933 and July 1937, culminating on 19 July with a national show in Munich,[196] in which a single photograph placed in the middle of the show served as an example of ideal German art and beauty – surrounded by what was regarded as modern trash. It presented Uta von Naumburg (fig. 26), one of the thirteenth-century dynastic portrait sculptures in the west choir of Naumburg Cathedral, as the prototype of the Aryan woman, a Teutonic Madonna.[197] Comparisons between representational art of the past and modern stylized – not to mention abstract – art had become a common practice of denigrators of the latter. The classic beauty of Uta's image resonated particularly among the Right wing that regarded the avant-garde as a Jewish plot against European culture. An irony of the Entartete Kunst affair was that the works condemned as degenerate and removed from German museums were then auctioned during 1939 at the Fisher Gallery in Lucerne. The first auction, on 30 June 1939, was accompanied by a catalogue of 125 items in which the works previously declared as worthless by the Nazis were lauded by the gallery in order to obtain the best possible price for them. Works by Gauguin, Van Gogh and Picasso were among those sold, most of them to American buyers.[198]

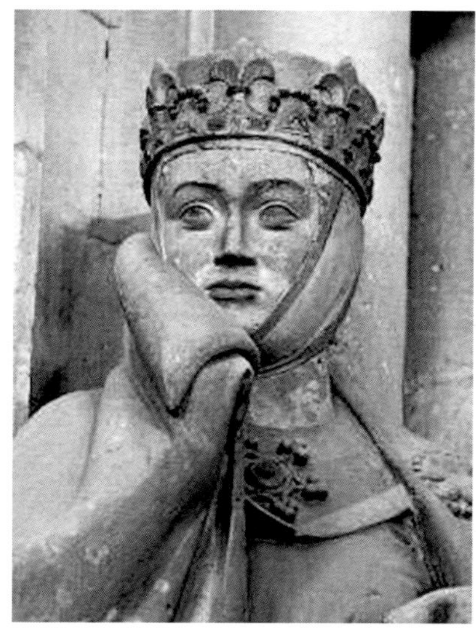

Fig. 26
Uta von Naumburg
Stone, life size
Sts Peter and Paul Cathedral, Naumburg

For those who did not see this exhibition during 1937, or had not drawn the 'correct' conclusion regarding what constituted 'degenerate', the publishing house of the Nazi Party produced *The Eternal Jew*,[199] a book of 265 photographs representing Jews in as unpleasant a manner as possible. On page 51, with the caption 'Neanderthal art', Epstein was shown, with the comment:

> In sculpture even more than painting, Jews display their absolute lack of talent. To get the attention that their vanity demands, they turn primitive. Here, Jacob Epstein-London looks thoughtfully at his disgusting work of a pregnant idiot (1931), which he calls 'Genesis' (birth).

The book commented on every famous Jewish or allegedly Jewish figure in cultural life. Thus the entry 'Charlie Chaplin' (pp. 67–68) stated that "the Galician Charlie Chaplin (whose mother was born Thonstein) emigrated to America .... The slapstick gang of this flat-footed, clumsy, impoverished yet eternally generous man with the huge shoes was a sensation for the non-Jews." The apparently non-Jewish Chaplin, who never made the slightest attempt to deny or approve the rumour of his Jewishness, responded in 1940 with his ingenious film *The Great Dictator*, playing in it the part of a Jew.

The reaction in England against Germany's attitude to modern art found its voice in 1938, when Ewan Phillips of Leicester Galleries (Epstein's main gallery) became involved

196 Clinefelter, *Artists for the Reich*, p. 68.

197 In the 1920s, local photographer Walter Hege photographed the twelve figures (in the Sts Peter and Paul Cathedral, also known as the Naumburger Dom, in Naumburg), concentrating on Uta in perfectly lit photographs. The photos were widely published, and Uta became a national idol, an icon. She is considered an outstanding female figure in the art world, placed by some art connoisseurs on the same level as Egypt's ancient Queen Nefertiti, Botticelli's *Venus* or da Vinci's *Mona Lisa*. Walt Disney used her as the model for the beautiful but sinister queen in his film *Snow White and the Seven Dwarfs* in 1937.

198 Karl Shwartz (the last director of the Jewish Museum in Berlin); a summation of the affair taken from the archive of *Ha'aretz*, Tel Aviv.

199 Diebow, *Der Ewige Jude*.

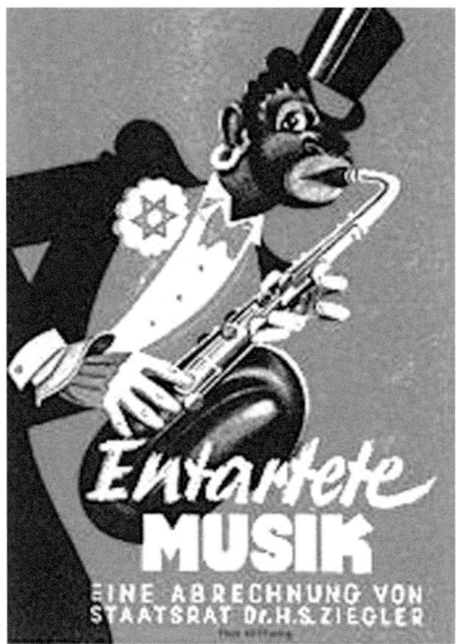

Fig. 27
Poster for the 'Degenerate Music' exhibition, Düsseldorf, May 1938

in an exhibition of contemporary modernist German art at the New Burlington Galleries organized by Herbert Read and Roland Penrose, countering Hitler's 'Entartete Kunst' exhibition in Germany.

A further step in the attack on Jewish creativity was taken in a week-long event in Düsseldorf, 22–29 May 1938. Concerts and lectures presented ideologically and ethnically 'pure' music on the one hand, while 'degenerate' music exhibits accompanied them from 24 May (fig. 27). The music condemned as 'degenerate' included works featuring Jewish or African characters or by composers of Marxist persuasion or of Jewish origin, including some well established in the classical canon such as Felix Mendelssohn, Gustav Mahler and Paul Hindemith, as well as avantgarde composers – Arnold Schoenberg, Alban Berg and Anton Webern, even Kurt Weill because he had been influenced by jazz music, which was considered degenerate because of its roots in Afro-American culture.[200] I have found no sign, however, of a reaction from the British music world of the time to 'degenerate' music.[201]

In politics, what is more, the official response to events was one of acceptance. In November, Britain's Minister of Foreign Affairs, Lord Halifax, visited Germany, initiating an official policy of appeasement,[202] attempting to feed the monster lest war break out; Mosley's political ideas had temporarily gained the upper hand.

An echo of a past relationship occurred in April 1938 with the retirement of J.B. Manson, who had worked in the Tate Gallery for 25 years, and been its director for eight. During the years of Manson's directorship, when British art was acquiring a considerable force and world status, the Tate eschewed the acquisition of modern art for its collections – that of Picasso or the Vorticists, or even Moore's work. Relations between Manson and Epstein, since their Parisian period (I/46), and mutual participation in The Camden Town Group, had deteriorated, and Manson's hostility to Epstein's stylized work had meant that no piece by him had been acquired by the Tate.[203] It was quite a while before Epstein softened towards him and, whether because he needed to exhibit during the war years or for old time's sake, he consented to partake in a joint exhibition with Manson (by then disgraced and alcoholic) and John Craxton (Leicester Galleries, 1944).

Other events of the period that may have captured the culture-loving Epstein's interest were Paul Hindemith and Leonide Massine's ballet premiere in London in July, and in October a prophetic event that foretold our more recent era of brainwashing media in which reality acquires a virtual dimension: Orson Welles drove almost an entire nation into panic with his radio broadcast of H.G. Wells's *War of the Worlds*.

LES FLEURS DU MAL

During 1938 Epstein produced an astonishing collection of drawings of his son Jackie, then about four years old [50]. The capturing of the "fugitive and endless expressions and changes of movement has been a rare experience", to which Epstein dedicated a whole paragraph in his autobiography (204–05). "It is the life, free, careless and apprehensive at the same time, of the little boy with his lively eyes, and his also expressive hands in their infinite and unconscious gestures that I wish to capture." These feelings

200 Though American swing music was filled with immoral, sexually related themes, behind the scenes Joseph Goebbels and his Propaganda Ministry created one of the swing era's most improbable jazz bands, Charlie and his Orchestra, led by Karl (Charlie) Schwedler and consisting of some of Europe's finest jazz musicians.

201 At the time, composer Béla Bartok considered the label 'Degenerate Music' as honourable, and in 1938 courageously demanded that the Nazi government should include his own compositions in the Düsseldorf exhibition. It took England's musical world half a century to recognize the value of those banned musicians, when the Decca Record Company set out to record its *Entartete Musik* project, restoring music by composers suppressed by the Nazis and since forgotten. See http://www.deccaclassics.com/series/prod_series?ID=ENTMUS.

202 The term is applied to the foreign policy of British Prime Minister Neville Chamberlain towards Nazi Germany between 1937 and 1939, judging this policy either to be condemned for allowing Hitler to grow too strong or accepted as a realisation that he had no alternative and acted in Britain's best interests.

203 Only the more naturalistic bronze *Visitation* (1925) had been in the Tate, presented by the Contemporary Art Society in 1927. Epstein commented on Manson in regard to *Genesis* in a letter to Moore of March 1931 (see p. 47).

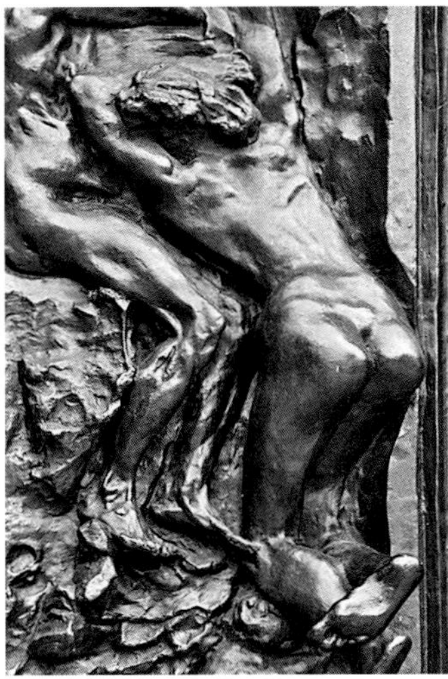
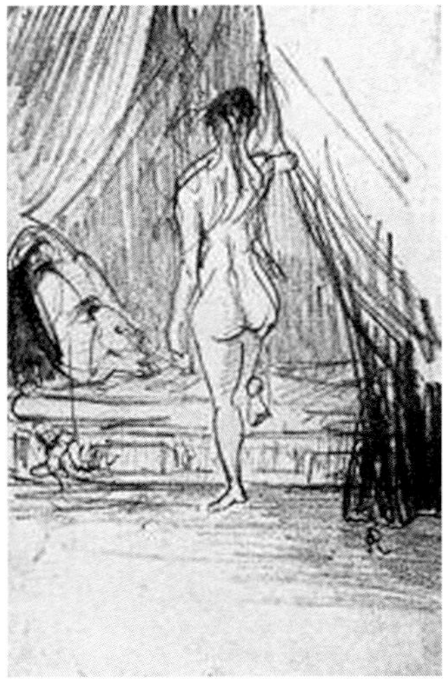
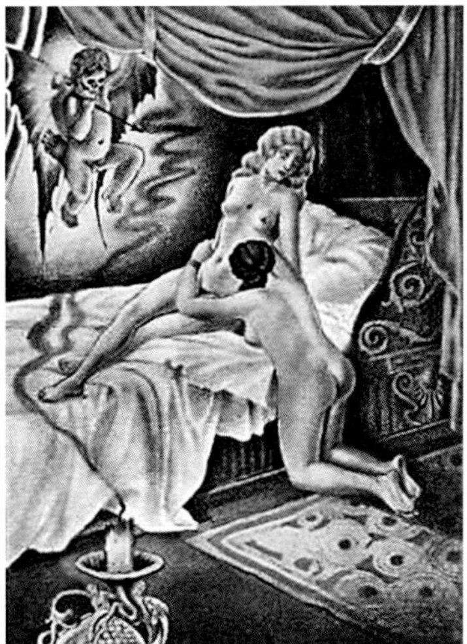
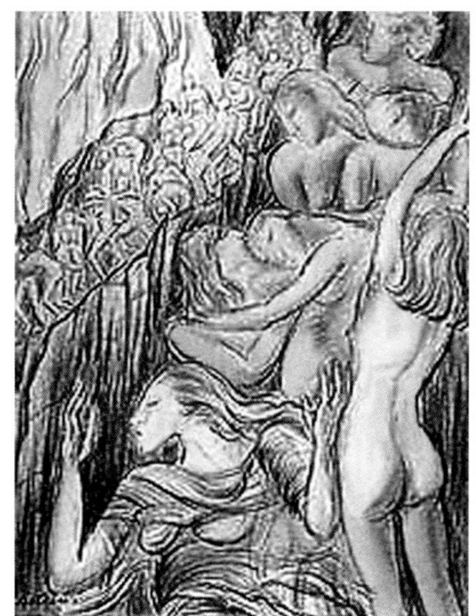

Fig. 28
Auguste Rodin
The Gates of Hell (detail), late 1890s
Kunsthaus, Zurich

Fig. 29
Illustrations for a passage in Baudelaire's *Fleurs du Mal*

a. Odilon Redon, 1890 edn, 219 x 154 mm
Carlton Lake Collection (Texas University)

b. Carlo Farneti, 1935 edn, Gibert Jeune, Librairie d'Amateurs

c. Jacob Epstein, *Damned Women*, pencil on paper, 570 x 450 mm, private collection

about the little boy to which he gave expression he summed up as "a period in my life, and [I was able to] mark out, through drawings, a plastic expression I am proud of". This optimism even infiltrated one of his otherwise sombre illustrations for a new English translation of Baudelaire's *Fleurs du Mal*, a commission undertaken in 1936 (see p. 92). "I believe only six or seven drawings were wanted, but ... I found the subject so absorbing I made sixty drawings" (188).

The published book included 22 drawings, and 37 were presented at an exhibition in December, with citations from the poems accompanying most of them. In the catalogue, for which Epstein wrote an introduction, 'Hommage à Baudelaire', he made a point of clarifying that the illustrations that had been done by others – stressing seductive mulattos, exotic negresses and "nostalgic eldorados" – did not altogether sum up Baudelaire. He, on the other hand, had been haunted "by the images of revolt, anguish and despair – disgust with the world and self" expressed in the poems. It was these dark sensations rather than eroticism and sensuality that ignited Epstein's imagination "to evoke upon paper this profound drama .... Man caught in the snare of sinful existence [and seeking] to escape '*la conscience dans le* MAL'". To a great extent these feelings characterized his response to the political and social upheaval of the period in which the drawings were done.

A comparison between Epstein's dramatic illustrations and others by other artists can be epitomized by surveying some varying treatments of a common theme, one explored influentially by Rodin in his *Damned Women* on the *Gates of Hell* in the late nineteenth century[204] – two naked women, one viewed from behind (fig. 28) – with its lesbian connotations. I illustrate Odilon Redon's drawn 'interpretation' (not an illustration) of 1889 (fig. 29a);[205] an edition published in Paris in 1935, in colour (fig. 29b); and Epstein's drawing (fig. 29c) of 1938, on which he remarked: "My technique [turning out somewhat like a lithograph] is justified by the austere and measured form of the poems".

How much of himself did Epstein invest in his drawings for *Les Fleurs du Mal?* From among Baudelaire's approximately 180 poems, he illustrated sixty, "solely to satisfy a craving of my own"; some of the choices, I suggest, hint at a personal response to "this Bible of the modern man", filled with "powerful and subtle images ... with splendid

204 The sculptural project was commissioned in 1880 and was meant to be delivered in 1885. Rodin would continue to work on and off on this project for 37 years, until his death in 1917.

205 One of nine small drawings, first exhibited at the Salon des XX in February 1890.

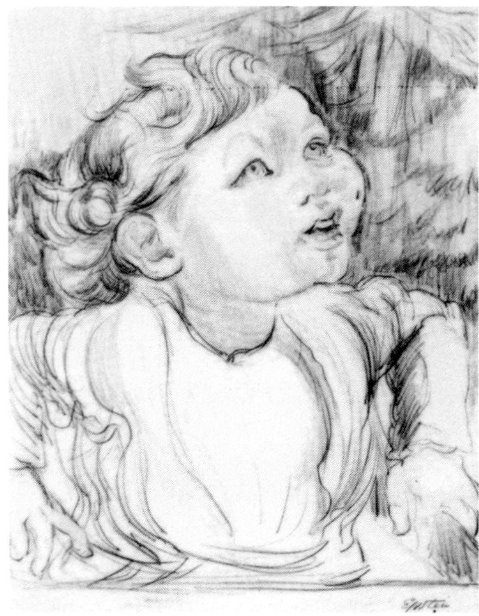

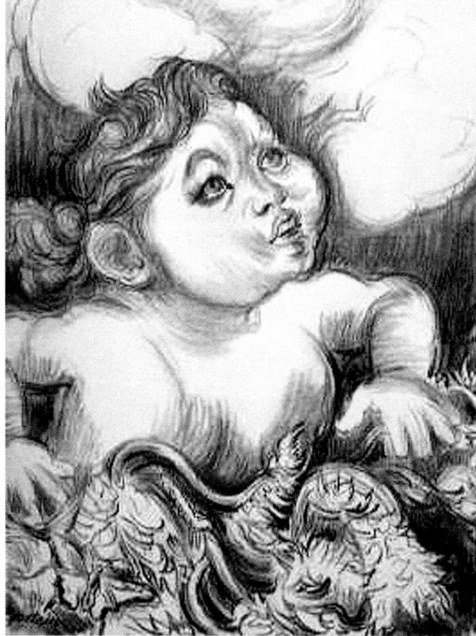

50
Jackie, 2nd portrait [about four years old], 1938
Pencil on paper, 570 x 430 mm
Private collection

51a
Illustration to Baudelaire, *Flowers of Evil*, 1938: *Bénédiction*
Pencil on paper, 570 x 450 mm
Private collection

and maleficent entities".[206] A full discussion on the artist and the poet is beyond the scope of this book, but one cannot avoid noting a crucial difference between the two personalities involved: in spite of being attracted to women, Baudelaire hated and mistrusted them and never attached himself completely to any one; Epstein, on the other hand, had been unashamedly attracted to two of his models, and deeply attached to two women – his first wife and his lover who later became his second wife – entrusting his life into their hands. I have selected among his illustrations for Baudelaire's poems those I regard as biographically important.

In one drawing, the artist seems to relate only to two stanzas in the long and complex poem 'Bénédiction', which describes the blessings thrust upon a little boy by an unseen angel. Epstein depicted an image of a baby boy with shining eyes who resembles his own son Jackie [50], regarded by him as a blessing, and merely nods to Baudelaire's acidic text by adding a snake-like flower close to the child's bosom as a symbol of the troubles that await him [51a]. Despite Epstein's depiction of the '*mal*' hidden among flora, in all probability his loving attitude to a boy would have never been espoused by Baudelaire. In this case, it seems, the artist preferred his own feelings over those of the poet.

Continuing with the subject of 'damned women' mentioned above, some of Epstein's choices among Baudelaire's poems referring to lesbian relationships seem to correspond to his personal interests. The illustration for 'Madrigal Triste' [51b] shows two figures. The one in the background has Kathleen's hair-style and slanted tearful eyes set within a dark aura, by contrast to the illumined aura she has in a drawing of 1929 (when she was pregnant with their third child), given to her as a token of love [52].[207] The first lines of this poem seem to echo Epstein's understanding of her distress and the state of affairs between them:

> *Sois Belle! Et sois triste! Les pleurs*
> *Ajoutent un charme au visage*
> Be beautiful! And be sad! The tears / Add a charm to the face.[208]

Women's relationships with other women was an issue that in all probability became relevant to Epstein's life through the crisis of Kathleen's response to Jackie's existence in 1935 (p. 85), leading to a stressful atmosphere that would have contributed to his wish, expressed in 1936, to escape as much as possible to Deerhurst (p. 93). The friendship between Kathleen and Beth Lipkin grew stronger, as did her friendship with Sally Ryan and Sally's companion Eileen in the period during which these drawings were in gestation, in 1936–37. These relationships introduced into Epstein's life an ingredient of sisterhood for which, as time passed, he seems to have developed a tolerance; at any rate it

206 Citations from the introduction Epstein wrote to the exhibition of the drawings; the book, Baudelaire, *Flowers of Evil*, was published in 1940.

207 Epstein and Buckle, *Epstein Drawings*, no. 48.

208 English translation of all Baudelaire's verse cited here and further on are by William Aggeler (*The Flowers of Evil*). See also http://fleursdumal.org/poem/190.

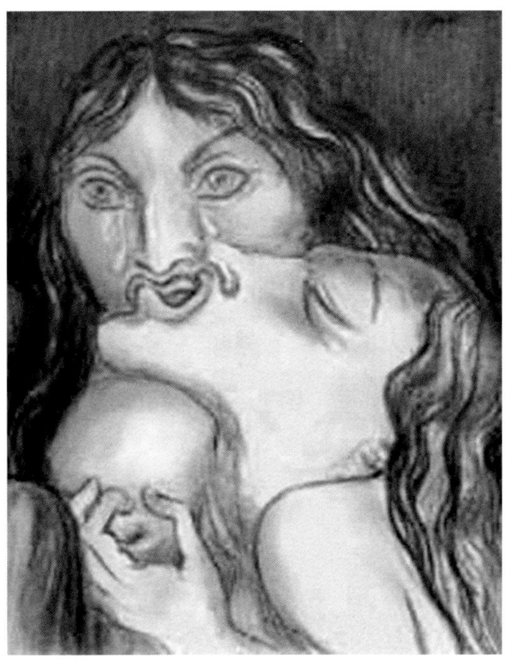

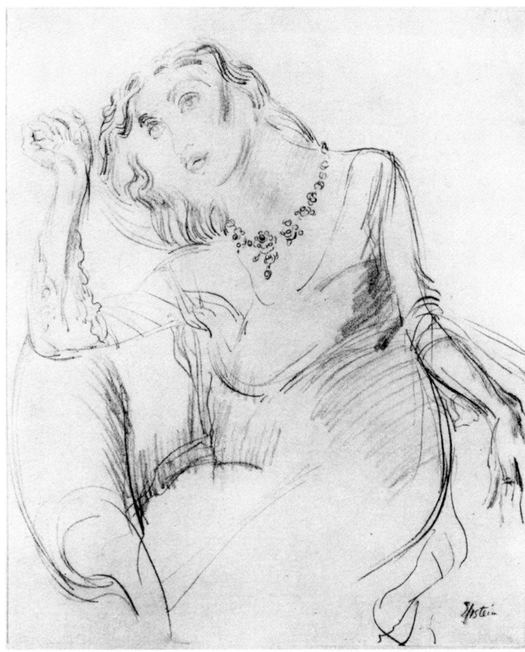

51b
Illustration to Baudelaire, *Flowers of Evil*, 1938, *Madrigal Triste*
Private collection

52
Kathleen [1929]
Pencil, 686 x 553 mm
GREC-NAGW

did not diminish Kathleen's attachment and devotion to him. Moreover, knowing the reason for her distress, which he could find beautifully expressed in 'Madrigal Triste' –

> *Quand ton cœur dans l'horreur se noie;*
> *Quand sur ton présent se déploie*
> *Le nuage affreux du passé*
> When your heart is drowned in horror / When there spreads out over your present / the frightful cloud of the past

– he may have realised that this sisterhood provided her with a kind of consolation.

Public reception of the drawings was not favourable when they were presented at the Tooth Gallery in December 1938,[209] as their dark mood and the images of "revolt, anguish and despair, disgust with the world and self" did not appeal to an audience that during the same year had witnessed their own world being turned upside down. In March, Nazi Germany had invaded Austria (the *Anschluss*), and during April Hitler demanded self-determination for the Sudeten Germans in Czechoslovakia; British Prime Minister Neville Chamberlain's visit to Hitler's mountain resort at Berchtesgaden resulted in the Munich Agreement (signed in the early hours of 30 September 1938) that forced Czechoslovakia to surrender territory to Germany. On the same day, returning to England, Chamberlain delivered a speech claiming that the agreement would bring "peace for our time" (misquoting the phrase "peace in our time" from *The Book of Common Prayer*, which also Disraeli had echoed when returning from the Congress of Berlin in 1878).[210] Chamberlain's policy was applauded at the time; he was even nominated in February 1939 for the Nobel Peace Prize (triggering Erik Brandt, a member of the Swedish parliament, to submit the nomination of Adolf Hitler, although, apparently under mild pressure, he retracted it after a few days).[211] In November Europe reverberated with the

209 Epstein (*Let There Be Sculpture*, p. 209), cites several critics, among them only one positive one.

210 Disraeli stated "I have returned from Germany with peace in our time".

211 Hitler's nomination and Brandt's retraction were discovered when the list of past nominations was released; see http://nobelprize.org/nomination/peace/database.html.

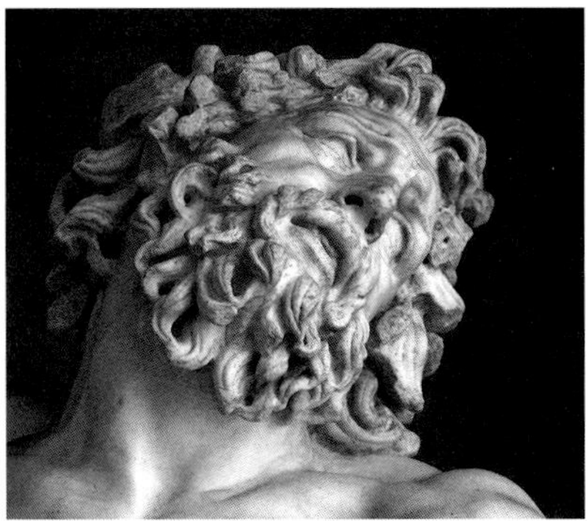

Fig. 30
Attributed to Hagesander, Athenodorus and Polydorus
Laocoön and his Sons (detail), 25 BC
White marble, life-size
Vatican Museums, Museo Pio-Clementino

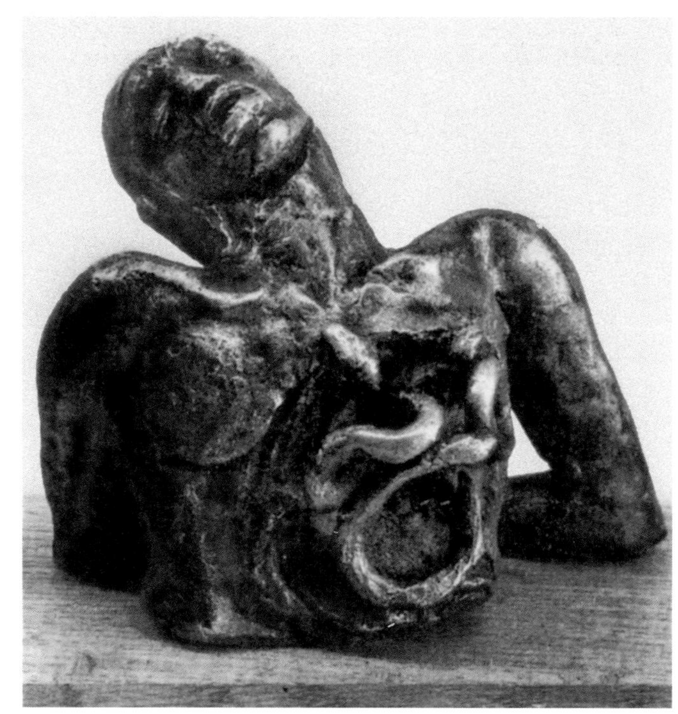

53
Le Serpent au Coeur (L'homme aux serpents), 1938–39?
Bronze, H. 10.9 cm
Private collection

smashing of shop windows belonging to Jews and the burning of synagogues, during Germany's *Kristallnacht*.

One might say, therefore, that when Epstein's Baudelaire exhibition was presented to the public in December, it had very few flowers with which to console its viewers, who found in Epstein's drawings too much of the *Mal*. His attempts "to represent the spiritual, religious, and ecstatic sense of the poems with their tragic and sombre shades" might have been successful artistically, but were – alas – unwanted. Criticism of the drawings centred on the distortion of bodies and faces, the nakedness and the disturbing eroticism, with more than a tinge of cruelty – no wonder that Epstein considered his drawings for Baudelaire "at the same time, amongst my best work and my greatest failure ... from the point of view of any intelligent appreciation" (188). To counterbalance one virulent critique of the whole series and its "misshapen females, sometimes decapitated, always repellent",[212] I cite a more intelligent contemporary appreciation:

> Epstein, more than any other contemporary sculptor, has been accused of insincerity and unnecessary distortion [of the figure], but comparing his drawings with, say, one of Rubens, even those who fail to understand his sculpture, must realise that there is no very great gulf in draughtsmanship between these two masters.[213]

The poems that had inspired Rodin to sculpture the 'damned women' motif in *Gates of Hell* apparently did not inspire Epstein to do any great sculptural work, other than one interesting small maquette entitled *L'homme aux serpents* [53], "a work thought [to be] related to the drawings".[214] The title may indicate a legendary figure such as the Trojan priest Laocoön, who was strangled by sea snakes because he tried to warn the citizens of Troy of the danger of letting in the wooden horse. The figure in Epstein's small

212 P. Jeanneret, *The Daily Mail*, cited in full in Epstein, *Let There Be Sculpture*, pp. 190–91.

213 Macnab, 'The Artist's Approach to Figure Drawing' (*The Studio*, 1939) p. 94.

214 Silber, *Sculpture of Epstein*, no. 299. I could not find a relation to such a subject among Baudelaire's poems mentioning snakes. There is only one copy of the maquette (whereabouts unknown).

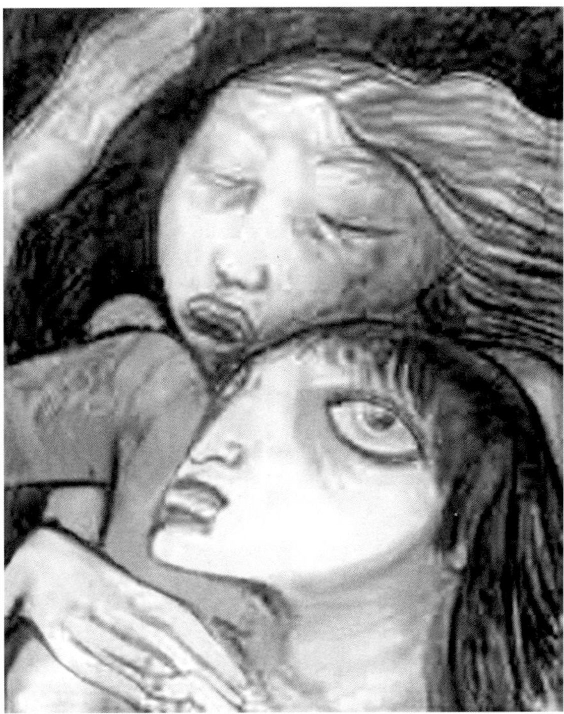

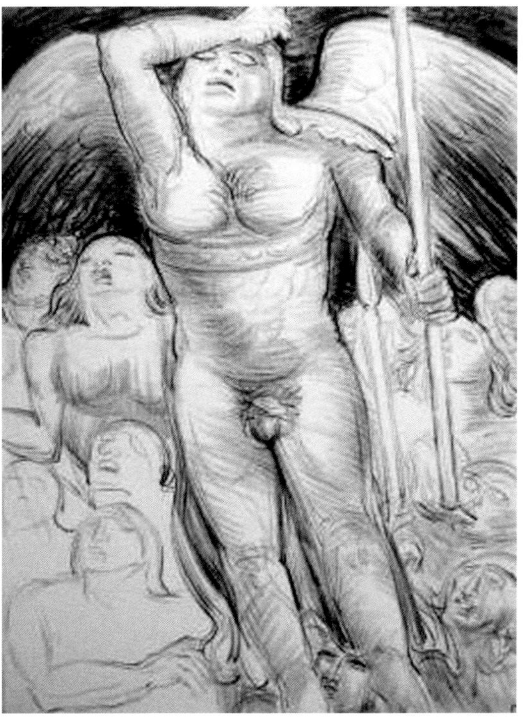

51c
Cain and Abel
Illustration for Baudelaire, *Flowers of Evil*, 1938 (not included in the book)
Private collection

51d
Cain's Ascension
Illustration from Baudelaire, *Flowers of Evil*, 1938

maquette echoes the neck and head movement and the relatively small opening of the mouth (described in the literature as screaming) of the Vatican's famous Roman group, *Laocoön and His Sons* (fig. 30).[215] Epstein's positioning of the snakes in a hole in the chest, where the figure's heart should have been, leaves one to wonder whether he intended to represent a personal state or, as befitted the period, a warning about humanity's prospects of letting 'snakes' into its midst.

Some of Epstein's illustrations for Baudelaire's 'Caïn et Abel' seem to have led on to several small maquettes and a large sculpture. In the catalogue of the Baudelaire exhibition Epstein cited only the poem's first lines:

> *Race d'Abel, dors, bois et mange;*
> *Dieu te sourit complaisamment.*
> Race of Abel, sleep, eat and drink; / God smiles on you complacently.

Among Epstein's many drawings for *Les Fleurs du Mal* there are two illustrations that may correspond to the subject of Cain and Abel (there is no record of this subject being among his 1931 illustrations of the Old Testament). The one with two figures, dark-haired and light-haired [51c], was not included in the edition. One may suppose that Epstein was seeking a way to warn against fratricide, both in the contrast between dark and fair and the hand positioned close to the throat.

Baudelaire's poem has two parts: the first conveys a positive attitude toward Abel and a harsh one toward Cain; in the second part, after Abel's death by "a pike", Cain – the lighter figure, as emanates from the following drawing that was included in the book – is regarded as the bearer of the future, and the poem ends with his task:

215 The interest of this sculpture (for theories of art on differences in representations of the same subject in classical art and literature) derives from the fact that in Virgil's second book of *The Aeneid* Laocoön is described as screaming terribly while he is being strangled, whereas his mouth in the sculpture is not opened wide enough for this to be the case. See http://www.victorianweb.org/art/illustration/beardsley/petracca.html

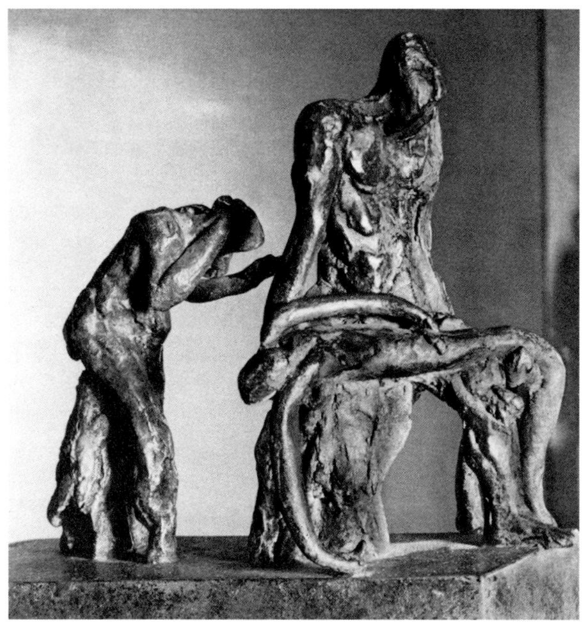

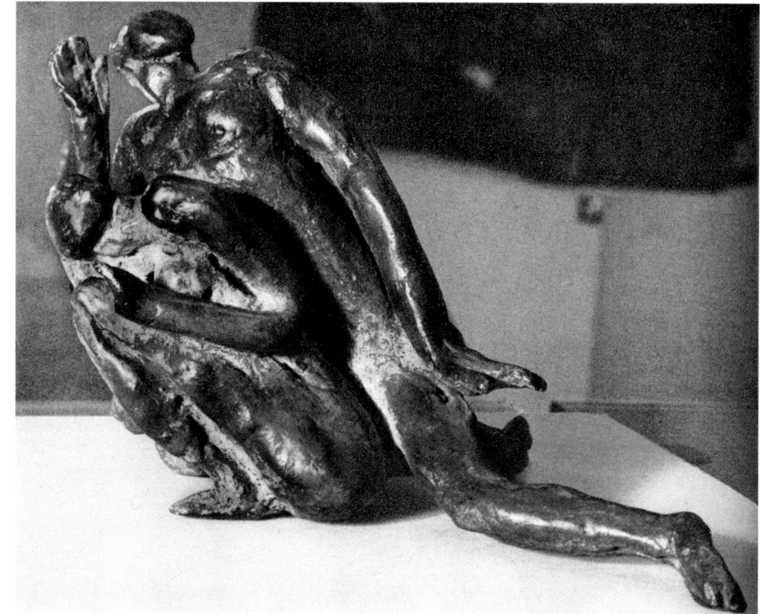

54a
Adam and Eve (maquette), 1938
Bronze, H. 11.5 cm
Watford Museum

54b
The Burial of Abel (maquette), 1938
Bronze, H. 23.3 cm
Watford Museum

> *Race de Caïn, au ciel monte,*
> *Et sur la terre jette Dieu!*
> Race of Cain, ascend to heaven / And cast God down upon the earth!

It is this very ending of the poem that Epstein's drawing included in the edition seems to illustrate – Cain's winged ascension, elevating him above the crowd (his descendants?) that surrounds him [51d]. The poem's exhortation to the race of Cain (who, ultimately, is a forebear of humanity) may also have ignited in Epstein a desire to express its very beginning in a large work – the first human formed in the image of God, Adam.

There are two preceding small maquettes that seem to reveal a continuity with Baudelaire's illustrations – *Adam and Eve* [54b] and *Burial of Abel* [54a], both conveying a sense of sorrow chiming with the mood of the period and the threat of impending fratricide. In the end, however, Epstein did not develop these maquettes into a full-size work, and they form no obvious link to the sculpture of *Adam* that followed soon afterwards.

During this entire period Epstein's financial affairs continued their unsteady path of a meagre income (about five commissioned portraits in this year), and in a letter from September to Sally Ryan he admits that he was glad

> to get your cheque of 200 pounds. The demands of debts pile up and my show of drawings still 3 months off. After 2 months the publisher of the drawings produced 1 miserable proof. I will continue on the stone for a while [*Adam*] and then see if there is a portrait I can do, but things are somewhere at a standstill .... partly it's being summer and also the political situation makes people damned cautious. What are artists to do?
> ... Are you thinking of doing any work? A change of place is sometimes good that way but I cannot imagine myself working in New York.[216]

216 Letter from Epstein to Sally Ryan, 9 September 1938, written on 'Hyde Park Gate' stationery (four pages); reproduced in http://www.schulsonautographs.com.

CHAPTER 4

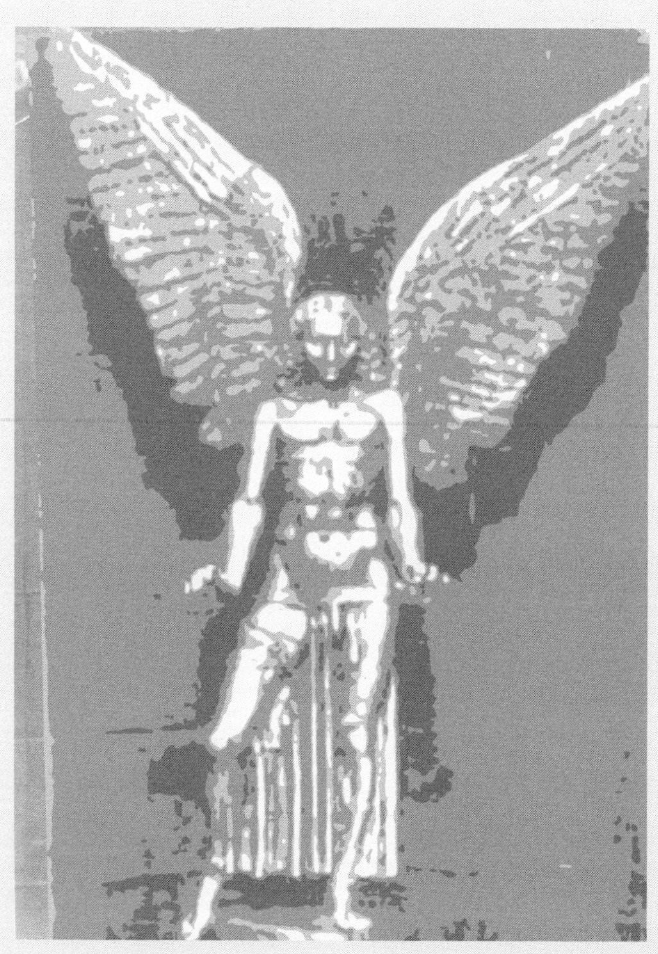

IN TIME OF WAR (1939–45)

ADAM

With a couple of months free before his Baudelaire exhibition and with no portraits in sight, Epstein "made a great spurt, working relentlessly" on the carving of *Adam* (195). He may have been intrigued by Baudelaire's poem in which Cain's task is to bring God down to earth to be with us. In Judaism, however, the direction is reversed – elevating Man to God's stature, for after eating of the forbidden fruit "the man has become as one of us" (Genesis 3: 22). The choice of this subject, on the threshold of an impending catastrophe, might have been a reminder that, despite the 'evil flowers' in human life, there is another side to the rationale for the creation of humanity.

The figure of the first-created human is a universal motif through which every culture presents the qualities that have been chosen to symbolize that culture's values. For the secular-minded at the beginning of the twentieth century, however, Genesis was merely a literary text, and Epstein's work demonstrates that he indeed regarded it as such.

Two of Epstein's works, a sculpture and a drawing, show Adam as a lone figure.[1] As usual in Epstein's practice, the sculpture was preceded by drawings, of which apparently only one has survived, drawn on realistic lines and showing an incomplete figure lying with one arm stretched upwards [55].[2]

Adam's reclining pose has a long artistic tradition,[3] and Epstein's drawing resembles Michelangelo's *Adam* in the Sistine Chapel specifically, but this was not the pose executed by him in stone. My discussion of the *Adam* Epstein eventually executed deals first with form, then with content.

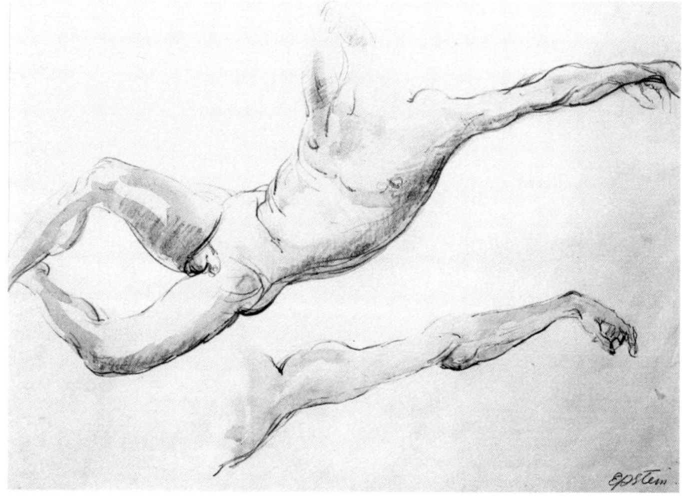

55
Figure study, male nude, 1934?
Pencil and wash, 450 x 533 mm
GREC-NAGW

1 The following discussion echoes several paragraphs of my article 'Epstein and *Adam* – Revisited', but I have added details and expanded its scope.

2 The association with *Adam* was made by Kathleen Epstein in Epstein and Buckle, *Epstein Drawings*, fig. 59.

3 See, for example, the mosaic in the nave of the Palatine Chapel in Palermo, 1158, depicting the creation of Eve (reproduced in D.T. Rice, *The Art of the Byzantine Era*, London 1977, fig. 150), and the same subject in a marble relief at the Duomo in Orvieto, by Andrea Pisano, 1308 (reproduced in J.P. Hennessy, *Italian Gothic Sculpture*, London, 1955, fig. 39).

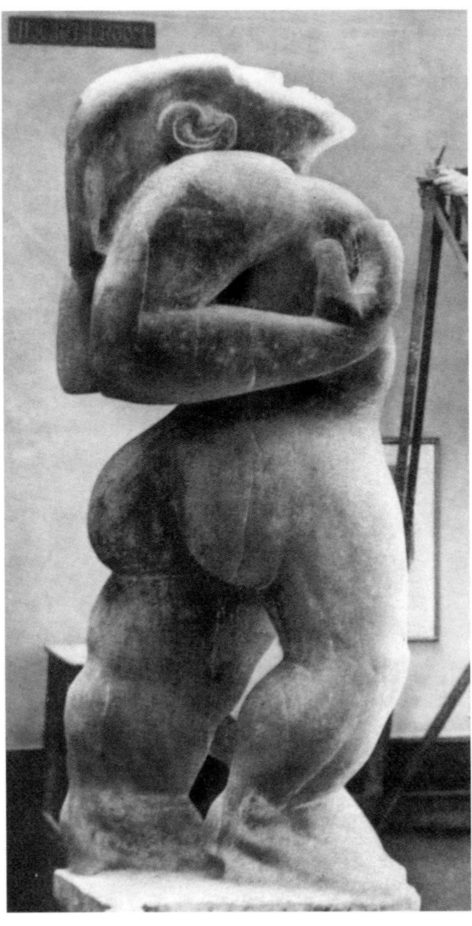

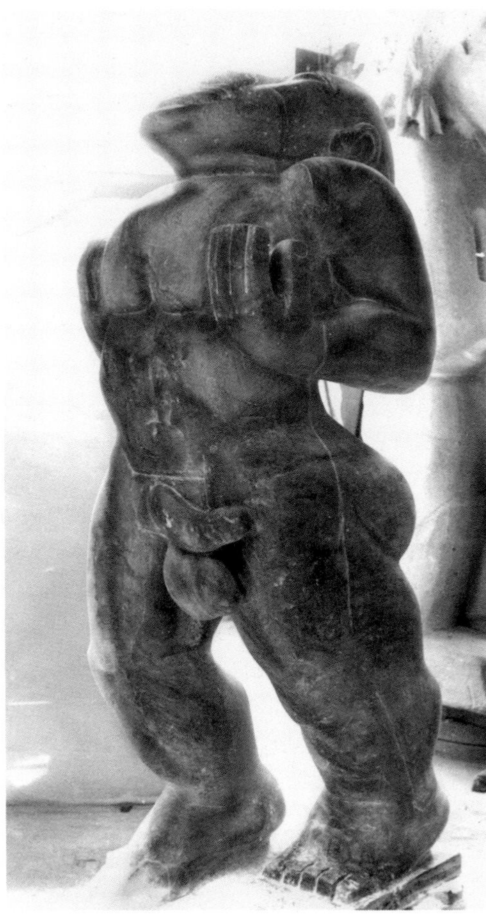

56a
Adam (side view), 1938–39
Alabaster, H. 218.5 cm; base 66 x 81.3 cm
Courtesy of Harewood House, Leeds

56b
Adam (front view)

The sculpture is a huge mass – "I seized a block of alabaster in my studio and saw in it Adam"[4] – configuring a nude male standing with his chest arched forwards, head bent backwards and hair falling down his back [56a]. This was Epstein's first colossal (larger than life-size) work seen in the round; all his other large carved works until then (*Behold the Man* as well as the Strand statues) were meant to be viewed essentially from one angle. Epstein explained viewers' impressions of his carvings of the 1930s as "colossal" by his retaining the mass of the block as much as possible:

> My method in carving is to work from edge to edge of the block in all directions. This gives me the greatest possible dimension within the block & although my stone is not very large, this method gives my sculpture a few larger appearances than the actual dimensions of the stone are so that it gives my carvings an always [...] dimension as 'colossal' although they are by no means of great size. Size is impression & for that reason quite small stones can seem 'colossal' .... Grandeur depends upon the feeling of mass imparted or sometimes lost in the stones.

Stylization into quasi-geometrical forms is also evident in Epstein's previous carvings, such as *Primeval Gods* (1931–33) or *Consummatum Est*, and so are the masses softened by the smooth surfaces to create a flow of forms. With the exception of *Genesis* (1930), these sculptures share an approach to the human figure influenced by so-called primitive or

4 This and the following are taken from a passage on *Adam* that was not included in Epstein's published autobiography (on light-blue pages of the draft, NAGW archive).

archaic art, in which the parts of the body are stylized into almost geometrical forms and are retained within the confines of the block. In spite of differences in design and style, *Adam* echoes pre-Columbian sculptures or those of Easter Island in their vertical mass. Unlike these static colossi, however, Epstein's work is full of movement: "I managed to get a tremendous movement within the compass of a not very wide, upright stone", with "an inner energy, comparable to a dynamo where tremendous energy is generated" (195).[5]

As in Epstein's previous alabaster work, *Consummatum Est* of 1937, the light colours of the stone were given to the head, conferring a spiritual aura upon it. Details in the figure are stylized in flat relief or by light incision [56b] – the fingers, the square plate of pubic hair, the navel, the breasts and the fingernails. The facial details [56c] are accentuated within their elliptic frame, but because of the height of the figure they are not fully visible to the standing viewer. However, the profile of the nose and the open mouth and its grimace, as well as the eye-sockets, are very much present in this (seen from the floor) seemingly faceless figure, thereby conferring on it an apersonal dimension of 'no-one/everyone' that results in universality.

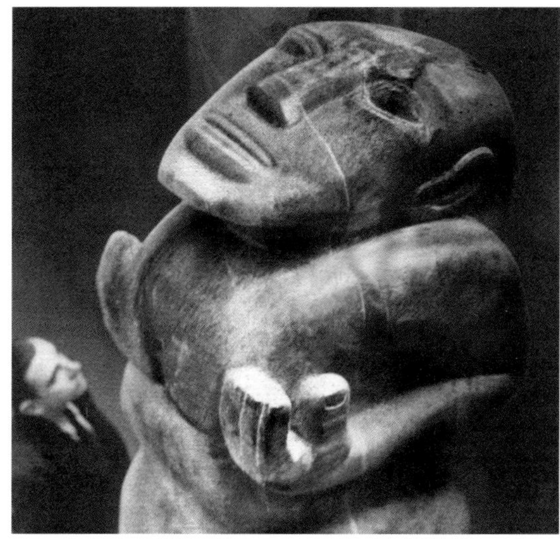

56c
Adam (top view)

The bent arms draw the elbows backwards, and the palms with their upraised fingers are close to the sides of the chest. In spite of the heavy volume of the block, the standing pose is not static: there is an internal movement implied by the slight lifting of the heels that emphasizes the effort expressed in the masses of the buttocks, and an external one indicated by the weight placed on the front parts of the legs, the left one of which, being the more backward, induces the phallus to incline sideways [56b].

The stylization of the phallus is unprecedented in sculpture. "Actually, I started at the work centrally, that is for pivot and central principal I carved the organs of sex; around this I built or conceived the figure."[6] This process of carving seems logical, because, once the issue of the organs protruding from the body is settled, the rest is related to that fixed centre. A literary interpretation is that "the prodigious phallus, nobly supported, sings to what poet Walt Whitman related as 'the song of procreation'":

> From my own voice resonant – singing the phallus
> Singing the song of procreation ... [7].

The image is perhaps justified by Epstein's written description of the movement as "inner energy, comparable to a dynamo where a tremendous energy is generated" (195). A relevant precedent, however, may be the inclined phallus of Adam in Michelangelo's fresco of *The Creation of Adam*. Michelangelo, however, drew a pose possible in life, organic to the naturalistic representation of the figure, without making the penis the focal point of the work (the touching hands are), whereas Epstein created an exaggerated movement for it that attracts the attention of the viewer, making it much more of a focal point and giving it, as he stated, "that centrifugal urge and dynamic outspreading feeling essential to an Adamic work".[8] As Epstein's drawing indicates an allusion to Michelangelo's work, it appears that, though rejecting a supine pose for his sculpture, he adopted the inclined phallus from this source. Epstein's accentuation of this organ in Adam parallels the curly pubic hair added in 1931 to his *Sun God* [30a], also influenced by Michelangelo – by his treatment of the pubic hair in his *David*. I suggest that in both cases the motivation was the same, to stress the procreative ability of its bearer – the

5 Evelyn Silber ('Body Language: Making and Viewing Epstein's *Adam*', p. 10) discusses Whitman and his poetry as an influence on *Adam*. She picks up the word 'dynamo' used by Epstein with regard to *Adam* in order to connect it with *Rock-Drill* (1913), to which Epstein considered attaching "pneumatic power" to set it in motion (70). In fact the inner energy of *Adam* has little to do with an attached external source, and I find other affinities and influences more significant.

6 Unpublished draft of Epstein's *Autobiography*: NAGW archive.

7 The first stanza of Walt Whitman's poem *From Pent-up Aching River*; as suggested in Silber, *The Sculpture of Epstein*, p. 54.

8 Unpublished draft of Epstein's *Autobiography*: NAGW archive.

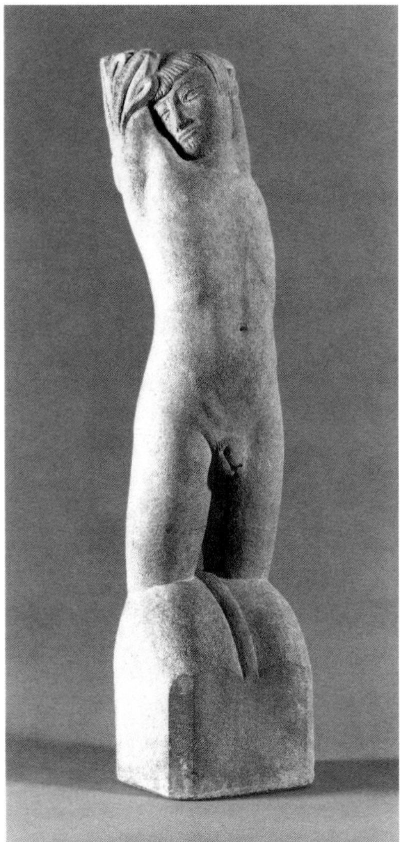

Fig. 31
Eric Gill
Adam, 1927–28
Bath stone, 72 x 16 x 15 cm
Art Collection, Henry Ransom Humanities Research Centre, The University of Texas, Austin

Sun God who gives life to the whole universe, and the human who procreates life in his own world. Epstein stated this clearly enough himself:

> My Adam is frankly sexual but of sexual impulses akin to the Godlike urge & creative dance movement of Beethoven's 7th symphony. I felt this Adam in myself for a long time before I began it[;] once conceived of the authentically set, wave of the idea & feeling it strongly in myself, I set to express it in stone ... not to lesser or low down that quality.[9]

A comparison between Epstein's and his contemporary Eric Gill's *Adam* is in order, as Gill's *Adam* [fig. 31] and *Eve* [fig. 3] of 1928 preceded Epstein's *Genesis* of 1930 and *Adam* of 1938–39. It is hard to determine the extent to which Epstein intentionally contrasted his work with corresponding work by Gill (and vice versa),[10] but in the case of *Adam* and *Eve*/*Genesis* it seems that the miniaturist charm of Gill's figures – in mannerist poses projecting a consciousness of the body – may have induced Epstein to present more substantial figures. On his own *Genesis* vis-à-vis Gill's *Eve*, Epstein stated that his was not a coquettish and fanciful erotic nude (see p. 39); and again his *Adam* is a forceful figure in movement as opposed to the banal pose of Gill's *Adam*, executed in accordance with the prevailing aesthetic convention that I have termed 'the harmony school' (see p. 33).

In referring to *Adam* Epstein commented for a second time on the inspiration of music on his art. Links between music and painting had already been suggested by others, arguing that as music was basically abstract and non-material it would lead to abstract works of art.[11] Abstract art, as discussed above (p. 46), did not appeal to Epstein, and his reverence for music lay in its influence on the soul, as so beautifully argued by Shakespeare (*The Merchant of Venice*, V, i):

> The man that hath no music in himself,
> Nor is not mov'd with concord of sweet sounds,
> Is fit for treasons, stratagems, and spoils;
> ...
> Mark the music.

Epstein instead related the influence of music to his non-abstract sculpture, in the first instance to *Consummatum Est*, which he had conceived under a feeling "of a tremendous quiet, of awe" during the playing of the 'Crucifixus' section in Bach's B minor Mass (176). For *Adam*, he mentions, only briefly, the music of Beethoven's 7th Symphony (195). However, a long paragraph in a chapter entitled 'I Listen to Music' in his autobiography is dedicated to another of Beethoven's works, the Mass in D Minor, discussing Arturo Toscanini's conducting practices and indirectly comparing the work of the conductor whom he is watching to that of the sculptor:

> I watch the conductor, who seems now to be possessed with dynamic energy and controls the music like plastic material. A wonderful sculptor, I think, moulding and conjuring the material in its varied and intricate shapes, lengthening out, scooping with tremendous curves, evening out great planes, broad sides of sound, compelling the advance and retreat with beckoning of the left hand, his expression determined, with dark eyes glowing with profound emotion of the work (233–24).

9 Unpublished draft of Epstein's *Autobiography*: NAGW archive.

10 Although there is an affinity between their work of 1909–10, I refer here mainly to Gill's later work for Broadcasting House – the panels of *Ariel* echo Epstein's *Rima*, and *Prospero and Ariel* echoes Epstein's *Day* at the Railway Headquarters (see I/195).

11 Kandinsky, *Concerning the Spiritual In Art*, Chapter IV: "[Painting] stands, in fact, at the first stage of the road by which it will, according to its own possibilities, make art an abstraction of thought and arrive finally at purely artistic creation": see www.gutenberg.org/cache/epub/5321/pg5321.txt (the translated pronouns needed to be altered). Abstract art influenced by music constitutes an important part also of Paul Klee's oeuvre.

Besides music, the *Adam* and its various intricate facets reflect other aspects of Epstein's wide cultural interests. The sculpture's movement, in particular, more than any other of Epstein's works, manifests his wide scholarship in various fields of the arts. The *Adam*'s backward-drawn elbows [56a] are elements he had previously used in differing accentuations in *Elemental* [39c] and *Sun Goddess Crouching* [40b]. Here the head bent backwards almost to horizontal and the elbows folded to bring the hands beneath the chest echo the movements of maenads from classical antiquity – for example, a Greek relief from the fifth century BCE (fig. 32) in which the figure extends one hand with the fingers upraised and the thumb detached in a deliberately contrived pose; or a figure in the round from the fourth century BCE (fig. 33) who tilts her head back – elements discernible also in *Adam*.[12] Kenneth Clark categorized movements and poses of this kind as representing "ecstasy", as expressing "something more than physical abandonment", as "images of spiritual liberation or ascension".[13] Such precedents enable interpretation of the movement in *Adam* as dance, which, surprisingly, has not been recognized in previous commentaries,[14] although Buckle suggested an allusion in *Woman Possessed* to the climax of Massine's choreography of Stravinsky's *Le Sacre du Printemps* (p. 66). Epstein himself did not elaborate on the movement in *Adam* beyond the vague phrase that "the movement lies not in the flung-out forms but in an inner energy" (195); in his unpublished draft he mentions "creative dance movements" but in the context of Beethoven's 7th Symphony, as noted above. *Adam*'s dancing pose requires some exploration also into dance in Epstein's own time.

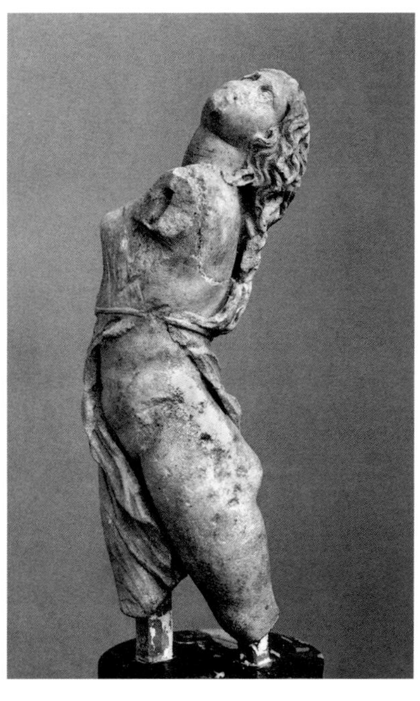

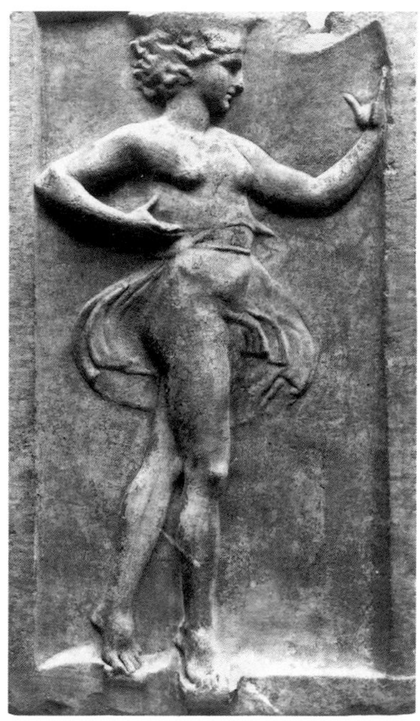

Fig. 32
Maenad, 5th century BC
Staatliche Museen, Antikensammlung, Berlin

Fig. 33
Maenad, 4th century BC
Marble relief, H. 45 cm
Staatliche Kunstsammlungen, Dresden

Interest in the art of ancient cultures at the turn of the twentieth century had included an awareness of ancient dance, which then became a source of influence. A search for new kinds of movement led contemporary choreographers to look at ancient Greek reliefs and vase paintings, from which they – Duncan, Fokine and Nijinsky[15] – formed their own interpretation of Greek dance:

> Duncan, like Fokine, understood Greece as the gracious billowy curves of the Parthenon friezes. Nijinsky, with his Faun, took an utterly different view. It is the severity of Attic carving, the simplicity and faith of pre-Pheidian sculptors, against the charm and elegance of Praxiteles, significant character against grace ... Pheidias and Michelangelo against Praxiteles and Giovanni da Bologna.[16]

Rodin had written:

> In no part is Nijinsky as marvellous and adorable as in *L'Après-midi d'un Faune*. No jumps, no bounds, nothing but attitudes and gestures of a half-conscious animal creature .... He possesses the beauty of the antique frescoes and statues; he is the ideal model for whom every painter and sculptor has longed.[17]

12 Extensive sources are mentioned in J.D. Beazley, *Greek Sculpture and Painting*, Cambridge 1932. Epstein could have found these sources in the British Museum Library, which he frequented, and where I found them (for example, K. von Stradonitz, *Die griechische Skulptur*, Berlin 1907).

13 Clark, *The Nude*, p. 359, fig. 214. The same movement of the head is evident also in a Greco-Roman relief of a Dionysian procession in fig. 217.

14 Arnold Haskell was the first recorded 'balletomane' in England who wrote books and articles on the modern ballet. As Haskell was aware of Epstein's knowledge in all fields of art, it would have been reasonable to expect him to recognize immediately the allusions that I have mentioned in his articles on art written after the publication of *The Sculptor Speaks* (1931), but I have not found any sign that he did.

15 Relevant to the discussion are Nijinsky's wife Romola's recollections, *Nijinsky*. A former art student, she saw the artistic connections between art and dance. Throughout her book she stresses Nijinsky's visits to and observations of art in museums, and the inspiration he drew from what he saw.

16 Nijinsky, *Nijinsky*, pp. 122–23.

17 Rodin's article, editorial page of *Le Matin*, 31 May 1912, cited ibid., p. 150.

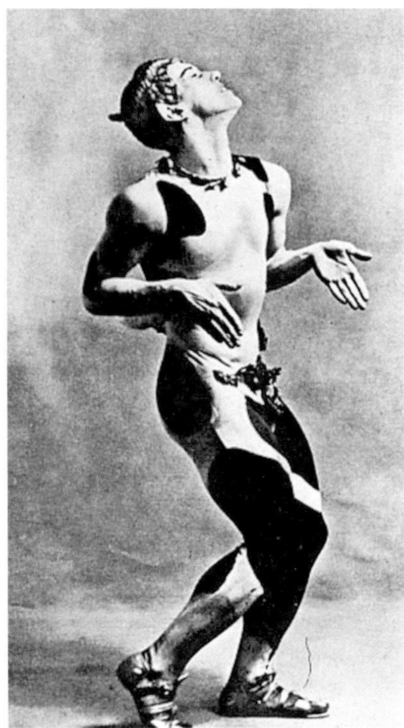

Fig. 34
Nijinsky in *L'Après-midi d'un Faune*, 1912

Epstein was in Paris during 1912–13 for the erection of the Tomb of Oscar Wilde,[18] and like Rodin he too had the opportunity to observe the sculptural values of the new ballet. A comparison between the movements of *Adam* and those of Nijinsky as the Faun (at a certain moment, fig. 34) reveals a similarity in the position of the elbows, the bending of the knees and the movement of the head – even the exposure of the teeth. Nijinsky, specifically and explicitly, aimed to show "the initial awakening of emotional and sexual instincts and their reaction ... similar to the half-voiced desires of those primitive creatures, *the ancestors of man*, part animal, part male human being".[19] This awakening is expressed in the Faun's dance at the very moment that he finds the maiden's forgotten scarf: "The Faun tilts back his head and bears his teeth in stylized laughter".[20] Epstein's *Adam*, manifesting the same type of movement as Nijinsky's dance – the tilting of the head, the grimace and the knee-bent pose with backward-drawn elbows – implies the same notion of ecstasy and sexual awareness.

Two famous precedents, which both Nijinsky and Epstein must have known, are the panels of *Adam* by Dürer and by Hans Baldung Grien; these are executed in a similar style, and their differences shed light on their differing approaches. Dürer's *Adam* (fig. 35) is a downward-looking, pondering and sad figure, as if recognizing wrongdoing; Baldung Grien, on the other hand (fig. 36), presents a somewhat proud Adam: one hand nests on his thigh, his elbow is bent back, his head is upraised, his chin juts forward and his smile projects satisfaction. His other hand, holding a branch, has an uplifted thumb that points to the phallus and metonymically alludes to erection.

Baldung Grien's expression of man's acquired notion of procreation seems to reflect "recognition of the power of man's sensual drive".[21] It is reasonable to assume that this, or another of Baldung Grien's paintings or prints in a similar vein, could have been Epstein's inspiration. His sculpture has a similar uptilted head and grimace, and bears similar implications: its pose projects pride in the achievement of acquiring carnal knowledge:

> I look upon my work as a healthy and serious force, not at all a reaction to present tendencies, because I am not influenced by passing sets of movements, but follow the bend of my own tendencies.[22]

In Baldung Grien's drawing this awareness is expressed through the erect thumb, which focuses the attention of the viewer on the site of the sexual organ; in Epstein's sculpture the accentuated focus is on the artistically unprecedented position of the same organ. Likewise, the self-awareness that Epstein's *Adam* projects, through its pose and composition, makes explicit the notion of rebellion; his sculpture presents Adam as without remorse after tasting of the forbidden fruit. While the brown lower parts of the sculpture allow the interpretation that this is Adam immediately after the Creation,[23] the perception that he is "Adam the begetter of Original Sin"[24] contradicts what has been said above, as does the idea that "The sculptor evokes a whole world of experience with extreme economy, condensing into a single flow of closed and open movement, flight, stillness, fear, isolation and questioning".[25] At the time, Epstein had been surprised by a charge of viciousness: "I do not know ... that this would be 'barbaric' work as has been alleged".[26]

The answer to the question of why Epstein did not choose for his sculpture the reclining pose chosen by Michelangelo and echoed in his drawing [55] may lie in the

18 The premiere was on 29 May 1912. Epstein, arriving in Paris in early June, saw one of the season's performances (*Let There be Sculpture*, p. 276). He told his daughter Kitty, herself a ballet fan, that he saw all the Russian ballets in Paris and London: conversation with the author, 1985.

19 Nijinsky, *Nijinsky*, p. 124 (my italics).

20 Buckle, *Nijinsky*, p. 240. The score, inscribed by Nijinsky with choreographic notation and with indications of staging, is in the British Museum: ibid., p. 462, note 74.

21 For a comparison between Baldung Grien's approach and Dürer's, emanating from different theologies, Catholic and Protestant, see J.A. Marrow and A. Sheslac (eds.), *Hans Baldung Grien: Prints and Drawings*, pp. 54–55.

22 Unpublished draft of Epstein's autobiography: NAGW archive.

23 Suggested in Buckle, *Nijinsky*, p. 244.

24 *Contra* Cork (*Epstein*, p. 58), "a man who knows he has sinned and implores forgiveness" – in other words this is Adam after the eating of the fruit – adding, "Epstein was certainly meditating on the biblical notion of the Fall". However, in the same breath Cork contradicts himself: "His sense of well-being is paramount, and guilt has not yet tempered his pride to a significant extent".

25 Silber and Friedman, 'Isolation and Defiance', in *Epstein: Sculpture and Drawings*, p. 238 (in which it is unclear where the 'fear' lies – in the sculptor, the sculpture or the viewer?).

26 Unpublished draft of Epstein's autobiography: NAGW archive.

gist of the traditional presentation, in which the Creator was the dominant figure and Adam, in a supine posture, was weak, or even lifeless, indicating dependence. Epstein's solitary figure, on the other hand, conveys independence, having moved onwards from the moment of creation and being borne on to a state of liberation and pride.

As an informed reader, Epstein must have realised that his *Adam* corresponded to Ovid's description of the first man's vocation in his *Metamorphoses* – "to look up to heaven and lift his head to the stars" (I, 86). This attitude could be interpreted as pride or hybris – one of the seven deadly sins that had pushed the Devil to rebel against the God-Father authority (Milton's *Paradise Lost*). Epstein, apparently, did not regard pride in one's own creative potential, work or artistic stance as a sin. Therefore, when he declared that "into no other work had I merged myself so much" (195), one can feel his identification with the proud primordial being he had created, as well as his personal pride in his creative power as an artist. It is no wonder, therefore, that from amongst his entire oeuvre he selected a photograph of *Adam* for the frontispiece of his autobiography, and that its title derives from the command of the biblical Creator: "Let there be Sculpture".

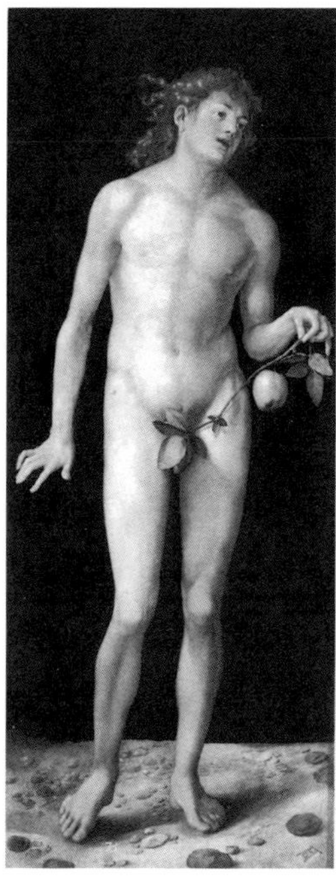

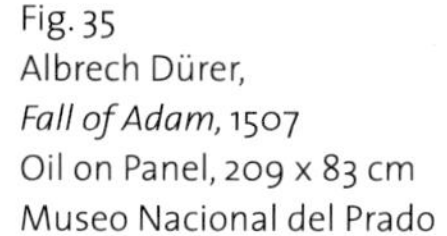

Fig. 35
Albrech Dürer,
Fall of Adam, 1507
Oil on Panel, 209 x 83 cm
Museo Nacional del Prado

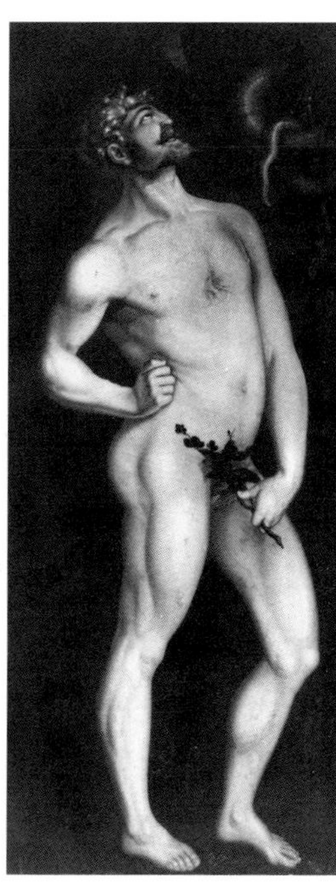

Fig. 36
Hans Baldung Green
Fall of Adam, 1525
Oil on Panel, 208.5 x 83.5 cm
Museum of Fine Art, Budapest

By January 1939 Epstein's financial affairs had deteriorated, and prospects for the coming year were even worse than usual: Silber's catalogue indicates that at the end of this year, of ten portraits executed, seven were of models and family members and only three can be regarded as commissions. In order to pay his taxes for the previous year he had to sell items from his collection of art: reluctantly, he chose to sell 28 Matthew Smith paintings. This must have been a painful decision not only because he admired Smith's art and was one of its few substantial buyers,[27] but also because Smith seems to have been Epstein's only lifelong artist friend,[28] and, unlike Epstein's other friendships, theirs existed concomitantly with both of Epstein's families. At this sad point when Epstein had to sell his collection, a brief note on Smith and his paintings is in order.

It was probably in 1916 that Smith (1879–1959) and Epstein first met, when Epstein took rooms in 23 Guilford Street, not far from Smith's Percy Street studio.[29] Smith admired Epstein's energy, his courage and stamina, "feeling himself lamentably deficient in both".[30] His early work, especially the Fitzroy Street nudes and the Cornish landscapes, possesses a muscular vigour and directness, and is remarkable for its immediacy. These qualities, which were quite alien to the predominant styles of painting in Britain at the time, can also be found in Epstein's work – both sculpted and drawn – and perhaps that is what attracted them to one another. Epstein began seriously to collect Smith's work in 1923, and by 1930 he had 28 works – the largest collection anywhere at that time. Superficially the two men could not have been more dissimilar, suggested Alan Bowness, the director of the Tate Gallery:[31] "Epstein was flamboyant and impulsive, Smith shy, timid, and hesitant; it was a contrast of hot and cold .... Smith's pictures are ... the kind of paintings that an Epstein should have produced, and this was no doubt why Epstein (who was a rather indifferent painter) liked them so much." Epstein added a little spice to Smith's art, in Paris in the 1930s, when Smith engaged Epstein's favourite model, Sunita, to model for him. After acquiring a wider artistic reputation with the 23 paintings he had shown at the Venice Biennale in 1938, Smith came to London to help Epstein to arrange his paintings for sale at the Leicester Galleries. In effect this was

27 Cyril Connolly, 'Matthew Smith: Job and Prospero', *The Sunday Times*, 1962, cited in *Matthew Smith*, exh. cat. 1983. 28

Alice Keene (daughter of Mary Keene, Smith's heir) mentioned that sooner or later Epstein quarrelled with all his friends (ibid., p. 19).

29 From 1930, Smith lived near Cannes, leaving France only when forced to return to England at the outbreak of World War II. During the war both Smith's sons were killed and, separated from his wife, he lived an increasingly solitary existence. After the war he lived a reclusive life in England, moving between seedy hotels or staying with Dorelia and Augustus John. A considerable number of his paintings were shown at the Venice Biennale in 1950. He was knighted in 1954

30 Keene, *The Two Mr Smiths*, p. 38.

31 Bowness, 'Three tributes – Epstein, Smith and Spencer', pp. 16–17. Epstein died in August 1959, Smith in September and Spencer in December of the same year.

Smith's first retrospective exhibition, even though the catalogue (no. 692, January 1939) presented the paintings only as from the collection of Jacob Epstein. The exhibition was very successful, and Epstein's financial situation was temporarily eased.

Thomas MacGreevy reviewed the show in a critique, thinly disguised as praise for Smith's abilities, that echoes Roger Fry's remarks on Epstein's art (I/162–63), and so shows up another element in common between the two friends:

> Matthew Smith sets out to be an all-round naturalistic painter ... he tackles pretty nearly all the genres and the results are almost uniformly triumphant – so triumphant that *one feels a little disappointed to find Mr. Smith remaining a splendid painter rather than a great painter* .... I think the trouble may be that Mr. Smith paints, to put it crudely, *with rather too much 'guts' and just a shade too little visual sense.* In view of the artist's immense vitality and mostly brilliant execution, it may seem ungenerous to cavil, but it is impossible not to feel that *he might be an unchallengeable master and yet is not*, that he avoids our question unnecessarily often.
>
> I should add that the pictures in this exhibition were from the collection of Mr. Jacob Epstein.[32]

In June, Epstein presented *Adam* at the Leicester Galleries (exhibition no. 704, June–July 1939). Its public reception was initially, as Epstein perceived it, relatively calm:

> Apart from the usual intended misunderstandings of section of the press, and the deliberate personal insults of the so-called 'Left Intelligentsia', the work was well received. Perhaps I have at last educated the public, if not to complete understanding, to, at any rate, a more tolerant attitude. Foaming at the mouth and foul abuse were for once absent (196).

Two positive reviews reflected what the critics outwardly saw and inwardly felt – "... earth-bound but reaching upwards because man knows no other destiny, and can put himself...to no better purpose";[33] and, on the formal qualities, "... conceived in stone, its nature has not been violated by the chisel, and the forms and volumes are so magically related one to the other, that there is an upward surge and flow which brings it to life – a kind of pulsating stone".[34] On the other hand, in addition to the usual derogatory comments – for example, "Bold experiment in Neo-Barbarism ... a brutish, simian rendering of the human form"[35] – the so-called 'leftist intelligentsia' expressed itself in the familiar jargon of the Fry-Bell school, stating that "there was apt to be *a discrepancy between content and form*",[36] and adding, "It is, however, a splendid piece of carving". In regard to his children's portraits, the note continued, "his genial *appreciation of their forms is free from the crooner's emotion* which he is prone to express in older persons".

Barely a month after *Adam* was exhibited, Charles Stafford of Golders Green, the director of several goldmining companies, purchased the carving, refusing to state its price and claiming that "it is the greatest work of imaginative art, left to his family as an heirloom".[37]

From this period on, the Epsteins' responses to events, their thoughts, feelings and tribulations, are recorded in letters to Oko, who had left for America just before the Second World War. They were written in various moods of agitation, anger and despair, as reflected also in the often indecipherable handwriting. They reveal the beginnings of

32 T. MacGreevy, 'Leicester Galleries (Matthew Smith)', *The Studio*, April 1939, pp. 174–76 (my italics, indicating remarks generally directed towards Epstein).

33 L.B. Powell, *The Birmingham Mail*, 9 June 1939; cited in Epstein, *Let There be Sculpture*, p. 199.

34 W. McCance, *Picture Post*, 24 June 1939; cited in Epstein, *Let There be Sculpture*, p. 329.

35 T.W. Arp, *The Daily Telegraph*, June 1939.

36 *The Times*, 8 June 1939. It was written by an anonymous critic that "might well have been Blunt or Nash or Bell": Gardiner, *Epstein*, p. 37 (my italics, indicating the new-speak of the Bell-Fry circle).

37 *News Chronicle*, 15 July 1939.

the saga that followed upon the sale to Stafford of *Adam* (and of other sculptures later on) and lasted almost until Epstein's death. Stafford gave the rights to display *Adam* during the summer of 1939 to Lawrence Wright of Blackpool, who opened for this purpose the Lawrence Wright Art Gallery.[38] Wright's intention was "to open 'high culture' up to the masses", and Epstein, who was finally convinced that his work was to be shown "in a manner befitting [*Adam's*] religious and artistic significance", gave the enterprise his full backing, allowing, in addition, the display of twelve of his bronzes, including busts of the young Paul Robeson and of Haile Selassie (the former Emperor of Ethiopia). Epstein himself arrived in Blackpool to open the exhibition in July 1939,[39] declaring the presentation to be his "passport to the future", and adding that "this statue is a religious one … it is conceived as an elemental figure, the father of us all … it should have been in the Tate Gallery". *Adam* received 20,000 visitors daily, it is reported, and as a consequence Wright wanted to commission Epstein to do an *Eve*, because "Adam is lonely – he must have a mate".[40] Epstein, apparently, did not take this 'commission' seriously, whether because he regarded his *Genesis* as an embodiment of Eve or because he suspected the good intentions of Mr Wright. He sent him a telegram in July requiring an advance of £5,000 to start an *Eve*, and added: "I also understand you will purchase the 14 bronzes now being shown in your art gallery for £15,000 – this sum to be paid immediately – as I consider my collection of bronzes to be the best in the world, particularly my *Kathleen* which I consider my masterpiece". No money or commission resulted from this exchange; but Stafford's *Adam* and the bronzes Wright had received were shipped to New York. Epstein's reaction was resentful:

> My last show on which I had counted so much was a failure although the "Adam" sold; but on the sale of the 'Adam' brings a long story. It sold for very little considering the amount of time and labour I had given it.
>
> It lead [sic] me into a series of adventures with crooks which I will write of later; one of the most disastrous consequences was the loss of a whole collection of bronzes 12 in number which if you see exhibited in N.Y. you will know have been stolen from me.
>
> The Adam is owned by one of the world's biggest swindlers … so vile a specimen of confidence man & crook. His name is Charles Stafford & he it is who has sent the Adam to America to be exploited on Broadway & Coney Island …. If everything is publicised by Mr. Stafford in the American press you can be certain they are lies.[41]

Epstein had already complained about the affair in an earlier letter to Oko, blaming the gallery for not handling the sale of *Adam* more appropriately: "All this comes down to the stupidity of the Leicester Galleries".[42] Eventually, in 1954, *Adam* (as well as *Consummatum Est*, and later on *Jacob and the Angel*) was sold by Stafford to William Cartmell of Louis Tussaud's Waxworks on Blackpool promenade,[43] and installed in the attraction's basement beneath a large heating pipe.

38 The following details were taken from the website of the Grundy Art Gallery, Blackpool, which organized the exhibition *Jacob Epstein and Blackpool* (26 June–11 September 2010) to commemorate the composer and entrepreneur Lawrence Wright's contribution to the town. See http://artsphere.co.uk/2010/08/jacob-epstein-and-blackpool/.

39 The event was filmed in the news (*Rebel Angel* – Central TV).

40 *The Times*, 17 July 1939.

41 Letter from Epstein to Dr Oko, 14 March 1940: HUCAC.

42 Letter from Epstein to Dr Oko, 7 December 1939: HUCAC.

43 Tulloch, 'Miracle or Monstrosity?

A BATTLE FOR A BOOK AMIDST A WAR

In January 1939, German Jews were being driven to emigrate; in February, France and England recognized General Franco's rule in Spain; in March Germany occupied Czechoslovakia and, when Germany demanded Gdansk from Poland, Britain and France agreed to support Poland if it should be invaded by Germany; April saw the publication of John Steinbeck's novel *The Grapes of Wrath*, recording in the United States the economic upheaval that Europe had also felt.

During a brief period in mid 1939, Epstein, alone among artists, was preoccupied with challenging the authorities of the British Museum regarding their treatment of the Elgin Marbles (206–14). The issue had arisen as early as 1921, when during one of his visits to the museum Epstein had noticed that workmen were 'cleaning' the marbles with some kind of sand and scrubbing brushes (206), and a plaster nose had been added to the statue of Demeter of Cnidus. Epstein protested in a letter to *The Times* (2 May 1921), but he was ignored and the cleaning of the patina on the sculptures' surface continued: "The discussion [was] ended by *The Times* itself, awarding the Museum officials 100 per cent marks, the maximum, for their custodianship, I suppose".

Two years later, the suggestion that raspberry juice should be squirted on to Demeter's head "was instrumental in finally convincing [the authorities] of the wisdom of removing the false nose". Further confrontation occurred in mid 1939, when cleaning and restoring the Elgin Marbles involved, as the Museum explained "some unauthorized cleaning of some marbles", which it excused by asserting that "that the effects are imperceptible to anyone but an expert".[44] On 25 May 1939, Epstein concluded the argument in *The Times* saying: "Putting me in my place seems to be of greater importance to the museum officials than the proper care and protection of the Greek marbles". In his autobiography Epstein commented that "so far, any damage done has remained a mystery, as the Marbles have not since been put on view" (207). When Epstein wrote this last comment, it was intended that the marbles should be hosted in the new wing, financed by Lord Duveen, in which they are now housed, but the war kept them temporarily out of sight in a shelter.[45]

The month of August 1939, besides bringing the good news of the birth of Epstein's first grandchild, Leda, witnessed the Molotov-Ribbentrop pact, which effectively divided eastern Europe between Hitler and Stalin. On 31 August Germany staged a "Polish assault" on the radio station in Gleiwitz, followed by the invasion of Poland. In accord with the pact signed in 1938 with Poland, on 3 September Britain declared war on Germany, and France followed six hours later, both quickly joined by the British Commonwealth countries of Australia, New Zealand, South Africa and Canada. World War II had begun. Switzerland proclaimed neutrality, and so too, for the time being, did Franklin D. Roosevelt for the United States. America was still neutral in 1940 when Chaplin's *The Great Dictator* was released – a stirring and controversial condemnation of Hitler, fascism and anti-Semitism. It was the only film made in Hollywood to do so, although this was a town that, according to Nazi propaganda, was ruled by Jews.

The final months of 1939 in the Epstein household were devoted to pursuing

44 In a speech in Parliament, given by Captain Crookshank, published in *The Times*, 20 May 1939.

45 For more on the issue of the treatment of the Elgin Marbles and Epstein's involvement see, for example, I. Jenkins, 'The 1930s Cleaning of the Parthenon Sculptures in the British Museum', at www.britishmuseum.org/about_us/news_and_press/statements/parthenon_sculptures/1930s_cleaning/press_scandal_of_1939.aspx and other articles on the British Museum website.

payment for his work being shown in Blackpool and to the completion of the sculptor's autobiography. Another matter of financial dispute was a bronze head of Dr Stephen Wise, which he had made out of personal interest, not as a commission, and which Simon Marks then asked him to lend to the Palestine Pavilion at the New York Fair.[46] Some time later, he was informed that the bronze had been given as a gift to Dr Wise by a group of his friends, headed by Louis Lipsky, at a great jamboree. In his complaint to Oko he states that he has put a price of £200 on the head, adding with dry black humour:

> It may be very pleasant for all concern & to have bronzes presented that don't belong to them[,] but in this case the owner (myself) feels that he ought to be paid. I am investigating the matter & have written to everyone concerned: Marks, Lipski & Wise [and] the whole 'mishpacha' & I hope to get payment or bust![47]

The ongoing saga of the autobiography (a battle for a book amidst the war) was nearing its final stages, and Epstein refers to the project in his December letter to Oko: "I am engaged on a sort of memoirs for Michael Joseph publishers House & am working hard to get it finished. I never imagined that literary work was so difficult. The difficulties for me are those sculpted." As mentioned earlier, Epstein wrote his preliminary notes on a relatively small pad of bluish paper, and the text was then typed up by Peggy Jean, revised (with suggestions by Margaret and, as claimed, some clandestine help from Kathleen on the chapter on music),[48] and then sent to the publisher for approval. The text was delivered at the end of December 1939 to the publisher Michael Joseph, who had obtained Epstein's agreement in the first place by stating that he would pay £2500, "that is 1500 for the British rights and an option of 1000 Pound Sterling for the American rights, the option to expire 8 weeks after the delivery of the book".[49] From then onwards Epstein spent long months in settling disputed points and awaiting actual publication.

Meanwhile, London was preparing itself for air raids in a war that people had previously refused to believe would happen. "You were right about the war coming," Epstein wrote to Oko; "I suppose I have got the English mentality by now, a sort of lazy mind that first accepts things & waits until something happens."[50] Epstein and Margaret remained in London during the week in order for him to continue his work. "London in a black-out looks wonderful but is damned uncomfortable. We gamble [sic] about in the darkness of doorways if the planes come over."[51] The members of his two families were scattered: little Jackie and his governess were sent to the Deerhurst cottage in Epping Forest; the Garman children were living in Harting near Petersfield with Kathleen's mother, who now had with her, besides Kitty, also Esther. Theo, after leaving his mother's house in London because "all the other people are moving along the row, and so we are very lonely",[52] also went later on to Harting, living in a cottage nearby. Kathleen remained in her London house in the King's Road, hosting her sister Helen and little niece Cathy, who had come back from Martigues. Following the death of Grandma Garman, the Garman children went to live with Kathleen's nanny, Ada Newbould, and later were joined by Helen's daughter Cathy; Kathleen came to visit them at the weekends (when Epstein was at Deerhurst). An indication of the cordial atmosphere among Epstein's

46 Dr Stephen Wise (1874–1949) was an American Reform-Rabbi and Zionist leader.

47 Letter from Epstein to Dr Oko, 7 December 1939: HUCAC. '*Mishpacha*' in Hebrew and Yiddish means family; the connotation here, however, is negative, similar to that of a mafia family. Louis Lipsky (1876–1963) was a noted Zionist leader, journalist and writer.

48 Gardiner, *Epstein*, p. 378; also from Kitty's conversation with the author, 1985.

49 Letter from Margaret to Oko, 17 April 1940, HUCAC, explaining the state of affairs with the publisher.

50 Letter from Epstein to Dr Oko, 7 December 1939: HUCAC.

51 Ibid.

52 Letter from Theo to Beth Lipkin, 7 July 1939, from 270 Kings Road, London: NAGW–BL/1/4/2/1/1.

second family is given in a birthday letter that Theo wrote to Beth Lipkin in Canada. He thanks her for her kind letters and her "present of handkerchiefs", as he had been left without any at all, and mentions that Kathleen had given him for his birthday "a lovely set of four chairs and a table to put in the studio in the new house next door [near the rest of the Garmans]".[53]

Jackie's stay in Deerhurst started quite pleasantly, and he joined his father on weekends to paint and explore the forest ("I knew every corner in it as well as I know the palm of my hand").[54] Later on the place proved to be less pleasant, as the surrounding airfields and the movements of troops in the area made it a target for enemy bombs; consequently, an Anderson shelter (a kind of bunker) had to be built in the living room.

"As buses were rare because of petrol rationing, the Epsteins were brought to Deerhurst on Sundays by a taxi driver they knew," commented Gardiner when referring to the Epstein's living expenses. Their retinue included a live-in couple (the cook Chai-Pi and her husband; she also served as a model), Nichols the handyman, and David Roche, who was in charge of the house.[55] All of these were on top of Epstein's other responsibilities toward his second family, whose expenses he left to Margaret's care. Thus, rushing to visit Kathleen before Christmas Eve, he asked Margaret (who enjoyed visiting auctions and picking up jewellery for the models) if she had bought a jade necklace for Kathleen (who was, after all, also a model), and, when she said she had not, as the asking price was too high, he angrily smashed the glasses on the Christmas table that had been set.[56] Margaret, apparently unmoved, said to Peggy Jean: "Extraordinary! To ask your wife to buy presents for your mistress!"

Editing of the autobiography was continuing and, as might be expected, there are differences between the handwritten drafts and the published book. The exhausting editing process that the Epsteins had to undergo is discussed further on, but for now I note two examples of chapters that were not included.[57]

The first was entitled 'Indian Sculpture'. Epstein had started to absorb formal elements of Indian sculpture into his work after July–August 1908, once he had completed his carvings for the British Medical Association.[58] At last he had some free time in which he was able to investigate the then cramped and cluttered Indian collection of the British Museum. In all probability he was guided to this section of the Museum by Ananda Coomaraswamy's books, *Medieval Sinhalese Art* (1908)[59] and *The Indian Craftsman* (1909),[60] which had had a great impact on London's intelligentsia. Through his books and also his personality, Coomaraswamy had aroused an interest in Indian art that went beyond what had so far been studied only by archaeologists, suggesting that artists were the best qualified to judge the significance of works of art considered as art. Although there is no evidence of Epstein being fascinated and swept away by Indian culture as others were (among them William Rothenstein, who went to India in 1909; I/96–97), influence of Indian sculpture on his work is manifest in two tropes that he acquired around this time – the Indian method (differing from the Western classical one) of showing the body through the garment, which would become a common feature of his female busts (see, for example, [26]), and the accentuated sideways movement of the hip as opposed to the 'S'-shaped African one that would appear in his work during the mid 1910s (see, for example, [7]). A first assimilation of these tropes is evident in his

53 Letter from Theo to Beth Lipkin, 7 July 1939, cited previous note.

54 Conversation with the author, 1989.

55 Gardiner, *Epstein*, p. 379.

56 This amusing anecdote is mentioned in both Gardiner, *Epstein*, p. 379, and Rose, *Demons and Angels*, p. 220, each with a slightly different accent, and both relying on Peggy Jean's report.

57 Unpublished draft of Epstein's autobiography: NAGW archive.

58 They bear Rodin's influence in the treatment of the bodies, whereas their presentation as a procession of naked figures in different poses was undoubtedly influenced by processions in Roman sarcophagus sculpture. There are examples of such processions also on sarcophagi in the British Museum (the Genzano Sarcophagus, AD 150–80, for example). Among the many expressions of it during the 2nd century, I imagine that the Sidamara Sarcophagus at the Istanbul Archaeology Museum might particularly have appealed to Epstein, a fragment of which – a life-size marble head of a child, with curling hair, broken off at the neck – had been detached in the previous century and brought to the Victoria and Albert Museum, London.

59 Coomaraswamy draws a parallel to the later Arts and Crafts movement in England. The books were printed at the Kelmscott Press of William Morris.

60 See http://www.dictionaryofarthistorians.org/coomaraswamya.htm. Some of Epstein's details of the way Indian craftsmen approached their subjects seem to be influenced by this book.

sculpture for Lady Ottoline Morrell's garden, started at the end of 1908 (I/84), and they are obvious in the carving *Maternity* [6], started in 1909. Epstein and Eric Gill had gone together in 1910 to look at Indian sculpture at the Victoria and Albert Museum and the British Museum.[61] But his study of Indian sculpture had enabled Epstein to look beyond its mere form, and in the draft he would comment on its underlying culture with a very personal emphasis.

Epstein first notes: "In ancient Buddhist & Brahmin work there existed fixed causes which defined and limited the proportions of the figures of Gods & humans ... [which is apparent] when we consider the great rock-cut temples of Elephanta, Elusa & Badani". Other cultures had a similar approach – Asian (Angkor-Wat), ancient Egyptian (Kanarak) and medieval (Chartres) – but "To us the religious fervour and zeal that could express itself is entirely foreign". Thus, "The living sculptor turns with nostalgic thoughts to these smooth & seemingly golden periods of sculpture & must lament that he is born in a time when taste like religion itself [is] degraded & withered vision". Identifying his art with something like this religious fervour, he found that "at moments of crisis [the artist] wakes up to find himself not only unwanted but shoved aside as unnecessary in the 'design for living'. This existence as a parasite easily dispensed with is one of the most degrading situations that the modern artist finds himself faced with."

Not dissimilar sentiments were expressed in a foreword that also remained unpublished,[62] in which he acknowledged that "We live in no ordinary times, & the methods & modes of new or old 'ideologies' can have far reaching effects". Here he was referring not merely to political ideologies, but rather to the phenomenon that "all those who have never been able to draw a line or do a stroke in art assume command", particularly in a situation of war. They then have "the amazing audacity to publish the view that without this experience of war the artist's life seems unfulfilled!" "The artist," Epstein claimed, "does not need the thrill of war, & never has needed it", as "the artist draws emotional stimulus from the contemplation of anything". He justifies his point citing other artists' attitudes: a letter from Van Gogh to his brother provides a complete answer to those who imagine the artist as a middling and empty mind that needs filling by war; and Blake said that one should "see a world in a grain of sand and Heaven in a wild flower". Epstein's protest might be regarded as an attempt to justify his lack of active participation in World War I, and he brings up the case of Cézanne: "When Cezanne was asked by some impertinent 'Daddy what did you do in the war [1870]?' he answered 'Do you know I was very busy just then painting my series of pictures called *Estaque*'."

The decision not to include a foreword, whether Epstein's or the editor's, also caused Epstein's intended motto for the book to be discarded:

> I would like to give this book the sub-title of 'The dream & The Poet'.
> I have dreamt & achieved & have experienced the pitfalls & disappointments of a poet.

After the bombing of England began in 1940, art galleries and museums started to look for safe places to store their treasures. John Rothenstein's stewardship at the Tate, and his preservation of the collection during the war years, was a major accomplishment. He travelled around the country, asking landowners to lend a helping hand and space

61 Eric Gill's diaries, 22 March 1910; 20 August 1910; 10 November 1910; microfilm in the TGA.

62 Unpublished draft of Epstein's autobiography: NAGW archives. It has three versions, and after comparing them I took details from the more inclusive one.

on their estates, often receiving it but always surprised at "how anti-Semitic the Gentry were".[63] Epstein's works were not included in his list, as at that time the Tate had only *Visitation* (1925) in its cellar, whereas Rothenstein's main interest had been in caring for the enormous number of paintings.

Margaret Epstein, for her part, made several efforts to ensure the safety of Epstein's sculpture. In an early cable to Oko she tried to enlist his help in convincing a third party, Hiram Halle,[64] to come to the rescue "by offering [him] to help any such scheme with suggestions … to get Jacob and his works safe for the duration".[65] Apparently Halle became a supportive friend, and in a later letter to Oko Margaret recounts that "Halle was very good he let us have a loan", which apparently did not solve their problems, "having loans to pay for expensive rents & income taxes and rates[,] with no assets no commissions no sales and all contracts smashed the moment war began. We will have to get out as soon as possible but storage will have to be done first."[66]

In January 1940 Britain's first period of rationing started (bacon, butter and sugar) and the Epsteins' financial situation declined further. There were no pubic commissions for any artist. By 15 February the conditions had worsened to a state in which Epstein cabled Oko:

> This is an appeal for help[,] I and mine Peggy and Jackie are in a really bad way[.] all my contracts have fallen through result of war[.] my book which I counted on has been held up and purchasing of sculpture finished here[.] dear friend can you raise one hundred pounds for me and cable it[?] could give you sculpture as guarantee or someday when I come to America I could add Benjamin portrait[.] cannot think of how better to appeal to you and Dorothy.[67]

The main issue that occupied the Epsteins' attention during 1940 was the publication of Epstein's book in England, but there were also problems in the US. The latter task had been kindly and patiently taken on by Oko, in addition to his handling Epstein's sculptures in the US for which payments were due. As we may deduce from various letters to Oko, the publication absorbed much of the energies of both Epstein and his wife as they attempted to keep their heads above water in their worsening financial situation.

Just prior to publication in England the need arose unexpectedly to find an American publisher, because the publisher who had had a two-month deadline (from January 1940) to sell the rights had not found a buyer; the option returned to Epstein, who asked Oko: "Do you know a publisher who would be keen?"

On 18 March Epstein complained that what he had begun with a positive attitude was ending with him spending "a good of time in writing" and finding that he had made a mistake in not insisting that his publisher publish what he had written. "I am asking Peggy [Margaret] to get together the book or a good portion of the book to send to you to look it over & tell me my chances [of publication] in America".

There were three problems with publication, Margaret explained to Oko in her letter of 17 April. The first was that their agent, Spencer Curtis Brown, being a good friend of the publisher Michael Joseph, had led them to think that they "don't really feel that

63 This detail was told by his daughter Lucy to the author, 1998. Needless to say, it does not appear in Rothenstein's memoirs of the period, *Dark Day, Hideous Night: 1939–1965*, p. 30. His avoidance of unpleasant aspects in people's attitudes to Jewish issues (also of his own origins) is astonishing. Thus, on Wyndham Lewis, who praised Hitler in his book of 1933, he writes: "About his opinions I will here say nothing" (p. 41).

64 Hiram J. Halle (1867–1944) was an American businessman, part owner of the Gulf oil company, inventor and philanthropist, as well as an amateur painter. He collected works of art, including Epstein's sculptures, among them his portrait, made in 1933–34.

65 Cable from Margaret to Dr Oko, 4 January 1940: HUCAC (my division into issues).

66 Letter from Margaret to Dr Oko, 17 April 1940: HUCAC.

67 Cable from Epstein to Dr Oko, 15 February 1940: HUCAC.

we have an agent for us". The main problem, however, derived from Epstein's stressed economic situation, for he, "in order to get the cheque, agreed to minor alterations" by the publisher, who "is not appreciative of literature or cost. He is only commercial. Pity we got him. We were fascinated by the big offer of £2500." The third problem related to the publication rights: the option of £1000 for the American rights had been included within the "big offer". By the time Margaret wrote her letter, however, this option had expired, leaving the Epsteins with the unpleasant task of searching by themselves for an American publisher. The sensible Margaret summed up the issue by saying "it's no use crying over spilt milk"; and therefore she sent with her letter "the 2nd copy of the manuscript of the book", explaining that "it is very nearly what the book will be, but not quite a replica because the publisher is going to change it by doing what he counts to do to it [sic] now that Epstein has in our desperate need signed to let him have it for a very much reduced rate of £1500".

Leaving all the procedural details to be reported in Margaret's letter, Epstein's letter of the same date (17 April), deals mainly with textual issues: he hopes Oko will like the manuscript, but if not "tell me what you think quite frankly; I've had a lot of criticism already and can stand some more". Epstein admits that he could not bring himself to write a "gossipy" book about himself; and he had written about people he had known, artists or sitters, because they had contributed to his art and not because they provided a "domestic" illustration of him. He tries to explain to Oko the rationale behind his text, admitting that "while it does not tell 'everything' (how could I also cover bravely above all things)", yet it covers his "sculpture life & that surely is all that need be known, or rather all that ought to interest people interested in sculpture or art"; and he states that "To have succeeded [in showing] the workings of one's mind is surely more interesting than the ups & downs of very private life, [and] that [is] of course where I came up against the publishers & the publishers' reader's opinion of the book".

Margaret was responsible for whatever had to be done in handling the process – the issue of provenance and dates of articles cited, for example – and also for ensuring that the American edition would not appear before the English one, as this could cause them to be "in a boiling cauldron". On the other hand, she was afraid that "after a period of 100 days or so after the English version has appeared[,] the American rights cease to be valuable as a marketable asset", and therefore she asked Oko to manoeuvre between these two imperatives, as the experiences in Blackpool "have made me perhaps too suspicious of any business people – even publishers can be honest [–] some[,] I hope".[68] She had been handling all the correspondence regarding the book and home affairs from her 'office', which was moved often, and sometimes "put under the bed in a box out of sight, and sometimes in the box room".[69]

In mid May 1940 the Epsteins sent the publisher Michael Joseph 56 permissions from authors; "Others will be sent as they come in", with the requested minor alterations that enabled citation of their articles. During the rest of the month Margaret was still engaged in obtaining permissions from various publications and writers on Epstein's work,[70] because she's "got to go by law", as she wrote on 20 May, mentioning that the postage on her letters had "became a costly business". She expresses her concern that the book would not come out in England, as "the times are not good for artistry publishers

68 Letter from Margaret to Dr Oko, 26 April 1940: HUCAC.

69 Letter from Margaret to Dr Oko, 7 June 1940: HUCAC.

70 Letter from Margaret to Michael Joseph, 15 May 1940: HUCAC. A letter which typifies what had to be typed individually and sent to all concerned is in TGA – 9012/1, sent to Samuelson, 5 May 1940.

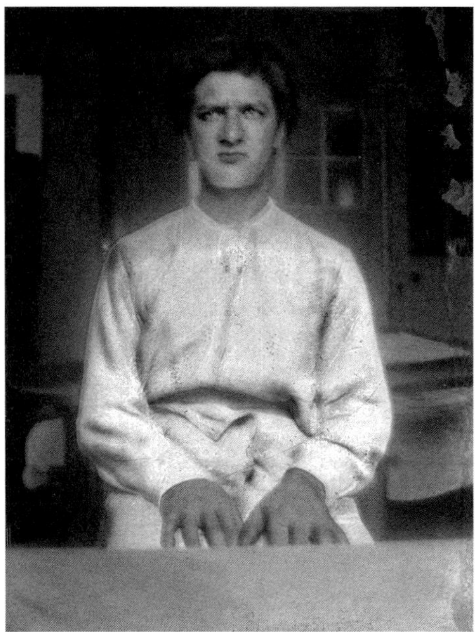

Fig. 37
Epstein as a young man
The background is that of a country cabin
NAGW archive

here", and comments on her husband's habits (which would frustrate researchers in the future) that had forced her to go "searching for the dates, [that] was the worst part of it because Jacob never puts dates".

Margaret's workload included organizing the photographs of Epstein's works. She sent Oko three albums of photographs in which Epstein's choices were marked in red. As "they are my collection of treasury",[71] she asks that they be returned to her once the publisher had finished with them.[72]

Her dealings with the photographs triggered in Margaret the idea of exploiting them further, as "of course you will not be able to use all the photographs but perhaps they could come out as a book of photographs later and we might make some money on that".[73] An underlined comment on the second page of her letter reads:

> Included also is a photograph of Jacob about 18 years of age when he was wild[,] over Greenwood Lake camping out or just before that, perhaps running off to hide & read Dostoyevsky [fig. 37]. You might be able to enlarge it & put it in.[74]

The same idea of a photograph album is expressed by Epstein in his letter of June 20, asking "Do you think a book could be made of photographs say 100 or 150 (or not) … [under the title] 'Let There be Sculpture'".

Two letters by Margaret addressed to Oko have long lists of corrections that needed to be made to the manuscript sent to him, and some of the reasons for this mentioned in the second one are quite amusing:[75]

1. In 1908–1912: in the lines that state that Ezra Pound wished Gaudier-Brzeska to make his portrait phallic, for the possibility of libel here where libel is frequent, 'Phallic' has been changed to 'virile'.
2. The details referring to a gallery keeper 'who was introduced to gallery keeping by Epstein and developed into a swindler' – just the 9 or 10 or 11 lines that point to him especially are crossed out in case he seeks fame and fortune in an action.
3. The change from 'rat-like little person called Konody' to 'razor nosed little person called Konody' is made to prevent his gay young widow from seeking fame & fortune … perhaps backed by somebody's money with an eye to libel being possible.[76]

In his letter of 18 September, Epstein describes the final stumbling block before the actual publication as being the publishers' fears about libel: "They have done their best to keep out all references to Roger Fry whose 'sacred' reputation they seem bent on protecting".[77] Epstein was angry about this, as the publishers' objections had arrived after they had already accepted the manuscript. Moreover, as he writes further on to Oko, "it seems the reader of Michael Joseph turned out [to be a] friend of everyone criticized in the book. Naturally he cuts out as much as he can." Margaret had summed up: "I wonder any frank book is ever able to see the printed stages nowadays!" So much was the book bowdlerized that their old acquaintance Feibleman wrote of his surprise regarding the final product:

71 The album and an index of photographs is in HMI, 36.2.1998, box 9.

72 Letter from Margaret to Dr Oko, 26 May 1940: HUCAC.

73 Letter from Margaret to Dr Oko, 7 June 1940: HUCAC.

74 Unfortunately, even after tracing Oko's son and grandson, I could not locate other photographs that no doubt existed. Epstein, *Let There be Sculpture*, p. 21, mentions a painter, Mr Wells, who "made photographs of visitors" during the summer, and the one reproduced here seems to be one of them, as the background is that of a porch and an entrance to a kind of chalet.

75 Letter from Margaret to Dr Oko, 27 August 1940: HUCAC.

76 Paul Konody (1872–1933) was a Jewish art critic for *The Observer* and *The Daily Mail* before the World War I. In *The Hidden Hand* (22 February 1924) he reviewed Epstein's portraits, saying that he is driven by "a curious perversity" to seek in his white models "features of the dark races". Perhaps this is why Epstein commented on his facial features.

77 Fry died on 9 September 1934. Despite the admiration he acquired amongst the Bloomsbury circle, Virginia Woolf, in her 1940 biography of Fry, did not hesitate to dwell on his shortcomings: "In spite of frillings that should have made his opinion worthless, it had weight …. far more zealous in his exploitation of new ideas and wild theories than enthusiastic about art itself. And this characteristic qualified him fully for his journalistic career when funds were low. This qualification repaid the bank account": Woolf, *Roger Fry*, p. 292.

> When his own autobiography was announced I became very eager, because I knew the kind of things he can say; but nothing of the sort was said in his book. It is a staid and rather dull factual account – one which leaves out most of the significant facts.[78]

Epstein's autobiography, *Let There be Sculpture*, became available to the British and also American public in December 1940. I cite one critique from each continent. For an American critic, "The book roared like a thwarted bull, and with as little humor .... Getting back at his critics, Epstein flayed the 'wretched lot of logrollers, schemers, sharks, opportunists, profiteers, snobs, parasites, sycophants, camp followers, social climbers and four-flushers' [who] infest the world of art – this jungle into which the artist is forced periodically to bring his work and live."[79] A noted British author and commentator, Sir John C. Squire,[80] wrote favourably of the book but resented Epstein's ignoring his artistic milieu, although "It's natural that an artist with an intensely personal message should be a little blind to personal messages of other artists"; therefore, for Squire, the book conveyed a certain of pettiness, not least because, other than Rodin, Epstein mentioned almost no other sculptor – "no mention of Zadkine or Dobson, and only a passing reference to Henry Moore". On the other hand, on the issue of Epstein's place in contemporary sculpture, another critic noted that Epstein "speaks with confidence and without mock modesty. He is a great man and he knows it."[81] This last statement, I suggest, is a simplistic formulation of what Epstein projected to the world, as his frustrations regarding his social position (as is evident from his 'Indian Sculpture' draft; see p. 125) were more complex. Modern art, as he perceived it, ignored the symbolic forms of tradition, exchanging them for meaningless forms, which from Epstein's point of view did not have what Squire termed "personal messages" to deliver. It is thus unsurprising that in his autobiography he did not comment on the work of contemporary artists, nor did he mention names; he merely described what his own art was about, and related it to those few artists whose work he revered.

NOT THEIR FINEST HOUR

There were other subjects that preoccupied Epstein in addition to his tribulations with the book, and on 18 March 1940 he wrote a long letter to Oko which reflected his oscillating moods.[82] The only positive details in it are that Peggy Jean's Leda, his granddaughter, "is a darling & I have already made 2 studies of her" and that Peggy Jean "is a happy wife & mother". Epstein mentions a bust sent to Dr Roitman in Cincinnati, writing that he had received for it the money which "came just in time to save me from several unpleasant & infested [sic] Creditors. Were things normal here I could meet all my debts & keep going but nothing is as it was."

His gloomy remarks on England's state of affairs probably do not vary from those that might have been made by other taxpayers: "Our rulers having handed us in an extra war demand [taxes] that we pay not very in piece as of flesh [sic; alluding to Shylock] but also the few pennies we make to keep ourselves in rations ... local rates have risen to breaking point". The rest of the letter conveys a sense of retreat, or a kind of surrender to mental exhaustion:

78 Feibleman, *Philosophers Lead Sheltered Lives*, p. 98.

79 Anon., *Time*, 28 October 1940: www.time.com/time/magazine/article/0,9171,764884,00.html.

80 In 1937 Sir John Collins Squire (1884–1958) became a reviewer for the *Illustrated London News*, where his favourable appreciation of Epstein's autobiography appeared on 12 December 1940.

81 Newton, 'Epstein', *Journal of the Society of Arts*.

82 Letter from Epstein to Dr Oko, 18 March 1940: HUCAC.

> I have of course an expensive place if I do outsell my things & selling is very much out of the question. I have tried to arrange an exhibition of sculpture in New York. That may be difficult a go[.] I must come across if I do. In fact there is no future here for me. The few persons who might have bought my things are scared stiff now.

In contrast to the above, one recalls his statement of 9 September 1938 to Sally Ryan: "I cannot imagine myself working in New York" (p. 112).

Margaret's letter of 17 April 1940 echoes the concerns expressed in Epstein's letter, but it relates mainly to her own fears and hopes in regard to leaving England:[83] "If we could find 1000 Pounds Sterling independent of Michael Joseph or of Spencer Curtis Brown our agent & go between, Epstein and Jackie and I might take the last boat to New York and stay for the duration [of the war, as] the bombs are to come"; and in a comment in the margin she adds: "Europe is not Healthy for Jews". Her worries emerge strongly in a letter dated 20 May, written after hearing that most of Rotterdam had been destroyed by bombs and nearly 1,000 people killed, and the rest threatened by typhoid – from which she calculates that in London casualties could amount to two million; she adds: "perhaps some kind millionaire Rev. will get 3 seats on the Yankee clipper for Jackie & Epstein and me soon to take us where there are no bombs".

To escape from bombs makes sense, but in Margaret's case it seems also to have been an escape from the unmentioned Kathleen. She reiterates her attempts to present Epstein's work abroad: "Knoedler's Gallery has been approached. They are willing to hold an exhibition in the autumn in New York"; and again, she repeats her hopes to escape to New York "for the duration [and] perhaps for always, who knows".

Epstein was now thinking along the same lines (although perhaps for different reasons), writing a long letter on the same day, 17 April, hoping that Oko would not think he was to turn him into a dealer, "& one without commission. I take it you are interested".[84] Negotiating an exhibition of work in the autumn, he hopes "to come over with Peggy & Jackie so that I can do portraits. It is on the portraits I count most." This latter statement would seem to demonstrate Epstein's sense of being lost, generally or artistically, when compared to what he had written to Kathleen during his visit to New York in 1927, namely, that he had no "ambition to do busts of professors and public men ... loathe the idea of doing such work".[85] On his financial problems Epstein wrote that "We just can't meet things here", as the war had brought about a terrible impasse in his life and that of Peggy (his wife's nickname), who was "very unusual this winter, a heathen cold winter that tired everybody". He tells about the forced sale of "my Matthew Smith collection", but he still has "the two largest canvases veritable masterpiece ... I am forced to sell them to keep going. My personal luxuries like my Matthew Smith paintings & my nature collections are in jeopardy."[86] As for the state of his art – "Sculpture here is at a standstill .... Artists are having a rough time & I am having a rotten time."

Suspecting that the collection of bronzes that had been "stolen" from him were now on exhibition in New York with *Adam*, Epstein adds a cynical comment on the low price he has had to accept in order to reimburse the Leicester Gallery for its advance, and at the end of the day he had lost while "the rogue who bought the statue has formed himself with my 'Adam' & the stolen sculptures into a company".

The most interesting and revealing part of this long letter, however, is the openness

83 Letter from Margaret to Dr Oko, 17 April 1940: HUCAC.

84 Letter from Epstein to Dr Oko, 17 April 1940: HUCAC.

85 Letter from Epstein to Kathleen, 1928: NAGW–NY-2-rtf.

86 Epstein's attempts to sell them by himself are expressed through his failure to convince Mr and Mrs Samuels of Liverpool to purchase them, and in a letter of 22 May 1940 he expresses his regrets that they haven't reached "any agreement" over Smith's *Reclining Nude*, which Epstein regarded as "a masterpiece": TGA.9012.1.

with which he expresses his innermost feelings about people's attitude to him and his art:

> My representation is great but as I am not the laud of artists (say in portraits) that is popular even my great sculptures cannot bring me a postcard home.
>
> I don't think there is anything antisemite in this. I am just not in the English taste; I have known this all my life & have ignored it. At last it stares me in the face.

In May 1940 the Olympic Games were cancelled and Winston Churchill became Prime Minister of Great Britain, succeeding Neville Chamberlain and telling the nation that he had "nothing to offer but blood, toil, tears and sweat". Epstein's long letter of June to Oko reported the crucial occurrences occupying the minds of the British people, mainly the retreat from Dunkirk that ended on 4 June, after which Churchill promised to fight on the beaches, fields and streets, urging the perseverance of the population so that future generations would remember that "this was their finest hour". The by now elderly Epsteins, as reflected in their correspondence of the period, seem to have had little perseverance, partly because of the daily bombings over London, partly on account of their dealings with a publisher who did not meet their expectations, partly worrying about their little boy and grandchildren and, I suggest, not least because they had become exhausted from confrontations with galleries that did not sell Epstein's works and from the worsening of their financial situation which, to say the least, had never been good. Nevertheless, it was much better than the Epstein's earliest period of constant poverty. I asked Peggy Jean whether Margaret had ever complained about the harsh times, and the answer was "No; she just said they were 'hard'".[87]

One is left to wonder to what extent their lack of perseverance might have also stemmed from the general mood in London towards "them people", as described by Epstein in the same long letter of June:

> For one thing the word-spread anti Jewish propaganda [can] only have terrible results & in certain circumstances Jews will be in the same trouble here as they are in Germany. So much for the tolerance of Mosley & Co!

And expressing a personal fear, he adds:

> I fear for Jackie. Peggy Jean & her little one I hope will leave as soon as they can arrange it. I hope it is not too late. I am planning with Peggy to get away with Jackie[.] I hope it is not too late.

He then explains to Oko that it is one thing to be absorbed in one's work in the US (where he "would like to be now"), while it is quite another thing to work in a country where the mob and its politicians would be compelled to make the Jews a scapegoat.

Epstein's artistic influence on Oko seems to have led the latter to accumulate a collection of "ethnographical works and fetiches" (mainly African) that remained in England when the Okos left for America. Margaret, realising that the Okos would not be in England again for some time, sent it to them as soon as it became possible, also because when one sells nothing, she explained in her letter,[88] income tax still has to be paid for artefacts held over a long period;[89] therefore "things happen to ones nerves and one

87 Peggy Jean's phone conversation with the author, 2001.

88 Letter from Margaret to Oko, 24 June 1940: HUCAC.

89 This is a point I was not aware of, and was explained by Beth Lipkin (1985) when I asked why Epstein had to dispose of art, and almost all of his Matthew Smith paintings: "Taxes", she said.

does not want to shoulder other people's responsibilities". This comment by Margaret, of wishing to stay out of Oko's affairs, seems somewhat ingracious in view of what is written in the rest of the letter (as well as in others), openly and constantly asking Oko to share the burden of the Epsteins' problems. Margaret's comment, at this stage of their relationship, may indicate that "things" indeed were happening to her nerves, and that she had lost her sense of perspective. The war too, was having its effect:

> When the book is out on your side and also on this side of the Atlantic I hope the war will have cleared and the enemy disheartened a bit by contact with desperate fighters real heroes defending their own.
>
> It must be encouraging for the censors who read other people's letters for the government to discover every wish of their own repeated [in this letter] with more or less to the scales [i.e. to same extent].[90]

A further indication of her state of mind is reflected in a letter sent on 22 June to the architect William Holden (with whom Epstein probably had had little contact, if any, since their dispute over the preservation of the BMA sculptures in 1937; pp. 101–02). It seems to convey the almost desperate situation that forced Margaret into asking his help in what could be considered an almost criminal offence, "to find a safe place" to keep Epstein's work, which is "in danger of being seized in lieu of debts". Holden replied by suggesting that she make an arrangement with a dealer which would clear the debt.[91]

The almost sole help from serious buyers during that period had been extended by the Liverpool couple Mr and Mrs Samuels.[92] They had purchased Epstein's work from the gallery during the 1930s, and in the 1940s they became friendly enough to come to purchase directly from Epstein himself. Thus, Epstein mentions in his letter[93] the casting in bronze of the *Cunningham-Grahame* portrait for them, and complains that he had not been able "to get my girl [Peggy Jean, by then married to an American] off yet" (to the US), as it depended on obtaining her birth certificate from France. Further on he writes: "I suppose the Matthew Smith arrived all right", indicating that he had managed to sell at least one of the Smiths that still remained in his possession. Later on Epstein arranged for the Samuels to meet Smith at his place and, as Epstein phrased it in his letter, they saw "what an innocent and unassuming person he is despite his great qualities & reputation as a painter". He also reminded them of his own exhibition of flower paintings, to be held on 17 September at the Leicester Galleries, which "I hope will bring me in some money for I'll need it" and that they would be sold for 25 guineas each. He sold the Samuels three of the paintings, charging them – minus the gallery commission – only £59.1.3, "which will just about pay for PJ's tickets". He wished to include their purchased paintings in the exhibition as "lent by you. That helps a show a lot if you can start it with something sold". Admitting to his shortcomings, he asks them perhaps not to advance the money, as "that would keep me from spending it which is what usually takes place".

The appearance of German bombers in the skies over London during the afternoon of 7 September 1940 signalled the beginning of the Blitz, and Epstein's exhibition of flower paintings at the Leicester Galleries, which he had counted on to bring in some income, was postponed by the owners, who feared that no one would come. The gallery nonetheless tried to maintain its activity, and the show was eventually presented later in that

90 Letter from Margaret to Oko, 24 June 1940: HUCAC.

91 As phrased in the abstract of the letter that is part of the Adams Holden & Pearson Papers, Series 15: personal and private correspondence of Charles Holden, 1917–1955 Order/Ref. no.: AHP\28\19\1-3, cited in *The Dictionary of National Biography, 1941–1950*, ed. L.G. Wickham Legg and E.T. Williams, Oxford 1959, pp. 762–63.

92 Letters from Esptein to Mr and Mrs Samuels are in the Tate archive, TGA.9012. 1-17.

93 Letter from Epstein to Mr and Mrs Samuels, 9 August 1940: TGA-9012/.2.

month, and was quite a success.[94] For the catalogue Epstein "found those 2 lines from the sonnets":

> How can this rage with beauty hold a plea
> Whose action is no stronger than a flower? [95]

Hardly four days after expressing his satisfaction with the reception of his exhibition of the flower paintings which "started off all right … a bomb dropped on Leicester Sq. & the blast has done some damage to the Gallery altho no actual damage to the paintings", he wrote to Samuels,[96] and the gallery owners were afraid to continue, in spite of his trying "to install courage into their rabbit natures". A little later, however, when the artist William Roberts came to the gallery,[97] he "found Brown and his assistants putting things in order and sweeping up broken glass. He [Brown] said to me 'We don't intend to close, Sir Kenneth Clark has asked us to carry on'."[98]

Meanwhile, the earlier cancellation of the exhibition had brought some friends to the rescue:[99] "Matt Smith bought the first picture & the Contemporary Art Society also bought & Moshe Oved (Edward Good), and [Mr & Mrs] Maisky". Epstein also turned for help to Samuels, asking him to send the previously rejected advance payment for the paintings (see p. 132), less the commission; owing to the considerable expense of arranging the show, "the little you've mentioned in your letter [as] it would help …. I look to you as a friend," he wrote,[100] adding a bitter comment on the gallery that he had dealt with for 25 years: although "they have made thousands of pounds out of my [works] they are still not my friend in an emergency & look cold bloodedly on my shows as just money making". He therefore asked the Samuels to find other buyers for his flower paintings, to be sold without commission. He needed money "as my girl is about to have a baby, it is useless counting on my savings for that[,] especially as I must carry on personally".

In order to solve his financial problems Epstein needed to seize any opportunity to sell his work, and so he sent two bronzes to New York ("One is a head study of Hornstein [his son-in law] called 'Ishmael' & the other 'Leda' at 7 months[,] Peggy Jean's lovely girl") for a retrospective exhibition in October at his old school, the Educational Alliance, while understanding that it was to be a "somewhat a fancy affair & is not a selling proposal".[101] However, he adds in his letter, "they are all for sale of course …. If I could sell them during the show I could ask you to look after them. Possibly you might find a buyer." Indeed he sets out his terms: "I have placed the prices of £200 & £100 on them but I would accept anything 'reasonable'". The rest of the letter gives a glimpse into Epstein's tax troubles, of the kind mentioned by Margaret in regard to Oko's collection (p. 131): "The government has allowed [the sculptures] out for a period of 6 months & if unsold by then they will have to come back to me", and he was worried about his other sculptures and drawings, as one bomb could destroy the lot.

After almost two weeks of the Blitz, Epstein expressed in his letter of 10 October his view of London at war, reporting that there had been no attempt by the Germans "at attacking military objectives & bombs are dropped in London & about London indiscriminately", trying to destroy the city. "It's not so bad during the day when planes can go off & bring them down or drive them off but at night it is more difficult & we all live in the cellars or in the shelters … our strange government are opposed to deep shelters; how

94 Letter from Epstein to Oko, 18 September 1940: HUCAC: "They sold readily at 25 guineas. I have now done about 150 new paintings".

95 Ibid. Shakespeare's sonnet 65 in fact reads: "How with this rage shall beauty hold a plea".

96 Letter from Epstein to Samuels, 19 October 1940: TGA.9012-6.

97 William Roberts (1895–1980) was a Vorticist artist – or Cubist, as he considered himself – whom Epstein knew well.

98 William Roberts, 'The Leicester Galleries'.

99 Letter from Epstein to Dr Oko, 10 October 1940: HUCAC.

100 Letter from Epstein to Samuels, 16 September 1940: TGA.9012.4.

101 Letter from Epstein to Dr Oko, 18 September 1940: HUCAC.

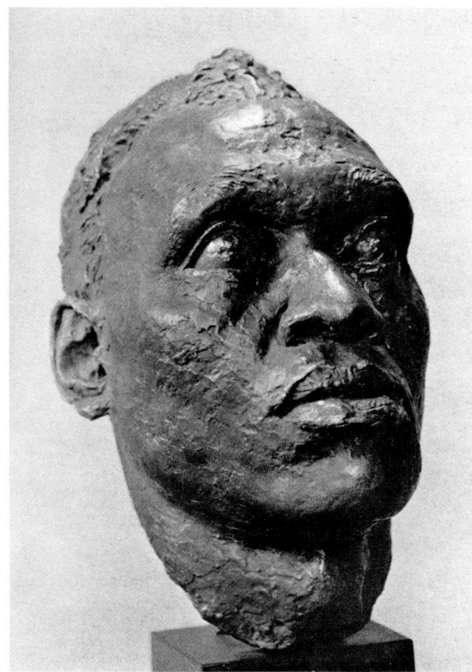

58
Paul Robeson, 1928
Bronze, 34.5 x 21.5 cm
York City Art Gallery

long the people will stand for this I don't know but this absolutely criminal attitude of the government is spreading an uneasy feeling." However, in spite being dissatisfied with the authorities, he ends his letter with an optimistic and a patriotic statement: "Of course we are not D---- as French & will put up a stiff fight: our air force is doing wonders."

In 15 October 1940, amid his problems with his autobiography, which "does not come out until November" but "has been accepted by the 'book club' as their trifle book of the month", thus helping sales, Epstein wrote to Oko about a totally new project:

> Despite everything I am working & now have an American negro boxer posing for me. I will use the study of him for a project & have [...] harboured a work concerned with negro slavery for which I have made sketches.

Two works – a drawing and a sculpture – are related to this subject of Negro slavery. Why the American-born Epstein should have seen fit to engage only now, in the late 1940s, with an issue with which he had been acquainted since childhood I can only speculate – possibly he was influenced by Paul Robeson's decision to come to live in England with his family.[102]

The Robeson-Epstein contact had begun in New York in 1927 (I/183–84, 186), during which time Epstein had done Robeson's portrait [58], and it continued after the Robesons arrived in England (1928–39). Paul Robeson had acquired fame and success both as a singer and as an actor. He played the role of Joe, specially written for him, in the London production of the American musical *Show Boat* (his rendition of 'Ol' Man River' is still widely considered the definitive version of the song), and in May 1930 he became the first black actor in nearly a century to play Othello, opposite Peggy Ashcroft's Desdemona, in an otherwise all-white cast.

Both Epstein and Robeson were socialists and when Fascism escalated in Europe they joined the anti-Fascist movement A.I.A (see p. 76); but while Epstein remained an uninvolved supporter Robeson became an ardent activist, who, by December 1937, had addressed four rallies for the Republican cause and visited Spain in 1938. Upon his return he set out to raise funds for the Spanish Republic as well as medical care for the returning wounded American veterans. During 1939 Robeson became increasingly involved with the struggles of British workers [fig. 38], entering the pits with miners to see for himself their working conditions and performing for them on numerous occasions.

From the sketches mentioned in Epstein's letter, only the one presented here appears to have survived [59], seemingly reflecting the crowd of Robeson's miners in the photograph as well as old engravings of slaves in ship-holds [figs. 39a–b] that no doubt Epstein had seen in books in his youth. But is this a 'good' drawing? Although it conveys a sense of inhuman crowding, it somehow remains on the plane of mere illustration, lacking what might be termed "the sense of horror"[103] conveyed in the less-crowded but similarly beam-framed shelter drawings made by Henry Moore [fig. 39c].[104]

It was only in his sculpture, I suggest, that Epstein succeeded in conveying a state that went beyond the rhetoric of the plight of the black man, because, being made during a period in which much of Europe was progressively being held in chains, his plight became the plight of every chained human being, of loss of freedom.

102 Buckle (*Epstein: Sculptor*, p. 267) offers no explanation. Neither does Gardiner, although he may have provided a hint by citing Epstein's correspondence with Paul Robeson's wife, who not only commissioned Paul Robeson Junior's portrait but also arranged to have two more copies made for other people (Gardiner, *Epstein*, p. 377). The Robeson connection is suggested here as the inspiration for the "negro slavery" works.

103 Drawings of concentration camps conveying a similar atmosphere of crowding would be made by other Jewish artists later on. There is no evidence of Epstein dealing with this subject.

104 Among the Tate's collection of Moore's shelter-drawings, I have chosen this particular one because the structure of the tunnel echoes Epstein's beam above the people's heads.

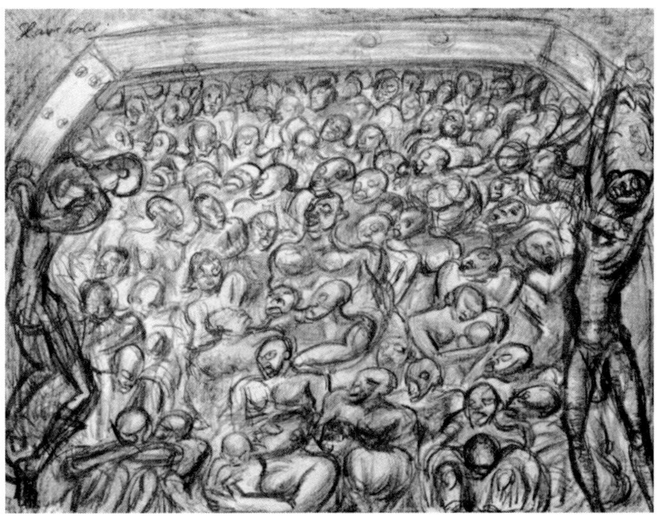

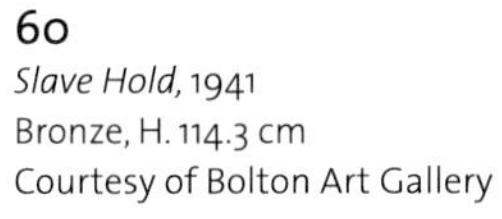

59
Den
Pencil on paper, 180 x 230 mm
Private collection

60
Slave Hold, 1941
Bronze, H. 114.3 cm
Courtesy of Bolton Art Gallery

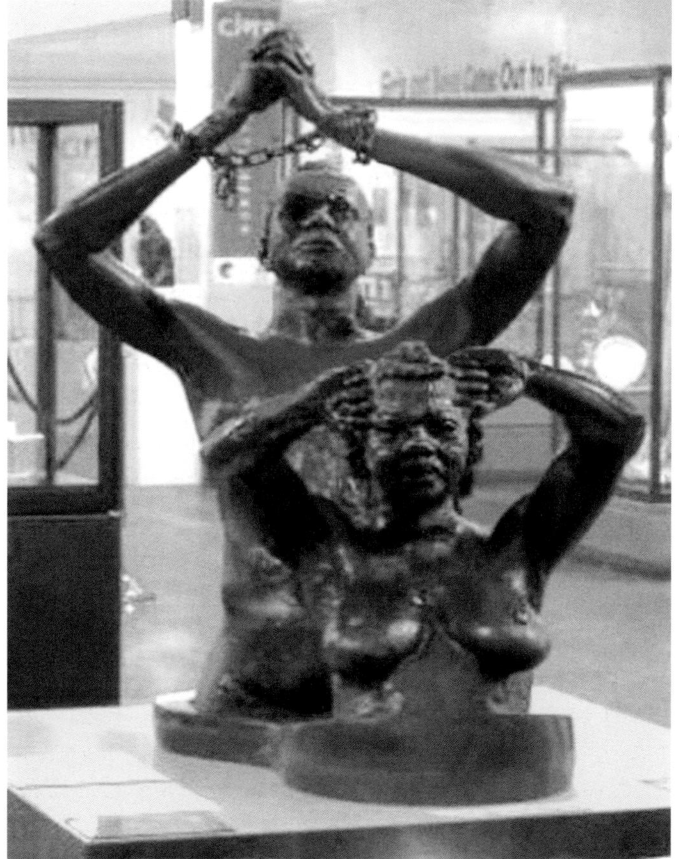

Fig. 38
Paul Robeson among protesting miners, 1939

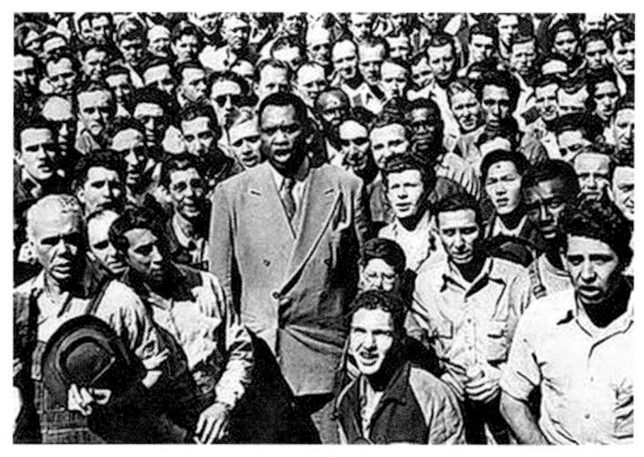

Figs. 39a–b
Old engravings of slaves in ship-holds

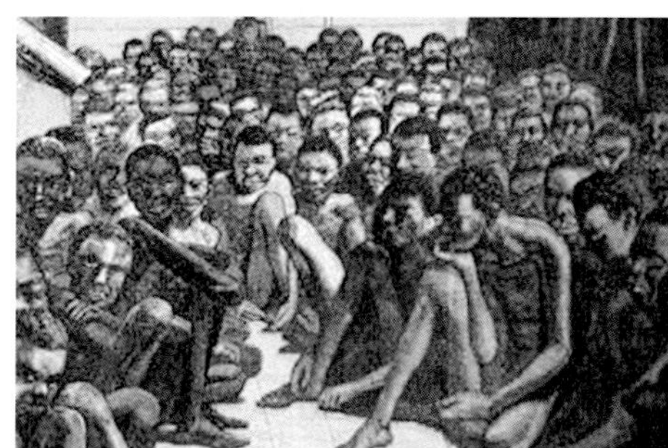

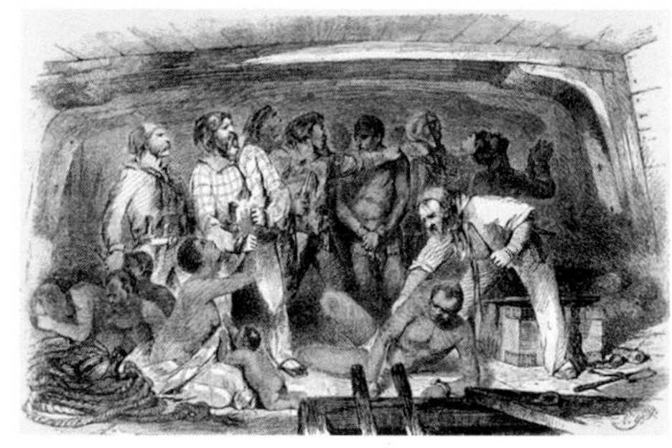

Fig. 39c
Henry Moore
Shelter
Pen and black ink, 47.7 x 43.2 cm
Tate

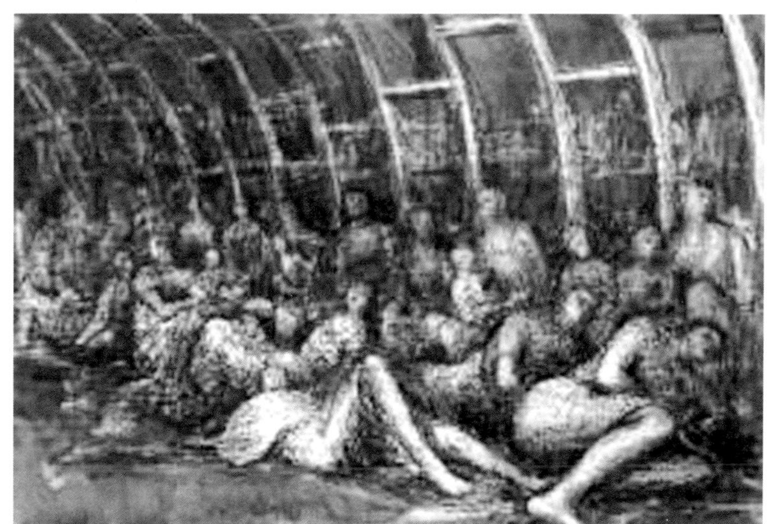

The bronze *Slave Hold* [60] features two figures, male and female, presented from the waist up, holding their chained hands above their heads. Although for the male figure Epstein used the new model mentioned in his letter, for the woman he seems to have drawn on the head of Betty Peters, a favourite model of his during the 1940s.[105] The expression of man's evil to man in this sculpture, reflected through the plight of the Negro race,[106] as well as the struggle against evil of Epstein's own race during this period, might have triggered in him a desire to find an expression for the fight against all evils, in a project that followed shortly afterwards.

Epstein's personal interests are mixed with general ones in his letter to Oko of 15 October, "sending a cutting to show how Hebrew books have suffered although Jewish literature has already been burnt in Germany"; he does not forget to comment on more painful and acute issues:

> the howling of warning sirens reminds me of German falcons overhead at only 8.30 in the morning. We are all safe so far, & I am trying to get with my work, but one naturally apprehension etc. [sic]
>
> I am having dinner with Matthew Smith tonight at the 'Church'. You know he has had a son killed while flying in Egypt & his younger son is also in the air force; so things are tragic here.

Epstein's personal treasures at home were not affected by the bombing, but those he had tried to protect in warehouses, including his collection of antiques, had been soaked in water "which has not done them very good [sic]. I am taking them out gradually from the vaults where they were flooded. I am now drying them & trying to get them back into condition again", he wrote in November.[107] After discussing a possible exhibition of his work in New York, to which he would like "to send my two large carvings 'Behold the Man' & the 'Consum[m]atum Est' & forty bronzes as well", and mentioning that the overall expenses of £300 "are beyond me", he adds some personal details:

> I wish Jackie were where it is safer. God above knows when all this is finished .... I have Jackie at Epping where I still go weekends. It is safer out there than here in London .... Peggy [Margaret] is all right .... Matt Smith was at Epping last week end & enjoyed it.
>
> The winter isn't very delightful to look forward to.

JACOB AND THE ANGEL

After Epstein's memoirs had finally been published towards the end of 1940, later works that he created during that year and after are mentioned in a 'Postscript' written for the new edition of 1954, entitled *Epstein: Autobiography*. However, the postscript provides very few details on his major projects and hardly any on personal matters. Some of his portraits and their sitters consttiute most of the matter of the postscript – Epstein perhaps unconsciously countering the usual tendency to regard them as less important. The task of a researcher seeking to understand Epstein's motives and actions, in light of the little

105 Silber, *Sculpture of Epstein*, no. 307. A date of 1939 is suggested for the portrait of Betty but, as it was presented with *Slave Hold* in the Leicester Galleries' exhibition no. 752 in 1942, it seems reasonable to relate it to *Slave Hold*.

106 Silber, in *Sculpture of Epstein*, claims that *African Mother and Child*, no. 303, made in 1939, was "intended as part of *Slave Hold*". Although Epstein, in stating its date as 1940 (PS/126–27), brings it close in time to the execution of *Slave Hold*, I fail to see any common context of motherhood and slavery.

107 Letter from Epstein to Oko, 9 November 1940: HUCAC.

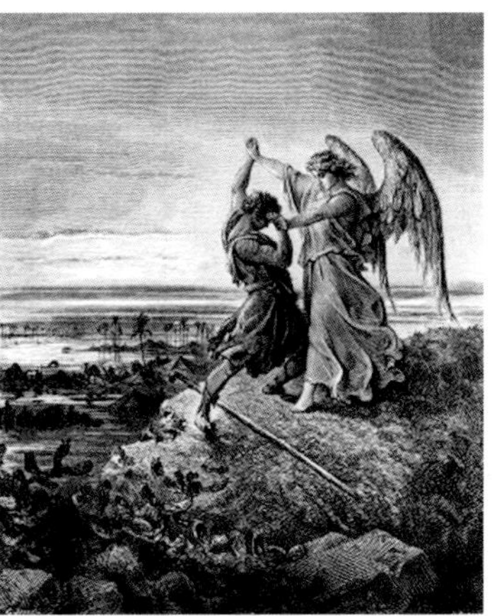

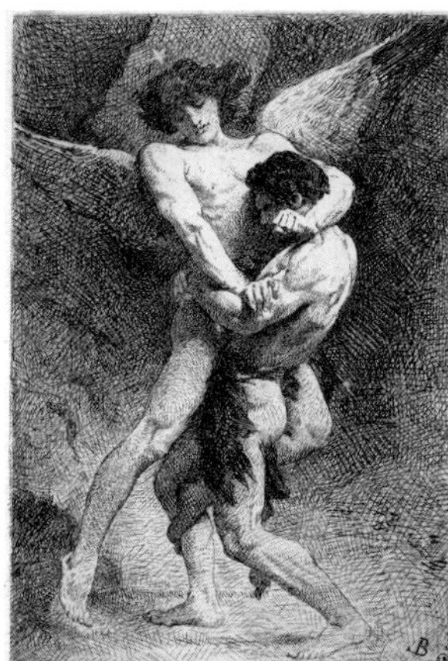

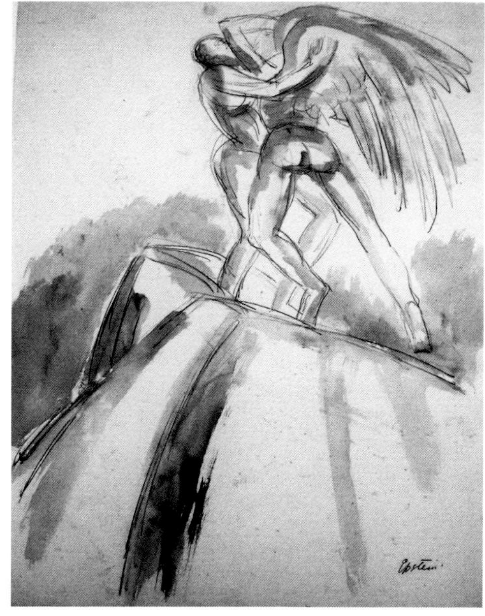

Fig. 40
Gustave Doré
Jacob wrestling with the Angel, 1866
Engraving

Fig. 41
Léon-Joseph-Florentine Bonnat
Jacob wrestling with the Angel, 1876
Pencil and black chalk on paper, 527 x 368 mm
Monchy-St Eloi, France

61
Jacob wrestling with the Angel, 1931
Watercolour and pencil; 570 x 430 mm
Private collection, on loan to NAGW

information provided, is not an easy one. It becomes harder still in the absence for the later years of the kind of correspondence he held with Oko, and even harder when one tries to relate the artist to the social and artistic panorama of a period for which there is so much information and, by contrast, it is easy to be carried away by details.

It is unclear when Epstein started to work on *Jacob and the Angel*. Oddly enough, I have not been able to find any comment on it made by Epstein himself – perhaps because it was carved concomitantly with his arduous negotiations over the text of his autobiography, in which only works already completed were mentioned. However, one wonders why it was not mentioned in the 'Postscript' of 1954.

Probably he started the carving towards late 1940, and on 10 June 1941 he was still working on it: this is indicated in a letter to Samuels, in which he writes of his disappointment with a Mr Margulies, who had spoken of purchasing a cast of *The Visitation* but did not carry it through: "For one thing I thought it would help me to finish my present great work 'Jacob and the Angel'".[108] He had barely finished it by the end of the year, "putting in some hard work on his new carving[.] It will probably be his last alabaster group he says here", commented Margaret in the margin of her October letter.[109]

When had Epstein first considered doing this sculpture? It is reasonable to suggest that, as with his other large works, he had been brooding on it for quite a while. In all probability he settled on the idea during 1940, perhaps in September when the Blitz started (it continued until May 1941), thus imbuing the subject-matter with relevancy – a war between the Nietzschean 'beautiful animal', offspring of the 'Aryan Sun',[110] and a peaceful entity that simply wanted to sit quietly in its tent. It is also reasonable to suggest that the first seeds of the subject were planted in his mind when, in response to the growing anti-Semitism around him, he included *Jacob wrestling* among his Old Testament illustrations in 1931. In this drawing [61] Epstein was obviously influenced by Doré's renowned engraving of the protagonists' combat (fig. 40) – the angel's light hair contrasting Jacob's dark hair, and in particular the setting for the figures on the edge of a cliff, the angel to the right as if trying to push Jacob over it. However, in accordance with his Symbolist practice of bestowing an allegorical meaning on naked figures (already applied by him in the Calamus drawings; I/57), Epstein stripped both Jacob and the angel, thus echoing a drawing by the Symbolist Bonnat (fig. 41), with whose work he had probably became well acquainted during his studies in Paris.[111]

108 Letter from Epstein to the Samuels, 10 June 1941: TGA-9012.9.

109 Letter from Margaret to Dr Oko, 9 October 1941: HUCAC. In it "he says here" probably means 'he says now, while I'm writing to you'.

110 Lulu, from the play *Erdgeist* (Earth Spirit; 1895) by the German dramatist Frank Wedekind, is "the true animal, the wild, beautiful animal" and, as Friedrich Nietzsche put it, "a blonde beast". She personified a primal form of woman in whom the barbaric is considered admirable for its sheer strength, daring, energy and willingness to take risks. 'The Aryan Sun' is an expression that I coined. See a brief mention on p. 57, and a more elaborate discussion in I/52.

111 Bonnat (1833–1922) was a professor at the Ecole des Beaux Arts in 1882, and appointed in May 1905 as director of the school. Epstein attended this school during part of the academic year 1903–04 (I/43–44). There is no information on contact between them, but Bonnat was quite popular with American students in Paris. He spoke Spanish and Italian and knew English well, to the relief of many monolingual Americans. He was friendly with Rodin, and his non-portraiture drawings were influenced by the Symbolists, as fig. 40 attests.

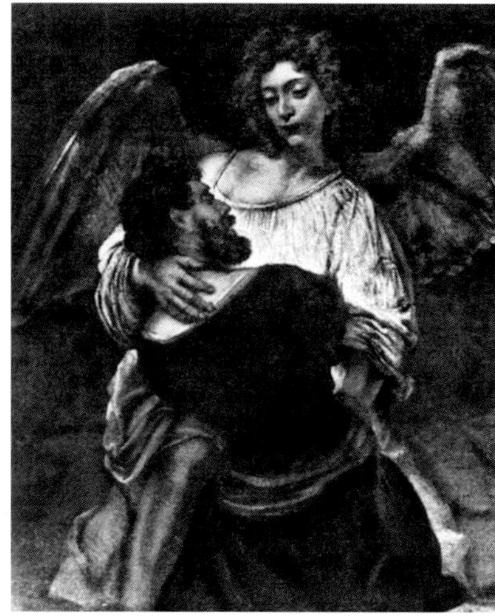

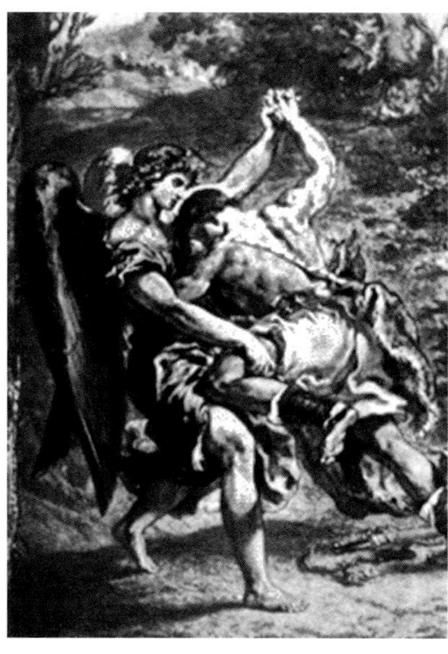

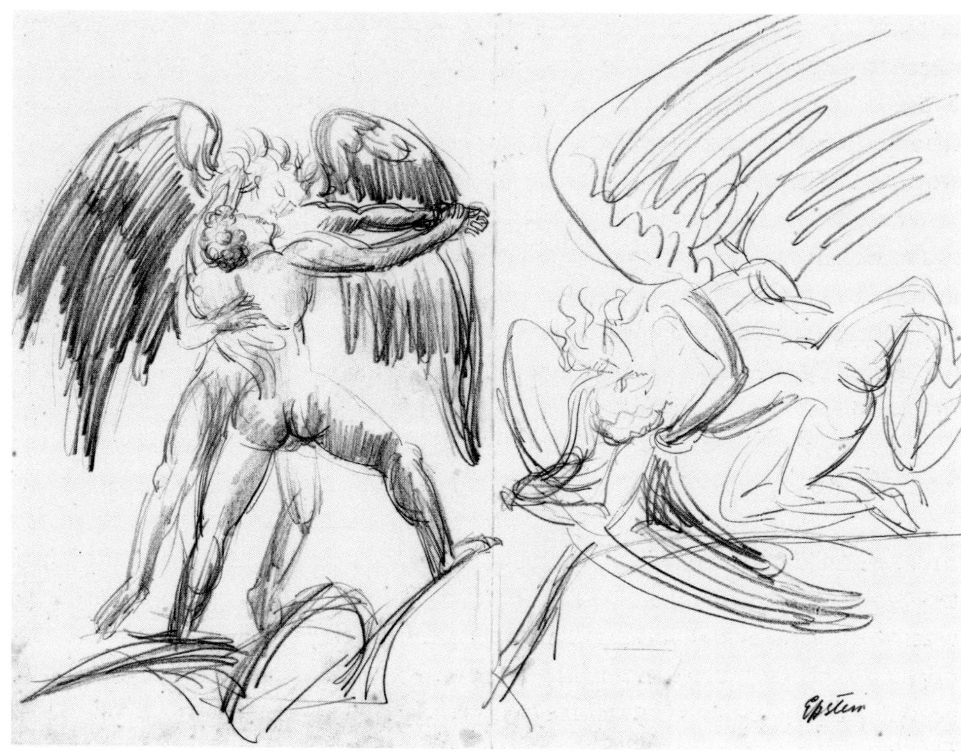

Fig. 42
Rembrandt van Rijn
Jacob wrestling with the Angel, 1659
Oil on canvas, 137 x 116 cm
Staatliche Museen, Berlin

Fig. 43
Eugène Delacroix
Jacob wrestling with the Angel (detail), 1856–61
Oil on wood, 71.4 x 48.5 cm
St-Sulpice, Paris

62
Studies for 'Jacob and the Angel', 1940–41
Pencil, 445 x 575 mm
Private collection

As Epstein did not usually date his drawings, it is not clear exactly when he made the two other sketches on this subject, both on the same page [62], which are generally related to the period of the carved sculpture despite acknowledgement that the drawings have no formal or conceptual denominators in common with it.[112] I consider them to be preliminary sketches that project his musings prior to the more minimalist approach that eventually characterized his illustrations of the Old Testament,[113] and I comment on them before discussing the sculpture itself.

This pair of drawings stimulated tantalizing speculations by commentators, such as: "whether standing or rolling on the ground, they seem to kiss';[114] and in this vein of implied sexual ambiguity, a more blunt interpretation regarded their standing pose with arms outstretched as expressing "impassionate dance, and then falling to the ground like lovers in a carnal embrace", recalling the Calamus "homoerotic illustrations".[115] In an attempt to shed light on this grey area between homo-eroticism and male friendship-comradeship, in which the intimacy is not necessarily a sexual one, I have argued against such simplistic interpretations of the Calamus drawings (I/56), and a similar reservation applies to these two drawings, too. Comparison to Rembrandt's painting on the subject (fig. 42) surely raises the question whether the effeminate angel's face looking longingly at Jacob, his hands tenderly clasping Jacob's waist and back in what can be interpreted as a loving embrace, really constitute or deserve the label 'homoerotic'.

The ambiguous connotation in Rembrandt's painting could equally well be perceived as a mixture of attraction and rejection between the two protagonists; the former emotion (which is not necessarily sexual) is evident in the faces and the embracing pose, and the latter in the retreating head and shoulders of the man. The struggle between them is depicted in physically contrasting movements of limbs: while Jacob's back seems to be forcibly pushed towards the angel by the angel's exposed knee and leg on it, Jacob's rejection is expressed by his hands pushing the angel away. Epstein's drawings, as well as the sculpture discussed below, echo the same sense of attraction and rejection rather than the expected vigorous biblical struggle, like the one depicted in another renowned work, by Delacroix (fig. 43).

With the exception of Bonnat's naked bodies, in all the other precedents noted (and as also seen in earlier illustrations of this struggle) the figures are dressed. Naked bodies involved in a physical combat are bound to touch one another, with their sexual organs too. Bonnat's solution to this was to add a kind of drapery to Jacob's loins seen in profile [fig. 40], whilst in Epstein's pencil drawings the problem does not arise as Jacob is seen from behind.

A more direct precedent, formal as well as contextual, and within Epstein's own work, for the carved *Jacob and the Angel* seems to be one of Epstein's drawings, entitled *Together They Fought*, for Moshe Oved's *The Book of Affinity*, in which he had illustrated a struggle similar to that in *Genesis* between a human and a superhuman being. Oved's fantasy-parable, briefly mentioned earlier (p. 73), had been written during the tumultuous years when Fascism and anti-Semitism were gaining political power in Germany, with ripples also in England. It was published in 1933, after Hitler had come to power and had begun his efforts legally to intimidate Jews, ultimately driving many of them into exile. This campaign against Jews, culminating in their outright persecution, is echoed also in Oved's book. For example, Chapter I/2 describes a mob storming a shop, "shouting deliriously, tossing flags, daggers, and all manner of weapons of destruction, exclaiming: "Jew! Bolshevik! Alien! Jew!" It is little wonder that Epstein felt an empathy with Oved's text, particularly as similar, if disguised, epithets had been aimed at him and at his art. The exposition of the book and the interpretation of each symbolic point are not our concern here, excepting one chapter in it, important for understanding the spirit that preceded Epstein's drawing of Jacob and the Angel as well as the carved work and his ultimate approach to it.

Chapter I/4 tells the story of a lamb's skull given to the protagonist by a wanderer who then vanishes. At a certain point the skull metamorphoses into a "lion cub, all blazing with flame", declaring itself to be "He-She, Standard bearer of Affinity, leading the procession of Eternity into Order";[116] moreover, whilst clasping the man tightly in its jaws it claims that with its fire it will smite the man with its paws. This is the very pose that Epstein depicted in the drawing (inscribed on the back: *Together they struggled*), using only brown ink lines and hatchings for the figures, which float in a grey cloud [63]. Notable in this drawing are the bristling fairer locks of the lion, its clenched jaws close to the human figure's inclined dark-haired head, as if devouring the chin, and its tight grip that causes the human's legs to float. A similar pose and details were executed in the carving.

'Affinity' means among other things 'attraction'. It is this sense that seems to be at work within the man in Oved's story, in his being attracted to the lion cub's "shining body" that lights up the darkness; and he seems to feel a kind of attraction also to the cub's humane ability to "play a tragic tune when stung deep and raw by big big bee of Jealousy". Finally, when the man has recovered, toughened by He She's blows and thereby having acquired the ability and power to order it to depart, he achieves a kind

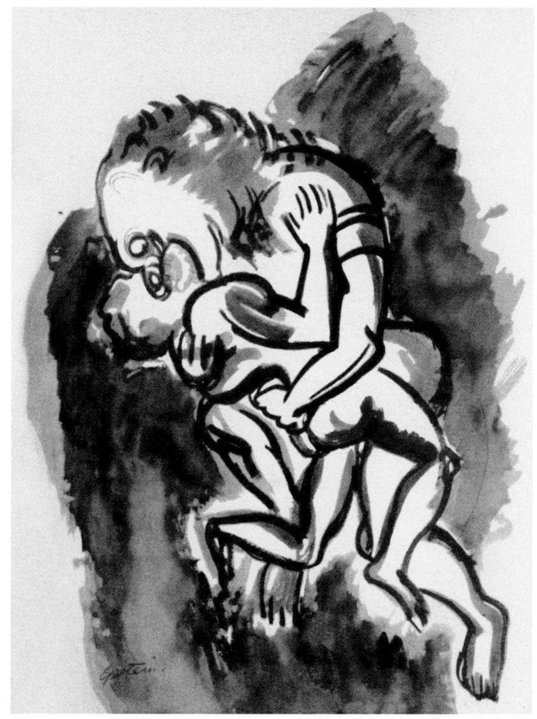

63
Together they struggled, 1933
Pen and wash
Mosheh Oyved, *The Book of Affinity*, p. 15

[opposite page]

112 Silber, *Sculpture of Epstein*, p. 54.

113 Unfortunately, there is no way to list all of Epstein's Old Testament drawings, and, since among those I could find there are several on one subject, there is room to assume that there might also have been others on the subject of Jacob and the Angel.

114 Silber, *Sculpture of Epstein*, p. 54.

115 Cork, *Jacob Epstein*, p. 63.

[this page]

116 The only 'he-she' entity in Jewish thought is God – as the creation of men and women in his image in Genesis 1: 27 may be interpreted. Oved's definition of its task, to lead into order, seems to follow and accentuate this interpretation.

of victory. Oved's story, therefore, has several similarities to the biblical story of Jacob's struggle, and was undoubtedly influenced by it and its end, in which, in spite of Jacob's injured thigh, the emissary (in Hebrew, 'angel') has to depart without imposing his will on Jacob.[117]

Jacob and the Angel [64c] is Epstein's second carved 'colossal' figure (larger than life-size) conceived in the round (*Adam* was the first). The two figures of the sculpture, a mature huge-winged one embracing, almost carrying, a helpless seemingly younger human figure, are struggling. Although the bodies are almost of the same height, the different masses of the bodies and heads and their details create the impression that the human is much smaller.

The contrasting elements of the heads are the most notable feature of the work: the angel's bright head, long face with thick lips and flying hair contrasts Jacob's darker short-cut curls and his small, smooth round face [64a]. Epstein repeated here what he had started in *Consummatum Est* and continued in *Adam*, using the lighter part of the stone for the head, thus giving it a spiritual aura. However, it is not Jacob who receives this aura but rather the winged figure, corresponding to the cub's "shining body" in Oved's text, and to the Aryan concept of "the beautiful blond animal" (see above, note 110). Another echo of Epstein's drawing is the sense that Jacob is floating, which is achieved through his being held under his armpits. However, this is just a projected sense because, in spite of the angel's effort to lift him (conveyed by Jacob's raised right heel), Jacob's left sole retains its hold on the ground. It is, I suggest, the barely raised heel of that sole that predicts Jacob's eventual mastery over the angel, by the very part of the body after which, in Hebrew, he is named.[118]

As in his previous monolithic works, in this one too Epstein sought to confine the figures and their movements within the frame of the block (thus not protruding from the figures' axis), leaving in it signs of its original form – in the barely touched wings, when viewed from the back [64b]; and, recalling the nakedness in his *Adam*, Epstein did not avoid displaying part of the angel's phallus; however, the viewer has to go arround the figure and look down in order to see it.

Commentators on the sculpture have had resort to common interpretations of Genesis 32: 24, perceiving the sculpture as an explicit and direct depiction of the biblical text and referring to previous representations of Jacob's struggle with a winged angel. There are two reservations in regard to this approach. First and foremost, Epstein had never before done this kind of sculpture in which the symbolism was so explicit; Epstein's symbolism, as argued (I/13), was an implicit one; and secondly, if one takes the text as a whole, Jacob, after over twenty years of hard labour in his father-in-law's household, was far from being a youngster when he struggled with his opponent. He would clearly not have had the figure's smooth young face after such years of toil, which were supposed to have left their marks on his complexion: as the text specifies, "Thus I was; in the day the drought consumed me. And the frost by night; and my sleep departed from mine eyes" (Genesis 31: 40). Had Epstein wanted to represent the text literally, he would have had to present a mature, wrinkled man, and also a bearded one, as the custom of the region would requireof a father of twelve. Instead, he presented an ageless figure, and thereby indicated that he had turned a mythological event taken from within his own culture into an implicit symbolism that served his own purpose.

117 I consider that a biblical interpretation is in the eye of the beholder: Cork (*Jacob Epstein*, p. 63) says that "Jacob failed to vanquish his opponent", probably because, according to the boxing code, he did not win by a knock-out. On the other hand, like me, one may regard the end result, holding the captured adversary, as a kind of victory, and, unlike Cork, not as being "reduced to holding on to his adversary's body and refusing to let go".

118 Ya'akov derives from Akev-heel, *Genesis* 25: 26: "and his hand took hold of Esau's heel; and his name was called Jacob".

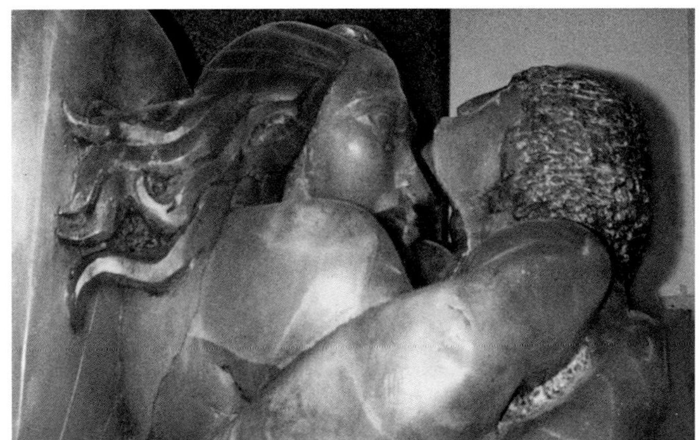

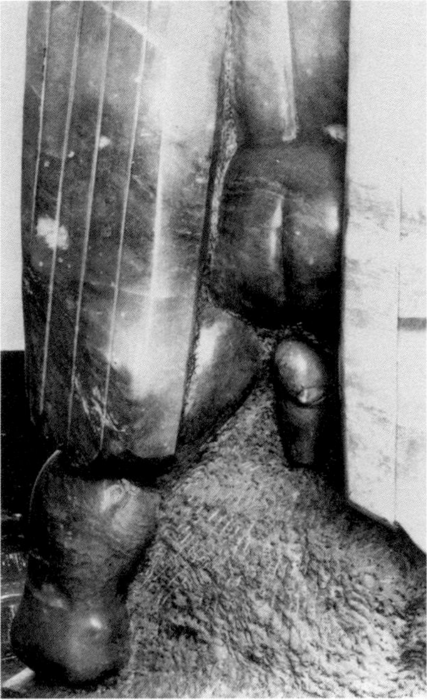

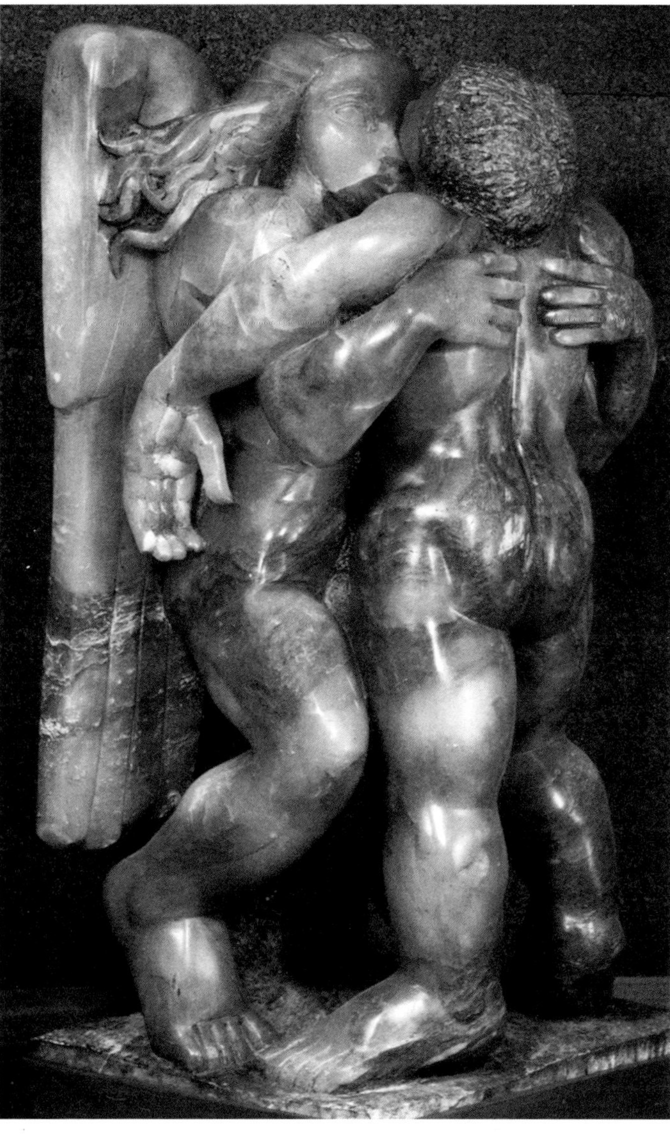

64c
Jacob and the Angel, 1940–41
Alabaster, H. 213 cm; base 109 x 117 cm
Tate

64a
Jacob and the Angel (heads)

64b
Jacob and the Angel (back)

Jacob's struggle, as reported in the Hebrew text, which Epstein knew well from reading his Bar-Mitzvah portion,[119] is reported as: "and there wrestled a man with him". The traditional Jewish interpretation regarded the "man" in the text as Esau's emissary, and viewed the struggle as an omen for the future in which the sons of Jacob would have to stand against hostile nations.[120] To express this meaning Epstein depicted the emissary (angel) in the traditional way, corresponding to representations, but with divergences. First and foremost the wings are a folkloric element he had used in the Tomb of Oscar Wilde, in which he had contended that they symbolized the task of "a messenger";[121] in *Jacob and the Angel* they are attributes of Esau's messenger. There is also present the more recent symbolism of the head of the *Sun God*, which he had perfected in 1931, redefining the long wavy hair. *Sun God*, as discussed above (pp. 56–57), had been a product of Epstein's engagement with what I have termed 'the Aryan Sun' (the attraction he and his contemporaries had felt during the 1910s towards the notion of the Aryan). With the victory of the Nazi movement, this notion had acquired frightening overtones:

119 Elaborated in I/19; briefly, Epstein's reading portion for his Bar-Mitzvah was *Genesis* 28–32: 3, which recounts Jacob's tribulations on his return to Canaan.

120 The renowned commentator Rashi (familiar to every Orthodox Jew), citing the oldest source, *Bereshit Raba* (77: 3).

121 Haskell, *The Sculptor Speaks*, p. 20.

the historic affinity of the Jewish cultural elite with, even devotion to, German culture had since the 1930s been effectively transformed by the Nazis into open Jewish-Aryan existential and cultural warfare. It seems almost to have been prerequisite that Epstein should take up his sun-god's head from the earlier period and rework it to fit this contemporary development.[122] As already suggested, Epstein's estrangement from these earlier ideas had begun in 1931–32, when *Sun God* as the creator of human life was superseded in his depiction of a 'begetter family' in *Primeval Gods*. The next step, I suggest, is expressed with all its ambiguity of attraction and rejection in *Jacob and the Angel*.[123]

While Epstein had been working on his carving, his personal affairs and the world around him were in turmoil. In January 1941 British troops marched into Abyssinia, liberating it from Italian conquest; in March Franklin D. Roosevelt signed the Lend-Lease Bill to lend money to Britain. An important event from a cultural point of view, and in particular for the music-loving Epstein, might have been the first performance in England of Benjamin Britten's *Sinfonia da Requiem*, op. 20. In April Germany bombed Coventry, destroying the ancient cathedral in which, when it was later rebuilt, Epstein's *Ecce Homo* and *St Michael* would eventually be placed. Meanwhile, in 1941, the sculptor had reached such a state that, in a cable to Oko, he had beg, "as a special favour" and "due to exceptional circumstances", for an advance on the American rights of his book to be cabled to him by the publisher Putnam.[124] In May the British cracked the German 'Enigma' code, almost at the same time that Adolf Hitler's deputy, Rudolf Hess, parachuted into Scotland, claiming that he was seeking a way to end the war, while the Germans launched their last major air attack on Britain (on Birmingham). On 15 June 1941 Jacob's father Max Epstein died at the age of eighty-three;[125] nowhere have I found any sign of Epstein's reaction to this, although one may assume that Margaret sent the family in New York the expected condolences. On 16 July 1941 Romanian troops that had fought alongside the Germans at the key battle for Kishinev entered the city, unleashing a pogrom on its Jews that continued for several days.[126] This was the same city in which the pogroms of 1903–05 had motivated Epstein to make *Kishinev*, the first sculpture he exhibited in England (I/74-5).

One bit of good news was that in August Epstein's son Theo (who had had to stop his regular studies after moving to live in Harting during the war years and had taken a correspondence course for a year) passed his matriculation in June – "first division, 'which is my best', say I with modest pride".[127] During September, however, the Epsteins' main concern was to salvage whatever they could from the hands of Stafford, who had taken together with his rightfully acquired *Adam* the collection of twelve bronzes loaned by Epstein to him in Blackpool to be exhibited in New York and was still holding onto them. Epstein, as Margaret reported,[128] regarded these portraits as his best and latest work and, still intending to go to America, he would have liked them to be "a nucleus of any exhibition". Therefore they were "trying to pull them out of hell fire as it were by paying the thief", and they made a deal with Stafford: "for the new carving [*Jacob and the Angel*] we got a clause put in the agreement that on payment of £300 in November we get the 12 bronzes returned to our agent [Oko] in America". Margaret asked Oko to store the twelve bronzes in the meantime, as "in fact you are the only one Epstein too mentions as the one he can trust with his work".

122 As the discussion attests, I do not accept the reading of the sculpture as a battle between Jacob's carnal and spiritual natures, resulting in him becoming more spiritual, nor it being "the divine intercourse in human, which the sculptor has presented by showing Jacob at the pinnacle of sexual fulfilment": Buckle, *Epstein: Sculptor*, pp. 256 and 263, citing a clergyman.

123 'Attraction' in the cultural sense suggested here is remote from the sexual attraction suggested by Cork (*Jacob Epstein*, pp. 63–64).

124 Cable from Epstein to Dr Oko, 17 April 1941: HUCAC.

125 Babson, *The Epsteins*, p. 57.

126 www.yivoencyclopedia.org/article.aspx/Kishinev.

127 Letter from Theodore Garman to someone named Peggy, 4 August 1941: NAGW archive, BL/1/6/1/2. It was written from Rosemary Cottage, in South Harting nearPetersfield, Hampshire, where the Garman children stayed during the war.

128 Letter from Margaret to Dr Oko, 18 September 1941: HUCAC.

What this transaction amounted to was the sacrifice of a large carving (which the public might not have liked) in order to get back the portraits favoured by potential customers in the US, where the Epsteins were still eager to go. The idea of entrusting the works to Oko gained ground in Margaret's next, very long, letter, which, among several other issues, emphasizes this intention.[129] She therefore provided Oko with a description of each portrait. This letter seems also to have been written as a response to Oko's questions regarding past events, and mentions forgeries in a 'PPS' about the photographs sent to Oko for the autobiography, noting that Epstein did not like the idea of their being shown around – especially to artists, as "He sees so many bad copies of his work here[;] he does not like that". Revisiting reactions to Epstein's work on the Hudson Memorial (R*ima*)[130] she expresses her own feelings and uses (p. 4, in pencil) expressions that Epstein had been careful not to use in his autobiography:

> all the lowest scum like whipped up beer and they talked and wrote about destroying it – the beautiful thing that Epstein had worked hard all winter to carve into the stone [p. 5. here in pen] against obstacles & harassments that only I know to the full .... I thought it the most beautiful thing anyone has ever done & Muirhead Bone thinks it marvellously fine ... [again in pencil] and here were the admirers of loathsome insipidities like [Frampton's] *Peter Pan* reviling Epstein's monument and threatening to lay hands on it .... [p. 6] It was a great fight [line in pen, followed by pencil] what a pity you missed it! I will send you photographs & cuttings. At present they look like an entangled jungle in the basement.

On pp. 7–8 of her letter she describes how easily Epstein could be manipulated – in this case by a Baltimore man himself called Jacob Epstein,[131] "a sort of dry goods millionaire", who was "tickled to deal [death]" at receiving goods for cut prices, calling Epstein a great sculptor, and getting his namesake to make a bust of him. After the work was done, "true to the methods that had made him great among dry goods kings of America, he drove a bargain with (our) Epstein" by which, for the lure of ready cash, "he easily got a very good scoop and (our) Epstein a loss[;] but Jacob Epstein of Baltimore was so happy after showing his paces as an artist at the commercially smart game, that my Epstein just let him do it".

Margaret repeats in this letter her obsession with what she assumed to be Kathleen's hold on Epstein, which, as before, she expressed without mentioning Kathleen's name or the existence of her children with Epstein:

> That would be the best thing if Epstein could get to America in the end of October to get him away from an entanglement that he wished to get out of but finds it difficult because she follows him everywhere and will not take no for an answer.
>
> She follows to the Forrest where he goes to get away from her and she watches the cottage and he cannot get out without being waylaid and she makes scenes and threatens suicide and then he always gives in although he is often convinced that she is only a good actress and that she really only comes for limelight.

129 Ibid. Pp. 1 and 2 mention issues regarding the bronzes. In the additional nine pages she pours out her soul , initially with a clear calligraphy in pen, moving to less and less clear writing in pencil, returning to pen on the last pages.

131 Silber, *Sculpture of Epstein*, p. 150.

Whether or not Margaret's report should be taken at face value, something had been going on with Kathleen, for Epstein had been escaping to his cottage every weekend, while she remained in London, visiting her children once a week in Harting. From a letter to her from Theo it emerges that her state of mind was moody:[133] "Why were you so pensive and sad when I left you on Tuesday night at the hut?"; and after suggesting that perhaps it was caused by his rude remarks about someone called Donald ("of which I was heartily ashamed afterwards [as it] had hurt your feelings"), he then concludes that she was "worried about Esther's health", adding: "I remember once before seeing that sad look of dejection in your eyes (which is such a rare thing for you) at Ada's when you allowed your thoughts concerning Esther to get the better of you".[134] Theo's religious beliefs seem to have taken a stronger hold of him during these tumultuous days, as he suggests to her: "Do not worry about her [Esther]. Faith moves mountains .... Without faith Jesus Christ would never have lived in this world or his sayings and teachings survived so that people might read them 2000 years after his death." But in their correspondence Epstein is not mentioned at all, probably because of Theo's reservations towards him (see p. 85). As Margaret's letter with her description of Kathleen's harassment is, like Theo's, from October, one wonders whether Kathleen's mood is indeed reflected in Margaret's description, however distorted it may have been. Perhaps the worries that led Kathleen to chase after Epstein might have stemmed from financial concerns during a period in which, from the little the Epsteins had, she, naturally, received even less.

I have found no record of Epstein's relationship to Esther or any of his other children during this very difficult period, either because they lived in the country and it was felt that they were safe, or more probably because he was still occupied with *Jacob and the Angel*; on 3 November he wrote to Oko that he was still working on his "large carving & hope to finish it by the end of December". Working was what kept him "from brooding too much on things", including his astonishment to "find that many of my acquaintances of my generation have turned out to be fascistic in tendency & would tell you of some curious & enlightening experiences [that justify their tendencies]"; but he leaves all this "for 'after the war'; if & when!". He manages to survive, he tells Oko, by selling portraits,[135] and he is grateful for "what [he] can get for them, knowing the prime collectors are giving artists a raw deal indeed", adding that the war seems to bring out all the pettiness there is in people. The happy news was that "Peggy Jean is expecting another child & her look [is] splendid".

November 1941 saw a counter-attack on Germany by the RAF – bombing Berlin, Mannheim and Ruhrgebiet – which put a stop to the German bombing of England. Perhaps this accounts for Epstein's somewhat more cheerful letter to Oko at the end of the year,[136] in spite of the sad news for Matthew Smith: "I see Smith occasionally although he is in a bad way mentally I'm afraid [after the death of his two sons in the war]. He has at last got started painting again; that will be his salvation." Salvation through art seems have applied also to Epstein, who wrote: "Inspiration in my studio has not been lacking. I have been happy working although often worn out & fatigued." After discussion of his bronzes in New York (to be exhibited there in 1942) he ends on a personal note on his first family, which only accentuates the lack of information on his second one:

132 Page 9 of the letter. There is no way to determine the truth of any of these details.

133 Letter from Theo to Kathleen, 28 October 1941:NAGW–BL/1/3/3/4.

134 Ada Newbould was the nanny with whom Kathleen's children stayed during the war. Information on Esther as a child is unavailable. When Theo wrote his letter in 1941, Esther had been about twelve years old, and nowhere is there an indication that at this stage she had health problems.

135 These were probably copies of old portraits, as Silber's catalogue indicates that during 1941 he had made six portraits, five of which were of models and family; thus only the one mentioned hereafter seems to have been paid for.

136 Letter from Epstein to Dr Oko, 20 November 1941: HUCAC.

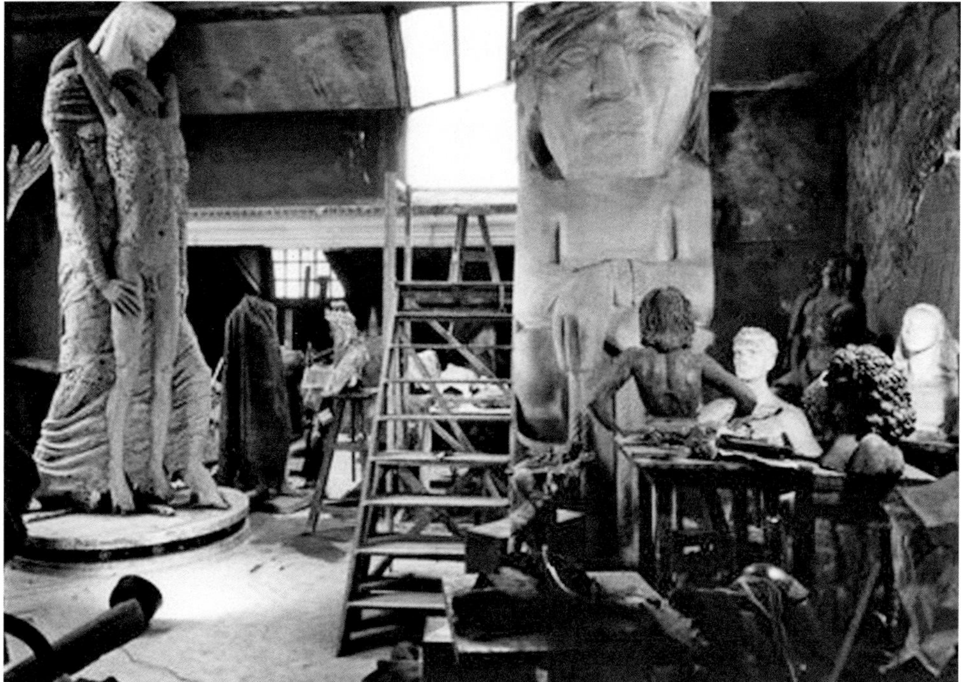

Fig. 44
Epstein's studio, with notably a plaster for *Social Consciousness* (see p. 196) and *Behold the Man* (see p. 83), 1950

> Peggy Jean will soon have her child & Hornstein is now a full chartered Doctor. Peggy [Margaret] is well & Jackie is a great boy with tremendous life in him; a handful of vim & mischief. Some day I hope to have him in America where he can have a chance. I imagine Benjamin [Oko's son] studying Spinoza or at any rate soon.

Sometime in 1941 Epstein made a bust of the composer Franz Reisenstein,[137] and needed a letter-carver to inscribe the name. Epstein invited David McFall, a young fellow in his twenties, one of a group of fine letter-cutters cultivated by Eric Gill (who died in this year), quickly to cut the inscription into the bust which had just been cast in plaster and was still wet and soft.[138] When McFall entered into the studio he was surprised by the number of portraits he saw, pondering: "Had circumstances driven him to turn out too many pot-boilers?"[139] Epstein, who had never been embarrassed by his portraits, regarding them as his 'children', had once expostulated when a tactless American lady asked him how many children he had: "What! Did you expect me to keep count?"

McFall's arrival at the studio was the start of a relationship that lasted for almost eighteen years, until Epstein's death. The young man was constantly called upon to help – "at eight o'clock in the morning if he needed me that day. He would say "How are you placed Mack-fal? … I would abandon my own work and head off for Hyde Park Gate without a second thought, and I do not recall that I ever refused him once." To his credit, McFall never pretended to be his regular assistant, adding that "as far as I know he never had one". Epstein's studio during that period is described by McFall:

> The Epstein studio was a nightmare of congestion [fig. 44], there were no facilities worth mentioning. Busts of the famous jostled for elbow room with the infamous. Pyramids of damp smelly chippings accumulated over the years

137 Not mentioned in Silber's catalogue. It could be the original version of the "unknown man" (no. 340), of which there remains a negative dated 1943. In 1934 Franz Reisenstein immigrated to England at the age of twenty-three to escape the Nazis, one of nearly 70 Jewish composers to do so in 1933–35 (see Haas, *Emigré Composers*). His status as a British resident was interrupted (and compromised) by his tour of South America in 1937–38, and so, despite a seven-year residency in London until the outbreak of war, he joined the thousands of German and Austrian Jews interned in requisitioned hotels on the Isle of Man.

138 McFall, p. 2.

139 The label 'pot boiler' has been given to Epstein's later work, discussed further on, and in a retrospective McFall, a sculptor himself who had been trained as a carver, used it, seemingly disapproving of the large quantity of Epstein's bronze portraits.

> crept towards an avalanche of coke dumped next to the clay bin. Modelling stands, buckets of partly prepared clay, step ladders and timber for armatures left little room for manoeuvre. All was dominated by the glowering presence of the Subiaco 'ECCE HOMO'.

By December 1941, and in spite of the book having been almost a year on the market, the Epsteins' problems with their publishers were still not over, as "we haven't seen the money yet we had hoped before Xmas but alas there is no sign of it yet";[140] and in regard to Epstein Margaret adds that it was always the same problem, that when he has money he does not have the new work to hold an exhibition (in this case in New York), and when he has the work he seldom has the money for the journey and all connected with it. Her main concern, if they were to reach New York, was for a place "where he can work & where he has models he wants". Her consolation, as well as Epstein's during those first years of the war (as expressed also in this letter), were their children. Peggy Jean was working hard at running her household, and she and her husband "have never a penny but that's better than getting stale & blasé & dissatisfied from having too much, which is often seen in London … they and Leda will never be more good looking or happier than they are now". Margaret becomes almost ecstatic when she writes about Jackie:

> Our little Jackie is fast growing up big, he is 4 stones and 4 feet and is very like Jacob. He has same kind of blue eyes and the same cheeks and the same hands. He is I suppose what Jacob was when he was little, a terrible mixture of goodness & bad moods, highly strung, a temper like a volcano one moment, and sweet & good hearted the next; curiously enough only interested in machinery and ships. Engines are his little Jackie's heart delight. He thinks of a submarine as a paradise.

On 10 February 1942 *Jacob and the Angel* was presented in Epstein's exhibition at the Leicester Galleries. The reactions to the sculpture varied; surprisingly, most of them showed more than a tinge of admiration: The *Daily Telegraph* critic described it as "a craftsman's tour-de-force"; the *Manchester Guardian*'s correspondent enthused over its "complex interweaving of rhythms" and the *Daily Mail* pondered whether it was "a miracle or a monstrosity".[141] The most interesting of all was the (unpublished) reaction from the camp hostile to Epstein, in a letter from Herbert Read to Ben Nicholson:

> I went to see the Epstein monster yesterday. I was rather unexpectedly impressed. It is much the best of his carvings, but it is rather objectless – it is difficult to see what angle it is meant to be viewed from, and where, in an interior, it could go.[142]

After the closing of the show at the Leicester Galleries the sculpture, which according to Epstein's agreement signed in 1941 (see p. 143) belonged to Stafford, made its journey to Blackpool, repeating both the journey and the commercial success of *Adam* carved in 1939. Thus it became, among Epstein's other sculpture there, another "objectless" figure "difficult to see from which angle it was meant to be viewed".

140 Margaret's letter to Sylvia, December 1941: Babson, *The Epsteins*, p. 54.

141 Stuart Tulloch, *Tate etc*, Issue 22 / Summer 2011.

142 Letter from Herbert Read to ben Nicholson, 20 February 1942: TGA -8717.1.2.3667. Contrary to this opinion, I see this sculpture both as being an object and as having an objective.

TWO LARGE BRONZES

I. *THE GIRL WITH GARDENIAS*

After the arduous work on his autobiography and on *Jacob and the Angel* Epstein needed some artistic relaxation, and he seems to have found it working on the inspiring features of his companion and model Kathleen. There is a rough drawing [65a] which, being utterly different from the sculpture eventually made, might testify to the process of thought that preceded it. On a lined piece of paper Epstein posed a woman wearing a long frock, leaning backward and about to climb some stairs. The sculpture retains the positions of the feet in the drawing but presents a different axis for the figure.

Retrospectively, writing about it in 1954 (PS/229), Epstein may have been able to relate to this period with a kind of benevolence acquired by the passing of time, blurring the somewhat bleak mode that had at that time characterized his daily life – unless he was referring to the easier work of modelling a figure after the arduous period of carving alabaster stone. "About 1942 I modeled a life-size figure of a lyric nature and I greatly enjoyed this happy period. I called it 'The Girl with Gardenias' [65b] and exhibited [it] as the central piece at my war-time exhibition in Leicester Galleries. Strangely enough, in view of the admiration and interest it later attracted at the Battersea Park outdoor exhibition in 1948 [when it was bought for the Aberdeen Art Gallery], this work was ridiculed and minimised by the art critics of the leading papers."[143]

Expressing his enjoyment at working on this figure (and, as hinted above, with its sitter) seems to indicate that in spite of whatever might have been her mischievous behaviour, or their disagreements, Margaret's references to Epstein's resentment of Kathleen were somewhat exaggerated. The pros and cons of their relationship also seemed to have been misunderstood; when Margaret mentioned that "he always gives in" to her (p. 144) she apparently ignored Kathleen's attraction to him both as a model and as a source of inspiration. For his part, Epstein could clearly distinguish between his personal feelings and the portraits he made (even those of Kathleen's stunning facial bone-structure): they were intended to convey the personality of the sitters and not his opinion of them. In the case of *The Girl with Gardenias*, however, there is a kind of discrepancy between Kathleen's slender, vigorous and youthful figure inclined forward and the mature face that, in spite of its slight smile, conveys what their son Theo had called a "pensive and sad" expression (p. 144).[144] It is these obviously contradictory elements in his sitter that Epstein may have purposely chosen to depict. Neither in them, nor in Kathleen's almost naked body, is there the "anomaly" suggested by Buckle,[145] who claimed that a middle-aged nude is artistically justifiable under "certain circumstances" (which he does not define), thus probably expressing the norms of propriety of his own time and era. Nowadays, however, perceptions are different, and a flesh-and-blood middle-aged woman with a young carved body is no longer a novelty. One could claim, therefore, that Epstein's sculpture is a-periodic in not catering to a particular trend. Surprisingly, in the light of their long attachment, this work is Kathleen's only representation in full figure,[146] and it immortalizes their relationship by the inclusion in her hand of her favourite flowers, which he used to bring her. Some time in 1942, during his work on her figure, her sister Helen's husband passed away in Martigues, and as always it was Kathleen who lent a helping hand. Helen

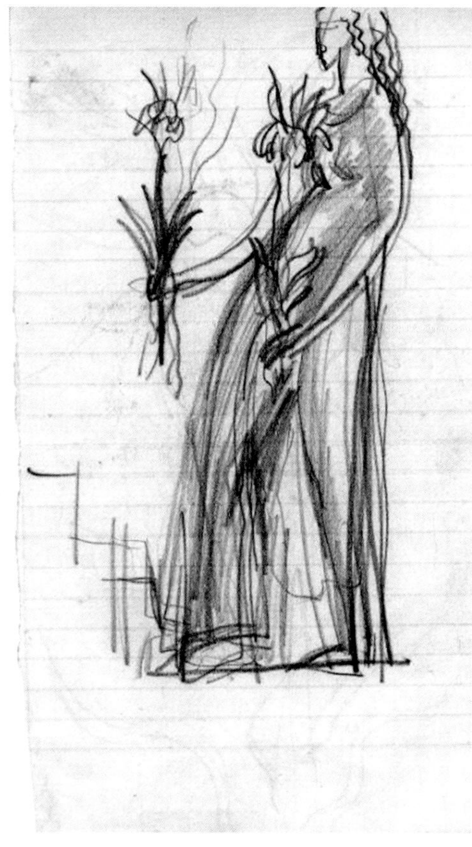

65a
The Girl with Gardenias/ Figure sketch, c. 1942
Pencil, 195 x 123 mm
GREC-NAGW

143 Silber (*Sculpture of Epstein*, no. 336) dates it to 1943, which might be more attuned with Epstein's custom of presenting his new works almost immediately upon completion; in this case it would date to even later – 1944.

144 There is a half-size version of this work, entitled *Kathleen, 6th portrait* (Silber, *Sculpture of Epstein*, no. 315; not exhibited) and dated 1941. It might be that this portrait was made *after* the whole figure had been accomplished and not beforehand, as suggested in the catalogue, and was thus made later than 1941.

145 Buckle, *Epstein: Sculptor*, p. 268.

146 "It came too late," said Beth Lipkin when I mentioned this work and Kathleen's mature face (conversation with the author held in 1985).

and daughter Cathy stayed with her in London until the liberation of France, and one can assume that Epstein tolerated, if not agreed, to their constant presence in Kathleen's house as, in all probability, they managed to keep out of the way when he came to visit.

1942 was a "happy period" for Epstein, both for the number of portraits – sixteen were made, of which about eleven had been commissioned – and for exhibitions: besides his 'stolen' portraits exhibited in New York at the American British Art Centre (see p. 143) and his own exhibition in February with *Jacob and the Angel* and other works at the Leicester Galleries, during July he held an exhibition together with Matthew Smith at Temple Newsam House, Leeds. This last event demonstrates once more the close relations between these two artists, who had another factor in common – Augustus John. Although John and Epstein had drifted apart, Smith remained friendly with both, and in the last period of his life he often stayed at John's house. It was at this joint exhibition that Dr Blake, an eye specialist, met Smith and bought Epstein's bronze of *Jackie – 11 Months*,[147] for which, in November, Margaret thanked him for sending a cheque.[148] Eventually Blake became the Epsteins' eye specialist, consulting with Margaret on Jackie's eyesight whenever he came down from Leeds to his clinic at 7 Harley Street in London. On 4 December Margaret sent a card thanking him in her confused manner, poetically divided:

'Dear Dr. Blake, here are three cards give I to the Eye Doctor par excellence if he is going south by Tuesday. Sincerely yours [signature]	On each of your two visits I have meant to give them to You. Once I forgot The second time I left it To Epstein & he forgot

In Margaret's letter of 4 February 1943[149] we have evidence of the mutual concern and cordiality between Epstein and Smith. Smith had severe problems with his eyesight and, as Margaret elaborates, "has not the best adviser in the way of a quack doctor just now. He is not for eyes. He is a kind of psychiatrist or sexual, no inhibitionist [sic]. Matthew Smith will probably never get over losing both his sons in the war, but he need not be the prey of such ugly birds." Margaret, not wanting Smith to suspect that he and the doctor had been deliberately being invited together to their house ("I only drag him in by long distance calling S.O.S for a birthday or New Year lunch"), suggested that Blake meet him subsequently as if casually. Therefore, he should "go up to him in the Café Royal and continue the friendship and then confidences would naturally ensue about the Yellow spots etc etc that haunt him in his eye sight". She justifies this careful handling of the matter by saying "perhaps I am rather too touchy on the subject .... I get all this of course indirectly. I have a great admiration for Mathew Smith's work of course, and personally he is naturally an angel, compared with most artists. Sometimes those who surrounded him are questionable in their influence, that is all." She concludes her letter by expressing her own and Epstein's fondness, wanting "to see everything good happen to him".

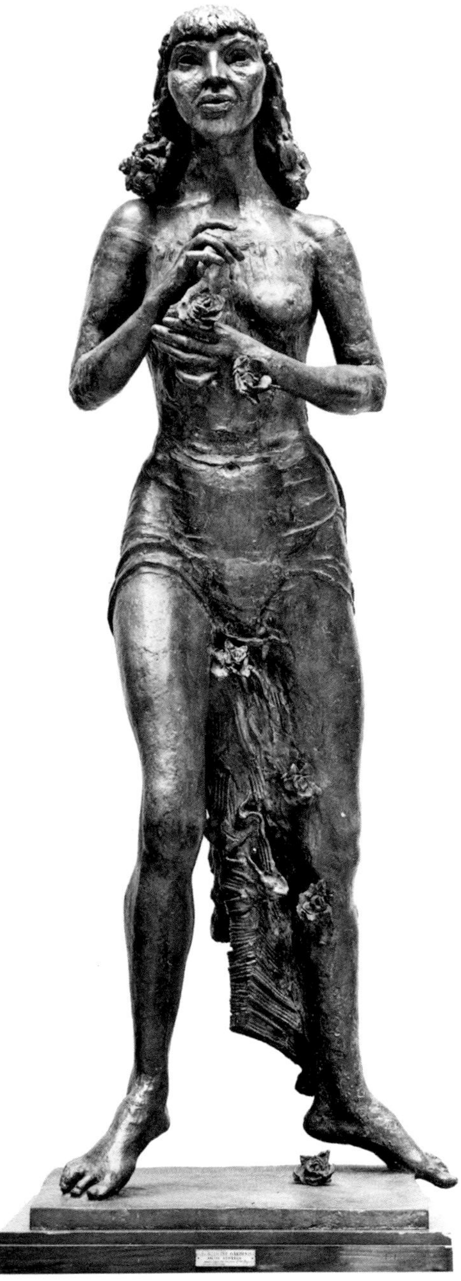

65b
The Girl with Gardenias, 1942 [1943]
Bronze, H. 190 cm
Courtesy of Aberdeen Art Gallery and Museums Collections

147 There are two bronzes of Jackie, and I believe that Blake's must be no. 260 in Silber's catalogue, of "provenance unknown"; no. 261 has several recorded owners, Dr Blake not being among them.

148 Margaret's letter to Dr Blake of 2, The Grove, North Lane, Roundhay, Leeds, 4 November 1942: HMI 24/1990.

149 HMI 24/1990/7.

Epstein's good friends of the late 1930s and 1940s, otherwise, seem to have comprised mainly Jews. This had not been the case during his earliest period in England, in which he had kept the company of non-Jewish artists and musicians, with no meaningful Jewish presence in his life other than the notable one of William Rothenstein. In addition to the anti-Semitic atmosphere that had since developed, the arrival of Jewish refugee artists in England during the mid 1930s altered his milieu to some extent, and he developed contacts with several who shared similar East European cultural roots. Perhaps there is indeed something in the culture of Jewish people that induces a kind of intimacy and closeness among them so different from the aloof and reserved attitude of the English. But, perhaps more surprisingly, as discussed later, during the same period the gentile Kathleen developed her closest social contacts (which were to last for the rest of her life) mainly with Jewish-Italian refugees. As for Epstein, he met the painter Joseph Herman when Herman arrived in 1943 from Glasgow to London to exhibit his work at the Reid and Lefevre Gallery; Herman and others formed a group that differed distinctly from Epstein's regular social contacts, perhaps because they could speak Yiddish among themselves – "With Adler (and Benno Schotz, Manger and Stencl) certainly because [Herman] spoke no English when he arrived in Glasgow in 1940. With Epstein, whom he met later, I suspect not, but I don't know this for sure."[150]

An event that took place involving this trio of friends (Herman, Epstein and Adler) and is described in print, suggesting that Epstein might have held little regard for Jewish customs, requires clarification: Adler and Epstein had a meeting at Herman's Hampstead studio on the eve of a Sabbath; to mark the occasion, beer bottles instead of candlesticks held the candles, and Epstein (so it is claimed) brought "his *tallis* as a tablecloth": thus they celebrated "in their own highly unorthodox fashion".[151] I doubt whether Epstein, unobservant even in New York, would have bothered to bring a *talith* (prayer shawl) with him to Europe in 1902, or had been keeping it in London. Herman's son David substantiated my doubts: although "not remotely religious, ever", yet "My father had a tallit, one of his most cherished possessions, which he always kept in his studio – a gift from Adler, I believe".[152]

As the war continued government patronage was given to artists through the War Artists Commission.[153] This resulted in some fine paintings from established artists like Paul Nash, Graham Sutherland, John Piper and Stanley Spencer, but did not elicit any great work from new painters, although 15,000 works of art were produced. Perhaps it is needless to say that Epstein was not among the artists who received commissions; nor were other 'misfits' such as Edward Burra (whose wartime paintings were a continuation of his Spanish Civil War works) or Francis Bacon (*Crucifixion*, 1945). Art during World War II in England generally conveyed people's sense of endurance and national pride, of which Henry Moore's powerful (black and white) shelter drawings (see fig. 38c) can be regarded as a paradigm. Moore, however, through his sculpture was unable to offer an immediately meaningful expression of the war years and their tribulations, any more than were others of his milieu tending towards abstraction and high stylization. By contrast it was here, where meaning and idea were so crucial, that Epstein and his kind of art found their place, offering an expression of hope and victory arising

150 David Herman, email to the author, 24 December 2011, referring to the painter Jankel Adler, the poets Itzik Manger and Abraham Nahum Stencl and the sculptor Benno Schotz.

151 Rose, *Daemons and Angels*, p. 221. Rose's footnote refers to another comment by Herman, but leaving the impression that this anecdote – for so it is – was also told by Herman.

152 "He valued his friendship with both men enormously – it was Epstein who introduced him to African sculptures, which became a great passion for almost half a century": David Herman, email to the author, 9 December 2011..

153 The following general data are taken from the introduction in Shaw and Shaw, 'The Cultural and Social Setting'.

from a desperate situation – with works such as *Jacob and the Angel* exhibited in 1942. This expression of a struggle between good and evil that ended well may have been wishful thinking at the time, especially since the positive ending of the biblical event was not achieved in reality for the people of the Bible. A new Nazi plan against the Jews had begun; having concentrated them in ghettoes, having sent them to forced-labour camps and killed those unfit for work, the Final Solution was undertaken, an attempt at the annihilation of all Jews for the simple fact of being Jews – the Holocaust.

II. *LUCIFER*

Epstein depicted the 'bad' partner in the struggle between Jacob and the Angel with the type of wings generally associated with angels in folklore, and continued to engage with different kinds of wings as attributes for future entities both positive and negative. His musings on his next subject involving wings, of which he wrote "needless to say I consider [it] a major work[,] one of those works the result of long meditation and sudden inspiration" ["sudden inspiration" crossed out],[154] resulted in an extant drawing, maquette, panel and, finally, a huge bronze sculpture representing Lucifer, commonly regarded as a rebellious fallen angel.

In the drawing *Lucifer and his Angels* [68] three winged figures are depicted from the waist upwards, their configuration varying in a peculiar way. The central figure is drawn clearly in dark lines, suggesting his identification as Lucifer, whereas the two at either side (apparently less important entities) are quite faint. The figure to his left turns its head toward him, its long narrow skull with almost no lips conveying an unpleasant aura; the figure to his right has delicate feminine facial features, and a hairstyle resembling Epstein's bronze portrait *Israfel* [66].

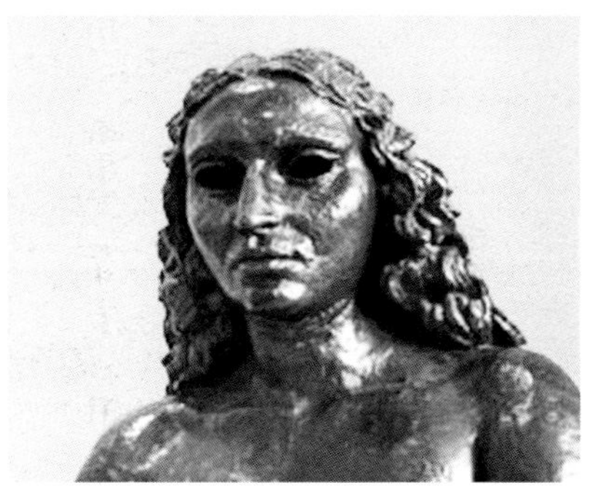

66
Israfel, 1930
Bronze, H. 53.3 cm
Private collection

67
Satan, Beelzebub and Belial (maquette), 1944 [1943]
Bronze, H. 190 cm
Formerly Shinman collection

68
Lucifer and his Angels, 1944
Pencil and wash, 445 x 578 mm
Private collection

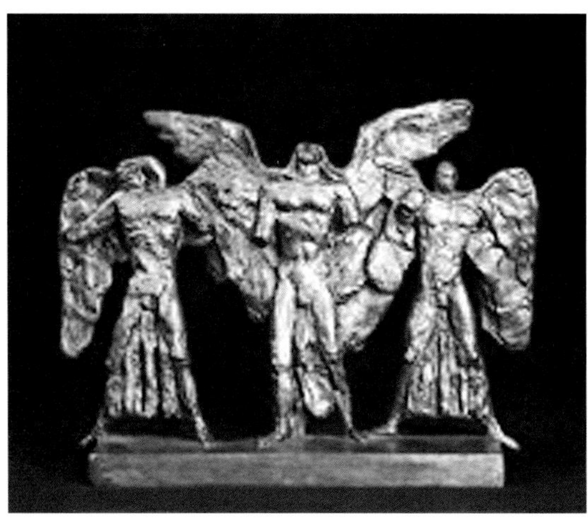

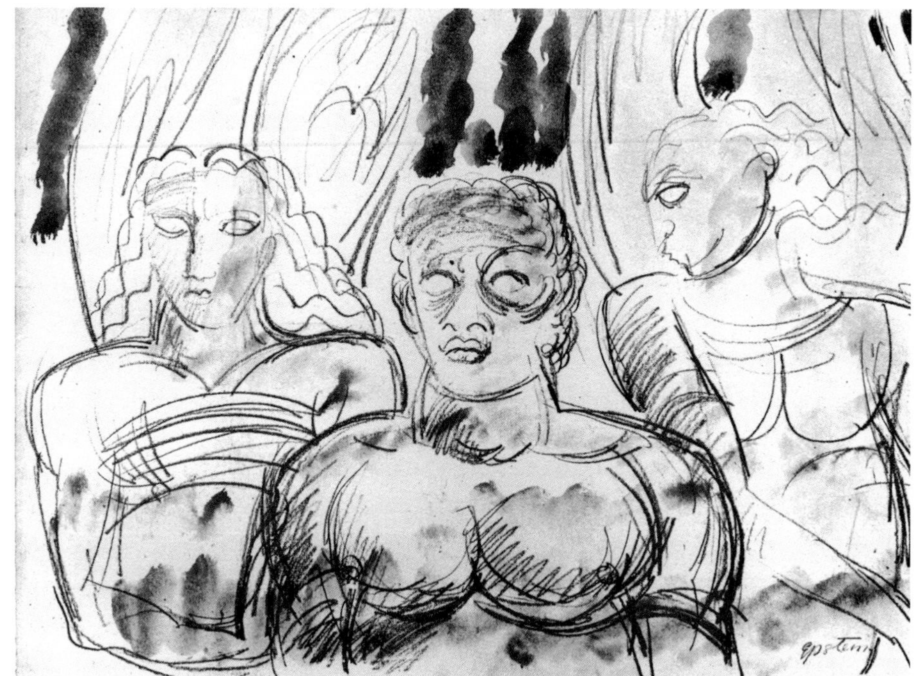

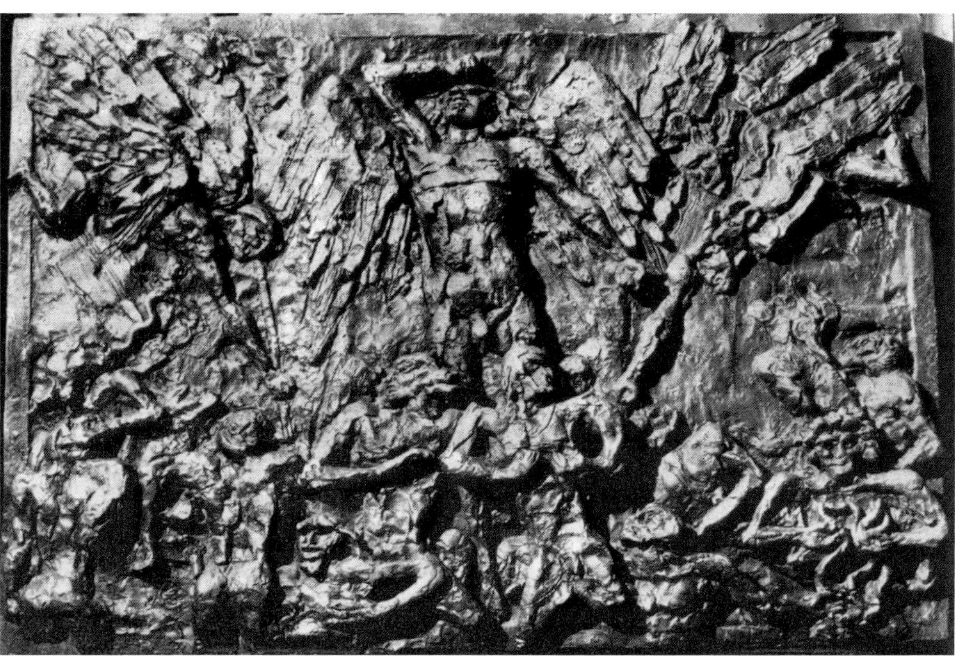

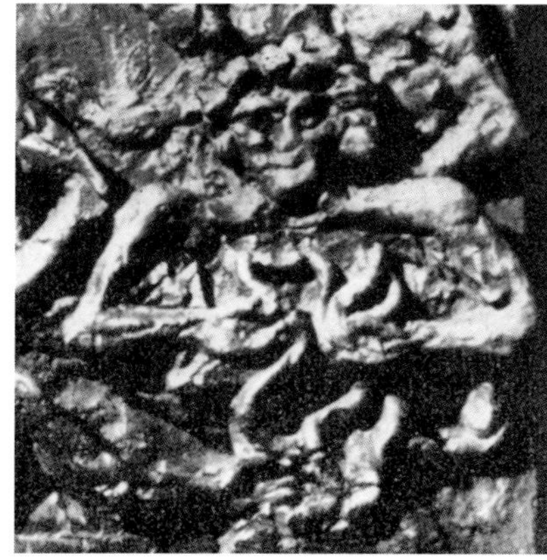

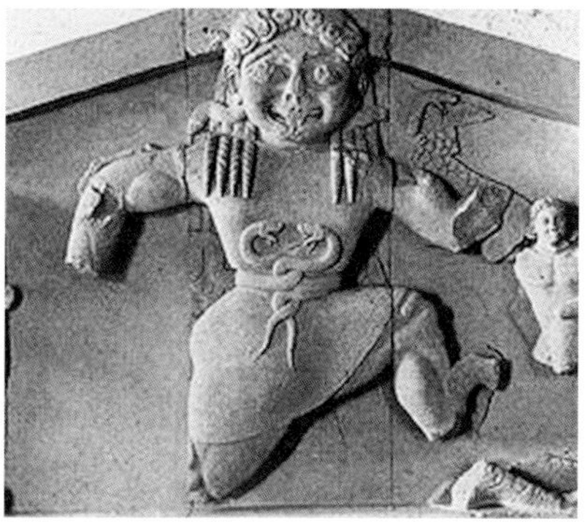

69
The Fall of Lucifer, 1944
Bronze relief, 62.2 x 89.5 cm
Formerly Shinman collection

69a
The Fall of Lucifer, 1944
Bronze relief, 62.2 x 89.5 cm
Formerly Shinman collection

Fig. 45
Medusa, centre of a pediment of the Temple of Artemis, Corfu
Mid 6th century BC

Epstein transferred the sketch of three winged figures into a preliminary maquette [67] exhibited in 1947 under the title *Satan, Beelzebub and Belial*,[155] in which the hand movements and the spread wings of the angels seem to elaborate on his maquette *Kneeling Angel* of 1924 (I/175). Epstein did not develop this preliminary maquette into a sculpture, and the concept of the three fallen angels seems to have been developed into a panel entitled *The Fall of Lucifer* [69], featuring a multitude of figures. This panel deserves more attention than it received when exhibited in 1944.

The composition has as its central axis the figure of a frontal naked winged man that extends from top to bottom of the panel, thus connecting its upper and lower areas. The figure is depicted with a cloth strip across his chest, his bent left arm raised to touch his head and his right arm stretched downwards – a mirror image of the figure in Epstein's drawing of *Cain* in *Flowers of Evil* (51d). However, whereas Cain's wings indicate a flight upward and his face conveys a sense of expectation in his search for God, the figure in the panel has a severe face gazing ahead at the horizon, with wings inclined downward.

The upper area on either side of the figure is occupied by two flying angels diving downwards, each with an outstretched arm with clenched fist directed at the figures occupying the lower part of the panel. The lower register is filled with a cluster of human figures, including a woman with snakes at the far right, in this case holding them close to her chest [69a]. In Minoan art, women with snakes represented the Goddess with the Snakes, and in ancient Greece suggested the evil Medusa. Although in the image shown here (fig. 45) the figure does not hold the snakes, there is a similarity between her archaic grimace and hair and that of the figure in Epstein's panel. Epstein's cluster of figures can thus be interpreted as the fallen entities that the angels in the upper part have driven down, particularly as their aspect is unpleasant. In contrast, the central figure of Lucifer, whose features are executed almost to perfection amidst the vague and sometimes grotesque images around him, does not display a mean or vicious

[opposite page]

154 Epstein's unpublished notes for his *Autobiography*: NAGW archive.

[this page]

155 Satan, who awakens all his Legions, is in the Christian theology Lucifer; the names, thus, are interchangeable. The three entities (according to various post-biblical written sources) belonged to the order of angels that surrounded God, but after Lucifer's rebellion they were all consigned to Hell (Milton, *Paradise Lost*; Book I).

expression. He is gazing ahead, more like a ship's captain seeking something on the horizon – a being seeking a purpose in its existence. This depiction, contrasting with the common depiction of Lucifer as the sorrowful sinner, I consider to be a preliminary stage in Epstein's developing conception of Lucifer, more fully embodied in his large bronze. As in the case of *Jacob and the Angel*, Epstein makes no comment about his motives in regard to *Lucifer*, only mentioning that the work took him almost a year (PS/231), and noting that after its completion he did Winston Churchill's portrait.

Lucifer is a combination of a male body and the female face of the portrait *Israfel* [67], done from his most renowned model, Sunita, in 1930. The figure [70a, 70b] is attired in a few frontal strips of cloth that tie at the back, thus exposing the front of the body, including the phallus; to some extent, the position of the feet on the ground resembles that of *The Girl with Gardenias*. On the whole, however, it seems that William Blake's drawings had once more exerted an influence on Epstein (the first instance, as discussed in I/91, had been in regard to *Sun God*); this time, however, it resulted in a slight reversal of meaning: Blake's painting of a naked Lucifer is entitled *Satan in his Original Glory*, thus relating to his first state of being in Milton's *Paradise Lost*, and the extrovert glory is manifested by the forward-looking gaze and the spread hands holding the orb topped with a cross, symbolizing his dominion over the world [fig. 46]; Epstein's portrayal is that of a figure with an inward gaze that has reached his own personal glory, altering Blake's movement of the hands and adding a tender, almost caressing, movement to the palms. Epstein regarded his pose as requesting the "Silence [that] is best before a visionary work".[156]

Commonly visualizations of Hell's occupants differentiate the negative beings by giving them bat-like wings, while the positive ones tend to have raised bird-like wings; thus Satan [fig. 47a] and Lucifer [fig. 47b] are portrayed with bat-like wings in Doré's popular engravings for Milton's *Paradise Lost*. Unlike Doré's depiction, Epstein's *Lazarus* has wings upraised and bird-like, like those of the angels [fig. 47b]. Their almost parallel lines in Epstein's *Lucifer* echo those of the carved angel in his Tomb of Oscar Wilde but, being moulded, they project a softer texture than those sharply carved ones. Epstein, it is clear, made use of a vocabulary of tried forms, developing his range of poses and styles into new forms of representation which, in turn, require new interpretations. The usual representation of Lucifer was that of a male, either naked or fully dressed, with outspread bat-wings and a strained face, as the poetry of Milton implied. What was Epstein trying to convey in his unorthodox angel-winged male-female *Lucifer*, who obviously does not express any sadness?

Among the unpublished notes for his autobiography Epstein writes of his own "puerilities" when it came to "the understanding of the awesome problems of evil & revolt", admiring the imagination that composed the sentence "How art thou fallen from Heaven, O Lucifer son of the morning" (Isaiah, 14: 12), and referring "to what Shakespeare called 'Proud Lucifer'". His sculpture, thus, was intended to be:

> An embodiment, a conception imaginative & of high daring, an expression of the beautiful of the darkly beautiful beloved of great poets; I search to have express[ed] it all in 'Lucifer'.

156 Epstein's speech at the unveiling of *Lazarus*, 26 June 1947: NAGW.

70b
Lucifer, 1944–45
Bronze, H. 315 cm
Birmingham Museum and
Art Gallery

70a
Lucifer (side view)

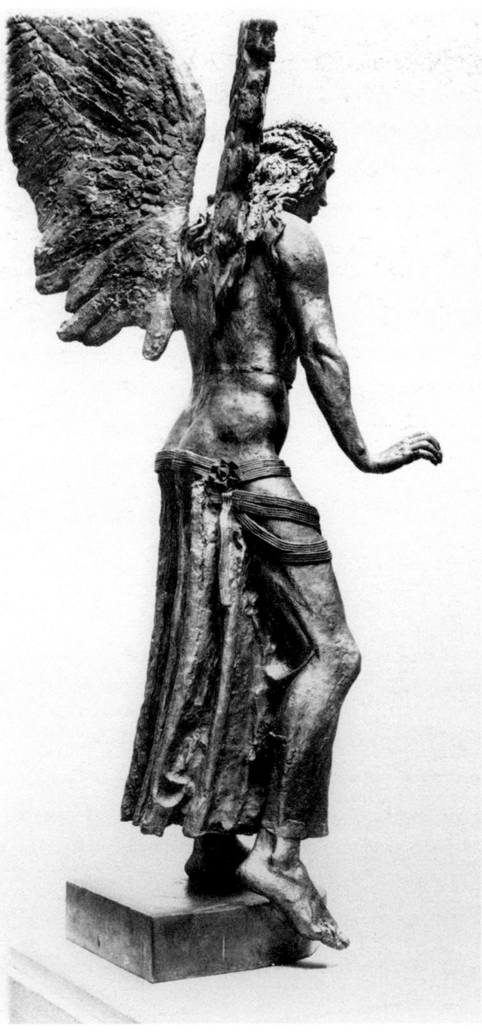

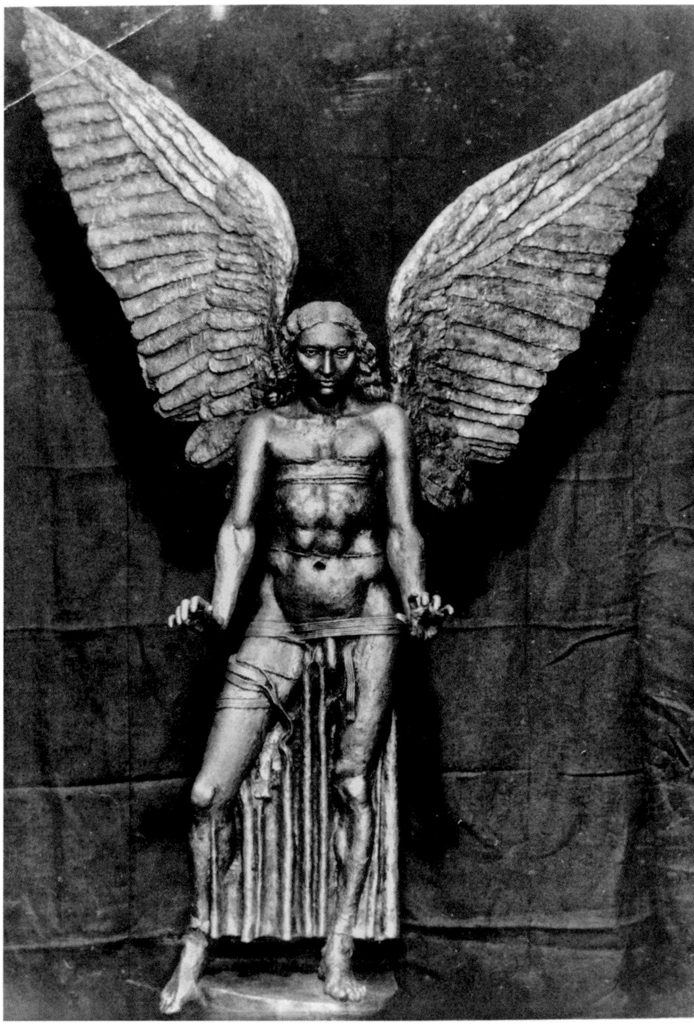

Fig. 46
William Blake
Satan in his Original Glory, 1805
Pen, ink and watercolour,
430 x 340 mm
Tate

Figs. 47a–b
Gustave Doré, *Satan Miserable* and
Satan is cast out the Hill of Heaven and is cast in Hell's Canyons
Illustrations to Milton's
Paradise Lost, 1866

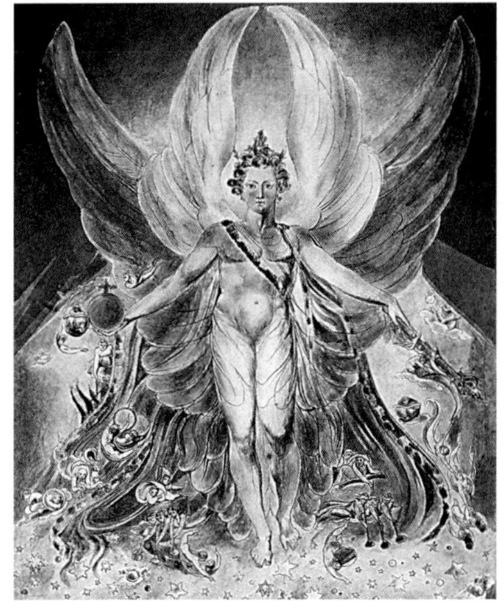

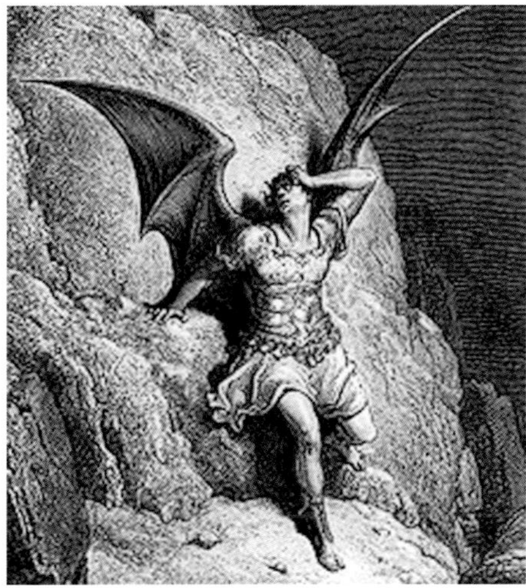

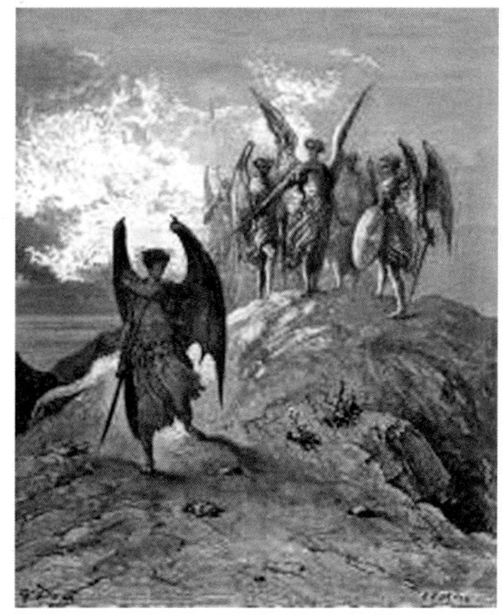

The Latin 'Lucifer' means 'light-bearer'; it was a title given to the dawn appearance of the planet Venus, the morning star, used to translate the Hebrew *Hêlēl Ben Shachar* (Isaiah 14: 12),[157] and there is no doubt that Epstein knew the Hebrew name. There were other facets to 'Lucifer' as the light-bearer of the morning star, of which Epstein, no doubt with Kathleen's guidance, would have become aware[158] – the Catholic liturgy's *Exultet* chant in praise of the Paschal candle refers to Christ as the Morning Star:

> *Flammas eius lucifer matutinus inveniat:*
> *ille, inquam, lucifer, qui nescit occasum,*
> *Christus Filius tuus qui,*
> *regressus ab inferis,*
> *humano generi serenus illuxit,*
> *et vivit et regnat in saecula saeculorum.*
>
> May the morning star which never sets / find this flame still burning: Christ, that morning star, / who came back from the dead, / and shed his peaceful light on all mankind, / your Son, who lives and reigns for ever and ever.

The Blessed Virgin Mary, too, is referred to as "star of the morning" and "light of dawning" in the popular hymn 'Mary Immaculate, Star of the Morning', associated with the Wednesday Novena to Our Lady of Perpetual Help:[159]

> Mary Immaculate, Star of the Morning
> Chosen before the creation began
> Destined to bring, through the Light of your Dawning
> Conquest of Satan, and rescue to Man.

In his customary practice of borrowing from literature whatever suited his personal notions, Epstein formulated an imaginative and highly daring conception of Lucifer, by combining from the liturgy the male-female elements of the morning star. By alluding to both Mary and Jesus, he was probably attempting to bestow something of their aura on Lucifer; indeed, I would go further and state that as Jesus and Mary were human beings, Epstein's *Lucifer* therefore represents humanity and its dualities.

Just as his *Adam*, also a paradigm of humanity that had usurped a certain kind of power from God, conveys no remorse and looks forward with hope, so does his *Lucifer:* he stands proud in spite of failing in his attempt to seize power; and his seizing of his own future is expressed by the hands that lean forward as if to hold back the descent of the inclined body. Hope intransigent in transgression-rebellion against whatever authority might be a personal attitude of some artists; Epstein, to a great extent, in his aspiration to reach the summit – in my opinion and as the title chosen for this book suggests – is also a light-bearer, a *lucifer*.[160]

Lucifer was shown at the Leicester Galleries in November 1945, in an exhibition entitled *Jacob Epstein; 'Lucifer' and paintings of flowers and landscapes of Epping Forest*. The sculpture, as Epstein reports briefly in the Postscript (PS/231), remained in his studio unsold. It was rejected by the Fitzwilliam Museum, Cambridge, despite its being recommended there by Professor Lawrence, the brother of Lawrence of Arabia, and by the Victoria and Albert Museum, which contended that it did not exhibit living artists.

The tribulations that Epstein had to undergo with these institutions can be deduced from similar, widely published proceedings that took place later on with the Tate

157 The British generally use the names 'Morning Star' or 'Day Star', but rarely the Latin form 'Lucifer'.

158 As attested by her daughter Kitty, who stated that Kathleen had introduced him to Christianity and its details: interview with the author, 1985.

159 In the Catholic Church, a 'novena' is a devotion consisting of a prayer repeated on nine successive days, seeking special graces.

160 A similar view, but accentuating the rebellious aspect, was transmitted by Silber, who titled her Epstein's exhibition booklet 'Rebel Angel' (Birmingham Museums and Art Gallery, 16 August – 30 November 1980), and by Central TV, whose documentary was entitled *Jacob Epstein: Rebel Angel*.

Gallery. Following Professor Lawrence's advice, Epstein wrote to Rothenstein, Director of the Tate,[161] inviting the Gallery trustees to view *Lucifer* in his studio, "in case they have not seen it [in the exhibition], preferably at daylight, as no important matter should be rest upon photographs". The almost unanimous rejection of the generous offer by Professor Lawrence and the trustees of the estate of Lawrence of Arabia to donate *Lucifer* was accompanied by the question "whether they would consider defraying the cost of a cast of Epstein's *Madonna and Child*, which the Board had long wished to possess, or its reproduction, for presentation to the Gallery instead of *Lucifer*".[162] To this Epstein's reply was no, on the grounds that its sale to Sally Ryan prohibited it, though that "concurs with my own feeling".[163]

The rejection by the Tate Gallery trustees was published in the press: "Tate Turns Down an Epstein Gift; 'Lucifer' Twice Rejected",[164] noting that the only trustee to support acceptance was Henry Moore, at the time in America, who had sent a letter of approval.[165] The insult of the newspaper story on 16 January was made even more insulting, in Epstein's view, by Rothenstein's letter to him afterwards, sent on 31 January. Epstein's typed response identifies Rothenstein himself "as one of the prime movers in the rejection of *Lucifer*" and condemns his "grotesque" gesture of condolence, declaring that his "reiterated sentiments about the 'generosity' of the gift are ludicrous". Moreover, Epstein continues, Professor Lawrence "has written to me of his disgust at what he terms your insulting action" – referring no doubt to the leak to the press of the rejection. The action had elicited "widespread dismay and condemnation", and Epstein enclosed in his own letter to Rothenstein several other letters that expressed it, among them that of the Artists International Association.

His restrained reaction to the rejection in his autobiography (PS/231) differed entirely from the one he had expressed at home, as reported by McFall:

> The rejection of this bronze – first by the Tate and then the Fitzwilliam – sparked off such a tantrum that Mrs. Epstein and I who were present were struck dumb and helpless by the sheer ferocity of Epstein's anger. He paced the floor like a menacing lion, shaking his fists at the ceiling and shouting at us, "I will not be overlooked, I will NOT be overlooked".[166]

That Epstein tended to such outburts is corroborated by John Finch, Margaret's aid, who had lived in the house in 1946–47: "Epstein would be quite vitriolic about someone or something he didn't like. He could be almost paranoid if he felt his work was unfairly criticized".[167]

Eventually (in 1947) *Lucifer* ended up in Birmingham, as Epstein wrote in a very dry tone. This was the fruit of Margaret and McFall's efforts to get it accepted by Trenchard Cox, then curator of Birmingham City Art Gallery. "We were given a full civic reception for the unveiling at which Epstein made a rambling and totally inaudible speech."[168] The typescript immediately recalls Epstein's letters to Oko, which mix together a jumble of different issues; they are comprehensible when read calmly, but are difficult to grasp when heard. In his speech Epstein attacked the artistic cliques' "closed-shop" approach, "with its well-studied literary blurb, pamphlets and books, exhibitions and criticism", condemning the lack of imagination and the absence of human interest in modern works.

161 Epstein's letter of 5 November 1946: TGA-8726/3/10.

162 The following data from Tate Gallery Records were kindly provided by Christopher Bastock from 'Minutes of a Meeting of the Tate Trustees Dec 5th 1946' (Vol. V, p. 121).

163 Epstein's letter of 4 January 1947: ibid.

164 *News Chronicle*, 16 January 1947.

165 Trustees present at this meeting: John Rothenstein (Director); Norman Reid (Assistant Director); Hon. Jasper Ridley (chair); Lord Justice Somervell; Lord Harlech; Philip Hendy; Henry Lamb; Hugo Pitman; Charles Wheeler. Trustees absent from this meeting: John Piper; Henry Moore; Rt. Hon. Lord Jowitt; Rt Hon. Vincent Massey; Allen Gwynne-Jones. Unfortunately, in the press-cutting that published the rejection (note 158), Sir Muirhead Bone is also noted, leaving the impression that Epstein's old friend and supporter had turned against him. Although Sir Muirhead had been a member of the board, at some point between September and October 1946 he had been forced to retire owing to ill health (Tate Gallery Records; data kindly provided by Christopher Bastock).

166 McFall, p. 2.

167 John Finch, letter to the author, 1 July 2009.

168 McFall, p. 2. Looking at the typed version of the speech, McFall's remark makes sense: after briefly apologizing for not being accustomed to speaking in public, Epstein moves on to describe his vocation as an artist and the official negative response to it (Birmingham being the exception), followed by an attack on Surrealist art and its clique of propagators who cause trouble for other artists; and finally he devotes a brief part to Lucifer; all this occupies half of his speech. The other half is wholly dedicated to Bernard Shaw's portrait and their exchange of opinions about it.

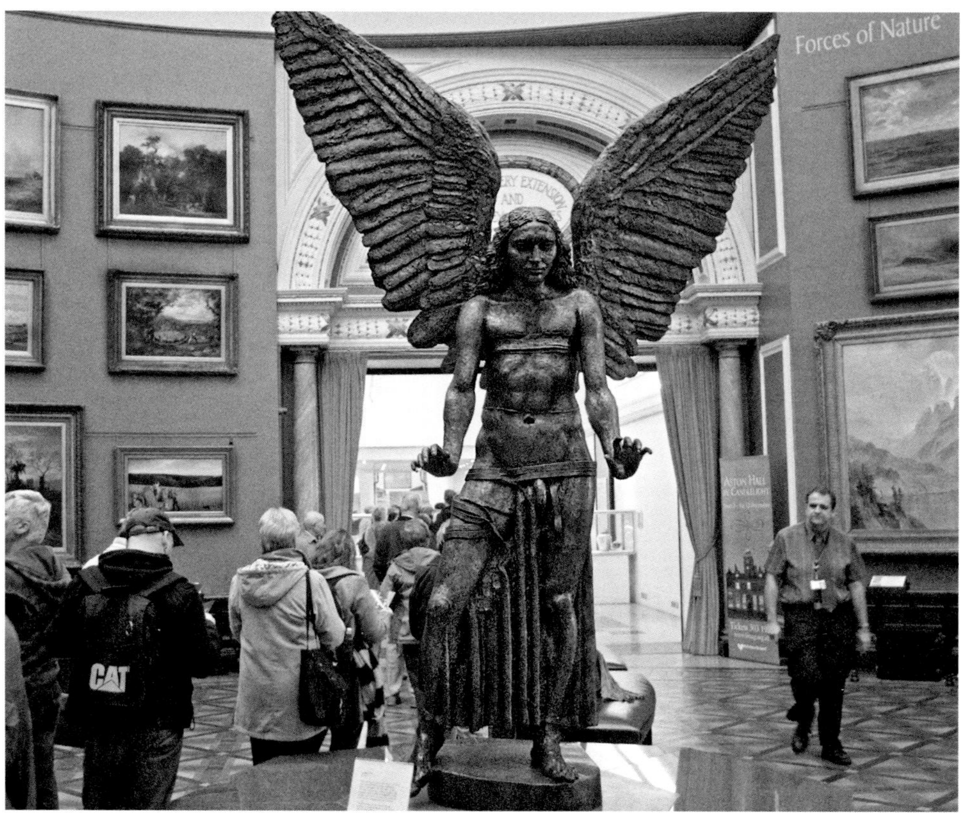

Fig. 48
Lucifer in Birmingham Art Gallery

For the occasion of the unveiling, *Lucifer* was displayed in the centre of the Round Room; but it was then relocated to the tea-room, standing incongruously at one end of it. That is where Stephen Gardiner and I, too, saw it in the mid 1980s. It now occupies anew a central place in the main gallery – as befits a great work (fig. 48).

CHAPTER 5

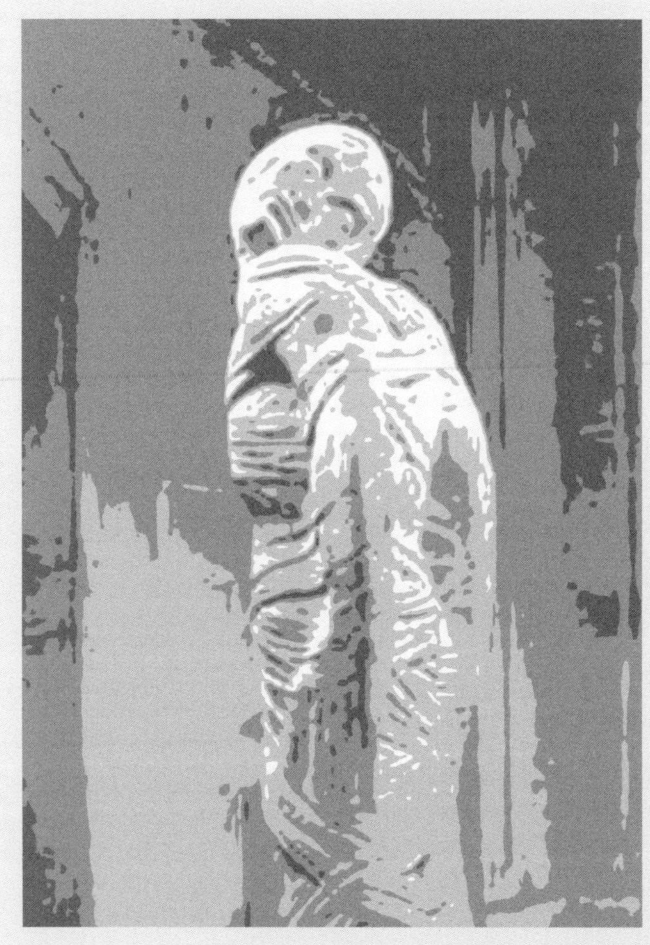

DEATH AND RESURRECTION (1945–50)

END OF A NIGHTMARE

On 28 April 1945 Mussolini was killed, and on 30 April Adolf Hitler committed suicide in his bunker. Several days earlier, on 15 April 1945, the British public had been shocked by BBC journalist Richard Dimbleby's report on the liberation of the Bergen-Belsen concentration camp by the British 11th Armoured Division.[1] Dimbleby concluded his message by saying his day at Belsen was "the most horrible of my life". On 19 April, eight days after the liberation of the Buchenwald concentration camp by the Americans, Prime Minister Churchill responded to General Eisenhower's request to send a group of Members of Parliament to see for themselves the horrors exposed in the camp near Weimar, thus proving to the British public that the case of Bergen-Belsen had not been a unique phenomenon but part of a systematic approach.[2] The frightening realisation was that in the German concentration camps throughout Europe an estimated nine million people had died, about six million of whom were Jews. Romanians, Slavs, homosexuals, Jehovah's Witnesses and various other minorities and disabled persons, as well as political enemies of the Nazi regime (particularly Communists) comprised the remaining three million. In total, the war casualties numbered twenty million soldiers and forty million civilians.

The composer Benjamin Britten played in the camps together with violinist Yehudi Menuhin, in the wake of which he composed his *Holy Sonnets of John Donne*, an exploration of the theme of innocence and corruption. William Golding's *Lord of the Flies*, on the origins of evil in society, was published in 1945, and Michael Tippett's oratorio *A Child of Our Time* was written between 1939 and 1941, also indicating a deep awareness of the moral dilemma of the times. World War II was perceived by most people as necessary and inevitable, whereas World War I had elicited a sense of outrage at the enormous cost and futile waste of life. Therefore, when Benjamin Britten composed his *War Requiem* to lament "the pity of war" in 1960 – at a time when the anxiety about nuclear weapons was at its peak – he set to music the poetry of Wilfred Owen of the earlier war and not of the later one.

Life for Epstein returned to its general course after the war, which ended for Europe on 8 May 1945. He started what would be a long-standing correspondence with Peggy Jean in America, and his letters constitute an important source for his opinions on various issues.

In July 1945 Epstein had to reject a suggestion by an old colleague and acquaintance, Horace Brodsky,[3] who was seeking the possible publication of Epstein's drawings. Epstein explained that he "could not manage to get any drawings together for a book;

1 60,000 prisoners were found alive, most of them seriously ill, and another 13,000 corpses lay around the camp unburied. See 'The 11th Armoured Division (Great Britain)', United States Holocaust Memorial Museum.

2 The results of their visit, quoting in their introduction Churchill's words on "finding the truth", were published in a slim booklet on 27 April, and sold to the public for two pence.

3 Horace Brodsky (1885–1969), Australian born, was a member of the London Group and an intimate friend of many artists, such as Jules Pascin, Jacob Epstein and David Bomberg, but in particular Henri Gaudier-Brzeska. His graphics were used to illustrated the literary works of Ezra Pound, Eugene O'Neill, Upton Sinclair and Theodore Dreisler.

they are too widely scattered & God alone knows where they are. Many are in America … it looks easy but actually is impossible".[4] This was regrettable, because presenting even only part of his output of drawings could have offered an important insight into his versatility.[5]

In the same month, in the elections held on 26 July, Churchill was ousted from office by the Labour Party, which won a resounding majority. A new understanding between the government and the people was needed, one that would compensate them for what they had suffered (60,000 civilians and 335,000 merchant seamen and combatants had been killed). The Welfare State came into being, with a National Health Service for all, and National Insurance covering every stage of life. Rationing, however, continued up to the mid 1950s. Churchill moved into a house opposite Epstein's and, other than on one occasion sending a policeman over to complain about the noise at one of the Epsteins' regular music recitals,[6] it seems that the neighbours developed a kind of mutual respect, out of which Churchill's portrait would later be commissioned.

On 6 August 1945 the world witnessed the horrendous consequence of the nuclear bombs dropped on Hiroshima and Nagasaki; alongside the horrors in Europe, this introduced the word 'holocaust' into common usage in the English vocabulary, a word that few Britons would have used before 1945. After eliminating the Fascist menace, a worried England now looked with suspicion at the victorious Communist Russia, not least because so many of the British intelligentsia were left-wing. Orwell's *Animal Farm* (published in England on 17 August 1945) offered a frightening parody of leftist ideology, but unfortunately I could not find any comment on it by the left-wing Epsteins. Similar anti-Communist feelings and paranoia had been at work in Britain after World War I, when Russia became a Communist state (I/160).

SCULPTURAL ENIGMAS

The catalogue of Epstein's works indicates that during 1942–43 there had been about thirteen commissioned portraits, constituting his main income. The hard work and mental effort involved in his large carving *Adam* of 1942 and the large bronze of *Lazarus* that started in 1943 (finally completed and exhibited in 1945), might have induced Epstein, somewhat out of context and perhaps as a means of relaxation, to make between 1943 and 1945 in the studio a series of about fifteen life studies of nudes,[7] all of them waving their limbs in all possible directions (was he studying limb movement?). Most of these figurines (all 50–60 cm) were presented at his 1947 exhibition and, as none seem to have found any expression in his following work, I shall not discuss them here. To some extent this series of nudes recalls Epstein's collection of 75 drawings of nudes made around 1925, both before and after his laborious work on the Hudson Memorial, and published later in a book (1927). Important for this discussion, however, are a series of seven maquettes (dated in Silber's catalogue as 1946) as well as two unrecorded maquettes.[8] Most of these were exhibited together with the series of nudes at *Jacob Epstein: New Sculpture* at the Leicester Galleries in February 1947, but were ignored by critics, probably because they were not developed further into sculpture.

Even as preliminary expressions of an idea, the maquettes may be regarded to a

4 Letter to Brodsky, 21 June 1945: TGA-949/2/5.

5 Other than *Epstein: Drawings* of 1962, which I have discussed in the 'Introduction' (p. 20), the only book of drawings published during his lifetime is that by Wellington, *Epstein, Seventy-five Drawings*.

6 Jackie Epstein, conversation with the author, 1989.

7 The models were Betty Peters, Mary Tracy and Juanita Forbes (Silber, *Sculpture of Epstein*, nos. 341–53, 366, 528).

8 They exist among a series of proofs of prints that depict Epstein works: NAGW–BL/7/2/24.1.

great extent – following the credo of this book – as reflecting Epstein's thinking, and this was often related to his personal life. This seems also to be reflected in their mythological titles and their literary content, which often serve as metaphors for the human condition. The exact date of their execution is unclear, but they seem to belong to the period in 1945–46, when relations between Epstein and Kathleen were unsteady. While the order of their execution is unknown, they are briefly mentioned here with Silber's catalogue numbers in an order that suggests a logical line of thought reflecting his personal concerns.

Nightfarer (no. 379) has no image available, and therefore Epstein's depiction of a wandering and perhaps restless man is for the moment unknown. One might expect that the idea conveyed would be that of a dark element intruding into the sculptor's life, one that came and left, perhaps unseen in the darkness, but whose presence had obviously been felt.

There is no image of *Jupiter and Semele* (no. 375) available either. Semele, according to legend, had been treacherously advised by Jupiter's consort, Juno, to ask him to appear to her in all his divine splendour. When he obliged, the awesome vision caused her violent death. One depiction of which Epstein had undoubtedly been aware since his Parisian days and interest in the Symbolists (I/57) was the painting of this subject by the French Symbolist Gustave Moreau. Epstein's representation of this divine physical love might perhaps have been a retrospective assessment of his love-affair with Kathleen, of the beginning of the relationship between the renowned artist and his adoring and adored model and of its less than smooth continuation. It is in this realm of musings, I suggest, that his *Narcissus* (no. 377; no image available) seems to belong: depicting the self-adoring being who underestimated the love of Echo, this work might have reflected the model's love for the self-centred artist during the first stage of their relationship. But the passing of time altered things, as Epstein may have expressed in what might be regarded as the next figurine, entitled *Pasiphae*,[9] the wife who bore several children to her husband King Minos of Crete. Cursed by Neptune, disregarding husband and children, she lusted for and mated with a white bull sent by the god. The two unrecorded maquettes seem to refer to this legend, as they both depict a mating couple: in one her lust is consummated with a human male [71a], while in the other it is with a bull [71b]. The legend stereotypes the female as an emblem of grotesque bestiality, while also suggesting excesses of sensuality and deceit. Pasiphae's passion resulted in her giving birth to the Minotaur, a creature with the head of a bull and the body of a man, a kind of monster partly disguised as a man, and not the father's natural son.[10]

The maquette *Neptune* [72] is a rough sketch that depicts the god who initiated the events suffered by Pasiphae.[11] This is not the god standing above the life-giving waters of the Trevi Fountain in Rome, but an emaciated elderly figure with horn-like protrusions sprouting from his head and a hooked nose and beard, sitting in an oriental pose with crossed legs on top of several human figures, his hands resting on the undefined mass (water?) that covers them.

Might the dual depiction of a woman's sensuality and deceit carried through excess into bestiality, in what might be regarded as the Pasiphae images, and the somewhat pathetic figure of *Neptune* indicate a particular state of affairs in Epstein's personal life? Two occurrences during the 1940s support this conjecture.

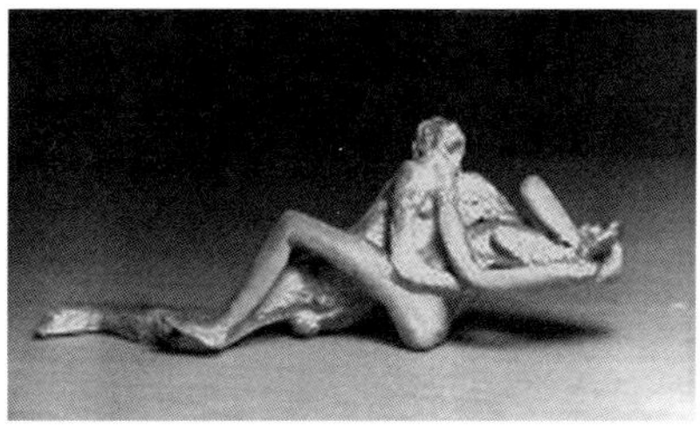

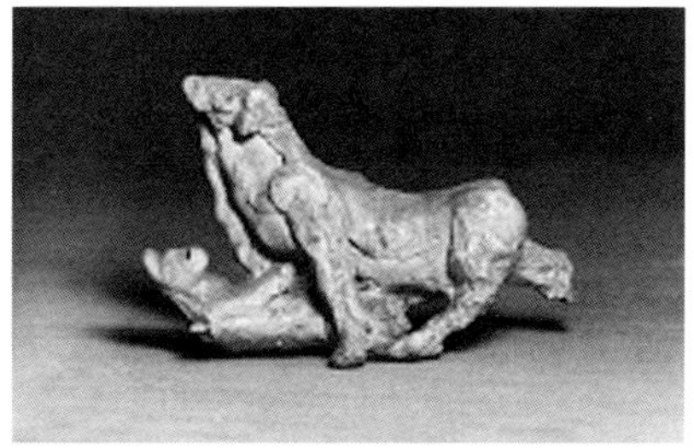

71a–b
Untitled (no records; made from film-print)
GREC-NAGW

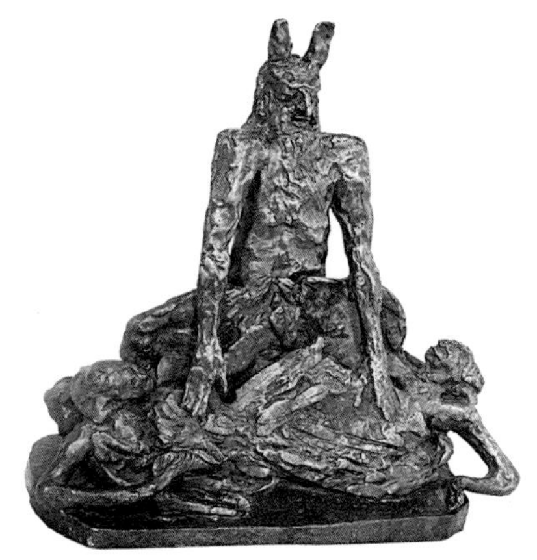

72
Neptune, 1944–45 [1946]
Bronze, H. 34 cm
Formerly Shinman collection

9 In Silber, *Sculpture of Epstein*, its title is given as "Pasiphae (no. 380; head of a child)", but she does not reproduce an image. In the light of what the text further suggests, I believe that her description is more appropriate for another work.

10 This brings to mind the rumour that supposedly Margaret spread, namely that Theo was not Epstein's son: Gardiner, *Epstein*, p. 314.

11 Silber, *Sculpture of Epstein*, suggests it is "related to the *Lucifer, Belial and Beelzebub*" maquettes (mentioned above, p. 151); if indeed this is the case, then (as there is no contextual relationship) it may indicate 1944–45 as the period of execution also for all the others.

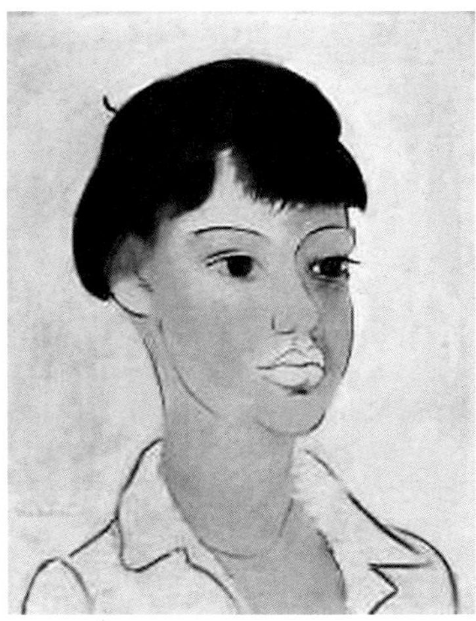

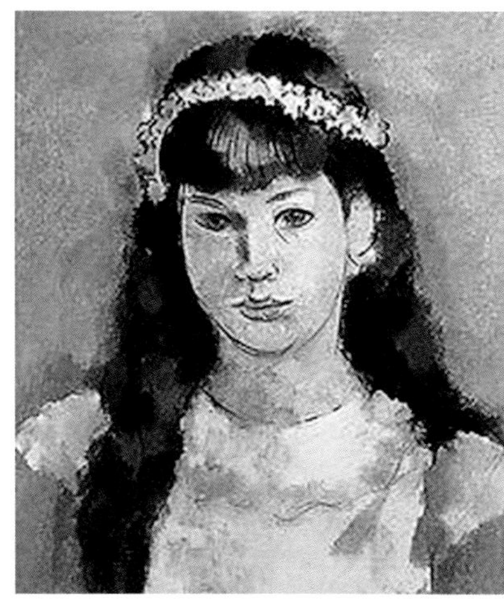

Fig. 49a
Fritz Mühsam
Theo, 1935 [1934]
Oil on canvas, 41.5 x 33.5 cm
GREC-NAGW

Fig. 49b
Fritz Mühsam
Esther, 1935 [1934]
Oil on canvas, 46 x 38.5 cm
GREC- NAGW

After the war started, many European refugees, including Jews, fled to England. Even as a young girl in her private school in the country, the kind-hearted Kitty remembered how horrified she had been by the stories told by a German refugee girlfriend; and with deep empathy, in spite of living in the atmosphere of her pious Christian grandmother, she told me: "It made me feel Jewish".[12] One such refugee was Fritz Mühsam (1880–1949),[13] a Jewish artist of Epstein's age who had lived in Paris during the 1930s. He fled to England, and up until the liberation of France he lived in London near Kathleen and her family,[14] which at that stage comprised mainly Helen and her daughter.[15] Besides the English couple John and Susan Lade, the other refugee acquaintances who lived nearby Kathleen in that neighbourhood were mainly what one might call "the Italian connection" – Ethel Calvocoressi, Mario Sarfati from Lake Garda and the Vivante family from Siena; it was through the Vivantes that Kathleen became acquainted with Marc Joffé and his baby son Roland, who was later on to become important in her life. From a letter written much later on, it appears that Epstein maintained his distance from these people during those years: "I only met Epstein two or three times .... [He] appeared rarely. Quite privately. But he was sharply felt as a distant presence, hardly mentioned except with a kind of awe."[16] But after Margaret's death, when John and Susan Lade helped to take care of Theo when Kathleen moved into Epstein's house, Epstein developed a warm relationship with the couple, taking them out to dine in his favourite restaurants.[17] The Italians returned home after the war, but Kathleen's warm contacts with them continued, and Italy was later to occupy an important part in the Epsteins' lives.

Mühsam returned to Paris as soon as it became possible. From his letter dated 20 October 1945, written after Helen had also returned to France, bringing him presents from Kathleen, it seems that he had also been in contact with Kathleen before the war, as he asks her: "But when will you cross the Channel Yourself??? Wouldn't it be lovely to meet old Paris *again* and the Chartres Cathedral?"[18] Kathleen's previous visit to France had been in 1935 (see p. 88) after discovering that Epstein's liaison with Isabel had resulted in a new son.

As Mühsam's letter indicates, they enjoyed each other's company; and that might have been the occasion on which he made Theo's and Esther's portraits (figs. 49a–b),[19] Kathleen having presumably given him their photographs.

12 Conversation with the author, 1985.

13 Personal data on Mühsam are almost non-existent, other than on sales of his paintings in various galleries. The following is my own conjecture from whatever could be found on the internet and from data in the NAGW.

14 Mentioned by Epstein's daughter Kitty Godley in 'The Garman Ryan Collection: As I saw it', p. 12. The data given by Kathleen's records in the NAGW are that "Mühsam was a Jewish artist, a friend of Kathleen and her family, and was one of many Dutch and German refugees who lived near them". In all probability he left Paris around 1938–39.

15 Gardiner, *Epstein*, p. 406.

16 Letter of Paolo Vivante to Cressida Connolly, 11 March 2002: NAGW – cc/1/5/2/2.

17 Gardiner, *Epstein*, pp. 405–06.

18 NAGW archive (my italics).

19 NAGW archive; dated – erroneously, I suggest – to 1934, a year before Kathleen's trip to Paris.

The renewed contact between Kathleen and Mühsam during his time in England appears to have been close enough for him to worry from afar about her children, writing "over the problem of dear Theodore's disease" and suggesting that she not count on "material means" but on Christian Science,[20] and even providing her with the address of a recommended practitioner. This is reminiscent of Theo's suggestion that Kathleen rely on her Christian faith (p. 144), and it may have been Mühsam's influence that moved Theo in this direction in 1941 when he was responding to Kathleen's concern about Esther's condition. Both children seemed to have been affected by mental problems that started at quite a young age. Esther was twelve years old in 1941. Theo's letter is the only source to point to her early problems. As for Theo himself, the family friend Gardiner suggests that his breakdown was the result of his hard work on a farm during the war (as a conscientious objector), combined with the effort invested in his matriculation correspondence courses while, concomitantly, pursuing his ambition to be an artist.[21]

After inquiring for news about her and the children, Mühsam ends his letter with "All my loving thoughts to you, Dearest Kathleen, from yours ever". The fact that Epstein is not mentioned suggests that the above-mentioned group which surrounded Kathleen in her home during the war years enabled her to have a parallel universe of which Epstein was not a part, and probably also did not meet, in spite of his daily visits between 6 and 7 pm, during which "no one was allowed in".[22]

Were the maquettes with their significant mythological titles conceived in 1945 and executed in 1946, a representation of Epstein's response to her close relationship with (the 'bull') Mühsam? Or with others? Kathleen's letters were not kept; if not destroyed by her, they were probably destroyed by Beth Lipkin. There is no way to know whether she had told Epstein about her new acquaintance in Paris when he had asked her in his letter of long ago about the new people she had met (p. 160). Although Gardiner knew her personally and claimed to have been a life-long friend, there is no mention in his biography of Epstein about the adoring Mühsam who painted her children, was her companion on her tour of Paris in 1935, and part of her social circle in the late 1930s and early 1940s.

It was probably through Kathleen's "Italian connection" mentioned above that she met during the war a handsome young Italian Cambridge undergraduate, whose name was not disclosed by the family.[23] The love affair started in England and later continued when she visited Italy on her own. In between she wrote him affectionate letters which she later destroyed, save for one which he managed to copy, attesting to this relationship and to her tender feelings for him.

Epstein's reaction? One may assume that, being in his mid sixties and realising that he was deeply attached to a woman still in full bloom and twenty years younger than himself, he came to terms with it; no less, I suggest, because Kathleen probably managed to keep her affairs quiet so as not to offend or ridicule him.[24] Epstein's next depiction, therefore, I suggest, was *Lovers on an Eagle's Back* [73]. As a subject it has no direct mythological connotation, although its configuration is still in the realm of legend. The depiction has been said to have been influenced by the comforting words of the prophet Isaiah (40: 31), that those who have faith "shall renew their strength; they shall mount up with wings as eagles; they shall run, and not be weary; and they shall walk, and not faint" (King James Bible). Although the prophet was referring to those who have faith in God, the secular Epstein had to rely on the faith he had in his and Kathleen's attachment

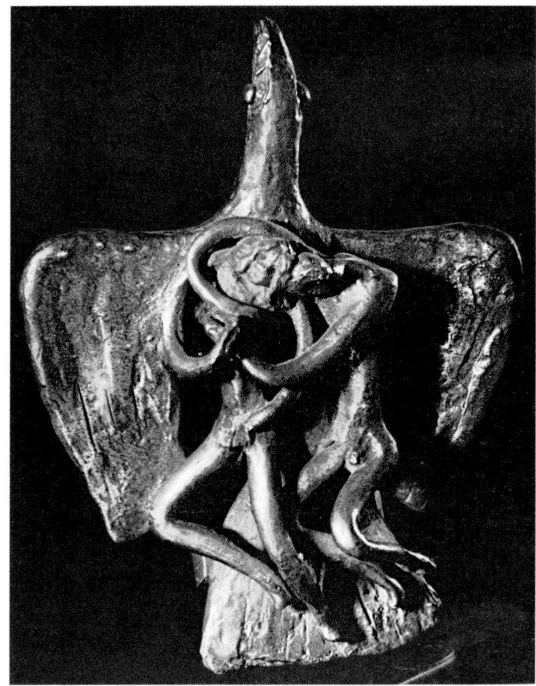

73
Lovers on an Eagle's Back, 1945 [1946]
Bronze, H.10.5, L. 20 cm
Private collection

20 It suffices to mention (in regard to Mühsam's recommendation) that Christian Science asserts that man and the universe as a whole are spiritual rather than material in nature and that truth and good are real, whereas evil and error are illusive aspects of material existence. Christian Scientists believe that through prayer, knowledge and understanding all things are possible for good through God; this does not contradict Mühsam's Jewish origins.

21 Gardiner, *Father and Son – Jacob Epstein, Sculptor, and Theo Garman, Painter*, p. 6.

22 Godley, 'The Garman Ryan Collection: As I saw it', p. 13.

23 Connolly, *The Rare and the Beautiful*, pp. 189–90. The source of the following is Kathleen's daughter Kitty.

24 One may wonder, though, whether he ever saw her photograph in the nude, taken during the mid 1940s (Connolly, ibid., p. 194, as in 1940; no photographer mentioned).

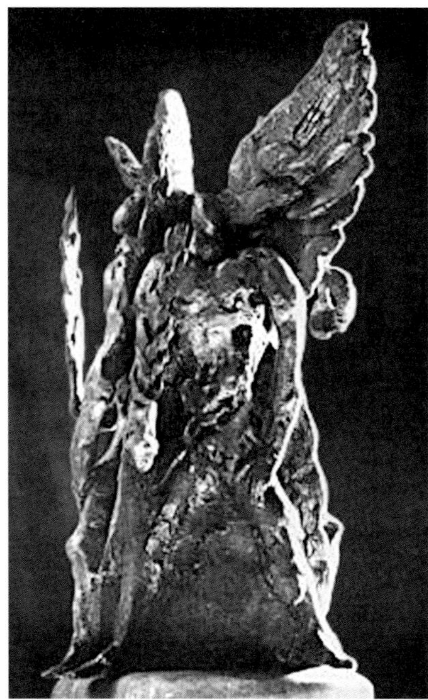

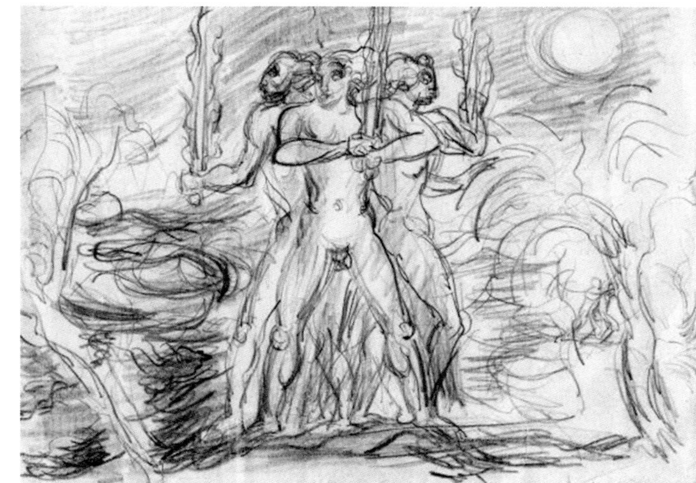

74a
Guardians of Paradise, 1947
Bronze, H. 25.4 cm
Private collection

74b
Three Naked Men with Blazing Swords
Pencil, 17.5 x 22.5 cm
GREC-NAGW

to one another, despite the sense of estrangement that their situation implied.

Epstein's representation of these lovers is quite strange, because the woman lies on her side with her back to her partner, and the only contact between them is that of the man's embracing arms. In contrast to Narcissus's estrangement from Echo in the previously mentioned myth, in this maquette it is the woman who distances herself, turning her back to him while he seems to be appealing for her attention.

The last in this series of maquettes as I would order them seems to express Epstein's eventual coming to terms with this frustrating state of affairs, by recreating a reality different from that which the lovers used to have. A preliminary drawing, *Three Naked Men with Blazing Swords*, points to awakening from a state of naivety in Eden and of expulsion from a place of former harmony [74b]. The maquette *Guardians of Paradise* [74a] seems to show the previous state of affairs conclusively at an end, with two winged male figures standing back to back while holding out flaming swords in one direction, preventing a return to Eden, in accordance with the biblical description. This maquette seems to finalize Epstein's attitude towards the entire series and towards his previous relationships with Kathleen: the biblical expulsion did not end the relationship between the man and the woman, but rather removed them together on to a different plane of reality, and, I suggest, the same happened in Epstein's case: he and Kathleen found for their love their own *modus vivendi*, based also on friendship and devotion.

MARGARET: SUNSET

As soon as the war was over, two important changes took place in the Epsteins' household which, at that time, included David Roche, an Irish cook who came each day, and Jackie's governess. The first change was due to Margaret's exhaustion resulting from her many responsibilities. Upon advertising for a secretary, she received over seventy applicants, finally hiring a young ex-serviceman formerly in the Merchant Navy, John Finch, because he "was the only one who didn't claim to have an artistic background".[25] Finch had started writing during the long night watches, and had come to London from a mining village believing at the time that if one wanted to be a writer one "had to live

25 Information kindly provided by John Finch in a detailed letter to the author, 29 June 2006.

in London". He was looking for a job, and "the Epstein job turned out to be it". He lived in the house, very much a member of the family, having a room on the top floor and eating with them in the living room, in which there was "a grand piano, a chair or two and a scrubbed top table", around which "Myself, Mrs E. (he [Epstein] always called her Peggy) and Epstein and Jackie would be sat". His duties included tidying up the mass of paperwork, typing letters, doing shopping etc., being a companion to Jackie, who was very "highly strung", and, to some extent, dealing also with the foundry in which Epstein's work was cast. In his introductory letter to me he described himself as "amanuensis to the Epstein Household in Hyde Park Gate in 1946/7".

The second change concerned the work process on Epstein's bronzes. The large number of portraits that needed casting (and they constituted his main income) left Epstein at the mercy of skilful and reliable plaster-moulders. If a sculptor has to do his own plaster-moulding it reduces his output by half, and there were occasional comments that in Epstein's case this might not be such a bad thing. When after one particular argument Epstein told his moulder to pack his kit and get out, shouting "and don't come back here", he turned to David McFall, "sweet and demure as a débutante, for he was a very funny mimic", asking who did his moulding. When McFall admitted that he did his own, Epstein wheedled him into casting his portrait of Jawaharlal Nehru for him – "as a special favour Mack-fal ... to save the NEHRU [1st version, 1946] ... just handle it as you do your own"; "and that is how I got hooked into the plaster bin", explained McFall.[26] The "NEHRU" portrait was indirectly initiated by Nehru himself, when he attended the Commonwealth Conference in London in July 1946, and phoned Epstein expressing a wish to visit him in his studio. Nothing was said about a portrait, but Epstein seized the rare opportunity and asked Nehru to sit for him. There were only three sittings, each lasting an hour before the conference, resulting in what Epstein regarded as a "non-comprehensive" portrait (PS/233). Epstein complained to Peggy Jean about the Jews' refusal to buy it.[27] In another letter he explained:[28]

> A friend had hoped to see my Nehru bust placed in Israel. Most strange
> to say the Israelians [sic] turned it down.
> I will show it in January at the Leicester Galleries with the London Group.
> It is a tragic bust. But Nehru seemed to me like that.
> The strange influence of Lady Mountbatten was painful to see.[29]

When Nehru next arrived in England, Epstein was able to create an impressive bust of his sitter.[30] McFall was to mould many other portrait busts and heads, and was therefore entirely qualified to state that the casts done during Epstein's lifetime "are superb workmanship because he was punctilious in checking his waxes at the foundry. This is why any posthumous bronzes are manifestly worthless."

These two educated and interesting individuals in the Epstein's household, McFall and Finch, a practicing artist and an author in the making,[31] became friends ("I knew David and used to go walking with him in Hyde Park, and one winter we skated on the Serpentine!") and remember fondly the atmosphere of the place and its inhabitants even when the habits of these inhabitants may have seemed peculiar. Finch provided me with the more intimate details on the life of the Epsteins, while McFall wrote mainly about the working atmosphere in the studio.

Margaret "used to wear three or four skirts and kept her keys about three skirts

26 McFall, pp. 5–6.

27 Letter from Epstein to Peggy Jean, 4 November 1948: TGA- 8716/12. This first version had been exhibited in the Leicester Gallery in February 1947.

28 Letter from Epstein to Peggy Jean, 12 November 1948: TGA-8716/12.

29 Michael Thornton ('The Royal Gigolo', *Daily Mail*, 3 September 2011; http://www.dailymail.co.uk/femail/article-1085883) writes: "During her years as Vicereine of India, she had a deeply passionate relationship with India's first Prime Minister Pandit Jawaharlal Nehru. There are those who suspect that Nehru, like both Mountbattens, had bisexual tendencies, and that Mountbatten (who had a ten-year-old 'open marriage' relationship with his wife), possibly in a last desperate attempt to maintain physical contact with her, may have joined them in a bizarre *menage à trois*". This 'bizarre' corresponds to Epstein's "strange" in his letter.

30 Silber, *Sculpture of Epstein*, no. 410; dated 1949, presented at the Leicester Galleries in 1960.

31 David McFall became a known sculptor and a member of the Royal Academy; John Finch wrote scripts for films and TV series.

down. If you needed the keys you went through a procedure where she lifted one skirt at a time, with a coy glance at each one, until she got there." As an ageing mother she tried very hard to cope with Jackie ("a 13/14 year old and very neurotic"), though she spoiled him terribly. "Twice I had to go and collect him from his school, which had given up on him .... Epstein wanted him to be an artist and used to bribe him by giving him a shilling for each painting he did. If Jackie was hard up he used to knock off a couple of paintings, usually of Spitfires and Hurricanes, but with no signs of talent at all."[32] Years later, a much older Jackie smilingly told me that once he had been "asked" to paint, saying jokingly "and I did!!"

As people tend to talk around the dining table, I always asked my interviewees about conversations during and after meals. Beth Lipkin (who later came with Kathleen to live in the house) used to join the meal, but immediately after finishing hers she would retire to her room, and thus was unable to report on conversations; Jackie stated that they were always about art, but owing to his basic lack of interest in the subject he could not remember any particular issue. John Finch, however, was able to provide a glimpse into Epstein and his cultural interests:

> I wish I could remember the conversations, but only that they were fascinating to a young would-be writer. Epstein and I talked mainly about books. I don't think he had much time for contemporary writing. He would occasionally read a book I recommended, but I can't remember him being enthusiastic about modern writing at all. We often discussed poetry.
>
> I wouldn't have dared discuss art, except that he was interested in some small sculptures I had picked up in West Africa during the war and would always like to talk about Africa.
>
> In politics he was unashamedly left wing (as I was) and we enjoyed talking politics. He had no time at all for the establishment, especially in the world of art. His favourite description of King George VI was "poor sap". He was also interested in hearing about the mining community from which I came.[33]

An ironic incident during this period was the Blackpool's side-show people's surprise visit to London, with the Epstein carving they had acquired, in March 1946. Their "peep-show" had been introduced by "a nasty little man in tuxedo and a red carnation blaring through a loud speaker [urging people] to come and see the most shocking thing in the world".[34] The "shocking thing" was Epstein's *Jacob and the Angel*, presented in a room full of drawings of Epstein's nudes. The *Art News* critic concluded his impression of the event: "People were coming, the owners are making a fortune, and the poor public, whether it realises or not, is seeing art". One may assume that Epstein was not amused; his views on this recent affair must have been similar to his attitude expressed toward the whole Blackpool affair (see p. 121).

During 1946 Finch observed Epstein's work on the portrait of Winston Churchill, whom both Epstein and he politically opposed. "One would have expected him to be critical of Churchill, who lived opposite, but if he was I never heard it." Aunt Sylvia, on the other hand and in her exaggerated manner, provides an amusing piece of gossip:[35] "Churchill always referred to my brother as 'that talented monster'. Churchill used to receive cases of liquor free, as gifts, and he would never give my brother any at all. That

32 Finch, email letter of 8 September 2009.

33 "An odd coincidence was that my grandfather knew the Moore family in Castleford, and my mother was born in a house just two or three miles from Moore's parents' house": Finch, email to the author of 1 July 2006.

34 G.R., 'A Peep at Epstein', *Art News*, March 1946 45–59.

35 Babson, *The Epsteins*, p. 59.

annoyed Jacob." When Epstein's American relatives were visiting him, "they noticed a big commotion in the street outside, about which Epstein remarked, 'Oh, T*hat man* is going out'; when they wanted to photograph Churchill, after explaining who they were, they got his reply: '*Oh*, T*hat man*'. Good neighbours, one would say." Finch would open the door when Churchill came for his sittings, and show him and his bodyguard into the studio, pondering on "God knows what he thought of the mess". The studio was heated by an old-fashioned solid fuel stove, which he and McFall kept going as it was always cold, "as was the rest of the house".[36]

Churchill had been deprecated his own artistic work, but Epstein thought "it was better than Churchill gave himself credit for", as he said to Finch upon returning home after Churchill had invited him to look at his paintings. The respect for one another's achievements appears to have been mutual, because when in 1954 Epstein was knighted he suspected that the recommendation to the Prime Minister had been at the instigation of Churchill, as he didn't know "anyone else who would be interested".[37]

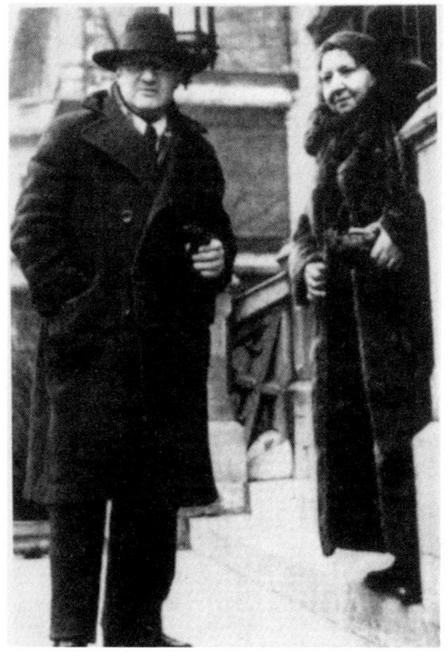

Fig. 50a
Epstein and Margaret in front of the steps leading up to the front door of their house
GREC - NAGW

Epstein had been working hard (on portraits), and his eyes "may be just tired but I should not like the state of *Diesel* [sic; referring to mask-like protective eyeglasses] to be habitual", as he wrote to Dr Blake, the family's ophthalmologist.[38] By the end of 1946 Epstein seems to have already been occupied with his next project, from which no preliminary drawings seem to have been kept. This is unfortunate, as the new subject – the first which, to my mind, combines in one figure notions from both the Old and New Testaments – had required a prolonged process of thought, "and was the outcome of an idea which haunted me for many years" (PS/231). It may have taken him quite a time, and in all probability also several sketches, before he started to transfer his vision into stone, probably at the end of 1947, after one of the worst periods in his life: on 3 March 1947 Margaret Epstein, aged seventy-four, died of a brain haemorrhage after slipping on the icy doorsteps of their house the day before. In fig. 50a they are seen in front of the steps leading up to the front door. Years later John Finch wrote the following stanzas in the long eulogy that describes his life with them:[39]

> The day you died it was I who found you, searching
> The house when you failed to follow us in from the cab.
> I found you at the bottom of the steps, unmoving;
> Then as we sought to get you inside, you struggled back
> To life, insisting on making it yourself, on being what
> You had always seen as your raison d'être; the guardian
> And comfort of the one you called, "The great man".
>
> We sat down to dinner, you insisting you were well
> And pulling back your veil to reveal that vanquished face
> As you looked down curiously at your soup, and
> I wonder now what you saw there; did you see
> The hills and the white sea-spray of the Western Isles
> From where you came and was it to there that you returned
> As your head dipped grotesquely into the bowl
> Before we could hold you?

36 Finch, email to the author of 1 July 2006.

37 Letter from Epstein to Peggy Jean, 20 January 1954: TGA-8716/30.

38 Letter of 17 June 1946: HMI-24/1990/14.

39 Kindly emailed to the author with permission to cite (1 May 2012); only two stanzas are reproduced here.

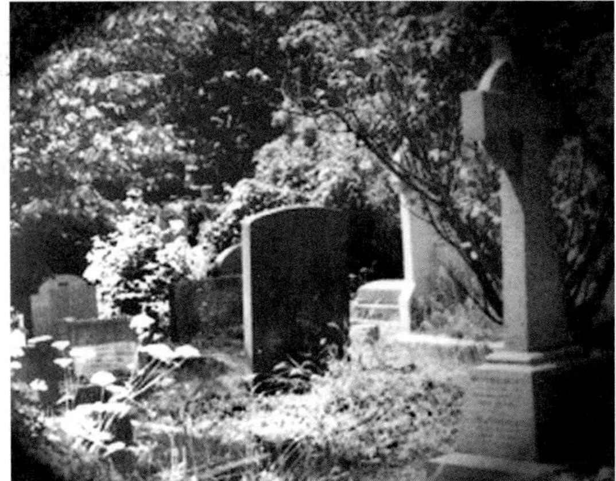

Fig. 50b
David McFall
Tombstone of Margaret Epstein, 1956
Highgate Cemetery, London

She was carried out to an ambulance, saying to McFall her last words: "Don't let Epstein see me like this – see that he has his gloves ...", while he was thinking, "a parallel with Rodin's Rose Beuret comes to mind".

The Epsteins' relationship was and remained a matter of wonder to those who did not know them personally, in particular regarding Margaret's tolerance of his infidelities.[40] John Finch, who lived with them for a period of almost two years, seems to be the only one to have written from an insider's position on their personal life together:

> Jacob and Margaret obviously had a close relationship, as they shared the same bed in a room where all the Benin sculptures were stored ....
>
> Despite his relationship with other women, he stayed with Mrs E who was in many ways quite grotesque when I knew her, stricken by the coarsening disease she had.
>
> To some extent I suppose it was because she 'managed' him and protected him from the rigours of ordinary life, but I don't feel that this was all there was to it, as it must have been obvious to anyone who stayed in the house that there was genuine affection there.[41]

Margaret's death led to a situation that can only be termed 'awkward'. She was interred at Highgate Cemetary and both Peggy Jean, who left for America after the funeral, and Jackie even much later had assumed that there was a tombstone; Peggy Jean even suggested incorporating Epstein's *Marble Arms* of 1923 (I/170, ftn. 27). However, for almost a decade her grave remained without a tombstone. Epstein, who hardly ever bothered with practical arrangements, may have asked Kathleen to deal with the matter (in the same insensitive manner with which he once asked Margaret to buy a Christmas present for Kathleen; p. 124), or he may have automatically expected her to see also to this matter too among his other affairs – which she did not, nor did anybody else. At the end of the day it was David McFall's respect for the deceased woman that brought the issue to a close: according to his diaries, in November 1956, when he was invited by Epstein to carve the letters for Epstein's figure of the South African Prime Minister Jan Smuts (erected in Parliament Square), McFall also carved and erected Margaret's headstone in Highgate Cemetery (fig. 50b). The assumption among McFall's circle is that he might also have paid for it himself.[42]

Peggy Jean came over from America to the funeral and to offer help. "They had a room upstairs – a bedroom – which was full of her collection of art and things ... it was full of vermin and mold when they opened it. Peggy Jean did not know what to take. Later everything had been thrown away."[43]

Margaret, as Peggy Jean testifies, had been hoarding stuff "like a squirrel" in that room; Epstein's work was in another one near the studio, and Margaret had occasionally sold items when money was needed.[44] But, as it was later found, she had neither recorded the work Epstein had done, nor reported its content to her daughter: "I never remember PJ getting a letter from Mgt. If she did, she didn't save it. They were always from Jacob."[45] The accumulated mess was such that "Kathleen wouldn't come near the house", and Peggy Jean had first and foremost to clean it up to some extent and to organize a filing cabinet for Epstein's papers.[46] Some of the mess still remained after

40 The issue is discussed in I/52, regarding Meum and the children, and in I/170, in regard to Kathleen.

41 Email letter to the author, 1 July 2009.

42 An email by Rodney Seddon and a conversation with Alexandra McFall-Dane, 2010. There are no direct records left in spite of McFall having been meticulous in keeping diaries, recording both work progress and social engagements. In any case, commenting on the issue of the gravestone might have been too embarrassing for the kind McFall to have recorded it.

43 Babson, *The Epsteins*, p. 54.

44 Peggy Jean's recorded interview with the author, 1993.

45 Email from her daughter Leda Sloat to the author 19 May 2010.

46 Peggy Jean's recorded interview with the author, 1993.

Peggy Jean had left, and, when she later asked for certain items, Epstein wrote that "there are inefficiencies about finding things in the house. You know that we had to have the rooms cleaned and especially the school room, which was an intolerable mass of stuff."[47] All the messy piles were taken by the cleaners while he was at work and Kathleen had been unable to watch them every minute, Epstein explained, adding that Jackie's mementos that were not part of the piles were taken too, and "must have been stolen", asking her not to tell Jackie as he would feel bad about it. Gardiner (p. 402) has a more colourful description, ending with Epstein's running into the street and ordering a rag-and-bone man to take everything away, without bothering to look at anything or sort it out.

Only after Margaret's death did the members of Epstein's two families develop the contacts previously forbidden: Peggy Jean met Kathleen, learned to respect her devotion to her father and began calling her Kitty as her father did; she grew fond of her step-sister Kitty and in particular of Esther, but never met Theo.[48] At the time Kathleen was living in her house at 272 King's Road with her children, her sister Helen and Helen's daughter Cathy, until Helen became involved with Mario Sarfati, an elderly Jewish lawyer from Lake Garda, and after a brief period she became pregnant and married him, moving to Italy.

After Margaret's funeral, when things began to settle, Peggy Jean took Jackie with her to America. "Our years at Cape Hatteras [North Carolina] were wonderful and we all loved it .... It was like living in wilderness .... Jackie would bring reptiles home for pets. My Dad [Norman Hornstein] let him"; and when in later years their daughter Leda asked Jackie if he missed England, he responded – '"not at all".[49]

Although Kathleen moved to live in Epstein's house only in 1949, she took over his affairs almost immediately after Peggy Jean's departure, and was "shocked to discover"[50] the chaotic financial problems and piling debts which had undoubtedly also influenced the financial support she had been given throughout the years, as well as contributing to the bad state of the house and its neglected interior. This certainly gave her a glimpse into the problems encountered by Margaret, not the least of which was the need to find new people to manage the problematic household because, as David McFall reported, "within hours of [Margaret's] death the persona of the household switched over. David Rush, the Irish cook [not having been paid for three months],[51] made off in haste for the Emerald Isle, "Miss Moggeridge [the pianist] retraced her steps, and I was asked [by an apologetic Epstein] for my latch-key of No. 18. Working there became very awkward, not to say impossible from then on."[52]

Despite being deprived of his easy access to the house, and the tension that grew between him and Epstein, to McFall's great pain, it was McFall who was called, and came, whenever help was needed in the studio. Epstein maintained their relationship in spite of Kathleen's resentment of anyone who had been close to or fond of Margaret (with the exception of Matthew Smith). Epstein and McFall would walk together in the park on Sundays. Epstein's insecurity was reflected one evening when they were walking together up Gloucester Road; upon passing a tramp sheltering in a doorway, Epstein said: "I'll finish up like that Mack-fal", to which McFall added in his memoirs: "and he meant it".

47 Letter to Peggy Jean, 14 June 1948: TGA- 8716/5.

48 Peggy Jean's recorded interview with the author, 1993.

49 Email from Leda Sloat to the author, 19 May 2010.

50 Gardiner, *Epstein*, p. 403.

51 Peggy Jean's recorded interview with the author, 1993.

52 McFall, p. 8.

LAZARUS

Margaret, who knew every work of her husband from his initial thoughts to the final concept, did not live to see Epstein working on and completing one of his most outstanding carvings, over which he had long been pondering. This was a work in which he immersed all his mental and physical powers during a great part of the year of her death and well into the next one,[53] particularly as it had been an unprofitable period during which he had done only six portraits, four of which were personal and only two were commissioned.

The origin of the stone on which he worked is complex. In his memoirs, in reacting to Silber's catalogue, McFall recounts: "Epstein had stored certain early pieces begun before the first world war in Harrods Depository and had been requested to retrieve them.[54] One of these, which came back to the studio, was a figure in Hopton-wood stone called MATERNITY, 23 (plate 5). This was the time-hardened stone which Epstein slowly and painfully transformed into LAZARUS with blunt chisels and wood rasps."

Even if one accepts McFall's description of a transformation being carried out on stonework, his indicating Silber's no. 23, pl. 5, is in error; this same *Maternity* of 1910 is 'alive and kicking' in Leeds Art Gallery.

A claim to have been the *Lazarus's* living model made by Aubrey Grandon[55] may suggest that, perhaps, there were no preliminary drawings and that Epstein carved directly, inspired by the living figure – chiselling away at the stomach, the back and the pose that, as told by Gordon to Gardiner, "was a hard stance to hold for a long time"; and this form of modelling continued for several months.

The carving of *Lazarus* was perhaps one of the rarest of occasions for which Epstein asked a colleague (McFall's) opinion on how to go on with a work, thus revealing uncharacteristic hesitation:

> To begin with LAZARUS had feet. They were the tortured feet of one who had survived untold agonies, feet which could walk no further .... But the lower legs were too short. Too short by far, like stumps. Querulously, he asked me what I thought. I knew that he knew the legs were too short – I hesitated, then decided that it was not the moment to be evasive. I replied quietly that there was only one remedy – and that was to carve out the feet so as to gain length for the legs. He didn't answer but I had confirmed his own conclusion.[56]

Another incident, in which Epstein almost died, is also related to the *Lazarus*: "As Epstein chiveyed [chipped] away at the feet, he reached a point when the stone became top heavy". As the tall and bulky stone lost equilibrium, Epstein, and also McFall, felt a very slight movement in the floor boards and Epstein, himself quite heavy and unable to raise himself at all, gasped "Mack-FAL!". "Miraculously a shortish timber of 3"x4" was lying within my reach and, in one almost acrobatic leap, I grabbed it and jammed it against a ridge of the embalming clouts – and so scotched the fall of LAZARUS. Epstein was pale with shock, he dropped his tools and shuffled out of the studio to retire upstairs."

53 "This work made in 1948", he wrote on the completed piece (231), whereas Silber suggests 1947–48. I tend to agree with her earlier date. In a letter to Peggy Jean (2 November 1948: TGA-8716/16) he writes that he is still working on the *Lazarus*.

54 Unfortunately, and partially owing to the new ownership of Harrods, this information cannot be verified.

55 Gardiner, *Epstein*, pp. 413–14.

56 McFall, pp. 8–9.

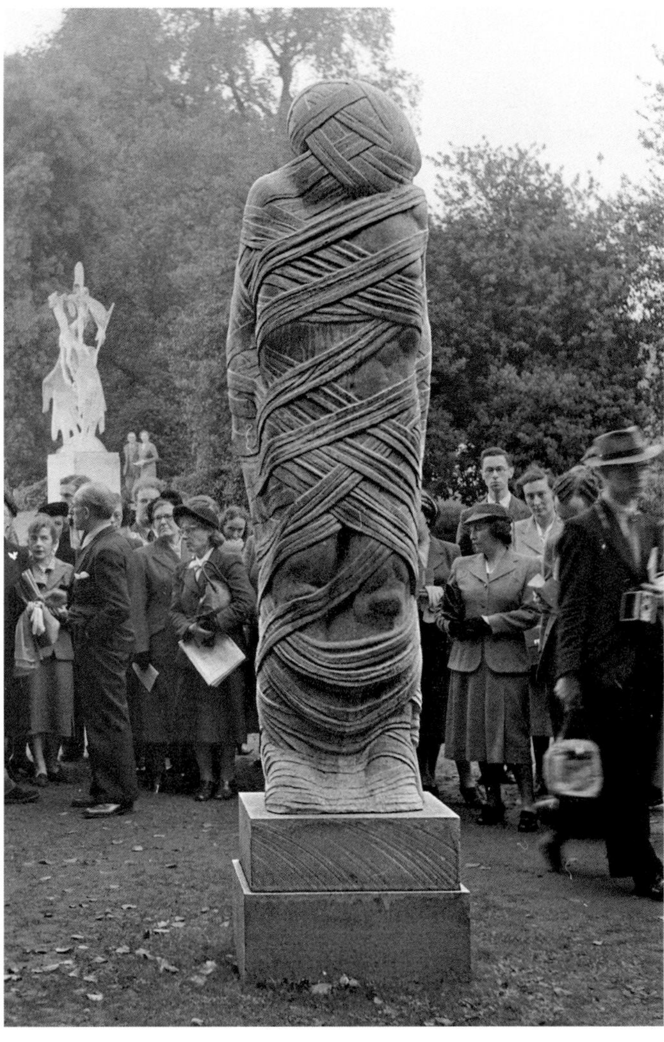
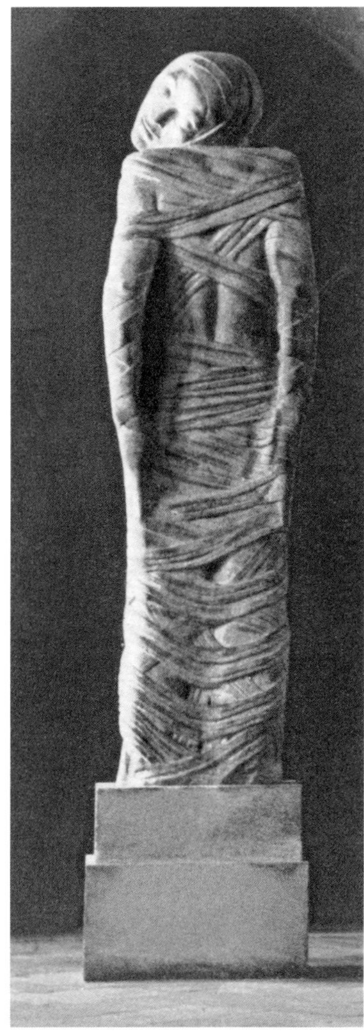
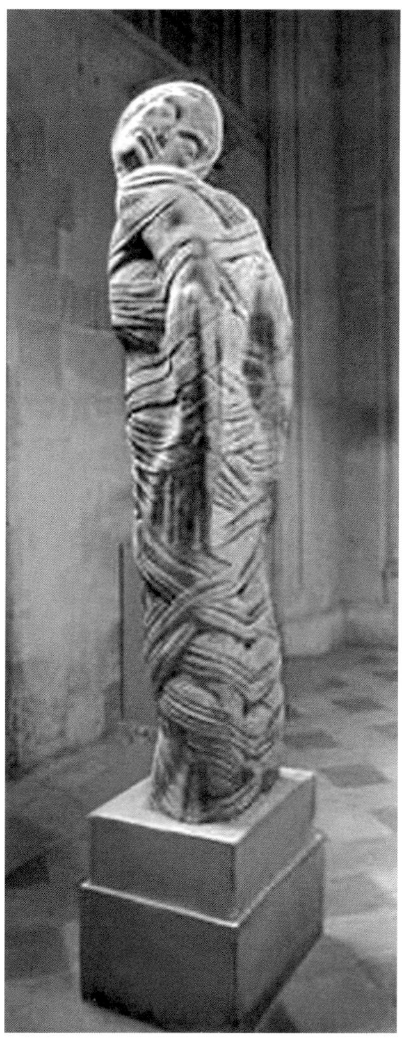

In the lack of preliminary drawings, the original final conception of the intended sculpture with the feet and its surroundings is unknown. The end result is nonetheless intriguing and unique, not only in Epstein's oeuvre but in the presentation of the figure in general.

Presentation, which determines the relations between object, base and the viewer, is of great importance for every work of art. I discussed this in regard to the final placing of *Ecce Homo* (p. 82), and the same issue affected *Lazarus*: its display in a gallery (1950), later on in the open space of Battersea Park (1951) and finally in New College, Oxford (1952) resulted in each case in a different impression on its viewers. Intriguingly, the aspect that has often left viewers bewildered is what is generally regarded as unimportant in this case, namely the frontal view. Almost every image of this sculpture has been taken from the back or side, and the front, which in almost all works of sculpture offers a kind of 'introduction', has been ignored to the extent that finding a photograph of the front proved unusually difficult. Might this strange phenomenon not stem from the fact that the front presents no facial features?

The front view, in which Lazarus's averted head hides his face altogether from the viewer [75a], reveals only the exposed knees of the figure through the shroud that covers the whole body and head; the side view [75c] accentuates the contorted pose that draws

75a
Lazarus (front), 1947–48
Hoptonwood stone, H. 254 cm
Presented to the public in Battersea Park, 1951

75b
Lazarus (back)
New College Chapel, Oxford

75c
Lazarus (side)
New College Chapel, Oxford

the shoulders forwards, and the back view [75b] concludes the strained movement with arms drawn back and face turned to the viewer. It is the unique and disregarded frontal viewpoint which, I suggest, requires the viewer who enters the portico of the church in New College, Oxford, to look at it first, and then to move slowly round it – gradually discovering all its compositional and formal aspects.

Epstein's depiction of *Lazarus* departs from the common West European iconography, which might have been epitomized for him by the precedent of a revered artist – Rembrandt. Both in two engravings and in a painting of *The Raising of Lazarus*, Rembrandt depicted Lazarus with head exposed, wearing a gown and rising from a stone coffin sunk deep in the earth.[57] Epstein seems to have turned for inspiration to earlier depictions in the East. Lazarus can be seen standing, with head covered and shroud enveloping his body, in many Eastern Christian icons that depict his rising from the burial cave of which the Gospel of John tells (11: 1–45). In the example shown here (fig. 51) he has his knees exposed in order to demonstrate that he still has living flesh – as in Epstein's sculpture.

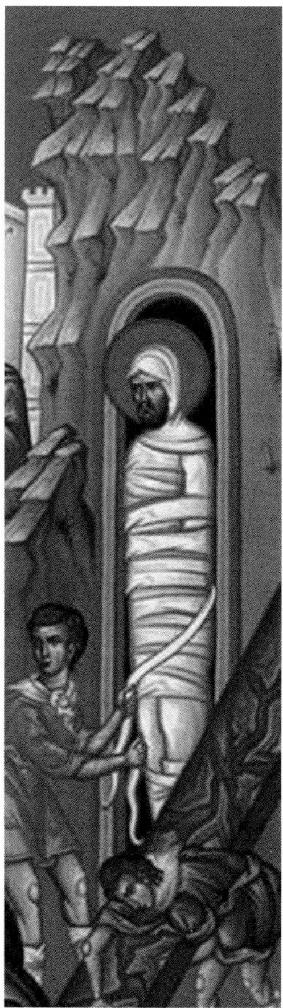

Fig. 51
School of Novgorod
Lazarus (detail), 2nd quarter 15th century
Oil on panel, 23 x 18 cm
Sergiev-Posad Museum, Russia

By this time Epstein had developed a wide repertoire of elements and poses and seems to have had recourse once more (as in the case of *Lucifer*) to earlier ideas: the erect body repeats the slight S movement of his sculptures of the 1910s, evident also in the gap between the exposed knees (hard to achieve in a straight pose); the head has a sideways movement sharper and stronger than that in the *Rock Drill*; the arms are drawn backwards like those in *Adam* and *Sun Goddess Crouching*. The position of the hands in *Lazarus* is even more emphasized: by being drawn sharply backwards they touch the buttocks and accentuate the stretching movement of the awakening body, an awakening indicated also by the phallus which is slightly discernible through the shroud. The sense of 'awakening' that I have attributed to the hand movements in both *Adam* and *Sun Goddess Crouching* seems to be at work also in *Lazarus*; all of these recall the movement originating in Nijinsky's dance of awakening in *L'Après-midi d'un faune*.[58] A later acknowledgement of the relation of Epstein's sculptural pose to dance was expressed by the French composer Olivier Messiaen (1908–1992): "In spirit my work is closest to the Sir Jacob Epstein's *Lazarus*".[59]

Epstein's saying that his *Lazarus* was the outcome of an idea that had haunted him for many years might suggest that its *raison d'être* was to express after World War II an ancient Jewish desire for salvation, prophesied by Ezekiel in his vision of the Valley of Dry Bones (37: 1–14). As there are no Jewish images of the phenomenon of resurrection, Epstein resorted to one inspired by early Christian art, which held in common with Jewish Orthodoxy the custom of using a burial shroud (coffins, as in Rembrandt's drawings, are not used in an Orthodox Jewish burial). This religious imagery might have served Epstein to express also his satisfaction with another revival: during 1947, the ancient desire of the Jews to return to their homeland in the land of Israel was in the process of being fulfilled, and in 1948 it was accomplished. Although not fond of certain Zionists who had tried to recruit him to 'the cause' and dictate his attitude, Epstein was very much a supporter of an Israeli state.[60] His note that *Lazarus* "was inspired in the happiest possible manner" (PS/231) seems to justify relating it to the new Jewish state.[61]

When *Lazarus* was exhibited at the Leicester Galleries in March 1950, it was subjected to much hostile criticism and was returned unwanted to Epstein's studio. There were nonetheless some positive comments from critics able to appreciate what he had

57 Rembrandt, oil on panel, 96.2 x 81.5 cm, c. 1630, Los Angeles County Museum of Art.

58 As I have observed in Nijinsky's choreography performed in 2004 by The Royal Ballet at Covent Garden. Unfortunately no photograph of a similar pose of the body exists.

59 Paul Griffiths, 'Poèmes and Haïkaï'. In his version of *L'après-midi d'un faune* in London (1929), Messiaen repeated Nijinsky's choreography, from which it seems that his perceptions on movement in Epstein's sculpture would be in accord with mine.

60 Peggy Jean Epstein in a recorded interview with the author, 1993.

61 A similar interpretation in Karl Schwarz, 'Jewish Sculptors'. The article was re-published in Roth and Narkiss, *Jewish Art*, but this interpretation was not included. The "many years" that Epstein spent pondering the idea do not correspond to the brief period of the Blitz, and therefore I would not concur with Cork (*Epstein*, p. 65), who regards *Lazarus* as an expression of the revival of London after the war.

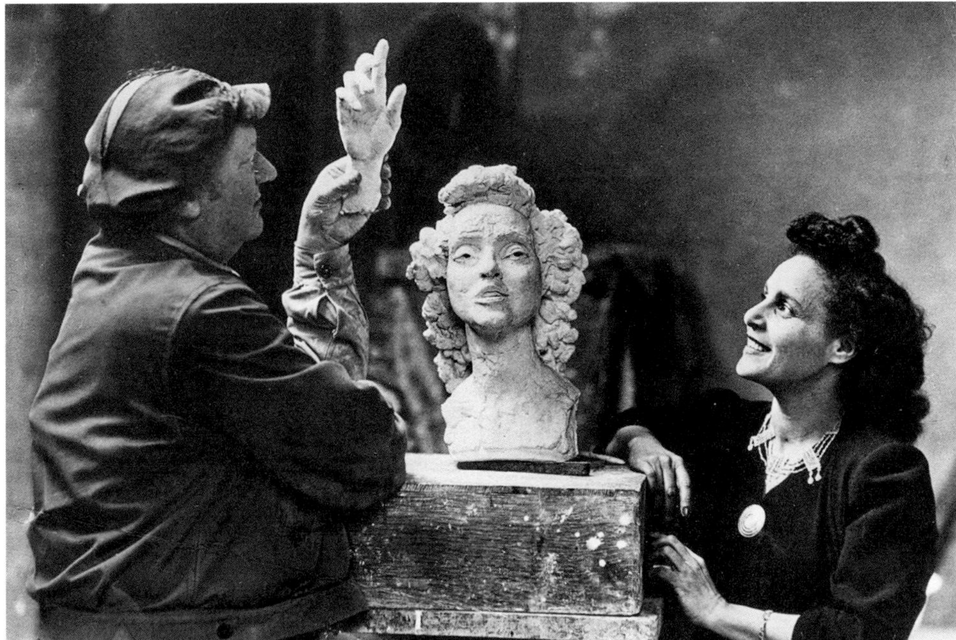

Fig. 52
Jacob Epstein and Bracha Zefira, 1948
Courtesy of the late Bracha Zefira

achieved: Wyndham Lewis wrote that it "perhaps is the most impressive of his series of giant carvings", and the art historian Eric Newton complained that no architect was using Epstein's work.[62] Eventually, after being exhibited at the Battersea Park Art Exhibition during the Festival of Britain in 1951, the carving was bought for the very modest sum of £700 by Alec Smith, Warden of New College, Oxford, and on January 1952 it was placed at the west end of New College Chapel: "We all travelled down with Matt [Matthew] Smith & the presentation of the statue in the chapel was most impressive. I got very little for this statue but I think the placing was worthwhile."[63] The event is described by Epstein (PS/232) as "one of the happiest issues in my working life .... How often does a sculptor find in these days the ideal setting for his work? ... When at last I actually saw the 'Lazarus' installed in the Chapel it seemed miraculous to me that the statue should harmonise so completely with the ancient stone walls. The lofty soaring arches seemed to continue the upward thrust of my figure."

In 1948–49 (before the exhibition of *Lazarus*, but still during the course of the events I have suggested as inspiring its creation), Epstein came into direct contact with the Israeli singer Bracha Zefira. Epstein's contacts with Zefira, who was not an official of the Zionist movement, contrast greatly with what seems to have been his lack of conversation with Chaim Weizmann (see pp. 77–78).[64] As a prominent Israeli singer and music-researcher of her Jewish Yemenite roots, who also possessed an encyclopaedic knowledge of Jerusalem's multi-ethnic musical diversity, including the liturgical music of various synagogues, she had a lot to discuss with the music-loving Epstein. She began a concert tour in Europe shortly before Israel's War of Independence, arriving to perform in London in 1948 with her companion, the historian Dr Joseph Nedava. Epstein came to her performances, visited her backstage, took her out to dine and asked her to model for him (fig. 52).[65]

During their sittings they talked about Israel: he was interested in the new socialist

62 *The Listener*, 23 March 1950; *The Sunday Times*, 19 March 1950.

63 Letter to Peggy Jean, 24 January 1952: TGA-8716/22.

64 Conversation with the author, 1989.

65 A note in the newspaper *Davar*, 16 June 1948, includes this photograph; the portrait, therefore, was done in 1948.

settlements and the bohemian atmosphere of Tel Aviv. She told amusing stories about her life as a Yemenite orphan adopted by a European Yiddish-speaking family, which made her a fluent Yiddish speaker, and also told him about her Yemenite customs – of which he was excited to hear, comparing them to the differing Western Jewish ones that he knew. In short, they discussed many subjects that, as far as I can gather from what has been written and told about him, he had never discussed and perhaps could never have talked about in his daily life. Zefira's companion, Joseph Nedava, doing a history degree in London, was in turn fascinated by Epstein and his interest in Israeli affairs and wanted to write a monograph on him.[66] The intimacy between Zefira and Epstein was such that Epstein felt comfortable to joke and tease her about the physical contrast between Nedava and her: she was relatively tall and dark complexioned, he relatively small, very thin and white-complexioned. "It cannot work!" Epstein said, and indeed eventually it did not.

Zefira was unaware of Kathleen's problems with her family at that time – a very ill son who demanded attention, a sister in Italy who also had health problems, and a daughter with a baby. She recalls that Epstein's behaviour changed whenever Kathleen left the house: "He would hurry to write a letter to his daughter in America and post it before she came back. Kathleen's only interest was in her daughter, only her daughter." In the end Zefira did not like her portrait because, she said, it had too much of Kathleen in it. She did not like Kathleen either, who reminded her of a snake; a similar perception was held by a nephew of hers, who recalls her glances as "being frightening, almost hypnotizing, like a snake".[67]

DAWN OF A NEW ERA

I. MOVING IN TOGETHER

Owing to the sorry personal circumstances mentioned above, Epstein held no exhibitions of new works after the one in February 1947, in which he presented Churchill's portrait surrounded by his nude studies. He continued his work on *Lazarus*, however, and was still working on it in November 1948,[68] and throughout the year of 1949, when Kathleen was in Italy, helping her sister Helen who had undergone an operation. Epstein wrote to her about "pain and tribulation" during his working on the *Lazarus* and on his injuries: "I turned to the carving and now I have hurt my left elbow with jarring it against the stone. It has become more and more painful and Dr Goffe is to see it on next Sunday morning."[69] He missed the opportunity during this period of acquiring the house in which he lived from the owner, who wished to sell it for £13,000. Epstein consulted his lawyers, Hattrell & Partners, who advised him it was a reasonable figure in the market then current.[70] Being as usual short of funds, however, Epstein failed to make the purchase, which would have enabled him to avoid considerable trouble later.

There were happier occurrences in his life towards the end of 1947, besides his work: his daughter Kitty married the painter Lucien Freud, and by July 1948 Kathleen's first granddaughter, Annie, was born. Kathleen, who also corresponded with Peggy Jean, wrote to her about it (Lucien was Peggy Jean's former schoolmate), mentioning that

66 If such a manuscript existed – neither Zefira nor the Nedava family have ever seen a completed version.

67 Connolly, *The Rare and the Beautiful*, p. 198.

68 Epstein's letter to Peggy Jean, 12 November 1948: TGA- 8716/12. I found no comment by him on the Olympics that took place in London during the summer of 1948; sports, apparently, did not occupy his attention.

69 Letter of 2 September 1949 (inserted in a folder of 1940): NAGW–BL/1/3/2/9.

70 Letter of 22 September 1947: NAGW – BL/1/1/2/5 .

his father had bought them a flat in St John's Wood;[71] the marriage gave Epstein an opportunity to make a bust of his new son-in-law.

Epstein started to write to Peggy Jean almost immediately after she had left with Jackie for America in September 1947, but his archived correspondence only starts in March 1948. He undoubtedly was delighted that Kathleen too was writing to her. Although at the time still living apart from him, Kathleen became more involved in Epstein's life, arranging his affairs, organizing his participation in various exhibitions, and becoming a driving force to such an extent that he admitted to Peggy Jean that there were things he could have never done without Kathleen.[72]

One of the issues Kathleen had to cope with was their dealings with Phillip Sayers, the Irish art dealer who had helped the Epsteins in 1929 with a loan for the lease of their house in Hyde Park Gate (pp. 15–16). Although he had been partly repaid with a portrait (1932) and in works of art taken over the years, Sayers was now pestering Epstein over the debt ("he is becoming exactly like a money-lender who is laying a trap for me to fall into so that he can get the better of me") and intruding into his private life, expecting to be treated like an intimate friend in the house and "calling Kathleen 'Darling' and trying to touch her which she resents".[73] Therefore Sayers's visits to the house were stopped by Epstein, who sent him his cheque, "although I am told he has overcharged me; but my income tax accountant is looking into that". Sayers's name first comes up in his May letter and recurs thereafter.

The financial difficulty caused by the payment to Sayers left Epstein in a sour mood, also because Sayers had taken some of his business to [Epstein's lawyer] Gootkin, and Epstein suspected that he was influencing him: "I am thinking of getting a different solicitor when he makes a will". Help during these financial ordeals came from Abel, the proprietor of Epstein's favourite restaurant, The Ivy, through his purchase of two bronzes, "one of you an early one & the one of Jackie (*Ragamuffin*)". Epstein had carried out this deal by himself and therefore, as might be expected, it was done somewhat carelessly: "I haven't settled about the precise sum but will see him on Tuesday to settle that side of it which I think will be all right as Abel is expected to be a wealthy man". The unpleasantness with Sayers ended with his departure for the US, but Epstein still needed his help in getting around England's financial restrictions in order to transfer money to Peggy Jean, who was supporting Jackie. Sayers proved to be untrustworthy in this regard, too, as in May Epstein wrote: "What angers me about Sayers is that I specifically asked him before he left for U.S.A. *to do something for Jackie* and he did absolutely nothing and he was in a position to do about and asked him to do".[74] The unpleasantness of Sayers's attitude toward Epstein's women continued when he finally came to see Peggy Jean and, apparently, made some crude remarks about Meum, Peggy Jean's biological mother (of whom she had learned only after Margaret's death). At the top of his reply to her Epstein wrote a response to her comment: "You were right about Meum, Sayers is obscene".[75]

Meanwhile Epstein's financial situation remained as shaky as ever, and he finished his long letter of May 1948 declaring: "I do not feel secure in any way although I am constantly getting things & working out portraits", because he constantly had "to sell a terrible lot to make £2000 asked in income tax";[76] "The Leicester has the work of years [*Ecce Homo*] & cost me a lot to get into its final shape". Despite all his financial problems,

71 Letter of 15 May 1948: TGA- 8716/58.

72 Letter of 18 April 1948: TGA 8716 /2.

73 Letter from Epstein to Peggy Jean, May 1948: TGA 8716 /4. This is the first of several letters on Sayers.

74 Letter from Epstein to Peggy Jean, May 1948: TGA 8716 /4; my italics. Sayers's explanation: "He claims that he did not get our letters and those he did get he said he never understood". One can sympathize with the last part, given both father's and daughter's illegible handwriting.

75 Letter from Epstein to Peggy Jean 14 June 1948: TGA 8716/5.

76 The same situation continued throughout his life, and also after his death. Thus, Jackie writes to Peggy Jean: "The Leicester Galleries have a small number of plasters which it is still possible to cast from, and they are handling the whole thing .... We are having a tax problem apparently and although there is some money there, I don't think it can be divided for a while" (25 January 1970: TGA 8716-63).

he was endeavouring to get her money "for your summer's holiday".

Jackie remained with Peggy Jean, who fulfilled Epstein's request to "hold on" to him as "it would be tragic [for him] to return here, being out of place in London, although I long to see him", particularly as, from what she had told him, "he seems to be getting on fine".[77]

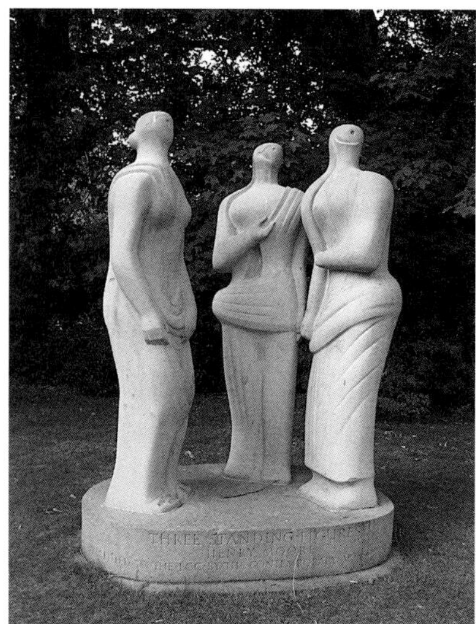

Fig. 53
Henry Moore
Three Standing Figures, 1948
Darley Dale stone, H. 213.4 cm
Battersea Park, London

What turned out to be a new era in Epstein's career after the war was announced to Peggy Jean in two letters giving his view of the Battersea Park exhibition of May 1948. What I say below relates mainly to Epstein's work, as there are extensive reports elsewhere of the exhibition itself, which pioneered the idea of taking sculpture to 'the people', giving ordinary citizens and not just the regular gallery-goers the opportunity to experience contemporary sculpture in relaxed surroundings.[78]

Epstein's submission of *The Girl with Gardenias* seemed less relaxed, at least from his point of view. In the committee for the exhibition his "friends F. Dobson & Henry Moore tried hard to ignore" him,[79] but, on the insistence of other members, who wanted his work, he had been included. This occasion brought about Epstein's first written expression of animosity towards Moore: the renewed clash of their contrasting approaches was undoubtedly due to this being the first artistic arena in which both of them had participated since their halcyon days in 1929 (the Transport Headquarters in St James – Epstein with *Day* and *Night*; Moore with *West Wind*).

After writing about the opening of the exhibition, to which he had gone with Kathleen and at which, to some extent, they were a centre of attention ("the photographers were busy photographing Kathleen & myself"), he continued his letter in a vein of bitterness, not only towards Moore but also towards Moore's influential supporters:[80]

> The whole show was really got to boost Moore[,] and his abstract work long prepared for this event was made the centre of the business. It has been bought by the contemporary Art society & is to be presented to the nation. It is a question as to whether it will be accepted. It is the only sculpture to be shown in the posters & of course Moore was made the hero of the opening[,] leading the members of the Cabinet, Cripps & Bevin[,] straight to this work and ignoring everything else.

Whatever may have been the merits of *The Girl with Gardenias*, it was not a new work specifically made for the occasion or for the surroundings, but dated from 1943 and had already been exhibited in a gallery in 1944. Moreover, in 1948, after the war and amidst a sense of national renewal, other artists' recent works were present, reflecting a variety of artistic directions. Epstein's opinion of them as "monstrosities" did not alter the fact that they were presenting something new.

Henry Moore's *Three Standing Figures* in this version of 1948 (fig. 53), though planned for another project and not for the occasion or position it now occupies in Battersea Park, is an early example of the monumental work with which he started along a new artistic path – one of huge, minimally styled works conceived from the outset as sculpture-in-nature. Epstein, no doubt, was aware of their novelty and therefore made a point of commenting in his letter that "The Rodin's & Maillol's & my things look in harmony with the trees & outdoors". Epstein's animosity to Moore was not merely personal, I suggest, stemming from his grounded or ungrounded suspicions that Moore was blocking his commissions,[81]

77 Letter from Epstein to Peggy Jean, 6 June 1948: TGA-8716/1.

78 The general details were taken from http://www.vads.ac.uk/learning/designingbritain/html/precincts.html; http://www.batterseapark.org/html/sculpture.html.

79 Letter from Epstein to Peggy Jean, 6 March 1948: TGA-8716/1.

80 Letter from Epstein to Peggy Jean, May 1948: TGA 8716-4. On Moore's sculpture in Battersea Park, discussed below, see www.henry-moore.prg/.../battersea-park/three-standing-figures-1947.

81 The Epstein-Moore entanglement was exacerbated by Moore's 'closed doors' policy, applied whenever his recommendation was needed for anyone outside his own milieu. In Epstein's letter to Peggy Jean of 30 May 1949 (TGA-8716-21) he tells of such an occasion, when David Cohn, once a great friend and "life-long intimate of Moore", had fallen out with Moore for the usual reason of Moore's refusal "to introduce him to his 'influential' friends; *always the same story*", as Epstein concludes the issue (my italics).

but arose also because Moore's work could be both modernist (in its stylization) and accessible to the public (in not requiring interpretation of content or aim). It is not surprising that people were impressed by Moore's new approach combining modernity and nature, to the extent of that they ignored both Epstein's more familiar art and Epstein himself:

> Bevin avoided me & so did Moore, they mingled around, very self important and posed for the photographers .... Kenneth Clark & of course that miserable little Rothenstein were much in evidence at the opening.[82]

In his views on the work of the younger generation of artists and the position in the art world they had acquired, Epstein could have taken comfort from others who were resistant to the takeover by "Moore & Co.". These included McFall, as well as "Lambert the sculptor [who] has sent me a friendly & sympathetic letter", protesting against the domination of the intellectuals and saying that what "the would-be intellectual sheep are now boasting about makes me sick".[83] "I think in the end they [the intellectuals] may not have it all their own way."[84]

On this very point where 'intellectual' art is concerned, it seems to me that Epstein deliberately avoided the art bandwagon, remaining within the boundaries of his own artistic language and his own interpretation of familiar subjects. Eventually Moore, too, in most of his future work would be confined within his own artistic mannerisms and subjects, which, unlike Epstein's, required only limited efforts of involvement and interpretation by the viewer. However, unlike Moore, Epstein misread the advances implicit in the constant experimentation of the era with forms, dimensions and media, advances which would eventually lead to an art that would express ideas using means and forms radically different from those of the past.

Epstein and Kathleen appearing together in the open-air public exhibition, and being photographed together, led to speculation in the press that they were married. A worried Kathleen immediately wrote to Peggy Jean that "we are not married .... Some day we might but things seem to me best as they are." Having reported to her about the major house-cleaning that had given Epstein "the feeling of security and isolation that he needs for his work", she pointed to her contribution to his mental welfare: "I make your father laugh quite a bit and we have a lot of fun between times".[85]

By the end of 1948 Kathleen had become heavily involved in nursing ailing family members – to the extent of refusing to go to New York with Epstein. She "seems to have a dislike of the American Scene which she cannot overcome. In this I hope to persuade her, but she is frightfully engaged with people who are all ill, and she sees them on hospital & help [sic]". The ailing individuals probably included Esther, but the most serious was Theo. Peggy Jean, looking back, remarked:

> With time he had grown harder to manage, becoming violent, slashing, and not liking Kathleen to leave him; he became antagonistic towards Daddy. In those days very little was done or treatment known for such disorders, except lobotomy, which neither Kathleen nor Daddy would pursue. They were afraid that he would become a vegetable and no longer be able to do his wonderful paintings. Theo resented Kathleen's leaving him to go to Epstein's house.[86]

82 Letter from Epstein to Peggy Jean, May 1948: TGA 8716-4.

83 Letter from Maurice Lambert of 14 May 1948: NAGW, BL/1/1/1/4.

84 Letter from Epstein to Peggy Jean, May 1948: TGA 8716-4. "Intellectuals" seems to have been Epstein's label for all those subscribing to abstract rather than concrete perceptions, whether artistic or literary.

85 Letter from Kathleen to Peggy Jean, 24 August 1948: TGA-8716/58.

86 Peggy Jean's letter (via an email from Leda) to the author.

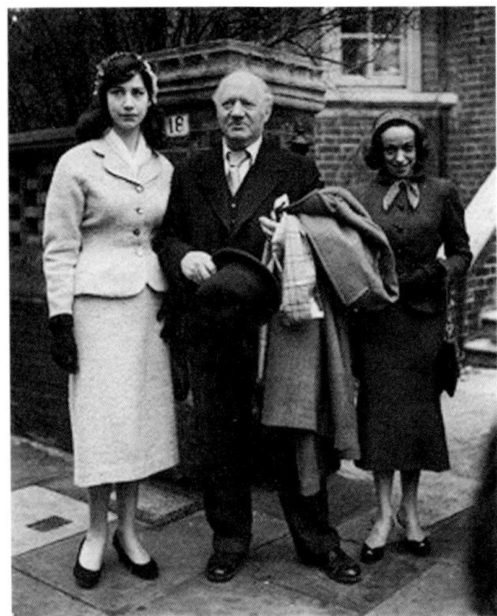

Fig. 54a
Jacob Epstein, Esther and Beth Lipkin, 1953–54

In a later letter Epstein recounted that "Kathleen's boy Theo gets worse & worse, all treatments have been tried with no success";[87] constantly and for reasons unclear to me Epstein continued to ignore the fact that Kathleen's children were also his.

Kathleen left her house at 272 King's Road in early 1949, leaving Theo behind, who continued to live there and paint; she found a companion for him (Anne Champernowne) and later sent them both to Florence to the Vivantes' house in Siena (p. 160), where Theo found inspiration for his paintings in the beautiful views of the city and its surroundings.[88] Kathleen moved into Epstein's Hyde Park Gate house, bringing Beth Lipkin with her: "After the war I came back to England and our friendship [Beth's with Kathleen] was renewed as if it had never been interrupted. I came to know Epstein well and Kathleen in particular very closely. They both asked me to stay with them although I already had my own home in Kensington."[89] Although I found Beth a gentle and straightforward person, I doubt whether this statement is the whole truth. I suspect that Kathleen had pressured Epstein, or even made it a condition of her moving into the house. Family gossip suggests that, although Epstein tolerated Beth's presence in their life, he himself could hardly stand her.[90] Her response to my question on the artistic or social topics discussed in the house appears to confirm that she had been an integral part of their life, but only up to a point:[91] Epstein spent his morning and much of the afternoon in the studio, and when he came out around 5 pm for supper they all attended the meal; afterwards she retired to her room, leaving them to themselves. Beth, keeping herself a bit behind the scenes (fig. 54a), belonged to Kathleen's domain only, where she was accepted by all of her children, who seem to have liked her (nicknaming her Buffy) and to have respected the importance of her companionship in Kathleen's troubled life.

In early January 1949, perhaps in preparation for Jackie's return, Epstein urged him to write "a long letter telling me everything you do", and later on, presumably responding to Jackie's reply, sent him a cookbook (!).[92] "Jacob came to visit us and had a ball. He'd get up early and go swimming in the rough ocean. I'd go with him," noted his granddaughter and Jackie's playmate Leda. "He would draw my brother and I. Mostly me, as my brother wouldn't sit still. My Dad and Jacob had long conversations about art and war. I asked Jackie late in life if he was homesick and he said no. It was such a wonderful place to live. He kept a stack of *Popular Mechanics* by his bed."[93] Epstein went to the US to fetch him, and while there he was asked to do the portrait of Patricia Hitchcock, daughter of the famous film-director. He was about to refuse, as she did not correspond to his type of model.[94] However, persuaded by Peggy Jean that he needed the money, he made quite an impressive bust of her (fig. 54b).

In July Epstein sent Kathleen what was probably his last letter of this trip to America, where he had gone principally in order to bring Jackie back home, "and that I'll accomplish".[95] After mentioning that he has moments of deep depression, that he cannot imagine himself living there and that she would hate America, he writes that receiving Kathleen's letter had made him feel better. He ends this long letter with a separate enigmatic paragraph with clearly Christian connotations, probably taken from some literary source with which they were both familiar:

87 Epstein's letter to Peggy Jean, 4 November 1948: TGA-8716/12.

88 Gardiner, *Epstein*, pp. 411–12.

89 Beth's letter to Gardiner, 12 January 1993: NAGW–BL/1/4/4/32/2.

90 Peggy Jean's recorded interview wit the author.

91 Conversation with Beth Lipkin, 1985.

92 Epstein's letters to Peggy Jean, 4 and 23 January 1949: TGA-8716/16 and 17.

93 Email from Leda Sloat to the author, 19 May 2010.

94 As told to the author by Peggy Jean in an email letter. This work is not registered in Silber, *Sculpture of Epstein*. The photograph was taken from http://www.hitchcockwiki.com/wiki/Hitchcock_Gallery:_image_2746. In the preview of the 2004 DVD release of Alfred Hitchcock's one and only romantic comedy, *Mr & Mrs Smith* (1941), Epstein has a brief appearance close to this bust.

95 Letter to Kathleen in Verona, 29 July 1949; NAGW–BL/1/3/2/8.

Now as you are nearing the doorway into the convent you perceive a dim figure, shrouded, with arms outstretched like the Christ on the Cross: it is impossible to make out whether this figure stands outstretched arms welcoming you or preventing you from entering; as you approach and when close to the figure, the arms fold around you and a voice says "welcome Beloved"; the voice is that of Epstein.

Towards the end of August Epstein and Jackie arrived back in London, and a contented Epstein wrote later to his daughter that Jackie was settling in,[96] receiving piano lessons from Kathleen (which an older Jackie was to regard as a sheer waste of time); what all this amounts to, and later proved to be, they had become very good friends. Jackie remembers that, when he returned from America after two years, the house was clean, well arranged and hospitable, with a light atmosphere, and with Beth Lipkin there.[97] In the same placid manner in which he accepted the personal peculiarities of his family, he accepted her too.[98] The musical evenings at the house resumed, as well as the gatherings of artists and friends at Sunday's open house. One important change was in regard to house pets: the "galore" of cats that Margaret cultivated[99] gave way to a Shetland sheepdog named Frisky, given as a gift to Jackie, who, at the age of fifteen, had developed the above-mentioned interest in cars and also in animals, but not in all of them: when Peggy Jean wrote to them about a huge fish they had caught, Jackie "was not impressed".[100] During this period of mid 1949 Kathleen started her prolonged involvement in her sister Helen's illness, which meant frequent visits to Italy. A lonely Epstein wrote about it to Peggy Jean in May: "Her sister is having the second operation on her brain in Milan .... [She] seems to depend entirely on her, especially for nursing after the operation. The nursing in Milan hospitals is done by nurses who seem to be totally incompetent. Also Helen's husband is a very old man who is too disturbed by events to be much good."[101] Epstein also suggested that Leda should perhaps come to London for a while, as Kathleen, "who went yesterday, will be away at least two weeks; perhaps longer, it is impossible to say at the moment". "There is plenty of room in the house [as] there is only Kathleen & myself." He did not count the presence of the new cook they had engaged, who, along with her son Victor (whose portrait Epstein made), occupied a room on the top floor.

Whether Kathleen returned after the two or more weeks or stayed in Italy for a longer period, in August (as the letters indicate) she was still there, and during her visits to the hospital she also devoted time to a little boy in need of help and attention. The immense pain and suffering she witnessed there, and probably also her deteriorating relationship with her Italian boyfriend (see p. 161), affected her to the extent that she had a slight breakdown. At the end of August she wrote a letter to Epstein that alarmed them all,[102] and the crisis is reflected in Epstein's two letters and Esther's response in September ("I cannot somehow imagine that you will ever return").[103] Both Esther and Epstein were also astonished by Kathleen's asking Esther to send her money. In his letter of 2 September, he wrote: "I was hurt that you should ask Esther to get money for you; to send you money is my privilege. I tried to give you money on the way to the station but you refused it and only took what I knew would be inadequate."[104] He expressed his longings and apologized for being unable to join her in Milan to see *The Last Supper*

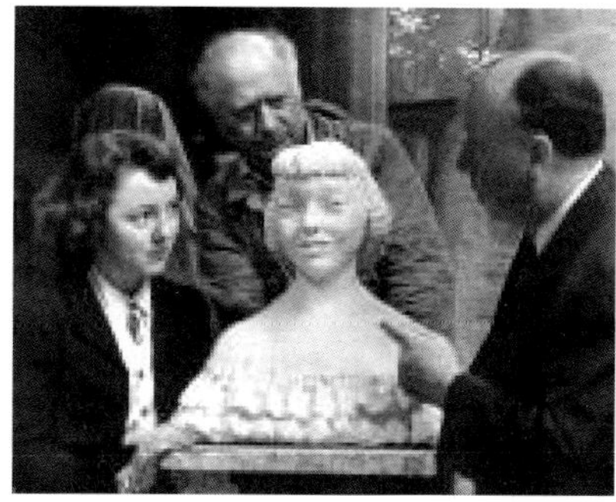

Fig. 54b
Alfred Hitchcock and his daughter Patricia with Epstein and her portrait

96 Letter from Epstein to Peggy Jean, 3 April 1950: TGA-8716/17. I suggest the correct date of the letter would be 1949, in the period immediately after Jackie had left America.

97 Conversation with the author, 11 March 1995.

98 To Jackie's credit, he continued to keep contact with Beth in her old age when she needed care, to the extent of moving with his wife Isabel into Kathleen's last house, which Beth had inherited, saying to me, "After all, she is family". Beth passed away in 2006, asking to be buried with Kathleen. As at the time Jackie had been unwell, Isabel arranged for Beth's ashes to be buried in Harting, where Kathleen, Esther and Theo are buried.

99 Aunt Sylvia's description: see Babson, *The Epsteins*, p. 29.

100 Letter from Epstein to Peggy Jean, 30 May 1950: TGA- 8716/21. It has been suggested that the real date was 1952, but this does not make sense as the letter mentions Jackie having his old room, so it must have been written soon after they arrived.

101 Ibid.

102 Apparently destroyed.

103 Esther's letter to Kathleen in Milan, Italy, 5 September 1949: NAGW– BL/1/3/5/2.

104 Undated letter from Epstein to Kathleen (2 September 1954?): NAGW–BL/1/3/2/23.

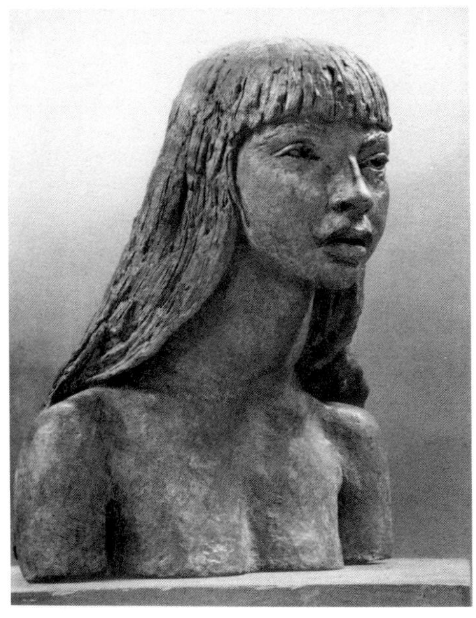

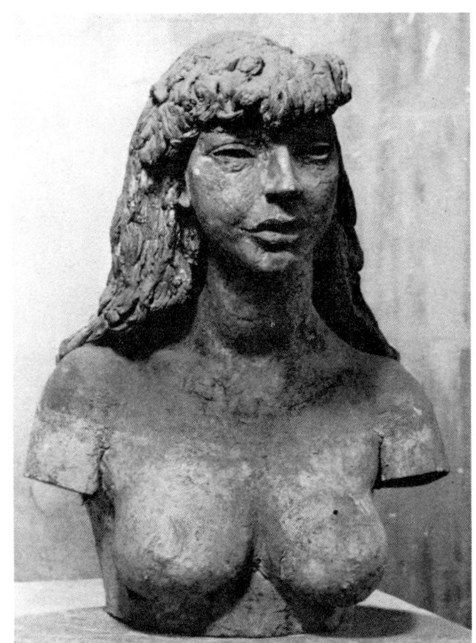

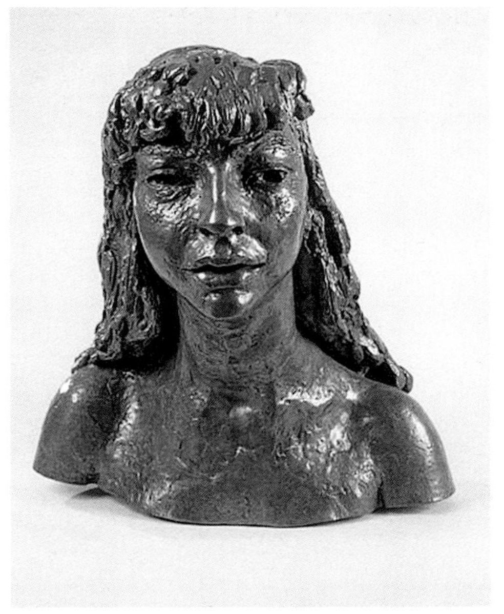

76a
Esther, 1st portrait, 1944
Plaster, H. 47 cm
GREC-NAGW

76b
Esther, 2nd portrait, 1948
Plaster, dimensions unknown
Provenance unknown

76c
Esther, 2nd portrait (2nd version), 1948
Bronze, dimensions unknown
Provenance unknown

and to view it with her, without the presence of other companions.[105] In this long letter in which he urges her "Come back. come back", he adds: "Only you understand only you attract me; with your loveliness you have always enraptured me", expressing his realisation that above all and in spite of all "You must love me or you would not do so much for me". No doubt he was referring to the efforts she had made in organizing his participation in September in the second post-war Edinburgh Festival with the portraits that she had chosen, and also in an exhibition in Glasgow the following month.[106]

Epstein does not say a word about their son Theo in this letter, and such information can only be gathered from Esther's letters, vividly describing household issues: "The cooking is most uniform, but Epstein and Jackie seem to be invited out nearly every night .... Kitty and I have both done our bit, with much emulation .... We all went down to Epping on Sunday. On our returning home we found Theo in No. 18 [Hyde Park Gate]. He was in a terrible state and the first thing he said when we came in, 'you see, she sent for me in that vivacious way', etc. etc. At last Epstein saw what he really is like. It was terrible because they were both so upset. Thank goodness there was no row but it was terribly tense all the same .... My usual Sunday morning lie in was cut short at 8 o'clock with the arrival of those three musketeers Jackie, Epstein and Frisky for breakfast."[107]

In his next letter Epstein empathizes with Kathleen's stress – "What you write about hospital is dreadful" – and he praises her for her fortitude: "Now I picture you doing an angels work", elaborating on this theme and trying to comfort her with the promise of depicting her ordeals:

> I see you with the half blind child: soothing it and bringing relief to its little troubled body. I see you as Charity herself in the hospital ward: "and the greatest of these is Charity". I would like to make a statue of you like this; my early statue in the Tate Gallery [1925, *Visitation*] would only be a fore runner of this statue, the most beautiful statue in the world, as you will have said it, and posed for it.

105 Ibid.

106 Kathleen's letter to Peggy Jean, 24 August 1948: TGA-8716.58.

107 This letter is undated, but from its content must follow on Esther's letter of 5 September (see note 103): NAGW–BL/1/3/5/11.

However, and in the same vein of Christian Charity, he mentions his own interest:

> I feel a child needing charity, my soul wounded and lonely, longing for a mothering caress: what a grotesque image; I so old and wanting love! I am of course ridiculous in all this and you must laugh with your light and witty laughter. Nevertheless I wait for you to come to me.[108]

He tried to cheer her up a bit by reporting that he had started "the head of Esther the beautiful", that his birthday party celebrated at the Caprice was "an occasion for us all to remember you with love", and this time he mentions "Theo [who] has moved into his new studio [in a hut at the back of the house]. The change of place might do him good." He ends his long letter by mentioning the prospect of another artistic project:

> Yesterday afternoon I met with H. Moore the architects of the 1951 showdown ... I will tell you of when you come back. I only want this hurried note to tell you how much I love you and how much you mean to me; I only long and pray for your return. By now Helen had her operation ... [ending his letter with] I long for you as I have never longed before and this is saying something that no words can express.
>
> Your Epstein.

By November Kathleen was back in London, and Epstein reported to Peggy Jean that "Today, Sunday, we reassumed four Epsteins, Kathleen Esther Jackie & I".[109] Some time after Kathleen's return from Italy Epstein fulfilled his intention to depict her as "Charity herself", and he probably did so immediately in order to please her. Therefore, in early 1950, inspired by the Christian connotation that he had given to Kathleen's tribulations, he made a small maquette (33 cm high) of a Madonna (with Kathleen's features) and Child.[110] It took about two more years before the maquette would be developed into a full-size work, entitled *Madonna and Child.*

1948 and 1949 were good years for Epstein in regard to work, as in 1948 he modelled about ten commissioned portraits and in 1949 about thirteen; with the inclusion of portraits of family members his output amounted to 26 portraits. Among these, a portrait of "Esther the beautiful" of which he had written and which he made in late 1948 raises a complex question, because in Silber's catalogue there are three distinctly different portraits of Esther, though projecting a similar aura. The first [76a] was made and exhibited in 1944, in which her straight hair with a fringe is combed meticulously backwards. Buckle shows a bust that he identifies as a second portrait of her (no. 482; p. 315), depicting her with an uncombed fringe, hair drawn back and less meticulously combed, and her breasts fully exposed [76b]. A third portrait, noted in Silber's catalogue (no. 398) as the second portrait of Esther and described as "head and shoulders only" [76c], reveals that at some point it was decided to crop Esther's bust into a shortened, bosomless version. Another portrait of 1949 [77], however, in Silber's catalogue described as a third portrait of Esther, bears a resemblance to her, but the flat chest differs from that in Buckle's second portrait. When I saw a copy of it at the home of Kitty Godley in 1985, she insisted that it was a representation not of Esther but of one of her friends who resembled her.

Shortly after Kathleen's return Esther moved in with Marc Joffe [fig. 55], who had come to England from France as a refugee before the war, socializing with Kathleen and

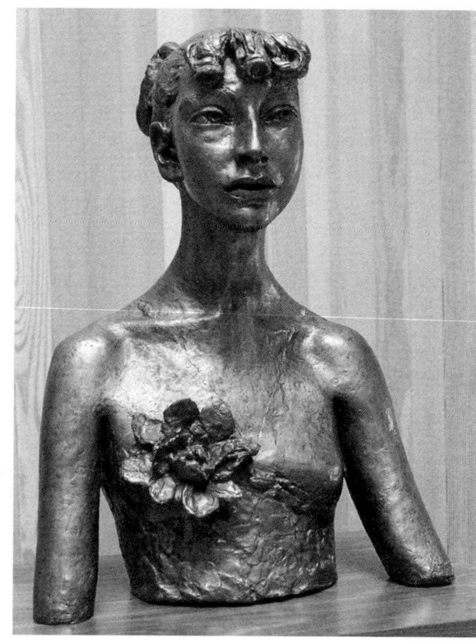

77
Esther, 3rd portrait (?), 1949
Bronze, H. 62 cm
GREC-NAGW

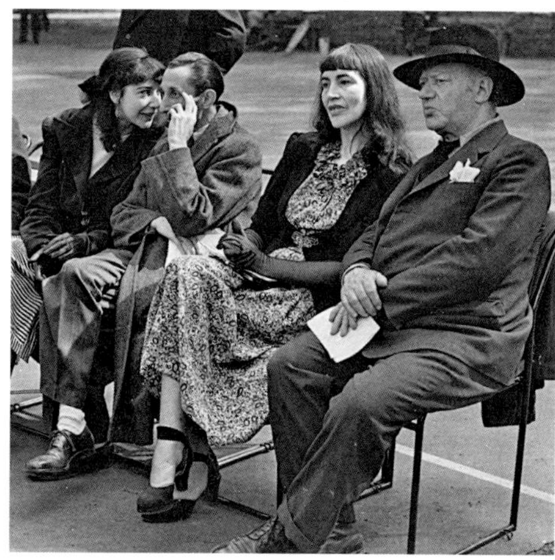

Fig. 55
Jacob Epstein and Kathleen, Esther and Mark Joffe
NAGW Archive

108 Letter from Epstein to Kathleen, undated (the upper part after "Darling" is cut off): NAGW–BL/1/3/2/23. By context this follows BL/1/3/2/9 (note 104 above).

109 Letter of 18 November 1949: TGA 8716-19.

110 In giving 1950 as the date of the maquette, I follow Silber's dating (*Sculpture of Epstein*, no. 437).

her Italian friends (see p. 160). He had married an Italian woman, whose interest in him was mainly to gain residency, and after a while she left him and their toddler Roland. When Esther heard that the child was in foster care in Kent she took him to live with her and his father, caring for him and for another two children, supporting herself as a nanny.[111] Jackie, who like everybody else loved Esther dearly, used to visit them, and as an adult he told me of the warm intimacy clearly discernible between the mature Joffe and the young Esther.[112]

Barely back in England, young Jackie was "beginning to talk of England as a 'dump' & to feel a yearning toward America", wrote Epstein, adding that Kathleen was very good with him.[113] At the time Kathleen was busy arranging to get Epstein's works sent to the US for an exhibition, and Epstein suspected that, had he intended to go to there, "K. would not be able to go with me. She has *her boy* who isn't at all well and he is planning to go to Italy to paint[,] and in that case I imagine K would want to go out to be with him part of the time anyway." Kathleen, however, remained in England, even though Helen's illness was worsening, sending Esther to Italy instead. "Sometimes we Kitty & her husband [go] to dinner at the Ivy or Caprice restaurant," Epstein told Peggy Jean, although these outings "to get away from the studio" were but a small compensation for him for not visiting them in America and having at their place "the sea bathing [which is] so good for me". Regarding his work, Epstein reported selling *Sun God* to Sally Ryan, and on having done "a great many new things and finished a very large carving" (*Lazarus*), and about a new commission for the 1951 Festival of Britain, that was "published in the press & has attracted a lot of attention".[114]

II. FESTIVAL OF BRITAIN

An article in a popular newspaper published in August 1950 celebrated Epstein's seventieth birthday. Entitled "Epstein, 70, wins the argument",[115] it declared that Britain's most controversial sculptor was finding after a lifetime of dispute that "people are beginning to believe him", even if this was because "they found younger sculptors to shock and annoy them". Epstein himself was represented in this interview as a calm individual who had stoically accepted this new situation: "Most of my critics have died; the rest have been inoculated by so many doses of my particular virus that they have got used to me by now". The importance of this article, however, lies in its report of opinions that he had rarely expressed before, particularly in writing, and not even in the 'Postscript' to his autobiography. Some of his remarks on art reveal him to have been even more distanced from the contemporary art world than he had been during the 1930s: "If I must have a label, I would say that I was a traditionalist .... I revere the antique. People who say I am revolutionary would say that antique sculpture is revolutionary." Bearing a grudge against modernists, abstractionists and surrealists, he defined the most recent works by Picasso, Paul Klee and Salvador Dalí as "ugly and incompetent" and worse, claiming that their success tended to "encourage the young to think that they can become great artists without the necessary study and training".

In the same month of August, the Epsteins' Epping Forest retreat 'Deerhurst', at 50 Baldwin Hill, was sold, which was probably a somewhat bitter birthday present for him;

111 Information from her letters in the NAGW archive, and Connolly, *The Rare and the Beautiful*, p. 199. Further details regarding Esther, as well as Theo, appear in Connolly's appendix (pp. 253–61).

112 Conversation with the author, 2007.

113 This, and all the following data, are from a letter to Peggy Jean, 20 January 1950: TGA-8716.

114 Ibid. (italics mine): once again Epstein does not acknowledge Theo as his son.

115 Milton Shulman, *The Evening News*, 15 August 1950.

I have found no explanation for it, as his financial situation had somewhat improved during the previous year. It may have been the number of works with which he was occupied, as well as the ones he expected in the future, that made Epstein realise he would not have the time to go there. Altogether, 1950 was a relatively good year: he made about seventeen portraits, five of which were of family members, and twelve paid for.

The Festival of Britain, celebrated in 1951, was already being planned in 1947, after the rise to power of the Labour Government. It was conceived as an attempt to reduce the nation's resentment of the austere economic measures that had had to be taken as a result of the abrupt ending of American aid immediately after the war, and to point to the advantages of the Welfare State, which, among other things, provided housing, free and equal education and a national health service. Owing perhaps to American resentment of anything that smacked of labour organization, or because US funding was needed for other parts of Europe (the Marshall Plan was initiated in April 1948), there was a mild estrangement between the US and England, worsened by British fears of being swamped by American culture. Concomitantly, there was fear of Russia's intentions, giving rise to the Cold War. Several other events also contributed to the atmosphere of suspicion and fear.

Replacing the League of Nations, the United Nations (UN) officially came into existence on 24 October 1945, with its General Assembly and Security Council meetings (before moving to the US) taking place at Westminster Central Hall in London from January 1946. In spite of the attempt through this organization to achieve reconciliation, in 1947 Churchill spoke of an "Iron Curtain" that divided Europe, and in 1949 George Orwell published *Nineteen Eighty-Four*, his bleak vision of a totalitarian society on the Soviet model. The East–West political and ideological divide would become military confrontation during the coming years in the war between North and South Korea (1950–53), each side supported by the countries that subscribed to their respective ideologies.

The British withdrew from India and Palestine; in 1952 the British influence in Egypt and north-east Africa was destroyed following the revolution of the young army officers who ousted Egypt's King Farouk, and the shrinking British Empire was to lose its last stronghold in the Near East when the Suez Canal was nationalized in 1956. Britain witnessed with resentment not only that American politics had replaced her world status, but also that American wealth had influenced the shift of artistic importance away from impoverished Europe.

In this atmosphere, amid Britain's suspicions of the intellectual influence of the US and USSR, both her former allies, the more abstract arts fared best, as abstraction reduced the possibility of ideological conflict that the more traditional and indicative forms of art might manifest. Art, however, occupied only a part in the intended Festival which, to a great extent, was planned to provide a showcase for the collective and individual achievements of Britons.[116] The exhibition, opened on the South Bank in London by King George VI on 1 May, was considered a "tonic for the nation". By September 1951 over eight million people had visited it.

The Festival committee included the art historian Kenneth Clark, the poet T.S. Eliot, the actor John Gielgud and the playwright Noel Coward, as well as representatives of

116 See http://vads.ahds.ac.uk/learning/designingbritain/html/festival.html; also: http://www.20thcenturylondon.org.uk/server.php?show=conInformationRecord.238.

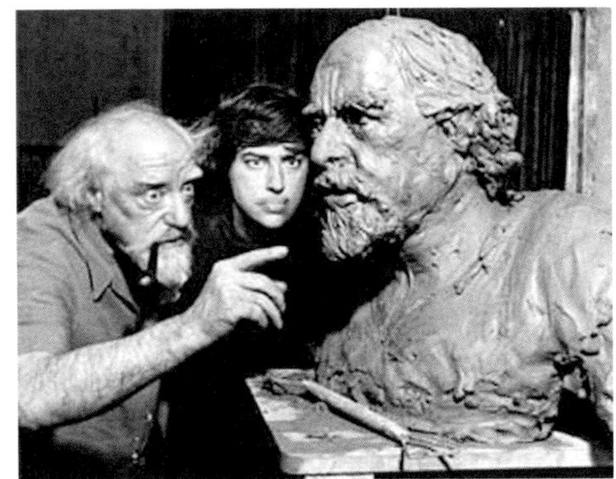

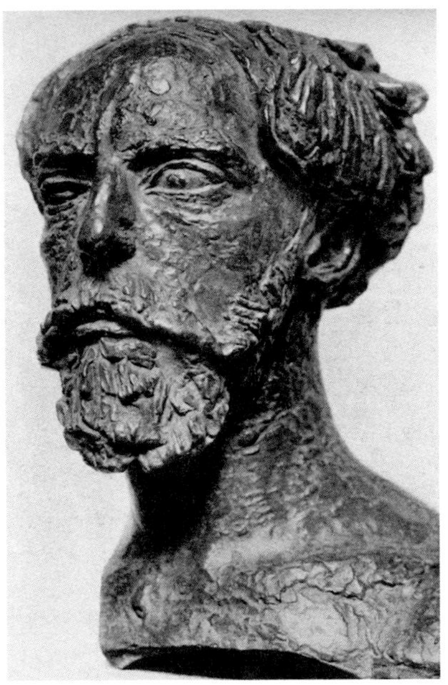

Fig. 56a
Fiore and Augustus John, 1950s
Courtesy of Dina Voisin of Fiore's Estate

78
Augustus John, 1916
Bronze, H. 35.2 cm
New Portrait Gallery, London

other disciplines. Thus it encompassed history, industry, science and the arts, exploring various aspects of cultural and everyday life in mid twentieth-century Britain. Members of the art world included, in addition to Henry Moore (featured in Epstein's September letter to Kathleen; p. 177), the Tate's John Rothenstein, with whom Epstein had had a turbulent relationship. Letters by Epstein suggest, however, that their relationship had somewhat improved, no doubt softened by Rothenstein's decision to hold an Epstein exhibition at the Tate after the closure of the Festival.[117]

Epstein, as he wrote to Kathleen in Italy, had been approached toward the end of 1949, as were others.[118] Some of the commissioned works were to be in Battersea Park in the open-air exhibition of sculpture running concurrently, and some were being shown in the various exhibitions that toured Britain's cities. Three of the works among those touring cities had been included on Epstein's recommendation of their creator, the Italian Fiore de Henriquez (1921–2004),[119] who had came to live in England in late 1949. Owing to her personality and exotic presence[120] she became very popular among high-society circles. She excelled in expressive allegorical sculpture, and as a portraitist she had many sitters from among the artistic and social milieu.[121] Epstein, who was not ashamed of declaring his respect for an artist (witness the case of Henry Moore in 1929), helped her to obtain the commissions of three enormous figures for the 1951 Festival of Britain. "He asked, 'How much do you want? Is £1,000 enough?' I almost vomited; I had hardly arrived, I had no money. He thought it wasn't enough: he said, 'How about two?' Still I couldn't speak. I think in the end I had £4,000. Imagine! And he was such a great sculptor. But of course, sculpture is not really the art of England – especially not from a woman."[122]

Another artist to fall under De Henriquez's spell was the painter Augustus John, who met her at a London dinner party in the early 1950s. Her compelling head of Augustus John [fig. 56a] is among her best portraits, and a comparison with Epstein's portrait of John made about 35 years earlier [78] explains the charm that Epstein, a master in capturing a sitter's personality, had found in De Henriquez's portraiture: her rough technique and expressive result convey the sitter's personality – which, it can be seen, had remained unchanged through the passing years.

In order to present a symbol of hope for the future at the festival, in his first public commission since *Day and Night* (1929) Epstein created a work on the theme that characterized the Festival – progress and achievement: "I conceived an idea of making a figure that should embody youthful courage and resolution, and the result was the bronze entitled *Youth Advancing*" [79a-b]. The slightly over life-size (208 cm) figure has an inclined pose, reminiscent of *The Girl with Gardenias*, accentuated by leaving only one foot on the ground.

As his completed carving *Lazarus* (1948–49) was also presented at the Battersea Park exhibition (before finally settled in Oxford), Epstein may have felt a need to present another facet of his talent in his other medium. With the Festival opening in May 1951, he needed to work quickly on the bronze figure during 1950, "giving up several portrait commissions in order to finish it off on time". This project started what would prove to be a long collaboration with the firm of Morris Singer in Clapham, who specialized in large-scale art works.[123]

Youth Advancing was placed at the entrance to the Homes and Gardens Pavilion in the South Bank Exhibition, but together with the compliments of the organizers on

117 Letter confirming Rothenstein's visit to Epstein's studio on 23 February 1951: TGA – 8726.3.10.

118 Among them was Robert Adams, Reg Butler, Lynn Chadwick, Frank Dobson, Barbara Hepworth, Karin Jonzen, F. E. McWilliam, Bernard Meadows, Henry Moore, Uli Nimptsch, and the young Eduardo Paolozzi (in his twenties). Their varied ages were topped by Epstein's seventy years.

119 See http://www.bodieslikeours.org/forums/archive/index.php/t-842.html.

[Continued on next page]

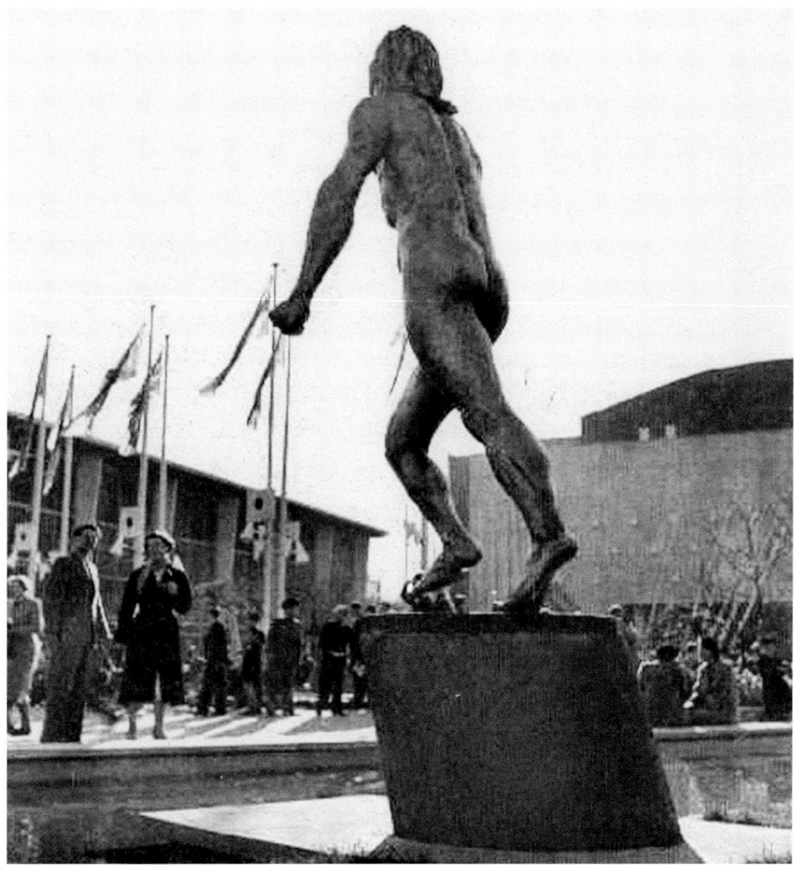

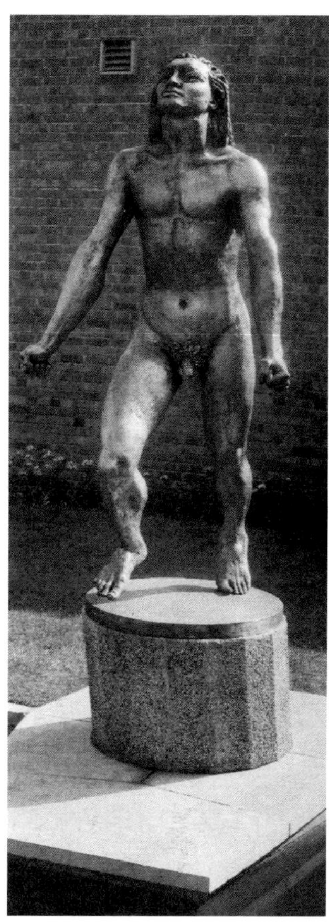

79a–b
Youth advancing (in situ; and back view), 1949–50
Bronze, H. 208 cm
(Now Manchester City Art Gallery)

his work came a review that surprised Epstein by referring to it as a "pot boiler".[124] I would suggest that it was not the mere portrayal that repelled the more experienced eye but rather the unpleasant rhetoric of the muscular naked body and the forward hand-movements that vaguely echoed both the German and the Soviet sculptures in the Paris exhibition of 1937 (pp. 103–04). To Epstein's credit, however, his figure not only conveys a hopeful resolution but also the face has a humane expression that is lacking in the Parisian works, which express an unyielding certainty.

The personal tension between Epstein and his former colleague Henry Moore that had begun in the 1948 Battersea Exhibition continued here too. Epstein's bronze was regarded as traditional, whereas Moore's work was situated within the contemporary artistic dialect, even if reactions to his work for the Festival were less favourable than to his work of 1948. Since he was a member of the committee, his large bronze *Reclining Figure* was given a prime location near the main entrance to the South Bank site. This latest addition to his long series on this subject, as one critic commented, had "too little contact with life to carry the imaginative conviction and dramatic power of its predecessors, [reaching] the stage of empty, if impressive, virtuosity, since he has been exploiting it now for twenty years".[125]

Many years after everything was over, commentators have still tended to undervalue more traditional creative expression and pay greater attention to the innovative artists of the time. Thus, in an exhibition entitled 'Symbols for 51' held in 1996 at the Royal Festival Hall, the catalogue points to the diversity of styles in treating the human figure

120 She was androgynous, which had been discovered at puberty, and which she kept secret from family and friends.

121 The introduction of the catalogue of a memorial exhibition (Wolseley Fine Arts, 29 September – 23 October 2004) states that, from 1948 to her death (2004), Fiore made in the region of four thousand portraits; Epstein's output was less than 10% of this number.

122 Jan Marsh, *Art and Androgyny*. I am greatly indebted to Dina Voisin of the De Henriquez Estate for information and permission to use photographs. We both deplore not having images of the rest of the sculptures.

123 Buckle, *Epstein: Sculptor*, p. 385; they cast the later sculptures, discussed below, the 'Liverpool Giant', *Social Consciousness*, *St Michael* and the Bowater House Group.

124 The same expression, dismissing the portrait-orientated works, is used by David McFall when describing, in retrospective, the number of portraits he found in Epstein's studio in 1946: McFall, p. 5.

125 Sylvester, 'Festival Sculpture'.

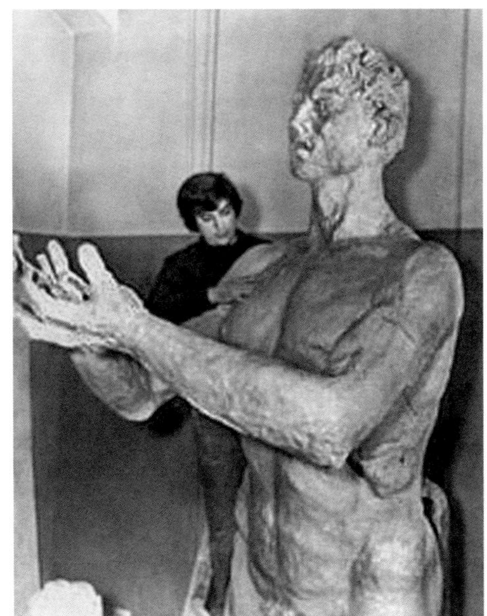

Fig. 56b
Fiore de Henriquez
The *Age of Stone* (?), 1956
Plaster, 400 cm
Now lost

in sculpture and to the many different guises of modernism typical of the period, such as the primitivism of Frank Dobson, Heinz Henghes and Anna Mahler, the moderate expressionism of Georg Ehrlich and Daphne Hardy, the surrealism of Reg Butler, F.E. McWilliam and Moore, and the constructivism of Hepworth's rotating sculpture.[126] Nonetheless, the more conventional styles are also mentioned – Jonzen's informal naturalism, and Peter Peris's realism: his *Sunbathers* that had that "contact with life" that has been missing in Moore's work. Epstein's figure, although perhaps displaying more realism than Peris's somewhat thin figures, was not regarded as falling into the categories of realism or naturalism, presumably because of the catalogue authors' disregard of symbolic sculpture intended as such, despite the 'symbol' in its title. Nonetheless Epstein's symbolic figure is described in this catalogue, which still remains today long after the exhibition ended, as (regardless of its unspecified style) "encapsulating the festival's optimistic spirit".[127] It is interesting to note the similarity between Epstein's approach and style in "encapsulating the festival's optimistic spirit" and that of his protégée Fiore de Henriquez, who, like him, chose symbolically to express the potential in English life.[128] She produced a group, twelve feet high [fig. 56b], of three plaster statues expressing "the skill of the British people" and representing *Effort*, *Industry* and *Communications*.[129]

Epstein reported on the display of *Lazarus* in the concurrently running exhibition at the Battersea Park in two letters sent to Kathleen in Italy. In the first he mentions that "It took all day to take it down and out" from the studio, which had interrupted the work on the bust (of Esther), which he intended to finish next week.[130] He also mentions a project that he had undertaken in America, *Social Consciousness*: "After that I'll like a respite to think of the Philadelphia sculpture and work on it". He also reports on incidents with neighbours and his son-in-law Lucien Freud's painting, which he regarded as ugly, "and I can't imagine looking at it with any pleasure; think of it hanging up on one's wall".

The next day, Sunday, he went to see his Lazarus in the park:[131] "To my disgust I found that this [new] proposed site was out in the centre of a field and not where I indicated it should go. I let the men get on with their job hoping the figures would look well; but it looked all wrong after they got it down: it stood out too far and was awkward."

After being approached by Epstein, the organizer, Barry Hart, agreed, "by Tuesday or Wednesday", to shift Lazarus to the place Epstein had originally chosen. Going around viewing other works, Epstein found "very few highlights, about half the pieces in the place. The kneeling figure by Lehmbruck seems to me the best thing there." Moore's work he described as "a horror", and horrific as well was "an assemblage of old iron" by Calder sent over by the Museum of Modern Art. Hart, so he reports, told him of the amount of trouble he was having with the abstractionists: "nothing satisfies them". The worst of them, apparently, was Moore: under protest, Hart had had to succumb to Moore's demand "to make a good place for his 3 graces at the lakeside [fig. 53]", for which a noble tree had to be cut down, "a tree 50 or 60 feet high". Hart, who had known Moore as a student, was astonished at his present stance.

126 Burstow, *Symbols for '51*.

127 Burstow, *Symbols for '51*, p. 9.

128 The sculpture is assumed to be *Effort*; http://www.peraltatuscany.com/fiore/section-2/50-66.html.

129 Another set of titles given (corresponding to the above titles) is *Age of Stone*, *Iron* and *Electricity*. Unfortunately, I could not discover their photographs either in her estate or in the Arts Council of Great Britain's archive, held in the Victoria and Albert Museum, which also hosts the records of the British Council.

130 Undated letter to Kathleen (some time between January to March, as the exhibition opened on March 1951): NAGW–BL/1/3/2/6.

131 Ibid.

CHAPTER 6

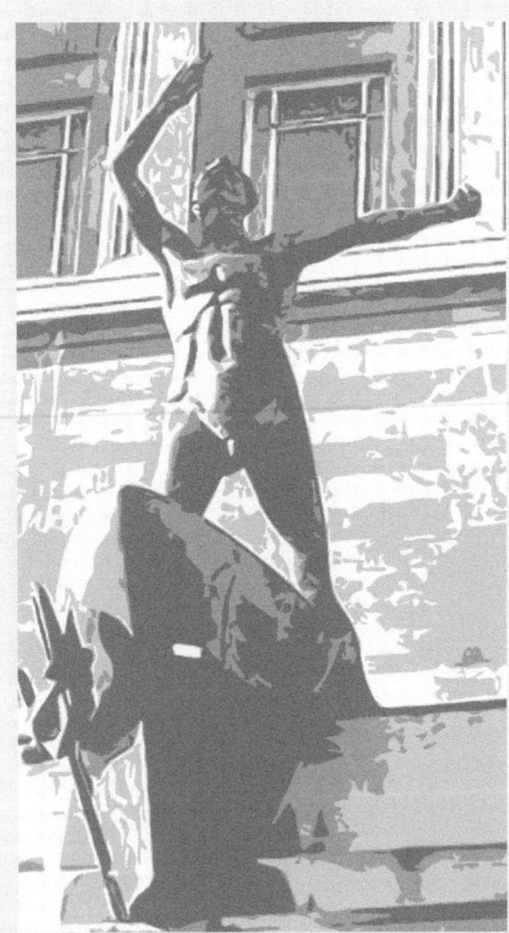

THE GRAND OLD MASTER (1951–59)

MADONNA AND CHILD

Overall, 1951 had been a good year. It marked a new era for Epstein of commissioned sculptures: after the *Lazarus*, there were to be no more large works executed solely for the artits's own pleasure or driven by his own urges. Sadly for this study, this means that less of the artist's inner feeling is expressed. Moreover, in these new commissioned works Epstein would not show much sculptural innovation but would re-use elements found in his previous works, albeit with different emphasis.

The two major commissioned projects of this period, *Madonna and Child* and *Social Consciousness*, were described as ambitious by Epstein himself. If the overlapping dates in Silber's catalogue are correct (1950–52 and 1951–53, respectively), Epstein must have been working concomitantly on both for quite a while.

Silber also numbers seventeen portraits made in 1951, in between these major works, all of them paid for. On the nature of Epstein portraiture, otherwise mentioned here only in passing, I cite Clifford Bax, who felt "such power and such technical distinction in his bronze portraits that to walk into a room when they are showing is like straying into the Albert Hall during a performance by a full orchestra conducted by Toscanini".[1] For me the experience can be compared to the electrifying impact of entering a room full of Rodin's naked bodies.[2] In a BBC interview, Epstein himself said of his portraiture:

> These are images of people and they are mental emotions rather than persons; but I believe I have been faithful to the natural form in my work ....
>
> I put everything I can into a portrait of any kind; study of the human being is frightfully important. Today portraiture is looked upon as a very secondary affair, and only valued commercially. That I deplore. I look at portraiture as requiring imagination as any other kind of work. And I will just [as well] put a portrait to represent me as a large architectural or so-called ambitious work.[3]

One interesting portrait, which he "had long wanted to carry out" (235), was that of T.S. Eliot, whom he had probably met while Eliot was a member of the Festival of Britain committee and who had been brought to his studio by "a mutual friend", in all probability the poet and playwright Ashley Ducks, who also commissioned Eliot's portrait in 1951. A cordial and enduring friendship developed between the two men, strengthened by the warm relationship that Kathleen had with Eliot's then companion (and in 1957, second wife) Valery. In 1958 Epstein lit the candles on Eliot's seventieth birthday cake,[4] and a later entry in Kathleen's diary for the 23 June 1959 notes dinner with him at the Garrick Club. Apparently Epstein found that marriage had made Eliot's face "so interesting that he wanted to do another bust".[5] (This is the second instance I have found in which Epstein commented on the altering effect of life changes on one's face; earlier he had used it as grounds for his constant refusal to let Kathleen drive!)

1 Bax, *Some I Knew Well*, p. 20.

2 I experienced such an impact at the exhibition of Epstein's portraits in the Israel Museum, Jerusalem, 2002.

3 A brief interview with the BBC of about 6 minutes, broadcast on the radio as late as 2 February 1958. The recording was recently interwoven with photographs by Geoffrey Ireland and turned into a short film: www.bbc.co.uk/archive/sculptors/12813.shtml or http://www.youtube.com/watch?v=D_gYH5GnBNY.

4 See the website of the NAGW, which owns the portrait of Eliot: www.thenewartgallerywalsall.org.uk/search/?do=%3E&title=Eliot&what=collection.

5 Letter from Valery Eliot to Gardiner, 20 March 1987: Gardiner papers, NAGW. She adds: "Alas, Jacob died before it could be done".

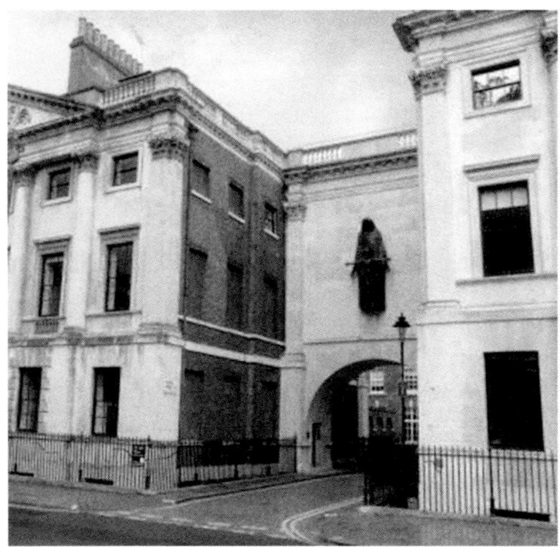

Fig. 57
Madonna and Child in its setting

It is not clear when exactly the modelling of *Madonna and Child* for the Convent of the Holy Child Jesus in Cavendish Square in London took place, and the only definite evidence consists of two articles of 1952 in *The Times*. On 10 January it noted that Epstein's group was almost completed (in a letter to Peggy Jean he remarked that he would have finished it sooner, "but have had to hold it up to do portraits to live on"),[6] and on 23 May it featured in an appeal by the architect Lewis Osman and Sir Kenneth Clark for contributions toward the casting. Factoring in the six months Epstein says he worked on it (PS/235) and the time spent in the arguments that accompanied its final approval, the work was probably begun in early 1951, just after Epstein had completed the commissioned *Youth Advancing*, so continuing the flow of commissioned works for public institutions.

Epstein says that the work was "commissioned by the Nuns of the Convent of the Holy Child Jesus" (PS/235), but it was initiated by the architect Louis Osman (1914–1996), who had been asked by the nuns to repair one of their buildings damaged in the war and to design a bridge to connect the two buildings that made up the convent.[7] The bridge continues the elevation of the two Palladian buildings, echoing the corner pilasters and aligning with their string-course and cornices, but providing a completely flat, plain façade, for which indeed a suspended sculpture rather than the more common carved decoration in low relief was a more suitable and elegant solution (fig. 57).

The architect was seeking a modelled group that would "project itself forward and upward so that it would seem to float in space against the background of the stone wall of the bridge", above the arch.[8] It was to be cast in lead, of which the sisters, from their war-bombed roofs, had rather a lot. Osman turned to Epstein, probably discussing with him the whole project some time in 1950, and asked for a Virgin and Child as befitted the name of the convent. As to the question 'why the Jew Epstein?', one could respond with Osman's opinion of him as "an artist deeply concerned with religious themes", and of his modelling style that linked him "with that of Donatello, right in the mainstream of Palladian art and Palladian theory". Uncommon, but apt, was also his remark that singled Epstein out from most of his colleagues: "I also knew him to be passionately fond of children".[9]

This fondness comes through from his numerous portraits of children, as well as in a letter of the period from Epstein to his granddaughter Leda that shows him to be a loving and respectfully interested parent:

> My dear Leda – thank you for writing me such a nice letter.
>
> I was very pleased to get it & showed it to Jackie. He didn't think your writing was very good, but I don't agree with him. Perhaps he is jealous ….
>
> Jackie is growing up tremendously; he is now taller than I am & weighs a lot. He has a motor cycle 1951 model & he rides long distances to school; in fact to a real aerodrome where he works on aero engines. He looks wonderful in his motoring kit with storm helmet & goggles & fur skinned jacket & leggings & over gloves all complete. I'm sorry I haven't a snap shot of him but I'll get one and send you.
>
> I am myself frightfully busy mostly doing portraits of children, all ages, all stages. Were you here I would model you, also Ian. I will look out a photo of myself to send you with this, if I can find one (fig. 58) ….

6 Letter from Epstein to Peggy Jean, 24 January 1952: TGA-8716/24.

7 The subject is eloquently summed up by Silber (*Sculpture of Epstein*, p. 209). For more on this, see Osman, 'A Bridge and Sculpture in Cavendish Sq.'.

8 Osman, 'Architect, Sculptor and Client'.

9 Ibid., pp. 10–11. On the attitude of Epstein's milieu towards children, see p. 7.

It would be wonderful if Jackie & I could come out for a holiday this next summer. I will try & manage it if I can.

Jackie has a dog called 'Frisky'; he is a Welsh sheep dog, very lovely & makes friends with everyone in the street, especially with the policeman who guards Mr. Churchill's house.

Give my love to Daddy & Mom & also Ian.

Your Eppy Daddy.[10]

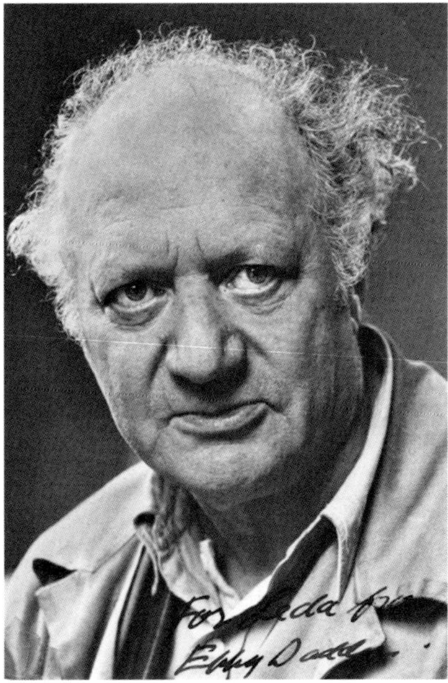

Fig. 58
Epstein's autographed photo sent to his granddaughter Leda

In addition to Osman's appreciation of Epstein's beautiful *Visitation* (1925), with its delicate sculptural treatment of the expecting Madonna, I cannot resist speculating on a tip, given to him indirectly by his renowned fellow architect Charles Holden, who had worked with Epstein on a similar concept of 'floating in space' for the angel on the Tomb of Oscar Wilde. Epstein had proven himself capable of achieving the desired effect of flotation, unlike Moore with his heavy, earth-bound expressions of Mother and Child made during the previous years. Osman could perhaps not resist the temptation of stamping a 'first' – it seems he wanted to be the first architect to utilize Epstein's "wonderful gift of modelled form [that] had not been used properly".[11]

Osman's request for a Madonna and Child may have challenged Epstein with a conceptual problem. He had already carved a mother and child in geometric form in the 1910s, and in 1927 had modelled *Madonna and Child* [1], a naturalistic bronze, which, beyond its title, had such a vague Christian association that the Russian ambassador considered acquiring it as a secular mother and child.[12] A different approach was required for this child, one exposing less of the body and making its Christianity explicit. The child Jesus is most commonly portrayed as an infant, seldom as a toddler or a young boy, so if he was to do this Epstein had very few artistic precedents to which to turn.[13] If Epstein was looking for a 'Christian' boy for inspiration, one of the rare sculptural works of which he may have known, or observed while visiting America, was the renowned *Child Jesus* made in the mid 1930s by Mary Aldrich Fraser (1868–1949; fig. 59).[14]

If Epstein was to follow her model, then the child's body in the configuration of the Cross had also to accommodate the figure of the mother. For this, I suggest he may have drawn on Murillo's *Two Trinities* in the National Gallery, in which Jesus, with outstretched arms, holds his parents' hands, and the even more apt, if rigid, hand-touching of Father and Son by Nicoletto Semitecolo in *The Holy Trinity* (fig. 60).[15] Epstein, however, gave his own composition a less rigid pose and a more human expression. The Christian affiliation of his group is made clearer still by the copper halo above their heads.

As there was no niche in the façade to accommodate a natural arrangement of the figures' feet, Epstein resorted to the sculptural solution of feet pointing downward, as they would in a Byzantine mosaic, thus forming a more strictly upright floating pose, undisturbed by protruding feet. An essential difference between his *Madonna and Child* of 1927 and the new sculpture was that the former was basically horizontal whereas this one was vertical. The impressive focal point in both compositions and their most eye-catching feature, I find, are the positions of the four hands. In the later work, the mother's pose, with down-stretched arms and frontal palms, as if anticipating catching the child's slender, cross-shaped figure, hints at his destiny, the Cross from which she will not be able to save him. Overall, Epstein managed to create a very personal composition of a type never seen in England before.

10 Letter from Epstein to Leda, 15 January 1951 (two years after Jackie returned home): TGA-8716.54-63.

11 See Osman, as in note 7 above.

12 For a full discussion of this work, see I/178–79.

13 Two such works – Jesus as a young boy – were conveniently accessible to Epstein in London: Murillo, *Two Trinities* (1681–82) in the National Gallery, and W.C.T. Dobson, *The Child Jesus going down with his parents to Nazareth* (1856), Tate.

14 In the Autumn 1936 issue of *Cathedral Age*, Mary Aldrich Fraser had an article entitled 'How the Christ Child Came', and in November 1937 an article by Helen M. Ewing in *Patchogue Advance* also indicated that the sculpture was made in the mid 1930s and later presented to Washington Cathedral. There is an original casting in the Cathedral, and similar castings and plaster models in the convent of St Anne in Kingston, N.Y., and the Church of the Good Shepherd in West Springfield, Mass. For this information I am indebted to Diane Ney, the Manager of Archives and Records of Washington National Cathedral.

15 In 1367 Semitecolo signed (as *Nicholeto Semitecholo da Venexia*) and dated one of a series of panels showing, among other scenes, a Holy Trinity.

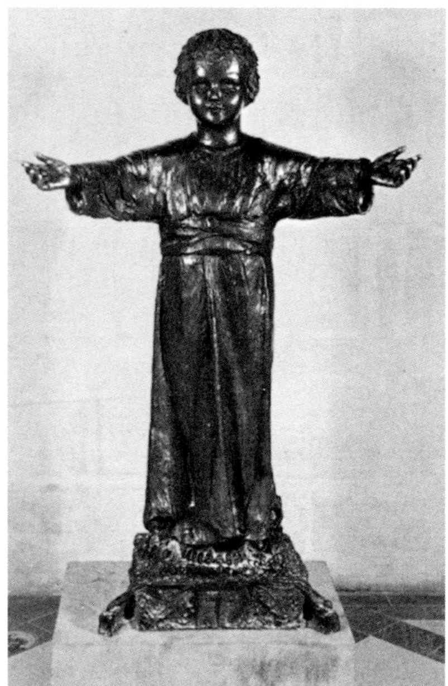

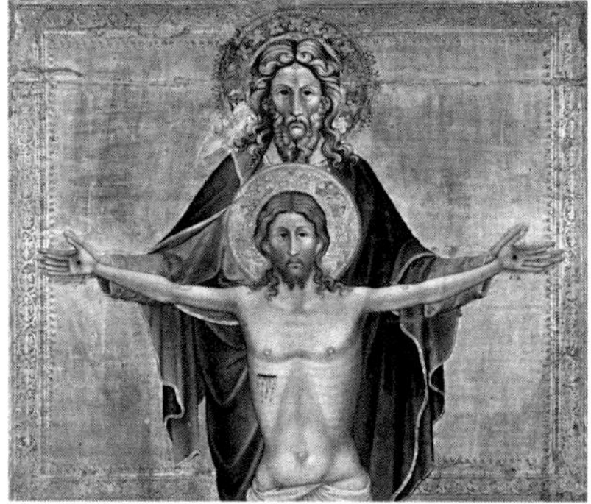

Fig. 59
Mary Aldrich Fraser
The Child Jesus, mid 1930s
Bronze, H. 120 cm
Courtesy of the Washington National Cathedral

Fig. 60
Nicoletto Semitecolo
The Holy Trinity, 1367
Tempera on panel, 65 x 72 cm
Padua Cathedral

Epstein first rendered his idea in a maquette (probably elaborating on the one with Kathleen's features that he had made in 1950; see p. 179), giving it to Osman "within a week" of their first discussion [82]. Osman presented the maquette to the nuns without mentioning the artist's name and the sisters approved it. Epstein started to work, undertaking it without any guarantee that he would be paid. After the large model was almost complete and, as mentioned above, only after Osman and Clark had applied for public support for its casting, did the nuns discover the sculptor's name. One wonders whether it was his being a Jew or the notoriety of some of his carvings, or both, that caused their dismay. Osman's threat to resign from the project if the sculpture was not accepted finally convinced them to agree to the almost completed work. Then, as Epstein reported, "The Mother Superior came to view it. She came with another Sister and they immediately showed the warmest interest in the work and asked to be allowed to contemplate it quietly and alone for some time. After that they returned several times bringing different nuns on each occasion" (235).

The nuns' only request, which Epstein does not mention, was to alter the face that bore Kathleen's eager expression looking forward to a more meditative one, looking at the child. Epstein consequently substituted the head with one based on the features of his pianist friend Marcella Barzetti [81], and the nuns gave their final approval.

The completed work [80] elaborates upon the vague details of the maquette, playing on contrasts: the horizontal lines of the child's draperies, reminiscent of a shroud, are set in the centre of the vertical folds of the mother's skirt, and this tension continues in the placing of Christ's outstretched hands in front of the down-turned hands of his mother. The work was unveiled on Ascension Day, 14 May 1953, and Epstein wrote in his autobiography that "No work of mine has brought so many tributes from so many diverse quarters". Years later, when he expressed his reservations concerning modern sculptors' preoccupation purely with form, he pointed to the *Madonna and Child* as combining form, idea and portrait: "This is what I mean by sculpture. My tendencies were always like this; it might not be known, but this is a fact."[16]

This very first sculpture by Epstein commissioned by and for a Christian institution recalls an earlier exchange: in July 1929, when discussing a proposed Roman Catholic cathedral in Liverpool, Archbishop Downey had said: "It would be calamitous if in an attempt to express the twentieth-century spirit you merely achieved something Epsteinish". On 31 July Epstein replied: "Perhaps Epstein can express Christianity as well as and better than any sculptor. Archbishop Downey does not wish to have any more imitations of Gothic or Byzantine sculpture. He can only then turn to Epstein. Who else is there? The Roman Catholic Church (the All-Embracing Church) employed Michelangelo, Raphael and other great artists of their day. Whom can they turn to to-day but the Jew Epstein?"[17] There is little surprise in Epstein comparing himself to the great masters of sculpture; he never underestimated his own abilities. He did not live to see the Metropolitan Cathedral of Christ the King in Liverpool present an 'Epsteinish' yet rigid terracotta *Madonna and Child*, made by Robert Brumby,[18] in the Lady Chapel (fig. 61). In a niche with an horizontal base, it nevertheless echoes Epstein's composition and seeks to convey a similar impact.

The work on the casting continued while Epstein was in the US, whence he wrote to Kathleen complaining that "life here is an interval life and when I meet you again I

16 Interview with the BBC: see above, note 3.

17 Cited from Haskell, *The Sculptor Speaks*, p. 39. The anecdote was told by Canon Mortlock in his address at Epstein's memorial service.

18 Ceramic designer Robert Brumby (b. 1934), whose church work has subjects in common with Epstein's, seems to follow him so far as pose and gesture goes. His *Christ in Majesty* (1965) at the Church of the Holy Family in Pontefract, for example, was influenced by Epstein's *Jesus* (1957) in Llandaff Cathedral.

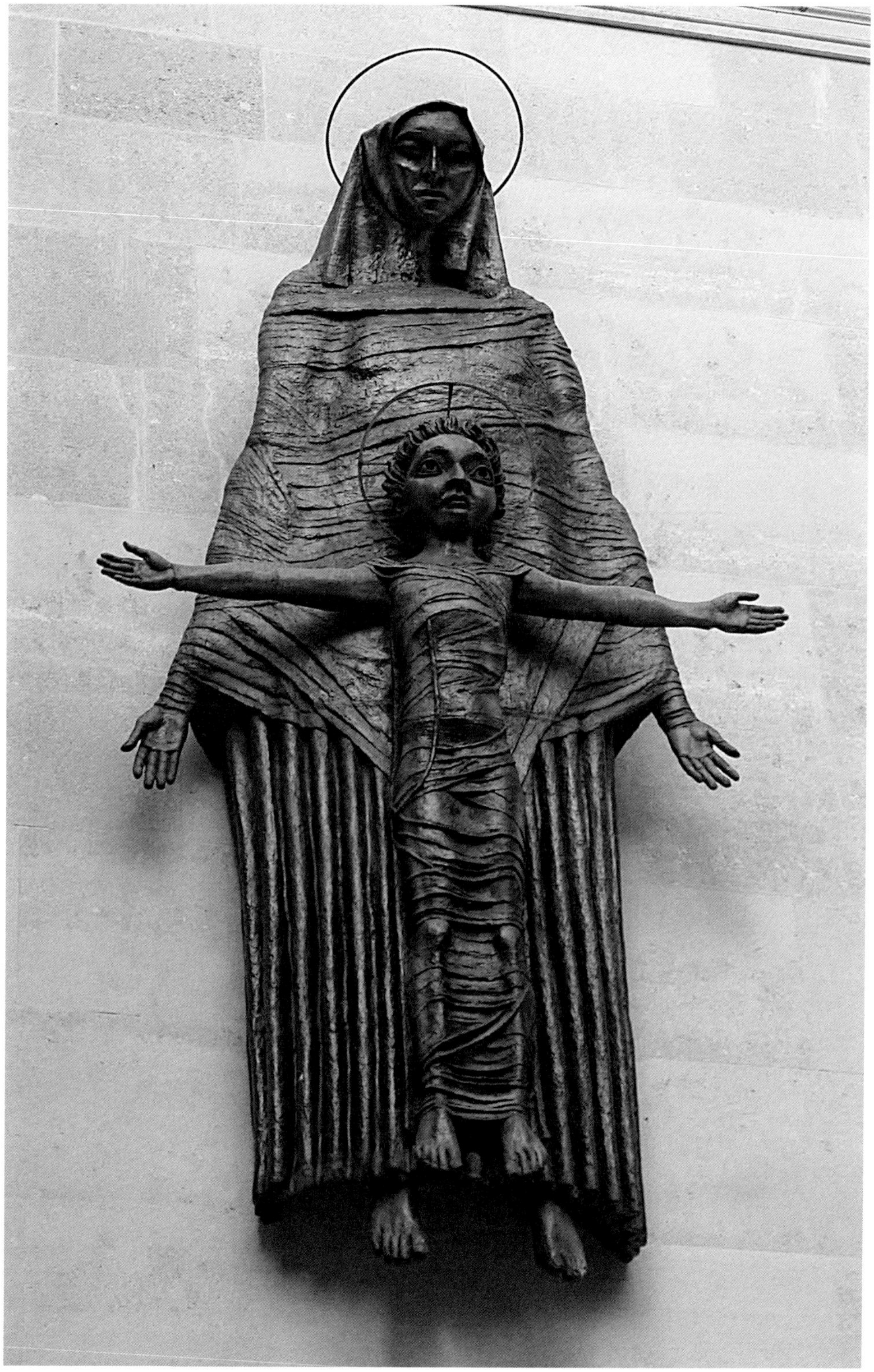

80
The Madonna and Child, 1951–52
Lead, H. 390 cm
Heythorp College (formerly Convent of the Holy Child Jesus), Cavendish Square, London

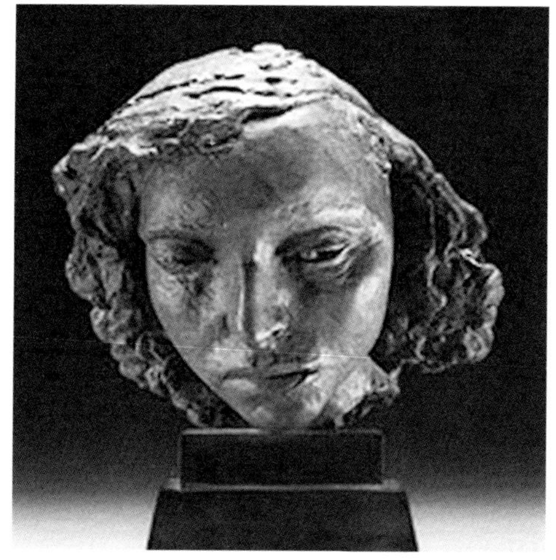

81
Marcella Barzetti, 1950
Bronze, H. 29 cm
Private collection

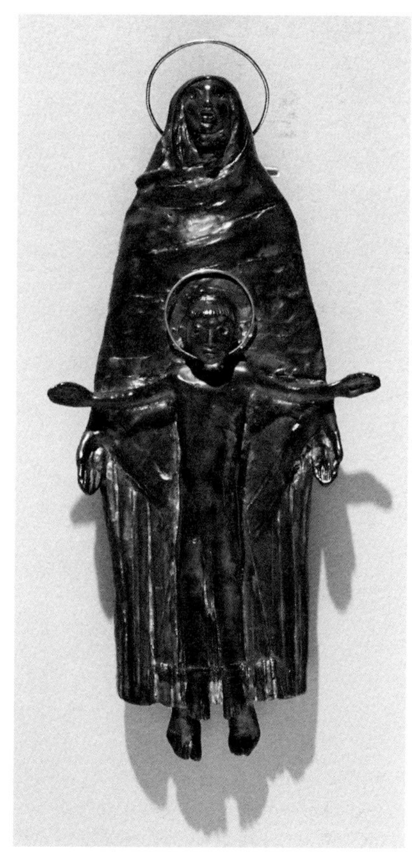

82
The Madonna and Child (maquette), 1950
Lead (halo in bronze), H. 33 cm
GREC-NAGW

will start to live again. How well we are together, but I feel [here] artificial, not right." He added regarding his work on the cherubs' heads [83] that Osman had suggested as door handles for the convent:[19]

> Both Gaskin and Parrot [the casters] have written me to assure me that everything is alright and the work is going forward. Parrot says the head and halo of the Christ is cast and the outer parts begun; also the little works [the four door-handles] are being finished. I have let Osman know he can expect them. The blighter doesn't deserve them, but I'm doing them for the Nuns and the children who I hope will enjoy them.[20]

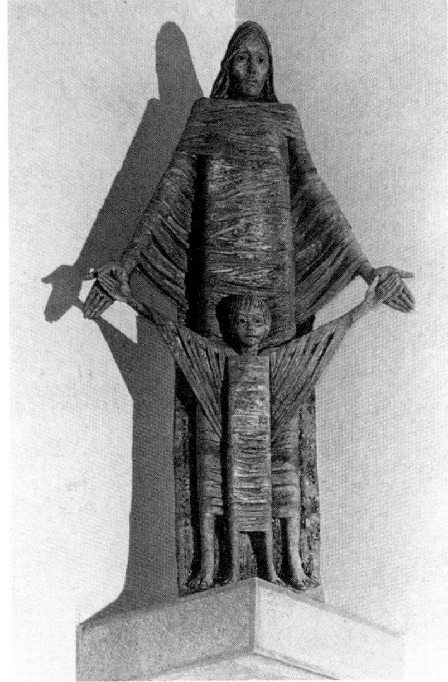

Fig. 61
Robert Brumby,
Our Lady and the Child Jesus, 1965
Terracotta, H.~300 cm
Metropolitan Cathedral of Christ the King, Liverpool

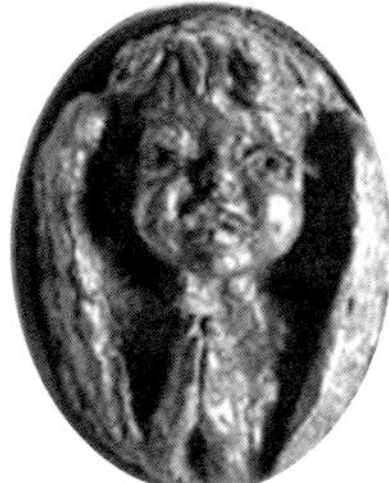
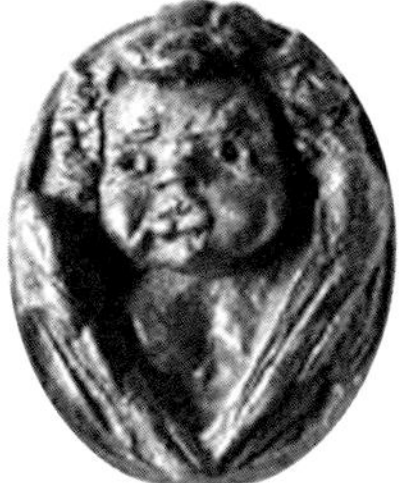
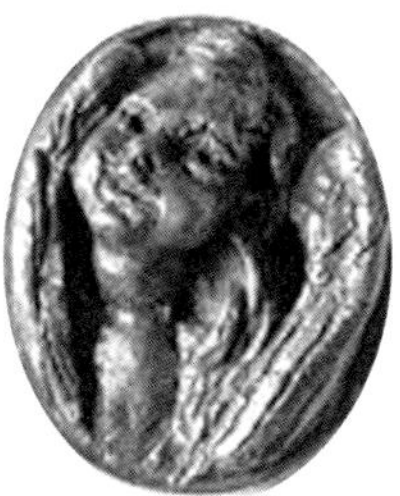
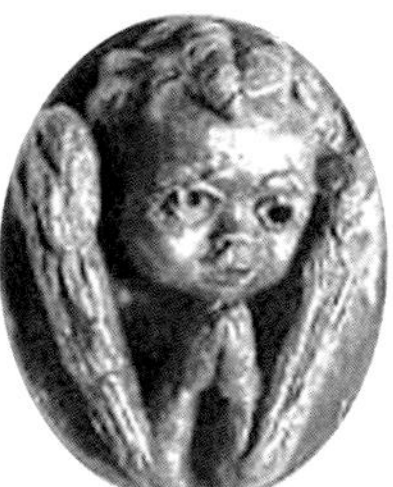

83
Four door handles with children's heads, 1952
Bronze, 11.5 x 9.5 cm (oval)
Heythorp College (formerly Convent of the Holy Child Jesus), Cavendish Square, London

Madonna and Child marked Epstein's entry into a fruitful creative decade of large commissioned works, which regretfully coincided with unpleasant and painful family affairs. The main line of his non-portraiture work would involve Christian subjects, but to these he would always give his own interpretation[21] rather than simply replicating the conceptions of those who commissioned the work. Following his successful expression of Christian notions with the Cavendish Square Madonna, eventually and after serious consideration, other Christian institutions also engaged him, in spite of his being a Jew. Right up to his final days he was working on sculpture for churches, some of which he was not able to complete before his death.

SOCIAL CONSCIOUSNESS

On 16 February 1951, after the completion of *Youth Advancing* for the Festival of Britain, and while Epstein was still engaged with *Madonna and Child*, he was approached for the second time by R.S. Ingersoll on behalf of the Fairmount Park Association in Philadelphia (FPA). He had first been approached in 1949,[22] but his reply had come too late and in the meantime six other sculptors had been invited to add their works to an already existing group of sculptures in the Samuel Memorial, "on a strip of land between the Schuylkill River and Kelly Drive".[23] When Epstein eventually saw the sculptures, he couldn't find "anything good to say of the sculpture already in place; all of it is lacking in any thrilling quality and some of it is decidedly poor and clumsy".[24]

The new project mainly involved sculptors living in America – Jacques Lipchitz, José de Creeft, Koren der Harootian, Ahron Ben Shmuel, Waldemar Raemisch and the

19 Buckle (*Epstein: Sculptor*, p. 376) adds that a few years later another set was cast for Coventry Cathedral. Two of the heads are members of Epstein's family – his granddaughter Anna Freud (Kitty's child) and grandson Ian Hornstein (Peggy Jean's son).

20 Letter from Epstein to Kathleen (before May 1953, when the sculpture was unveiled): NAGW–BL/1/3/2/18. For a comparison of the images with their portraits, see Buckle, *Epstein: Sculptor*, p. 525.

21 Epstein's previous sculptures – *The Risen Christ* (1917) and the ones discussed above, *Behold the Man, Consummatum Est* and also *Lazarus* – were made on his own initiative and bore entirely his own interpretations.

22 Silber, *Sculpture of Epstein*, p. 212. The following general details are taken from her thorough report of events in the FPA archive; I summarize them here as a foreword to the work itself.

23 For information on the site and on the work of the participating sculptors, see www.fpaa.org/samuel_garden.html.

24 Letter from Epstein to Kathleen, "Wednesday" [8, 15 or 22] August 1951: NAGW–BL/1/3/2/11.

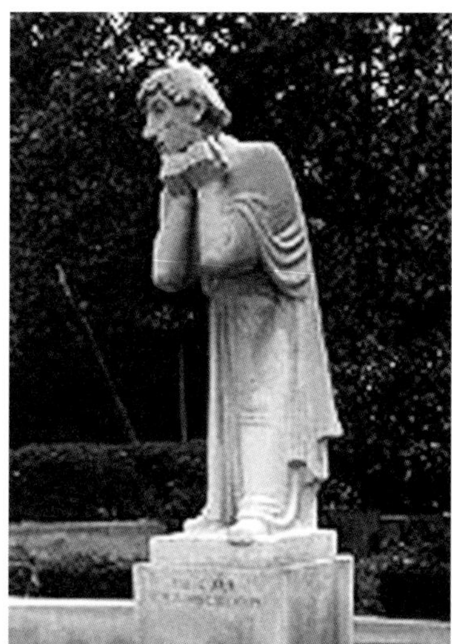

Fig. 62a
Waldemar Raemisch (1888–1955)
The Preacher, 1952
Granite, H. 270 cm

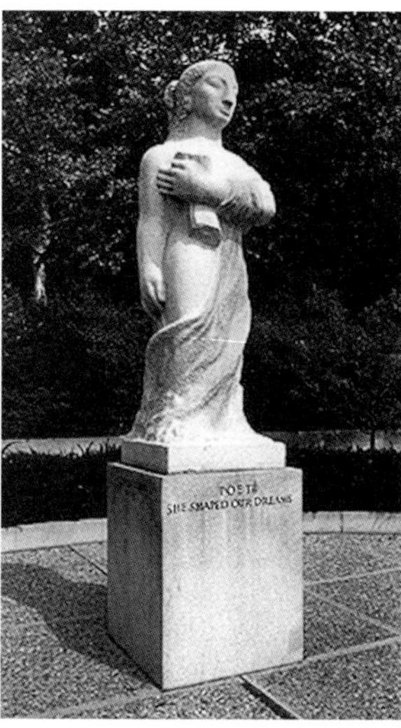

Fig. 62b
José de Creeft (1884–1982)
The Poet, 1954
Granite, H. 280 cm

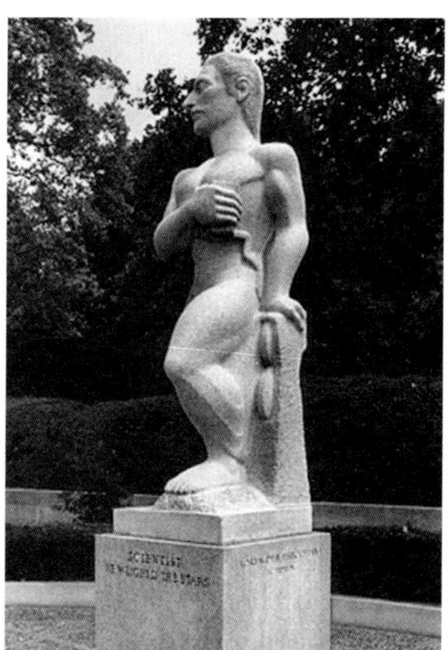

Fig. 62c
Koren der Harootian (1909–1991)
The Scientist, 1955
Granite, H. 280 cm

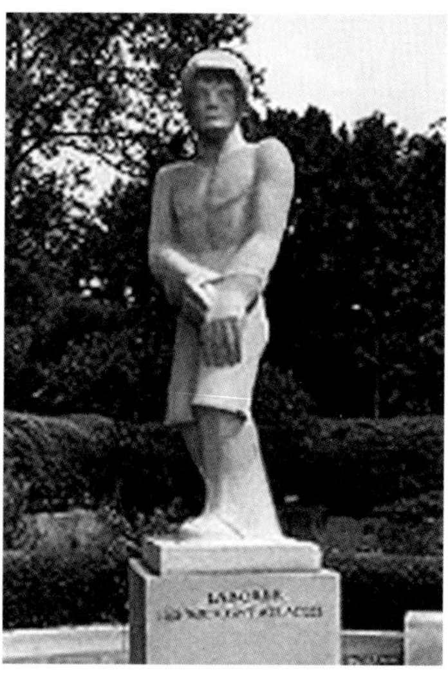

Fig. 62d
Ahron Ben Shmuel (1903–1984)
The Labourer, 1958
Granite, H. 280 cm
All The Samuel Memorial, Fairmount Park, Philadelphia, Courtesy of the Association for Public Art (Gary McKinnis © 1992)

European Gerhart Marcks.[25] Their sculptures were intended to take their place beside earlier works that were "emblematical of the history of America", with titles such as *The Miner*, *The Slave*, *The Migrant*, etc. The new titles were suggested by the sculptors themselves, each presenting a single figure (on an equal granite base approximately 105 cm high) that symbolized a particular occupation or status (figs. 62a–d).

Gerhard Marcks's proposed work, of a man holding his female companion's shoulder,[26] was rejected by the committee as they "did not believe he adequately captured the concept in a manner as would be suitable or could take its place among the other statues".[27] Therefore, at the recommendation of Sally Ryan,[28] Ingersoll approached Epstein again in 1951.

The original maquette that convinced the committee to give Epstein the commission has not been traced.[29] He is reported, however, to have made three tentative models in plasticine, described by Buckle as a warrior with a sword [84a], a seated woman [84b] and a mourning woman standing [84c]. The trio were cast by Kathleen into one unit after Epstein's death [84d], and attributed to the project on the basis that a seated woman was included in the final work, also positioned in the centre.[30] While respecting Kathleen's account and assuming that the other two figures were the result of Epstein's original ponderings on this project, it is hard to see 'Consciousness' in a man holding a sword, or to regard the gesture of the standing woman as particularly 'Mourning', or to understand how they are related to the figure entitled *Seated Woman*. The relations between the three maquettes gain meaning only if they are expressing some unifying idea, as a triad; Epstein, as has been constantly argued, was led by 'idea' throughout his oeuvre.[31]

A clue to finding a meaning may be the man with the sword, an unusual figure to have come from Epstein's pacifist mind. Such a figure must therefore be symbolic, expressing in some way a positive notion. The source for such an idea may have been

25 Gerhard Marcks (1889 –1981) was a German sculptor renowned also for his drawings, woodcuts, lithographs and ceramics. Several of his works were included in the 1937 Degenerate Art exhibition.

26 The only sculpture that seems to correspond to this description is a monumental bronze statue of two dressed figures, entitled *Oedipus and Antigone* (1960), installed at Luther College in Decorah, Iowa, in 2000.

27 The Samuel Memorial Committee, Minutes of the Meeting of the Board of Trustees, 28 June 1951 (information from Laura S. Griffith, Assistant Director of Fairmount Park Art Association). Gardiner (*Epstein*, p. 428) says they rejected him, "having failed to arrive at a theme 'which would be interpretive of the thought'"; Silber (*Sculpture of Epstein*, p. 60) gives the reason as not conveying "practical Christianity". I speculate that part of the reason was that Marcks's work, with its deeply sensual nature, did not suit the committee's conservative taste.

28 Letter to Epstein from Ingersoll's co-chairman Henry Marceau, 19 March 1951; cited in Gardiner, *Epstein*, p. 429.

29 Information from Laura S. Griffith (see note 27).

30 Buckle, *Epstein: Sculptor*, p. 346. All three are c. 35 cm high: Silber, *Sculpture of Epstein*, no. 450.

31 An intriguing comparison is with the three-figure group in Chaplin's *City Lights* (1931). According to the Mayor in the film, it represents "peace and prosperity" (Chaplin's cynical political jibe?). The group (by art director Charles D. Hall?) has elements like Epstein's maquettes – man with sword; seated woman; upward-moving hand of the third figure. But the differences between the film's classical, pompous and extrovert sculpture and Epstein's humanist work are considerable.

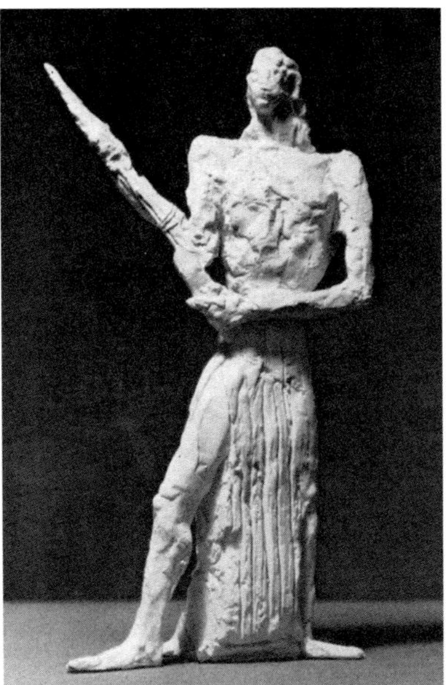
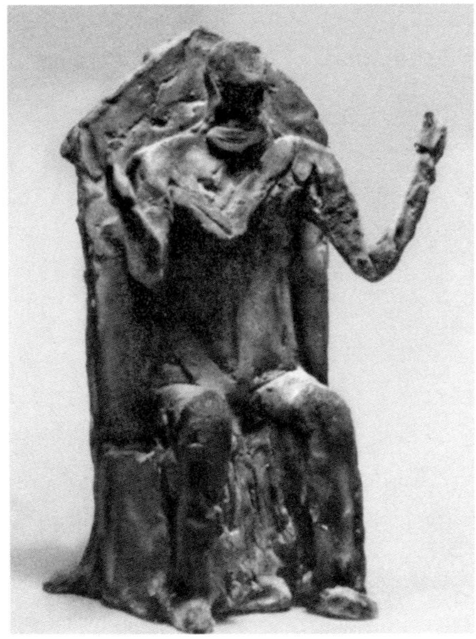
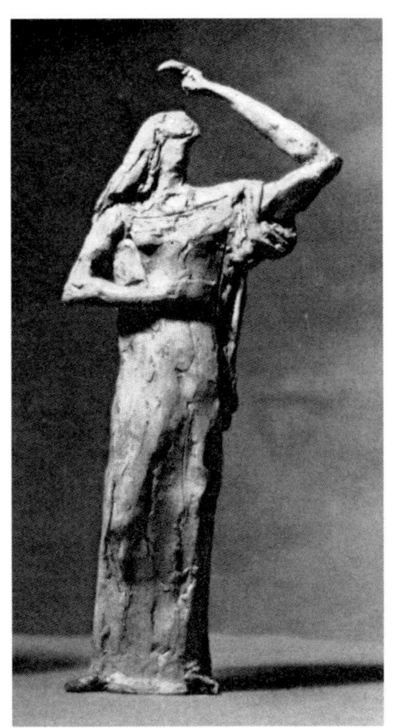

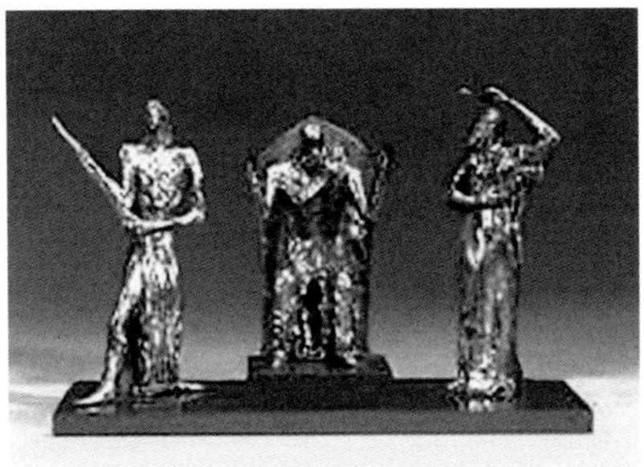

84
Four preliminary maquettes for *Social Consciousness*, 1951–52
Bronze
a – man with a sword
b – seated woman: 32.5 x 35 cm
c – woman raising her hands
d– triad of all figures: H. 35 5 cm

'Paradise and the Peri', the fourth chapter of *Lalla Rookh* by the Irish poet Thomas Moore,[32] in which 'consciousness' is expressed by the three gifts – a drop of blood, a sigh and a tear – that a wandering soul (*peri*, a term from Persian mythology) must bring with him in order to enter Paradise. Moore's version of the theme of three gifts seems a likely source for Epstein, at least indirectly, particularly as it also featured in Robert Shuman's cantata *Das Paradies und die Peri* (1843), which the music-lover Epstein must have known.[33] "Sometimes a poem or a piece of music will evoke a complete image in the most striking fashion," wrote Epstein in his autobiography (P/S, 237).

The first gift is related to a soldier who refuses to join forces with a tyrant who had conquered his land. Instead he attempts to kill the conqueror (although with his last arrow and not with a sword, as in Epstein's maquette). The *peri* brings to heaven a drop of blood; the gift thereby symbolizes 'resistance':

> The Tyrant lived, the Hero fell!
> ... Of morning light she caught the last
> Last glorious drop his heart had shed
> Before its free-born spirit fled!

The second gift, symbolizing 'devotion', is a sigh stolen from the lips of a dying maiden, who, rather than surviving the plague and living in exile from her dying lover, has chosen to join him:

> Again the peri soars above,
> Bearing to Heaven that precious sigh
> Of pure, self-sacrificing love.

In Epstein's maquette, this notion of unconditional love seems to be expressed by the standing figure waving her finger upward, as if vowing to hold fast to her intention.

The third gift in the poem is the tear of an evil man, who, upon seeing a child praying in the ruins of the Temple of the Sun at Baalbec in Syria, regretted his bad deeds:

32 An oriental romance by Irish poet Thomas Moore, published in 1817.

33 The motif recurs in a famous Yiddish tale by Y.L. Peretz, *Three Gifts*, adapted to suit Jewish European history. There is no doubt in my mind that in his New York youth Epstein had read or heard about it, as this story had acquired an almost iconic status in the Jewish world. Until recently it was on the curriculum in its Hebrew translation in Israeli schools.

And hope and feeling which had slept
From boyhood's hour that instant came
Fresh o'er him and he wept – he wept!

Although Epstein's third maquette, given the sex of the final sculpture for Philadelphia, is commonly referred to as a seated woman, the gender of the figure in the maquette is, in fact, unclear (the treatment of the chest is vague and neutral and the long skirt is not necessarily that of a woman), which enables interpretation of it as a repentant man raising his hands.

The repentance in the poem occurs within a temple – that of the Sun God – for which a substitute in the maquette seems to be the unusual throne, reminiscent of a temple or church entrance. This idea is given credence by the addition of a figure at the back of the seat, echoing the 1930s addition to the back of *Sun God* to form *Primeval Gods*. The pose of the figure, standing with legs astride and arms spread, even resembles that of *Sun God* [30a]. Unlike the simpler seated figure, whose gender is equivocal, the naturalistic figure at the back of the chair is certainly male [85]. Its title, *Young Bacchus*, was given by Kathleen, probably because of the vine leaves that surround him.[34] One has to question, however, why Epstein would have used the back of a maquette professed to be for *Social Consciousness* to toy with a totally unrelated subject. I would substitute this title, therefore, with that of *Sun God*. If Kathleen's dating of it to 1956 were correct it would mean that it was made long after *Social Consciousness* had been installed, implying that Epstein had used one of his maquettes (which had surely dried out by then) to muse on another subject that had no connection with the sequence of his work of the period.

As it is, the maquette actually sent to the commissioners is not available, and there is no evidence that the Thomas Moore triad, Resistance, Devotion and Regret, was ever presented to them. Indeed such a concept and its literary source might well have been too meaning-loaded for the commissioners, and these literary notions might not have suited the national consciousness in McCarthy's America, amidst its 'Second Red Scare',[35] which lasted from 1947 up to 1957 (no doubt heightened by the war in Korea, and focused on the threat of national and foreign Communists influencing American society and culture, infiltrating even federal government circles). Epstein remarked on "the joker McCarthy"[36] on the back of a later letter sent to him by Douglas Moore and Luis Kronenbur, proposing his honorary membership of The American Society of Arts and Letters and announcing his election to the American Academy.[37] The blunt words fit the old timer and all-time socialist Epstein, particularly as there can be no doubt about his attitude to McCarthy's censorship and persecution of American artists of every kind.

In any case, it seems that Epstein now revised his concept for the commission, remaining, however, with a triad with a seated figure at the centre[38] (the one I suggested symbolized regret for the abuse of one's fellow man). His triad was to express a public 'social consciousness' with a Christian tone that better befitted his clients.

The three figurines apparently made during Epstein's intended "respite to think of the Philadelphia sculpture and work on it"[39] are said by Buckle to give us a glimpse into the working method of Epstein's that he terms "relaxation" – his toying with forms and subjects that diverge from or perhaps have nothing to do with his finished works. I have already interpreted several such maquettes as relating to events in his life [e.g. 32, 47,

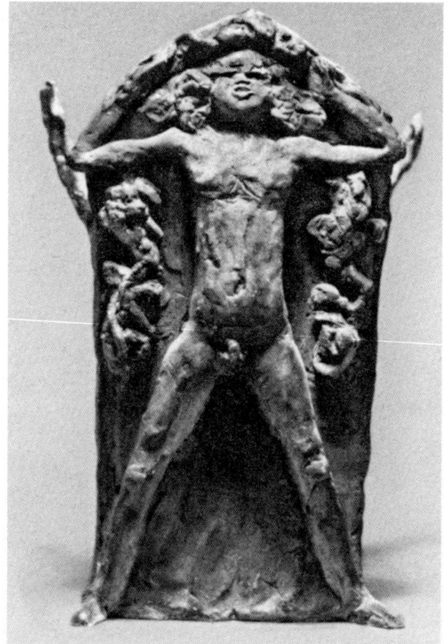

85
Sun God [?] [*Bacchus*] (verso of 84b), 1951–52
Bronze, 32.5 x 35 cm
Formerly Shinman collection

34 Silber, *Sculpture of Epstein*, no. 494.

35 The first one being from 1919 to 1920, following the Bolshevik Russian Revolution of 1917 and the intensely patriotic years of World War I, combating workers (socialist) revolution and political radicalism.

36 Archivist Neil Lebeter suggests, in an email to the author, 18 November 2011: "I don't think that it is Epstein's handwriting; it appears to be quite different. It could be Kathleen's perhaps, though it is not entirely clear."

37 Letter from Douglas Moore and Luis Kronenbur to Epstein, 9 May 1955: NAGW–BL/1/1/2/8: "We trust we may have the pleasure of conveying to the members your acceptance of their invitation".

38 Silber's deduction (*The Sculpture of Epstein*, p. 59) from his correspondence with the committee.

39 Letter from Epstein to Kathleen, undated, NAGW–BL/1/3/2/6.

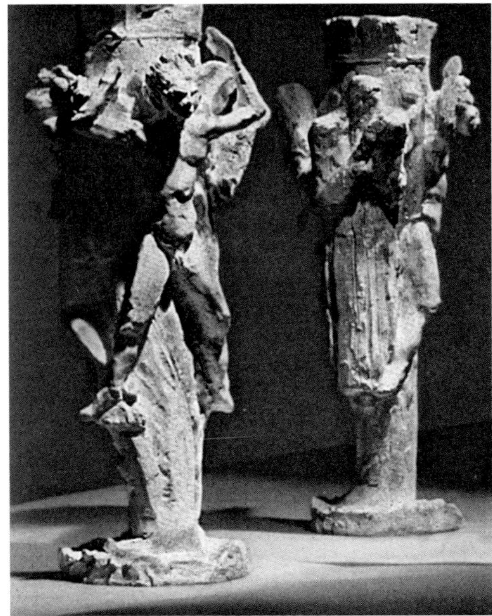

86
Two mace heads, 1951–52 [1953]
Plaster, dimensions unknown
Private collection

73]. For the maquettes made during the 1950s (as listed in Silber's catalogue), however, I cannot find a context, either within his sequence of work or in his personal life; nor is any reasonable explanation of them given by Buckle (who was the first to record details of the maquettes from "Lady Epstein's memory").[40]

Two mace heads dated by Buckle to 1953 [86] are said to be related to an unrealised project in Singapore of which nothing further is known.[41] Although it is hard to comment on the one at the back of the photograph, the one at the front presents a detailed and almost realistic floating figure of a naked young man with legs apart, his back against a column. The figure's facial features are carefully modelled, an uncommon detailing in Epstein's work, here made possible by its greater than usual height. This figure is closely related to the *Bacchus* [85] on the back of the chair of the undetailed seated-figure maquette (Regret?) associated with *Social Consciousness* (1953).

At the end of a prolonged correspondence with the Fairmont Association it was decided to settle on five figures. The contract, with a fee of $17,500 – an amount exceeding anything that Epstein had previously been offered – was signed in June 1951, but Epstein could not travel immediately to see the site because trouble at home tied him to London. His landlord was seeking to evict him from his house because the lease had expired. Epstein turned for help to the American-born lawyer Fanny Holtzmann, the most glamorous, unpredictable, brilliantly accomplished female lawyer of her time, well received in London's highest social circles.[42]

Holtzmann had come to live in England and, thanks to her sharp legal mind and integrity, soon found her place and gained the trust of the upper classes. One sketch portrays her as a vision of curly-haired, fawn-eyed defencelessness, while others claimed to detect a closer kinship to Machiavelli. She was invited to Chartwell for the intimate family celebration of Winston Churchill's eightieth birthday, and counted Noel Coward, Eleanor Roosevelt, the Grand Duchess of Russia and George Bernard Shaw amongst her friends. In 1932–34 she presented before a British court Princess Irina Alexandrovna Youssoupov and her husband Prince Felix's claim against the MGM production of the film *Rasputin*, and won for her clients an unprecedented sum. It is not surprising that the one-time Hollywood investor, right-wing supporter of Germany and American ambassador to London Joseph P. Kennedy was her bitter enemy.

Epstein's trust in her was justified. She arranged it so that he could remain in the house for the rest of his life, and as payment she only asked him to do her bust. The sitting, so we are told by Epstein's sister Sylvia, was handled in accordance with the peculiar personality of the sitter: "When she came to the studio to pose she asked whether she would strip to the waist, and received the reply that it's up to her". She did, and Epstein produced a bust of a plain woman with an intelligent face, false teeth and "voluptuous breasts".[43] However, a photograph of the sitting does not correspond to Sylvia's vision of a bare bosom (fig. 63). The never exhibited bust remained in Holtzmann's possession.[44]

In August 1951, having completed Holtzmann's bust, Epstein visited Philadelphia to inspect the site, reporting: "I was greatly impressed by the fine natural surroundings of rocks and trees and river, and I realised that something on a heroic scale was called for. I planned a group of five figures, two of them thirteen feet high, flanking a central figure

40 Buckle, *Epstein: Sculptor*, p. 7; see my remark in 'Main Sources'.

41 Buckle, *Epstein: Sculptor*, p. 363. Silber (*Sculpture of Epstein*, no. 470) quotes him, giving no provenance or details other than a reproduction, and no explanation as to the nature of the project.

42 Babson, *The Epsteins*, p. 60. Tales of Holtzman's legal wizardry were whispered from her native Brooklyn to the chancelleries of the Orient. See Berkman, *The Lady and the Law The Remarkable Story of Fanny Holtzmann*.

43 Babson, *The Epsteins*, pp. 60–61. The anecdote sounds like one of Aunt Sylvia's exaggerated stories or someone playing a joke on her. Her niece Martha saw the bust in Epstein's studio and remarked on the false teeth but said nothing of the "voluptuous breasts".

44 Not recorded in Silber, *Sculpture of Epstein*. Its whereabouts is unknown, and Holtzmann's family in the United States have never seen it.

with outstretched arms and upward glance, 'seated in the adamant of time'" (P/S, 237).

His letter to Kathleen reports a more problematic situation, encumbered with arguments about the right scale and site:

> It seems my work is to be in pendant to that of Lipshitz. I am getting somewhat fed up with Lipshitz and all his works. Unfortunately Ingersoll is a wholehearted admirer of Lip .... They wish me to see Lip's model [for the project] in N.Y. and I had to tell Ing. that his model could in no way influence my work and I didn't care to see it.[45]

Unlike the contributions of the other sculptors, Jacques Lipchitz's *Spirit of Enterprise* (fig. 64) comprises two figures – a muscular pioneer surging forward, one hand shading his eyes as if scanning the horizon, the other holding a caduceus, standing behind a great eagle (the American symbol) with outstretched wings, echoing the pioneer's movement forward and acting as his companion.[46] Lipchitz's work was lower in height than Epstein's intended figures and, as both works were to occupy adjacent sites, height, as Epstein continues in his letter to Kathleen, became an isse:

> The architects also insist on a small scale size.
>
> Alone with Ingersoll I tried to impress him with the waste of time and energy that this scale model involved; also that the original size of the whole thing has been altered by them ... the whole raw matter is to have something that they can play about with and that of course makes them feel important; moving the model here[,] there[,] higher lower[,] in the end they feel that they are 'creating' the work.
>
> I could see that the committee gets a great kick out of fussing over the whole business, which is beginning to weigh a little heavily on me.

Lipchitz's first work was destroyed by fire, however, and Epstein's group was the first to be installed. Lipchtiz's second version was completed and set in position only some time afterwards. Ultimately, by erecting Epstein's group on a very low base and Lipshitz's on a higher one, the two works were made to rise to almost the same height, about four metres.

Besides reporting on his woes, in this long letter to Kathleen Epstein tells her of the collections he had seen, and in particular Ingersoll's:

> The more I see of his collection in the garden the less I like it. His Maillols are indifferent, there is that ugly Italian horse and his rider and [the] Lipshitzes are horrid in every way. A small Brancusi I like but it is being ruined outdoors and I've advised him to put it in the house .... There is plenty of room here [in this garden] for a new work of mine. Ingersoll would like something large and I think the 2 *slave hold* figures would be acceptable to him. I gather he paid about £1200 for the Marini horse which I can see across the garden as ugly as ever.
>
> Ingersoll expressed surprise at the little he paid for my bronze at the Leicester. He expected to be asked around £1000 for it. That is what the Leicester does for me with Americans.

Epstein also retails anecdotes about various English individuals who had visited America before him: "Clive Bell when [he stayed] here stopped in this house as a guest; funny

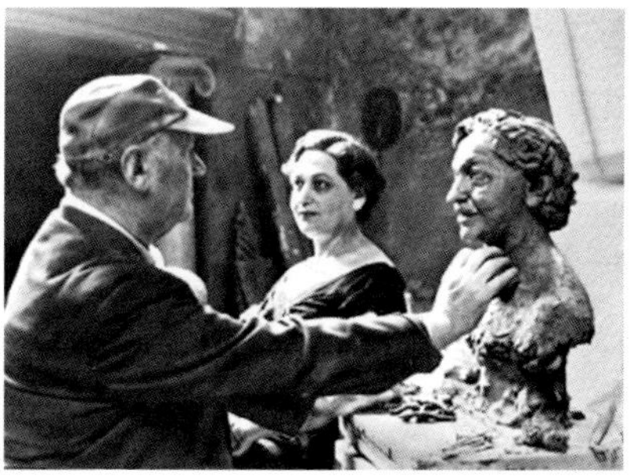

Fig. 63
Epstein and Fanny Holtzmann, 1951
Photograph courtesy of Niall Fairhead

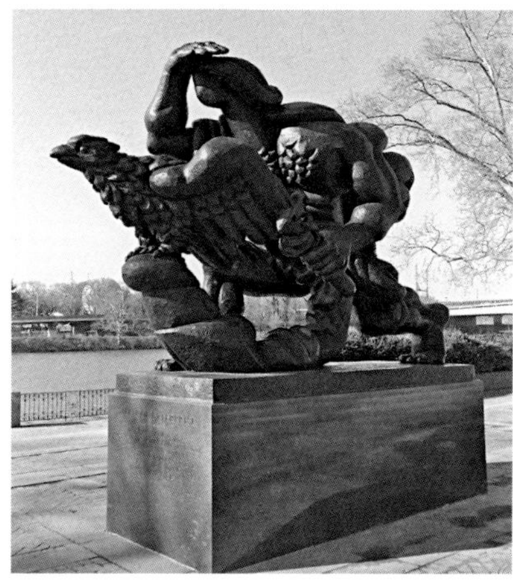

Fig. 64
Jacques Lipchitz
The Spirit of Enterprise, 1950–60
Bronze on granite base, H. 345 cm, L. 487.5 cm
Fairmount Park, Philadelphia
Courtesy of the Association for Public Art (photographer Howard Brunner © 1992)

45 Letter from Epstein to Kathleen, "Wednesday" [8, 15 or 22] August 1951; NAGW–BL/1/3/2/11. Order of passages altered.

46 Information from http://www.fpaa.org/child/map_45_lip_spi.html.

87
Social Consciousness, 1952–53
Bronze, H. 371 cm (maximum)
Courtesy of the Philadelphia Museum of Art, West Terrace

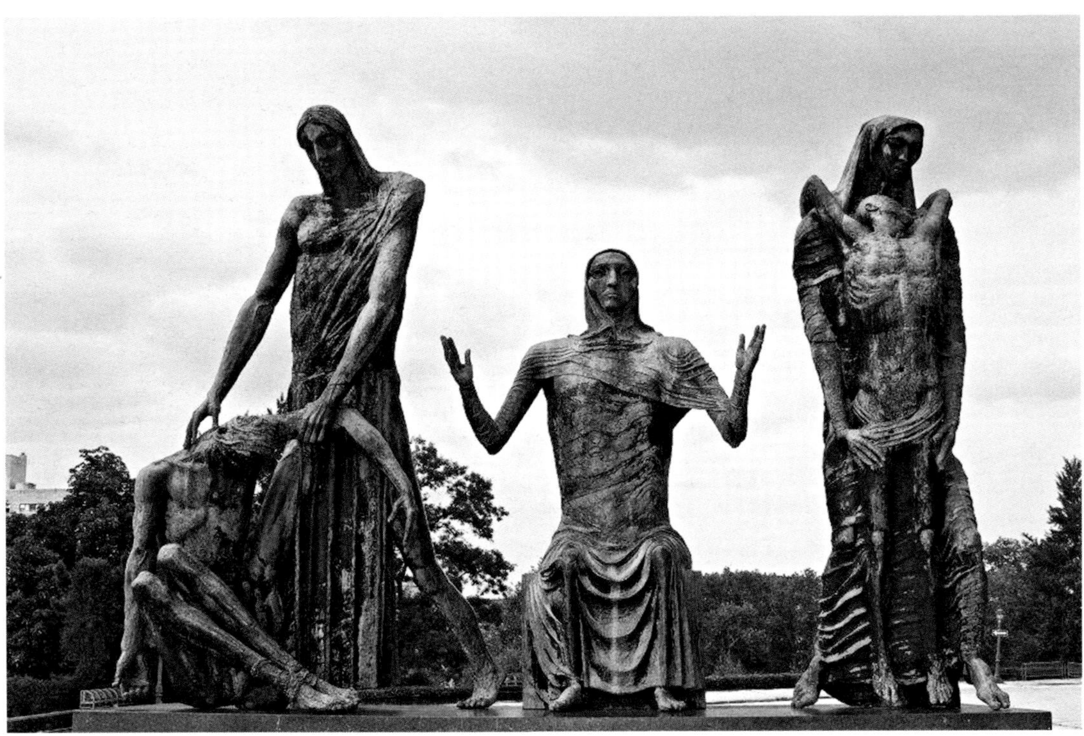

idea perhaps in the same room that I'm in. I'm told [Edith] Sitwell was disliked when lecturing here. It seemed to the Americans that she 'looked down her nose' at them." And he does not forget his family: "When I get to N.Y. I will wire Peggy Jean and make some arrangements to go down to Haterras. N.Y. is too oppressively hot to stay and I will get as much bathing in the sea as I can get .... Tell me how Kitty and Esther are and I will send a note to [Roland?] Joffe. Don't forget Epstein and don't think harshly about him."

Work on the final design did not start until late 1952 and, to accommodate the huge scale of the sculptures – a height of about ten feet for the central one and 12–13 feet for the flanking figures[47] – the Royal College of Art lent Epstein a studio, where he began work in November. The work process was followed by the photographer Geoffrey Ireland and published in a book.[48]

Epstein's works (alternative titles in parentheses) were intended to express "the human and compassionate side of the group" and "to bring the three parts into a coordinated whole".[49] Ultimately, however, the viewer encounters a composition of three separate entities. To the viewer's left is a group of two figures called *The Great Consoler* (or *Compassion*) – a standing Good Samaritan supporting a naked fallen man, as Buckle describes them. The central figure, *The Eternal Mother* (or *Destiny*), is a woman seated on a stone stool with her hands raised as if pleading. To the right is another female figure – previously intended to represent Death – who, as her current title, *Succor*, indicates, assists the frontal figure of a young, lifeless male, whose arms fold around her neck and whose hands helplessly hang down her back [87]. There is little novelty in the execution of these figures, as Epstein seems to have returned to previous poses and elements [88a–b]. The man's pose, with arms outstretched and drapery folds at the back, echoes that of *Lucifer*; the front folds of the skirt of the central seated woman display the same horizontal strips as in *Madonna and Child* (1927) and also in the carved version of a seated

47 Letter from Epstein to Ingersoll, 14 March 1952: FPA.

48 Ireland, *Epstein 1956*.

49 Letter from Epstein to Noble, 18 April 1952: FPA.

woman in *Night* (1929). The standing woman seems to reflect a development of his latest *Madonna and Child*, as if the protective mother of the child now has to contend with his end; her head is the same, modelled on Marcella Barzetti; her hands similarly convey the dependence of what could be the adolescent Jesus; and the toes of both figures are downward-pointing, almost floating. All three plasters were ready by September 1953, and the cast was completed in February 1955.

Epstein, however, could not escape the shadow cast by Lipchitz's intended work, which today dominates the central terrace. Worried that the scale of Epstein's sculpture "would not balance" Lipchitz's more compact composition, the committee planned to install Epstein's group on the terrace above East River Drive. As Lipchitz's group – begun anew after the fire – was not ready, *Social Consciousness* was installed on the west terrace of the Museum of Art.[50] This location allows the viewer, walking around it, to see the rough treatment of details of all three figures, which leaves one to wonder whether the group might not have been better placed in a spacious park and viewed from afar.

Epstein, who attended the unveiling on March 1955 and saw it temporarily placed on a wooden plinth, was nonetheless pleased with its location. This is the only work that Epstein executed in America and for his 'America', whose social attitude was so different from his own. His awareness of this brought to a closure his intellectual debt to the great American poet who had influenced him in his youth (I/22–23). In 1972 the wooden plinth was replaced by a stone one (538 × 252 cm) and, according to Epstein's wish (PS/237), inscribed:

> A *grand, sane, towering, seated* Mother,
> I *Chair'd in the adamant of* Time.
>
> *Walt Whitman, America*

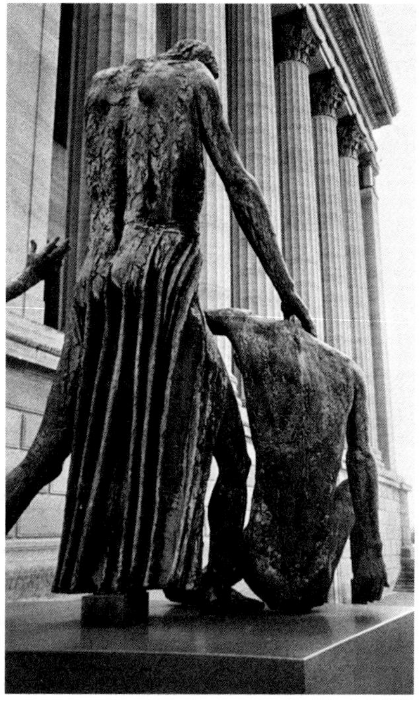

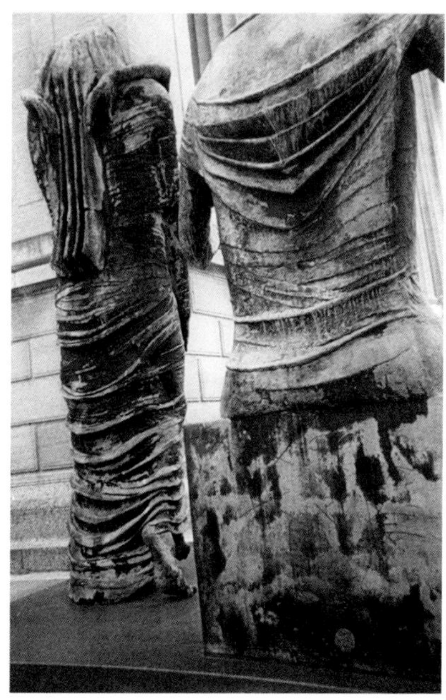

88
Social Consciousness (details)

THE BEST AND THE WORST OF TIMES

During 1952–53, apart from his commissions, there were other problems and issues to deal with. In January 1952, having had to reject orders for the portraits that were usually his bread and butter, Epstein had written to Peggy Jean: "Here lots of things are happening. The New Year I got an Internal Revenue bill for £1500. This must pay by succeeding installments of £500 each."[51] On top of that was the cost of Jackie's buying himself another car, "second hand but a good make, so he raced into a taxi. I have to pay £12 for the damage. There seems to be endless trouble with car involved insurances etc."

In March he wrote to her about the intended exhibition of his work at the Tate from September to November. His continuing animosity toward Moore's milieu is articulated in words that he was probably careful not to utter in public. He had discussed the exhibition "with Rothenstein, now Sir John! And you can imagine how agreeable it is to have to deal with the old hypocrite."[52] Epstein was nonetheless delighted to have his work exhibited at the institution that had previously rejected all of his large works. Before the opening he wrote to Rothenstein how happy he was that the occasion necessitated giving *Visitation* (of 1925; usually kept in the Tate cellars) "a brush up".[53] However, his suspicion that there was a lack of good will from the Tate was not allayed, and

50 The issue is eloquently summarized in Silber, *Sculpture of Epstein*, p. 312.

51 Letter from Epstein to Peggy Jean, 24 January 1952: TGA-8716/24.

52 Letter from Epstein to Peggy Jean, 8 March 1952: TGA-8716/23.

53 Letter from Epstein to Rothenstein, 1 September 1952: TGA-8726/3/10.

during the exhibition he reported to Peggy Jean on its success despite "the hostility of Rothenstein the director" and also of "the Arts Council, although they have arranged the show [who] are equally unfriendly and were really forced into holding the show as they had exhausted the interest in Moore and co. and everyone here was completely fed up with the 'abstractionists'."[54]

Following the opening of the exhibition, Matthew Smith gave a dinner party for Epstein at his favourite restaurant, the Caprice. According to Kathleen, "Smith loved a celebration, and festive meetings with him were apt always to become little festivals of paintings and wine-drinking".[55] In his letter to Peggy Jean Epstein added about the exhibition: "The critics have had to pay me some kind recognition,[56] forced out them as you can see by [life force?] in the *Lucifer*". He had not, on the other hand, "been spared by the scribbling hostilities [in] support [of] the Kenneth Clark & co [attitude]".[57] A critique published in *Apollo* praised his bronzes at the expense of carving, arguing that the exhibition presented Epstein

> primarily as a modeller – which might be the right evaluation … the expressive hands are as remarkable as they are contrary to 'sculptural' ideas.
>
> Epstein had suffered from the complete domination of theories other than his own during the period of his maturity as an artist. Meantime he has gone on being Epstein; and now that the early abstractionists have gone too far, there seems a chance that Epstein's integrity will serve him best.[58]

Although Epstein's artistic integrity had certainly kept him from succumbing to the modern trends of his time, it had also caused him, I suggest, to frown upon and judge for the worse the advantages that new forms, expressing personal yearnings and nightmares, had opened up for the impending era of 'visual culture'. This post-modern tendency to visualize all sorts of existence was to replace Epstein's era of 'visual art' – the tradition of visualizing mainly literary subjects.[59] Like a Don Quixote fighting his windmills, Epstein felt he had to fight against the very concrete issue of 'the modern' that threatened his artistic world. In 1952 he wrote: "I have recorded & broadcast on [the radio to] be heard next Sunday. They will be about the 'modern' movement in sculpture and I haven't held any pinnacles [pulled any punches] …. I wonder what the reaction will be."[60] His views were also recorded in a television programme:[61]

> The human side is totally neglected and forgotten, and my idea had always been to express human ideas and aspirations. Mechanical forms are all right on motorcars and aeroplanes, in dynamo and machinery of all sorts. But I cannot see why those forms should be repeated in sculpture or in painting.
>
> The human spirit is not confined to mechanism [mechanical] apparatus. I would say that sculpture involves the relation of masses but there must be thought and motivation if it is not mere exercise.
>
> I have never tried to create purely abstract forms. I want greater richness and meaning instead of impoverished invented forms. And there must be generating force or something in a work of art; not a mere exercise.
>
> What I most deplore is the loss of any deep human feeling. I come back to this, and I feel that my long experience and practice justify me in protesting.

54 Letter from Epstein to Peggy Jean, 8 March 1952: TGA-8716-23.

55 Letter from Kathleen to Peter Jones, assistant director of the Art Council, Welsh Committee, 22 May 1966: NAGW–EA/1/1/2. The letter contained a brief paragraph she wrote for Matthew Smith's exhibition catalogue.

56 See, for example, Pierre Jeannerat, 'Epstein's Final Triumph, Official Approval at 72', *The Daily Mail*, 25 September 1952.

57 Letter from Epstein to Peggy Jean, 8 March 1952, TGA-8716/23.

58 'Current Shows', *Apollo*, November 1952, p. 136.

59 The above very brief definition is based on 'What is Visual Culture?' in Mirzoef, *The Visual Culture Reader*. As the trend was yet to arrive it is outside the scope of Epstein's life and also outside the scope of this book. However, I felt that a brief explanation of Epstein's inability to open up to new tendencies (not uncommon among ageing people, set in their ways) was pertinent.

60 Letter from Epstein to Peggy Jean, 8 March 1952: TGA-8716/23.

61 BBC television programme *Monitor*, first broadcast 2 February 1958 (http://www.bbc.co.uk/archive/sculptors/12813.shtml). The date of the broadcast does not conform to that in a letter written by Epstein to his daughter in 1953–54, while he was working on his American commission *Social Consciousness*. To my question whether there was a previous recording the reply was negative, as the "production file for this episode of Monitor has not been retained. It is likely that this would have been the only place that a full version of the interview would be": Jessica Hogg, Archives Researcher, BBC Written Archives Centre, January 2012.

Another unpleasant altercation with Sir John Rothenstein occurred in 1952, this time not of Rothenstein's making. A reporter writing about Rothenstein's visiting Epstein's studio with his daughter Lucy fabricated a story, claiming that Lucy "joins the Star-studded Gallery of Epstein's heads",[62] and hinting that Kathleen was to be replaced by a younger model. Epstein was furious and an apologetic Rothenstein had to explain that he had no hand in this.[63] Epstein's hostility towards Rothenstein continued and, in a later letter to Peggy Jean, in which he mentions the threat of the rising water of the Thames to the Tate's basement, he commented, "it would have been no loss if the recent acquisitions [of mainly abstract art] had got drowned including the precious director".[64]

Epstein's exhibition at the Tate drew a crowd of 70,000 and, as Buckle somewhat sarcastically commented, "the show resulted in a purchase for the Gallery of a small bust made over 40 years ago (*Mrs McEvoy*)".[65]

By the end of 1952 Epstein had made nine portraits, six of them private commissions and the rest for public bodies. His public portraits included a notable number of people who had died, these commissions being characterized by a prolonged period between the decision and the signing of a contract. For example, after discussing and choosing a sculptor, on 23 April 1953 the Field Marshal Smuts Memorial Committee met and agreed that Epstein be appointed, for a fee of £10,000,[66] to model a full-length figure of the South African Prime Minister, to be placed on a pedestal in London's Parliament Square. He was given photographs and full freedom of expression. Epstein told his son-in-law, Norman Hornstein (Peggy Jean's husband), in a letter that it might be years before he could get started, as after seven months of deliberation by the committee there was still only the announcement "Nothing is decided", despite his having of his own accord "made a sketch of my monument & have also worked on a head in scale". He discusses somewhat sarcastically how he should present Smuts:[67]

> To start with I was asked to do Smuts in uniform, at the same time showing him as a great statesman, also as a great author & vice chancellor of universities! A tall order.
>
> Now it seems not even this site [Parliament square] is certain. Also I will be confined to showing the great field Marshall only as a great statesman. In what costume? Evening clothes? No one can tell me yet [as] Parliament members have gone off on their holidays; the sculptor is left without a contract & with no funds[,] which have to be voted by Parliament.

Every commission by a public body involved a politics of negotiation that is usually beyond the scope of this book. In this case, however, the delay of the contract affected Epstein's financial situation, particularly as his show at the Leicester Galleries in June 1953 "was not a success .... If it wasn't for two American girls who had their portraits made I would have been on the rocks."[68]

The completed work of Smuts was cast in 1955,[69] and was therefore probably started in 1954. David McFall had cast it as light as possible in order to transport it. "We had to get the big head of Smuts over to my studio for casting," recalled McFall, "and we all but lost it in the shifting around. The plaster was knocked over and shattered into fragments, Epstein complained that I had made it eggshell thin."[70] The interest in this

62 Eve Chapman, *Daily Mail*, 13 October 1952.

63 Lucy (née Rothenstein) in a conversation with the author, 1989.

64 Letter from Epstein to Peggy Jean, 25 February 1953: TGA-8716/28.

65 Buckle, *Epstein: Sculptor*, p. 357.

66 Information on the subject is taken from a file of the Memorial Committee (WORK 20/222) containing some black-and-white photographs, including some of the work of the South African sculptor Coert Steynberg, who had been considered as a potential sculptor. See http://yourarchives.nationalarchives.gov.uk/index.

67 Letter from Epstein to Hornstein, 22 July 1953: TGA-993/13.

68 Letter from Epstein to Hornstein, 22 July 1953: TGA-993/13.

69 Silber, *Sculpture of Epstein*, no. 483.

70 McFall, p. 11.

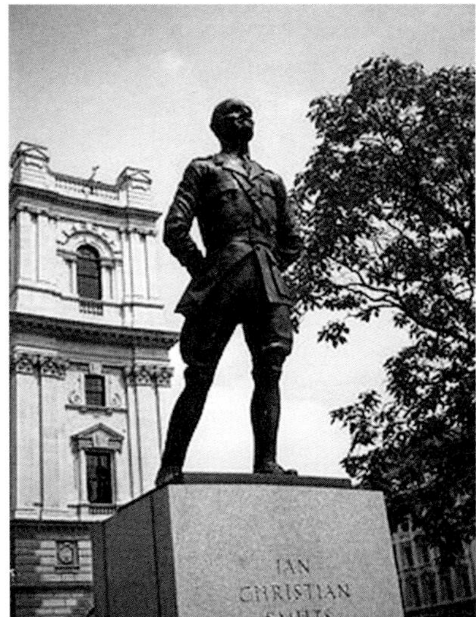

89
Field Marshal John Smuts, 1953–55
Bronze, over life-size
Parliament Square, London

particular portrait lies in its full-length figure [89], as, except for that of Kathleen [65], none of his commissioned portraits had been presented in such full or in such realistic detail. However, the slight forward inclination of Kathleen's figure acquires in the *Smuts* a greater one, to the extent that it was nicknamed 'the Skater'. The stone plinth of South African granite arrived in early 1956, and David McFall was called upon to carve the lettering.[71] The unveiling on 7 November 1956 was performed by the Speaker, as Churchill was occupied with the events of the Suez Canal. It is noteworthy that Churchill's own official statue, by Ivor Roberts-Jones, commissioned much later on behalf of the government and erected in Parliament Square in 1973, has an 'Epsteinish' movement unlike the stiff poses of the other dignitaries occupying the square.

In May 1953, while Epstein was preoccupied with the Smuts project, Wilson Parker and A.J.J. Ayres of the Royal Society of British Sculptors proposed to award him a Gold Medal for distinguished services to sculpture. Epstein, remembering his application for membership having being refused "many years ago,"[72] during a period in which he had needed support, turned it down, saying "they had waited too long".[73] Epstein was also preoccupied at the time with Jackie's ear problems and the order that he should report for military service. All in all, he had so much on his plate that he failed to reply or even to think about the subjects that his son-in-law Hornstein had raised: "I hope someday to be able to turn my thoughts & time to *Venus* [1915; I/118]. At the moment that seems altogether out of the question."[74]

During this period an honorary degree was bestowed on him: "The DCI conferred on me at Oxford was a great occasion" (fig. 65). The pleasant event on 22 June, at which the degree was bestowed on him by the Vice-Chancellor of Oxford University Sir Maurice Bowra,[75] was followed by a laudation of the carvings and portraits of this "artist of rich innovation". Three days later, somewhat amused by some of the other recipients of honours, he wrote to Hornstein:

> You see me in the company of the abhorred Morrison & still more horrible Maxwell-Fife [David Maxwell Fyfe], who recently sent a young man to the scaffold because he was in the company of a burglar who shot a policeman. Maxwell-Fife's face was like a large piece of solid lead with consistency of a pudding. I'm glad it is all over.[76]

A month later he let Peggy Jean know that, because of his work load, he would not be able to come in July for his annual holiday visit.[77]

An uneasy period in Epstein and Kathleen's life had started with a happy arrival – that of Annabel, a new granddaughter born to Kitty and Lucien Freud. Her birth, however, had been followed almost immediately by the break-up of the Freuds' marriage, caused by Lucien's affairs with other women (including the art student Katherine McAdam, who had been his daughter's babysitter, and with whom he fathered four children over the following years). In 1953 the couple divorced and Freud immediately married Lady Caroline Blackwood. Kitty came to live at Hyde Park Gate, leaving there for good after her marriage to Wayne Godley in 1957.

Kitty remembers Epstein sitting at a table laden with African effigies, holding them between his fingers as if to absorb forms and movements, hardly speaking. Their warm relationship and his paternal interest were misrepresented by Aunt Sylvia: "Kitty was

71 Rodney Sidon's addition from the diaries in an email of 31 August 2011 to the author: "David McFall did the inscriptions on Sir Stafford Cripps' bust (1954/4), Mrs Epstein's headstone (1956/10) and the Smuts statue (1956/11)".

72 Epstein wrote (I/ 57–58) that he was nominated by Harvard Thomas for membership of the RSBS (1908–09) and rejected. The Society officially represents British sculptors; thus "Jacob Epstein, who became a naturalized British citizen in 1911, could not become a member of the Society of British Sculptors unless the Council Members decided to grant him an Honorary Membership", explained Dr Emmanuel Minne (RBS archivist and art historian, 21 May 2006). This may also explain why the society has no records of the event, as from the outset full membership was not possible. The Society of British Sculptors became the Royal Society of British Sculptors in 1911.

73 Gardiner, *Epstein*, p. 441.

74 Letter from Epstein to Hornstein, 26 June 1953: TGA-993/12.

75 Gardiner, *Epstein*, p. 444.

76 Letter from Epstein to Hornstein, 26 June 1953, TGA-993/12. I cannot identify the company members noted by Epstein.

77 Letter from Epstein to Peggy Jean, 22 July 1953. TGA-993/13.

very extravagant – she used to run up big department-store bills, but Jacob always indulged her – whatever she wanted".[78] These "department-store bills", however, were mainly for food and clothing for her babies, and the expense (perhaps unknown to Sylvia) of consultation fees to doctors for her mental stress.[79] While she and her babies were living under his roof, Epstein had the opportunity and pleasure to sculpt her little daughters Anna and Annabel.[80] He evidently managed to draw inspiration for his sculpture from whatever troubles his private life presented, an ability that would sustain him as an artist during the impending woes.

October 1953 was a typical month in Epstein's life, with a mixture of good and bad news. The bad was an unpleasant reminder of the fate of his large carvings that had gone to Blackpool and were now being offered for sale. A note on the intended sale appeared in *The Times* and there are many references to the issue, of which I cite a particularly upsetting (or ironically amusing) one, published in America, the last line of which probably rubbed salt in Epstein's wounds:[81]

> Sandwiched between 'Fine Chippendale' and 'French Books' in the London *Times* last week was an ad that was enough to make an old sculptor turn in his chisel. The ad: 'Epstein's masterpieces. *Adam, Jacob and the Angel, Consummatum Est*, For Sale. Offers Wanted.' The statues were three of Jacob Epstein's most famous works: a hulking, dumbly defiant alabaster giant that makes the first man look scarcely human; a muscle-bound Jacob hugging a brutish-looking angel; and a recumbent, mummy like figure of Christ, with crude but powerfully eloquent hands upturned in protest.
>
> The three sculptures, along with a gracefully sprawling nude called *Eve*, had moved from owner to owner till they came to rest at a side show at Blackpool,[80] a more sedate version of Coney Island, full of slot machines, peep shows and freaks.
>
> The Epsteins used to draw up to $4,000 a week, but when receipts fell off, the owner decided to sell out.

The other distressing news was that of the death of Muirhead Bone (fig. 66) on 21 October 1953. Bone had been Epstein's friend since his arrival in London in the mid 1910s, and had remained his supporter throughout the hard times with both the Hudson Memorial (*Rima*) in the mid 1920s and the BMA decorations in the mid 1930s. I have not found evidence of their continuing contact but I have not found any derogatory comments from either of them, despite their disagreements during the late 1930s (p. 102).[82]

In 1953 Epstein made twelve portraits. One was of his dog Frisky but the rest were commissions, making it quite a good year from a financial point of view. In addition to sales in London, he also attempted to sell abroad through his brother Irving, who, after the death of his supportive older brother Lois, had taken over Epstein's interests. An article in *The New Yorker* 'Talk of the Town' made a point of this while reporting on his coming exhibition: "Talk story about Jacob Epstein, an English sculptor, whose bronzes are on display in the office of his brother, Dr Irving Epstein, who sells them for him".[83] During 1954 Epstein was living and working amidst various family disasters. The year,

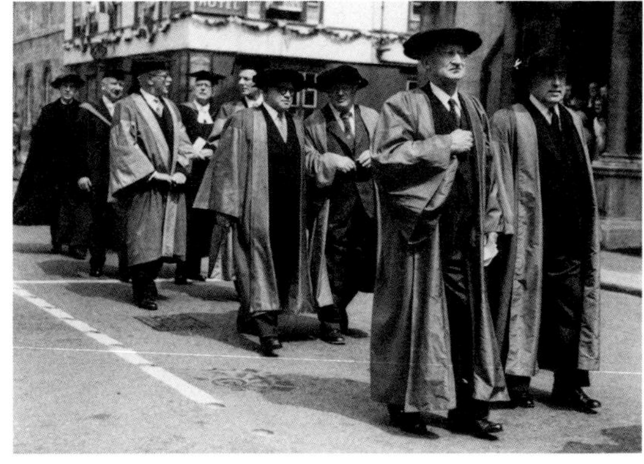

Fig. 65
Jacob Epstein (third from right) amidst the procession of Ph.D candidates, Oxford, 1953

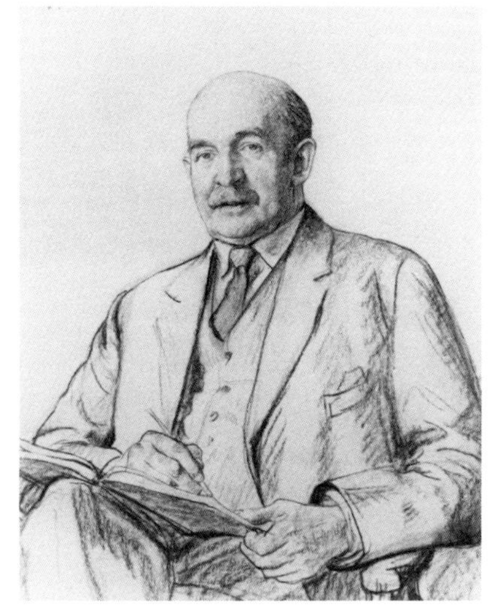

Fig. 66
Francis Dod
Muirhead Bone, 1931
Chalk, 37.8 x 27.9 cm
National Portrait Gallery, London

78 Babson, *The Epsteins*, p. 58.

79 Kitty's response to a draft given by the author for her comment.

80 Silber, *Sculpture of Epstein*, no. 453.

81 'Art: The Reward of Adam', *Time*, 12 October 1953. See http://www.time.com/time/magazine/article/0,9171,860068,00.html#ixzz1PB5CMu73. In early 1954 the three carvings were purchased by the town's Louis Tussaud's Waxworks. Joined by the artist's earlier work *Genesis* (1931) in 1958, they were kept by Tussaud as long as they drew crowds.

82 Unfortunately, this is the only tribute I can pay to Epstein's constant supporter. Bone's unsorted archive is with his son Quentin Bone, awaiting another researcher.

83 G.T. Hellman, 'The Talk of the Town: Jacob and Irving', *The New Yorker*, 16 May 1953, p. 24.

like the previous one, had started well. After the announcement of the 1954 New Year's Honours List, Epstein received a letter in a brown envelope that he nearly failed to open, thinking it was a tax bill.[84] The letter announced his award of a knighthood from the Queen, an investiture set for 16 February 1954. Epstein immediately wrote to Peggy Jean about it,[85] mentioning that the Queen would be away and the Queen Mother was to replace her. He wonders if a dark lounge suit would be correct, adding: "Thank Goodness no top hat and rubbish of that sort". His good friend Matthew Smith also received a knighthood.

On the same day he wrote to Hornstein about Jackie's conscription.[86] Epstein appealed to his doctor son-in law to provide a certificate of his defective hearing, which Hornstein did. In his next letter Epstein mentions that Jackie "is to have a further test for his ear soon", adding, with fatherly concern: "For Jackie the whole thing is most upsetting", causing him stress that "is the limit anyone is allowed. If he is taken into the army I don't know quite how he will react to it. With his freedom gone & under order, it is impossible to know how he will take it." Finally he adds:

> What [for] the ordinary boy would be taken perhaps as a matter of course would be taken differently by someone who is as 'spoilt' as Jackie is. His activities for the past 2 years [are] something extraordinary & I don't think you would approve of it for a moment .... As well he is a reckless driver.

These letters of January to Peggy Jean and Hornstein were written and sent just two days before the death of Epstein's eldest son Theo. On 22 January Theo's Chelsea art school had apparently misunderstood as theft his borrowing of a sculpture for his paintings, and sent the police round to fetch him. In order to avoid his arrest, with which his fragile mental condition would not have coped, Kathleen had arranged for an ambulance to take him to hospital. Theo, unaware of what was going on, struggled against his enforced hospitalization and, while trying to escape from some male nurses, suffered a fatal heart attack.[87]

On Epstein's feelings one can only speculate, as it was not until late in the year that he mentioned the event "that was too terrible" to Peggy Jean.[88] To this period, perhaps, belongs his undated letter to the ailing Meum, Peggy Jean's biological mother, who from her hospital bed had congratulated him. "I don't want honours, you know that," he replied, and toward the end of his letter – "I never thought I would be as lonely as I am" [I/154].

Epstein attended the investiture on 16 February 1954 with Esther, as Kathleen was too distressed to attend. The event was filmed and included in a documentary, *Rebel Angel*, showing him with his tall, beautiful daughter, who resembled her mother in her delicate figure and height. Both were taller than Epstein.

It is of little wonder that he had no patience for the people who bothered him during this period. "He was not the easiest of men to get on with," commented James Laver, who had been asked by the BBC to do a broadcast on Epstein's work when he received his knighthood. "I was so anxious to say what he wanted said, that I took my script to his studio and asked him to check it. After it had been broadcast I telephoned to ask if he had heard it. 'Yes'. And did you like it? 'No'."[89]

84 Haskell, *Balletomane at Large*, p. 61.

85 Letter from Epstein to Peggy Jean, 20 January 1954: TGA-8716.30.

86 Letter from Epstein to Hornstein, 20 January 1954: TGA-8716.33

87 Gardiner, *Epstein*, p. 447.

88 Letter from Epstein to Peggy Jean, 13 November 1954: TGA-8716.35.

89 Laver, *Museum Piece*, p. 236.

Epstein submerged himself in his work and, while waiting for the casting of his commissioned works to be finished, he did portraits – five commissions altogether – and thus had the funds needed to expand his collection. On 6 July he acquired at Sotheby's a rare Sumerian statuette of a standing woman in prayer, made of zinc during the Third Dynasty of Ur.[90] The money was also needed now for other purposes, as Kathleen was sending money to help her sister Helen in Italy.[91] Theo's shocking death added to the already fragile mental equilibrium among the Garmans, and an added shadow was cast by Esther's relations with Marc Joffe.[92] Whether for reasons related to Theo's death or not, Joffe left her, and Esther, with young Roland, came to live with the Epsteins. During the same period there was yet another sad event, when a student friend committed suicide because Esther had refused to marry him. A bleak mood descended on them all. As a distressed Kathleen was unable to go to Italy to help her sister Helen, Esther went in July instead, staying with their old friends the Vivantes (p. 160) and touring Italy, intending to return in September. The Vivante girls, she wrote, naively pestered her about her family relations, "convinced that Anne and Annabel and Roland all belong to me – 'And had Roland got a Daddy?' Yes. 'Why didn't he come to Rome?' Because he is busy. 'Yes of course, busy looking after Anne and Annabel'." Esther added a remark on the "complications in the tangle of relationships" in her family.[92]

Epstein's complexed attitude to people also arises in Esther's letter, when she reports on the arrival of a family from St John's Wood at the home of her Italian painter friend, "a Jewish art dealer with wife and grown up son and daughter … [who] for some reason hated me. I can only suspect that Epstein at some time or another had been rude to the Gallery, and I'm certain that he must thoroughly have upset their sense of propriety … they left the place mortified at finding what they obviously regarded as 'a bit of Chelsea' waiting for them in the bosom of this charming Italian family."[94]

Esther returned home, writing on 10 September to Joffe, who had been reproaching her: "I cannot say I read your letters with great enjoyment". Shortly after, Esther attempted to commit suicide, but was found in time and hospitalized. She wrote to Kathleen saying she felt much better, probably after she had had a long talk with Dr McDonald: "At least I am up today and perhaps they will decide on some treatment". She found the place to be "lovely and quiet there and nurses are sweet and kind …. There seems to be plenty to do here. Drawing classes, basket making, weaving etc. etc."[95] Her adaptation to life after leaving the hospital seemed to have started well, when she took a job at a bookshop and moved into her own place. But on 1 October, "in the first night out in her new room she gassed herself", Epstein wrote to Peggy Jean six week later, finding only then the mental strength to write about his double loss, of Theo and of "Esther, who was so beautiful and well loved by all".[96] Esther was buried close to Theo in Harting, the village in which she had been raised by nanny Ada Newbould, and where all the Garman children had spent the war years.

Within six months Epstein and Kathleen had lost two of their children. Seventy-four years old and scarred by professional and personal hardships, Epstein had his work to plunge into – four large projects were discussed towards the end of 1953, commissioned during 1954 and executed over the next two years.

Kathleen was, to some extent, left to herself. "After her two children's deaths, Lady Epstein converted to Catholicism," wrote Epstein's sister, summing up the issue.[97]

90 Gardiner, *Epstein*, p. 450.

91 Gardiner, *Epstein*, p. 451.

92 On Theo and Esther, see 'Appendix' in Connolly, *The Rare and the Beautiful*.

93 Letter from Esther to Kathleen, postal date 5 July 1954: NAGW–BL/1/3/5/5.

94 Ibid.

95 Letter from Esther to Kathleen (September 1954, after her return from Italy and hospitalization): NAGW–BL/1/3/5/13.

96 Letter from Epstein to Peggy Jean, 13 November 1954: TGA-8716.35

97 Babson, *The Epsteins*, p. 58. Her sister Mary (with her poet husband Roy Campbell) had converted to Catholicism in the early 1930s, and several others of the artistic milieu did the same during the 1950s (John Rothenstein, for example).

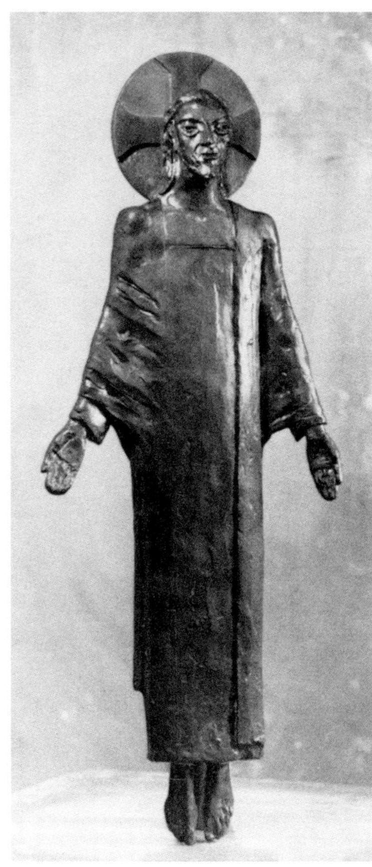

90
Christ in Majesty (maquette), 1954–55
Aluminium, H. 63.5 cm
Private collection

Catholicism could be conceived as a more demanding doctrine than the 'lighter' Christian denominations of Anglicanism or Protestantism. One might ask, therefore, why Kathleen took this step, and how – if at all – it influenced life and work in Epstein's household. The reason, perhaps in addition to the intellectual influence exerted on her by her friend T.S. Eliot,[98] seems to be the aspect of consolation inherent within the Catholic doctrine, namely, the Sacrament of Penance. The intent of this sacrament, which involves confession, is to provide healing for the soul through absolution (forgiveness) mediated by a priest, and so regain the Grace of God lost by sin. Kathleen was probably in great need of this kind of comfort, whereas the secular Jewish Epstein had his work to sustain his spirit. Both found their own ways of engaging with religion, but only up to a point. In spite of his work on Christian subjects, Epstein did not convert to any form of Christianity, and the only Catholic influence on their daily life that I have been able to trace was abstention from eating meat on Fridays.[99] Epstein accompanied Kathleen to Christmas Mass because he loved the music, and this was the only period in which the Jewish national symbol, the Temple Menora (seven-branched candelabrum), in their entrance hall was lit.[100]

THE GREAT PUBLIC WORKS: FIRST STAGE

I. *MAJESTAS*

A common denominator of most of Epstein's late projects is that their commission was raised in 1953–54, work on them was begun in 1954–55 and they were completed in 1955–57, some of them being in hand at the same time. Their uneven timetable, often affected by Epstein's personal affairs and smaller commissions, necessitates discussing them in a somewhat arbitrary sequence, determined by the approximate starting date of each project, the first of which was *Christ in Majesty*.

In October 1953 the architect George Pace, who had been charged with the restoration of the war-damaged cathedral in Llandaff, commissioned Epstein to decorate its new cylindrical organ-loft with a figure of Christ in Majesty. It was originally intended to be in gilded plaster, but in the end they both agreed that the sculpture should be cast in aluminium, which would be lighter on the structure of the giant arch supporting the cylinder and possessed "far greater durability, and would also have the soft silvery colour", which was in better accord with the building.[101]

The maquette [90] and the final sculpture repeat several elements of *Madonna and Child* – the down-pointing toes that do not require a horizontal stand and, more importantly, the downwardly open palms of the grown man echoing the hands of the mother when he was a child. Christ in Majesty (*Majestas*) in the Western Christian tradition is usually presented seated on a throne with a book in his left hand, and two raised fingers.[102] The downward hands of Epstein's free-standing Christ may derive from the figures of Romanesque church façades such as one on the central tympanum of Abbey of Vézelay (fig. 67). Epstein's Christ is a similarly stiff figure that has to be viewed from below; the face is therefore the only part in the sculpture with accentuated, detailed features [91].

98 According to his preface to *For Lancelot Andrewes: Essays on Style and Order* (1929), Eliot regarded himself as Anglo-Catholic in religion.

99 Spence, *Phoenix at Coventry*, p. 70.

100 Jackie in conversation with the author, apparently unaware of the nearby Jewish festival of Hanukah in which candles are lit. He added that Kathleen was careful to keep religion out of the house, but made no comment when he saw (in the preliminary draft I gave him) my mention of his aunt Sylvia's remarks on Kathleen's Catholicism or on Jackie's choice of a Catholic wife for himself.

101 Silber, *Sculpture of Epstein*, no. 475.

102 Seen in abundance in manuscripts. See, for example, the *Christ in Majesty* in the Westminster Psalter, 1200, British Library, MS Royal 2 A XXII. The gesture of Christ's right hand is not the gesture of blessing, but an "orator's gesture".

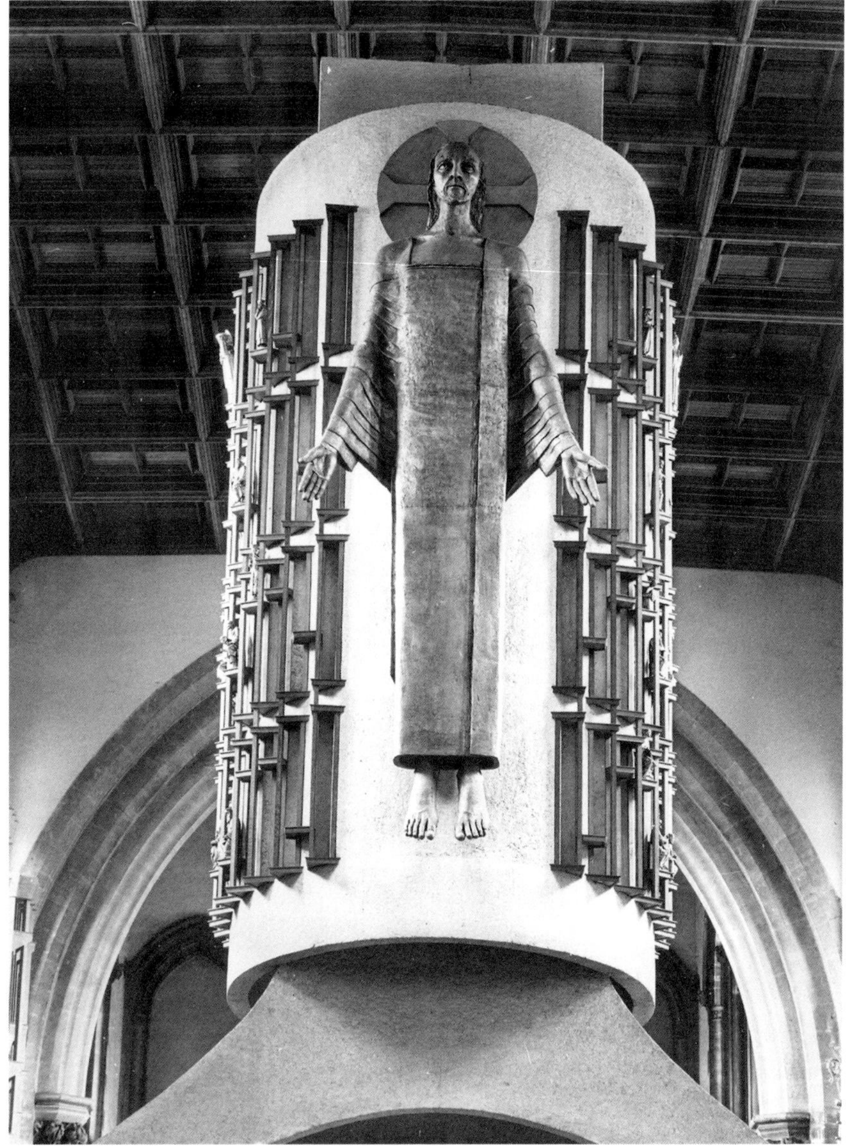

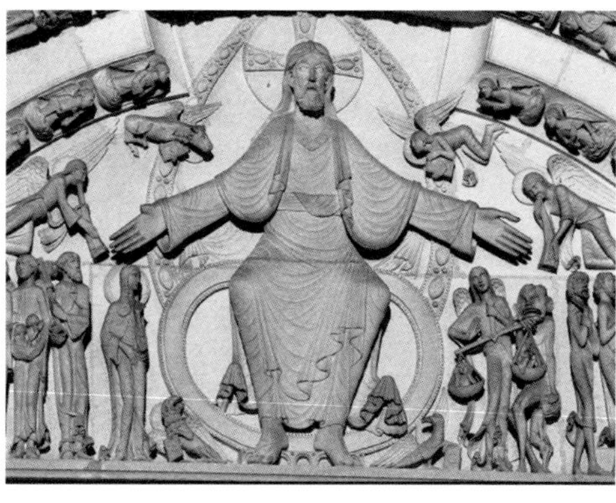

Fig. 67
Central tympanum of the façade, Abbatiale de Vézelay, Burgundy

91
Christ in Majesty, 1954–55
Aluminium, H. 430 cm
Courtesy of Llandaff Cathedral

The treatment of Christ's robe is unique, and I have found no similar sculptural pre cedent. It differs from Epstein's previous figures in its lack of folds, thus corresponding to the nearby flat arch and acquiring the simplicity of a modern flat architectural pilaster; the only signs of low-relief folds are in the sleeves, accentuating the plain surfaces around it. Surprisingly, Buckle (who could have discussed it with Kathleen) does not comment on the face of the figure. On whom was it modelled? Studying the portraits done by Epstein at the time, I venture to suggest that he drew on the features of the Labour Member of Parliament Sir Stafford Cripps [92], accentuating the cheek-bones and sharpening the nose but featuring the same high forehead and receding hair, combed back, and retaining Cripps's upright posture [93]. If this indeed is the case, then Epstein would have managed to intimate his socialist beliefs through the features of the socialist statesman.[103] (Jesus, as may be deduced from the Gospels, was himself a social reformer.)

The actual work seems to have started in mid 1954, soon after Epstein had finished the bust of Cripps, commissioned in late 1953. Upon completing the bust in March 1954,

103 Sir Richard Stafford Cripps (1889–1952) was a British Labour politician, and between 1947 and 1950 the Chancellor of the Exchequer. In this position, Cripps was responsible for laying the foundations of Britain's post-war economic prosperity.

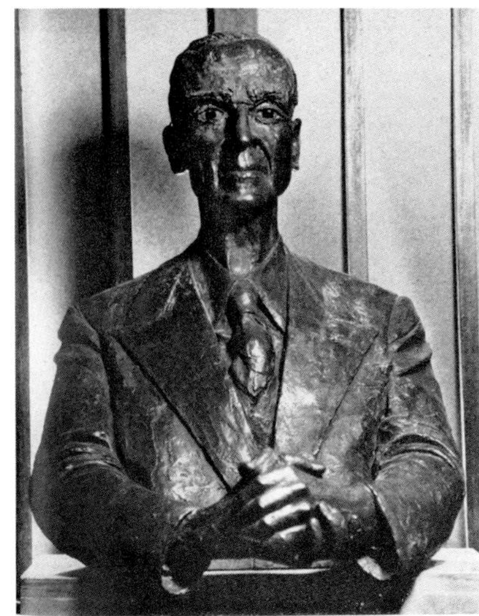

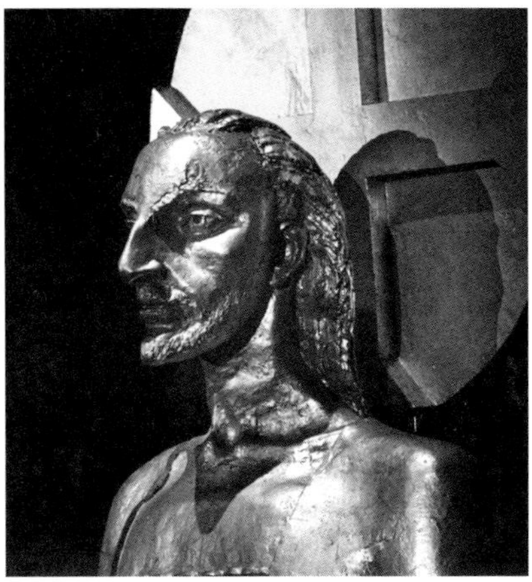

92
Sir Stafford Cripps, 1954 [1953]
Bronze, life size
St Paul's Cathedral, London

93
Christ in Majesty, 1954–55 (detail)

he contacted his letter-carver and moulder David McFall, requesting him to carve an inscription on the pedestal.[104] McFall's diaries indicate that on 5 May 1954 he went with Epstein to St Paul's Cathedral to look at the crypt where it would stand. The inscription, *If man neglects the things of the spirit and puts aside the full armour of God, he will seal the doom of future generations*,[105] was carved in Epstein's studio and, when completed, the statue was installed in the cathedral and unveiled on 28 May 1954.

This collaboration seems to have renewed the professional contact between Epstein and McFall, which had become only occasional after Margaret's death. As the figure for Llandaff neared completion, McFall was asked again to help:

> He was at work on the Llandaff MAJESTAS and he wanted me to make up the nimbus. To see him wading through the ferns in overcoat and scarf, impresario's hat and with arms outstretched – 'Make it this size Mack-fal – or this size mebby' extending his arms full span! I chalked out three concentric circles on my studio floor to help him decide, but in the event this didn't save me from having to do it all twice over.[106]

Opinions of the arch on which Epstein's work is located vary. The construction was hailed by critics of the time as graceful, but Epstein regarded it as a "bulky and alien parabolic structure spanning the medieval nave".[107] Gardiner, himself an architect, agreed with Epstein, and felt that "a shallow arch would have been stronger, and would have allowed the sculpture to assume complete charge of the composition". My feeling is that in "spanning the medieval nave" the arch brings the figure of Christ closer to the congregation, and a sense of accessibility is established (fig. 68). The original intention was for the arch to be decorated with a mosaic depicting the Last Judgement (a common setting for the Majestas), which would have reduced what Epstein had called its "bulky" impression, but the mosaic did not materialize, and as it is the bare arch draws the viewer's attention upwards, to the figure – as if towards heaven. The figure of Christ is more commonly found at the very end of a nave, and the gilded plaster version of Epstein's *Majestas*, donated by Sally Ryan to the Riverside Church in New York City, is an example of this. Placed in the more traditional location, this Christ is distant and unattainable (fig. 69). According to Aunt Sylvia, "the Llandaff parishioners were very upset [about the second version], understanding that they were to have the only one [but] they were unable to stop the gift".[108] Epstein, however, approved of the gift and its place above the organ, asking Sally to let the Revd Robert McCraken and his committee know how happy he was knowing it was there.[109]

The next big project had been commissioned in 1954 to adorn the main entrance to the new John Lewis store in Liverpool, but, because of the Llandaff project and trips to America – the last one, in March 1955, for the unveiling of *Social Consciousness* – it took some time before Epstein was able to commence work.

A series of pleasant (and in some cases humorous) events followed. In January 1955 Epstein became a member of the prestigious and intellectual private men's club the Athenaeum.[110] The club, as its recent website declares, was founded as a meeting place for "men who enjoy the life of the mind". Roger Fry had been one of its members, contributing to its publication devoted to "literature, science and fine arts". The extent of Epstein's involvement with the club, however, is unknown.[111]

104 Letter from Epstein to McFall, 8 March 1954: http://davidmcfall.co.uk/Documents/1954.

105 Words of Cripps: ibid.

106 McFall, p. 11.

107 Comment to Gardiner made by Epstein: Gardiner, *Epstein*, p. 442.

108 Babson, *The Epsteins*, p. 63, citing Epstein's sister Sylvia.

109 Letter from Epstein to Sally Ryan, undated. See: David Schulson Autographs Catalog (http://www.schulsonautographs.com/artists.htm).

110 Membership certificate from Athenaeum conferred on Jacob Epstein, 17 January 1955: NAGW–BL/3/1/3.

111 The club refuses to provide information until 70 years after a member's death. However, I suspect that Epstein's involvement had been restricted to the interests of his member-friend T.S. Eliot.

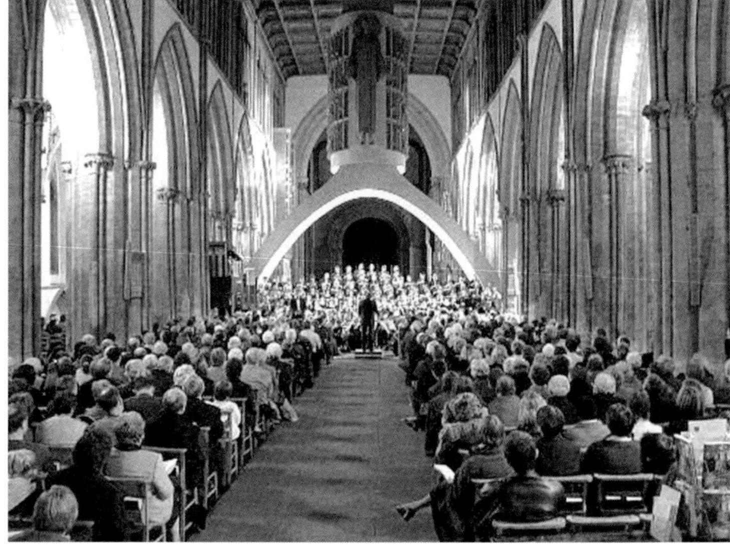

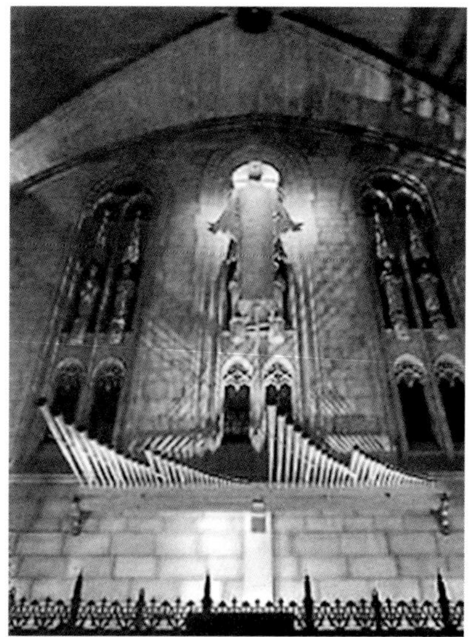

Fig. 68
Epstein's *Majestas* in Llandaff Cathedral's populated space
Courtesy of the Dean and Chapter of Llandaff Cathedral

Fig. 69
Epstein's *Majestas* on the wall at Riverside Church, New York
Gilded plaster, H. 430 cm

On 3 February Epstein's daughter Kitty married Wayne Godley, at the time a musician (probably to Kathleen's delight) but who later became a professor of economics, lecturing at Cambridge University. This happy event might have lightened the heavy weight on Kitty caused by the deaths of her brother and sister. Epstein made a portrait of his new son-in-law, as he had done of the previous one, Lucien Freud,[112] no doubt fascinated by his handsome features.

Almost immediately after the wedding, on 7 March, Epstein went to America to attend the unveiling of *Social Consciousness*: "Oh, they had a big celebration when it was unveiled. They had dinner in his honour and a big parade",[113] he told his sister Sylvia, as well as bemoaning various aspects of American society and the fact that he thought that Gertrude Whitney (a society sculptress) "was a big fake .... She would have other artists do things and put her name on the work". In a later letter to Kathleen he was dismissive of another element of New York art society:

> At Ingersolls [in Philadelphia] Mrs. Webster Plass and Fagg turned up; they were arranging a show of her African sculpture for Brooklyn. What a blessing this African business is for people who without it would be quite ignored.[114]

His dismissal of culture in America extended to other spheres and, while staying at Peggy Jean's place in the south, he wrote to Kathleen that he has been

> reading Mauriac [François] *Flesh and Blood* which I've found here. How well written this is compared to American novels I've looked at, although there seems no reason for the novel ending as it does. I have a thick anthology of American poetry. I can't make the moderns out except that they wish to be original and obscure; they certainly achieve obscurity. No wonder Dylan Thomas is popular here. Hornstein says [that there] are 2 poets to every reader of poetry here.[115]

Another mention of Hornstein hints at Epstein's earlier disapproval of him:

> Hornstein seems to me to have improved, changed a great deal. I think he has

112 Silber (*Sculpture of Epstein*, no. 502) dates Godley's portrait to 1956, two years after their marriage, relating it to Epstein's work of 1956 for which it served. Although Epstein had enlarged Godley's portrait for one of his large projects, I question this late date of the "natural size" not only because Lucien Freud's portrait had been done soon after Kitty married him but also, as discussed further on, because Epstein seems to have used Godley's features in an earlier work of 1956.

113 Babson, *The Epsteins*, p. 59.

114 Letter from Epstein to Kathleen, 30 July 1955: NAGW–BL/1/3/2/16.

115 Letter from Epstein to Kathleen, 11 March 1955: NAGW–BL/1/3/2/18.

> grown stronger and better in character. He is obviously very busy in this out of the world place .... Getting a livelihood is all anyone cares for here, and if I were to believe everything Hornstein tells me I would imagine the people round here to be a lot of degenerates.

Writing about the rate of crime published in the newspapers and seeing around him a place in distress, Epstein says about the south that "the smile has disappeared".

He ends his letter with his personal longings: "My life here is an interval life and when I meet you again I will start to live again. How well we are together, but I feel artificial, not right." In Kathleen's letter to him she seems to have added the letters KBE after his name, because he adds a note below his signature: Your K.B.E. amuses me! I can see your ironical smile as you write it! I can enjoy it! It's better than a C.H. anyway."[116]

By April Epstein was back in London, in time to see a note in the press on 22 April that McFall had been nominated an Associate of the Royal Academy. Epstein, who had a bad relationship with the institution and had rejected their offer of membership (p. 200), did not respond generously toward the man who had consistently helped him:

> One morning he phoned me early .... The phone fairly rattled with mirth before he could get a word out .... "I can't let this day pass Mack-fal – it's the funniest thing I ever heard" etc. He'd seen in *The Times* that I had been elected to the Academy. This mattered less than nothing to me, I had no ambitions in that direction and thought no more of it. But he went on about it until I got annoyed and offered to decline my election. This only made the joke even funnier! "Why Mack-fal you can't do that – you can't do that." "You did", I retorted. "Ah, that was different." He could be a 'corker' when he chose.[117]

Epstein's abrupt closure of the issue ignored the "important facet of it, that David could have got from the Academy commissions of portraiture of Royal Academians, and other sculptures from their related or dependent institutions".[118] One such portrait came much later (1958), when McFall was commissioned to do a sculpture of Churchill in Woodford Green.[119] Epstein had done Churchill's portrait in 1946, but McFall's commission was on a different, much larger scale, of the full figure:

> I knew he would never forgive me. In fact, when I asked him if he would look at my effort, he feebly asked where it was. (It was cast by Gaskin [Senior] and he must have seen it standing in the foundry yard – it was eight feet six inches high ...). Alas for the frailties of famous men!

In the same month of May Epstein's good friend Matthew Smith suffered another double loss. His wife Gwen died, and his once great love and muse, the painter Vera Cunningham, died of cancer. On 9 May Smith responded to Kathleen's letter about Vera, expressing remorse for not being there for Kathleen during her double loss:[120]

> It is so good of you to have written .... Thank you for the story you told of her. I remember it well as she was at that time, it was perhaps always in her to be like that, but none of us dare tell her that she was dying .... It seems so tragic and I keep thinking about it .... I feel so unhappy and realise more than ever how great your sorrow is and I have never done anything to help you.

116 The Order of the Companions of Honour is an order of the Commonwealth. It was established by King George V in June 1917, for outstanding achievements in the arts, literature, music, science, politics, industry or religion.

117 McFall, pp. 12–13.

118 An explanation provided in a conversation with the author by his widow Alexandra.

119 Churchill's constituency as a Prime Minister (1924–45).

120 Letter from Epstein to Kathleen, 9 May 1955: NAGW–BL/1/3/10/16. His own double loss was the death of both his sons in the War.

Closely attached to Smith and absorbing another tragedy into her life, Kathleen grew restless. In early June Epstein told Peggy Jean that Kathleen was nervous, and that he did not know what to do to quiet her. "Marry her," was the advice, and indeed he did.[121] They married on 27 June 1955, with Beth Lipkin as one of the witnesses and with no reporters around to disturb their privacy.[122]

In a letter to his daughter written the following day he tells that he had wanted to do so for a long time, but that Kathleen had not wanted the publicity: "Our odd position has been a source of embarrassment for a long time and now I hope things will be better".[123]

Not long after their marriage Epstein left for America by himself, for his usual visit to Peggy Jean in the summer and to enjoy their proximity to the ocean. Kathleen, who disliked America, went with Beth Lipkin to visit her sister in Italy. In his first letter to Kathleen from the period Epstein describes the sea voyage, on which for the first two days he had not been recognized, but soon after a "deluge" had followed, including a gala dinner to which he was invited by the captain, and, later on, when he disembarked, assembled journalists questioned him not about his work but about why Kathleen had not travelled with him.[124] He signs off, as usual, by writing that he misses Kathleen, and adds that they will go to France and possibly Italy upon his return.

After staying with his brother Irving and his wife on Long Island, and going with them to visit Ingersoll in Philadelphia, Epstein went to see Peggy Jean's new home in Southport, North Carolina, for a rest, and found there a contented Peggy Jean. In a long letter to Kathleen, after discussing money matters, he writes: "I am sending you some newspaper notices of the exhibition of sculpture which has been widely noticed in the papers and has made me known even in my quiet hotel here".[125] He then describes his impressions of the New Yorker who would become the founder of the Hirshhorn Museum and Sculpture Garden at the Smithsonian Museum in Washington.

Accompanied by his brother he met Hirshhorn at his office, where "one feels in art gallery of some kind" as he had "several of Moore's concoctions among a lot of other junk including heads and busts of the great collector himself.[126] Also some fake African." Hirshhorn played the great movie mogul, "seated at a table with 2 telephones in front of him … went on talking business into his phones. I got up to leave and he then deigned to take notice." They discussed a head of Somerset [Maugham] and how much Hirshhorn owed Epstein for a copy of *The Visitation* (1925):

> Our conversation [about prices] was heated. The great one had in front of him numerous copies of 'Time' which carried an account of him with a photograph. I asked him how much he had paid for that. This sent him into tantrums of rage and he became even more obscene in his calls. He yelled, danced, sang, became hysterical. His office was filled with one after another of his adherents including his lawyer whom I congratulated on keeping his boss out of jail!

In his last July letter to Kathleen he concludes the Hirshhorn affair: "I am determined never to go near Hirshhorn again. I will give him his statue and collect what is owing me and then finish forever. His behaviour was atrocious and if it wasn't for Irving being there I would have flung out of his despicable office."[127] The letter, sent after receiving Kathleen's letter detailing their financial situation, had opened with:

121 Conversation with the author.

122 Rose, *Daemons and Angels*, p. 259; there is no mention of others.

123 Letter from Epstein to Peggy Jean, 28 June 1955, TGA-8716.43.

124 Letter from Epstein to Kathleen, 17 July 1955: NAGW–BL/1/3/2/14.

125 Letter from Epstein to Kathleen, 22 July 1955: NAGW–BL /1/3/2/15.

126 In the following letter (23 July 1955, NAGW–BL/1/3/2/15) Epstein describes his discovery of his first portrait of Annabel (Freud) next to a head of Picasso by Henry Moore; he demanded that Hirshhorn call in one of his office workers and ask her which one was best. She chose the sculpture of Annabel.

127 Letter from Epstein to Kathleen, 30 July 1955: NAGW–BL/1/3/2/16.

> How wonderful to get a letter addressed to me as your husband and to think of you as my wife. I must of course resent those strangers who came to you and asked you if you are happy; I wonder what they mean. Some papers have hinted none too delicately that my leaving for America was a sort of Hollywood desertion! If only we were left alone to live our lives!

But Epstein could not ignore the facts she mentioned, and continues:

> I am appalled at the financial situation. And will have to take some active measures to get things straight. As you write we did not go into it very closely. I mean the mounting debts; I hate you stinting yourself, Beth and Frisky. What a good thing we haven't a cat .... I don't think I can get any more funds here, but if you go into the front room from our bedroom and look under the bureau next door you will find £250 in £1 notes. I was keeping that for homecoming in case there was -------. Now if you need to use that £250 use it.

By now, he seems to have taken for granted Beth Lipkin's presence in their lives, and knowing that she had gone to Italy with Kathleen he adds: "I think I would like to meet you at Le Havre. I so hate travelling by train and it would be nice to travel with you, and of course you will have Beth with you."

Epstein's thoughts about his intended work and artistic transactions make up the most interesting part of the letter:

> I feel quite tranquil about the Trades Union Council and if I don't get it I won't mind.
>
> Some day I would like to get back to doing my own work and work again from people I like to work from; that includes children ....
>
> I should ask the Leicester Galleries to send back the *Shalom Ash* as they are only keeping it apparently for an American speculator to see if he would make money out of it or get honours for himself by getting it bought, possibly, and for that I don't think it is worth waiting indefinitely .... I look forward to seeing Chartres with you.

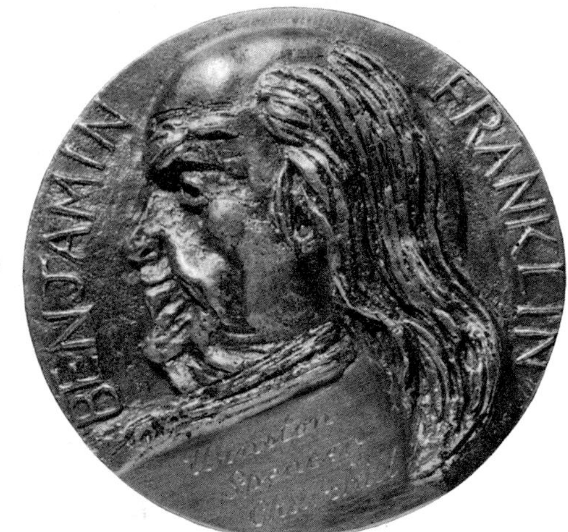

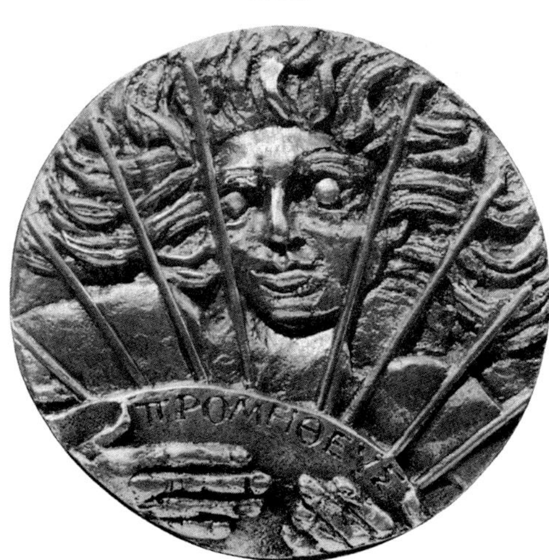

94
The Franklin Medal, 1955
Gold, dimensions unknown
Formerly Winston Churchill; Eleanor Roosevelt; bronze copy, formerly Shinman collection

While still in America Epstein received a special commission from the Philadelphia City Council – no doubt impressed by his work on *Social Consciousness* – to design the Franklin Medal, celebrating the 250th anniversary of Benjamin Franklin's birth, to be awarded to Winston Churchill and Eleanor Roosevelt.[128] Epstein needed to work on it in late 1955 so that it was ready for presentation on 11 January 1956.

Franklin's portrait was to be on the obverse [94a]. For the reverse, among Franklin's many facets and occupations, Epstein decided upon a symbolic expression of his scientific achievements (his many inventions and his experiments in electricity, especially the lightning rod) by alluding to the legend of Prometheus, the god who had stolen the heavenly fire and brought it to earth for mankind's benefit. He depicted a god-like figure harnessing the sun's rays to his chest [94b]. Prometheus's head on the medal seems to be a naturalistic elaboration of the head of Epstein's carving of *Sun God* [30] (1932), but with a smiling face and hair softened into a wavy design.[129]

128 One of the many media announcements on the issue: "EPSTEIN TO MAKE MEDAL; Accepts Job for Philadelphia Franklin Celebration", *The New York Times*, 16 July 1955, p. 16.

129 Silber (*Sculpture of Epstein*, no. 489) states it as bronze, whereas *The New York Times* (note 128) states the medium as gold.

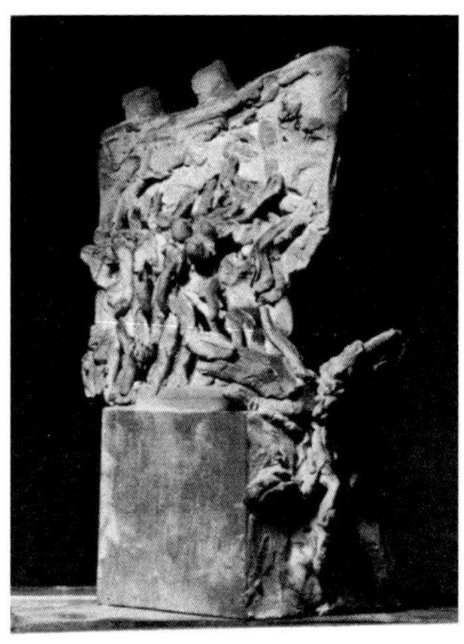
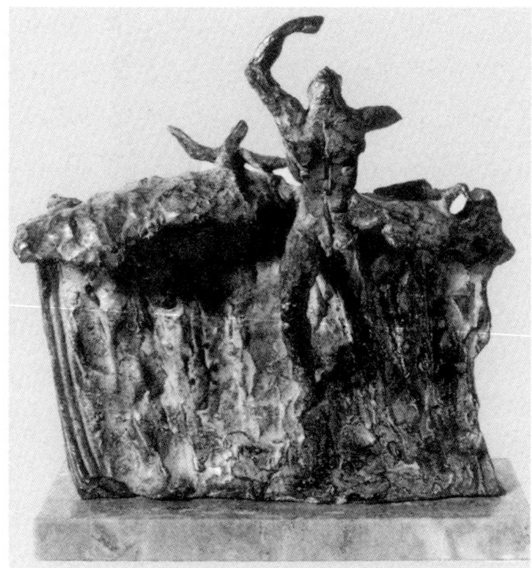
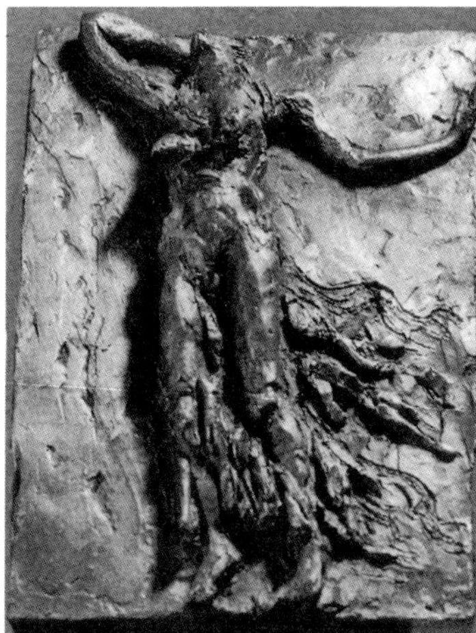
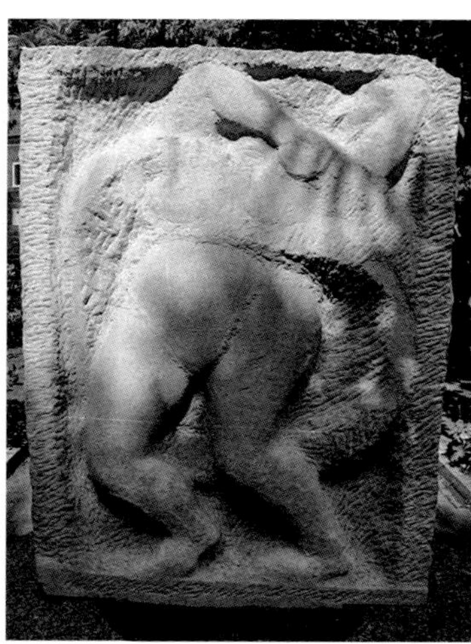

II. *LIVERPOOL RESURGENT*

Back in London in August 1955, Epstein had to juggle the schedules of his major projects. Although all had been commissioned by the end of 1954, the execution period of each varied (he was working on two during 1956). The first to be discussed is the one he worked on during 1955, *Liverpool Resurgent*, to adorn the wall of the main entrance of the new John Lewis store in Liverpool.

Liverpool's dockside location appears to have influenced Epstein's approach, and several maquettes introducing the element of water were made, although in the final piece water was manifested only in the symbolic ship-like design of the figure's pedestal. As a whole, the work was intended to symbolize "Liverpool rising from the flames of war" (the John Lewis store had been destroyed by bombing on 3 May 1941).[130] In October Epstein began to work on a ship's prow with figures [95].[131] No notes on its size are available, and the poor photograph makes it hard to decipher the figures. The independent figure standing in front of the ship and waving its arms, however, seems to be a prototype for the one finally executed.

In *The Wave*, another maquette toying with water as an expression of resurgence – and therefore thought to belong to the same period – a figure with similarly triumphant waving arms rides the crest of the wave [96].[132] In both maquettes the arm-waving of the naked male elaborates upon a similar pose displayed by his first nude in bronze of 1951, *Youth Advancing* [79b].

This arm-waving is also evident in a metope-like relief entitled *The Muse*, presenting a woman draped in a floating garment that exposes her naked body [97], standing in front of what appears to be breaking waves. It is hard to interpret this metope, claimed in Silber's catalogue to have been made in 1956, like *The Wave*; but, as all of these maquettes seem to reflect Epstein's musings on water as a metaphor (as preliminary suggestions for Liverpool), I consider both this and the rest to have been made in the same period of 1954–55. *The Muse* may resolve the dating of an unfinished carving entitled *Woman taking off her Dress* [98], posed as it is in a metope-like square relief. The carved figure has a similarly bent arm, indicating perhaps that Epstein may have intended to develop the subject of a woman with a floating wave-like garment from bronze to carving.

95
Ship's prow plinth with figures, 1954?
Plaster, dimensions unknown
Provenance unknown

96
The Wave, 1954? [1956]
Bronze, H. 30.5 cm
Private collection

97
The Muse, 1954? [1956]
Bronze relief, H. 29.9 cm
Private collection

98
Woman taking off her Dress,
unfinished and undated
Stone, 144 x 108 x 20 cm
Cheyne Walk, London

130 Silber, *Sculpture of Epstein*, no. 476, citing a *Liverpool Echo* report of the unveiling that took place on 20 November 1956.

131 Information given by Silber, *Sculpture of Epstein*, nos. 476–77. She bases the date on Epstein's letter to Hornstein of 20 October 1955.

132 Silber, *Sculpture of Epstein*, no. 493; following Buckle she dates it and the plinth to 1956.

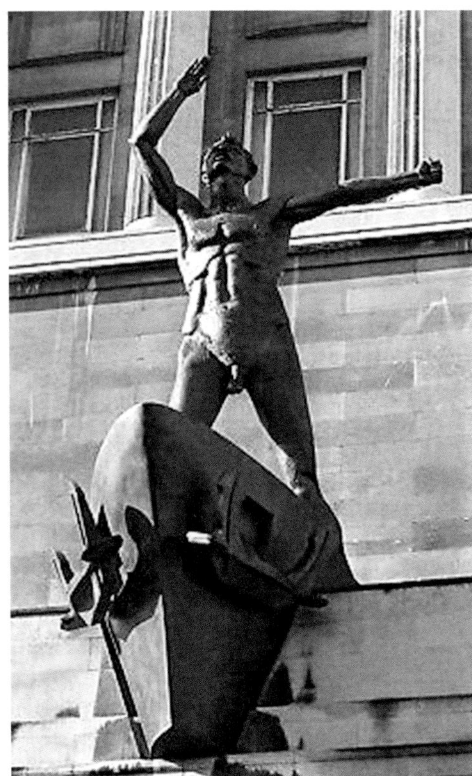

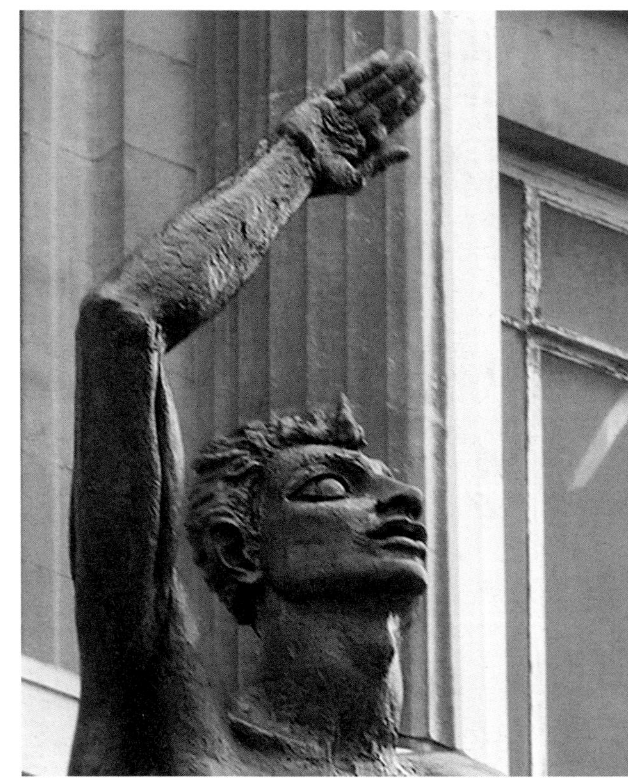

99a–b
Liverpool Resurgent, 1955 [1954]
Bronze, H. 540cm
John Lewis, Liverpool

In this discussion I have pointed to several pieces of information regarding the series of maquettes from this period that I regard as questionable. The first is the dating of many of them, such as the triad associated with *Social Consciousness* and the so-called *Young Bacchus*, *The Wave* and *The Muse*. These are all dated by Silber to 1956, wrongly, in my opinion, along with the maquette for the Trade Union Congress Memorial, which indisputably was done in 1956.

Buckle's claim that Epstein made the maquettes as "relaxation" of his exhausted fingers in the evening in the seems unlikely. Epstein was working in the studio all day until about 5 o'clock, and evenings were devoted to concerts, dining out and seeing friends. In 1956 he was engaged in the carving for the Trade Union Congress commission, which was so arduous while his health so poor that he had to employ an assistant, something he had never done before. One may assume that when coming home from such hard work, the last thing Epstein would have done would be to relax by means of further engagement of his hands.

Casts of all these maquettes were originally sold by Robert Jackson of Nantwich, Cheshire, and many of them belonged to the collection of Lady Cochrane and were sold by her family through Sotheby's on 14 December 1966.[133] All of them seem to be preliminary expressions of their respective subjects, created during the same period as their corresponding large works.

On the commission for the John Lewis store, Buckle (p. 366) reports that "the sculptor decided to model a gigantic male nude striding forward on the pew of a ship, a kind of figure head", and that for this he made a small maquette [95], but it was decided that

133 "Mr. Jackson had come under a certain amount of criticism from certain members of my family to the effect that he was a little too good at selling works of art, the origin of which was sometimes open to question .... Mr. Jackson was alleged to have had a close personal and business relationship with Lady Epstein which, after Sir Jacob's death, might have resulted in more than the official number of copies of some of the sculptures being cast and sold. According to my father, this was one of the main reasons for the sale of his mother's collection of Epstein sculptures": Sir Marc Cochrane, email, 20 December 2011.

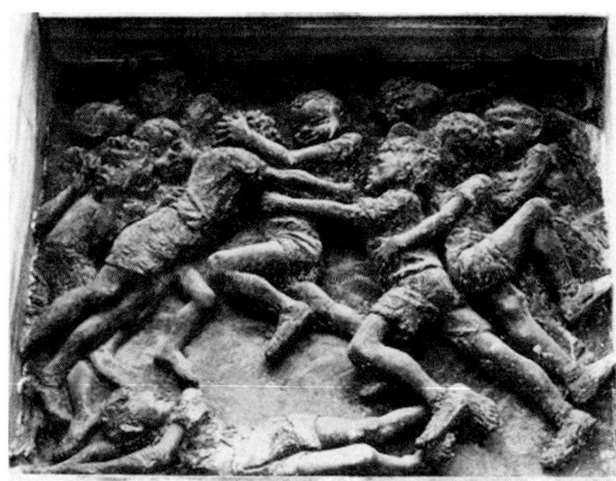
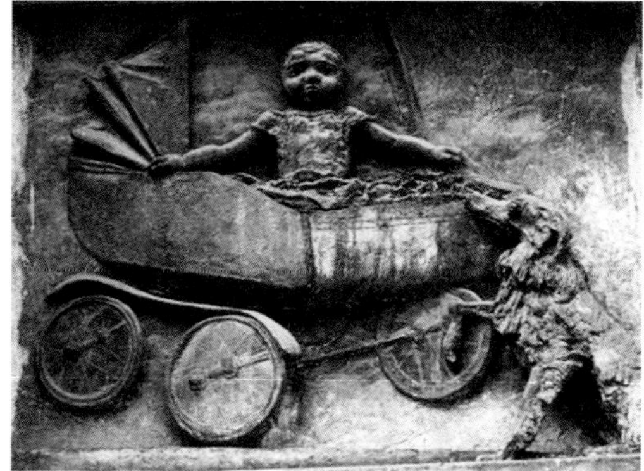
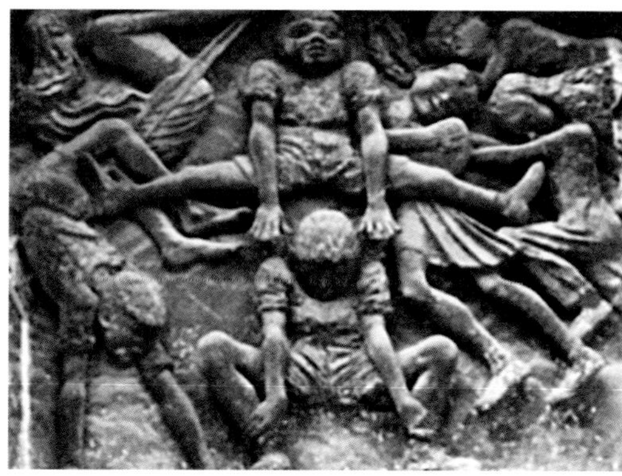

the base would be more plain. It is not known which of the maquettes were presented to Lord Woolton, the Managing Director of John Lewis, and documentation on this commission is not available.[134]

Liverpool Resurgent [99a] – a figure standing astride the boat with one leg forward and waving his arms – seems to echo Epstein's *Youth Advancing*. However, while the *Youth* is a life-size figure with a quite slender torso, downward-falling arms and clenched fists expressing resolution, the Liverpool figure is triple life-size (5.40 m in height), has a strong torso and upward-raised victorious waving arms, which seem to echo those of the German figures at the 1937 Paris International Exhibition (p. 103). In view of its position high above street level, these measurements were almost obligatory if the details, including the sharp facial elements, were to be visible to passers-by. There is no indication of the model for this figure or the face, but one can assume that Epstein again drew upon one of his earlier portraits. The face, with its receding hair-line and the relaxed lips [99b], may be a stylization of the features of his son-in law Wayne, whose portrait was previously dated to 1956.[135]

The huge nude was modelled in sections at the Hyde Park Gate studio, then put together, finished and cast in plaster at the Royal College (by Epstein's specialists at plaster moulding, Bill Olds and Jan Smith).[136] The unveiling took place on 20 November 1956.[137]

An interesting part of the impressive entrance to the John Lewis store is that of the three panels with reliefs of children [100a–c], made after his preparatory drawings.[138] Children are not very commonly depicted for public buildings of this or any other era, but Donatello's renowned carving of putti dancing in the Cantoria of the Cathedral of Florence [fig. 69] offers one precedent – in particular the boys' hand movements.[139] Epstein clearly enjoyed doing children's portraits: "I am myself frightfully busy mostly doing portraits of children, all ages, all stages", he once wrote to his granddaughter Leda (p. 186). The two side panels at the entrance depict children, mostly in profile, amidst a lot of movement and arm waving: on the right panel they are playing – a girl sits on a swing and a boy does a handstand, while the central frontal figure is leap-frogging, his round cheeks reminiscent of a portrait of Epstein's son Jackie as a boy, entitled *Ragamuffin*; on the left panel they are quarrelling, and on the central one Epstein depicted his granddaughter Annabel in a pram with his dog Frisky sitting beside her. The panels were Epstein's suggestion and made at his own expense.[140]

100
Children (three successive reliefs, from left to right: *Children fighting*; *Baby in a pram and a dog*; *Children playing*), 1955–56
Cement fondu, 101 x 183 cm
John Lewis, Liverpool

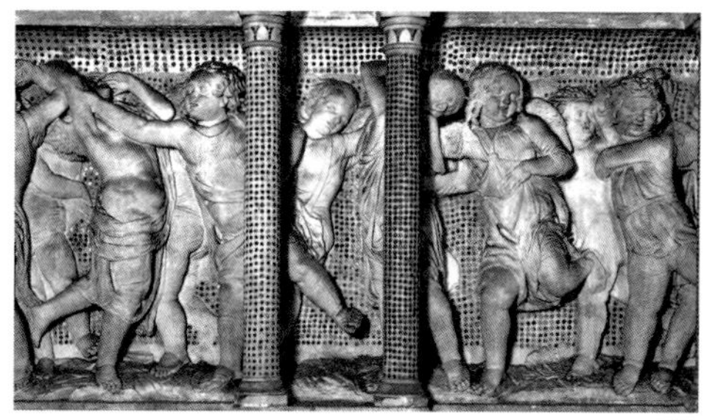

Fig. 70
Donatello
Putti dancing, 1433–39
Marble, 348 x 570 x 98 cm
Cantoria of the Cathedral, Florence

134 Comprehensive research was carried out by Evelyn Silber ('Epstein's Liverpool Colossus'). My further attempts to find photographs did not bear fruit, as the store's archive is in storage at the Liverpool Record Office, where, owing to lack of funding for cataloguing, it is not accessible.

135 See note 112 above.

136 A brief record on the commission is presented in Cavanagh, *Public Sculpture of Liverpool*, pp. 164–68. Particular details cited by him are taken from Evelyn Silber's research.

137 The building's new owner, Merepark, recently unveiled its £37 million plans to develop it into "a boutique hotel and offices, with retail surviving on lower floors" (John Siddle, *Liverpool Echo*, 29 May 2010).

138 The collection of Dr and Mrs Martin Evans (Epstein's relatives in the US); Silber, 'Epstein's Liverpool Colossus', p. 103, note 50.

139 Silber, *Sculpture of Epstein*, p. 59.

140 Buckle, *Epstein: Sculptor*, p. 391, cites Epstein's letter of June 1955 to Peggy Jean, a letter that is not part of the TGA list.

THE GREAT PUBLIC WORKS: SECOND STAGE

I. THE TUC WAR MEMORIAL

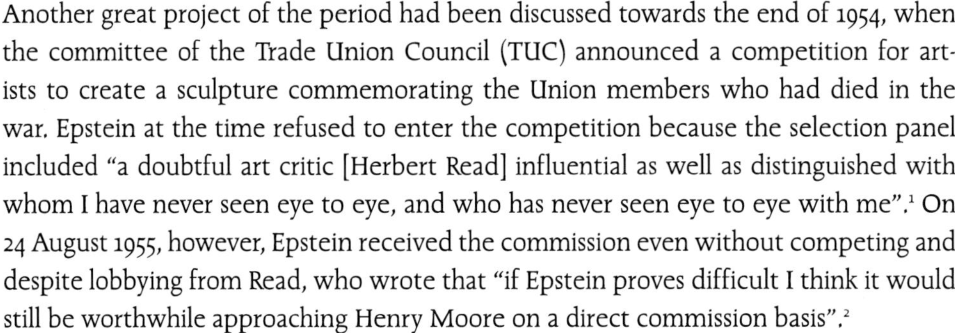

Another great project of the period had been discussed towards the end of 1954, when the committee of the Trade Union Council (TUC) announced a competition for artists to create a sculpture commemorating the Union members who had died in the war. Epstein at the time refused to enter the competition because the selection panel included "a doubtful art critic [Herbert Read] influential as well as distinguished with whom I have never seen eye to eye, and who has never seen eye to eye with me".[1] On 24 August 1955, however, Epstein received the commission even without competing and despite lobbying from Read, who wrote that "if Epstein proves difficult I think it would still be worthwhile approaching Henry Moore on a direct commission basis".[2]

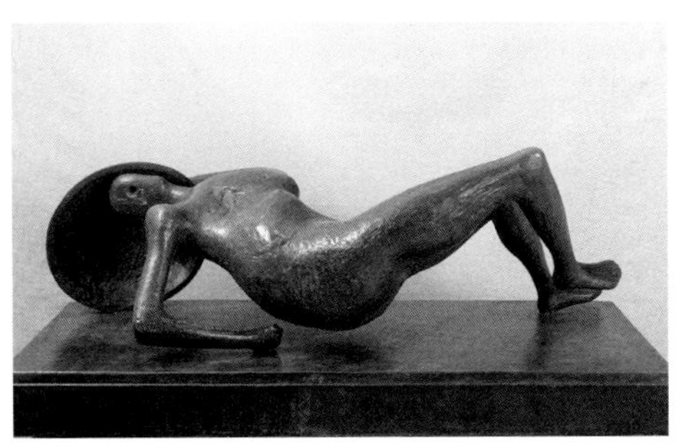

Fig. 71
Henry Moore
Falling Warrior, 1955–56
Bronze, L. 147 cm
Memorial Court, Clare College, Cambridge

In all probability, it is to this period of the competition – commemorating the dead – that Moore's *Falling Warrior* of 1955–56 (fig. 71) belongs. In this unique work, with neither precedent nor duplicate, Moore raised his oft-repeated solid reclining figure from the floor, giving the pose a sense of momentary balance and tension. Although different in subject, the fleeting pose has some affinity with that of Epstein's *Woman Possessed* (1932),[3] as both works seem to stem from the classical precedent of the *Dying Niobid* (fig. 9, p. 66).

After receiving the commission, Epstein presented to the committee a plaster maquette of *Mother and Son* [see 103].[4] The contract, signed on 7 November 1955, required Epstein to start working on the carving as soon as the stone was on site; he was given a year to complete the work and his fee was to be £15,000.[5] The maquette depicts a standing woman wearing a gown and a head covering, clasping to her belly the horizontal body of a man in a helmet, enveloped in what seem to be bandages; with her uplifted face she seems to be seeking a kind of salvation. Michelangelo's *Pietá* immediately comes to mind. A similar idea had been expressed in an earlier work and its maquette, *Night*, of 1929 [101, 102].

As with *Night*, the transference of the idea between one medium and another produced an end result that was not exactly what the commissioning body was expecting. Charles Holden, who had initiated the commission of *Night*, was well acquainted with Epstein's approach and had obviously been aware of the difference in his treatment of media (I/189). Epstein himself, discussing the bronze *Visitation* and the carved *Genesis*, had said that in the bronze he sought to convey a particular atmosphere, in the carving he meant to create a symbol.[6] The differences between the maquette as cast in bronze [101] and the final carving [104] do not therefore stem merely from the transference into another medium, but rather from Epstein's wish to make the carved figure into a representation of the sacrificial son (as also in *Night*, I/193).

A sense of awe at the carnage of World War II is realised in the sculpture in the mother's mutely condemning face looking straight out at the world, while her son's limp body with its drooping arm is held close to her chest [104b]. Her expression is similar to that of Epstein's *Risen Christ*, made in the wake of World War I. Exaggerated features in the white carving, set in front of a huge green wall and on a very tall pedestal in a courtyard, are perceived to be in natural proportions by the viewer, who observes them from afar, more or less at eye level and through the windows of the building [104c].

1 Epstein's letter to Sir Vincent Tewson, Secretary General of the TUC, 11 December 1954. Documentation of this project is in the TUC archive, file 28,433. For this information, I am indebted to Katherine Eustace ('A Question of Property'), who mainly discusses the question of who owned the rights to the maquette and whether or not there had been foul play by Epstein. According to her, apparently not.

2 Letter from Read to Tewson, 31 January 1955, TUC archive, file 28,433.

3 Silber (*Sculpture of Epstein*, p. 52), interprets Moore's pose as "poignantly crumpling in defeat" against Epstein's "ecstasy of momentary victory".

4 Eustace ('A Question of Property', p. 60) claims that Epstein presented a bronze maquette to the committee, and that "later on in 1956 he made also a sketch model in plaster – h. 57 cm". This seems odd, as a plaster version usually precedes the bronze. The plaster that remained with Epstein enabled him to produce two bronze copies (h. 54.5 cm), causing the TUC's suspicion of foul play on Epstein's part regarding rights. This is dismissed by Eustace and explained as Epstein's misunderstanding of the legal expression "for the time being", which differs from its use in ordinary life (pp. 61–62). The dispute was settled by Epstein giving the plaster to the TUC.

5 Silber, *Sculpture of Epstein*, no. 490. Full details on the project are in the TUC archive, file 28,433.

6 Haskell (*The Sculptor Speaks*, p. 63) discusses the difference between *The Visitation* (1925) and the carving *Genesis* (1930).

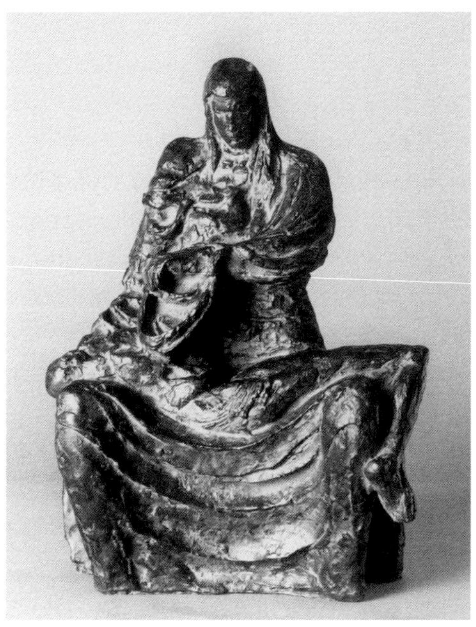

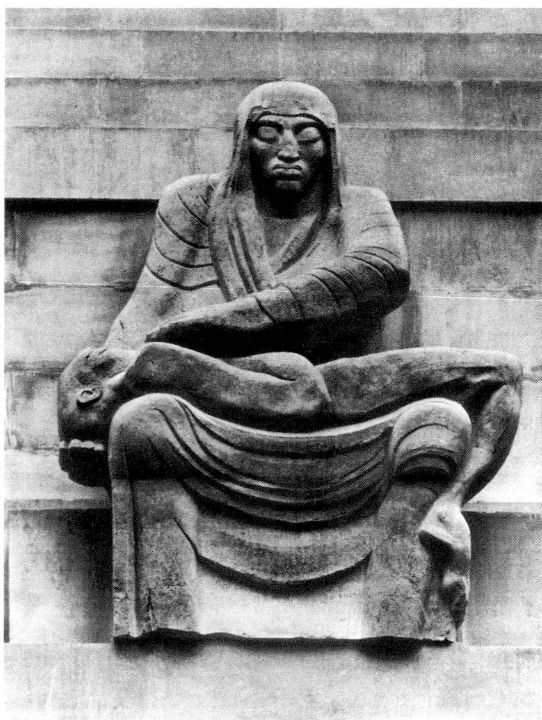

101
Night (maquette), 1928
Bronze, H. 53.5 cm
Private collection

102
Night, 1928
Portland stone blocks, 275 x 275 x 100 cm
London Underground Railway Headquarters, Westminster
Courtesy of the Transport Museum, London

103
Mother and Son (maquette), 1955
Bronze, 57 cm
Courtesy of Bolton Art Gallery

104a
TUC War Memorial (sculpture on stand), 1956–57
Roman stone, 300 x 150 x 120 cm
TUC building, Great Russell Street, London

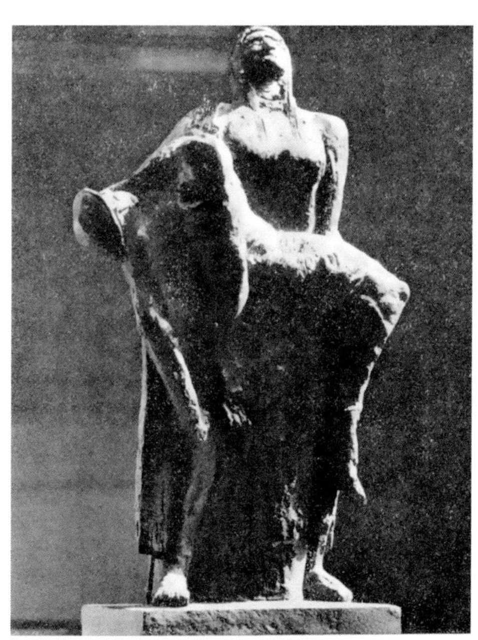

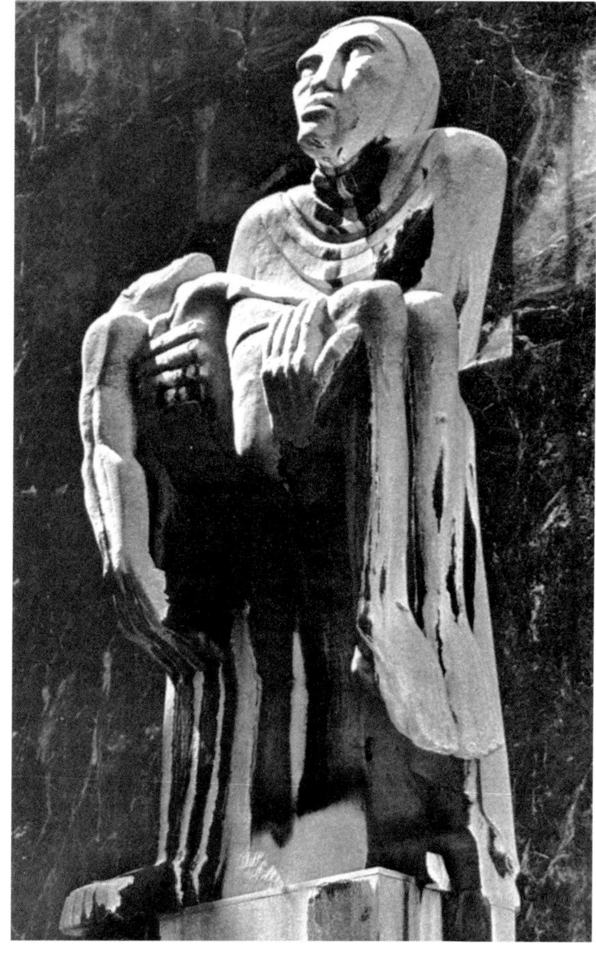

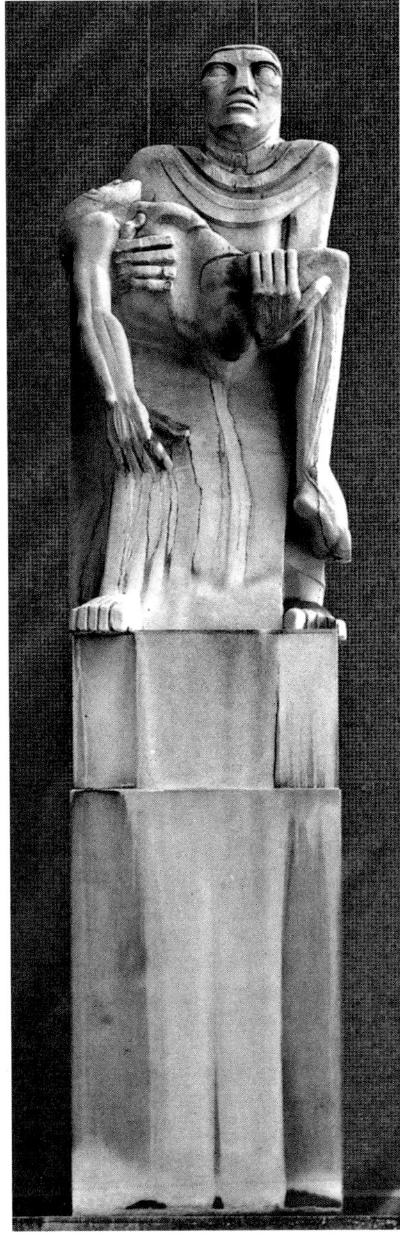

104b
TUC War Memorial (sculpture on stand), 1956–57
Roman stone, 300 x 150 x 120 cm
TUC building, Great Russell Street, London

This commission is a good illustration of the differences between Epstein and Moore. Moore's views on his *Madonna and Child* of 1943–44 exemplify his differing attitude: "The Madonna and Child should have an austerity and nobility, and some touch of grandeur (even hieratic aloofness) which is missing in everyday mother and child idea".[7] While some of these notions are equally evident in Epstein's treatment of the subject of the Madonna and Child, austerity or aloofness had never been qualities he would have cared to express in any of his works, not even in the most stylized ones of the 1910s. One wonders if it was not that very lack of reflection of human feeling in Moore's work that ultimately led the committee, looking for a sort of *Pietá*, to choose Epstein, particularly after seeing the nobility sculpted in the expressive and un-austere representation of his Madonna in Cavendish Square.

While waiting for the TUC work to begin, Epstein was kept busy: "I am full of work .... In the meantime I am finishing the model for the Liverpool – making the prow of an ocean liner for the figure to stand on."[8] On personal matters he reports: "Kathleen is busy looking after the house & myself. We have occasional music parties & we get some fine performers who are very pleased to come & play."

The stone was brought to its site in February 1956 and by the beginning of March Epstein was already working on it, under almost the same conditions as he had worked on *Day* and *Night*. "I have this stone in a hut in position in the open court of the building and lock it up when I leave,"[9] he wrote to Peggy Jean in a long letter, admitting the shortcomings of his age. At seventy-five, for the first time in his working life he needed to employ an assistant in chipping the lumps of stone, which was "as hard as granite and tools just break on it", finding himself "tired out at about 1.30" and in need of a lunchbreak and rest. Perhaps in order to prove this point, he enclosed in his letter "2 snap shots of Matthew Smith & myself .... You can see from the photos how old we are both looking; Matt very much more frail than I." About his workload he added: "I am now inundated with requests for work on buildings, large works which I don't know I will ever be able to accomplish. I was for so long without any commissions [that] I don't feel like turning down anything that comes my way; but it is all coming late."

For some reason, the helper is nowhere mentioned as being his long-time supportive colleague David McFall, who, according to his own records, had been working on the site since April.[10]

As mentioned above, Epstein was engaged concomitantly in several projects during 1955–56. Their chronology can be deduced from his letters to Hornstein. In June 1956 he summed up the state of his recent works: "At the moment I am working chiefly in stone on the site of the new TUC building in Great Russell Square. This will be a fine building in many ways & my work consists of a group in the great courtyard," while at the same time his "Christ for Llandaff Cathedral is being sent off" (at that date he was referring to the maquette, as the commission was agreed upon in mid 1956), and "the great work for Liverpool is in process of casting .... With all this I have to think of at least 3 commissions for London!"[11] In the same letter, after criticizing the new trends of American artists whom he called "charlatans", and deploring "most especially our being influenced by American fakirs like Calder & Pollock who dribbles paint directly

7 James, *Henry Moore on Sculpture*, p. 220.
8 Letter from Epstein to Peggy Jean 19 October 1955: TGA-8716/47.
9 Letter from Epstein to Peggy Jean, 30 April 1956: TGA-8716/50.
10 Not all his help seems to be recorded by the modest McFall, who never boasted about it. He records: "14 April 1956 Epstein TUC"; "17 August 1956 TUC" (Rodney Sidon citing from McFall's diaries, email to the author of 31 August 2011).
11 Letter from Epstein to Hornstein, September/October 1956(?): TGA-871/22.

out of a can", he complains that the effect these pundits "have on our intelligentsia is disheartening", concluding: "I am continuing steadily in my own way".

While continuing in his own way with the great project for Llandaff, Epstein had to come to terms with a new personal woe – Peggy Jean's divorce. As far back as 1949, when he went to America to bring Jackie back home, he had noticed some tension and had written about it to Kathleen:[12]

> This morning he has gone beyond himself in abuse of Peggy Jean shouting at her at the top of his voice and accusing her of running a dirty house .... I felt like interfering this morning but I hate ruptures and so I kept silent .... He is making Peggy Jean's life a misery. But what can I do? ... He behaves much more brutally than I would ever have imagined and I am shocked at his behaviour. [After describing some unpleasant little events, he adds:] All this perhaps sounds petty but what future there is here for any lasting happiness I cannot see.

When he visited them in 1955, however, he saw an improvement and a happy Peggy Jean (p. 207). The news about the divorce, therefore, came as rather a shock, and, after inquiring whether there was room for reconciliation, he wrote: "You seemed all of you happy when I was there a short time ago. I must have be singularly blind not to have noticed something .... Do please let me know what the trouble is."[13] The trouble was Hornstein's falling in love with his secretary, who had replaced the overworked Peggy Jean in his clinic. "As a child I saw my mother do all for her husband," recounted their daughter Leda: "He was hard to live with ... demanding.[14] I think he may have had depression from the war."[15]

In order to ease his sense of guilt and, as Epstein put it, "to exonerate himself from any blame ... making you the guilty party", Hornstein wrote to Epstein an eighteen-page letter, in which "he abuses you abuses me abuses men & portrays himself a martyred saint. Were I younger, I would come over & give him a good *thashmis*."[16] In a harsh tone Epstein continues:

> He describes you as having ruined his brilliant career. I seem to be as next to blame (in his eyes) as anyone & he even scorns my sending you financial assistance! ...
>
> I do not intend to answer his letter. There is too much dirt in it .... I never let him know of my personal feelings about him so as not to cause him to think I was in any way discontented & so cause friction. I always felt he was rude in his actions and I resented it but said nothing.

Two days later Epstein received another letter from Hornstein, complaining about Peggy Jean's lawyer and threatening that, if she did not agree to his own lawyer, he would "slow" her life and defame her name and would involve Epstein in it too. "How he will do this he does not say & I don't know how the devil he can bring me into it, but he knows by threatening me he can bring you to hell".[17] Over the next three years Epstein had to watch Peggy Jean endure the very unpleasant and painful process of their break-up,[18] involving financial disputes that required his help. In spite of the long bitter divorce process, the aftermath, according to their daughter Leda, was more positive:

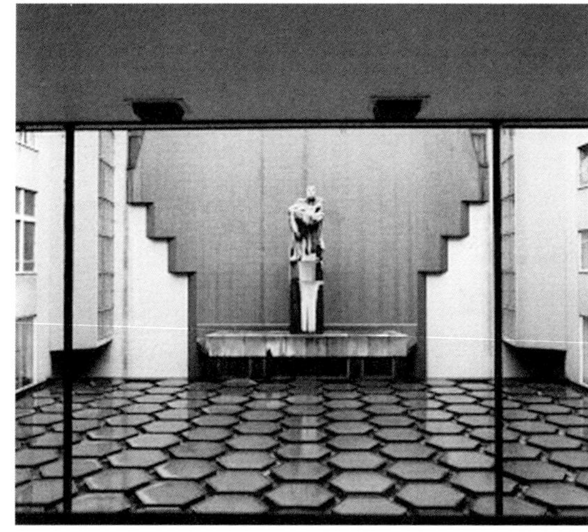

104c
TUC War Memorial, seen from afar, through window-frame

12 Letter from Epstein to Kathleen, 29 July 1949: NAGW–BL/1/3/2/8.

13 Letter (only part remaining) from Epstein to Peggy Jean, September/October 1956 (?); TGA-8716/23.

14 Email to the author. In the same vein, on 27 August 1951 Epstein wrote to Kathleen that he had had long debates with Hornstein about literature and that Hornstein always thought that he was right: NAGW–BL/1/3/2/13.

15 "After my dad died I came across a book of poems he wrote while in the war. They were horribly depressing and intellectual. Think I still have them, but I didn't want my kids to read them and I might have thrown them away": email from Leda Sloat to the author.

16 Letter from Epstein to Peggy Jean, 23 October 1956: TGA-993/1. The word *thashmis* is used in Jewish literary sources as a euphemism for sexual intercourse; Epstein means he will teach him a lesson. It is quite a surprise that after so many years as an outsider to Jewish tradition Epstein should use this childhood expression. I wonder whether Peggy Jean understood it.

17 Letter from Epstein to Peggy Jean, 25 October 1956: TGA-993/2.

18 Letter from Epstein to Peggy Jean, 10 February 1959: TGA-8716 53. He writes: "I hope things are not too hard with you & let me know how your divorce turns out".

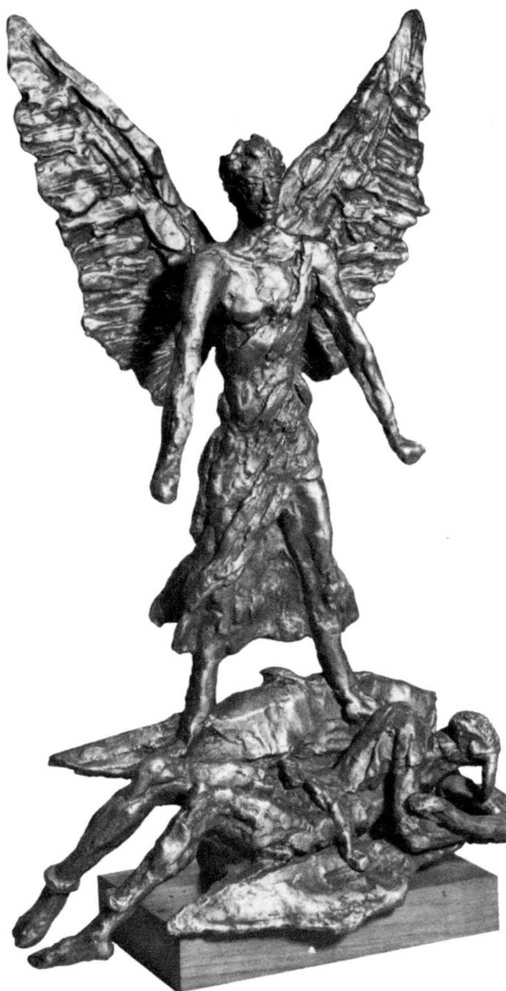

105
St Michael and the Devil (maquette), 1956
Bronze, H. 53.5 cm
Formerly Shinman collection

"My Dad remained friendly with my Mom and took care of her medically. I know he felt guilty about the new love."[19] Whatever his family problems – his worries about Peggy Jean, about Jackie's lack of professional direction or about Kitty's divorce – Epstein always remained a caring and financially supportive father.

In his letters to Peggy Jean, in between dealing with family affairs, Epstein always commented on his work. Thus, in a letter of October in which he was concerned about her divorce, he wrote about his being "in the midst of terrific preparations for unveilings of both of the Smuts & the Liverpool commissions .... At the unveiling of the Smuts there were 1500 invited guests."[20] It was only in November 1956, after the pedestal stone had arrived from South Africa, that David McFall was invited by Epstein to carve the letters on the Smuts Memorial (p. 200).

II. *ST MICHAEL AND THE DEVIL*

During a reception at Birmingham's Art Gallery in the winter of 1953, the architect Sir Basil Spence, having given his address at the Town Hall, had occasion to see Epstein's *Lucifer* dominating the gallery hall. It was the second great work on a Christian subject of Epstein's that he had seen, after viewing with Bishop Gordon the *Madonna and Child* in Cavendish Square. "Epstein is the man for us," said the Bishop, referring to their search for a suitable sculptor – "someone who could do justice" to the figure of the saint of their Coventry Cathedral.[21] Sir Basil agreed, convinced that "if Epstein could portray evil with such forcefulness he could portray the opposite in St Michael". While *Lucifer* is certainly forceful, one might disagree that it was 'evil', or that is exuded "evil from every finger".[22] A different take on *Lucifer* has been suggested above (p. 154), but it was to Epstein's advantage that Sir Basil saw *Lucifer* in a different light.

The process of obtaining this commission was arduous and longer than that of the *Madonna and Child*.[23] It began with an alarmed Reconstruction Committee remarking "But he is a Jew", to which Sir Basil replied "So was Jesus Christ". After some discussion and delay Sir Basil approached Epstein, whom he described as having an "expressive face and lively kind eyes (although they could flash daggers at times)", and "marvellous workman's hands with short strong fingers, rather like those of a great pianist". Sir Basil found that Epstein's attitude to honest professional opinion on his work was cordial – he accepted Spence's criticism on "some vertical lines on the drapery" of *Majestas*; he also observed how Epstein would take serious notice even of a child, saying "through innocence you find truth". In spite of Sir Basil's support, the committee felt that it also required the backing of the Cathedral Council, and it asked that a maquette be submitted to both institutions and to the Provost and that a preliminary talk with the sculptor happen before the work was undertaken. Kathleen invited Sir Basil and the Provost to lunch, in which "a long theological discussion on the significance of St Michael developed". As no details of the theological discussion are reported, one wonders whether, and how, Epstein referred to the Jewish Orthodox notion of Michael as a prince who had to fight the Prince of Persia to defend Israel (Daniel, 10: 13)[24] – wholly unlike the Christian notion of rebel angels described by Milton. No wonder, therefore, that after a theological discussion the Provost asked Epstein what his beliefs were, and

19 Daughter Leda Sloat writing to the author in 2011.

20 Letter from Epstein to Peggy Jean, 23 October 1956: TGA-993/1.

21 Spence, *Phoenix at Coventry*, pp. 67–76 (Chapter 12: 'St Michael, Patron Saint, and Epstein').

22 Ibid., 68.

23 The Llandaff Cathedral Archives indicate that Epstein was formally commissioned in October 1953 (Silber, *Sculpture of Epstein*, no. 475). The work was done during the last part of 1954.

24 See http://www.jewishencyclopedia.com/view.jsp?artid=560&letter=M#1833. It is only in post-biblical writings (Gen. Raba, xlviii. 9) that the names of the angels are mentioned as being introduced into the culture by the Jews from Babylon; Michael is specially designated in early Jewish writings, and very frequently in the Book of Enoch as "the prince of Israel", and also in later Jewish writings, particularly in Cabalistic works, as "the advocate of the Jews".

Epstein – politely and smartly – replied: "My beliefs can be clearly seen through my work". As his work projected deep human interest, Epstein was accepted.

Seven months after the commission Sir Basil renewed contact with Epstein, having read in a newspaper in January 1957 that he had declared *St Michael* to be his greatest work.[25] When he came to Epstein's studio he saw the maquette [105] and also the start of the full-size figure; the roughed out torso and the head – an enlargement of his son-in law Wayne Godley's portrait of 1956 – were already done. To Sir Basil's claim that the committee wished to see the maquette and approve it before continuing to the full-size piece, Epstein replied: "I am not working for the Committee any more, I am working for myself".[26] The following day the project was approved, as the Provost and Bishop were impressed by the head and did not request to see anything else. Photographs shown to the council and the church committee were unanimously approved.

In March 1957, still worrying about Peggy Jean's problems ("I suppose Hornstein would be pleased if you walked out & let him get away with it & so relieve him of all liability as far as you are concerned & also the children … don't discuss me with him"), and concerned about Jackie being "at a loose end" after having left the army, Epstein reported to Peggy Jean:[27]

> I have started a big work, the group for Coventry Cathedral & old assistant [McFall?] is helping me with the castings of the first portion; as the whole work is to be about 25 or 30 feet high, you can imagine I am busy.
>
> This work engages me entirely & I have a host of world patrons writing me letters & knocking at the door insisting that I do their work [namely portraits].[28] As I do all the work myself, it is out of the question; I keep fairly well although the operation has left its mark on me unfortunately.

For some reason, this is the only source to mention an operation that Epstein underwent in 1956, while working on the TUC Monument. It is hinted at in Buckle's notes on Epstein's health problems (379) – "how precarious was the state of Epstein's heart at this time" – although he does not mention an operation.

Epstein commented on the same personal issues again in April,[29] on Peggy Jean's situation – "I'm glad the children are well, good that they will stick to you. I hope that you can get proper financial support & not let Hornstein get away with his responsibilities. Let me know about this" – and on Jackie – "I'm pleased to tell you that Jackie has at last got tired of loafing & has got himself a job. It is of course to do with cars & if things turn out well & he sticks to it he will be able to make quite well as far as money goes. I have never denied him money as he knows …. I hope it takes him away from racing cars, which was nothing at all that would be good for him; in fact altogether dangerous."[30] As usual, Epstein then turns to news of his work – on the presentation of the Llandaff figure ("next Wednesday") that raises "a good deal of interest in London"; on the Archbishop of Wales, who would preside at the consecration of the nave and the dedication of the new work; and on the two days that he and Kathleen would spend in Wales for this occasion. And more:

> It is odd that most of my work is for religious establishments; that is because of the *Madonna & Child* in London, no doubt.
>
> I have survived the bad period when only Moore & Co. were thought to be

25 Silber, *Sculpture of Epstein*, no. 503.

26 Spence, *Phoenix in Coventry*, p. 71.

27 Letter from Epstein to Peggy Jean, 6 March 1957: TGA-993/3.

28 Between 1956 and 1958 he had modelled about fourteen commissioned portraits.

29 Long letter from Epstein to Peggy Jean, 2 April 1957: TGA-993/4, pp. 3–4.

30 Eventually Jackie became a racing-car engineer and a world famous racing-ring specialist. Unfortunately for them both, Epstein did not live to see it: http://www.lolaheritage.co.uk/news/news307/307_old.htm.

> sculptors worth looking at & I was ignored & neglected. As well I have commissions for portraits from Oxford & Cambridge & it is a great satisfaction to work for places where about you do with [sic] – & not be at the mercy of silly people.

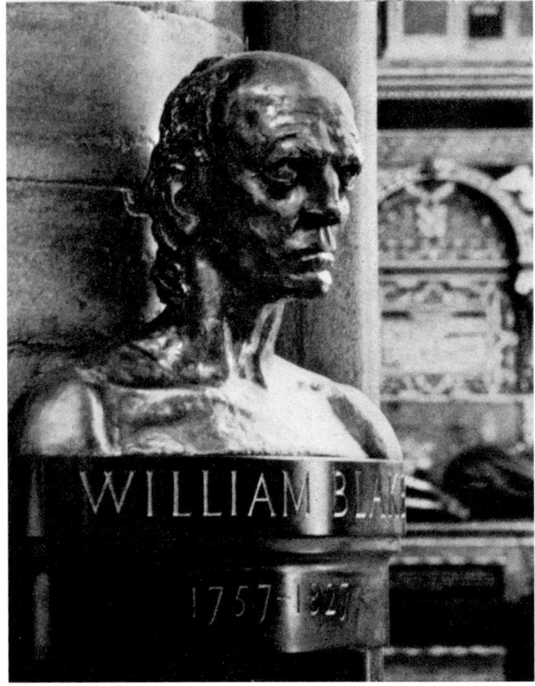

106
William Blake, 1956
Bronze, H.54 cm
Poets' Corner, Westminster Abbey, London

Epstein's private life in mid 1957 had two aspects. On the one hand it was a happy and satisfying period of work, mingled with the comfort of having Kathleen close by and the pleasure of both of them travelling in Europe; on the other hand, there were continuing worries about Peggy Jean's divorce and an ensuing sense of helplessness. In July 1957 he discussed with her a more convenient solution – Florida, where three months residence would entitle her to sue for divorce.[31] He himself was not going to the US that year; he was planning to go with Kathleen to Italy, "& we have thought of Scotland"; "some day I hope to persuade Kathleen to visit U.S.A. with me. At present she is all against it." Meanwhile, he felt

> often dead tired & worn out and I must stop soon, I know, or I might be stopping forever. You know I have this commission to do, the group for the new Coventry Cathedral [*St Michael*]. The architect asked me to do a large work & I needn't any encouragement to do just that. The whole of my sculpture will be 25 Ft. high & be cast in bronze .... My portraits are in such demand that the large works don't leave me with much time to do them.

In spite of his heavy workload he managed to dine twice a week in Soho, "which has been transformed by the Maltese into one big brothel. Something like what the Puerto Ricans did to sections of N.Y.", adding that, until the plans for a holiday materialized, he rested at weekends by going out "of a Sunday to Epping Forest for the day, but avoid our old house on the hill as the memory of that is too sad".

An enjoyable trip to Scotland in the summer holidays, on which Epstein and Kathleen took young Roland Joffe (by then a student at Carmel College, a Jewish public school), ended with Epstein suffering a heart attack that left him unable to move, and Roland staying with him by the roadside while Kathleen went to fetch a car to take him back to their hotel.[32] This must have been the period in which he had an operation,[33] although it did not deter him from continuing his work.

In October 1957 Epstein accepted an urgent commission by the Blake Society to do William Blake's portrait for the Poets' Corner in Westminster Abbey, to be completed within about six weeks. It seems that Epstein's success in producing portraits of the deceased from photographs had convinced the commissioners of the society that he was the right man for the job. Unlike his previous subjects, who had been photographed from all sides, Blake had been represented mainly from the front and in profile in drawings. There seem to be very few contemporary images of him,[34] and those noted here in their chronological order are my selection, assuming a path for Epstein's search.

First and foremost is the life mask by James Deville, made when Blake was fifty-six (1813), so that the phrenologist could have a cast of Blake's head "as representative of the imaginative faculty".[35] The mask failed to please Blake's family and friends, who said that the unnatural severity of the mouth was caused by the discomfort of the process, "as the plaster pulled out a quantity of his hair". This was corrected by Deville himself a decade later, in a head he produced based on the mask [fig. 72]. It seems that it was this figure

31 Letter from Epstein to Peggy Jean, 2 July 1957: TGA-993/5. Epstein's custom was to oscillate between subjects and, therefore, I have edited the order of the issues presented here.

32 Buckle, *Epstein: Sculptor*, p. 398.

33 I have not found specific information on this operation, other than Epstein's remark (in retrospect) in a letter sent to Peggy Jean on 25 November 1957: TGA-993/16.

34 Buckle (*Epstein: Sculptor*, p. 400) tells that Epstein "got together all the portraits he could, including sketches by Stothard" (Blake's contemporary collaborator in designing some of his engravings). Unfortunately, I have not found Stothard's portrait.

35 Information provided by the website of London's National Portrait Gallery, which has the Phillips painting and the mask.

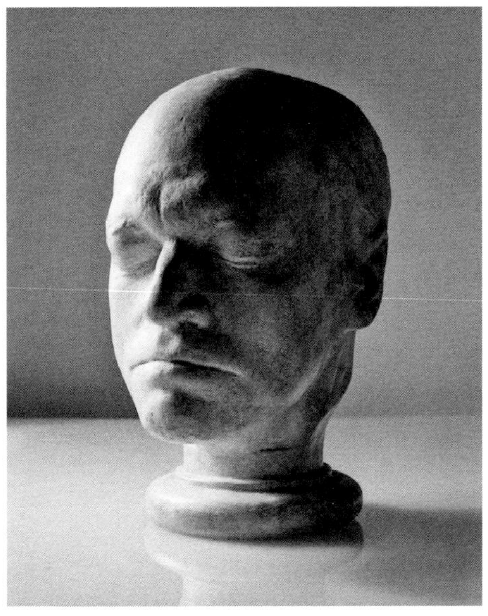

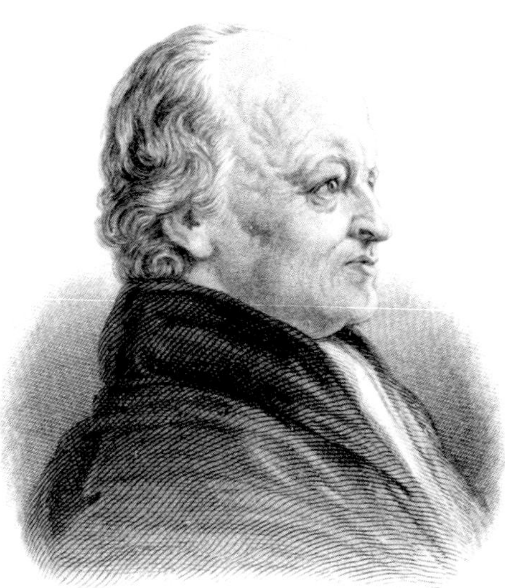

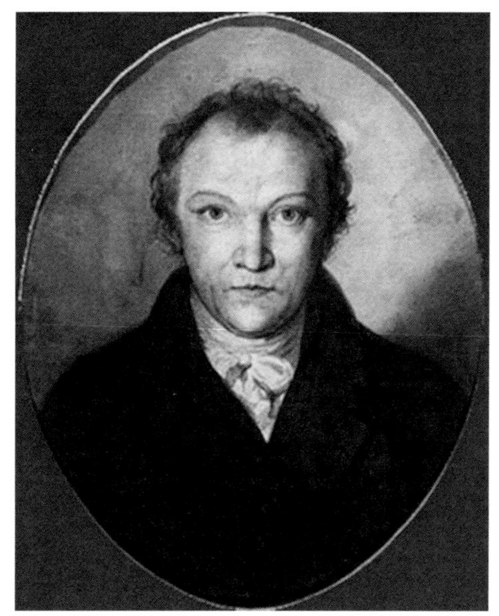

that served Epstein as a starting point. By elaborating on John Linnell's curls drawn in a pen draft (probably preparatory for his oil painting) [fig. 73],[36] Epstein added the missing hair about which the family had complained, and took notice of the less severe mouth that Blake himself depicted in his self-portrait [fig. 74]. Epstein's representation seems to do justice to the great artist, whom he admired, and a different viewpoint of the portrait accentuates the sharp-looking, penetrating eyes.

"I have been a student of Blake all my life," Epstein explained. "I had no hesitation about what I should do."[37] This included the addition of the exposed shoulders which gave the poet a less formal air, more attuned with his free disposition, while at the same time retaining the respectability conveyed in the painted portraits.

The base, in "black Jerusalem stone", was donated by Epstein, having been given to him by Sir Patrick Geddes when he returned from the Holy Land before the war.[38] The Blake Monument was unveiled at the end of October 1957 in a religious ceremony that was "most impressive", as Epstein reported to Peggy Jean;[39] and, although a large crowd of dignitaries attended, Epstein (perhaps hurt, perhaps offended) mentions the lack of professional critics and the absence of "rogues like Kenneth Clark, Herbert Read, Henry Moore, John Piper & many others who did not approve of my doing the work! So they did not come."

A month after the dedication Epstein was occupied with the large work for Coventry, which "progresses & perhaps by the end of the year I will have the plaster model ready & it will then be erected at the moulders. The studio is too small to set up the whole thing .... I have a moulder to assist me & you would be surprised to see the size of the Coventry work."[40]

The figures which both Epstein and Sir Basil wanted to be "understood by all" derived from traditional presentations of the subject, in which the angel is hovering above the subdued devil at his feet, held down by the sharp head of the spear.

Gustave Doré's familiar depiction [fig. 75] is but one example, demonstrating the

Fig. 72
James Deville
William Blake, 1823
Plaster cast, H. 29.2 cm
National Portrait Gallery, London

Fig. 73
John Linnell
William Blake, 1820
Pen on paper
Private collection

Fig. 74
William Blake
Self-portrait, 1802
Monochrome wash
Private collection

36 John Linnell's portrait of Blake, 1821, in the John Linnell Archive at the Fitzwilliam Museum. See www.fitzmuseum.cam.ac.uk/gallery/Linnell.

37 *The Daily Telegraph*, 25 November 1957.

38 Buckle, *Epstein: Sculptor*, p. 400. Sir Patrick Geddes was a renowned town-planner, who, in the early 1930s, during the British Mandate in Palestine, designed the centre of Tel Aviv, known nowadays as 'the white city'. Although I do not doubt the story, I question the 'Jerusalem' epithet, probably given by Kathleen, as Jerusalem stone has light brown colours. The black basalt (a volcanic stone) is common mainly in the north-east of the country – eastern Galilee and along the Syrian-African Rift. The main point here, however, is it being from Palestine and, regardless of its origin, the epithet befits the poet who wrote a poem entitled *Jerusalem*.

39 A letter and press-cutting from the *The Daily Telegraph*. 25 November 1957: TGA-993/16.

40 Letter from Epstein to Peggy Jean, 25 November 1957: TGA-993/6.

different kind of wings for the 'good' and 'bad' guys – discussed with reference to *Lucifer* (p. 152) – and Epstein was undoubtedly familiar also with Raphael's depiction of the subject in the Louvre.[41] A notable sculptural precedent, corresponding to these two-dimensional depictions, is Herbert Gerhard's bronze for the Michaelskirche, Munich (1588), and its copy in 's Hertogenbosch in the Netherlands (1620). The common denominator of most of the precedents is the obvious element of struggle; Epstein, on the other hand, presented a victorious aftermath.

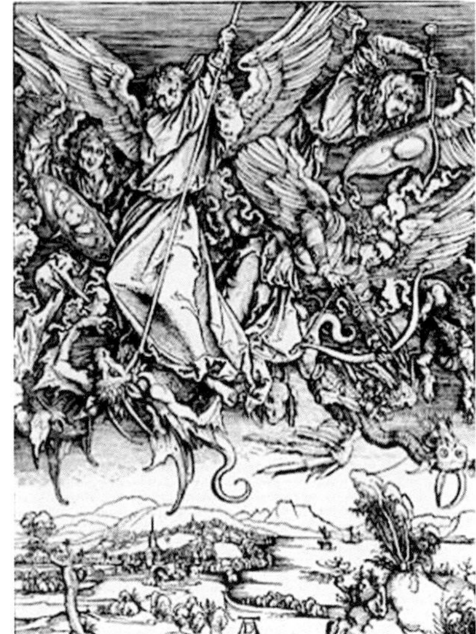

Fig. 75
Gustav Doré,
St Michael and the Devil, 1866
Engraving from Milton's *Paradise Lost*

Victoriously, the angelic figure of Michael hovers above the reclining Devil, holding a spear in his right hand, his legs apart, forming an X with his hands and wings spread diagonally upwards [107a]. Like El Greco's figures, Michael's narrow body and elongated limbs convey a sense of spirituality, contrasting with the well-built, masculine and sensual figure of the Devil,[42] stripped of his wings and lying chained below Michael's toes, which almost touch his head. The serenity of the forward-looking angel and the beautiful facial features are contrasted with the protruding eyes of the devil and the ugly horns springing from his skull [107b]. Interestingly, however, in the depiction of the lips the same expression is displayed in both figures [107c].

Given that the sculpture was intended for a church destroyed by war and re-established after victory, Epstein's emphasis seems befitting. It is in his impressive presentation of the devil's attractive body, however, that lies Epstein's interpretation of the victory in the recent war against evil. It was the seductive aspect of the Nazi devil that had lured Europe towards it; the victory, therefore, is the spiritual victory of the good within the human condition.

Because of its great size [108] and because the large art-college studio was no longer availble,[43] the figures had to be worked on in sections (like the separate head that Sir Basil had earlier seen; p. 219) during the last months of 1957 and throughout 1958. "It looked very odd to see a most evil devil twelve feet long with a kitchen table growing out of his backside," recalled Sir Basil Spence, commenting on the "very curious objects for support" that Epstein used.[44]

Just before his death, in 1959, Epstein completed a bust of Sir Basil Spence in seven sittings.[45] "It started with a lump of clay the size of an apple," described Sir Basil, "building up slowly with successive layers and carefully moulding the form to the accompaniment of bursts of Hebrew or 'stay there' when he dubbed a lump of clay in position." His description echoes that of the sculptor Clare Sheridan many years ago (I/155), indicating that Epstein retained throughout his life for his portraits the modelling process – building from the centre outwards with layers of what Peggy Jean called "sausages" (small cylinders of clay) – which he himself had developed.[46] I think Sir Basil may have confused the linguistic outbursts Epstein made when when he did something wrong. They could not have been in Hebrew as at the time the renewed language still lacked a lexicon of profanities; it was probably Yiddish, the language with which Epstein had grown up in his parents' home.

The unveiling of the work, attended by Kathleen, took place on 24 June 1960, after Epstein's death.

"On the whole I am in good health. Of course since my operation I have to be careful. I have never really regained my former strength & lifting is out of the question. Walking

41 *St Michael and the Devil*, 1518, oil on canvas, 268 x 160 cm, Musée du Louvre, Paris.

42 Buckle (*Epstein: Sculptor*, p. 407) comments that there was no model for the angelic torso; Gordon Bagnal-Godfrey posed for the Devil.

43 He left it at the beginning of 1956: letter from Epstein to Peggy Jean, 4 February 1956: TGA-8716-49.

44 Spence, *Phoenix at Coventry*, p. 72.

45 Ibid., p. 73.

46 A demonstration of the process had been exhibited by the artist Michael Gillespie – a fine bronze-caster, working for Jacob Epstein in his later years to produce numerous bronze heads – and can be seen on *Rebel Angel – Central TV*.

108
St Michael and the Devil, 1956–58
Bronze, overall 1066 cm
Coventry Cathedral

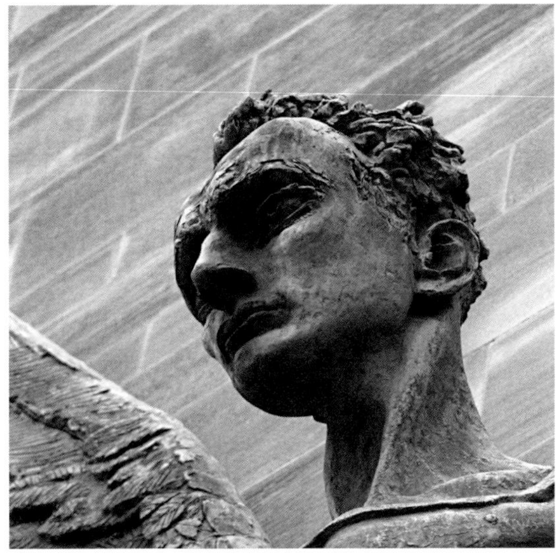

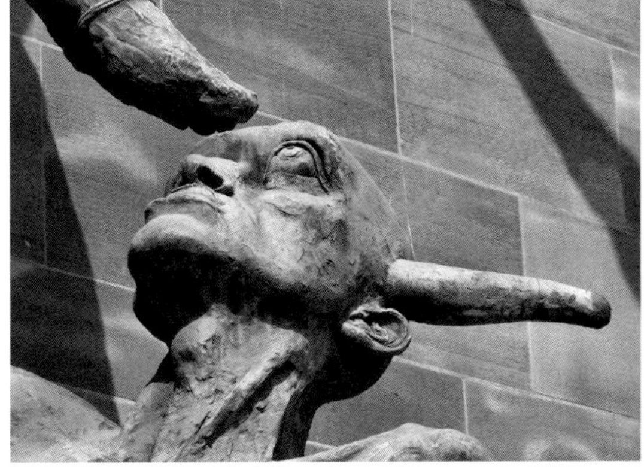

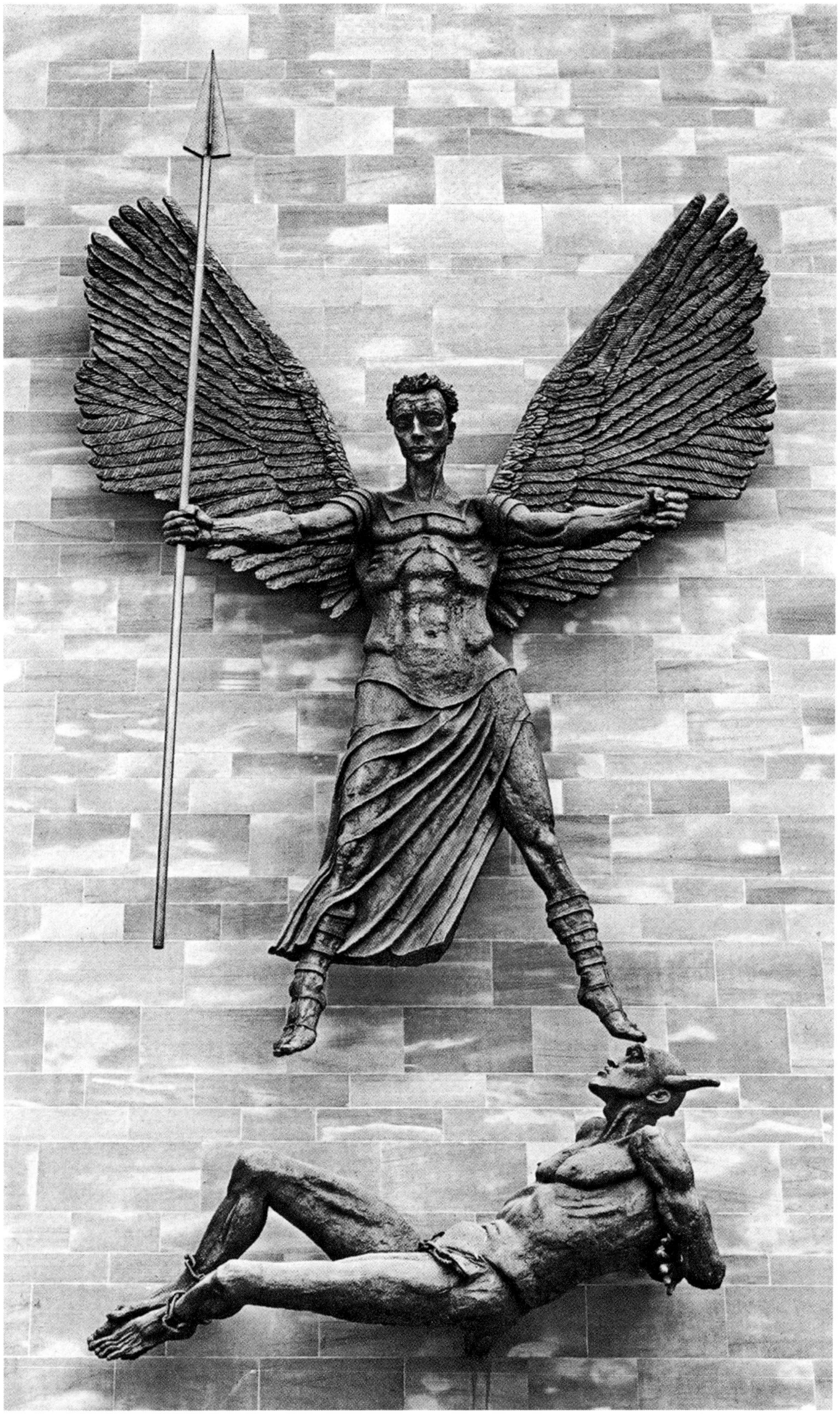

also tires me & you remember what a good walker I was," Epstein told Peggy Jean at the end of the year.[47] His failure to regain his former strength continued into the beginning of the following year, and it is reflected in his subsequent letters; the handwriting is narrower and smaller:

> Actually I don't feel frightfully fit. I think I have overdone the work somewhat, & I feel terribly tired. I don't feel bad in the studio but outdoors away I easily get fatigued. I don't like seeing doctors as I'm afraid they might recommend something that would hold up the work & I've two [projects] to do & be halted just now.... I have a moulder to assist me, but apart from moulding I must do everything myself. I have portraits to do but apart from that there is this big work for outdoors.[48]

The outdoor work had been commissioned for presentation to the Crown by the property developer Lord Harold Samuel, who had built Bowater House (for the Bowater Organization headed by Sir Eric Vansittart Bowater) between 1956 and 1958, at the forefront of the post-war redevelopment of London. Epstein, by now a proven and trustworthy 'public' sculptor, was given in mid 1957 a free hand and choice of subject for the commission. As Epstein never named it, it has had several titles over the years – once called the Bowater House Group (Silber, Buckle), or the Pan Group, it has recently been re-titled *Rush to the Green*.

Concomitantly with this great project, in February 1958 Epstein had been engaged with a portrait of Princess Margaret. Apparently the commission was given in November 1957, and at the time a somewhat reluctant Epstein wrote to Peggy Jean that a royal command was not paid for, adding: "So where would I be with my time taken up with Royalty and no compensation[?]".[49] However, in an undated letter from this period Epstein writes to Sally Ryan that in fact the bust was "not a Royal Command but a commission from the College of North Staffordshire of which the Princess is President".[50] During the sittings he had conversations with Her Highness and, not seeing eye to eye with her on several issues, Epstein wrote to his daughter in a mellower tone: "Royalty lives in an altogether different world than we commoners do, and it is impossible to understand their mentality. As they are never contradicted and treated like gods any criticism or answering back is out of the question; as you know I am no courtier. I listened to H.R.H. but of course never agreed to alterations which I thought unreasonable."[51]

Kathleen reports that a first version,[52] unseen by anyone, was by the royal household's demand taken away from the studio because it did not please Princess Margaret, who commented that it was "Hardly a portrait of the prettiest girl in England".[53] This, I suggest, was a response typical of some of his sitters, when they failed to see the personality that emerged from what they regarded as an unpleasing presentation of their features. In fact, Kathleen had time to cast in bronze the princess's first version; the casting is not recorded in Silber's catalogue as such, but I venture to suggest it to be no. 508, titled by Kathleen *Kitty, 3rd portrait* [109] and dated 1957, but never exhibited.[54] Its outline is similar to the sculpture eventually executed – the short hair and the fringe, the elongated face (in real life Princess Margaret's face impressed one as being rounder), and the expressive eyes [110a], which Epstein had commented were "especially remarkable".

Despite his deteriorating health, an upset Epstein made the recorded portrait with the 'official' ribbon [110b], but the sittings came to an end when Epstein was taken

47 Letter from Epstein to Peggy Jean, 25 November 1957: TGA-993/6.

48 Letter from Epstein to Peggy Jean, 11 January 1958: TGA-993/7.

49 Letter from Epstein to Peggy Jean, 12 November 1957: TGA-8716.52.

50 David Schulson Autographs Catalog: http://www.schulsonautographs.com/artists.htm.

51 Letter from Epstein to Peggy Jean, 28 February 1958: TGA-993/8. The handwriting is bad and the issues of the conversation are hard to decipher, in parts almost impossible.

52 Gardiner, *Epstein*, p. 468.

53 Ibid. However, according to Kathryn Jones, Curator of Decorative Arts for the Royal Collection, there is no record in the Royal Collection of this item or any images of it.

54 Silber, *Sculpture of Epstein*, no. 508. As HRH's first portrait had been cast, I suspect that Kathleen did not want to obliterate her husband's work and therefore titled it with her daughter's name. However, a comparison with Kitty's acknowledged 2nd portrait with short hair (Silber, *Sculpture of Epstein*, no. 387) shows differences of features and a totally different personality than that conveyed by the supposed 3rd (see also the line of her portraits in Buckle, *Epstein: Sculptor*, p. 397). The fact that this 3rd portrait had never been exhibited seems to justify my speculation.

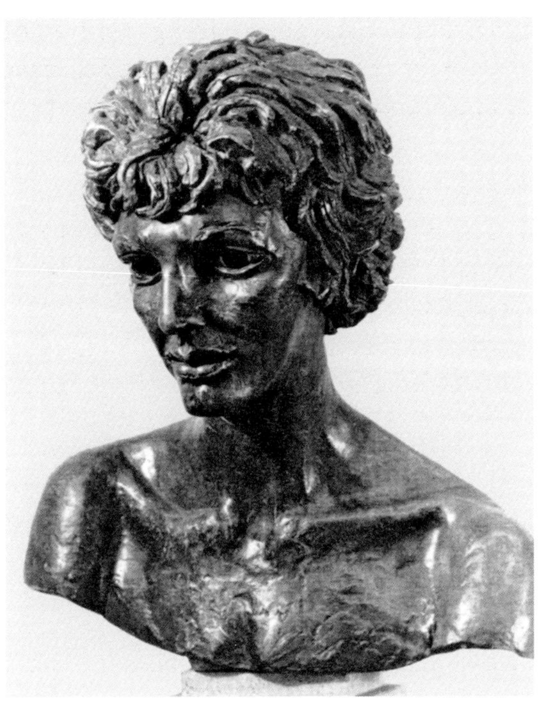
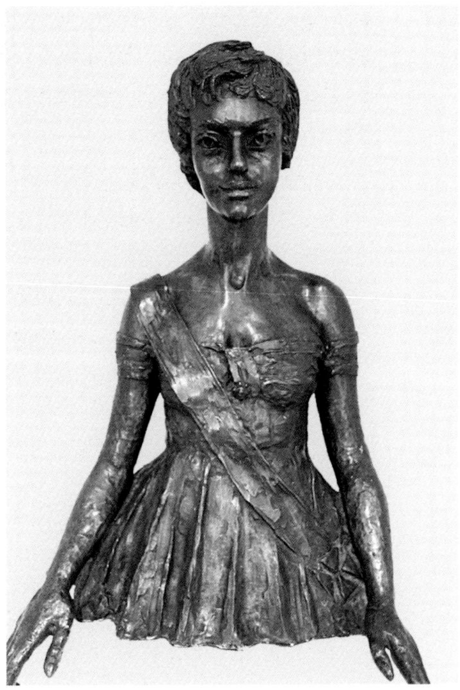
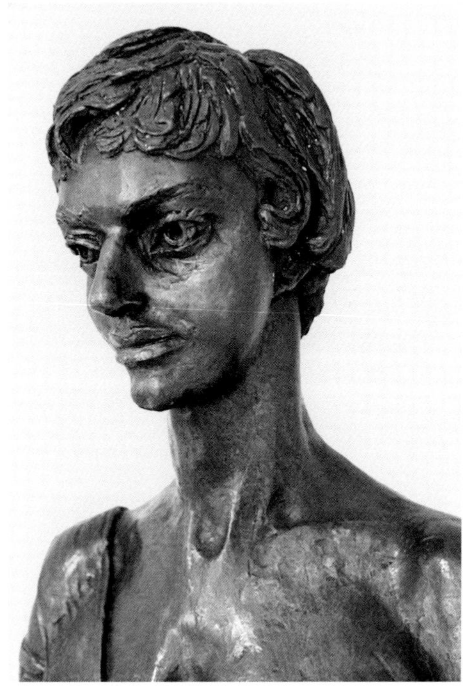

ill in March: "I finished a bust of Princess Margaret just before I went into hospital. I hope to get sittings again after her trip to U.S.A. & extend the bust to include the hands".[55] They were never resumed, however, and the recorded bust with the hands was in all probability done from photographs, a practice with which Epstein was by now well acquainted. The casting of Princess Margaret's official bust was made in 1959, after Epstein's death.

109
Princess Margaret, 1st portrait [?]
[*Kitty, 3rd portrait*], 1958
Bronze, H. 49.5 cm
Formerly Shinman collection

110a–b
Princess Margaret, 1958
Bronze, H. 92 cm
Courtesy of Keele University

On his hospitalization, which prevented his presence at several events, and during which Kathleen visited him twice a day "to make certain he didn't sign himself out", he commented to Peggy Jean:

> I had a bout in Hospital. I got so bad I had to consult a specialist & he diagnosed heart trouble & immediately arranged for hospital treatment. I was in London Hospital for 3 weeks but have now happily returned home, I suppose I overdid the work for I no soon finished our large work [St Michael] then another … I must go slow & not do any big work.[56]

The first event he missed reopened an old wound. *Genesis* was put up for auction by its owner, Sir Alfred Bossom. Persuaded by Epstein, Bossom had attempted to offer the statue to the Tate, which, still unconvinced by Epstein's success and status, turned him down. The successful bidder bought it for a mere £4,200, and Epstein was horrified at the news; the low price seemed a particular insult, and he noted that while the Tate could not find even such a low sum to purchase his work, it could easily afford nearly £20,000 to acquire a Cézanne.[57] The disregard for Epstein and his art by the artistic establishment was evident also in the Art Council's catalogue of the *Contemporary British Sculpture* exhibition in London (1958) and at the Brussels World Exhibition (17 April – 19 October 1958), the works for which were selected by the Belgian Executive Committee and inter

55 Letter from Epstein to Peggy Jean, 16 April 1958: TGA-993/9. In this letter, too, ill health is evident in his handwriting, which becomes harder to decipher.

56 Gardiner, *Epstein*, p. 469.

57 The above and following details are cited from the article on the exhibition *Jacob Epstein and Blackpool*, Grundy Art Gallery, Queen Street, Blackpool, 26 June – 11 September 2010: www.artsphere.co.uk/2010/08/jacob-epstein-and-blackpool. See also Gardiner, *Epstein*, p. 469.

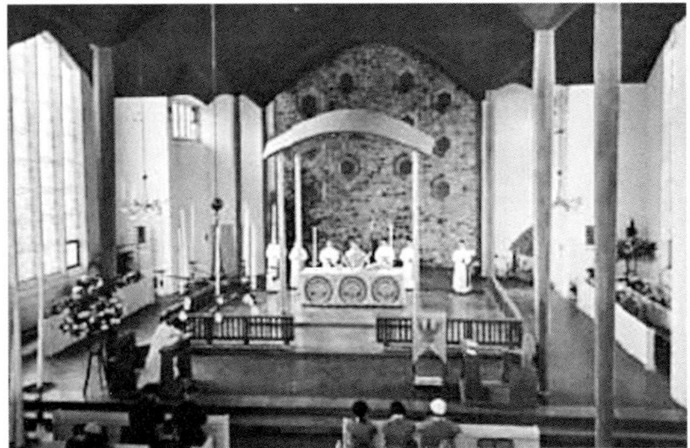

Fig. 76a
Church of the Ascension in Crownhill, Plymouth (interior), in 1958

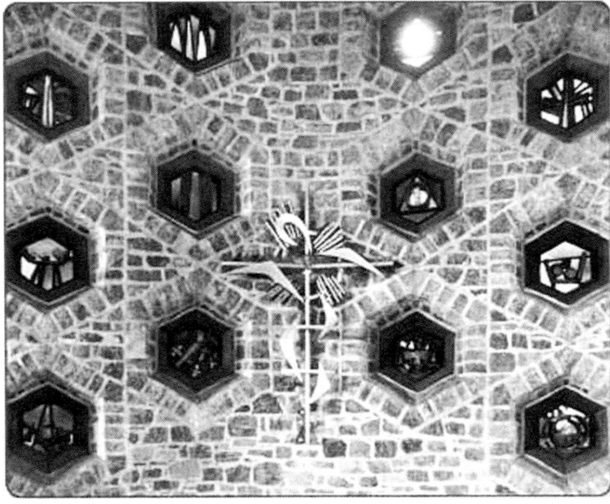

Fig. 76b
Church of the Ascension, central wall with the hexagonal windows
Courtesy of the Parochial Council, Church of the Ascension

national experts (London was represented by Sir Herbert Read). Among the artists chosen were Alexander Calder, Barbara Hepworth, Henry Moore, Kenneth Armitage, Reginald Butler and Francis Bura,[58] and, although portraits were also presented, none of them were by Epstein.

In his letter to Peggy Jean on the sale of *Genesis*, Epstein attached a newspaper clipping that reported: "The room had a crowd of 300 seated people with dignitaries such as Duncan Grant and Lord Rothschild and son Jacob; others were standing near the wall. The buyer, William Cartmell of Louis Tussauds, acquired *Genesis* with the intention for exhibition at Blackpool." After the bidding had finished, Kathleen, who had been present at the auction, rushed to speak to Cartmell, who is reported to have said, 'I've never been to Sotheby's before. I'm more used to going round the murder trials to get ideas for the Chamber of Horrors at the waxworks". "Unfortunately ... Blackpool," Epstein commented to his daughter,[59] and infuriated he added: "What I object to is that it has been bought by these people who will show it in a cheapjack and vulgar manner. Any artist would be upset to have his work subjected to this sort of indignity." Thus, during the Easter season of 1958, *Genesis* joined *Adam*, *Jacob and the Angel* and *Consummatum Est* in a collection of anatomical and freak-show oddities at Louis Tussaud's, where 10,000 visitors were expected daily.

Another event of which he read in the papers on March 27, from his hospital bed, was the unveiling of the TUC memorial, "to trumpets ... quite a do". The reception by many was positive: "As a work of art, Epstein's work appears to be almost painfully moving. It is a tragic monument on a grand scale," reported the *Daily Telegraph* on 28 March, thus contradicting the majority of the thirty-five TUC Council members, who disliked it, calling it "a monstrosity ... [the] sooner it joins *Genesis* in Blackpool the better".[60] Epstein's response was: "The architect of the building is pleased & so am I".[61]

In his long and news-loaded April letter to Peggy Jean, Epstein wrote about the house, which had just been sold, and of the new owner, who had had to comply with Holtzmann's arrangement (p. 194), which enabled Epstein to stay ("At any rate I've that guaranteed"): "I have a terrible lot to do & Kathleen insists I take a good rest before beginning again". As part of his recuperation, Kathleen arranged a series of trips. On 27 April 1958 they went with Beth Lipkin to Venice, returning on 15 May, and at the beginning of September Epstein went by himself to Plymouth to see the site of an intended project, a church; afterwards, on 6 September, he went with Kathleen and their friends John and Valery Cowie to the Continent, writing to Peggy Jean in early October that he had "had a great trip in a car through France & Italy with Kathleen & visited a number of Cathedrals", and was studying stained glass, as he had "a commission to design a sculpture and window for a new church in Devon".[62]

The subject of the new work comes up again in his letter of the end of October, when he says that he had been making "a special study of stained glass" while halfway through the Bowater House group, which he thought would be "quite a new thing for London & I think will give Londoners something to talk of". Concomitantly, probably owing to the success of previous examples, he was commissioned to do another posthumous portrait: "As well I am designing a statue of Lloyd George for the House of Commons. So you see, I am busy as usual." In a P.S. remark he adds: "Kathleen is well & of course does all my business".[63]

58 Langui, *50 Years of Modern Art*.

59 Letter from Epstein to Peggy Jean, 16 April 1958: TGA-993/9.

60 Gardiner, *Epstein*, p. 470.

61 Letter from Epstein to Peggy Jean, 16 April 1958: TGA-993/9.

62 Letter from Epstein to Peggy Jean, 10 October 1958: TGA-993/9.

63 Letter from Epstein to Peggy Jean, 27 October 1958: TGA-993/10.

The commission for several hexagonal stained-glass windows,[64] for which he had drawn inspiration during his visits to the churches of Europe,[65] and which also included an intended sculpture of the Ascension of Christ,[66] came from the new Church of the Ascension in Crownhill, Plymouth. The church had been designed by the architect Robert Potter of the firm Potter & Hare.[67] This now listed building became a benchmark for the Liturgical Movement, with its unique central altar set further inside the building (fig. 76a), intended to be "at the heart of the 'gathered people of God'". To some extent (as I have suggested; p. 206), Epstein's *Majestas* in Llandaff does just that in a conventional church interior.

Epstein's sculpture was to be placed on the granite wall amidst twelve hexagonal windows in four rows, each having an image of a saint. However, unlike the existing arrangement (fig. 76b), in which all the hexagons point upwards, in Epstein's studies half of them point sideways, as he attempted to introduce variety into an otherwise standard grouping of windows.

Represented in the studies – pencil, watercolour and gouache drawings on six-sided paper sheets, each 62 × 71 cm – are "Saints Barnabas, Peter, Philip, Matthew, John, Thomas and Judas";[68] Gardiner (472) mentions another saint, James, Son of Thunder,[69] thus bringing the total to eight drawings. The twelve windows might indicate a wish to present the Twelve Apostles, and therefore Judas Iscariot is also included in the list.[70] The inclusion of St Barnabas (not one of the canonical twelve apostles, but mentioned by Paul) may indicate the influence of Epstein's churches tour – where he had seen perhaps an isocephalic procession of Christian saints, like the renowned one in the lower register of the apse mosaic in the Basilica of St Paul outside the Walls in Rome. Unfortunately, Epstein died before he could realise the sculpted figure and the drawings for all the windows. Except for *St Peter*, it seems that Epstein had yet to transfer the first drawings into the more rigid lines and planes that befit glass. Each image, even in its crude state, seems to have been given its own style –probably an attempt to indicate the different natures of the saints. Some remained as preliminary drawings of naturalistically detailed faces.[71] It is hardly surprising that Kathleen, who was aware of their uncompleted state, "would not release them to the new architect Robert Potter".[72]

The intended *Ascension of Christ* never materialized as a full-scale sculpture. What remains is a maquette depicting a man in a floating pose, his hands, neck and head raised upwards [111]. The movement seems to be influenced by Raphael's *Transfiguration*, one of the earliest depictions of the subject that frees the Christ figure from the rigid pose of the hands (fig. 77). The upward arm movement was followed also by the English artist John Flaxman (1755–1826) in his illustration of Christ in Glory for *Compositions from the Divine Poem of Dante*.[73]

This was Epstein's second non-symbolic execution of an adult Christ, the first one being that in Llandaff, and it is interesting to note the differences. As facial details are hard to decipher from a maquette, there is little point in trying to guess who might have posed for this portrait of Jesus. The hairstyle – two locks reminiscent of the Jewish ringlets (*peyoth*) lying on his chest – is different from Llandaff's severely back-combed style. Epstein seems reluctant to from a constant Jesus-type, and this is evident also in the peculiarity of the maquette's attire: the diagonal folds, which emphasize the upward movement, have a transparent effect, accentuating every part of the body, including

64 Gardiner mentions twelve hexagonal windows (*Epstein*, pp. 470 and 472 and note) and specifies two of them – "one of James, Son of Thunder, the other of Peter" – adding that the illustrations are in "a catalogue, untitled but dated 16.12.1958, recording that the stained glass was being made in France and that the windows would be in position, August 1959".

65 Gardiner (*Epstein*, p. 471) gives full details of Epstein's visits to places and the people he met; I have chosen to concentrate on what is related to his work.

66 Silber, *Sculpture of Epstein*, no. 513.

67 On the architect, see www.telegraph.co.uk/news/obituaries/religion-obituaries/8195099/Robert-Potter.html. On architectural aspects of the church, see: www.plymouthdata.info/Churches-Anglican-Ascension.htm.

68 See www.artfact.com/auction-lot/sir-jacob-epstein-seven-studies-for-stained-glass-1-c-283u205um.

69 Gardiner, *Epstein*, p. 519, note 472: "illustrations in a catalogue, untitled but dated 12.12.1958 [?]".

70 As far as I know, the inclusion of Judas in such a context is unusual. After Jesus's crucifixion he was exchanged by the remaining eleven Apostles for Matthew.

71 I am indebted to Bryn Sayles, Modern and Post-War British Art, Sotheby's, for enabling me to have black-and-white images of the drawings. They were auctioned by Sotheby's on 3 June 1966 (lot 167) as "Jacob Epstein's *Studies for stained glass windows with Saints*, works on paper (28 x 24 in.) executed *c.* 1958–59".

72 Kathleen's refusal to release the sketches does not concord with Gardiner's information on the reportedly completed project, taken from a catalogue (note 69 above) relating that the stained-glass windows were eventually made "in France". The present windows were finally designed by Geoffrey Clarke. I am grateful to Jean England, who, on behalf of the church, told me that Epstein drew up sketches for three of the windows before he died: email to the author, 16 October 2011.

73 In 1793 Flaxman created 110 line drawings of Dante's *Commedia* in a commission for Thomas Hope, an English aristocrat. This collection of works was reissued in 1807 under the title *Compositions from the Divine Poem of Dante*: www.worldofdante.org/gallery_flaxman.html.

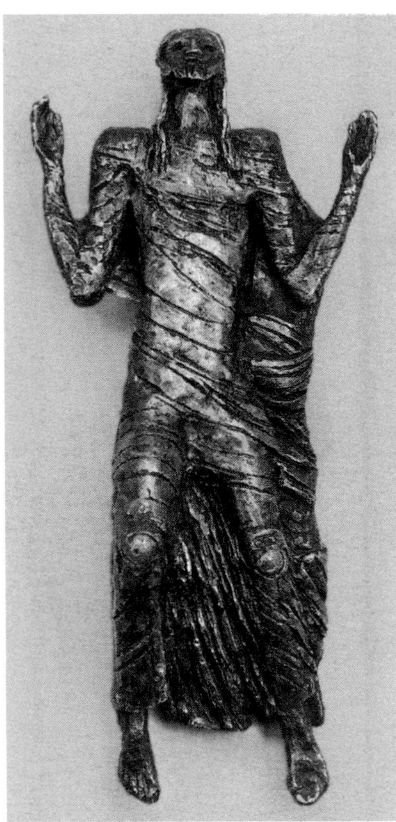

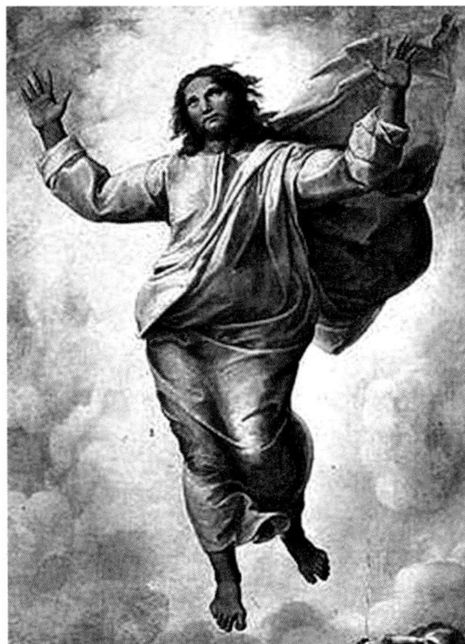

111
The Ascension of Christ (maquette), 1958–59
Lead, H. 34.9 cm
Private collection

Fig. 77
Raphael
Christ in glory (detail), 1516–20
Tempera grassa on wood, 410 x 279 cm
Pinacoteca, Vatican

the genitals, and thus representing Jesus as a vital human being rather than the commonly portrayed neutral, covered, symbolical figure, like that in Llandaff. Despite these small differences, this intended work essentially offers no novelty or enrichment of his artistic vocabulary. In preventing him from executing the sculpture, therefore, old age prehaps saved him from becoming a kind of industry, like Moore with his later repetitive works.

The last year in Epstein's life was loaded with both work and social activity: "I am as always up to the neck in work, large work which never seems to finish & also portraits over which I don't take too much time".[74] Amusingly, he writes that he had heard from his American niece Martha [Clamage] that "her whole family have taken to sculpture, even her father who is a dentist; it would be better if they all stuck to what they had been doing before & leave the sculpture to me". In regard to his sculpture he adds:

> This year the Carnegie Institute show; a terrible show full of abstractions & crazy things. Needless to say the prize of £500 went to Henry Moore for Britain. My piece – a bust of Kitty sold out just same [price]. The art world gets crazier & crazier & nothing can stop it. I seem the only sane person practicing sculpture.

But there were also quiet moments of rest in the little garden of their house, where Kathleen's most striking features were caught by the camera, explaining – if there is still a need to explain – Epstein's continuous fascination with them (fig. 78).

Besides the portraits there was what he defined as the "large work" that consumed him and his time, the Bowater House group, referred to here by its recent title of *The Rush to the Green*. During the long period on which he worked on it, he found the need to return to the Continent: on 22 April 1959 the Epsteins left from Paddington to Paris, spending a week there, passed mainly in the Louvre, with Epstein's brother Irving and his wife; on 28 April he and Kathleen continued on to Venice, returning on 18 May to London, and dining with Matthew Smith on 31 May.[75] The evenings of June and July were busy: they attended, amongst others, Claudio Arau's concert, a John Haul recital and met twice for "dinner with T.S. Eliot at the Garrick Club" – and during the days Epstein continued his work on *The Rush to the Green*.

74 Letter from Epstein to Peggy Jean, 20 January 1959: TGA-993/11.

[opposite page]

75 Kathleen's diary for 1959, NAGW. The Louvre is mentioned by Beth Lipkin, interviewed by Gardiner (*Epstein*, p. 473).

76 Gardiner, *Epstein*, p. 468.

77 Carew, *The Nine Lives of Paton College*, pp. 11–12: www.mun.ca/memorial_history/bios/EVBowater.html.

78 'Robert Bowman Modern presents works by the key modern British sculptors', *All Art News*, 29 January 2011. The maquette presented (and sold to a private collector) belonged to Lady Samuel.

79 Letter from Epstein to Peggy Jean, 27 October 1958: TGA-993/10.

80 I am greatly indebted to Prof. Mira Friedman for drawing my attention to this work.

81 I am indebted for this information to Francine Bouré, *documentaliste* at the Musée des Beaux-Arts, Paris; letter of 28 March 2012.

82 *"L'intelligence exacte de sujet est une des qualités les plus rares de la statuaire contemporaine … fuyait au soleil couchant parmi les nudes"*: 'Les Salons de 1898', *Gazette des Beaux-Arts*, 1898, vol. 20, p. 135, repr. p. 133. Another critique published in 1899 is 'Contemporary Sculptors and Medalists' (www.oldandsold.com/articles27n/french-art-24.shtml). A recent publication on St-Marceaux is 'Une famille d'artiste en 1900 les Saint-Marceaux', in *Les dossiers du Musée d'Orsay*, Paris 1992.

III. *THE RUSH TO THE GREEN*

The commissioned group – its subject left to Epstein's discretion – was intended to face the south side of Hyde Park and stand on a high pedestal on a traffic island between flanking roads coming out from under Bowater House, built in the late 1950s.

The maquette [112] presents a family group of father, mother, child and dog, being driven ahead by the god Pan playing his pipes. The five figures are arranged so that their tops form an uneven hyperbolic upper line: the small, symbolic figure of Pan is at one end, the tall parents at the centre, and the small child and dog close the composition at the other end. The mother, leaning on a thin beam, is the tallest figure in the composition, while the father is the central one. The gestures are directed toward the park, away from the built-up area and towards the green, creating "a vision of people escaping from the prison of offices and hard work to the freedom of nature".[76] This notion befitted Sir Eric Bowater – "an indefatigable worker and organizer, a fact to which the great Bowater organization bears witness, [he] nevertheless had a flair for knowing how to relax"[77] – and he approved Epstein's subject and its maquette. To commemorate the commission, Lord Samuel requested that Epstein cast four bronzes of the maquette, for Lady Samuel and their three children.[78]

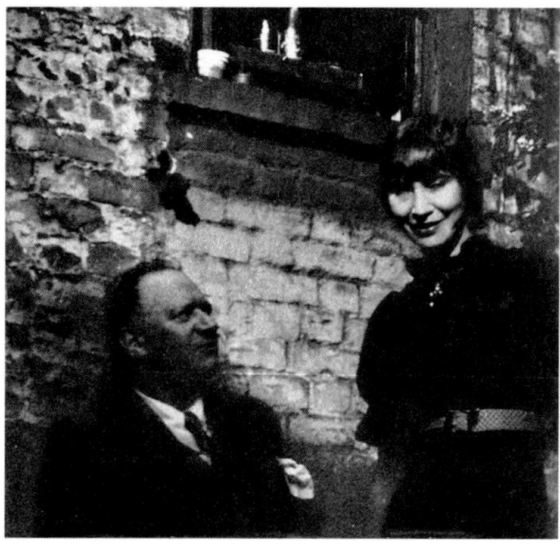

Fig. 78
Jacob Epstein and Kathleen at their garden, date unknown

The figures, all depicted in the nude, lean foward at an impossible angle, almost in a state of flight. This kind of momentary balance is found in other works by Epstein – in *Liverpool Resurgent*, for example – but in no other work had it reached the extreme of this exceptional group, which, as he stated, would "give Londoners something to talk of".[79]

Epstein, I suggest, drew inspiration for the extremely inclined bodies from European precedents in the Louvre – seen perhaps on the recent trip to visit his brother, or during his early studies in Paris in 1903–04 – such as the classical figures of the Borghese *Gladiator*, with its forward movement accentuated by the outstretched hand, and of *Apollo and Daphne*. His recent visit to the Louvre may have brought to mind a work he might have known during his Paris studies, *Vers l'inconnue* (also named *Nos Destinés*; fig. 79) of 1898 by the sculptor Charles René de St-Marceau (1845–1915),[80] an outdoor work, exceptional for its period, that had been destroyed in 1942 as it had become excessively weathered.[81] At its unveiling and until its destruction it was considered a superb work: its "precise understanding of subject is a quality very rarely found in contemporary sculpture".Its vision, "fleeing to the sunset among the nudes", is said to have been suggested by a swift flying cloud.[82] The sculpture, indeed, shows a group of nudes above a cloud with arms stretched forward, surging ahead.

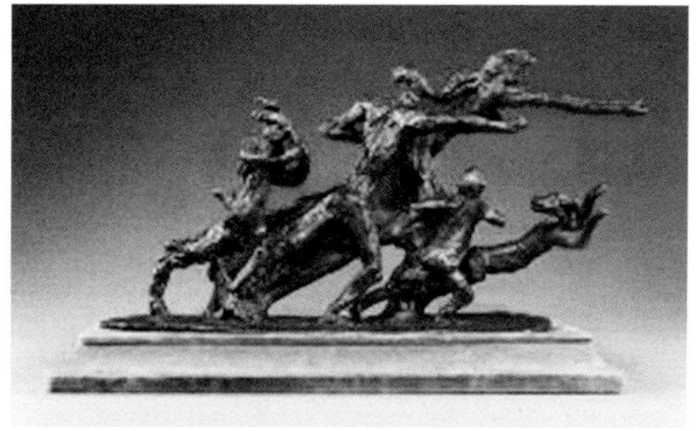

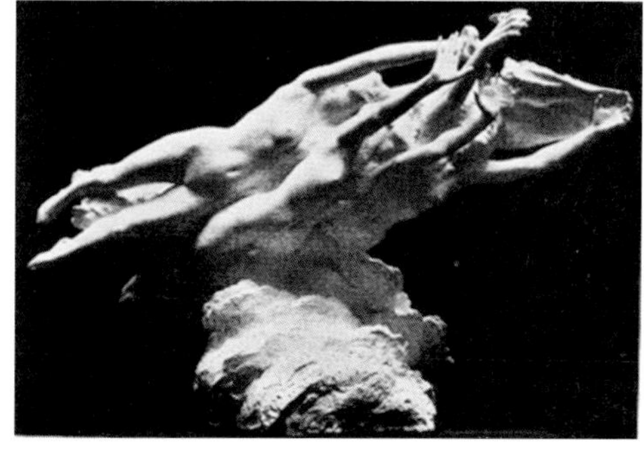

112
The Rush to the Green (The Bowater House Group; maquette), 1958
Bronze, H. 28; base 33.7 x 10.8 cm
Private collection

Fig. 79
Charles René de St-Marceau
Vers l'inconnue, 1898
Marble
Now destroyed

An echo of some of its elements can be seen in one of Epstein's preliminary drawings for the group [113], in which a floating figure apparently leaning on a solid body resembles the woman leaning on a figure at the front of St-Marceau's group. Another common element is that of a drape or veil, which in the Paris sculpture was held by the figure in the back of the composition and in Epstein's drawing partly covers the figure's chest. This seems to be an early drawing, in which, in all probability, the final concept had not yet been achieved. Thus, although Epstein was not considering a clothed group, in the silhouette above, drawn in a light circumscribing line, a pencil stroke on the buttocks might be interpreted as underwear.

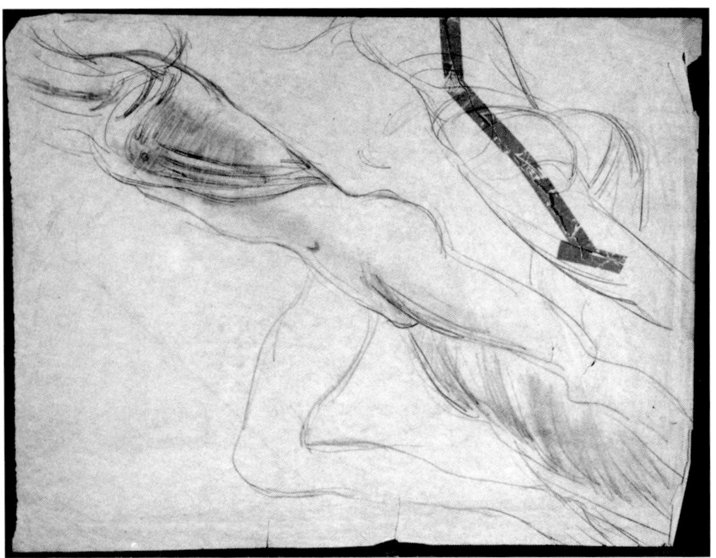

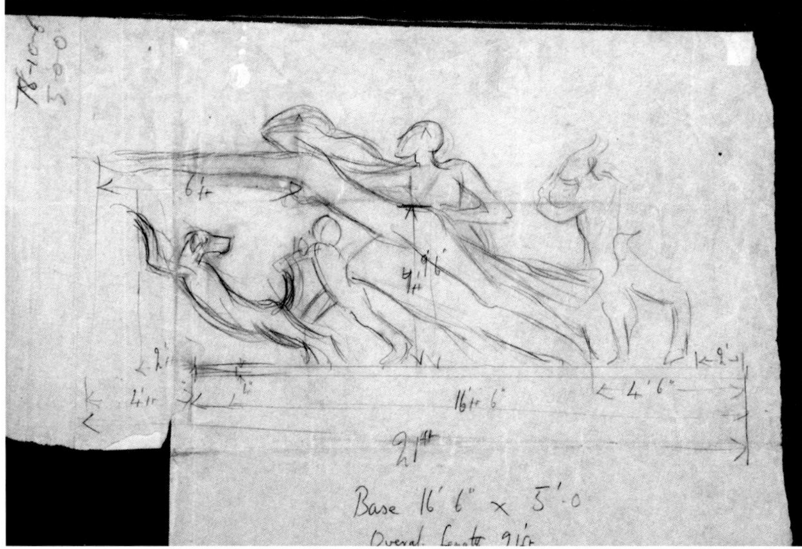

113
Two studies for the figure of the mother from 'The Rush to the Green' (Bowater House Group), 1958
Pencil on paper, 420 x 535 mm
Henry Moore Institute, Leeds

114
Study for 'The Rush to the Green' (Bowater House Group), 1958
Pencil on paper, image 256 x 150 mm
Henry Moore Institute, Leeds

The second drawing [114] shows a more final conception (with lists of wood and nails added in the cut-off surrounding page). The composition of the group and its participants are detailed and measurements are given. The central point where the man's chest and the woman's lower back meet is indicated. In a development on from the maquette, the woman is leaning on some kind of support, and her arms are stretched forwards.

In the transference from maquette to sculpture Epstein softened the stiff and almost military hand movements of the man and the woman, and altered the position of the limbs of each member of the group, creating a more interesting arrangement when seen from street-level.[83] The central beam that holds the composition together and is so crucial to its equilibrum is narrower than in the maquette, therefore not distracting the viewer's attention from the figures around it. When I saw *The Rush to the Green* years ago, still in its original position in front of Bowater House, my impression was of an enigma that required careful inspection by moving slowly around it (as in the case of *Lazarus*). This seems to be what Epstein intended – a many-figured, non-frontal, non-heraldic group on a wide base that requires careful all-round observation [115].

When approaching the group from the passage under the buildings, the first figure seen is the god Pan – with his horns, large pointed ears and goat's legs – playing his pipes and looking straight ahead, and, as in the drawing, slightly distant from the others. Whereas in the maquette he is a small figure, in the sculpture he is given a grown man's height. Perhaps Epstein wished to break the symmetry that would have been created by small figures starting and ending the composition, as in the maquette, or perhaps he worried that a small Pan might not be noticed in a front view of the group.

In front of Pan is a running man, his chin tilted forward, his left arm folded behind and his right one stretched forward. He veers slightly to the right, behind a small boy, whose head is raised and whose arms are folded in a chiastic relationship to those of his father. The woman to the left of the boy has her face raised up to the sky; she leans on

83 Silber (*Sculpture of Epstein*, p. 60) has a different opinion: "In the maquette there is a natural cadence and rhythm to the group, but the finished work does not live up to its promise, the impetus of the group acquiring a hard uniformity while losing its rhythmic subtlety".

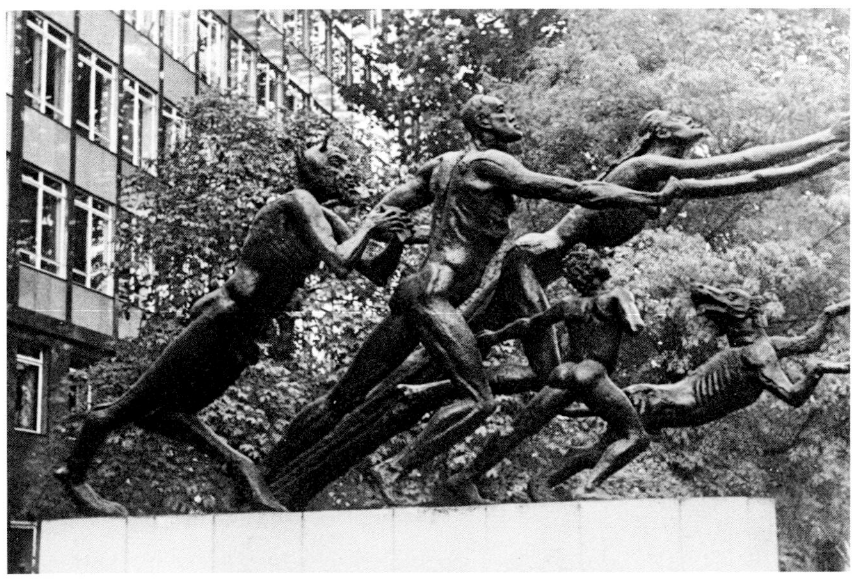

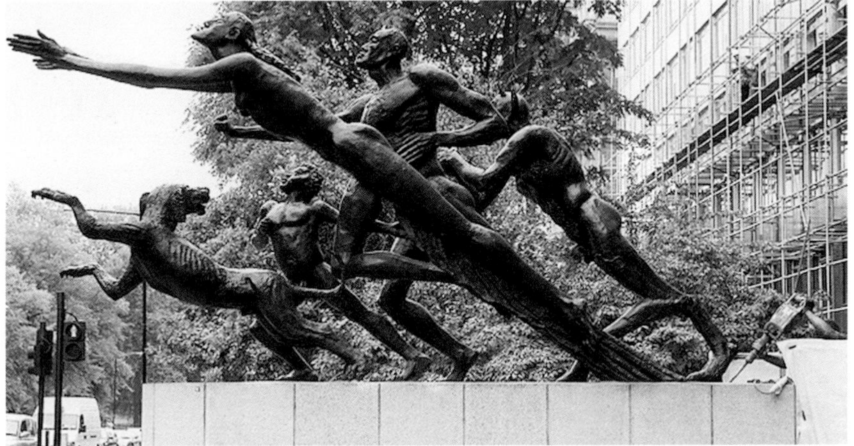

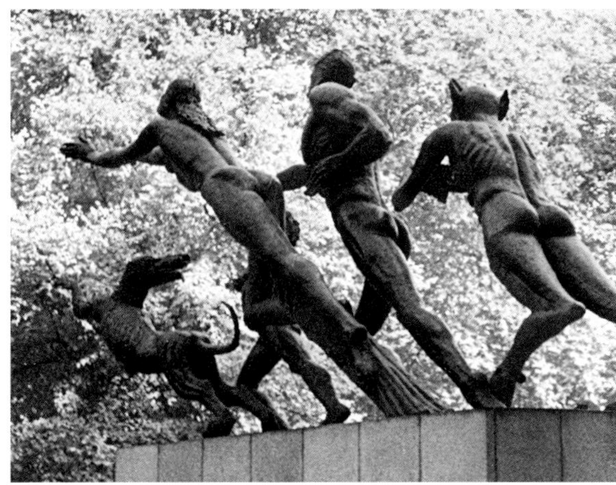

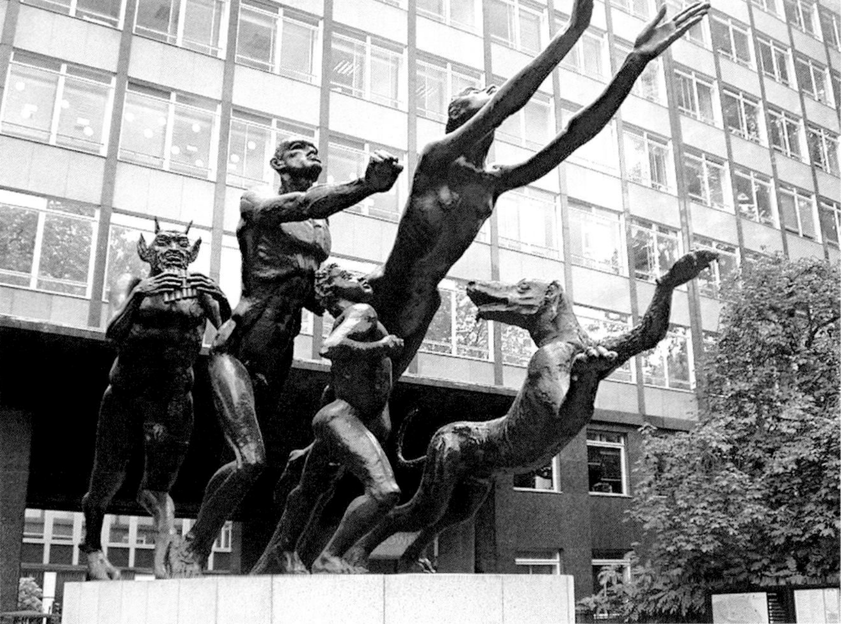

115a–d
The Rush to the Green (The Bowater House Group), 1958–59
Bronze, figures about life-size
115.a view from the man's side
115.b view from the woman's side
115.c view from the back
115.d view from the front
Photographs 1985

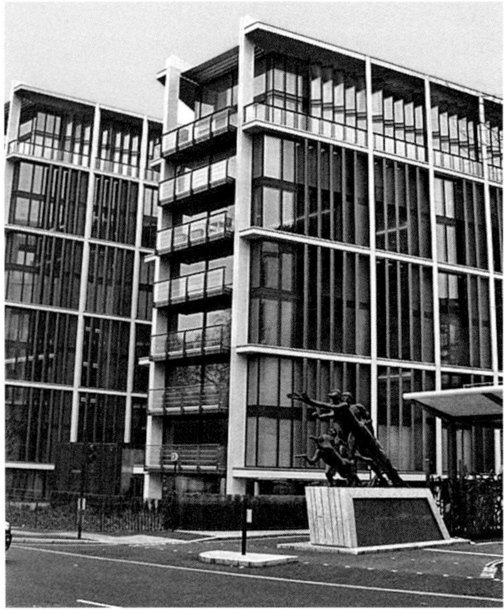

Fig. 80
The Rush to the Green (Bowater House Group), 1958–59, in its present setting, One Hyde Park

the piece of wood between her legs, while her arms are stretched upwards rather than forwards as in the drawing and the maquette. The dog, at the front, turns its head back towards the group, its right front leg is bent as if emulating the boy's movements, and its left leg is stretched forwards and upwards.

The group as a whole, with its thin, elongated figures – reminiscent of El Greco and of Epstein's illustrations for Walt Whitman's *Calamus* poems (I/57) and his figure of St Michael – conveys a sense of spirituality, of harmonious uninhibited freedom and of sheer joy of a family group.

The Rush to the Green seems to be the culmination of Epstein's development of the momentary pose that surges forward – the axis here inclined to the point that the figures defy gravity – and of his move from "the organic flexibility" of the human physio-gnomy to the somewhat rigid stylization befitting a symbol – from *The Girl with a Gardenia* [65], followed by *Lucifer* [67], *Youth Advancing* [79] and *Liverpool Resurgent* [99].

There is more to this sculptural composition than a mere development in pose and feature, no doubt due to its being Epstein's own chosen subject and not, like the previous large bronzes, a commissioned subject. The sulpture of 1959 seems to bring to a close what had been started long ago, in 1908, when a young and unconventional sculptor had depicted a series of naked figures in different postures for the decoration of the BMA building. Epstein's career began with naked figures and ended with naked figures, after their maker had gone through a life full of tribulations and bereavements that echo the words of an ancient sufferer who, at the end, had nonetheless found some consolation in his own nakedness: "Naked came I out of my mother's womb, and naked shall I return thither" (Job, 1: 21).

The sculpture was erected in April 1961, two years after Epstein's death, which may explain the lack of derogatory articles written about it at the time (from which Gardiner would otherwise probably have been somewhat pleased to cite). Epstein's colleague and helper David McFall , however, stated that his own work load at that time meant that he "was not available to participate in [Epstein's] final flights of fancy, such as the Bowater group, which is generally looked upon as a monumental disaster".[84]
The end of the twentieth century brought changes to the original site of *The Rush to the Green*. Epstein's sculpture was removed when Bowater House was demolished to be replaced by a new apartment building (fig. 80)[85] and the group was installed anew on South Carriage Drive. The impression it now leaves depends on the eye of the beholder. One view is that the "new 'street furniture' in aggressively safe Elfin fluorescent yellow" diminishes "the original impetus of *Rush to the Green* .... But, being a resilient family, the Rush-Greens will no doubt adapt to their straitened circumstances and their pushy new neighbour, and continue to work some of their old magic on unsuspecting passers-by.... The great god Pan pipes them on, but keeps a weather-eye open on his tough old face."[86]

84 McFall, p. 13.

85 One Hyde Park, Knightsbridge, London, by Richard Rogers, 2011. The photograph presents the side facing Hyde Park, *The Rush to the Green* on the right.

86 I quote from Dr Nick Maroudas's eulogy on Epstein's public sculpture in London, 11 January 2012, 'Epstein's London Sculptures'.

EPILOGUE

On the evening of 18 August 1959 Kathleen's diary recorded "drinks with Matthew Smith at the Cloisters [his one room apartment at Chelsea Cloisters, Sloane Square], 6 pm", a visit in which they brought to the ailing painter a tiny Renoir landscape to have beside his bed.[87] Next day the Epsteins, accompanied by Beth Lipkin and the dog Frisky, went to Epstein's favourite restaurant, and upon finishing their meal Epstein insisted on walking home across Kensington Gardens. John Finch, much later and from afar, described the event with details (which he took from Gardiner's biography) in a poem addressed to Margaret:[88]

> And one day softly singing Schubert and happy
> With his love by his side he walked home through Hyde Park
> To die.
> And as he sang – oh sad thought …
> Were you listening?

The last hours in Epstein's life are told both by Buckle and by Gardiner, each conveying a slightly different finale. Buckle's account (p. 414) was dictated by Kathleen and published in her lifetime, and naturally it includes elements emphasizing Epstein's attachment to her: "He had once said that he was afraid Kathleen might not be with him when he died", and in this, adds Buckle, "as in many other ways, he was lucky", because when she followed him upstairs to his bed afterwards he declared, "All's well. The group is finished". Epstein's eyes were open, and he "saw Kathleen when she came in to find him lying on the floor by the bed. He died a few seconds later." Gardiner's account (474–75) repeats most of the description above, altering some details (in italics):

> When later going into the house, he went into the studio, where Kathleen *discovered him under the Bowater group, flat on his back, at work on one of the figures' toes. "It's finished" he said …. Now I'm off."* Kathleen followed him upstairs and *listened to him singing as he lay on in bed. Then he said: "Kitty – I'm going".*

This description is "a total fabrication and insulting to him", wrote Beth Lipkin to Gardiner, "I certainly gave you no such account in my interview".[89] There is also one quite different record, a verbal one, given by Peggy Jean, who cited from Kathleen's letter to her relating that she and Epstein were sitting in their little garden having toast and eggs, when Epstein turned to her and said: "I've done it", and then went upstairs to his room; Kathleen heard a noise, and it was the end – an immediate one.[90]

Kathleen, through Buckle and Gardiner, maintained that Epstein had completely finished the group before he died, whereas in fact a few additions were still required (mainly on one hand and several fingers) and David McFall, his trusted colleague, was called in for the job.[91] McFall, however, with his usual modesty, never let it be known, thus helping Kathleen to maintain the legend of Epstein's dying immediately upon its completion.

Epstein died on 19 August 1959. At Kathleen's insistence he was buried in Putney Vale Cemetery, and I suspect that the practical Kathleen – knowing that she would be

87 Gardiner, *Epstein*, p. 474.

88 Only the last part of his poem is dedicated to Margaret.

89 Letter from Beth Lipkin to Stephen Gardiner, 12 January 1993; NAGW–BL/1/4/4/32/2.

90 *Rebel Angel* – Central TV.

91 Told to the author by Jackie Epstein in an interview in 1989. It is to McFall's credit that he never boasted about it to anyone, nor revealed it in his memoirs.

required to leave the house in the upmarket neighbourhood of Hyde Park Gate – had arranged that particular place so as to be close to her intended homes in the less expensive southern areas of London, the last one in Putney itself. It is perhaps deplorable that she did not consider burying him in the prestigious Highgate Cemetery (now a tourist destination), where Margaret had bought a plot for him.

The Jewish executor of Epstein's estate, Sir Barnett Janner, the solicitor who had drafted Epstein's will, insisted on a Jewish burial,[92] either having heard himself or citing Jewish individuals who had heard Epstein expressing this wish.[93] Years later, Jackie could not understand how Janner "had the nerve to interfere in such a private matter"; it required some explanation to clarify to him what a Jewish burial meant for Jews.[94] At the time, however, Kathleen refused, claiming that the *sculptor* Epstein was not exclusively a Jew.[95] Therefore, as Buckle concluded the issue, he was buried in the "non-denominational" part of Putney Cemetery.[96] It was a very private ceremony taking place at "24/8 Putney Vale Cemetery, 11.50 am", as recorded in Kathleen's diary, and attended by family members and Peggy Jean, who flew in from the US; only a dozen mourners from England, among them Matthew Smith, were present. The service at the graveside, which was stated to be "neither Jewish nor Church of England", was conducted by the Dean of Canterbury Cathedral, Dr Hewlett Johnson.[97] After the funeral, the family had dinner together.

For 10 November, Kathleen arranged a commemorative event for the public at Westminster Abbey, and the address was delivered by Canon Mortlock (see p. 84), the Rector of St Vedast, Foster Lane, in the City, which is an Anglican church but in the Catholic tradition to which her friend T.S. Eliot adhered. In his address Mortlock said: "Epstein had executed a number of outstanding religious [Christian] works. How a member of the Jewish faith had become an interpreter of such works was one of the sublime mysteries".[98] As this research has attempted to show, the mystery stemmed from Epstein's knowledge of, and attachment to, his own roots, which embraced also Jesus, and from his conscious choice to express them. It was only after his death that the racial factor was openly admitted in the public's attitude towards him. "It is not difficult to understand why Epstein, more than any other single artist in Great Britain during the first half of the twentieth century, was chosen to represent all that was most perverse in the modern movement. In the first place – one hates to admit it – anti-Semitism raised its Caliban face", stated the obituary in *The Burlington Magazine*, adding in a footnote that "the thinly veiled anti-Semitism of some early criticism is too disgusting to bear".[99] The obituary in the magazine that (under the late editor Roger Fry) had not approved of Epstein and his work revealed a mild "change of heart"; it noted that the main criticism against him was his use of an unfamiliar idiom of alien forms, which he then transformed into formal harmonies for expressionist purposes, namely the expression of emotions. Within artistic circles of the early twentieth century, and in particular the Bloomsbury crowd to which Fry belonged, this was considered a vulgarity and as such inexcusable; moreover Epstein had used his alien idiom to express themes and ideas, including Christian ones, "which were too dear to the hearts of Englishmen". Another obituary elaborated on this racial aspect, but referred it to the nature of his work:[100]

> It is impossible to judge his work fairly without references to its racial flavour. Not only was he at his best and most sympathetic in dealing with compatriots,

92 Jackie's report to the author. Sir Barnett Janner, headed the firm Davies Janner Solicitors; he was at the time also a member of the Board of Deputies of British Jews.

93 Barry Feldman, letter to the author, 1 May 1995: "Epstein expressed a wish to be buried in 'a Jewish cemetery in the country' to several of his Jewish friends, among whom I cite the late Alexander Margulis, the former Chairman of the Ben Uri Society .... I don't know whether Epstein's wish was known to his widow, but I suspect that it was."

94 Author's conversation with Jackie, 1985.

95 Kathleen's resentment of this point was strong, and extended further: she resented the fact that the first memorial exhibition took place (November–December 1959) at a Jewish institution, the Ben Uri Art Gallery. The curator Barry Feldman "had to contend with a strong opposition from Lady Epstein. Not only did she refuse to lend any of Epstein's works, but she went out of her way to persuade others to refuse": Barry Feldman's letter to the author, 1 May 1995.

96 The issue is more complicated, because according to the law a person has to be registered as a member of whatever Jewish community in order to be buried in its respective Jewish cemetery; Epstein never officially joined any Jewish community, but one may assume that had the family complied with his wish he would have been an exception to the rule.

97 *The Times*, 28 August 1959.

98 Ibid.

99 *The Burlington Magazine*, vol. 101, November 1959, 'Editorial', p. 369.

100 *The Times*, 28 August 1959.

> but he tended to give a Semitic character to Gentile subjects, and a good deal of what aroused hostility in his work was due to his racial preferences in physical types – his large-eyed and heavy-lipped young women for example. No doubt he owed something to his admiration for Negro sculpture, but Shem rather than Ham presided over his work in general.

Needless to say, almost every newspaper devoted in their obituaries at least a paragraph to Epstein, summing up the main contention discussed in my earlier book: Epstein was recognised as the father of modern sculpture in Britain and, as Henry Moore described it: "He took the brickbats, he took the insults … and as far as sculpture in this country is concerned, he took them first".[101] There was also an attempt to explain the recent change in public opinion of him:

> The one time rebel, who had been accused of everything from charletanism to sacrilege, had become a respected pillar of his adopted country's aesthetic life, almost, if not quite, a member of the establishment. Was this the old story of the man with a chip on his shoulders who mellows under the influence of success and ends up a completely traditionalist? No, says Sir John Rothenstein, director of the Tate, it was Epstein who changed the British public.[102]

There were also some less positive comments, like the one in *The Daily Herald* (22 August 1959): "But he remained a rebel and a joker to the last" (referring, as did McFall, to *The Rush to the Green*).

In the aftermath of Epstein's death there was a suggestion of turning his house into a public museum, but this failed owing to a lack of sponsors and funding.[103] Epstein's estate (net £40,473) was made public in July 1960, naming his beneficiaries: he left the Egyptian mask entitled 'Queen Nefertiti' to his wife, and "such single piece of my sculptures which is my own work" as he might choose to his brother, Dr Irving Epstein (Evans), of Long Island, America. The residue of the property was equally divided between Lady Epstein, his two daughters and his son.[104]

Following his death, the first memorial exhibition took place in November–December 1959 at the Ben Uri Art Gallery, curated by Barry Feldman, and other galleries followed. On March 1960 a large and impressive exhibition, *The Epstein Collection of Tribal and Exotic Art* was mounted by the Arts Council; its content was then sold, of which several items went to the British Museum. From 10 June to 19 July 1960 the Leicester Gallery exhibited *Fifty Years of Bronzes and Drawings by Sir Jacob Epstein, 1880–1959*. The catalogue had an introduction by Arnold Haskell, who had known Epstein well since the early 1930s, and in which he mentioned: "What has struck me most over this long period has been Epstein's complete consistency and the inconsistencies of so many of his critics, and his absolute integrity as man and artist".

Kathleen, left with the task of evacuating the big house and sorting out the issue of the plasters and works she could not possibly keep, started negotiations to send Epstein's plasters to Jerusalem, a project initiated by the chairman of the Jerusalem

101 James, *Henry Moore on Sculpture*, p. 194.

102 *News Chronicle*, 22 August 1959.

103 *The Times*, 16 November 1959; Gardiner, *Epstein*, p. 478.

104 *Evening News*, 19 July 1960.

Museum board, Billy Rose. In a long letter he explained the project of a new National Museum of Israel on a hilltop in Jerusalem,[105] which was to include, besides his own sculpture collection, also plasters by Jaques Lipchitz and contributions from other supporters internationally. Kathleen agreed to donate the plasters to the growing collection of the new enterprise, conditional upon their being given a special arrangement, as was published in the media: "Epstein Pavilion for Jerusalem", proclaimed *The Times*, somewhat smoothing over (below, in italics) the failure of public bodies in England to do right by Epstein's art:

> Plans to convert the late Sir Jacob Epstein's studio into a memorial museum have been *abandoned* in view of an offer by Mr. Billy Rose, the American showman, to finance the building of a pavilion in Jerusalem, Lady Epstein said last night. The Pavilion that will form part of a new wing at the Bezalel National Museum will provide a permanent home for most of the original casts, one or two carvings and a selection of drawings.[106]

The negotiations for the transfer of the plasters took quite a long time, being finally accomplished in 1965.[107] It involved two co-executors of Epstein's estate (Sir Barnet Janner and H.F. Matthews, as well as another firm of lawyers that Kathleen chose to consult),[108] and the promise that "the plasters would be displayed in a specially constructed pavilion as a memorial to Sir Jacob Epstein", and that they would be repaired in London at their expense "subject to Lady Epstein's supervision". Furthermore "Lady Epstein would also be consulted as to the most effective way to display the life works of Sir Jacob Epstein".[109] During that period, the most important exhibition ever held of Epstein's work was a retrospective presented in Edinburgh in August 1961, moving to the Tate Gallery in London in November. It included the large carvings salvaged from Blackpool for a reported £30,000 at the initiative of Lord Harewood and Mr Jack Lyons. After the exhibition they were spread among various collections and museums. Kathleen suggested that Rose come to Edinburgh during the Festival in order to see the exhibition but he hesitated "to make this trip across the ocean without some sort of tentative commitment", be it only an approval in principle from Lady Epstein and the co-executors.[110] I have found no evidence that Rose saw the exhibition, but I am certain that he would not have been happy with the results of his efforts to gain for the museum in Jerusalem some of its first international treasures, at a time when the museum still held so few. The construction of the museum took some time, and in 1966 Kathleen asked the then chief curator to relay to Jerusalem's mayor Teddy Kolleck an invitation to visit her when he arrived in London, as she would like "to hear about the progress of the Museum" as well as show him paintings that "he might be interested to see".[111] As the opening of the main museum building had been in 1965, Kathleen was apparently referring to the promised pavilion. Jackie Epstein, who only later on in life became involved with the Epstein estate, asked me to inquire into the matter after I mentioned that I had not seen any Epstein Pavilion. I relayed the museum's explanation to the family, namely that the spirit of the times had changed, and in recent years the Museum's policy (and the same applies to other major museums in Israel) is no longer to dedicate special space to the work of one artist permanently. However, many of the plasters were restored and presented in the first exhibition of Epstein's work in Israel,

105 Billy Rose, letter to Anthony B. Lousada, 26 June 1961.

106 27 January 1962; my italics. The name and nature of the museum are incorrect – it was not 'a new wing', but a new concept that incorporated the collection of the Bezalel National Museum with archaeological items, etc. Copies of all the letters on the issue of the gift to the museum were kindly provided to me by Jackie Epstein.

107 Letter from the co-executor Barnett Janner to Jackie Epstein, 2 March 1965, thanking him for the final agreement regarding the gift and the destruction of damaged plasters.

108 Stephenson Harwood & Tatham. The long letter cited above was actually sent to Mr Lousada of this firm, attempting to convince Kathleen through him of the seriousness of the project that by virtue of the objects it would hold would be of international importance.

109 Ibid.

110 Ibid.

111 Kathleen's letter to Karl Katz, Chief Curator of the Israel Museum, 17 February 1966: photocopy kindly provided by Jackie Epstein.

held in 2002, within the museum's 'Focus on the Collection' series, and published in a catalogue.[112] The two plasters of the BMA building stood at either side of the entrance, leading down the stairs to the main hall of the exhibition, which had about 60 portrait-plasters [fig. 81]; however, as the curator stated, given their delicate state they could not be on permanent display. On the other hand, Epstein's *Torso from Rock Drill* and his *Doves – First Version* are currently included in the permanent display of the Early 20th-Century Art Gallery, and *Visitation* continues to be on view in the Museum's Billy Rose Art Garden.[113]

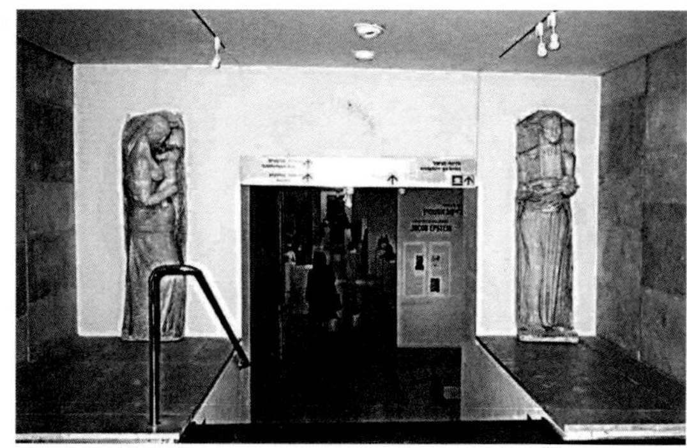

Fig. 81
BMA plasters at the entrance of Epstein's exhibition, 2002, curated by Adina Kamien-Kazhdan at the Israel Museum, Jerusalem

At a certain stage Kathleen needed money because her financial problems had continued much as they had been when Epstein was alive. Although being herself "in better health at the moment", she had the extra burden of her almost blind sister (Helen) who was staying with her, and she therefore started to produce copies of the portraits, as Jackie reported to Peggy Jean:

> The Leicester Galleries have a small number of plasters which it is still possible to cast from, and they are handling the whole thing. It does not amount to very much but I think it will bring us something and it can all operate whether Kathleen is there or not. We are having a tax problem apparently and although there is some money there, I don't think it can be divided [among the children] for a while.[114]

It took some time for the art market to notice in 1971 that "There are too many Epsteins around. And they are all genuine. Lady Epstein, the sculptor's widow, has been taking fresh casts from her husband's original moulds."[115] A week later another article continued the subject: art dealers were asking questions but "Lady Epstein was unavailable for comment". In a meeting with all concerned, she admitted that she had made two more of Churchill "as a result of special requests".

> Q. Had [she] sanctioned casting of other Epstein's work between 1959 and June 1968?
> A. Yes.
> Q. How many?
> A. I think that is very unreasonable request!
> Q. At our suggestion: "roughly – was it ten or twenty or ..."
> Lady Epstein cut the discussion short with "oh, many more than that, hundreds." We could not persuade her either to estimate the posthumous casting or to reveal how much was paid for them.

In my conversation with Jackie on the issue, he resented the implication that Kathleen had made too many copies of some portraits (the above "hundreds" was, perhaps, not a very appropriate joke for the occasion), saying that Epstein had given a clear indication of how many should be produced of each portrait (Jackie stated it as a maximum twelve for public figures and six for the rest); unfortunately I found no such indication in his will. At the time, the affair resulted in reduced prices for Epstein's works, as had happened with his maquettes (p. 212). However, as Gardiner rightly commented,[116] a plaster could be made also from a bronze and then a cast made from that plaster; the fact that the plasters not donated to Israel were destroyed does not alter this possibility.

112 Kamien-Kazhdan, *Jacob Epstein: Focus on the Collection*.

113 'We are pleased to expose the collection of plasters virtually on the Museum's website, visited yearly by millions": http://www.imj.org.il/imagine/collections/results.asp?searchType=simple&words=epstein&ArtistE=on.
In spite of my personal disappointment that The Israel Museum, Jerusalem, did not keep to its commitment, I believe that the Epstein estate bears part of the blame because the issue had been neglected for so many years by its custodians; things perhaps might have been different had it been followed up earlier.

114 25/1/1970; TGA-8716/63.

115 'The case of the multiplying Epsteins', *The Sunday Times*, 21 and 28 February 1971.

116 Sheila McGregor (ed.), *A Shared Vision*, Walsall 1999.

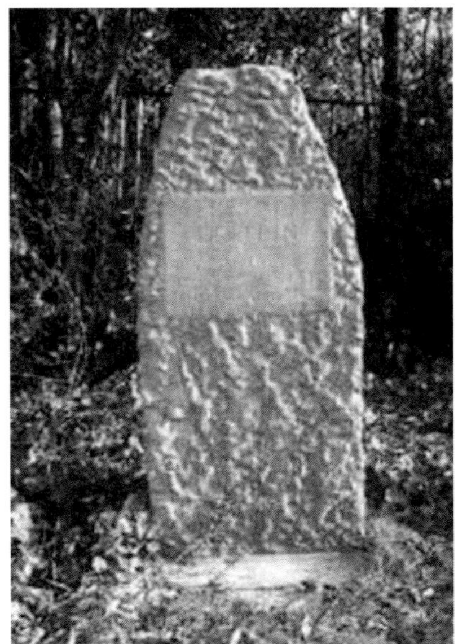

Fig. 82
Epstein's tombstone, Putney Vale Cemetery,

Kathleen's efforts to establish a permanent legacy for Epstein's works bore fruit when she collaborated with Sally Ryan in accumulating the Garman-Ryan Collection, buying art of other artists in addition to works by Epstein that they had.[117] On 29 June 1968, Sally died, bequeathing in her will everything related to art, including prints, her library and her own works, to "my friend Lady Kathleen Epstein", ordering the executors of her will to pay all necessary taxes and the shipping expenses for sending it all to her home in England.[118] Sally left half a million dollars to Kathleen, with a list of works that were in Kathleen's house (then at 18 Elm Park Road, London SW3) and works sent from the US.

In 1972 Kathleen donated the collection to the town of Walsall, where it was initially presented in the old library. It is now settled in its permanent home, the New Art Gallery Walsall, which also hosts also the largest archive of Epstein's papers and photographs. Kathleen died on 17 August 1979, twenty years after her husband.

"Epstein designed his own tombstone", Beth Lipkin told me (fig. 82). As at the time I had not seen Margaret's grave (fig. 50), I could not comment on it. The similarity between the simple unadorned tombs leaves room to suggest that, in addition to McFall's initiative, the design might have been Epstein's. The last contact with Epstein's affairs of his devoted colleague and helper David McFall was unpleasant and, I suggest, unjust:

> I was not invited to attend either his funeral or the memorial service at St. Pauls Cathedral. An omission of stupefying meanness. I went the day after the burial to his graveside and saw Matthew Smith's bouquet of yellow chrysanthemums. The message read simply "Jake from Matt". I was not responsible for the stone cairn subsequently placed over the grave which bears his name inscribed in lower-case minuscules. God be my witness – I would have carved his name in CAPS:
>
> JACOB EPSTEIN SCULPTOR 1880–1959
> [instead of JACOB EPSTEIN Sculptor]".[119]

Not long afterwards, on 29 September 1959, Matthew Smith too died.

Just before the fiftieth anniversary of Epstein's death, I proposed to the municipalities of Jerusalem and Tel-Aviv that a street be named after Epstein. Jerusalem rejected the idea while Tel-Aviv embraced it, and I am grateful to its Name Committee, headed by Haviva Avi-Gay, and in particular to the late Lydia Davidov, who provided small reproductions of the street signs with Epstein's name to be given to members of his family.

On the fiftieth anniversary of Epstein's death, on 19 August 2009, a group of people was assembled by the Ben Uri Gallery and its director David Glasser to celebrate 'Epstein's Day', touring Epstein's public sculptures in London under the guidance of Richard Cork. The day ended in an evening gathering at the Fleming Collection Gallery, which, so befittingly for the occasion, happened to be holding an exhibition by Muirhead Bone, Epstein's long standing friend and supporter (pp. 101–02). The event included a brief launching of my previous book on Epstein's formative years, followed by Richard's comprehensive speech on Epstein and his work.

117 Sally's will – NAGW.
118 Gardiner, *Epstein*, p. 479.
119 McFall, p. 14; the original caps are cited.

In my own brief speech I explained my insistence on visiting Epstein's grave as the first step of the tour, recalling my first visit there in the mid 1980s, when I could hardly find it and there was no public sign to direct the visitor to the grave of one of England's most important artists – a state of affairs that unfortunately still exists. I vowed to myself then, standing alone under the gentle obligatory London drizzle, to return once more after I had earned the right to do so.

And indeed I came back, but not alone. I was there with my completed book and with the attendance of a crowd that truly appreciated his work. When people started to leave, the family members – Epstein's daughter-in-law Isabel, his granddaughter Leda, great granddaughter Amy – and I with my husband remained around the grave. And before my husband recited the ancient Jewish burial prayer the *Kadish*, in Hebrew (for Epstein) and in English (for the rest), I placed some small stones on the grave which, according to the Jewish Orthodox custom in funerals, commemorate the destruction of the Holy Temple.

Similarly, small stones were placed a year later on Epstein's Jewish daughter's grave, Peggy Jean, by Epstein's granddaughter Leda Hornstein-Sloat (fig. 83).

I have fulfilled my promise.

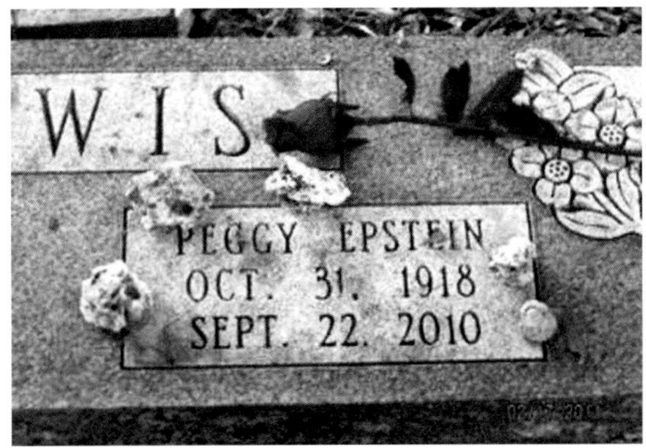

Fig. 83
Peggy Jean's grave

BIBLIOGRAPHY

In view of the enormous number of articles in the printed media on Epstein – and lately on internet sites – mainly books that have direct relation to Epstein, or add important general information, have been included in this list. See pp. 11–12 for a discussion of the the most relevant publications that have appeared hitherto on the sculptor, and for the archival, filmic and oral sources used in this book. Ephemeral notices appearing in the press of the time are cited in full in the text; so are also occasional internet sources or books primarily of general interest.

Ackroyd, P., *T.S. Eliot*, London 1985

Babson, J.F., *The Epsteins: A Family Album*, Aylesbury 1984

Barker, E., 'The Primitive Within: The Question of Race in Epstein's Career 1917–1929', in Silber and Friedman, *Sculptures and Drawings*

Baudelaire, C.P., *Flowers of Evil*, ed. James Laver, drawings by Jacob Epstein, London 1940

Baudelaire, C.P., *Flowers of Evil*, trans. William Aggeler, Fresno, CA 1954

Bax, C., *Some I Knew Well*, London 1951

Berenson, B., *Aesthetics and History in the Visual Arts*, London 1948

Berkman, E.O., *The Lady and the Law: The Remarkable Story of Fanny Holtzmann*, Boston, Mass., 1976

Berthoud, R., *The Life of Henry Moore*, London 1987

Black, R. *The Art of Jacob Epstein*, New York 1940

Blunt, A., 'Epstein and Religious Art', *The Spectator*, 15 March 1935

'From Bloomsbury to Marxism', *Studio International*, November 1973

Bone, J., 'Mr Epstein Alien Sculpture', *The Guardian*, 23 July 1929

Bowness, A., 'Three tributes – Epstein, Smith and Spencer', *Arts*, February 1960, pp. 16–17

Brown, O., *Exhibition: The Memoirs of Oliver Brown*, London 1968

Buckle, R., *Jacob Epstein: Sculptor*, London 1963

Nijinsky, New York 1971

Burke, T., *London in My Time*, London 1934; http://gutenberg.net.au/ebooks04/0400651h.HTML#c02

Burnham, J., *Beyond Modern Sculpture*, London and New York 1968

Burstow, R., *Symbols for '51, The Royal Festival Hall, Skylon and Sculptures for the Festival of Britain*, exh. cat., Festival Hall, London, 2 March – 21 April 1996; http://vads.ahds.ac.uk/learning/designingbritain/html/festival.html

Carew, S.J., *The Nine Lives of Paton College*, London 1974

Carey, J., *The Intellectuals and the Masses: Pride and Prejudice Among the Literary Intelligentsia 1880–1939*, London 1992

Carpenter, H. (ed.), *The Letters of J.R.R. Tolkien*, London 2006

Carving Mountains: Modern Stone Sculpture in England 1907–37, exh. cat., Kettle's Yard, Cambridge

Casson, S., *XXth Century Sculptors*, Oxford 1930

Some Modern Sculptors, London 1929

Cavanagh, T., *Public Sculpture of Liverpool*, Liverpool 1997

Clark, K., *The Nude: A Study in Ideal Form* [1953], New York 1959

Clinefelter, J.L., *Artists for the Reich: Culture and Race from Weimar to Nazi Germany*, New York 2005

Compton, S.P., *British Art in the 20th Century: The Modern Movement*, exh. cat., Royal Academy, London, 1986

Connolly, C. (Cressida), *The Rare and the Beautiful: The Art, Loves and Lives of the Garman Sisters*, London 2004

Connolly, C. (Cyril), 'The Sculptor Paints', *The Architectural Review*, vol. 81, March 1932, p. 101

Enemies of Promise, London 1948

Cork, R., *Vorticism and Abstract Art in the First Machine Age*, I, London 1976

Jacob Epstein, London 1999

Craven, T., *Modern Art: The Men, the Movements, the Meaning*, London 1935

Dickson, R., and S. MacDougall, *Forced Journeys: Artists in Exile in Britain c. 1933–1945*, exh. cat. Ben Uri Gallery, London 2009

Diebow, H., *Der Ewige Jude*, Munich 1937

Eliot, T.S., *After Strange Gods: A Primer of Modern Heresy*, London 1934

Elliot, David, 'The Battle for Art', in *Art and Power: Europe Under the Dictators 1930–1940*, exh. cat., ed. D. Ades, T. Benton, D. Elliott, I. Boyd Whyte, Hayward Gallery, London 1995, pp. 31–35

Epstein, J., *Let There Be Sculpture: An Autobiography*, London 1940

Epstein, J., *Epstein: An Autobiography*, London 1955

Epstein, K., and R. Buckle, *Epstein Drawings*, London 1962

Epstein, exh. cat., intro. John Rothenstein, Arts Council exhibition, Tate Gallery, London, 1952

Eustace, K., 'A Question of Property', *Apollo*, no. 145, May 1997, pp. 60–62

Farr, D., *English Art, 1870–1940*, Oxford 1978

Feibleman, J.K., *Philosophers Lead Sheltered Lives*, London 1952

Felsenstein, F., 'Epstein as a Book Illustrator', in Silber and Friedman, *Sculpture and Drawings*

Friedman, T., 'Epstein and the Theatre', in Silber and Friedman, *Sculpture and Drawings*

Gardiner, S., *Epstein: Artist Against the Establishment*, London 1993

'Introduction', in *Father and Son – Jacob Epstein, Sculptor, and Theo Garman, Painter*, exh. cat.,

The Fine Arts Society, London, September 1989

Gaunt, W., 'Epstein's Bible Drawings', *The Studio*, no. 103, 1932, pp. 290–91

Gayford, M. 'Isabel Rawsthorne', *The Daily Telegraph*, 25 July 1998

Getsy, D.J., 'Fallen Woman: The Gender of Horizontality and the Abandonment of the Pedestal by Giacometti and Epstein', in *Display and Displacement*, ed. Alexandra Gerstein, London 2008

Giedion-Welcker, C., *Contemporary Sculpture: An Evolution in Volume*, Zurich 1955

Gilboa, R., *Mythic Motifs in Jacob Epstein's Sculptural Work* (English abstract of M.A. Thesis, Tel-Aviv University, 1984): http://independent.academia.edu/RaquelGilboa

Papers/1105767

'Epstein and Adam – Revisited', *British Art Journal*, vol. iii, 2004, pp. 73–78

... And There Was Sculpture: Jacob Epstein's Formative Years (1880–1930), London 2009

Gill, E., Diaries (microfilm in Tate Gallery Archive)

Godley, K., 'The Garman Ryan Collection: As I saw it', in *A Shared Vision*, exh. cat., ed. Sheila McGregor, New Art Gallery, Walsall, 1999, pp. 9–15

Golding, L., 'Epstein', in *Great Contemporaries*, London 1935

Grafly, D. 'Gill and Epstein', *American Magazine of Art*, vol. 27, 1934

Griffiths, P., 'Poèmes and Haïkaï: A Note on Messiaen's Development', *Musical Times*, vol. 112, September 1971, pp. 851–52

Haas, M., *The Emigré Composers*, Jewish Music Institute, University of London, 2004

Hale, K., *A Slender Reputation: An Autobiography*, London 1994

Harrison, C. *English Art and Modernism 1900–1939*, London 1981

Haskell, A., *The Sculptor Speaks*, London 1931

Black on White: an Arbitrary Anthology of Fine Drawings, London 1933

'Epstein's "Behold the Man"', *The Studio*, vol. 109, 1935, pp. 272–73

In His True Centre, London 1951

Balletomane at Large: An Autobiograhy, London 1972

Henry Moore: Early Carvings 1920–1940, exh. cat., essays by H.A. Garrould, T. Friedman and D. Mitchinson, Leeds City Galleries, 1982

Hinks, R.P., *Myth and Allegory in Ancient Art*, London 1939

Holmes, C., *Anti-Semitism in British Society 1876–1939*, London 1973

Holroyd, M., *Augustus John: The New Biography*, London 1997

Horrie, C., 'Revealed: the fascist past of the Daily Mirror', *The Independent*, 11 November 2003

Ireland, G., *Epstein: A Camera Study of the Sculptor At Work*, intro. by L. Lee, London 1957

Isaacson, W., *Einstein: His Life and Universe*, New York 2007

James, P.B. (ed.), *Henry Moore on Sculpture*, London 1966

Jason, N., and L. Thompson-Pharoah, *The Sculpture of Frank Dobson*, London 1994

Jewish Art, exh. cat., intro. C. Spencer, in Glasgow Museum, Glasgow 1979

Kamien-Kazhdan, A. (ed.), *Jacob Epstein: Focus on the Collection*, exh. cat., Israel Museum, Jerusalem, 2002

'Unveiling Moore's Enigma', in *Henry Moore: Focus on the Collection*, exh. cat., Israel Museum, Jerusalem 2005

Keene, A., *The Two Mr Smiths*, London 1995

Langui, G., *50 Years of Modern Art*, London 1959

Laver, J., *Museum Piece*, London 1963

Lehman Hare, T., 'Much Ado About "Genesis"', *Apollo*, March 1931, pp. 176–78

Lewison, J., 'Going Modern and Being British', in *Blast to Freeze*, exh. cat., Kunstmuseum, Wolfsburg, 2003

Lovatt, E., 'Epstein's Bible', *Jewish Renaissance*, vol. viii, April 2009

Lucie-Smith, E., *Art of the 1930s: The Age of Anxiety*, London 1985

McCarthy, H., 'Democratising British Foreign Policy: Rethinking the Peace Ballot, 1934–5', *Journal of British Studies*, vol. 49, no. 2, 2010, pp. 358– 87

Mannin, E., *Confessions and Impressions*, London 1930

Maroudas, N., 'London's Epstein Sculptures', *Spike Magazine*, January 2012; http://www.spikemagazine.com/category/spike-contributors/nick-maroudas

Marsh, J., *Art and Androgyny; The Life of Fiore de Henriquez*, London 2005

Matthew Smith, exh. cat., Barbican Art Gallery, London, 1983

Mellers, W., and R. Hildgard, 'The Cultural Setting', in Boris Ford (ed.), *The Cambridge Cultural History of Britain, VIII: Early 20th Century Britain*, Cambridge 1992, pp. 3–44

Mirzoef, N., 'What Is Visual Culture?', *The Virtual Culture Reader*, 2nd edn, London 2002

Mosley, O., *My Life*, London 1950

Muggeridge, M., *The Nineteen Thirties*, London 1940

[unsigned], 'Famine in the North Caucasus'; 'Hunger in the Ukraine'; 'Poor Harvest in Prospect', *The Manchester Guardian*, 25, 27, 28 March 1933

Neve, C., *Leon Underwood*, London 1947

Newton, E., 'Epstein' , *Journal of the Society of Arts*, 26 June 1942, pp. 519–21

Nijinsky, R., *Nijinski* [London 1934], New York 1972

Orwell, G., *The Collected Essays, Journalism and Letters*, vols. I–II, New York 1968

Osman, L., 'A Bridge and Sculpture in Cavendish Sq., London', RIBA *Journal*, vol. 40, August 1953, pp. 414–16

'Architect, Sculptor and Client', *Architectural Association Journal*, vol. 70, 1954, pp. 7–19

Overy, R., *The Morbid Age: Britain Between the Wars*, London 2009

Oyved [Oved], M., *The Book of Affinity* [London 1933], New York 1935

Parkes, K., *The Art of Carved Sculpture*, London 1931

Platt, S., *Art & Politics in the 1930's: Modernism Marxism Americanism*, New York 1999

Posèq, A.W.G., 'The Hanging Carcass Motif and Jewish Artists', *Jewish Art*, vol. xvi, 1990–91, pp. 139–56

Soutine: His Jewish Modality, Lewes 2001

Priestley, J.B., *English Journey* [1934], Harmondsworth 1984

Radford, R., *Art for a Purpose: The Artist's International Association 1933–1953*, Winchester 1987

Ramsden, E.H., *Themes and Variations*, London 1953

Rathborne, M., 'Gladstone, Disraeli and the Bulgarian Horrors', *History Today*, 2004; http://www.historytoday.com.print.7581

Read, H., 'Introduction', in *Contemporary Prose and Poetry*, vol. 2, 'Surrealism', July 1936, pp. 13–13

Read, H., *Henry Moore: Sculpture and Drawings*, London 1944

Read, H., *The Meaning of Art*, London [1931] 1951

Read, H., *Contemporary British Art* [1946], Harmondsworth 1964

Read, H., *The Philosophy of Modern Art*, London 1965

Read, H., 'British Art 1930–1940', *in Art in Britain 1930–40 Centred around Axis, Circle and Unit One*, exh. cat., Marlborough Gallery, London, 1965

Read, Herbert, *The Origins of Form in Art*, London 1967

Redfern Gallery, London, exh. cat., May 1932: *Illustrations to the Old Testament by Epstein*

Reid, L.B., *The Man From New York: John Quinn and His Friends*, New York 1960

Roberts, W., 'Dealers and Galleries: The Leicester Galleries', in *Five Posthumous Essays and Other Writings*, Valencia 1990; http://www.users.waitrose.com/ ~ wrs/dealers.html

Rose, J., *Demons and Angels: A Life of Jacob Epstein*, London 2002

Rose, W.K., *The Letters of Wyndham Lewis*, London 1965

Roth, C., and B. Narkiss (eds.), *Jewish Art: An Illustrated History*, New York 1961

Rothenstein, J., 'Introduction', in *Epstein*, exh. cat., Arts Council Exhibition, Tate Gallery, London, 1952

Dark Day, Hideous Night, 1939–1965, London 1966

Rutter, F., *Evolution in Modern Art*, London [1926] 1932

Sacks, G., *The Intelligent Man's Guide To Jew-Baiting*, London 1935

Schinman, E.P. and B.A. (eds.), *Jacob Epstein. A Catalogue of the Collection of Edward P. Schinman*, Farleigh Dickinson University Press, 1970

Searle, Adrian, 'Henry Moore: Smooth Operator', *The Guardian*, 22 February 2010

Shaw, R., and G. Shaw, 'The Cultural and Social Setting', in Boris Ford (ed.), *The Cambridge Cultural History of Britain*, IX: *Modern Britain*, Cambridge 1992, pp. 1–44

Silber, E., *The Sculpture of Epstein with a Complete Catalogue*, Oxford 1986

'Body Language: Making and Viewing Epstein's Adam', in *Finding Adam: Epstein and*

Harewood: An Extraordinary Story, Harewood 2011, pp. 8–26

'Epstein's Liverpool Colossus', in *Patronage and Practice: Sculpture on Merseyside*, ed.

Penelope Curtis, Tate Gallery, Liverpool, 1989, pp. 101–10

Silber, E., and T. Friedman, *Jacob Epstein: Sculpture and Drawings*, exh. cat., Leeds City Art Galleries and Whitechapel Art Gallery, London, 1987

Spence, B., *Phoenix at Coventry*, London 1962

Sylvester, A.D.B., 'Festival Sculpture', *The Studio*, vol. 142, no. 702, 1951, pp. 75ff

Symons, J., *The Thirties. A Dream Revolved*, London [1950] 1975

Trier, E., *Form and Space: Sculpture of the Twentieth Century*, London 1968

Tulloch, Stuart, 'Miracle or Monstrosity? Jacob Epstein's *Jacob and the Angel*', *Tate Etc.*, issue 22, Summer 2011

Underwood, E.G., *A Short History of English Sculpture*, London 1933

Van Damm, S., *We Never Closed: The Windmill Story*, London 1967

Van Damm, V., *Tonight and Every Night*, London 1952

Wagner, A.M., *Mother Stone: The Validity of Modern British Sculpture*, London 2005

Watson, F., *Art Lies Bleeding*, London 1939

Wellington, H., *Epstein, Seventy-Five Drawings*, London 1929

Wilcox, T., *Day in the Sun: Outdoor Pursuits in Art in the 1930s*, London 2006

Wilenski, R.H., *The Modern Movement in Art*, London 1927

'People You Would Like to Know – Jacob Epstein', *Woman's Journal*, March 1930

The Meaning of Modern Sculpture, London 1932

Wittkower, R., *Sculpture: Processes and Principles*, Harmondsworth 1986

Woolf, V., *Roger Fry*, London 1940

Zilczer, J., 'The Theory of Direct Carving in Modern Sculpture', *The Oxford Art Journal*, vol. 4, no. 2, 1981

CHRONOLOGY OF JACOB EPSTEIN

The following presents chronologically events in the life of Epstein (hereafter JE), books published in which he features, and works considered in the text. In addition, there is an estimation, based on Evelyn Silber's catalogue, of the number of portraits commissioned or private (of models and family) made each year.

1929

The Epsteins settle in a London house at Hyde Park Gate, and keep a cottage, no. 49 Baldwins Hill, in Epping Forrest.

APRIL Esther, Kathleen Garman's daughter by JE, is born (conceived August 1928).

MAY The Underground Building sculptures *Day* and *Night* are unveiled.

JULY JE starts an action against International Depositories Ltd. for forging his work.

OCTOBER *Rima* (the Hudson Memorial in Hyde Park) vandalized by hooligans with tar.

WINTER Starts *Genesis* in Baldwins Hill.

PUBLICATIONS Hubert Wellington, *Seventy Five Drawings*, London 1929 – mainly of Sunita.

1930

FEBRUARY The stone for *Genesis* is moved to his London studio and the work is carried out there.

4 MAY – 4 NOVEMBER Epstein, Moore and Skeaping present British sculpture at the Venice Biennale.

17 OCTOBER An action brought by JE in July 1929 (on forged works sold as Epsteins) is decided against him (141).

PUBLICATIONS Alfred Rosenberg, *Myth of the Twentieth Century* (Nazi doctrine on art), published in Germany.

WORKS ~ 10 portraits, of which four models, six commissions.

1931

FEBRUARY *Genesis* presented at the Leicester Galleries.

JE writes the introduction to Moore's second one-man show (April 1931) at the Leicester Galleries, which presents one of his first reclining figures.

Isabel Nichols becomes JE's model and eventually comes to live at the Epsteins' house.

PUBLICATIONS Arnold Haskel, *The Sculptor Speaks*, London 1931; Herbert Read, *The Meaning of Art*, London, 1931.

WORKS *Sun-God* 2nd stage; *Primeval Gods*; Old Testament watercolours; *Kathleen, 3rd portrait*; illustrations to the Old Testament
~ 12 portraits, of which two models, ten commissions.

1932

23 FEBRUARY – 19 MARCH 'Illustrations to the Old Testament' presented at the Redfern Gallery.

Moseley forms the British Union of Fascists.

PUBLICATIONS L.B. Powell, *Jacob Epstein*, London; R.H. Wilenski, *The Meaning of Modern Sculpture*, London.

WORKS *Elemental, Woman Possessed, Chimera; Isabel, 2nd portrait; Kathleen, 4th portrait.* ~ 10 portraits, of which seven models, three commissions.

1933

JANUARY Hitler and the Nazi Party rise to power in Germany; German refugees reach London.

JE, John, Moore, Gill and Ben Nicholson help to form an Artists International Association, to establish an army of artists opposing the advance of "philistine barbarism".

Augustus John uses his influence to free a number of German and Austrian artists who had been interned by the British government.

FEBRUARY The Leicester Gallery presents the first exhibition of young avant-garde British artists who formed the group 5 & 7 – including Moore and Hepworth.

APRIL The Mayor Gallery presents the first Surrealist exhibition in London.

MAY *Carvings and Bronzes by Jacob Epstein* at the Leicester Gallery.

SUMMER: The Epsteins move from their old cottage into one across the road, 'Deerhurst', no. 50 Baldwins Hill; Isabel joins the family for the summer holidays, during which JE draws floral watercolours.

Kathleen goes to Martigues in the south of France to help her sister Helen.

SEPTEMBER Albert Einstein arrives in England.

NOVEMBER Artists International Association (AIA) protests against Fascist victories in Spain, forming a "refugee committee" trying to help artists to be admitted in England.

DECEMBER Christmas exhibition at the Tooth Gallery of JE's *Bible Illustrations* – a sell-out.

WORKS Watercolours of Epping Forest; illustrations for Moshe Oved's *The Book of Affinity*.
~ 10 portraits, of which seven models, three commissions.

1934

FEBRUARY JE and Isabel conceive a child.

APRIL The first and only exhibition of the group Unit One, held at the Mayor Galleries, stamping the importance of the new path of English avant-garde art.

19 OCTOBER Jackie, JE's son with Isabel, born at Surbiton General Hospital.

PUBLICATIONS Herbert Read (ed.), *Unit One*, London 1934.

WORKS *Ecce Homo (Behold The Man)*; ~ 10 portraits, of which two models, eight commissioned.

1935

JANUARY The quarterly review *Axis* starts to appear, propagating abstract art.

MARCH Kathleen realises that Jackie is Epstein's natural son.

APRIL The battle to save the MBA sculptures in the Strand starts.

'Non-Aryan' writers prohibited from being published in Germany.

SEPTEMBER The swastika is made the official symbol of Nazi Germany and the Nuremberg Laws deprive German Jews of citizenship.

WORKS *Kathleen, 5th portrait*; the drop-curtain (30 × 25 feet) for the ballet *David* for the new Markova-Dollin Ballet Company.
~ 12 portraits, of which seven models and family, five commissioned.

1936

7 JANUARY Opening of the ballet *David*.

King George V dies and Edward VII is crowned king.

MAY Haile Selassie, 'Emperor of Abyssinia' [Ethiopia], leaves Ethiopia following the Italian conquest, and Epstein is asked to do his bust.

1 JUNE JE signs a contract to do illustrations for Baudelaire's *Fleurs du Mal* with the American publisher George Macy and undertakes to produce them by July 1937.

11 JUNE TO 4 JULY The International Surrealist Exhibition is held at the New Burlington Galleries in London.

AUGUST The Berlin Olympic Games open.

JE's daughter Peggy Jean is sent to New York and returns in October.

4 OCTOBER Oswald Mosley's Blackshirts march in the Jewish-populated East End of London, disseminating anti-Semitic and anti-Communist slogans.

NOVEMBER German invitation to the London Group to exhibit British Art in Germany is rejected.

JE's older brother, Lois, dies.

DECEMBER JE's exhibition of flower drawings.

WORKS ~ 7 portraits, all commissioned.

1937

MARCH JE and Margaret with daughter Peggy Jean in Paris for their yearly Easter visit; Peggy Jean meets Norman Hornstein and they get married in October.

APRIL The destruction of the Basque town of Guernica.

12 MAY Coronation of George VI. A renewed attack on the MBA statues starts immediately after the coronation, ending in mutilation of the sculptures.

25 MAY – 25 NOVEMBER The Paris Exhibition opens, featuring 38 rival displays.

19 JULY The opening in Munich of the exhibition *Entartete Kunst* (Degenerate art).

WORKS *Consummatum Est*; ~ 8 portraits, of which three models and family, five commissioned.

1938

APRIL JE receives an honorary degree from Aberdeen University.

SEPTEMBER Prime Minister Chamberlain signs the Munich Agreement and returns, stating that the agreement will bring "peace in our time".

NOVEMBER *Kristallnacht* – burning of synagogues in Germany.

DECEMBER Exhibition of JE's 37 drawings illustrating Baudelaire at the Tooth Gallery.

WORKS Maquettes of *Adam and Eve; Burial of Abel;* illustrations for Baudelaire's *Fleurs du Mal;* carving of *Adam* initiated.
~ 9 portraits, of which three models, six commissioned.

1939

JANUARY JE sells his collection of Matthew Smith's drawings owing to financial difficulties.

JUNE *Adam* exhibited, and in July sold and given to a showman to be presented in Blackpool.

AUGUST The Molotov-Ribbentrop pact, practically dividing East Europe between Hitler and Stalin.

23 AUGUST Leda, JE's first grandchild, is born.

31 AUGUST Germany stages a "Polish assault" on the radio station in Gleiwitz, followed by the invasion of Poland, and on

3 SEPTEMBER Britain and France declare war on Germany.

DECEMBER JE hands his autobiography to the publisher Michael Joseph.

WORKS ~ 10 portraits, of which seven models and family members, three commissioned.

1940

JANUARY England is bombarded; rationing of food and, later on, the Blitz on London.

The children are sent away from the city; the Epsteins and Kathleen remain, visiting them at weekends.

MAY Churchill becomes Prime Minister of Britain; the German Enigma code is broken; Hitler's deputy Rudolf Hess parachutes into Scotland.

PUBLICATIONS JE's *Let There Be Sculpture* published in London in December, and immediately afterwards also in the US.

WORKS *Slave Hold;* starts *Jacob and the Angel;* flower paintings; ~ 6 portraits, of which two models and family, four commissioned.

1941

JANUARY British troops liberate Ethiopia from the Italian conquest.

APRIL Germany blitzes Coventry.

25 JUNE JE's father, Max Epstein, dies.

SEPTEMBER Carver and sculptor David McFall starts working for Epstein.

NOVEMBER British air counter-attack on German cities stops German bombing in England.

WORKS ~ 6 portraits, of which five models and family, one commission.

1942

10 FEBRUARY *Jacob and the Angel* exhibited.

MARCH 'Reinhardt Operation' starts, sending Jews to three death camps in Poland – Belzec, Sobibor and Treblinka; it is the beginning of the 'Final Solution' for the Jews – the Holocaust.

PUBLICATIONS Robert Black, *The Art of Jacob Epstein*, New York.

WORKS Drawings on the theme of Lucifer; start of *The Girl with the Gardenias;* ~ 16 portraits, of which five models and family, eleven commissions.

1943

WORKS *The Girl with the Gardenias; The Fall of Lucifer* (relief); *Lucifer.*

1944

MAY JE's exhibition of April deferred; opens in May with *The Girl with the Gardenias.*

WORKS Series of nude studies (exhibited in 1947); ~ 7 portraits, of which two models and family, four commissioned.

1945

APRIL Mussolini killed; Hitler commits suicide.

Bergen-Belsen concentration-camp liberated by British troops, and for the first time the British public is exposed to the encompassing and horrific results of the Holocaust.

8 MAY End of war in Europe.

JULY Labour wins election; Churchill ousted from office.

AUGUST Nuclear bombs dropped on Hiroshima and Nagasaki, ending World War II.

NOVEMBER JE's *Lucifer* presented at the Leicester Galleries and rejected as a gift by both the Tate and the Fitzwilliam Museum, Cambridge.

WORKS Series of maquettes with personal connotations, not developed into sculpture. ~ 7 portraits, of which six commissions.

1946

John Finch enters the Epsteins' life, helping Margaret Epstein with her correspondence and serving as amanuensis to the household.

MARCH The Blackpool peep-show of Epstein's work comes to London.

END OF YEAR *Lucifer* is given to Birmingham Art Gallery.

WORKS Portrait of Winston Churchil; conceiving *Lazarus.* ~ 13 portraits, of which seven models, six paid for.

1947

FEBRUARY JE presents his *Churchill*, and nude studies made in 1944.

3 MARCH Margaret Epstein dies. Son Jackie is sent to live with Peggy Jean in the US.

JE's daughter Kitty marries Lucien Freud.

WORKS *Lazarus;* ~ 6 portraits, of which four models, two commissions.

1948

MAY *The Girl with Gardenias* shown at the first 'Sculpture in the Open Air', Battersea Park.

WORKS ~ 12 portraits, of which ten commissioned.

1949

Kathleen moves with Beth Lipkin to 18 Hyde Park Gate, leaving her home in 217 Fulham Road to the 25-year-old Theo.

LATE AUGUST JE visits New York and brings Jackie back to England.

SEPTEMBER JE participates in the second post-war Edinburgh Festival with his portraits.

OCTOBER JE participates in exhibition in Glasgow.

WORKS ~ 14 portraits, of which one family, thirteen commissioned.

1950

JE starts *Youth Advancing* for the Festival of Britain.

MARCH *Lazarus* presented at the Leicester amidst portraits.

AUGUST The Epping Forest retreat 'Deerhurst', no. 50 Baldwins Hill, is sold.

WORKS Maquette of a Madonna (who has Kathleen's facial features) and a child. ~ 17 portraits, of which five family, twelve commissioned.

1951

JE begins *Madonna and Child* for the Convent of the Holy Child Jesus in Cavendish Square, London.

FEBRUARY JE starts negotiations with Fairmount Park Association in Philadelphia for a composition later developed as *Social Consciousness.*

1 MAY The Festival of Britain opened by King George VI.

Epstein presents *Youth Advancing* at the South Bank Exhibition, and *Lazarus* at the Battersea Park exhibition.

JUNE JE signs a contract with Fairmount Park Association, visiting Philadelphia in August, to see the site for *Social Consiousness.*

WORKS Three maquettes, a preliminary concept for *Social Consiousness.* ~ 17 commissioned portraits.

1952

JE is lent a studio at the Royal College of Art to work on *Social Consiousness.*

JANUARY *Lazarus* installed at the west end of New College Chapel, Oxford.

SEPTEMBER–NOVEMBER JE's retrospective organized by the Arts Council is held at the Tate Gallery.

WORKS ~ 9 portraits, of which three family, six commissioned.

1953

APRIL JE receives the commission for a posthumous figure of Field Marshal John Smuts.

MAY JE rejects the Royal Society of British Sculptors' proposal to award him a gold medal for distinguished services to sculpture.

14 MAY Unveiling of *Madonna and Child.*

22 JUNE JE receives an Honorary PhD from Oxford University.

OCTOBER JE's large carvings that went to Blackpool are offered for sale.

Muirhead Bone dies.

WORKS *Field-Marshal John Smuts;* two maquettes of *Mace Heads.* ~ 12 portraits, one of his dog Frisky and the rest commissions.

1954

22 JANUARY JE's son Theo dies of a heart attack.

16 FEBRUARY JE is knighted; investiture by Queen Mother at Buckingham Palace.

1 OCTOBER JE's daughter Esther commits suicide.

WORKS Three large works discussed during this year, executed during the following three years: *Liverpool Resurgent* for the John Lewis store in Liverpool; the Trades Union Council's memorial; *Christ in Majesty* for Llandaff Cathedral; ~ 5 commissioned portraits.

1955

MARCH JE attends the unveiling of *Social Consciousness* in Philadelphia.

MAY JE nominated as a member of the American Academy of Arts and Letters.

27 JUNE JE marries Kathleen Garman and almost immediately travels alone to Philadelphia; on his return, a visit with Kathleen to Paris.

AUGUST JE receives the commission for the TUC memorial.

WORKS JE's *Franklin Medal* given to Churchill and Eleanor Roosevelt; starts elements for *Liverpool Resurgent;* ~ 5 commissioned portraits.

1956

FEBRUARY–MARCH JE starts Trade Union Congress Memorial.

MAY Commissioned to do *St Michael and the Devil* for Coventry Cathedral.

JUNE Works on *Christ in Majesty* for Llandaff Cathedral.

JULY–AUGUST JE is troubled by Peggy Jean's divorcing Hornstein.

NOVEMBER Unveiling of *Liverpool Resurgent.*

WORKS ~7 portraits, of which one family, six commissioned

1957

MARCH JE starts work on *St Michael and the Devil* (unveiled by Lady Epstein on 24 June 1960).

APRIL The presentation in Llandaff of *Christ in Majesty*; a commission for the Bowater House Group (*Rush to the Green*).

SUMMER Holiday in Scotland, ending with JE's heart attack, requiring an operation.

OCTOBER JE receives an urgent commission to do William Blake's portrait for Poets' Corner in Westminster Abbey.

NOVEMBER Commissioned by the College of North Staffordshire to do Princess Margaret's portrait.

PUBLICATIONS Geoffrey Ireland, A *Camera Study of the Sculptor at Work.*

WORKS ~ 8 commissioned portraits.

1958

JE in hospital with pleurisy and thrombosis; convalesces in France and northern Italy.

MARCH Unveiling of the TUC group.

APRIL *Genesis* sold to Cartmell of Blackpool.

APRIL AND SEPTEMBER Trips in Europe.

WORKS Starts several works: *Rush to the Green*; *Princess Margaret* bust; glass windows and a maquette of *The Ascension of Christ* for the new church of the Ascension in Crownhill, Plymouth. ~ 3 commissioned portraits.

1959

19 AUGUST JE almost completes *Rush to the Green* (erected April 1961) before succumbing to coronary thrombosis. Buried in Putney Vale Cemetery, grave no. 1347, class A, block AS.

10 NOVEMBER Memorial service held at St Paul's Cathedral.

NOVEMBER–DECEMBER First memorial exhibition at the Ben Uri Art Gallery, London.

WORKS ~ 7 commissioned portraits.

1960

MARCH A large and impressive exhibition, *The Epstein Collection of Tribal and Exotic Art*, mounted by The Arts Council.

10 JUNE – 19 JULY *Fifty Years of Bronzes and Drawings by Sir Jacob Epstein, 1880–1959*, exhibition at the Leicester Gallery.

1961

AUGUST A retrospective exhibition of JE's sculpture presented in Edinburgh, moving in

NOVEMBER to London's Tate Gallery.

2009

19 AUGUST 'Epstein Day', celebrating the 50th anniversary of Epstein's death, arranged by the Ben Uri Gallery, London.

INDEX

PHOTOGRAPHIC CREDITS

Illustrations in this book fall into two categories: Epstein's own work, indicated by [no.]; photographs and other artists' work or photographs, indicated by [fig. no.]. All Epstein's works have received publication clearance from the Epstein Estate – Tate Enterprises.

For the readers' convenience, some bronze sculptures (which almost all exist in several copies), are noted in the main text as belonging to public galleries, and thus may differ to what is given here as sources of photographs and publication rights.

Efforts, which are solely the author's responsibility, were made to trace and contact all owners and copyright-holders and to obtain their permission to publish the illustrations in this book. However, lapse of time and change of owners resulted in what perhaps may amount to a breach of rights when owners could not be found; although their involuntary contributions deserve credit that could not be given, I do hope that the mere publication would constitute a kind of compensation.

Epstein had been meticulous about the photographs of his works in books published while he was still alive and, as much as I could, I have tried to follow his choice of images, which were mostly taken by the photographer Paul Lieb (from 1918 until WW2) and deposited in the Conway and Witt Libraries, The Courtauld Institute of Art, London. In some cases the deceased owners of collections, dispersed to unknown owners, left behind catalogues from which I have taken images (notably the Shinman Collection); I am morally indebted to the recent owners. Other sources were publications over 70 years old (rights expired) as well as images taken from internet sites which have a good repository of copyright-free photographs, mainly of public sculptures, stated below.

I apologize for any errors or omissions in the following alphabetical list, and would be grateful to be notified of any corrections that should be incorporated in future reprints or editions of this book.

First and foremost I am greatly indebted to the New Art Gallery – Walsall (given in the short form GREC-NAGW) for providing so many images gratis, as well as to other institutions and private people who exempted me from publication fees. My gratitude is expressed by stating their contribution as 'courtesy' in the captions of the relevant images in the main text or, if not possible, here below.

BRITISH SOURCES

Aberdeen Art Gallery & Museums Collections – (courtesy) 65b; 101
A.C. Cooper (courtesy) – 32; 39
The British Museum – fig.7
Ben Uri Gallery, London – fig.12
Birmingham Museums and Art Gallery – 13; 36; 70a-b
Boundary Gallery, London (courtesy) – 38; 51c
The Courtauld Institute of Art – (Conway Library) 5; 39c; 42c; 47; 48a-b; 104c; fig. 3; (the De Lazlo Collection of Paul Laib Negatives, Witt Library) 56c
Bolton Art Gallery – 60
GREC-NAGW – 2; 3; 4; 10; 11; 12; 33; 35; 49a; 52; 55; 65a; 71a-b; 74a; 76a; 80; (private collection, on loan to NAGW) 19; 29; 61; fig. 16; fig. 37; fig. 65;
Griffith, Robert – (courtesy) 43
Henry Moore Institute – 113; 114; fig. 19; fig. 53
Keele University – 109a-b
Leeds City Art Galleries – front cover; 6; 31
LLandaf Cathedral, Wells – 91
Museum of London – 75a; 79a-c
National Gallery, London – fig.14
National Portrait Gallery, London – fig. 44; fig. 54
Nottingham Castle Museum – 40; 57
Tate Gallery – 7; 8; 46; (Archive) fig. 2
TUC images – 104a-b
Victoria and Albert Museum –23
Wintworth Art Gallery, Manchester – 15a-b

NON-BRITISH SOURCES

Germany: Glyptothek, Munich – fig. 9; Staatlische Kunst Sammmlungen, Dresden – fig.33; b.p.k Photo Agency (Staatliche Museen, Berlin) – fig. 32; fig. 42
Italy: Bargello Museum, Florence – fig.17; Pinacoteca di Brera, Milan – fig.20; Museo Pio-Clementino, Vatican – fig. 30; fig. 77
National Gallery of Australia, Canberra – (Ccourtesy of A.C. Cooper) 32
America: Riverside Drive Church, New York – 1; fig. 69; Metropolitan Museum of Art, New York – 30a-b; fig. 10; Association for Public Art, Philadelphia – (courtesy photographer Gary McKinnis © 1992); fig. 62; fig. 64.
Canada: Dalhousie University Art Gallery: 49b (donated by Col. Th. L. Bullock, 1971)

PUBLICATIONS

Baudelaire, *Fleurs du Mal*, Paris 1923 (ill. Odilon Redon) – fig. 29/II
Baudelaire, *Fleurs du Mal*, Paris 1925 (ill. Carlo Farneti) – fig. 29/III
Baudelaire, *Fleurs du Mal* (trans. James Lever; illustrations by Jacob Epstein), London 1940 – 51 a,b,d
Buckle, Richard, *Epstein*, London 1964 – 76.b (pl. 482); 86 (pl. 572)
Robert Black, *The Art of Jacob Epstein*, New York, 1942 – 1; 56a-b; 58; 78; 103
Encyclopædia Britannica – 48a
Franz Eher, Nachf. *Der Ewige Jude*, 1937 – fig. 26

Kathleen Epstein and Richard Buckle, *Epstein: Drawings* – (private collections) 18; 21; 34; 66
H. Hapgood, *The Spirit of the Ghetto*, p. 260 – 17
Arnold Haskell, *In His True Centre*, London 1951, p. 59 – fig. 5
Kladderadatsch, 49, 1933,7 – fig. 23b
Moshe Oved, *The Book of Affinity*, New York 1935 – 41; 63
Redfern Gallery catalogue (London 1932) – 22; 24; 24a; 25
E.P and B.A. Schinman (eds.), *Jacob Epstein. A Catalogue of the Collection of Edward P. Schinman* – 14; 16; 20; 24a; 37; 39b; 50; 59; 68; 69; 72; 85; 94; 105; 110
Evelyn Silber, *The Sculpture of Epstein* – (no. 299) 53; (drawing 26) 62; (no. 398) 76c; (no. 473) 93; (no. 477) 95
Vaughn, William, *William Blake*, London 1984, no. 18 – fig. 6
A.W. Wagner, *Mother Stone* – fig. 4

PRIVATE COLLECTION

14a-b; 25; 26; 27; 28; 45; 54a-b; 67; 73; 74b; 84a-d; 90; 102; 111; 112

AGENCIES AND PHOTOGRAPHERS

A.C. Cooper Ltd, London – (courtesy) 32; 39a
Niall Fairhead – Images (courtesy); © Alpha Photo Press Agency (UK) Ltd. fig. 63
Amy Sloat Wain – 87
Author's – 64; 75b; 88; 115; fig. 1
Bridgeman Library (UK) – fig. 60
Roger Lovette – (courtesy) 75c-d
Mike Pitts – (courtesy) fig. 48b
Bonhams, London – (courtesy) 96; 97
RMN, Grand Palais, © – fig. 15; fig. 41

INTERNET SITES

http://www.myspace.com/englishblake/photo – figs. 72; 73
http://commons.wikimedia.org/wiki/File:William_Blake,_Self_Portrait – fig. 74
http://encyclopentopia.com/term/Jacob_Epstein – 89; 107; 108
http://streetsofliverpool.co.uk/liverpool-resurgent/ – 99a-b; 100
http://www.flickr.com/photos/11561957@N06/5611554200 – 99a-b
Royalty-Free – 82; 83; 89; 98; 107; figs. 13, 13a (Corvis; photograph by Phillip Colman)
http://www.historum.com (S-3848-.2) – fig. 38
http://www.faculty:colostate-pueblo.edu – fig. 39a-b
http://www.icon-art.info/masterpiece.php?lng = en&mst_id = 3332 – fig. 51;
http://www.mutualart.com/Artwork/MARCELLA-BARZETTI D12FABD9ABCDFBA3; 81
http://www.westminster-abbey.org/our-history/people/william-blake – 106
http://www.spikemagazine.com/londons-epstein-sculptures-hyde-park.php – fig. 80a-b